D0941615

THE BIBLE AND THE
ANCIENT NEAR EAST

Essays in honor of
William Foxwell Albright

EDITED BY G. ERNEST WRIGHT

WINONA LAKE, INDIANA

The Bible
and the Ancient Near East

EISENBRAUNS 1979

Reprinted by
EISENBRAUNS
Winona Lake, Indiana

This reprint has been authorized by The Biblical Colloquium

Copyright © 1961 The Biblical Colloquium

ISBN 0-931464-03-X

FOREWORD

The essays in this volume are presented in affection and respect to a great scholar, teacher and friend. The work of William Foxwell Albright during the past forty and more years has been an exceptionally learned stimulant, not infrequently controversial, on the very front lines of Near Eastern scholarship. The catholicity of interest which it represents, its radically empirical emphasis in historical method, its full employment of fresh linguistic, philological and archaeological data to challenge older views and to form the bases of new syntheses—these are at the root of its heuristic importance. So concentrated has been the interest in, and the respect for, the primary data that the historical evaluations of this or that conformation of evidence at first glance appear to shift frequently, if not bewilderingly. Yet such an impression can exaggerate the true situation, unless it is realized that a single new fact discovered on the historical frontier can frequently challenge a given reconstruction, if one is open to its meaning. Furthermore, where the evidence has been sufficiently extensive to permit safe generalization, Albright's systematizing constructions have provided the framework within which subsequent scholarly work must move. Examples of this are his archaeological chronology of Palestine, and his studies in the history of Canaanite, Hebrew and Jewish paleography. Among other syntheses of great importance, even though they are still debated, are his history of the Canaanites (see Appendix I), his work in the Egyptian syllabic vocabulary, his reconstruction of the Mosaic era of biblical history, his synchronistic studies of Near Eastern chronology, including South Arabia, his philological studies of ancient Hebrew poetry in the context of the Northwest Semitic milieu, and many other constructions alluded to in the chapters which follow and in his bibliography (see Appendix II).

The purpose of this volume is to describe the course taken by scholarly research since World War I in the various areas of Near Eastern study to the end that a perspective may be gained of the progress made and of the problems demanding solution. The original plan of the book called for certain chapters to be included which dealt with such subjects as topographical research, and Canaanite, Aramaean and Iranian cultures. Contributors who had planned to write on these topics were forced, by a variety of factors not under their control, to withdraw from the project. As a result, certain of the remaining material has been expanded and Appendix I introduced.

We who have contributed deem it an honor to present these studies to a great colleague and teacher on behalf of his friends and debtors without number throughout the world.

I wish to thank Frank M. Cross, Jr., and David Noel Freedman for special assistance in the preparation of this volume. Particular mention should also be made of Patrick W. Miller, assisted by James S. Ackerman, John S. Holladay, Jr., John G. Janzen, Alan W. Jenks, Werner E. Lemke, and Paul A. Riemann, members of the Old Testament and Near Eastern Languages and Literatures departments of Harvard University, who prepared the index and assisted in the proofreading of the appendices. Nancy R. Lapp, who prepared the Albright bibliography for publication, must also be given special mention.

It is a matter of regret that this volume has been so long in preparation that certain of the chapters were completed long before others. For this reason, and to be fair to the authors, each article is dated.

G. ERNEST WRIGHT

Cambridge, Massachusetts
January 1, 1960

CONTENTS

ABBREVIATIONS

*(except as specially noted
in the footnotes to the various chapters)*

AASOR—*Annual of the American Schools of Oriental Research*
AfO—*Archiv für Orientforschung*
AJSL—*American Journal of Semitic Languages and Literatures*
ANET—J. B. Pritchard, ed., *Ancient Near Eastern Texts* (Princeton, first
    edition, 1950; second edition, 1955).
BASOR—*Bulletin of the American Schools of Oriental Research*
BHT 16—"Geschichte und Altes Testament," *Beiträge zur historischen
    Theologie,* Vol. 16, 1953. Albrecht Alt zum 70. Geburtstag dargebracht.
BJRL—*Bulletin of the John Rylands Library*
BWANT—*Beiträge zur Wissenschaft vom Alten und Neuen Testament*
BZAW—*Beihefte zur Zeitschrift für die Alttestamentliche Wissenschaft*
CBQ—*Catholic Biblical Quarterly*
FSAC—W. F. Albright, *From the Stone Age to Christianity* (Baltimore, first
    edition, 1940; second edition, 1946. Anchor edition of Doubleday & Co.,
    1957).
GKC—*Gesenius' Hebrew Grammar,* edited and enlarged by E. Kautzsch.
    Second English edition tr. and revised in accordance with the 28th
    German edition (1909) by A. E. Cowley (Oxford, 1910).
HK zum AT—W. Nowack, ed., *Handkommentar zum Alten Testament*
HTR—*Harvard Theological Review*
HUCA—*Hebrew Union College Annual*
JAOS—*Journal of the American Oriental Society*
JBL—*Journal of Biblical Literature*
JBR—*Journal of Bible and Religion*
JCS—*Journal of Cuneiform Studies*
JNES—*Journal of Near Eastern Studies*
JPOS—*Journal of the Palestine Oriental Society*
JQR—*Jewish Quarterly Review*
OTMS—H. H. Rowley, ed., *The Old Testament and Modern Study* (Oxford,
    1951)
RA—*Revue d'Assriologie*
RB—*Revue Biblique*
RES—*Revue des études sémitiques*
UH—C. H. Gordon, *Ugaritic Handbook* (Rome 1947)
VT—*Vetus Testamentum*
ZA—*Zeitschrift für Assyriologie*
ZAW—*Zeitschrift für die Alttestamentliche Wissenschaft*
ZDMG—*Zeitschrift der Deutschen Morgenländischen Gesellschaft*
ZDPV—*Zeitschrift für die Deutschen Palästina-Vereins*

THE BIBLE AND THE
ANCIENT NEAR EAST

CHAPTER ONE

Modern Study of
Old Testament Literature

JOHN BRIGHT

IT IS FITTING that a volume prepared in honor of William Foxwell Albright should begin with a chapter on Biblical literature and criticism. For, while it is possible that future generations will remember Professor Albright less as a Biblical critic *sensu stricto* than for his countless contributions to linguistic science, archaeology, and the whole field of ancient Oriental history, it is probable that few men of our times have affected the course of Old Testament studies more profoundly than he. More than this, he has awakened an interest in, and imparted an understanding of, the Bible to the many students who have sat at his feet, as the present writer would like gratefully to testify.

Any attempt to describe in brief compass the course of Biblical criticism over the past thirty-five years must of necessity be selective. It is manifestly impossible to take up the various books of the Bible one by one and to review the history of discussion regarding them. No attempt to do so will be made here. We shall, rather, confine ourselves to a description of some of the more significant trends which have manifested themselves in certain major areas of Old Testament study in the period with which we are concerned. Both because some selection must be made, and because it has always been—and remains— the most crucial battleground of Biblical criticism, the bulk of our remarks will be devoted to recent discussion of the Pentateuch (Hexateuch) problem, with studies that relate to other parts of the Bible drawn in as space allows. By happy coincidence, it is precisely upon the problem of the Hexateuch that the contribution of Professor Albright to Old Testament criticism has made its most decisive impact.

One should begin by warning the reader that it is impossible to make general statements regarding any phase of Biblical criticism today without running the risk of oversimplification. The whole field is in a state of flux.

It is moving, certainly, but it is not always easy to say in what direction. Sometimes it gives the impression that it is moving in several mutually canceling directions at once. Even upon major points there is often little unanimity to be observed. As a result, scarcely a single statement can be made about the state of the field that would not be subject to qualification. Indeed, perhaps the only safe generalization possible is that the critical orthodoxy of a generation ago, with its apparent certainties and assured results, has gone, but that no new consensus has taken its place. Nevertheless, in spite of confusion and disagreement, certain significant trends can perhaps be charted.

I

As regards the Hexateuch problem, one could have spoken thirty-five years ago of a consensus of scholarship. The critical studies of previous generations had erected a massive and seemingly well-tested structure which, though vigorously combated by theological conservatives, and still debated at many points, was accepted in principle by virtually all the scholarly world. In spite of rumblings of discontent which were beginning to make themselves heard, it seemed likely that the structure would stand. All that the future seemed to hold for it was further refinement, testing, and application. As late as 1928 no less a scholar than A. S. Peake could say: "The net result of the recent critical movement, it seems to me, is that we are left in the main very much where we were a quarter of a century ago. Reactionary and radical conclusions still have their representatives, new theories make their appearance from time to time. They probably contain their elements of truth and necessitate minor readjustments. . . . The relative dating of the codes advocated by the Grafians will, I am convinced, remain, and the absolute dating will also, I think, not be seriously altered. And in the other departments of Old Testament criticism I anticipate a similar maintenance of what I may call a central position."[1] As we shall see, this prediction has turned out to be both right and wrong.

The critical orthodoxy of the day rested on two pillars: an analysis of the documents and a theory with regard to the development of Israel's religion. It is important that the two be distinguished, for they do not necessarily hang together. Both had been erected through generations of study and had been joined in classical fashion in the work of J. Wellhausen.[2] The story of development of the Documentary Hypothesis has been told many times and need not be repeated here.[3] The Documentary Hypothesis represented an attempt to account for the variations of style, differences of viewpoint, reduplications of narrative, and the like, to be found in the Hexateuch—phenomena which had been observed as far back as the 17th century. It had its explicit beginnings in the work of Jean Astruc (1753), J. G. Eichhorn (1780–83), and others who had suggested that Genesis at least was composed of two parallel documents. By the second half of the 19th century, after generations of scholarly debate, it was becoming the accepted opinion that four major documents could be discerned running through the first six books of the Bible. Through the work of E. Reuss and his pupil K. H. Graf (1865–66), these had been, in good part on the basis of the development of religion observable in them, arranged in the order to which we are accustomed: J (ninth century), E (eighth century), D (seventh century), P (*ca.* fifth century). This theory of the documents was taken over by Wellhausen from Graf, with generous recognition,[4] and given brilliant vindication.

To the theory of documents there was added at this time, most notably by Wellhausen himself,[5] a reconstruction of the history of Israel's religion. This had its ultimate origin in the philosophy of Hegel as applied to the religion of Israel by certain scholars of the school of W. M. L. De Wette (1780–1849), notably J. F. L. George and W. Vatke.[6] It was held by proponents of this school that an evolutionary pattern was observable in all of human history, and in the history of Israel no less than elsewhere. It was assumed that Israel's religion developed from the most primitive forms to the highest within the Old Testament period, undergoing a fundamental change of character along the way. The religion of the Hebrew ancestors was customarily described as an animism, or polydaemonism which evolved first into a national henotheism and, finally, as a result of the work of the prophets, into the ethical monotheism of the exilic and postexilic periods. The documents of the Hexateuch were ranged along this line of march according to the level of religion exhibited in them: J and E (like the narratives of Judges and Samuel) reflecting the pre-prophetic period; D (and the Deuteronomic histories), the reform activity of the seventh century; P (like Chronicles), the circumstances of the postexilic community. The historical worth of these documents—centuries removed, as they were, from the events of which they purport to tell—was held to be minimal. Indeed they were valued almost exclusively for the light they cast on the beliefs and practices of the respective periods in which they were written, not as sources of information regarding the period of Israel's origins.

This was the theory which dominated Old Testament studies a generation ago. The prevailing intellectual climate, in which philosophies of an evolutionary bias—whether Hegelianism or Positivism or whatnot—were the mode, and in which a general confidence in man's progress was abroad, prepared the way for its victory. To the mind of the day it offered an explanation both of the problem of the Pentateuch and of the history of Israel's religion that seemed reasonable and satisfying. By the early decades of the 20th century the virtual unanimity of scholarship in Europe and America had, in some cases with qualifications, been won over to it. It found embodiment in scores of histories, commentaries, introductions, and handbooks, many of which are still in use today. It is probable that thirty-five years ago few could have believed that it would ever be superseded.

Yet, secure as this critical orthodoxy may have seemed then, forces were already at work which would eventually undermine it. These forces were various, many of them lying beyond the scope of this paper. Not least of them was the fact that the philosophical understructure upon which the whole scheme rested, and which lent to it an aura of self-evidence, fell into discredit. After two total wars and countless other unmentionable horrors, few are left today who would find a melioristic evolution a sufficient explanation of human history—and, by the same token, of Israel's history. Deprived of its philosophical rationale, the critical structure was left vulnerable. Further, within the realm of criticism itself, there was certainly a reaction against the ridiculous extremes to which documentary analysis was sometimes carried, extremes which taxed all credulity and threatened to discredit the whole procedure in the eyes of sober-minded people.[7]

More positively, the amazing access of knowledge regarding the ancient Orient—and Israel—which recent years have brought has served to throw the critical theories of yesterday into question and to show that a revision of them is required so drastic as to amount to virtual abandonment. This is a subject which lies outside our present concern, but mention of it must be made because of its enormous bearing on critical issues.[8] When the founders of Biblical criticism did their work, very little, if anything, was known at first hand of the ancient Orient. The great antiquity of its civilization was not even guessed, the nature of its various cultures and religions scarcely understood at all. It was natural, therefore, for the early critics to view Israel in isolation against a foreshortened perspective, to posit for her earliest period the crudest of beliefs, and so to telescope the entire evolution of religion from primitive forms to ethical monotheism into the space of a very few hundred years. Such a course is, in the light of the data, no longer possible. As the milieu in which Israel began has emerged into day, it has become evident that inherited notions of the nature of her early religion must be revised; such terms as polydaemonism and henotheism are seen not to apply at all. And, what is more to the concern of this paper, it has become plain that the narratives of Israel's origins found in the Hexateuch, far from reflecting the circumstances of those later ages when the documents supposedly were written, reflect precisely—whatever one may say of their historical worth—those of the second millennium B.C. of which they purport to tell. And criticism has, willy-nilly, been forced to take account of this fact.

Further, as Israel's own early history and constitution have been better appreciated, the fallacy of telescoping her religious development into too late a period has been underlined. To mention but one thing, the realization of the place of the tribal league (amphictyony) in the life of early Israel has been of capital importance.[9] No longer can it be assumed, as once was the custom, that Israel was first given unity, and therewith a structure within which an organized cultus and bodies of law could begin to develop, only with the rise of the monarchy. Nor can the notion of covenant be dismissed as a late idea. The tribal league was itself a society founded in Yahweh's covenant; and it was within that league that Israel's distinctive institutions, her cultus and her legal tradition, were given their normative form. And the great traditionary saga of Patriarchs, Exodus, and Conquest, which comprises the bulk of the narrative portions of the Hexateuch, and from which both J and E seem to have drawn their material, was presumably likewise given definitive shape at this time.[10] That insights such as these necessitate revision of inherited notions of the development of Israel's religion goes without saying; but they also have the greatest bearing on the criticism of the Hexateuch as well.

It is generally agreed today, therefore, that a new approach to the Biblical traditions is required. The older critics, it has long been realized, proceeded too largely on the assumption that the Hexateuch was the product of a purely literary activity, which came into being by the editing together of written documents. They conceived their task, therefore, almost exclusively as that of unraveling these various strands that they might study each in isolation. While the possibility was granted by some of them that the documents might contain older material, this recognition was in practice allowed little play; the documents were evaluated as the creations of the ages in which they were written, and this led inevitably to the discounting of their worth as historical sources. But no sooner did new discoveries begin to pour in than it became evident that a new evaluation was in order, for it began to be clear, in the light of parallels, that at least some of the material of the Hexateuch did not originate with the authors of the documents at all, but had been adapted by them from traditions much more ancient. As early as the turn of the century, indeed, certain scholars had begun to turn their interests from documentary analysis to the study of individual units of tradition within the documents. The pioneer was H. Gunkel, who was the first to apply the methods of form criticism to Biblical studies, and who early gave attention to certain traditions in Genesis in the light of Babylonian parallels.[11] He was followed in this by H. Gressmann, who applied similar methods to the study of the traditions of Moses.[12]

It was in the work of these two scholars that the reaction against the conventional criticism may be said to have begun. And as each succeeding year has brought further discoveries, that reaction has gained in intensity. It is today quite evident that to date the documents by no means dates their contents or passes verdict on their value, and that documentary analysis is only the beginning of the critic's task. As one observes, for example, the remarkable way in which the Patriarchal narratives of J and E—though presumably written down in the tenth century and after—reflect conditions that obtained a half millennium or more earlier no other conclusion is possible. Attention must be given, therefore, to the history of the traditions in their pre-literary form. It has become clear that while one may assign to the various documents absolute and relative dates, their material can be ranked in no neat chronological progression, nor can the documents themselves be used to support an equally neat picture of the evolution of Israel's religion. But this has meant that Wellhausenism, in its classical form, has all but ceased to exist, while the Documentary Hypothesis itself has been forcibly placed in a new light.

III

Such a statement, it must be emphasized, by no means implies that the Documentary Hypothesis has been abandoned. It rose independently of the views of Wellhausen and his school and stands or falls independently of them. And, so far at least, it seems in general to have stood. With certain exceptions to be noted, one can say that the virtual unanimity of scholarship still adheres to the classical documents, with those documents ranged in the classical order. Here the prediction of Peake, quoted above, seems in the main to have been correct. Debate has continued lively enough on numerous points of details; but one senses no general tendency to alter the conventional theory in its essentials.

1: For example, the dates of the various documents cannot be said to have been a closed question. Especially as regards D, the early part of our period witnessed a warm agreement on the subject, with the generally accepted date (seventh century) called into question from two sides: by those who would place its composition after the exile, and by those who would push it back to the days of Solomon or before. The former view was pressed by such scholars as G. Hölscher and F. Horst in Germany, R. H. Kennett in England, and G. R. Berry in America.[13] The latter was supported by scholars in Great Britain and on the continent, such as W. Staerk, T. Oestreicher, and A. C. Welch.[14] And more recently, E. Robertson has placed the composition of Deuteronomy as far back as Samuel.[15] But both attacks may be said to have played themselves out without appreciably denting the established position.[16] The postexilic date has won few adherents; the seventh-century date continues the commonly accepted one—but with this concession: it is now quite widely recognized that much of the *material* of D had a long history behind it, possibly reaching back to the legal tradition of the ancient amphictyony as handed down by Levitical circles in northern Israel.[17]

Nor does one note any widespread mood to alter radically the dates conventionally assigned to the other documents. P is still given a postexilic date[18]—though, once again, as we shall see below, it is now commonly agreed that much of its material is centuries older. In the case of J, conventionally dated in the ninth century, one notes a tacit agreement on the part of an increasing number of scholars to place its composition in the tenth century, before the death of Solomon.[19] E is still usually placed a bit later than J,[20] though it has frequently been pointed out that the material of E is in many cases more archaic than that of J.[21] On the relationship of J and E one can record little agreement, with some holding them to be independent of one another,[22] others regarding E as a tradition dependent on J,[23] and still others holding that both go back to a common body of tradition.[24] But these disagreements, it will readily be seen, are minor ones and represent no drastic alteration of the theory of documents as conventionally held.

2: Debate has also continued with regard to the extent of the various documents, so much so that one can speak of no consensus. But it must be said again that none of this aims at an abandonment of the Documentary Hypothesis, upon which there is general agreement, but only at its further refinement. For example, the documents J, E, and P, conventionally traced through Joshua, have been extended by not a few through Judges and Samuel, and even into Kings.[25] Equally as many, however, would argue that the material of these latter books is drawn from special sources.[26] At the other extremity, there has been the attempt to extend E, usually begun in Genesis 15, backward into the primeval history of Genesis 1–11.[27] Of far more sweeping significance have been the arguments of M. Noth, which in the writer's view are fundamentally sound, to the effect that J, E, and P extend only through Genesis-Numbers, while in Deuteronomy-Kings we have a great historical work based on the Deuteronomic law—which is incorporated in it—tracing the history of Israel from Moses to the fall of Jerusalem. We should, therefore, for critical purposes at least, no longer speak of a Hexateuch or even of a Pentateuch, but of a Tetrateuch and a Deuteronomic corpus.[28]

The last thirty-five years have also seen several attempts to isolate yet other documents than the conventional ones. With some scholars, indeed, a five-document theory has replaced the usual four-document one. The feeling that there are two strata in J (J^1 and J^2) is not new; it was elaborately developed in the work of R. Smend in 1912,[29] and has since been taken up by a number of scholars. In more recent years a number of attempts have been made to find within this material a fifth separate source. Among these have been that of O. Eissfeldt, who traces, mostly in the material assigned to J^1, a source L (Lay Source) running from Genesis 2 to the death of David; that of J. Morgenstern, who finds a source K (Kenite) extending from the birth of Moses to the beginning of Judges, which he believes to have been the basis of Asa's reform and to date to the early ninth century; and that of R. H. Pfeiffer, who finds a source S (Seir) in parts of Genesis which he believes was first composed in Edom in the tenth century.[30] It is interesting that both Morgenstern's K and Pfeiffer's S overlap in good part Eissfeldt's L, which indicates a measure of agreement among these scholars. So far as one can judge, however, none of these proposals has commanded a wide following. Perhaps this is because though there is no doubt material in J that sits loosely there, it is so fragmentary that it can be assembled into a separate document only if one posits that large portions of it have been lost. Perhaps it is better to reckon with strata in the transmission of the material of J before it received fixed written form, or with the supplementation of that document with further material from living traditions. And perhaps the same may be said of the strands which some scholars have found within P.[31]

IV

But though the Documentary Hypothesis continues to command general acceptance, it must be said that there has been a reaction against it. With some, this seems to be no more than an attempted corrective of the more absurd extremes of documentary analysis; with others it announces itself as a rebellion against literary criticism as such. While it does not seem at the moment that any such tendencies are going to sweep the scholarly world, one senses at the same time, even among adherents of the conventional criticism, a certain loss of interest in documentary analysis, a feeling that it has been pushed quite as far as it will go and that the future of Old Testament studies does not lie along the lines of a further refinement of it.

1: Such a trend manifested itself in Germany between the wars in the work of P. Volz and, to a lesser degree, of W. Rudolph.[32] The former, who confined his examination to Genesis 15–35, concluded that both E and P should be dismissed as independent narrative documents. We have here, he held, only one narrative, that of J. The so-called E represents no more than a new editing of J; and P likewise added no new narrative, but, at the most, further edited J. One can see that this, as far as Genesis is concerned, is in effect an abandonment of the hypothesis of documents for one of supplements. Rudolph, who worked independently and subsequently carried his studies through the rest of the Hexateuch, agreed with Volz regarding E, while holding that P is an independent document. In effect, he retained the Documentary Hypothesis, but reduced the number of documents by one. It must be said, however, that Volz and Rudolph seem to have gained little following,[33] most scholars apparently feeling that the material of E is sufficiently distinctive to be called a separate source, though admittedly great parts of it have not been preserved. As for P, it is difficult to deny its separate identity.

2: Another scholar to announce his abandonment of the Documentary Hypothesis in its conventional form is J. Pedersen.[34] Pedersen does not, up to a point, deny the validity of the source-critical method. Though he refuses to regard J and E as parallel narratives (to do so is to misunderstand the ways of ancient narrators), he concedes that bodies of material corresponding to the symbols JE, D, and P are to be found in the Hexateuch and can be isolated. But to range these in chronological order as is usually done is, he holds, impossible, for all contain material both early and late. P is indeed postexilic, but many of its laws are centuries older; D *may* contain laws that reflect the cultic struggle of the seventh century, but it, too, gained final form after the exile; and even JE, though most of its material is very old, likewise contains touches that hint of a later age. In other words, the documents can be isolated; but they do not lie in chronological sequence, but parallel. That this signals a radical break with an evolutionary interpretation of Israel's religion is certain, and is so stated by Pedersen himself. Whether it also serves to rob the history of that religion of all motion and to reduce it to a flat-surface phenomenological description is another question.[35]

3: By far the most sweeping attack on the conventional criticism has been launched by the Uppsala School in Sweden, particularly by I. Engnell.[36] Our concern here is not with Engnell's views with regard to cult and ritual, which owe much to the so-called "Myth and Ritual School" in Great Britain and to S. Mowinckel's work on the Psalms,[37] but with his attack on the problem of the Hexateuch. And here Engnell not only rejects Wellhausenist notions of the evolution of Israel's religion but, going far beyond the positions of Volz and Pedersen outlined above, announces his break with the Documentary Hypothesis itself. Like H. S. Nyberg and others before him,[38] he assigns a major role to oral tradition in the transmission of the Biblical material. As for the Pentateuch, save for much of the legal material, most of it was transmitted orally until the postexilic period, when it gradually found written fixation. To try to trace parallel documents through the Pentateuch is to impose our modern Western notions upon a literature which is neither modern nor Western. Variant accounts, repetitions, and the like in these books are to be explained by the "law of iteration," or repetition, in oral transmission. Like Noth, Engnell separates the Tetrateuch (Genesis-Numbers) from the Deuteronomic corpus (Deuteronomy-Kings). In the former we have what may, for want of a better name, be called a "P-work," in the latter a "D-work." But D and P do not stand for documents, but as symbols for the traditionary circles which brought these works, respectively, to final form. To separate a J and an E within the "P-work" by literary-critical methods is impossible. Material corresponding to these symbols may be observed there, but it represents no more than strata of tradition already so fused in the oral stage of transmission that a separation of them cannot be carried out.

This is not the place to attempt a critique of this position.[39] But one senses that, though it furnishes a healthy corrective to the excessive niceties of the conventional criticism, most scholars outside the immediate circle of Uppsala seem to feel that it carries matters too far. To be sure, oral tradition deserves more stress than the older critics accorded it, for, after all, all the early traditions of Israel arose orally in the first instance and were transmitted orally for a greater or lesser period of time; and, even after written form had been imparted, oral transmission continued side by side with it, supplementing, combining, and reshaping. But is not oral tradition given too exclusive a role here? Writing was, after all, known throughout the entire history of Israel, and it is unbelievable that the tradition did not in many cases attain a written form far earlier than Engnell seems to think. And are not his protests against

Wellhausenism directed against a view of Israel's religion to which almost no one adheres any more? And has Engnell gotten rid of source criticism, or merely moved it into another area and given it a new name? If material corresponding to the symbols D and P (and, by subtraction, to JE) can be found, does not the task of separating it still remain, whether one calls it literary criticism or not? While it is still too early to assess the effect of the Uppsala position on Hexateuch studies, one may venture to doubt that it will cause the majority of scholars to abandon the Documentary Hypothesis, however much it may constrain them to modify their understanding of it.

v

Yet, if the Documentary Hypothesis still commands acceptance, it must be repeated that stress in current research no longer falls upon literary criticism,[40] but upon the history of the individual units of tradition before they found their way into their present position in the various documents. In other words, the approach forecast by Gunkel and his school, now allowed new possibilities by the access of linguistic and archaeological data, has continued to be developed and broadened. The schools of A. Alt and of Albright himself have been especially active in this regard. And, while one cannot speak of a unanimity of results, the effect has been to push a vast quantity of material, even in the latest documents—poems, lists, laws, and narratives—back to a *Sitz im Leben* in the early periods of Israel's history. And this, it need hardly be said, has made a much more affirmative picture of early Israel, her institutions and religion, possible.

So numerous have such studies been that only a few examples can be given here. The work of Alt and Noth on certain of the lists in Joshua 13–19, commonly assigned to P and once regarded as postexilic and historically worthless, has been especially fruitful.[41] These scholars showed that the border lists of the tribes (Joshua 15:1–12; 18:12–20, etc.) have their origin in, and authentically reflect, the period before the rise of the monarchy.[42] Alt also dated the city lists in the same chapters (e.g. Joshua 15:21–62) to the reign of Josiah,[43] but a more recent study by F. M. Cross and G. E. Wright makes it likely that these go back to the ninth century, with the system itself possibly older yet.[44] In like manner, Albright has ably demonstrated that the list of Levitic cities in Joshua 21, though cast in the framework of P, had its origin in the days of the united monarchy.[45] New evidence is also making it plain that not only the lists but certain of the narratives of P are likewise of most ancient origin.[46] As studies of this sort pile up, it is becoming increasingly difficult not to believe that the bulk of the material of P is of pre-exilic, even of quite ancient, origin.

Form-critical studies of the various bodies of law in the Pentateuch have been equally significant. The notion that Israel's legal tradition was a relatively late development has long been untenable—indeed has been since the discovery of the Code of Hammurabi in 1901, and now *a fortiori* with the addition of the yet older laws of Lipit-Ishtar, Eshnunna, and Ur-nammu, to say nothing of the Assyrian and Hittite codes. It early began, therefore, to be suspected that many of the laws of the Book of the Covenant (Exodus 21–23) go back to Mosaic days if not before.[47] The fundamental study of Alt, which applied form-critical methods, was epoch-making in this regard.[48] Separating the laws according to form into the categories "apodictic" and "casuistic," Alt reasoned that the latter, abundantly paralleled in other ancient codes, represented laws taken over by Israel after her settlement in Palestine; while the former, which he found without parallel, represented Israel's own peculiar contribution. The later study of H. Cazelles,[49] likewise based on form-critical analysis, even placed the Book of the Covenant in the Mosaic or immediately post-Mosaic period. While all might not be willing to go so far, there seems to be a growing agreement, especially as the early amphictyony and the place of law in it is better understood, that the legal tradition of Israel had its roots in that amphictyony, not in some later period.

In this connection, too, mention should be made of a penetrating study by G. E. Mendenhall of the covenant forms in the Biblical tradition in which, among other things, striking formal similarities are pointed out between the structure of the Decalogue and that of certain Hittite suzerainty treaties.[50] The conclusions of this study seem, at least to the writer, to have important bearing both on the date of the Decalogue and on our entire understanding of the constitution and faith of early Israel. As for the Decalogue, while one cannot speak of any unanimity regarding its date today, one senses that more scholars are ready to place it in the earliest period than once was the case.[51] It is probable, too, that fewer and fewer scholars would argue, as once was customary, that the law codes of the Pentateuch lie in a straight-line development, with the laws of D growing out of those of the Covenant Code, and those of P in turn out of those of D. On the contrary, it is increasingly recognized that not only does the Covenant Code express the legal tradition of the amphictyony but the laws of D—whatever the date of that document's composition—likewise reach back to that tradition, probably as transmitted in northern Israelite circles;[52] while the laws of P, though preserved in a post-exilic form, reflect the cultic tradition of Jerusalem which, via the temple and the tent-shrine of David, itself goes back ultimately to the amphictyony. The various bodies of law, therefore, represent less a straight line of evolution than parallel developments of an ancient tradition.

Important studies have also been made of certain poems in the Pentateuch and elsewhere in the light of the new linguistic evidence from the Ras Shamra texts. Professor Albright and certain of his pupils have been especially active in this regard. If their conclusions are to be accepted—and the writer is prepared to do so—quite a number of poems, some of them formerly regarded as quite late, are now to be placed in Israel's earliest period (tenth century and before). Among these are: the Balaam poems of Numbers 23–24, the Blessing of Moses (Deuteronomy 33), the Song of Miriam (Exodus 15:1–18), and parts of the Psalm of Habakkuk, as well as certain of the psalms in the Psalter (e.g. Psalms 29, 68).[53] Add these, and others, to those poems commonly conceded to be of early date (e.g., Judges 5; Genesis 49; Joshua 10:12 f.; II Samuel 1:19–27, etc.), and quite a respectable body of literature becomes available for the study of earliest Israel's beliefs at first hand. Some have, to be sure, vigorously criticized the whole method employed here.[54] But, while it is yet too early to see what the full implications of such studies will be, and while of course extravagant claims are not in order, there indeed appear to be fruitful possibilities for future research in this area.

VI

Aside from studies such as the foregoing, which represent but a sampling of those that could be mentioned, the last few years have witnessed several significant attempts to apply the methods of form criticism, not merely to shorter units of tradition but to the whole field of tradition history: in other words, to write the history of the traditions before they reached normative written form in the documents. Of these, two may be singled out: those of von Rad and Noth.

Von Rad, whose views are developed in a series of works,[55] finds the basic theme of the Hexateuch already adumbrated in certain cultic credos which he isolated within the Deuteronomic work (Deuteronomy 26:5–9; 6:20–24; Joshua 24:2–13), and which he assigns to Israel's earliest period. It was the Yahwist (J), however, who placed his stamp on the entire Hexateuch. He it was who filled out the *schema* of the old cultic credo with a host of traditions and blocks of traditions known to him, adding to the whole the Sinai traditions (which had had a separate history), filling out the Patriarchal traditions, and placing at the beginning his account of primeval history (in Genesis 2–11). The Yahwist thus gave the Hexateuch its definitive shape, a shape not essentially altered by the addition of the material of E and P. Whatever may be said of von Rad's work—and this is no place to attempt a criticism—his isolating of the ancient credos and his finding in them the major theme of the Hexateuch's theology is of the profoundest consequence for the understanding of the faith of early Israel.

The work of Noth is on an even more ambitious scale.[56] Noth finds in the Pentateuch five major themes, all of which were present in the tradition from which both J and E derived, thus in the period of the Judges. These themes, he believes, represent traditionary blocks, each of which had its separate development through a complex history of transmission, until finally all were gradually linked together in the normative traditions of the amphictyony. He sees it as his task, by a rigid application of form-critical method, to trace each of these themes to its most original element, and then to describe the way in which it was filled out to its present form. Again, this is not the place for criticism.[57] But, though Noth's work is a masterpiece of logical erudition and contains much of lasting value, one feels that it exceeds the objective data and presses form-critical methods beyond their rightful limits. Its evaluation of the historical worth of the traditions is extremely negative, as is its view of the function of archaeological data as a possible control upon them. It raises the question if, just as literary criticism reached limits of nicety beyond which it could not go without subjectivism, similar limits do not impose themselves on the tracing of the history of tradition in its predocumentary form.

To sum up, it is evident that criticism has come a long way from the position of thirty-five years ago. While the Documentary Hypothesis continues to be held, it is clear that it can no longer be used as a support for the neatly evolving picture of Israel's faith found in earlier treatments of the subject. None of the documents represents a free composition, the contents of which can be dated at a fixed point in Israel's history. Or, to put it otherwise, the documents themselves can be so fixed, but their material has been torn loose from the neat chronological scheme almost altogether. What the future of Hexateuchal criticism will be, none can say. But it is safe to predict that the present interest in the individual units of tradition, in so far as this is followed with objective methodological control, gives promise of an ever better understanding of the history and institutions of early Israel.

VII

Want of space forbids more than a few general remarks regarding current criticism of other parts of the Old Testament. Here, too, much of interest has taken place as trends somewhat parallel to those noted above have run their course.

1: As for the prophetic books, the situation is not what it was thirty-five years ago when classical Wellhausenism, as exemplified in the works of such critics as B. Duhm and K. Marti, controlled their interpretation.[58] It was then the custom to view the prophets as the great pioneers of Israel's faith who, by their attack on ethical abuses and the worship of false gods, prepared the way for ethical monotheism. They were commonly thought to have been irreconcilably hostile to the cult. Under the influence of evolutionary notions, which posited that the more refined an idea, the later it must be, passages of an eschatological or universalistic nature—and, by the more extreme critics, passages reflecting hope of whatever sort—were customarily deleted from the books of the pre-exilic prophets as postexilic additions. The task of the critic was seen primarily as one of separating the genuine words of the prophet from the handiwork of later annotators and editors. Since material was often excised with a high hand because it fitted poorly in its context, or because of allegedly inferior style, or because its ideas were conceived to be unworthy of, or too advanced for, the prophet in question, the result was not infrequently a shredding of the prophetic books.[59]

In saying that fashions have changed, one must not create the impression that there has been a uniform trend toward conservatism. In some areas— Ezekiel, for example—a radical criticism unknown thirty-five years ago has manifested itself, though one hopes that saner counsels will prevail.[60] Nevertheless, one senses, overall, a far more constructive approach to the prophets than formerly was the case. As the Wellhausenist view of Israel's religion has lost ground, and as a more positive understanding of early Israel's faith and constitution has been gained, together with an appreciation of the role of the earlier prophets as representatives of the amphictyonic tradition, a new evaluation of the work of the prophets has resulted. One sees them no longer as pioneers but as reformers. As the relationship of the prophetic orders to the cult has been better understood,[61] a re-examination of the relevant passages has been forced and the prophetic criticism of the cult placed in a more balanced perspective. Further, as the element of promise indigenous to Israel's faith has been appreciated, and the importance of the cult as a seed bed of eschatological notions understood,[62] there is less and less disposition to relegate all passages expressing Messianic notions, or hope of whatever sort, to a late date. Finally, a closer attention to the literary forms of prophetic address, together with a grasp of the role of oral tradition in the transmission of their oracles, has issued in a decidedly more conservative approach to the text of these books and a greater reluctance to indulge in reckless excisions on the basis of style alone.[63]

2: In few areas have the last thirty-five years brought more sweeping changes than in the criticism of the Psalms—a subject that deserves far fuller treatment than is possible here.[64] In an earlier day, scholars were concerned to relate the various Psalms to the historical situations that presumably first gave rise to them. Since indices of this sort in the Psalter are few and vague, this turned out to be a futile endeavor, and one productive only of complete disagreement, so that a given Psalm might be assigned by equally competent scholars to dates at opposite ends of Israel's history. But since the level of religion in the Psalms seemed to the classical critics for the most part to be too advanced for an earlier period, the tendency was to relegate more and more of them to dates beyond the exile, until it became the fashion to place virtually all of them there, with a number even as late as the Maccabean period.[65]

The last generation, however, has witnessed no less than a revolution. The author of it was first and foremost H. Gunkel, who applied form-critical methods to the study of the Psalms, classifying them into various types and studying the *Sitz im Leben* from which these sprang.[66] Gunkel's work marked such a turning point that one may divide all study of the Psalms into pre- and post-Gunkel phases. There has been no worth-while commentary since his that has not built upon the approach which he developed. Scarcely less important has been the work of S. Mowinckel who, whatever one may think of his theories regarding the so-called enthronement festival, showed clearly the rootage of the Psalms in the cult of pre-exilic Israel.[67] The fashion of regarding the Psalms as largely postexilic has all but vanished; to date any of them in the Maccabean period seems little short of impossible. The bulk of them are of pre-exilic origin, and some of them are very archaic indeed. So understood, the Psalms now assume capital importance for the understanding of the cult and religion of Israel under the monarchy. That this requires many a revision of older notions of the development of Israel's faith goes without saying.

We may conclude our remarks with a reiteration of the statement with which we began. Old Testament criticism today is in a state of flux, a period of adjustment to new data and new insights. The old critical consensus has gone, without as yet having been replaced by any new one. Yet the observer may well find himself optimistic. In spite of clashes of opinion, in spite of blind alleys into which criticism has now and then strayed, one senses on every hand a tendency toward a more balanced evaluation of the literature than was the rule thirty-five years ago, a more realistic understanding of how that literature arose and, withal, a more constructive use of it as a tool for recreating the life and faith of ancient Israel. The consequences of all this for the study of Israel's history, and of Old Testament theology, lie outside the province of this paper—but they are enormous.

Richmond; January 1, 1957

NOTES TO CHAPTER ONE

1. A. S. Peake, "Recent Developments in Old Testament Criticism" (*BJRL* 12 [1928] pp. 3–30) p. 28 f. Peake referred, of course, primarily to the Documentary Hypothesis, not to the reconstruction of Israel's religion set forth by Wellhausen and others.
2. J. Wellhausen, *Geschichte Israels,* I (Berlin, 1878), Eng. tr. by Black and Menzies, *Prolegomena to the History of Israel* (Edinburgh, 1885; reprinted by Meridian Books, New York, 1957).
3. The fullest recent treatment is H. J. Kraus, *Geschichte der historisch-kritischen Erforschung des Alten Testaments* (Neukirchen, 1956); even fuller is H. Holzinger, *Einleitung in den Hexateuch* (Freiburg & Leipzig, 1893); in English, cf. Carpenter & Harford, *The Composition of the Hexateuch* (London, 1902); briefer and more popular, J. Coppens, *The Old Testament and the Critics,* Eng. tr. by E. A. Ryan & E. W. Tribbe (Patterson, N. J., 1942).
4. Cf. Wellhausen, op. cit. p. 3 f.
5. Not only by him, however; cf., for example, A. Kuenen, *De Godsdienst van Israel* (1869–70), Eng. tr. 1874–75 (3 vols., London & Edinburgh, 1882–83); B. Stade,

Biblische Theologie des Alten Testaments (2 vols., Tübingen, 1905, 1911); B. Duhm, *Die Theologie der Propheten* (Bonn, 1873); etc.

6. See Wellhausen's own acknowledgment, op. cit. pp. 4, 14.

7. As an extreme example, cf. the commentary of P. Baentsch on Leviticus (*HK zum AT*, Göttingen, 1900), where one will find seven subdivisions in P alone, plus numerous sub-subdivisions and redactors. Cf. C. R. North, *The Old Testament and Modern Study*, H. H. Rowley, ed. (Oxford, 1951), p. 56, on the point.

8. It is precisely here that Professor Albright's greatest contribution to Biblical studies has been made. For a synthesis of his views, see *FSAC;* also, *Archaeology and the Religion of Israel* (Baltimore, 3 ed., 1953); in briefer and preliminary form, "The Ancient Near East and the Religion of Israel" (*JBL* LIX [1940], pp. 85–112).

9. Cf. especially M. Noth, *Das System der zwölf Stämme Israels* (Stuttgart, 1930).

10. Cf. M. Noth, *Überlieferungsgeschichte des Pentateuchs* (Stuttgart, 1948), pp. 1–44.

11. Cf. H. Gunkel, *Schöpfung und Chaos in Urzeit und Endzeit* (Göttingen, 1895); idem, *Genesis* (*HK zum AT*, 1901; 3 ed., 1922).

12. Cf. H. Gressmann, *Mose und seine Zeit* (Göttingen, 1913). Gressmann also made available for comparative purposes a valuable collection of ancient texts and pictures of material remains: *Altorientalische Texte und Bilder zum Alten Testament* (2 vols., Berlin and Leipzig, 2 ed., 1926–27).

13. Cf. G. Hölscher, "Komposition und Ursprung des Deuteronominus" (*ZAW* 40 [1922], pp. 161–255); F. Horst, "Die Anfänge des Propheten Jeremia" (*ZAW* 41 [1923], pp. 94–153); idem, "Die Kultusreform des Königs Josia (II Rg. 22–3)" (*ZDMG* 77 [1923], pp. 220–38); R. H. Kennett, *Deuteronomy and the Decalogue* (Cambridge, 1920); G. R. Berry, "The Code Found in the Temple" (*JBL* XXXIX [1920], pp. 44–51); idem, "The Date of Deuteronomy" (*JBL* LIX [1940], pp. 133–39). For full bibliography on the question and discussion, cf. H. H. Rowley, "The Prophet Jeremiah and the Book of Deuteronomy" (*Studies in Old Testament Prophecy,* H. H. Rowley, ed. [Edinburgh, 1950], pp. 157–74).

14. Cf. T. Oestreicher, *Das deuteronomische Grundgesetz* (1923); W. Staerk, *Das Problem des Deuteronomiums* (1924)—books to which I have no access (but cf. Oestreicher, *ZAW* 43 [1925], pp. 246–49); also, A. C. Welch, *The Code of Deuteronomy* (New York and London, 1924); idem, *Deuteronomy, the Framework of the Code* (London, 1932).

15. E. Robertson, *The Old Testament Problem* (Manchester, 1950).

16. Cf. the symposium in *JBL* XLVII (1928), pp. 305–79 for a resumé of the arguments, with J. A. Bewer presenting the case for the early date, L. B. Paton for the late, and G. Dahl for the commonly accepted one.

17. Cf. especially G. von Rad, *Deuteronomium-Studien* (Göttingen, 2 ed., 1948), Eng. tr. *Studies in Deuteronomy* (London, 1953); also G. E. Wright, *Deuteronomy* (*Interpreter's Bible,* Vol. II, New York & Nashville, 1953).

18. Y. Kaufmann is an exception to this statement: cf. "Probleme der israelitisch-jüdischen Religionsgeschichte" (*ZAW* 48 [1930], pp. 22–43), idem, "Das Kalender und das Alter des Priesterkodex" (*VT* IV [1954], pp. 307–313). But Kaufmann seems to confuse the question of the origin of P's material with that of the date of P itself.

19. I know of no full-length discussion of this point, but one sees it assumed in one treatment after another: to mention only a few, cf. M. Noth, op. cit. (in n. 10), pp. 40–44; G. von Rad, *Das Erste Buch Mose* (*Das AT Deutsch,* Göttingen, 1949, 1952), p. 16 f.; G. E. Wright, *God Who Acts* (London, 1952), p. 73. I find myself in agreement with this.

20. E. Sellin, however, put E also in the tenth century: cf. *Introduction to the Old Testament,* Eng. tr. W. Montgomery (New York, 1923), pp. 55 f., 66.

21. E.g., R. Kittel, *Geschichte des Volkes Israel,* Vol. ɪ (Stuttgart, 7th ed., 1932), pp. 249–59; Noth, ibid., p. 40, n. 143.

22. Recently, with caution, A. Bentzen, *Introduction to the Old Testament,* Vol. ɪɪ (Copenhagen, 1948), pp. 48 ff.

23. E.g., S. Mowinckel, "Der Ursprung der Bil'amsage" (*ZAW* 48 [1930], pp. 233–71); E. Jacob, *La Tradition historique en Israël* (Montpellier, 1946), pp. 118–21, whose position approaches that of Volz (see below).

24. E.g., Kittel, ibid.; Noth, ibid., pp. 40–44; Albright, *FSAC,* p. 183 (Anchor ed., p. 241). I should myself side with this view.

25. E.g., O. Eissfeldt, *Einleitung in das Alte Testament* (Tübingen, 1934), pp. 288–340; G. Hölscher, *Die Anfänge der hebräischen Geschichtsschreibung* (1942)—a work which I know only through Eissfeldt's critical review, *Geschichtsschreibung im Alten Testament* (Berlin, 1948).

26. E.g., L. Rost, *Die Überlieferung von der Thronnachfolge Davids* (*BWANT,* ɪɪɪ:6. 1926); H. M. Wiener, *The Composition of Judges II, 11 to I Kings II, 46* (Leipzig, 1929).

27. Cf. S. Mowinckel, *The Two Sources of the Predeuteronomic Primeval History (JE) in Gen. 1–11* (Oslo, 1937); Hölscher, loc. cit.

28. Cf. M. Noth, *Überlieferungsgeschichtliche Studien I* (Halle, 1943). I. Engnell has adopted a similar position; cf. below.

29. R. Smend, *Die Erzählung des Hexateuchs* (Leipzig, 1912)—a work I have never seen. Smend was not, however, the first to believe that J is composite.

30. Cf. O Eissfeldt, *Einleitung in das Alte Testament* and, in more detail, *Hexateuch-Synopse* (Leipzig, 1922)—a work to which I do not have access at present; J. Morgenstern, "The Oldest Document of the Hexateuch," *HUCA* ɪᴠ (1927), pp. 1–138; R. H. Pfeiffer, "A Non-Israelite Source of the Book of Genesis," *ZAW* 48 (1930), pp. 66–73; idem, *Introduction to the Old Testament* (New York, 1941), pp. 159–67.

31. E.g., G. von Rad, *Die Priesterschrift im Hexateuch* (*BWANT,* 4 Folge, xɪɪɪ [1934], who finds a P^A and a P^B, plus other material. That P is not a unitary composition is widely recognized: e.g., Noth, op. cit. (in n. 28), pp. 180–216 and table on p. 217.

32. P. Volz and W. Rudolph, *Der Elohist als Erzähler: Ein Irrweg der Pentateuchkritik?* (*BZAW* 63 [1933]); W Rudolph, *Der "Elohist" von Exodus bis Josua* (*BZAW* 68 [1938]).

33. E. Jacob, op. cit. (in n. 23), pp. 118–21 seems to be one of the few exceptions, at least as far as E is concerned. See the criticisms of Volz and Rudolph in Noth, op. cit. (in n. 10), p. 23 f.

34. Cf. J. Pedersen, "Die Auffassung vom Alten Testament," *ZAW* 49 [1931], pp. 161–81; idem., "Passahfest und Passahlegende," *ZAW* 52 [1934], pp. 161–75. The same views are reflected in his *opus magnum, Israel: Its Life and Culture* (4 vols. in 2, Copenhagen, 1926, 1940).

35. Cf. the trenchant criticism of C. R. North in *The Old Testament and Modern Study* (H. H. Rowley, ed.), pp. 76 ff.

36. The bulk of Engnell's output (all, so far as I know, that bears on the Hexateuch problem) is in Swedish and, therefore, known to me at second hand. Cf. the summary and criticism of C. R. North, ibid., pp. 63–82; G. W. Anderson, "Some Aspects of the Uppsala School of Old Testament Study," *HTR* 43 [1950], pp. 239–56. Engnell's comparative method may be grasped from his *Studies in Divine Kingship in the Ancient Near East* (Uppsala, 1943); for a sample of his method with a Biblical text, see *The Call of Isaiah* (Uppsala, 1949).

37. Cf. S. H. Hooke, ed., *Myth and Ritual* (London, 1933); idem, ed. *The Labyrinth* (London, 1935); S. Mowinckel, *Psalmenstudien,* ɪɪ and ɪɪɪ (Oslo, 1922, 1923).

38. H. S. Nyberg, *Studien zum Hoseabuche* (Uppsala, 1935).

39. Cf. that of C. R. North, ibid.

40. This is not, again, to say that certain very recent works have not carried on the task of literary criticism in the old-fashioned manner; cf., e.g., C. A. Simpson, *The Early Traditions of Israel* (Oxford, 1948).

41. E.g., A. Alt, "Das System der Stammesgrenzen im Buche Josua" (1927), now reprinted in *Kleine Schriften zur Geschichte des Volkes Israel* (2 vols. [Munich, 1953], Vol. I, pp. 193–202); M. Noth, "Studien zu den historisch-geographischen Dokumenten des Josuabuchs," *ZDPV* LVIII (1935), pp. 185–255.

42. Contested, I think unsuccessfully, by S. Mowinckel, *Zur Frage nach dokumentarischen Quellen in Josua 13–19* (Oslo, 1946).

43. A. Alt, "Judas Gaue unter Josia" (1925), now reprinted op. cit. (in n. 41), Vol. II, pp. 276–88.

44. F. M. Cross and G. E. Wright, "The Boundary and Province Lists of the Kingdom of Judah," *JBL* LXXV (1956), pp. 202–26.

45. W. F. Albright, "The List of Levitic Cities," *Louis Ginzberg Jubilee Volume* (New York, 1945), pp. 49–73.

46. E.g., the work of M. R. Lehmann on Gen. 23: "Abraham's Purchase of Machpelah and Hittite Law," *BASOR* 129 (1953), pp. 15–18.

47. Cf., for example, L. Waterman, "Pre-Israelite Laws in the Book of the Covenant," *AJSL* XXXVIII (1921/22), pp. 36–54; A. Jepsen, *Untersuchungen zum Bundesbuch* (*BWANT,* 3 Folge, V [1927]).

48. A. Alt, *Die Ursprünge des israelitischen Rechts* (1934; see now op. cit. [in n. 41], Vol. I, pp. 278–332).

49. H. Cazelles, *Études sur le Code de L'Alliance* (Paris, 1946).

50. G. E. Mendenhall, *Law and Covenant in Israel and in the Ancient Near East* (Pittsburgh, The Biblical Colloquium, 1955).

51. For a summary of discussion and arguments for a Mosaic date, with full bibliography, cf. H. H. Rowley, "Moses and the Decalogue," *BJRL* 34 (1951), pp. 81–118.

52. Cf. especially the works in n. 17 above.

53. Cf. W. F. Albright, "The Oracles of Balaam," *JBL* LXIII (1944), pp. 207–33; F. M. Cross and D. N. Freedman, "The Blessing of Moses," *JBL* LXVII (1948), pp. 191–210; idem, "The Song of Miriam," *JNES* XIV (1955), pp. 237–50; Albright, "The Psalm of Habakkuk," *Studies in Old Testament Prophecy,* pp. 1–18; T. H. Gaster, "Psalm 29," *JQR* XXXVII (1946–47), pp. 55–63; Albright, "A Catalog of Early Hebrew Lyric Poems," *HUCA* XXIII (1950–51), pp. 1–39.

54. Notably S. Mowinckel; cf. *VT* V (1955), pp. 13–33; idem, *Der Achtundsechzigste Psalm* (Oslo, 1953).

55. Especially G. von Rad, *Das Formgeschichtliche Problem des Hexateuchs* (*BWANT* IV:26 [1938]); cf. also the works of von Rad cited in notes 17 and 19 above. For a summary in English, cf. G. E. Wright, *JBR* XVIII (1950), pp. 216–25.

56. M. Noth, *Überlieferungsgeschichte des Pentateuchs* (op. cit. in n. 10).

57. Cf. my work, *Early Israel in Recent History Writing* (London, 1956); also Albright, *BASOR* 74 (1939), pp. 11–23.

58. For a fuller review of recent trends than is possible here, the reader may be referred to the article of O. Eissfeldt in *The Old Testament and Modern Study,* (H. H. Rowley, ed.), pp. 115–61.

59. Cf., for example, B. Duhm, *Das Buch Jeremia* (*KHC;* Leipzig and Tübingen, 1901), who found roughly two thirds of that book non-genuine.

60. For a survey of discussion here, with bibliography, cf. H. H. Rowley, "The Book of Ezekiel in Modern Study," *BJRL* 36 (1953), pp. 146–90.

61. E.g., A. R. Johnson, *The Cultic Prophet in Ancient Israel* (Cardiff, 1944). But this insight must not be pushed to the point of making the great prophets cultic functionaries, or of obscuring the uniqueness of prophetism in Israel: so A. Haldar, *Associations of Cult Prophets among the Ancient Semites* (Uppsala, 1945).

62. The work of S. Mowinckel has been especially influential: recently, *He That Cometh*, Eng. tr. G. W. Anderson (Oxford, New York and Nashville, 1956).

63. Cf. H. S. Nyberg, op. cit. (in n. 38); H. Birkeland, *Zum hebräischen Traditionswesen* (Oslo, 1938); S. Mowinckel, *Prophecy and Tradition* (Oslo, 1946); and especially G. Widengren, *Literary and Psychological Aspects of the Hebrew Prophets* (Uppsala, 1948).

64. Cf. the sketch of A. R. Johnson in *The Old Testament and Modern Study*, pp. 162–209.

65. Classically in the commentary of B. Duhm, *Die Psalmen* (*KHC;* Freiburg, Leipzig and Tübingen, 1899).

66. Cf. H. Gunkel, *Ausgewählte Psalmen* (Göttingen, 2 ed., 1905); idem, *Die Psalmen* (Göttingen, 1926); and H. Gunkel and J. Begrich, *Einleitung in die Psalmen* (Göttingen, 1933).

67. Cf. S. Mowinckel, op. cit. (in n. 37); also H. Schmidt, *Die Psalmen* (Tübingen, 1934).

CHAPTER TWO

Biblical History in
Transition

GEORGE E. MENDENHALL

THE FREQUENCY with which scholars have published surveys of "the present state of Biblical studies" since the close of World War I is a good indication of the changes which have taken place in the field. Whatever else may be said of the field of Biblical history and religion, any charge that it is stagnant would be least justified, and the surveys referred to above show that scholars have seriously attempted to convey to one another and to the public at large their views concerning significant trends. Any period of rapid change, however, can reasonably be expected to result in wide divergence of opinion, in lively discussion that verges on polemic and conflict, and above all, in reluctance on the part of some in the field to give up positions long regarded as unassailable truth. Furthermore, scholarly positions regarded as established by general consensus of an earlier generation of scholars have become common property among educated people, who remain unaware that they are no longer up to date in their views of the origins and history of Biblical religion.

Today, little can be said concerning Biblical history and religion (beyond specific historical "facts") which will receive general assent among the specialists in the field. If the ability to command general assent among those who are competent be the criterion of the scientific, it must now be admitted that a science of Biblical studies does not exist. Certainly, each scholar feels that the views he now holds represent a steady progress beyond those of a past generation,[1] but that is not the point. A survey of the entire field shows rather such divergence of opinion and such disagreement on nearly every important issue that a consensus of opinion cannot be said to exist.[2] The situation may well be summed up by the observation that one eminent scholar could maintain in 1951 that no new trends could be discerned in the treatment of Israelite history,[3] while other scholars were "gasping" at the position taken in recent works by highly competent men.[4] The "fluidity" in this field referred to by Rowley[5] may with perhaps less courtesy but more accuracy be called chaos. This is true pre-eminently, of course, with regard to the interpretation of Israelite history which must inevitably come to grips with the problem of describing the changes in Israelite religion which all admit took place. Yet it is also true that there is very great difference of opinion with regard to specific facts as well, for example, the dating of various portions of the Hebrew Bible (see the preceding chapter).

How did the field arrive at such an impasse? It is here submitted that there were three main factors behind the disintegration of the scholarly synthesis produced by Wellhausen and his successors, all of which were foreseen at the close of World War I. These are: (1) the breakdown of source analysis as the primary method of reconstructing Israelite history and religion; (2) the introduction of new methods and new data; (3) the changes in the *Zeitgeist,* both in the academic and the world scene. The greatness of W. F. Albright's work might be best summed up by observing that he has been most sensitive to all three of these factors and has, during the period in question, led the way in producing both new historical facts and new interpretations of the total course of Israelite history. The history of Old Testament studies since World War I is to a very large extent the history of his academic productivity, and the transition which Biblical studies now are experiencing can be seen as having taken place in his own work during the first decade following World War I.[6] It is not surprising, then, that the controversy which inevitably attends important discontinuities in human culture and common understandings should have centered largely about his work; the controversy is itself the most sincere witness to the importance of Albright's work.

THE FACTORS INVOLVED

1: At the close of World War I it was widely felt that Biblical studies stood at the close of an era—that of the traditional (i.e., in scholarly circles) literary, or "higher" criticism. Two articles published in the *Zeitschrift für die Alttestamentliche Wissenschaft* by Rudolf Kittel and Hugo Gressmann emphasized this and pointed the way to future progress.[7] The program outlined in these two articles has been astoundingly accurate. In the writer's opinion, at least, the argument that the period of source analysis was at an end, having accomplished its task so far as it was capable of doing so,[8] has been well borne out by subsequent study.[9] The classical sources, J, E, D, P, described by Wellhausen and others, are still generally accepted by most scholars, however much Wellhausen's conclusions may have been modified in detail by subsequent critics. It is not generally understood, however, outside the circle of specialists at least, that the reconstruction of the history of Israel and its religion, which Wellhausen carried out on the foundation of his literary analysis, has almost entirely broken down (again in the writer's opinion). This Kittel had already declared.[10] For Wellhausen, as for most of his followers, the history of writing and the history of Israel were nearly identical. It was assumed that a document of a particular period could be utilized by the historian only for evidence of the period in which it was written. Consequently, the J document, for example, was used as evidence for the religion of the ninth century B.C. to which it was assigned, even though it purported to tell of events which were, for the writer of the document in question, in the far remote past.[11] This "hyperskepticism" did not result in a "history," for it lacked foundations, and the builders lacked yardsticks.[12] We have seen, rather, that the writing down of traditions in the ancient world comes at the end of an era, not at its beginning.[13] Writing is used to preserve, not, as in the modern scholarly world, to create. Consequently, the history of writing, or written documents in the ancient world is not the key to history, but only a necessary prolegomenon to the reconstruction of ancient history. The value of literary analysis for history and its success in convincing the scholarly world today depend upon the isolation of more adequate criteria for judgment than has evidently so far been produced by its adherents. The results, consequently, must be judged to fall in the category of hypothesis, not of historical fact. For the reconstruction of history itself, something more than literary analysis is needed, valuable and necessary as hypotheses are.[14]

2: In the same articles mentioned above, Kittel and Gressmann both suggested that the future of Old Testament studies lay in the utilization of new methods and new data. Specifically, more adequate controls were to be found in the data to be produced by the archaeologist,[15] in the insights to be gained by the study of the cultural history of the ancient Near East,[16] and in a more adequate concern for the history of Old Testament religion and the religions of the ancient Near East, which would lead ultimately to the construction of a theology of the Old Testament.[17] Old Testament studies have, since 1920, been characterized by an increasing concern with these materials. It is, consequently, not correct to say that the great changes in the field have not been foreseen, though it is of course true that specific archaeological discoveries came as surprises to nearly everyone.[18] There was at the beginning of our period a deliberate and well-founded rejection of a one-sided and antiquated methodology which had done good service and brought forth its products, but which could not be asked for further well-founded results, since by its very nature it lacked historical perspective and was no more than the preliminary tool of the historian.[19] The isolation of a source in the Pentateuch or elsewhere could give no more historical information than the fact that it was reduced to written form,[20] at some more or less fixed chronological period, by a person with some particular view of Israel's past. It could not produce criteria for the evaluation of the sources it isolated, beyond a possible demonstration that a later source used an earlier. During the period in question it became perfectly clear that even the very late Hellenistic writings utilized traditions which are known from much earlier documents of the ancient Near East,[21] sometimes 2000 years before. Since some religious traditions of the ancient world can be traced over periods of many centuries, we can see how the ancient scribe conceived of his task; we can at least have preliminary insights into the circumstances under which changes in the religious (or legal) traditions took place. Even here we cannot mechanically transfer into Israel all the characteristics of the Babylonian scribe, but we shall at least have some comparable material which would be far more adequate than that on which 19th-century assumptions were based—very largely, it would appear, on the model of the Hellenistic historian.

In addition to vastly increased knowledge of the processes of transmission by writing in the ancient world, we have vastly increased knowledge of religious, political, and social characteristics of that world. As a result, ancient Israel can no longer be treated as an isolated, independent object of study; its history is inseparably bound up with ancient oriental history, whether we are concerned with religion, political history, or culture. The process of cultural borrowing can be seen far more clearly than ever before, and new problems of interpretation have arisen as a result.[22]

It is still as true today as it was in the days of Kittel and Gressmann that results will be obtained by the utilization of new evidence produced by the archaeologist, rather than by continued attempts to analyze sources in the Hebrew Bible. Since the data resulting from excavation include written sources in many languages,[23] the language of the Hebrew Bible itself can be understood now far better than a generation ago. New linguistic criteria for dating specific parts of the Hebrew Bible are being produced, so that the history now being reconstructed is on a far more objective basis than could have been the case before.

In addition to new data, new methods are being introduced. Perhaps none of the traditional academic disciplines is now unchanged since 1920. Linguistic analysis has arisen since that date. Anthropology has made tremendous progress; the archaeology of Palestine was not placed on a firm foundation until the decade between 1925 and 1935, largely as a result of Albright's work.[24] The pioneering work of Max Weber, though it cannot be used uncritically as a history of Israel, is nevertheless the source of much stimulation to OT scholars and has opened up a field of research. To sum up, it is true in Biblical studies, as in nearly every other discipline, that works produced before 1930, other than a few "classics" in the field, are not frequently cited and used in modern research. (This, of course, does not include the original publication of texts, lexicons, and archaeological data of various kinds.) The impact of other disciplines, especially the social sciences, upon Biblical history has not yet been fully felt; here again, Albright has been in many respects a pioneer.[25] The future will no doubt see further application of other disciplines and their methods to the study of ancient Israel, but this process has tended to be rather slow, since most scholars are more interested in the immediate religious concerns of their subject matter.

3: The writer is convinced that very important changes in the field of Biblical history and religion have taken place because of changes in the world in which we live. Perhaps it is simpler and easier to describe the changes in the academic world as they impinge on the Biblical historian and theologian. The generally accepted account of Israel's history and religion produced by Wellhausen and popularized during the late 19th and early 20th centuries survives, to be sure, today. It is especially among non-specialists that it is accepted as indubitably valid, and particularly among those who would claim the label "liberal," religious as well as secular. Yet, Wellhausen's theory of the history of Israelite religion was very largely based on a Hegelian philosophy of history, not upon his literary analysis. It was an *a priori* evolutionary scheme which guided him in the utilization of his sources.[26] Such evolutionary schemes have been rejected nearly everywhere else.[27] Though we can see that an "evolutionary" development of human civilization does take place over a very broad expanse of time, new theories arise in attempts to interpret evidence, not as schemes to decide for us what shall or shall not be used. Hypotheses are basic to research, to be sure, but they should arise on the basis of some sort of evidence, not simply be transferred from a philosophic system. In the days of Wellhausen it is hard to see what other procedure could have been followed because the recovery of cultural history of the ancient Near East was in its initial stages. Yet it is difficult now to see what excuse there is for accepting an evolutionary pattern which would have ancient Israel develop from a primitive animism or even polytheism to ethical monotheism within a period of five or six centuries, when we now have very abundant evidence to show that the religious community of ancient Israel emerged not at the beginnings of history, but at the end of a very civilized, sophisticated, and cosmopolitan era. Though there are many scholars who still hold to the evolutionary pattern of Wellhausen, many adjustments in detail have been made, and it is at least a justified suspicion that a scholarly piety toward the past, rather than historical evidence, is the main foundation for their position.[28]

The changes in the *Zeitgeist* in the world outside are felt more directly, perhaps, but it is more difficult to be objective in describing their influence. This story goes back to the early 20th century, if not before. Attacks on the value of the Old Testament, of course, took place in the second century of the Christian Church by the gnostic Marcion. Similar attacks were leveled against it by men in other fields before World War I, notably Delitzsch and Harnack.[29] It was not until the radical attack on the whole Jewish community and its religious tradition that matters came to a head, with the rise of Nazism. (Similar tendencies had long been current outside Germany, which denied any value for modern Christianity in the Old Testament.[30]) The impact upon Biblical studies came about because of the fact that these attacks derived much of their ammunition from the older tradition of Old Testament studies itself.[31] The evolutionary theory, bent on demonstrating primitive beginnings to make way for evolutionary development to the lofty heights of ethical monotheism, led inevitably to the conclusion that such "silly, savage, senseless" religious traditions were of value only to the antiquarian—in Germany, of course, the conclusions were not so gentle. To put it bluntly, the Old Testament scholar found himself and his field under strong attack and found also that for any justification for popular concern with his field he would have to point out its value in a more positive way than had been done before. It is not likely that earlier generations of Old Testament scholars would have been willing to admit that the Old Testament was without value for modern man, but it is here maintained that an almost inescapable conclusion from the results of their research was that the evolutionary history of an ancient people is important and necessary only to the eccentric and the pedant. Christian theologians (and non-theologians) drew the further conclusion that since the whole evolution culminated in the rise of Christianity, the Old Testament was not necessary even to the Church. Only one further step was lacking: that the New Testament itself was superseded by modern Western civilization. The history of that civilization from 1912 to 1957, the widespread feeling that there was a breakdown of values, the loss of the facile optimism of the 1920s, called in question the whole process.

The result was a return to the problem of an Old Testament theology. The German Church found a reality and a value in the Old Testament which the scholars evidently had not bothered to point out, or had not seen.[32] Since Eichrodt's monumental work, an increasing number of works have appeared in the attempt to communicate to the present day the religious and theological permanence of at least certain aspects of Old Testament faith.[33] The Church and the scholar are not so far apart as formerly was the case. There is little reason to believe that Church dogma is increasingly dictating conclusions to Old Testament scholars, though some have expressed such fears.[34] Today the Biblical scholar finds himself fighting on at least three fronts; he must be faithful to his historical evidence, yet be concerned to do justice to the religious faith of the past, stated and implied in his records, neither idealizing nor bearing false witness. At the same time he finds himself involved in the problem of restating to modern man what the ancient prophet, poet, and historian intended to convey.[35]

It is no wonder that many scholars in the field tend to eschew the problem of constructing a history of the religion of Israel and of the history of Israel. Faced as they are with a chaotic mass of mutually exclusive views of that history, they have for a long time tended to concentrate on the demonstration of specific historical facts or details, the meaning and importance of which in any larger historical framework are not examined. No one, of course, will quarrel with the concern to ascertain the facts, but it is still true that a miscellaneous collection of facts does not constitute history. Particularly in the English-speaking world, very little has been done in Israelite historiography since 1931, apart from necessary textbooks for colleges and seminaries. The only exception is Albright's *From the Stone Age to Christianity*.[36]

Perhaps the most important gap in the field of OT history and religion is the lack of an adequate hypothesis to replace that of Wellhausen. If the Hegelian hypothesis of the 19th century is rejected by nearly all historians of the present day, it hardly seems adequate for ancient history for which our sources are relatively so much more limited. Hypotheses are basic to sound research and are eminently practical; they are constructed, not as a substitute for facts but to suggest possibilities and to guide future investigation. They should not dictate conclusions. The Biblical historian by his very subject matter is bound to take into consideration large time spans (large, that is, in comparison to the time spans usually dealt with by his colleagues in European or American history). The *Zeitgeist* here is against him. The lack of enthusiasm with which the historian has greeted the hypotheses of Toynbee, Spengler, and others concerning the rise and fall of civilizations is a frightening prospect to deter all but the most foolhardy. It is much easier to follow the accepted pattern of the 19th century, especially since it has received some academic respectability, mostly through default, and to be content with pointing out a few inadequacies here and there which will show that one is keeping up to date. The few attempts in the direction of a new general theory made during the past three decades have met with little success.[37]

THE PRESENT SITUATION

In contrast to the situation in 1920, we now have far different conceptions of nearly every period of Israelite history as the result of a number of important discoveries made during the past four decades. It will not, of course, be possible here to take into consideration every important new fact or insight. Rather, there will be presented here a selection of the most important results in a schematic pattern which is intended as a presentation of a new hypothesis for the history of Israel as well as of its religion. The obvious charge can be met in advance: that only those facts which fit the hypothesis are taken up and others ignored. The answer is twofold: first, this is inevitable for any hypothesis which must deal with such a long span of time as that which is the responsibility of the Biblical scholar; second, the following is not intended as a presentation of eternal truth but simply as a stimulus to future work, to see "whether it be so." It will be obvious to all acquainted with the writings of W. F. Albright that every page is dependent upon him, but its weaknesses and inadequacies are due to the present writer alone.

A. Praeparatio:[38] Since 1929 scholars have become increasingly aware that the narratives of Genesis dealing with the forefathers cannot any longer be dismissed as Canaanite myth.[39] However much these narratives may have been refracted in the process of centuries of oral transmission, they nevertheless preserve with such vividness and accuracy cultural features which we know to be characteristic of the pre-Mosaic period that scholars today must take them seriously as historical sources, at least potentially. A seemingly endless stream of details has shown us that the cultural milieu of these narratives lies in the Bronze Age,[40] especially the period from 2000 to 1400 B.C.[41] The consequences for the historian are enormous in implications. No longer does the cultural and religious history of Israel begin with a *tabula rasa* in the time of Moses. The religion of ancient Israel did not necessarily begin from scratch, so to speak, but rather it had behind it (or at least very rapidly took up) traditions which show a continuity extending over at least half a millennium. Furthermore, the very beginnings of this cultural continuity took place in a region which we now know to have been in close contact with the high civilizations of Mesopotamia for several centuries preceding the migrations which mark the beginnings of Israelite traditions, associated with the name of Abraham.[42] The historian is faced, then, with the problem of accounting for this continuity of tradition which precedes the rise of the Israelite religious community in the time of Moses. So far, the only serious solutions suggested are those of Albright and Noth. The former suggests that there was actually a tribal (or ethnic) continuity as maintained in Biblical traditions, though the process has been much simplified in the Biblical account.[43] Noth, on the other hand, appeals to cult centers to which such traditions were "bound," evidently little concerned with the fact that places do not preserve traditions (other than the possible tendency to be treated as sacred sites); instead, people do.[44] The disappearance of the whole of Early Bronze Age traditions in Palestine is indication enough of the fact that cultural discontinuities are almost certain to result in discontinuities of tradition as well, unless the earlier is valued and borrowed by the new, incoming group.[45] Why, then, were these traditions, current in Palestine long before the time of Moses, taken up into the Israelite religious traditions? The simplest, and therefore the best answer in the absence of further evidence is that these traditions belonged to various elements of the population of Palestine which were later to become Israel. Who were they? We know that Palestine before the time of Moses was a melting pot of all sorts of ethnic and cultural traditions.[46] We know, further, from the recovery of ancient Canaanite myth and legend,[47] that these pre-Mosaic traditions have nothing to do with the Canaanites apart from certain possible influences on the form and motifs of these old narratives,[48] which would indicate only contact with Canaanite culture some time before they were reduced to writing (probably first in the tenth century B.C.). Again, the simplest solution of the problem lies in the Biblical tradition itself, namely, that these groups included some at least who traced their origins to Upper Mesopotamia. The Amarna Letters again state clearly that the population of Palestine included a group called the Sutu[49]— who appear frequently in the Mari letters as an element in the population of that area. We cannot, of course, identify the proto-Israelites and the Palestinian Sutu; we can say that there is every reason to accept as well founded the fact that such migrations from the Euphrates valley and environs to Palestine had taken place, and that long before the time of Moses. With them had come all sorts of cultural traits which originated in Mesopotamia: legal and religious traditions are those for which we have the most evidence.[50] The most impressive absence of specifically Canaanite cultural traits in the Patriarchal narratives indicates that these groups had refused assimilation into the Canaanite culture.[51] The Biblical narratives emphasize this also, though it is, of course, possible that it is also a reflection of a later religious concern.

This is enough to indicate the sort of historical problem with which we must now deal. The starting point was the introduction of new evidence from Ras Shamra and Mari, which excluded from the realm of probability certain theories about the Patriarchal narratives previously held, and which, together with many details from other sources, called for a new theory to account for the new evidence. Though many scholars have accepted the historical foundations of the Patriarchal narratives as far back as 1937,[52] still many OT scholars either deny or ignore the new evidence. Still fewer have been willing to follow up the implications of the new materials, for if those who made up the twelve tribes of Israel included some at least who had first been in contact with Mesopotamian civilization, then for a period of centuries lived in a land surrounded by a cosmopolitan complex of many cultures in process of amalgamation, then it follows that they can hardly have been childlike, cultureless, traditionless barbarians. It follows that the earliest stages of the religion of Israel need not have been as primitive as earlier scholars had thought—not on the grounds of evidence, but on the basis of an *a priori* theory of how religion *must* evolve.

On the contrary, the present hypothesis would suggest that a new religious community under such circumstances as we now know to have been the case in ancient Israel arises when there is a felt dissatisfaction with the *status quo*. The new religion takes up all of the older tradition which is compatible; it preserves all which is felt to be of permanent value. Much of the old becomes irrelevant and is eventually lost. It is here suggested, then, that we may expect very many religious and cultural traits of Israel before the time of David to go back to pre-Mosaic times and to find their parallels in the written literature of Upper Mesopotamia and North Syria especially.[53]

B. The Creative period: Just as Wellhausen had accepted the Mesopotamian connections of the patriarchs,[54] so he accepted the designation of the period of Moses as the "properly creative"[55] period of Israelite religion, and as the period when its history began. This has never been seriously questioned by any important group of scholars. The issue here is: what was created? The admission by nearly all scholars that a new religious community came into existence in the time of, and as the result of, Moses's message and mission has had an unusual degree of unanimity, equaled only by the reluctance or refusal on the part of most scholars to commit themselves to any definite position concerning the nature of that religion. In other words, it looks for all the world like a religious community without any religion. The religion consisted of nothing but "seeds," which were ultimately in the course of centuries to produce the fruit of ethical monotheism.[56] Or, on the other hand, the religion consisted of a slogan ("Yahweh is the God of Israel, and Israel is the People of Yahweh"), plus much primitive superstition.[57] Albright's conclusion that the Mosaic faith was a highly developed monotheism has been enthusiastically attacked.[58] The controversy cannot be solved since the issue is not an historical one; it is rather a question of definition. Once it is admitted that the term may legitimately be applied to a religion which does not have a philosophical theology (which opponents of Mosaic monotheism do not seem inclined to do), then there is no control over the term. The usual position taken that there must be explicit denial of the existence of other gods before there can be monotheism is reduced to nonsense by the fact that things called "gods" existed in every pagan temple in the ancient Near East. Deutero-Isaiah found a way out of the impasse, but there is only the 19th-century theory to support the position that what he said would have been a surprise to Moses. What Deutero-Isaiah said was consistently communicated in action in the normative religion of the pre-exilic period. Nor can seeming exceptions to this prove anything: a consistently monotheistic religious community has never existed, else condemnations of idolatry would be pointless. Monotheism was not an issue in the earliest period; monolatry was. Monotheism could very easily lead to syncretism by the normal process so dear to the heart of the modern sophisticate, of identifying the one God with the various gods of other religions. Monolatry, on the other hand, demanded obedience to the will of the one God, which excluded both recognition of other gods and syncretism, though it did not exclude cultural borrowing.

The creative period can best be handled through an examination of the religious community itself. Since we know that the formation of co-operating groups by covenant was customary long before the time of Moses,[59] and, apart from the state and its monopoly of force, alternative solutions of the problem of forming groups which could trust each other are virtually unknown in the ancient world, the denial of the old school that this was a covenant community could be upheld only on the assumption that early Israel was held together by close blood ties; that is, it consisted of kinship groups. This has also been consistently denied, and the result was historical absurdity.[60] The problem of accounting for the almost unbelievable toughness of the new community, maintaining its unity and identity against seemingly insurmountable odds, cultural as well as military, was seemingly not felt to be a problem by older scholars. The problem becomes acute with the recognition that even covenant coalitions in the ancient world were usually as ephemeral and unpredictable as those in more recent memory. When we see further that Israel had no centralized government for the first two and a half centuries of its existence, any too simple solution must be regarded with extreme skepticism.

It is surely grotesque now to regard a religion as "primitive" which could survive against such odds, in the face of powerful drives toward syncretism, of powerful military opposition, of great cultural diversity within the community itself, and of radical changes in its own cultural traditions.

In view of the most persistent continuity of religious tradition, which preserved even historical and cultural features going back to the Middle Bronze Age, we are justified in cautious extrapolation from what we know of later times into the time of Moses. This will be carried out in detail elsewhere.[61] If pre-Mosaic traditions succeeded in surviving, it follows that the traditions of the creative period itself ought to be on a far higher level of reliability. Probably there has been a general trend toward a more conservative treatment of these narratives.[62] Several scholars have argued for the Mosaic origin of the Decalogue from different points of view.[63] The problem of describing the religion of this period from records which are recorded and interpreted in a much later period cannot be solved by appeal to evolutionary theories or *a priori* hypotheses. It is becoming quite clear that the solution of the problem will come from the treatment of details which seem to be incidental or accidental. Narratives which contain names, specific forms of cultic action, patterns of thought, or other concrete cultural features which can be checked by extra-Biblical sources can thus be controlled, at least to some extent. This has already been done for the Patriarchal narratives, and, if the writer's thesis concerning the covenant form is correct, the period of Moses is likewise on the way to becoming historical.[64] In view of the tremendous importance of the covenant tradition in subsequent Israelite history,[65] the whole course of Israelite religion appears in new light. The creative period referred to by Wellhausen includes something more than the creation of a *Volk*. Together with the community there emerges a *structure* of religious belief and action consisting of specific, concrete elements in a concrete relationship to each other. Each element in the structure (history, law, covenant form, etc.) has its own history; the structure may fall apart and be rebuilt in a different fashion. Nevertheless, the separate elements are never completely lost, but are for the most part of permanent and lasting value. Each element which forms a part of the religious structure of the creative period may have its own long and complex pre-history as well (*e.g.* no doubt, the Sabbath). What is created in this period is the community itself. The structure of its religion incorporates much that is already familiar to those who make up the community, and, in addition, that intangible, inaccessible to the historian, experience of the Holy.

C. *The adaptive period:* This period has likewise been illuminated by radically new insights coming particularly from Martin Noth and Albrecht Alt.[66] Relying upon forms of organization known from early Greek history, Noth has reconstructed in very useful and convincing fashion the federation of twelve tribes which continued during the period of the Judges. Albrecht Alt has brought some order into the problem of early Israelite legal traditions and has emphasized the importance to the early federation of the covenant renewal ceremony preserved in Deuteronomy 27.[67] When this work on the political and legal content is combined with the work of Albright and his students on the early poetry of this period,[68] the period of the Judges ceases to be something vaguely floating like a mirage in the mists of antiquity and begins to have concrete form and content. It must be emphasized that the new results have come through the application of methods other than the traditional source criticism, notably form criticism (Alt on law, Noth on tribal organization) and linguistics (Albright and his school). In addition, the stimulus brought by the sociologist Max Weber has likewise been important.

The problem which has not yet been adequately solved is that of continuity between the Mosaic and the federation periods. Here hypothesis is inescapable. By the term "adaptive," it is intended that there was an important continuity of a religious tradition which not only could be but was adapted to an economic, political, and social situation, one which was radically (if not totally) different from that of the creative period. From Moses to Joshua there must have been a change from a nomadic to a sedentary, agricultural economic basis; the simple organization of clansmen in the time of Moses gives way to a much more complex territorial organization of "tribes"; the group which escaped from Egypt seems to become lost in the population of Palestine which joined the religious federation, so that we cannot say what tribes or what parts of them actually were engaged either in the Exodus out of Egypt or in the initial stages of the Conquest. We cannot escape the conclusion that the group known as "Israel" grew suddenly from a small religious group of clansmen to a large organization, dominating most of the hill country of Palestine and much of Transjordan in a relatively short time. This could not have been by natural reproduction; the group was enlarged by the accession of much of the population of this area, to whom the religious community of Israel was much preferable to the social and political system under which they had lived previously (partly at least under Canaanite domination).[69] This period then, saw, the addition of many features to the Yahwistic tradition, which were both unnecessary and perhaps undreamed of in the wilderness period. To mention certain examples: the deity of the federation must have become associated with economic functions. Agriculture as the economic basis of life was incorporated into the religious tradition, with particular cultic and religious features continued perhaps with little change from pre-Mosaic times. The agricultural calendar became a part of the Israelite tradition. Everything which was of importance in the life of the federation inevitably was incorporated into the Yahwistic tradition, which meant that the latter in its totality was something much different from the time of Moses. Much of the Mosaic tradition no doubt was lost, ceasing to have any functional importance under the new circumstances of life. The center of the Mosaic religion, the covenant, continued to be the foundation of the tribal organization.[70] Much more detail could be added, and much more remains to be pointed out, but the adaptation of Mosaic tradition, and the great amount of what might be called cultural borrowing from pre-Mosaic times, cannot be reasonably doubted. Relatively little of the Mosaic period continued in a fixed, normative tradition, which could not and was not changed and adapted to fit the needs of a new period. Even the covenant bond gradually gave way to a commonly accepted view that it was a blood tie which held the people together, since the religion became less effective as an actual unifying factor.

There was an even greater adaptation of old traditions introduced with the monarchy. The fall of Shiloh prepared the way by introducing a vacuum, and something had to take the place of the old federation and its sanctuary which had served as the unifying center. Again we cannot go into detail, but kingship as an institution was borrowed from the pagan neighbors of Israel.[71] The problem of adaptation was acute. The first king, Saul, fell a victim to opposing traditions: that of the old federation with its religious standards and obligations, and that of kingship which needed power, military and financial, to survive and function effectively. The harmonization of the old and the new was carried out in a marvelously astute way by King David, but his successor, Solomon, carried innovations so far that schism resulted. The older religious tradition was taken over and connected inseparably with the kingship through the Temple of Solomon and the Ark of the Covenant. The old structure of the religion, however, by which each individual was obligated directly to Yahweh under the covenant, could no longer be tolerated by the king. No longer could each one do "what was upright in his own eyes." The rather thoroughgoing individualism of the earlier period had to give way to the political needs of the state, and the authority of the king had to be supported by religious institutions and personnel. Consequently, much of the older tradition was disvalued during the period of the monarchy and survived only in outlying villages and among religious conservatives, especially the prophetic party. Only in the North, after the schism, did the kingship fail to reach any permanent solution of the problem of obtaining religious guarantees for the political stability.[72]

With the division of the Israelites into two political units following the death of Solomon, the period of far-reaching adaptation of the old traditions came to an end, at least temporarily. The South held consistently to its religious (and political) conviction that Yahweh had chosen the dynasty of David to rule in perpetuity. The North, on the other hand, saw a perpetual conflict between the opposing traditions. We know far too little about the political constitution of the northern kingdom, but no radical innovations in the Yahwistic tradition seem to have taken place by deliberate decision. The problem of military, political, and religious organization had been solved well enough in the South, so that no further changes were felt to be necessary (but see below). The adaptive phase came to an end, and the radical changes which are characteristic of the period from Moses to Jeroboam cease to take place.

D. The traditional period: Nations, like universities, are not run simply by presidents, but by precedents. Once an organization comes into existence, all aspects of national life fall into well-defined patterns of thought and action by which the continuity of the group is thought to be assured. In the ancient world the whole system is, of course, closely bound up with religion, which both guarantees the integrity of the community and gives legitimacy to the culture in which and by which it exists. It is unfortunate in the extreme that historiography came to an end early in the period of the monarchy. The writers were concerned only to record the history of the period leading up to the establishment of the monarchy. With this, history came to an end. They had arrived, and all was well. Not until several centuries had passed, and the nation (both North and South) had been destroyed, was the problem of history rediscovered and historiography undertaken anew.

The emphasis upon the prophetic movement, with which Old Testament scholars have with good reason been concerned, had resulted in a loss of perspective. The prophets represent only one aspect of the Yahwistic tradition. Recently, the religious significance of the kingship has come into its own, and various solutions of this problem are available to the interested.[73] Whatever solution one accepts, the religious significance of the royal cultus (or cultic tradition) should certainly not be underestimated. Furthermore, the violent conflict between the prophets and the kings, which increased in severity as the end drew near, is a good enough indication that the prophets represented a body of convictions which flew in the face of traditions regarded as final, sacred, and inviolable. The prophets were proclaiming the necessity of change in the unchangeable.

The traditional period in Israelite religion is thus to be defined as one in which the primary task of the community is felt to be the preservation and transmission of a tradition which was necessary to the preservation of the group. One may freely grant that there is not too much evidence of a concern for the preservation of Yahwistic tradition during the monarchy. This is precisely the point. The traditional period tends rather to take religious tradition for granted. The main concern is for the functioning of the group— its political, economic, and social aspects. The inevitable result is increasing unconcern for the specifically religious (over against the cultic which flourishes) obligations, and economic motivations take the upper hand. Yet we do see considerable evidence for the existence of opposing traditions during the whole of the monarchy. One can hardly believe that the repeated condemnations of the kings by various prophets from the time of Saul to that of Zedekiah proceeded merely from the individualistic opinions of the prophets themselves. Such condemnation requires a powerful and authoritative tradition to back it up.

The conflict between the opposing traditions, royal and prophetic, came to a climax in the North with the contest on Mount Carmel. The attempt on the part of the Omrides to break with the past is indicated both by the creation of a new capital at Samaria and by the deliberate suppression of the Yahwistic prophets. The prophets and their tradition had proven too unadaptable to make stable government possible. Consequently, the dynasty attempted to solve the problem by establishing a new religion—that of the Tyrian Baal, Melqart.[74] With the rebellion of Jehu, the old reasserted itself, supported even by the most thoroughgoing primitivists, led by the head of the Rechabites.[75] In all the furor and violence of the whole period, there is no reason, no evidence, for the belief that anything important was added to the religious tradition.[76] The conflict arises out of the concern of the conservatives for the preservation of a tradition, not for the sort of adaptation which could incorporate the new into the existing framework of the religion and still preserve a continuity. The rigidity of the tradition made it seem necessary to the Omrides to reject it *in toto*. The tranquillity after the rebellion of Jehu seems to indicate that some sort of working compromise had been reached for a time. The conflict of traditions seems to have ceased being much of an issue until the rise of the prophets in new form with Amos.

The difficulty during the time of the so-called "writing prophets" was not that the religion was too primitive; it was rather too content with assurances that the continuity of traditional religious forms (especially sacrifice) was an adequate fulfillment of religious obligation. It has recently been emphasized that in spite of the relatively few references to the old religious law in the prophets, they are nevertheless dependent upon old tradition.[77] Albright has emphasized the "primitivistic" tendencies on the part of some and has placed these tendencies in the context of similar trends all over the Near East, especially during the seventh century.[78] Though they were interested in reform, they were not "social revolutionaries," nor were they religious revolutionaries. "They were, first and last, religious reformers. . . . Their task was not to preach a new . . . theology, but rather to demand a return to the purer faith of their forefathers."[79] The emphasis upon the absoluteness of religious obligation under the old covenant form furnished the foundation for their own highly creative message for their own time, and also the foundation for their passionate conviction that the downfall of the nation was inevitable. We do not see here a woodenly mechanical attempt to copy the remote past, and this has misled many scholars into thinking that their message was almost entirely the introduction of completely new religious concepts. Had that been the case, repentance, or "returning to Yahweh" would have been the last of their desires. On the contrary, their message consisted largely of the fact that a group which was called into existence (chosen) to serve Yahweh ceased to have any excuse for being when it *ceased* to serve.[80]

Thus the prophets added much of value to the tradition through their message to their own time, but they did not succeed in ushering in a new period in the history of Israel and its religion. It is here that we have perhaps the crux of the conflict between the older school and more modern conceptions of Israelite religion. The classical hypothesis of Wellhausen maintained that there were no conditions attached originally to the relationship between Yahweh and Israel.[81] Not until the prophets Elijah and Amos did ethical considerations become associated with the religion. Torah was simply a matter of the priestly technique of casting lots, rather than a complex of procedural techniques whereby a group attempts to maintain certain norms of action which were ultimately religious in origin, and which were felt to be necessary for the preservation of the group. The old traditions of the period of the Judges, which we must now take much more seriously than was done before 1920, emphasize strongly the existence of certain profound concerns connected with religious morality which were protected even at great cost. It is here submitted as a useful hypothesis that those concerns for a religious ethic (or morality) had rather been lost during the period of the monarchy, when the most pressing problems had been largely solved, when a measure of security was achieved, and when the religion became reduced to a set of easily transmissible forms which ceased to have the functions which originally they had at the center of the Yahwistic faith. Ethical and moral concerns were a matter of royal law, for the courts to decide, and the religious tradition of the time declared (contrary to earlier Yahwistic tradition) that whatever the king did *wás* just. That law had itself become secularized, following foreign patterns which met the needs of merchants and money lenders, but which failed to protect those who were most in need of protection. Even the priests who were expected to know something of the old religious norms had forgotten them, or at least had accommodated themselves to the existing situation.

E. *The Period of Reformation:* In spite of the reforming efforts of the prophets, it is evident that their message had little effect on their own time. An abortive attempt at reform was carried out by Josiah, not on the basis of the prophetic message but as the result of discovery. An old lawbook found in the Temple furnished at least partly the program for a return to old traditions. The reform seems to have ended with his death. Other than the small group of prophets and their adherents, the syncretistic, secularized way of life continued. The real reformation of the religious community did not take place until Jerusalem lay in ruins. With this event, as we know now, all corporate existence in Palestine ceased (except for the brief survival of a reduced group for a few years).[82] Reformation was necessary, for the old social, religious, and political forms of organization and continuity were gone.

That which is most characteristic of a reform period is the concern for traditions of the remote past, and this is strikingly evident in all our sources for this period. The period of the exile, and that following, was one of the systematic collection and recording of all old traditions which were felt to be of possible value. At the same time there was a deliberate rejection of the monarchical traditions, except for those having to do with the Temple cultus.

The period of the monarchy was one characterized by consistent and almost total unfaithfulness to the demands of Yahweh. The customary law of the kingship was ignored as irrelevant and secular. But, on the other hand, that which is true of almost any reformation in the history of religion holds true here as well: namely, that in the return to past tradition no distinction is made between that which we have termed the creative and the adaptive periods. It was known that a great transition had taken place after the reign of David, consequently everything earlier than Solomon was attributed to the creative period, that is, to Moses. Consequently, all premonarchial legal tradition (and some parts of it which were later) became known as the Law of Moses. In other words, all religious traditions of legal norms which could be accepted as normative by the reformed community were attributed to the creative period.

The procedure by which the exilic and postexilic scribes worked is essentially similar to that of the prophets. Though it seems quite certain that they did copy for preservation certain written records, yet the normal process of preserving took place simultaneously with a reinterpretation of the old traditions to meet the contemporary need. Canonization of a tradition in fixed and final form had not yet taken place, but once the task was complete, the Pentateuch was in existence, and no further changes could be made. Further developments in law could take place only by the increasingly Hellenistic process of interpretation of written documents. The normative religious traditions were henceforth unchangeable. They had reached finality.

We have thus reached the close of an era. The insistence upon the fact that the exilic and postexilic periods represent a reform movement rather than the creation of a new religious tradition need not imply that there was no creativity in it. Quite the contrary. It was a highly creative period, characterized by most of the features pointed out for the Mosaic period. A new community was formed in Jerusalem under the Persian Empire. Its political and religious structures were far different from those of the monarchy. Above all, the canonization of the Pentateuch is an innovation in the history of religion which furnished the foundation for the development, for all future times, of Judaism, Christianity, and Islam. One suspects that this also may have had accidental historical grounds, and the implications were not necessarily seen at the time canonization was taking place.[83]

The subsequent history of the Yahwistic tradition does not concern us here. The writer feels impelled to point out, however, that the creation of new religious communities, their tension with the environment in which they found themselves, the problem of adaptation to changed circumstances, and the solution of crucial problems did not cease with Ezra. The dialogue between historical event and religious faith has been continuous, and it is here maintained that the history of religion does show such recurrent patterns that, on a very broad scale at least, the reaction of religious communities becomes almost predictable in formal terms. It is also submitted that what may be true and universally recognized as reliable procedure in the study of a particular religious community at that period of its history here called "tradition" must not be assumed to be true of all other periods in the history of that community. In other words, a traditional period furnishes us no adequate analogy for drawing conclusions about a religion in its creative or adaptive phases. Above all, the individual cannot be explained on the basis of community life alone. The creative individual in religion is almost always in conflict with his community unless the latter is itself in the creative or adaptive periods. What the community does to the creative individual in its midst is perhaps the best criterion for typological classification of the community itself. At best, the community stipulates the boundaries within which it will tolerate creativity. At worst, it will punish any significant deviation from precedent. Where the gap between tradition and individual or community needs becomes too great, reformation takes place, but usually by schism. And one might say that within the framework of the community of scholarly piety, the present state of Biblical studies may perhaps be taken as an illustration of the point.

Ann Arbor; Spring, 1957

NOTES TO CHAPTER TWO

1. Cf. H. H. Rowley, *The Old Testament and Modern Study* (Oxford, 1951), p. xvii.
2. Ibid., pp. xvi–xvii.
3. Ibid., p. xxi. No article on the history of Israel was included in the volume for this reason.
4. W. A. Irwin, *JNES* xv (1956), p. 193, in a review of Gordon, *Introduction to Old Testament Times*. Cf. also his review of Orlinsky, *Ancient Israel,* in *JNES* xv, p. 55: "His story of the patriarchal period and of the work of Moses differs only slightly from what an informed fundamentalist might have written." Nevertheless, Irwin seems to grant very significant changes in Biblical history, loc. cit.: ". . . the Biblical story is far other than· the pious guesswork or fraud that the scholarship of fifty years ago believed."
5. Op. cit., pp. xviii–xix.
6. As an illustration, compare Albright's treatment of Genesis 14 in 1919 and 1926, *An Indexed Bibliography of the Writings of William Foxwell Albright,* prepared by H. M. Orlinsky (New Haven, 1941), p. 21.
7. R. Kittel, "Die Zukunft der alttestamentliche Wissenschaft," *ZAW* 39 (1921), pp. 84–99; H. Gressmann, "Die Aufgaben der alttestamentliche Forschung," *ZAW,* NF 1 (1924), pp. 1–33.
8. Gressmann, op. cit., p. 8: "Die Literarkritik hat die Aufgaben, die sie leisten musste und konnte, im allgemeinen erschöpft . . . neue, weittragende Aufschlüsse sind von ihr nicht mehr zu erhoffen."
9. The writer feels that this conclusion is justified for several reasons. First, subsequent work has not succeeded in commanding the general assent which Wellhausen's analysis still holds; quite the contrary, for more recent attempts at analysis have tended to lead to mutually exclusive positions. Cf. Eissfeldt, *Geschichtsschreibung im*

alten Testament (Berlin, 1948). Second, whole schools of scholars have repudiated even Wellhausen's analysis on grounds that the entire procedure is fallacious. See J. Pedersen, "Die Auffassung vom alten Testament," *ZAW* NF 8 (1931), pp. 161–81, and the treatment of the oral-tradition criticism of various Scandinavians by C. R. North in *OTMS*, "Pentateuchal Criticism," pp. 59 ff.; and as well the contribution by John Bright in Chapter 1 of the present volume. It is significant that most of the important new results in historical studies have little to do with literary analysis.

10. Op. cit., p. 84: "Es ist kein Zufall, dass seine 'Geschichte Israels' . . . alles andere eher war als eine Geschichte."

11. Cf. Wellhausen, *Prolegomena to the History of Ancient Israel* (trans. by Black and Menzies, Edinburgh, 1885), p. 360: ". . . The patriarchal legend has no connection whatever with the times of the patriarchs."

12. Kittel, op. cit., p. 86 f.: "Es fehlte dem Gebäude das Fundament, und es fehlten den Baumeistern die Massstäbe."

13 Cf. Kees, on the dating of the Pyramid Texts, *Handbuch der Orientalistik*, I² (Leiden, 1952), pp. 30–38.

14. Cf. Olmstead, A. T., "History, Ancient World, and the Bible," *JNES* II (1943), pp. 5–6: "So far as it goes, most literary criticism is sound and its conclusions are normally accepted by the historian. At this point the literary critic stops; he has attained his objective when he knows his author." See also Albright, *BASOR* 74 (1939), p. 12: "The ultimate historicity of a given datum is never conclusively established nor disproved by the literary framework in which it is imbedded: there must always be external evidence."

15. This was already emphasized by Gressmann, op. cit., p. 14.

16. Ibid., p. 8 f.: "Auf das literarkritische ist das vorderorientalische Zeitalter gefolgt." This has unfortunately been too frequently done in a woodenly mechanical way, on the assumption that any similarity between Isarel and Babylonia (especially in cultus) justifies a wholesale assumption that anything true in Babylon may also be assumed to be true in Israel.

17. Kittel, op. cit., p. 94 ff. Gressmann, op. cit., p. 11.

18. The "generation of activity" to which Rowley refers (op. cit., p. xvi) was foreshadowed in the two articles here being described.

19. Cf. note 14.

20. Even here, the traditional techniques of literary criticism are giving way to more objective techniques of linguistic analysis as criteria for dating. See Albright, *JBL* LXIII (1944), pp. 207–33.

21. Cf. Jacobsen, *The Sumerian King List* (Chicago, 1939); O. Eissfeldt, *Sanchunjaton von Berut. . . .* (Halle, 1952), on Canaanite religious traditions; M. B. Rowton, *BASOR* 119 (1950), pp. 20–22, on Josephus' use of old Tyrian chronicles. In view of the fact that these Hellenistic writings come from a time when the ancient oriental traditions were rapidly dying out, earlier historical traditions must be handled much more soberly than was the case a generation ago.

22. Cf. for example, Wilson, *The Burden of Egypt* (Chicago, 1951), p. 316: "It is only when a culture has worked out a certain degree of its own salvation that it may borrow forms of expression from others." However, when a new people emerges in the midst of history, it cannot escape borrowing from the past at the very beginnings of its history. Its culture is from the first the reinterpretation of certain aspects of the past.

23. It is not widely enough known that in the time of Moses the Canaanites were familiar with at least eight languages recorded in five completely different systems of writing.

24. Albright, *Archaeology of Palestine* (Pelican Books, 1949). See Chapter 4 in this volume.

25. This is illustrated only in part by the references to publications in these disciplines to be found in this author's *FSAC,* and *Archaeology and the Religion of Israel* (Baltimore, 3rd ed., 1953).

26. Albright, *JBL* LIX (1940), pp. 92–93. Cf. the critique of 19th-century anthropology by J. H. Steward, "Cultural Causality and Law," *American Anthropologist* 51 (1949), p. 2: "If the 19th century formulations were wrong, it was not because their purpose was inadmissible or their objective impossible, but because the data were inadequate and insufficient, the methodology weak, and the application of the schemes too broad."

27. See F. M. Keesing, *Culture Change,* (Stanford, 1953), p. 20: "This is *par excellence* the decade (i.e. 1920–1929) of historicalism. . . . The voice of evolutionism is muted to the work of a few diehards, notably Frazer." Compare also the significant remarks on pp. 14, 25, and 39.

28. The bitter controversy between fundamentalism and "higher criticism" lives on in this form.

29. See H. J. Kraus, *Geschichte der historisch-kritischen Erforschung des Alten Testaments* (Neukirchen, 1956), pp. 274–83, 350–57.

30. Ibid., p. 392: ". . . das Neue Testament beständig das Alte voraussetzt, um das ihm selber Eigene negativ kenntlich zu machen." This is a quotation from Kierkegaard which E. Hirsch placed at the beginning of his work on the Old Testament and the Gospel. Kraus points out that this attitude continues in the work of Bultmann (loc. cit.).

31. Kraus, op. cit., p. 393: "Nie sollte es die alttestamentliche Wissenschaft vergessen, dass die nationalsozialistischen und deutsch-christlichen Herolde einer neuen völkischen Religion den Kampf gegen das 'alttestamentliche Fremdelement' mit Waffen geführt haben, die ihrem eigenen Forschungsarsenal entnommen worden waren."

32. Ibid., p. 393.

33. W. Eichrodt, *Theologie des alten Testaments,* (Leipzig, 1933–39, 3 vols.). For discussions of the rise of Old Testament theology, see especially J. D. Smart, "The Death and Rebirth of Old Testament Theology," *Journal of Religion* XXIII (1943), pp. 1–11, 125–36; and C. C. McCown, "The Current Plight of Biblical Scholarship," *JBL* LXXV (1956), pp. 12–18. (An excellent presentation of the theological presuppositions of the critic who maintains that Biblical scholarship must be free of theological presuppositions.)

34. McCown, op. cit.; R. H. Pfeiffer, *JBL* LXX (1951), pp. 1–14.

35. It is here that the modern controversy centers. Apart from the stratosphere of discussion about demythologizing, scholars disagree violently as to what message the Bible conveys. See L. Waterman, "Biblical Studies in a New Setting," *JBL* LXVI (1947), pp. 1–14; and G. E. Wright, *God Who Acts,* Chicago, 1952. On the one hand, there is an emphasis on moral obligation; on the other, historical experience which becomes the foundation of religion.

36. Martin Noth's *Geschichte Israels* (Göttingen, 2nd ed., 1954), excellent as a factual account of Israel's political history, deliberately disregards the problem of religion and culture. Steward (op. cit.) also calls attention to the fact that since the 19th century, anthropologists have been little interested in the formulation of "regularities" or generalizations in cultural data. [Noth's 2nd ed. appeared in English translation in 1958. See also now John Bright, *A History of Israel,* Philadelphia, 1959, a major work which has rapidly become the standard text in English—Ed.]

37. These include Edward Robertson, *The Old Testament Problem, A Re-investigation* (Manchester, 1950); Y. Kaufmann, Tōlˁdōt hāˁᵉmūnā hayyiśrāˀēlīt (*History of Is-*

raelite Religion, Tel Aviv, 1937–48, 7 vols. See *Bibliotheca Orientalis* x, 186–92.) Both of these suffer from the same fundamental weakness of Wellhausen. In Kittel's words, "Veraltet war sie, weil sie Israel als für sich stehende, isolierte Grösse behandelte, was in den 70er Jahren noch verständlich, in den 80er und 90er aber nicht mehr erlaubt war."

38. Cf. Albright, *FSAC*, Chap. III.
39. E. Meyer, *Die Israeliten und ihre Nachbarstämme* (1906), pp. 249 ff.
40. For recent treatments of the Patriarchal period see Albright, *FSAC*, pp. 179–89 (Anchor ed., pp. 236–49); O'Callaghan, *Aram Naharaim* (Rome, 1948); R. de Vaux, *RB* 53 (1946), pp. 321–48; 55 (1948), pp. 321–47; 56 (1949), pp. 5–36; G. E. Wright, *Biblical Archaeology* (Philadelphia, 1957), pp. 40–52.
41. New data appear every year. See now E. A. Speiser, *BASOR* 144 (1956), pp. 20–23. It is no accident that it is those who have been most thoroughly trained in the literary and cultural history of the Middle and Late Bronze Ages who have treated the Biblical narrative with the greatest respect.
42. Cf. Albright, *JBL* 58 (1939), pp. 91–103; *FSAC*, p. 112 (Anchor ed., pp. 154–55).
43. *Archaeology and the Religion of Israel*, p. 99.
44. See the discussion by John Bright, *Early Israel in Recent History Writing* (Chicago, 1957), pp. 100–4.
45. A good illustration of this process can be seen in Mesopotamia during the transition from Sumerian to Old Babylonian culture. Certain aspects of Sumerian religious tradition were valued, readapted, and preserved. Others died out. Cf. Kramer, S. N., "The Oldest Literary Catalogue," *BASOR* 88 (1942), pp. 10–19.
46. *FSAC*, pp. 153–54 (Anchor ed., pp. 204–6).
47. *Archaeology and the Religion of Israel*, Chapter III.
48. Contrary to earlier unfounded views. Cf. Albright, *BASOR* 71 (1938), pp. 35–40.
49. Knudtzon, *Die El-Amarna Tafeln*, p. 45; R. Bowman, *JNES* vii (1948), pp. 68 ff.
50. Cf. note 40.
51. Contrast the rapid assimilation of Amorites in Mesopotamia to the Sumero-Accadian culture!
52. Among others, see Dhorme, *La Religion des Hébreux nomades* (Brussels, 1937), p. 69.
53. This has already been done to some extent. Cf. J. P. Hyatt, "Yahweh as 'The God of my father,'" *VT* v (1955), pp. 130–36. This will be discussed at length elsewhere.
54. Art. "Israel," reprinted in translation by Black and Menzies, in *Prolegomena to the History of Ancient Israel*, p. 429.
55. Ibid., p. 432.
56. Cf. T. J. Meek, "Monotheism and the religion of Israel," *JBL* lxi (1942), p. 37.
57. See G. E. Wright, *The Old Testament Against its Environment* (Chicago, 1950), p. 12, on Oesterley and Robinson, *Hebrew Religion* (New York, 1930): "One fourth of this book is given over to the description of the animistic and magical background of Israel's religion."
58. Meek, op. cit. Compare Albright, *Archaeology and the Religion of Israel*, p. 175: "In essentials, however, orthodox Yahwism remained the same from Moses to Ezra," with Meek, op. cit., p. 35: "A world concept politically, a world view is the necessary prerequisite to the idea of a world god. In the time of Moses the Hebrews were just learning to take their first steps in the direction of nationalism and were still a long way from internationalism. They could not possibly reach up to a world concept or a world god." This conflict is not one for the historian, but for the theologian, for radically opposed views of what religion *is* clash here head on.
59. Cf. Mendenhall, *BASOR* 133 (1954), pp. 26–30, and literature there cited; *Law and Covenant in Israel and the Ancient Near East* (Pittsburgh, 1955).

60. Wellhausen, "Israel," loc. cit. p. 432; Noth, *Geschichte Israels*, p. 45.
61. The writer expects to publish a fuller treatment of the problem in a future issue of *JBL*.
62. See the discussion of H. H. Rowley, *From Joseph to Joshua* (London, 1950).
63. Rowley, ibid., pp. 158–59, and literature cited in his note 1, p. 159.
64. See *Law and Covenant in Israel and the Ancient Near East*.
65. Cf. John Bright, *The Kingdom of God* (New York, 1953), pp. 26–27 and note 14; and Eichrodt, op. cit. (n. 33).
66. Noth, *Das System der zwölf Stämme Israels* (1930); Alt, *Die Ursprünge des israelitischen Rechts* (*Kleine Schriften* I [Munich, 1953], pp. 278–332).
67. Op. cit., p. 327 f.
68. Albright, *JBL* LXIII (1944), pp. 207–33; *JAOS* 67 (1947), pp. 153–60; Cross and Freedman, "The Blessing of Moses," *JBL* LXVII (1948), pp. 191–210; and "The Song of Miriam," *JNES* XIV (1955), pp. 237–50.
69. This must have been true particularly of the region around Shechem and in the extreme northwest of Palestine.
70. It is, at least to the present writer, impossible to conceive of a tribal federation without a covenant at this time, and equally impossible to conceive of a covenant which would not be intimately connected with Yahweh, and consequently with the Mosaic tradition.
71. Ultimately from Egypt probably via the Canaanites: see J. Begrich, *ZAW*, NF 17 (1940), pp. 1–29; and R. de Vaux, *RB* 48 (1939), pp. 394–405.
72. Alt, "Das Königtum in den Reichen Israel und Juda," *VT* I (1951), pp. 1–22.
73. See now for the most recent summary, A. R. Johnson, *Sacral Kingship in Ancient Israel* (Cardiff, 1955).
74. Albright, *Archaeology and the Religion of Israel*, pp. 156–57.
75. II Kings 10:15–16.
76. Wellhausen's view that Elijah first introduces ethical concerns (Naboth's vineyard) into Yahwism can be upheld only by throwing out all the evidence from earlier times.
77. Albright, *Journal of Bible and Religion*, VIII (1940), pp. 131–36; N. Porteous, "The Basis of the Ethical Teachings of the Prophets," in H. H. Rowley, ed., *Studies in Old Testament Prophecy* (Edinburgh and New York, 1950), pp. 143–56.
78. "Primitivism in Western Asia," in Lovejoy and Boas, *Primitivism and Related Ideas in Antiquity* (Baltimore, 1935), pp. 421–32.
79. Albright, *Journal of Bible and Religion*, VIII (1940), p. 131.
80. Amos 3:2.
81. *Prolegomena . . .*, p. 417: "The relation of Jehovah to Israel was in its nature and origin a natural one; there was no interval between Him and His people to call for thought or question."
82. See Albright, *FSAC*, pp. 246 f. (Anchor ed., pp. 322 ff.).
83. One wonders, for example, whether the final canonization, at least, if not the collection of the old legal traditions, is not connected with the Persian Empire and its conceptions (whatever they may have been) of law. Cf. George Cameron, "Ancient Persia," in R. D. Dentan, ed., *The Idea of History in the Ancient Near East* (New Haven, 1955), pp. 91 f., where he emphasizes the Persian concern for the codification of Egyptian religious and customary law.

CHAPTER THREE

The Hebrew Language in its
Northwest Semitic Background

WILLIAM L. MORAN

THE LAST THREE DECADES may justly be called a new epoch in the study of the Hebrew language. What sets this period apart in the history of Hebrew studies is the great increase it has brought to our knowledge of earlier and related dialects. The history of any language is always illuminating; obscurities can become luminous when seen in the light of their historical development. For the student of an ancient language, however, whose only source is the written word, and this in a relatively small body of material, such an historical perspective is often indispensable. The limitations of his material and the lack of native informants force him to the comparison of related, especially earlier, dialects. Only thus can he hope to grasp with greater precision the structure of the language, or to isolate and understand the function of those archaic speech forms which are so frequent in literary texts, especially in poetry. For the Hebraist, besides, such a procedure is the more necessary in that his texts have been the object of a long tradition, in the course of which dialectal and archaic elements have necessarily been obscured.

It is in the light of these problems that the importance of the new sources for the Northwest Semitic background of Hebrew is easily understood. Writing in 1822, Wilhelm Gesenius, "the father of modern Hebrew grammar," was confronted with "a total lack of historical data for the earlier (pre-Biblical) history of the origin and development of Hebrew."[1] A century later, in 1922, in the historical grammar of Hebrew published by H. Bauer and P. Leander,[2] of pre-Biblical Hebrew one still finds little history and much reconstruction. However, apart from the justifiable criticisms of both their reconstruction and their method, the task these scholars set themselves is to be appreciated in the light of the material available to them. Through the discoveries of the intervening century, among which was Gesenius's revolutionary decipherment of the Phoenician inscriptions, they were in an incomparably better position than Gesenius to write a history of the Hebrew language. Nevertheless, with the notable exception of the Amarna letters, there had occurred no significant break in the darkness which hung over Hebrew and related dialects in the second millennium.

The Amarna letters, it is true, had made a considerable contribution. Over two hundred of these letters were sent by vassal Canaanite kings to the Egyptian court in the early 14th century B.C. Composed by Canaanite scribes little conversant with the Babylonian language they were employing, besides containing numerous Canaanite glosses to Babylonian words, they constantly betray in form and idiom the native Canaanite speech of their writers. Discovered in 1887 at Tell el-Amarna in Egypt, and given a first-rate edition in 1907,[3] they advanced greatly our understanding of the early history of Hebrew, thanks especially to the studies of Böhl, Dhorme, and Ebeling.[4]

However, for the period of pre-Biblical Hebrew, there was still, for purposes of linguistic analysis, the same total lack of genuinely Canaanite texts which had confronted Gesenius.[5] The Amarna letters, moreover, instructive as they are, do attempt to pass as Babylonian, so that one cannot accept uncritically every feature of the language as genuinely Canaanite. The possibility must be left open for barbarisms inherited from other, both non-Babylonian and non-Canaanite, traditions. Besides, in order fully to exploit the indications of the vowels in the syllabic cuneiform, one ordinarily needs the guidance of some fairly comprehensive conception of what Canaanite speech was in this period.[6]

The last three decades or so have seen the situation changed profoundly. Owing especially to the great increase in archaeological activity between the two wars, many new sources of the greatest importance for Hebrew began to appear. They were to throw special light on two periods in the development of Hebrew, the first *ca.* 1900–1700 B.C., the second the Amarna period in the 14th century B.C.

For the earlier period mention should first be made of the publication in 1926 of *Die Ostkanaanäer* by the German Assyriologist, Theo Bauer.[7] Under the direction of B. Landsberger, he collected all of the personal and geographical names scattered through the Old Babylonian documents which had previously been recognized to reflect a West Semitic speech, and therefore of some relevance for early Hebrew.[8] Bauer's collection alone was an invaluable service, and to this he added the first systematic grammatical analysis of the names.

Also in 1926, Kurt Sethe published his decipherment of the execration texts.[9] Written in Egyptian, and dating from *ca.* 1925–1875 B.C., these texts were inscribed on vases with the names of potential rebel vassals, who, in the conceptions of sympathetic magic, were to be smashed with the smashing of the vases. Among these names were those of some thirty

Palestinian and Syrian chieftains, together with their respective localities. All were clearly of the same type and reflected the same language, with possible minor dialectal variations, which Bauer had studied in the cuneiform sources.

Complementing and doubling Sethe's material were the Brussels statuettes published by Posener in 1940.[10] Written on small figurines instead of vases, and of a later date (second half of the 19th century B.C.), they were likewise execration texts and, from a linguistic viewpoint, identical with the earlier texts. Finally, from Egyptian sources, an important contribution is an 18th-century list of Egyptian slaves (the Hayes list), recently published by Albright, in which are found over thirty Northwest Semitic names, mostly of women.[11]

We thus have from Egyptian sources around one hundred fifty personal and geographical names from Syria and Palestine between *ca.* 1900–1750 B.C. While in itself this is a meager source for purposes of linguistic analysis, still from the substantial identity of these names with those found in the incomparably richer cuneiform sources, we can safely project, with minor differences, the more detailed Mesopotamian picture into Syria and Palestine, while the Egyptian material, with its more accurate representation of the consonants, can at times be of great help in resolving the ambiguities of the cuneiform script.

Since Bauer's *Die Ostkanaanäer* in 1926, further publication of Old Babylonian letters and economic documents has added not a little to the stock of relevant personal names, but this contribution appears insignificant when compared with the results of excavations at Mari, Alalakh, and Chagar Bazar. Since 1933 ancient Mari, modern Tell Ḥarîri, on the middle Euphrates, has been, and will continue to be for many years, the principal source for early Northwest Semitic.[12] Because of its position, Mari was, by the standards of the time, a rich and powerful city, which, before its destruction by Hammurapi of Babylon, was coveted and ruled by two rival dynasties, whose native speech was close to, but not identical with, the Hebrew of the Patriarchal Age. A. Parrot and his staff have unearthed at this site over twenty thousand tablets, of which so far, apart from scattered publications in various journals, seven volumes with approximately eight hundred texts have been published.[13] From these documents, both letters and economic texts, we have over five hundred personal and geographical names pertinent to a reconstruction of early Northwest Semitic.[14] Moreover, though not to the extent found in the Amarna letters, the lexicon and idiom of the Mari letters are at times non-Babylonian, so that through them we gain further insights into the Northwest Semitic speech of this period.[14a] With but a small part of the Mari texts available, further publication can only increase the already tremendous importance of Mari for Northwest Semitic studies.

In ancient Alalakh of northern Syria, which was excavated between 1936–49 under the direction of Woolley, we have another important source.[15]

Aside from an occasional interesting lexical item such as LÚ(.MEŠ) *ma-si/zi,* "men of the corvée" (Heb. *mas*),[16] Alalakh's contribution is also one of personal names, about a hundred from a period contemporary with the First Dynasty of Babylon, with a smaller number from the 15th century.[17] Another roughly contemporary onomasticon is revealed in the Chagar Bazar texts from northwestern Mesopotamia.[18]

Our primary need now is a study like Theo Bauer's which, utilizing all the new material, will present us with a complete grammatical analysis of the language.[19] Only thus shall we be able to see what is involved in the discussion, if not to agree on the solution, of the problem of naming this language. Bauer called the language East Canaanite, here following Landsberger, who still, *"faute de mieux,"* retains this designation.[20] At first M. Noth preferred proto-Aramaic and, though he has subsequently abandoned the term itself, he has continued to urge connections with later Aramaic.[21] This is the linguistic relationship also stressed by J. Lewy, though he would insist that the speakers of the language be called Amorites.[22] By distinguishing Arabic and Canaanite theophorous elements in the onomasticon, E. Dhorme distinguished two linguistic groups.[23] Albright's position is more nuanced. Though he has frequently used Bauer's term, often with a parenthetical addition, "East Canaanite (Amorite)," still he does not agree with Bauer, as is clear from his review of *Die Ostkanaanäer.*[24] For him the language is one of five principal dialects distinguishable in the second millennium, identical with neither (South-) Canaanite nor proto-Aramaic.[25] Yet he can also write that "the Aramean language sprang from a West Semitic dialect spoken in northwestern Mesopotamia in the early second millennium B.C., a dialect which seems to have left clear traces in the Mari documents,"[26] thus drawing our language closer to Aramaic than to Canaanite. Most recently A. Caquot has cut the Gordian knot by refusing to call the language anything more than early West Semitic.[27] In his opinion the language evidences a stage of early development to which the later divisions of West Semitic cannot be applied.[28]

The answer to this problem is obviously of importance to the Hebraist. If Bauer's "East Canaanite" is justified, then the Mari and related material is of greater immediate relevance for the history of Hebrew than if, as the writer believes, we should avoid both "Canaanite" and "Aramaic" as misleading and see rather in this language an ancient and venerable uncle of both Canaanite and Aramaic, who was, it should be stressed, a colorful personality with an individuality bordering on eccentricity.[29] In this case we should adopt, as henceforth in this paper, one of several candidates, all with historical credentials, such as "Amorite" or "Khanean."

Turning to the second period illumined by the discoveries of the last thirty years, that of the 14th century B.C., we come to the revolutionary aspect of our topic—the discoveries at ancient Ugarit. As at Amarna forty years earlier, it was the chance discovery of an Arab peasant which led to the excavation of this site on the northern Syrian coast.[30] But excavation here by French archaeologists revealed cuneiform tablets written, not only in Babylonian[31] but also in an alphabet which, on decipherment by H. Bauer, Dhorme, and Virolleaud, disclosed a hitherto completely unknown Northwest Semitic dialect. More important, the contents of the tablets were principally epic literature. Contacts with Biblical literature were immediately apparent, and today there are few areas of Biblical studies unaffected by the discoveries at Ugarit. Prosody, textual criticism, literary history, Biblical theology—all have a pre- and post-Ugaritic date.

Not the least affected was Hebrew grammar. While the relationship of Ugaritic with Canaanite and, therefore, with Hebrew is a matter of increasing discussion,[32] no one denies its invaluable contribution, both directly and indirectly, to our understanding of the Hebrew language. Since it could be overlooked, the indirect contribution should be stressed. For it is because of Ugaritic that we have returned to earlier known material, and to new discoveries. It was Albright who, in a series of articles, indicated the new possibilities, especially in the Amarna letters, that Ugaritic had opened up.[33] The significance of Ugarit can be justly estimated only if this further contribution is also recognized.

In what follows we present a summary of the discoveries of the last thirty years which we owe to the sources described above. Unsatisfactory as this is from the viewpoint of linguistic description, it has the merit of avoiding, so far as possible, undue and unproved assumptions in the very complicated problem of Northwest Semitic relationships. At the same time, it should, we believe, show how few areas of Hebrew grammar have remained unaffected by the discoveries of these three decades.

Behind the phonemic structure of the Hebrew transmitted to us in the Biblical text there is a long history, of which we mention here only the more important developments in the earlier stages. Proto-Hebrew and related Northwest Semitic dialects possessed at one time, allowing for dialectal divergences, about twenty-five to twenty-seven consonants. Though the evidence for the period *ca.* 1900–1700 B.C. is not without its gaps and ambiguities,[34] later evidence indicates that *ca.* 1400 B.C. is a *terminus post quem* for the developments which resulted in the twenty-two consonant Hebrew alphabet. This date follows from the now famous ABC tablet at Ugarit.[35] If we bracket both those consonants which later coalesced with other consonants and the demonstrable Ugarit additions at the end, this tablet gives us the Hebrew alphabet of later centuries in exactly the same order: *'a, b, g,* [h]*, d, h, w, z, ḥ, ṭ, y, k,* [*š*]*, l, m,* [*ḏ*]*, n,* [*z*]*, s, ', p, ṣ, q, r, t,* [*ǵ*]*, t,* [*'i, 'u, š*]. Since the Ugarit additions are placed at the end of this alphabet, it is clear that the order of the other consonants must be borrowed from elsewhere. Were the other bracketed consonants also Ugarit additions, some principle governing their place of insertion should be observable; as Gordon has rightly stressed,[36] there is no such principle. The source, therefore, of this alphabet must be sought elsewhere, which, in view both of the general historical and cultural situation, as well as of known prior alphabetic activities, must be in the Canaanite speaking area to the south.[37] This only confirms what Albright has maintained for years on the evidence of the Egyptian transcriptions: before the earliest Phoenician and Biblical texts, Canaanite possessed a larger number of consonants than the later Phoenician alphabet indicated.[38]

In Hebrew, as elsewhere in Canaanite, *ḥ* coalesced with *ḫ*, *ṭ* with *ṣ̌*, *ḏ* with *z*, *ẓ* with *ṣ*, *ġ* with *ʿ*; the period of these shifts probably began in the 14th century.[39] However, diverging from the rest of Canaanite, Hebrew went its own way in preserving proto-Semitic *ś*. While the Jerusalem Amarna evidence on etymological *ṭ*, *ś*, and *ṣ̌* is not without its difficulties, the writer agrees with Goetze,[40] against Harris,[41] that the apparent anomalies are to be explained as due to the syllabary which the Jerusalem scribe employed, rather than as reflecting a complicated and unparalleled development. Goetze's view receives confirmation from several other peculiarities of the Jerusalem Amarna texts which set the Jerusalem scribe in another scribal tradition than that found in the other Canaanite Amarna letters.[42]

We have already seen dialectal divergences in the earliest attested evidence for Northwest Semitic. The picture after that is one of increasing variation and the gradual emergence of more dialects.[43] In addition to the consonantal differences just noted, vocalic changes took place. While the originally long vowels were in general stable, *â* became *ô* in most of the Canaanite speaking groups south of Ugarit in the period between 1700–1375 B.C. Short vowels were much more susceptible of mutation, and after the Amarna period final short vowels were generally lost, including the case endings of the noun (*-u, -i, -a*). The diphthongs were contracted (*au > ô, ai > ê*) before the Amarna period from Ugarit as far as Jerusalem. In the early period *au* still existed,[44] whereas for *ai* there is no clear evidence.[45] The Jerusalem dialect of Hebrew, however, retained the diphthongs and thus diverged dialectally from the Hebrew of the northern kingdom. There, as we know from the Samaria ostraca, Hebrew followed the pattern of Phoenicia, which in view of Israel's geographical position is understandable. In general, Palestine repeatedly appears as a linguistic "backwoods" in the development of Canaanite. Many changes occurred in Canaanite which either never reached Palestine, or only after a considerable interval.[46]

The loss of case endings in the noun, just mentioned above, is nothing new, but what is new is that there are not nearly so many remnants in Hebrew of the early case endings as had been previously thought. One established view was that the so-called *he locale* in expressions like *šamaima,* "heavenwards," preserved the earlier accusative ending *a*. This has been conclusively disproved by Ugaritic, where we also find, for example, *šmmh*. In the purely consonantal script of Ugarit the final *h* cannot be a *mater lectionis* indicating the vowel *a*, but must also be consonantal.[47]

Another remnant of the case endings has been thought to be the explanation of the *i* ending called the *hireq compaginis;* this, too, at least in the majority of cases, must be seriously questioned. In Exodus 15:6, "Thy right hand, O Yahweh, is fearful [*ne'dārî*] in strength," in *ne'dārî* we must deny at least any immediate connection with the genitive, for, as has been pointed out,[48] the grammatical difficulties which have led scholars to prefer the easier reading, *ne'dārā,* admit of an easy solution if we revocalize the consonantal text as *ne'dôrî,* that is, as an infinitive absolute. The basis for such a revocalization is to be found in similar infinitives, also with a similar *i* ending, in both the Jerusalem and the Byblos Amarna letters.[49] So, too, in Genesis 49:11, "He tethers ['*ôsᵉrî*] his ass to the vine," we would revocalize the apparent participle as an infinitive absolute (*'āsôrî*).[50] Not only is the participle with the *hireq compaginis* almost exclusively confined to appellatives,[51] which does not fit here, but an infinitive absolute used in narrative with subject unexpressed is quite normal, which is not true of the participle.

The presence in Amarna, moreover, of three participles with an *i* ending suggests that the *hireq compaginis* with participles in Hebrew is also not a remnant of the older genitive.[52] Speculation as to the precise function of this final vowel is, of course, impossible on the basis of three examples, but some connection with the *hireq compaginis* is hard to avoid. Since, whatever its function, the vowel in Amarna cannot be a remnant of the genitive in a period when case endings are still in use, the archaizing participles in Hebrew are not to be considered differently.

Ugaritic, with corroboration from Amorite and Amarna, has clarified or revealed several particles in Hebrew, the existence of some of which had been forgotten in later centuries. The most important of these is enclitic *mem,* which has cleared up scores of grammatical and logical inconcinnities of the Hebrew text. It is found in Mari names like *'Abdu-ma-Dagan,* "Servant of Dagan,"[53] and in a variety of uses in Amarna as well as in Ugaritic. After H. D. Hummel's completely convincing study on the subject,[54] a skepticism which prefers to suspect the text rather than accept a linguistic feature attested in Amorite, Ugaritic, and Amarna (Jerusalem!) should be virtually impossible.[55] The *motnê-m qāmau* of Deuteronomy 33:11 clearly belongs with Ugaritic *takmê-mi/ma ḥâmîti,* "the top of the wall,"[56] and Jerusalem Amarna's *ûbilī-mi ḥarrānāt šarri,* "the porters of the royal caravans."[57]

From Ugaritic, too, we learn of the particle *l* (vocalization uncertain) with different uses. The first and commonest is the asseverative *l* (probably *la*), found also in Amorite, as, for example, in *Sumī-la-'ammu* (*Su-mi-lam-mu*),[58] *'Ammī-la-'addu* (*Am-mi-la-du*),[59] *La-'aḥī-ṣaduq* (*La-ḥi-ṣa-du-uq*).[60] Thus, in Psalms 89:19 we have "For truly is Yahweh (*l-YHWH*) our shield, truly the Holy One (*l-qᵉdôš*) of Israel our king."[61] It is also found before a verb, as in Albright's ingenious solution to the hitherto hopelessly obscure Hab. 3:6, "While everlasting mountains broke up, Eternal hills collapsed, Eternal orbits were shattered (*l-tḥt'n*)."[62] A second use is with vocatives, pointed out by Albright in Psalms 68:34, *l-rôkēb,* "O Rider," by coincidence occurring with the same word in Ugaritic.[63] A similar use of the particle is perhaps the best explanation of the *l* in the name *Remaliah: Rûm-l-Yāhû,* "Be exalted, O Yahu."[64]

Ugaritic has thrown light on several other particles. This is true of the particle *kî* in Genesis 18:20 (*kî rabbā, kî kāb^edā,* "indeed great, indeed excessive") and in several other places, where, as in Ugaritic, we find the verb thrown to the end of its clause.[65] Moreover, in the light of Ugaritic,[66] now confirmed by Amarna,[67] where the conditional particle *hm* retains its original deictic force of "behold" or the like, Patton has collected a number of cases of Hebrew *hm(h)* where the apparent personal pronoun becomes intelligible when taken as a deictic particle.[68] The evidence for the conditional particle with this force confirms the earlier explanation of the so-called "*waw* of apodosis," found also at Mari[69] as well as in the Canaanite of the 14th century, as deriving from the original paratactic construction in Hebrew conditional and temporal clauses.

Examples where the Hebrew prepositions *b^e, l^e, 'al* have been clarified in the light of Ugaritic are now legion, and many of the old textual emendations now seen to be quite unnecessary. For it is now clear that where our idiom demands "from," Hebrew (Canaanite) and Ugaritic idiom employed "in," "in regard to," and "upon."[70]

To the Hebrew pronouns Ugaritic has added the indefinite interrogative *mn,* discovered by Albright in Deuteronomy 33:11, *umiśśôn^e'au mn y^eqûmun,* "and from his enemies whoever rises up."[71] It has also provided the first evidence in Northwest Semitic, outside of Hebrew, for the use of *'^ašer* as a relative pronoun: *'tr 'it bqt wšt ly,* "Find out what there is available, and then place [it] at my disposal."[72] The archaic use of the demonstrative in expressions like *ze Sînai,* "the one of Sinai," now finds parallels both in Ugaritic *đ-p'id,* "the one of mercy," an epithet of El, and in Mari names like *Zu-ḫatni(m),*[73] *Zu-ḫadim,*[74] *Zu-sumim,*[75] and possibly *Zu-ša-abi.*[76]

However, important as these discoveries have been for our knowledge of Hebrew, the major advances have been in the area of the verb. The Hebrew verb, it is true, still remains the source of most grammatical *cruces,* but progress within the last thirty years, if not bringing definitive solutions to all the problems, has at least focused the problems more clearly.

We may mention first the discovery of the unsuspected role of the infinitive absolute in Hebrew. The largest share of the credit for this discovery must be given to the long Phoenician inscription from Karatepe in Cilicia, though Ugaritic and Amarna are not without some contribution.[77] The use of the infinitive absolute instead of a finite verb was not unknown to Hebrew grammar, but it was not given due consideration nor, as a result, brought to bear on the solution of certain problems of the Hebrew text. It was Karatepe and, in its light, Ugaritic and Amarna, which demanded a serious investigation of the infinitive absolute in Hebrew and the extent of its use. This

Huesman has given us in two articles,[78] demonstrating that the substitution of the infinitive absolute for the finite verb was a fairly common construction.

Amarna and Ugaritic have shown the antiquity of the construction, and the relevance of the former, with its final *i* vowel added to the infinitive, for *ne'dārî* in Exodus 15:6 and *'ôsᵉrî* in Genesis 49:11 we have already seen. The infinitive with the additional *i* vowel is also used paronomastically in Amarna,[79] and we would suggest that the same construction underlies the text of Genesis 30:8. The text *naptûlê 'ᵉlôhîm niptaltî* has had different explanations, but all agree in taking *naptûlê* as a noun. Yet a *naqtûl* formation is otherwise unknown in Hebrew. It seems much simpler to revocalize, leaving the consonantal text untouched, *niptôlî 'ᵉlôhîm niptaltî,* and translate, "Greatly (lit. "with contending"), O God, have I contended," that is, to see in NPTWLY an infinitive absolute. While this has the slight difficulty of separating the infinitive from the finite verb—*'ᵉlôhîm,* however, may be secondary—it is far easier to accept than an anomalous *naqtûl* formation.

Another feature of the verb that is now clear regards the prefix of the Pi'el and causative conjugations. This had formerly been thought, at least in the Pi'el, to go back to *yu* as in Arabic and Akkadian. But in Ugaritic it is *ya* both in the Pi'el and in the causative.[80] In the earlier material the situation is not clear with regard to the Pi'el. The hypocoristicon *Ibassir*[81] is, on the evidence of all the Semitic languages, a Pi'el, and since the only evidence we have is for *ya > i,* we would reconstruct a more original *Yabassir.* Another group of forms (*Yamatti,* etc.) that might possibly be cited in this connection will be discussed below. But in the causative the prefix is clearly *ya: Ia-ki-in,*[82] *Ia-ri-im,*[83]   *Ia-ás-ki-in,*[84] *Ia-ú-ṣí,*[85]   *Ia-au$_x$(PI)-ṣí,*[86] *Ia-ás-li-im,*[87] *Ia-ši-ib,*[88] possibly *Ia-am-li-ik.*[89] Further, in view of the participles *Me-mi-ḫi-im*[90] and *Me-bi-šum,*[91] we would take *-emiḫ* in *Mu-ti-e-mi-iḫ*[92] as deriving originally from a causative *yamiḫ,* and *Ia-bi-šum*[93] as another causative.

In connection with the causative, it is to be noted that Amorite evidences a somewhat surprising antiquity for the performative *mē-* in the participles of the so-called hollow verbs. At Alalakh we have *Me-ki-in,*[94] and at Mari *Me-ki-nu-um,*[95] both identical with the Hebrew participle *mēkîn.* At Chagar Bazar we have *Me-mi-ḫi-im* and possibly *Me-ḫi-ri.*[96] However, it is possible that the origin of *mēkîn* in Hebrew is not the same as in this dialect, for we also find *Me-pí-ḫu-um,*[97] *Me-eḫ-ni-yu-um,*[98] *Me-ki-bu-um,*[99] *Me-ès-ki-nim* (genitive),[100] *Me-es₅-ki-ru-um,*[101]   *Me-es₅-li-mu-um,*[102] *Me-en-ḫi-mu-um,*[103] as well as *Me-bi-šum* already mentioned above. These forms show that *meqtil* was the regular form of the causative participle in Amorite, though the origin of the preformative remains obscure.[104]

An anomaly of the Canaanite verb in the 14th century, without parallel in the other Semitic languages, is the third plural masculine form *taqtulû(na),* along with the usual *yaqtulû(na).* While the existence of the form in Ugaritic might be doubted if one confines himself to the obscurity of a script which generally does not indicate vowels, still in view of the clear Amarna evidence for the form we should have no indication in extending *taqtulû(na)* from Byblos to Ugarit.[105]

The relevance, however, of this form for the explanation of certain *t* preformative forms with plural subjects in the Bible is still not settled. Albright, while admitting the Amarna and Ugaritic evidence, has not extended its application to the Hebrew forms, preferring to see in them a third feminine singular with plural subject taken as a collective.[106] Since this construction is attested in Hebrew,[107] it is virtually impossible to decide the question because of the ambiguities of the Hebrew text. However, it would be most surprising if in archaic or archaizing texts the Amarna-Ugaritic form never occurred, so that in the writer's opinion the existence of the form in Hebrew must be considered highly probable, though lacking conclusive proof.[108]

Two more discoveries bring us to the central problem of the Hebrew verb.[109] The first regards the imperfect, in so far as it derives from the earlier indicative *yaqtulu*. That Hebrew one time possessed an indicative is not new, but its usage has never been determined from texts of Canaanite provenience, and the date of its appearance in Canaanite placed much too late. Usage and date can now be fixed with considerable accuracy as the result of a re-examination of the Amarna letters.

In the largest single group of texts, those from Byblos, we can establish two principal uses of the indicative in the 14th century: first, as a present-future, and second, as a past iterative. The first is found in over two hundred examples; the latter, with twenty-three examples, is much rarer, but sufficiently well attested. One passage may be quoted, since it illustrates very happily the use of the "tenses" at Byblos: *miya mārū Abd-aširta ardi kalbi šar māt Kašši u šar māt Mitanni šunu u tilqûna māt šarri ana šāšunu panânu tilqûna ālāni ḫazānīka u qâlāta annû inanna dubbirū rābiṣaka u laqû ālānišu ana šāšunu anumma laqû āl Ullaza šumma ki'amma qâlāta adi tilqûna āl Ṣumura u tidûkūna rābiṣa u ṣāb tillati ša ina Ṣumura,* "Who are the sons of 'Abd-aširta, the slave and dog? Are they the king of the Kassites or the king of the Mitanni that they take the royal land for themselves? Previously they used to take the cities of your governors, and you were negligent. Behold! now they have driven out your commissioner and have taken his cities for themselves. Indeed, they have taken Ullaza. If you are negligent this way, they will take Simyra besides, and they will kill the commissioner and the auxiliary force which is in Simyra."[110]

Especially striking here is the use of the verb *leqû* in the perfect and imperfect. Three times we have *tilqûna,* once as a present, once as a future, once as a past. In the last instance it describes repeated action: previously the sons of 'Abd-aširta had made a practice of capturing cities ruled by a royal governor (Canaanite king), keeping clear of a city where a royal commissioner was stationed. However, when the latest single enormity is contrasted with former practice, there is an immediate shift from the imperfect indicative *tilqûna* to the perfect *laqû.*

While, admittedly, this passage is something of a *tour de force,* it does not convey a false impression of the general picture which emerges from a careful study of every example of the indicative in the Byblos letters. Moreover, there is no reason why, allowing for minor differences, we should not consider Byblian usage as comparable with that of contemporary Hebrew. Whatever, therefore, the previous history of the Canaanite verb, we can say that by the 14th century the imperfect indicative with the above usage was not starting to develop, as Harris thought,[111] but was already well established as part of the verbal scheme.

The second discovery is that of the origin of the Hebrew cohortative. The origin of *'eqtᵉlā* and *niqtᵉla* has long been a moot point of Hebrew grammar. Of the many views proposed, that of H. Bauer[112] and Joüon[113] turns out to be correct: the cohortative is a remnant of the earlier "subjunctive." This follows as an obvious corollary once the use of *yaqtula* in Byblian Amarna is established, since the use of the cohortative is substantially identical with that of *yaqtula* in Byblos.

Of the seventy-nine occurrences of the subjunctive form which can be analyzed, over seventy per cent fall into a jussive-purpose use, slightly more than fifteen per cent occur in conditional sentences. The statistics in themselves are very significant. Of equal or greater importance are two other aspects of the usage. First, the scribe shifts between *yaqtulu* and *yaqtula* within the' same letter, even within the same sentence, in a clearly defined pattern of usage. Thus, *yûdana šeʾim mûṣa māt Yarimuta ša yûdanu panânu ina āl Ṣumura yûdana inanna ina āl Gubla,* "Let grain, the product of Yarimuta, be given; what used to be given in Simyra, let it be given now in Byblos." Second, besides many illustrations of this sort, the syntax of purpose clauses is to be noted: after an indicative in the main clause, an indicative in the purpose clause; after a jussive or an imperative in the main clause, another jussive, imperative, or *yaqtula* in the purpose clause. This rule can be established quite independently of *yaqtula,* the use of which, therefore, in purpose clauses must be significant and reflect Canaanite idiom. In brief, the existence of a form corresponding to the Arabic subjunctive is beyond doubt for the 14th-century Canaanite of Byblos, and since the Hebrew cohortative squares with Byblian usage, its origin is now clear.

For the 14th-century Hebrew we would, therefore, reconstruct the following verbal scheme: punctual *qatala,* durative *yaqtulu,* jussive *yaqtul,* "emphatic" jussive *yaqtula.* That the Hebrew perfect goes back to the Amarna period has long been known, but what has not received due attention are the parallels to the *waw*-conversive with the perfect.[114] Yet in the Byblos letters there are thirty-three cases where the perfect is used with reference to the future. Of these, twenty-four are preceded by the conjunction *u,* "and," and are comparable, therefore, to the well-known construction of Hebrew; of the remaining nine, eight are in the protasis of a conditional sentence, the ninth in a temporal clause. For example, *dûkūmi eṭlakunu u* IBAŠŠĀTUNU *kīma yatinu u* PAŠḪATUNU, "Kill your lord, and then you will be like us and have peace";[115] *šumma ṣābu piṭati* IBAŠŠAT *kali mātāti nilqu ana šarri,* "If there will be an archer-host [at our disposal], we will seize all lands for the king";[116] *allu paṭārima awīlūt ḫupši u* ṢABTŪ *Ḫapirū āla,* "Behold! if the serfs desert, then the 'Apiru will seize the city";[117] *u la* KAŠID *irēšu u ušširtīšu,* "As soon as the request arrives, I will send him."[118]

However, besides such cases, we also have examples like *u laqû ālānišu,* "and they have taken his cities," where the underlying Canaanite *waw* does not convert the tense; above in discussing *yaqtulu,* we cited *u tidûkūna,* "and they will kill," not *u dâkū.* A clue toward resolving this apparent conflict in "tense" usage is probably to be found in the fact that, with the exception of the two perfects in the last passage cited above, all of these perfects occur in sentences which are implicitly or explicitly conditional. And the exceptions are more apparent than real, since they occur with a temporal clause, the general structure of which is identical with that of conditional sentences. This restriction to conditional sentences, where optative and precative elements are well attested, would seem to corroborate H. L. Ginsberg's insight[119] that the development of the *waw* conversive with the perfect in Hebrew was favored by one of the original functions of the perfect, namely, as an optative or precative. This much seems clear: Byblos shows us an early stage of the far more developed Hebrew usage.

The history of the Hebrew verb earlier than the Amarna period is most obscure. It has been frequently pointed out that the use of the verb in Ugaritic finds much closer parallels in Hebrew poetry, especially the early poetry, than in Hebrew prose.[120] Valuable as this observation is, the central problem remains of finding a clear pattern of complementary distribution for *yaqtul, yaqtulu,* and *qatala*—and if one holds the existence of *yaqattal(u),* for this form too. It is clear that the Ugaritic tense system is not that of contemporary Byblian Amarna. But what is it?[121] The writer would make no pretensions of knowing, and so must content himself with pointing out some material from the new sources which must be taken into account by anyone attempting a solution.

First, the following names are to be considered: *Ia-ma-at-ti*-DINGIR,[122] *Ia-na-ab-bi*-DINGIR,[123] *Ia-na-bi*-DINGIR,[124] *Ia-na-bi-im,*[125] *Ia-ba-si-ᵈDa-gan,*[126] *Ia-ḫa-at-ti*-DINGIR,[127] *Ia-ḫa-at-ti-*ᵈUTU,[128] *Ia-za-at-ti*-DINGIR,[129] *Ia-ba-an-ni*-DINGIR.[130] These names are extremely important because they raise anew the question of the existence of the so-called present-future in early Northwest Semitic. The only alternative explanation would be that the verbs in question are to be considered Pi'els.[131] Arguments can be made for both views, none of which is decisive, though the writer leans to the present-future.

Along with these forms are to be taken into account the clear cases (six) in the Mari letters where we find the form *iparrasu* and *iprusu,* not in subordinate clauses as Akkadian grammar demands, but in main clauses.

Finet has called them *"subjonctif d'insistance ou d'emphase,"*[132] but this is a *pis aller,* as is seen from his having recourse to the barbarous Akkadian of Idrimi for parallels. Certainly the simplest solution is to take these forms as momentary lapses of the scribes into their native idiom; if so, we would have further evidence, first, of the *yaqattal(u)* form in early Northwest Semitic, and secondly, of *yaqtulu* used in past narrative as at Ugarit.

Finally, the very meager evidence for the perfect in the early period is to be considered. Against Noth, who has persistently argued the opposite, it should be stressed that the perfects which he alleges are all statives,[133] which is something quite different in a discussion of tense distribution. Genuine perfects are to be found only in *Da-ni*-DINGIR,[134] *Su-mi-ra-pa*,[135] and possibly in *Qa-ra-*^{d}EŠ$_4$.DAR[136] and *Ma-la-ak-ì-lí*.[137] Whether this is to be explained as due to the normal content (prayers of petition rather than statements of fact) of the names, or to the recent emergence of the perfect, must be a cardinal point in any discussion of tenses.

Rome; January, 1957; revised, April, 1958.

NOTES TO CHAPTER THREE

1. Wilhelm Gesenius, *Hebräische Grammatik*[5], Halle, 1822.
2. Hans Bauer und Pontus Leander, *Historische Grammatik der Hebräischen Sprache* I, Halle, 1922.
3. J. A. Knudtzon, *Die El-Amarna Tafeln* I, Leipzig, 1907 (abbreviation *EA*); II (Glossary and remarks with collaboration of O. Weber and E. Ebeling), 1915.
4. Böhl, *Die Sprache der Amarna Briefe,* Leipzig, 1909; Dhorme, *RB,* 10 (1913), pp. 369–93; 11 (1914), pp. 37–59, 344–72 (reprinted in *Recueil Édouard Dhorme,* Paris, 1951, pp. 405–87); Ebeling, *Beiträge zur Assyriologie* 8, 39–79.
5. The proto-Sinaitic inscriptions had not been deciphered, and the valuable material in Max Burchardt, *Die altkanaanäischen Fremdworte und Eigennamen im Aegyptischen* (Leipzig, 1910), could not be fully exploited until the orthographic principles governing Egyptian transcriptions were determined; this was Albright's contribution in *The Vocalization of the Egyptian Syllabic Orthography,* New Haven, 1934.
6. Albright and Moran, *JCS* 2 (1948), pp. 239–40.
7. *Die Ostkanaanäer, Eine philologisch-historische Untersuchung über die Wanderschicht der sogenannten "Amoriter" in Babylonien,* Leipzig, 1926.
8. Dhorme, *RB,* 5 (1908), p. 216.
9. *Die Ächtung feindlicher Fürsten, Völker und Dinge auf altägyptischen Tongefässscherben des mittleren Reiches,* Berlin, 1926.
10. *Princes et Pays d'Asie et de Nubie,* Bruxelles, 1940. On the personal names of the execration texts, see Albright, *JPOS* 8 (1928), pp. 223–56; *BASOR* 81, pp. 16–21, 83, pp. 30–36; Noth, *ZDPV* 65 (1942), pp. 9–34; Moran, *Orientalia,* NS 26 (1957), pp. 339–45.
11. *JAOS* 74 (1954), pp. 222–33. The dates for the Egyptian texts given here follow those of Albright in this article.

12. Bibliography up to 1950, *Studia Mariana*, Leiden, 1950, pp. 127–38.

13. Translations and transliterations in *Archives royales de Mari (ARM)*, I–VI, Paris, 1950–54 (at the time of writing *ARM* VII has not appeared); cuneiform texts, *Textes cunéiformes de Louvre*, XXII–XXVIII; *Répertoire analytique des tomes I–V (ARM* XV), Paris, 1954.

14. The names occurring in *ARM* I–V are to be found in *ARM* XV, 120–60; for a study of these names, see especially Noth "Mari und Israel," *BHT* 16, pp. 127–52.

14a. Much of this material, with references to earlier studies, may be found in A. Finet, *L'accadien des lettres de Mari*, Bruxelles, 1956.

15. Sir Charles Leonard Woolley, *Alalakh*, Oxford, 1955; for a popular account by the same author, *A Forgotten Kingdom*, Penguin Books, 1953.

16. D. J. Wiseman, *The Alalakh Tablets*, London, 1953, 246:6, 13 (autograph *JCS* 8 [1954], p. 16), 259:15 (autograph ibid., 19), 265:7 (autograph ibid., 21), 269:18, 19. Cf. also ᴸᵁ*za-ki-ni* (all references in Wiseman, *The Alalakh Tablets*, p. 159; correct references in 256 to lines 19 and 27), which is Amarna *zu-ki-ni (EA* 256:9), *zu-ki-na (RA* 19 [1922], 103:69), and Heb. *sôkēn* (cf. Dhorme, *RB* 33 [1924], pp. 16–17).

17. Index of personal names, Wiseman, op. cit., pp. 125–53. (This index must be used with caution, being incomplete and not free from error in readings and datings; for corrections of dating, see Oppenheim, *JNES* 14 [1955], p. 197, n. 1, and Wiseman, *JCS* 8 [1954], p. 3.)

18. C. J. Gadd, *Iraq* 7 (1940), pp. 35–42.

19. We may expect this in a forthcoming monograph by I. Gelb. The writer would acknowledge his indebtedness to Professor Gelb for many discussions of the Amorite language, and in particular for the observation of the extent of the *me*-preformative in the causative participle (see below).

20. Landsberger, *ZA*, NF 1 (1926), p. 238; *JCS* 8 (1954), p. 56, n. 103. Recently, Dietz Otto Edzard, *Die "Zweite Zwischenzeit" Babyloniens*, Wiesbaden, 1957, p. 43, has given a qualified acceptance of Landsberger's view, though more from the historical than the linguistic viewpoint. Kupper, *Les nomades en Mésopotamie au temps des rois de Mari*, Paris, 1957, pp. 243–44, sees the problem as one remaining to be solved, and an important problem "car l'insuffisance de la terminologie ne peut que nuire à la rigueur et à la clarté de la synthèse historique."

21. *Die israelitischen Personennamen im Rahmen der gemeinsemitischen Namengebung*, Stuttgart, 1928, pp. 41–49; *ZDPV* 65 (1942), p. 34, n. 2; *BHT* 16, op. cit., p. 152.

22. *ZA*, NF 4 (1929), pp. 243–72.

23. *Recueil*, pp. 82–165, especially 104.

24. *AfO* 3 (1926), pp. 124–26.

25. *Atti del XIX Congresso Internazionale degli Orientalisti*, pp. 448–50.

26. *FSAC²*, p. 182 (Anchor ed., p. 239); cf. also *CBQ* 7 (1945), p. 18.

27. A. Caquot, *Annales archéologiques de Syrie* 1 (1951), p. 216.

28. Goetze's view, which connects the language with Ugaritic especially, should also be noted (cf. *Language* 17 [1941], pp. 134–37). This scholar would call the language Amorite.

29. Note that there is evidence of at least two dialects in this period, the distinguishing feature being a different scheme of sibilants. In cuneiform sources, with the exception of Alalakh, etymological *ṯ* is represented by *š, ś* and *ṧ* by *s*; in Egyptian sources, etymological *ṯ* is represented by *s, ś* by *s* (at least probably, on the evidence of the Hayes List and later material), *ṧ* by *š*; cf. Albright, *BASOR* 110, p. 15, n. 42. This is the general scheme, but there are many complicating factors in assessing the Egyptian evidence and, above all, that of Alalakh, where the confusion of the sibilants may reflect either actual differences of dialect, or

simply the practice of the *Hurrian* scribes. Note also *ARM* ɪɪ, 57:9, *sa-al-gu₅* (etymological ṭ!). The problem is not merely philological, but has important historical aspects, far beyond the scope of this paper.

30. For a brief review of the discoveries, translations, and bibliography, cf. G. R. Driver, *Canaanite Myths and Legends,* Edinburgh, 1956; also H. L. Ginsberg, *ANET²*, pp. 129–55.

31. For the Akkadian texts, cf. J. Nougayrol, *Le palais royal d'Ugarit,* ɪɪɪ, Paris, 1955; ɪv, 1956.

32. Literature reviewed by Moscati, "Il semitico di nord-ovest," *Studi Orientalistici in onore di Giorgio Levi della Vida,* ɪɪ, pp. 203–6.

33. *BASOR* 86, pp. 28–31; 87, pp. 32–38; 89, pp. 7–17, 29–32; cf. also Albright and Moran, *JCS* 2 (1948), pp. 239–48; ibid., 4 (1950), pp. 163–68.

34. Noth, *ZA*, NF 5 (1930), pp. 219 ff., questioned Bauer's assumption that the phonetic shifts producing the consonantal scheme of Hebrew had actually occurred in Amorite. Goetze, *Language* 17 (1941), p. 134, n. 60, equating *Ia-ás-ku-ur* with *Iaḋkur*, would find evidence for the preservation of ḋ. We would point rather to *A-ad-ku-ur* (*JCS* 9 [1955], p. 47) and *Ia-ad-kur*-DINGIR (*Sumer* 5 [1949], p. 143, no. 8), whereas we would relate *Ia-ás-ku-ur* to a stem *śkr* (cf. Albright, *JAOS* 74 [1954], p. 228, n. 38), with which cf. also *Sa-ki-ra-am, Sa-ku-ra-nu, Sa-ki-ru* (*ARM* xv, p. 154) and *Sa-ki-rum* (*RA* 49 [1955], p. 16, i, 14, and note that the ḋkr stem in the last mentioned tablet is written *Za-ku-ra-a-bu, Zi-ik-ra-*ᵈES₄.DAR, etc. [ibid., pp. 30–31]). Kupper's (op. cit., p. 73, n. 2) comparison with *škr*, "intoxicated," seems highly improbable to the writer. For etymological ḋ, cf. also *Da-ki-ru-um* (Bauer, *Die Ostkanaanäer,* p. 16) and *Za-ki-ru-um* (ibid., p. 41).

35. Virolleaud, *Syria* 28 (1951), pp. 21–23.

36. *Orientalia* NS 19 (1950), p. 375; for problems raised by the ABC tablet, see Speiser, *BASOR* 121, pp. 17–21.

37. Albright, *BASOR* 119, p. 24, and Speiser, op. cit., pp. 20–21.

38. *BASOR* 118, pp. 12–13.

39. Z. Harris, *Development of the Canaanite Dialects,* pp. 35–36, 40–41, 62–63.

40. Goetze, *Language* 17 (1941), p. 128, n. 15 (however, *a-si-ru/ri* in *EA* 287:54, 288:21, has nothing to do with a stem *'ṭr*); p. 129, n. 19.

41. Op. cit., pp. 33–34, 62–63.

42. Thus the Jerusalem scribe (1) never employs the *y*-preformative in the verb; (2) uses *muššuru,* as in letters of Hurrian provenience, instead of *wuššuru* with the Canaanite scribes; (3) Ass. *lamnu* rather than Baby. *lemnu,* another Hurrian text feature; (4) Ass. *ezābu* rather than Baby. *ezēbu.* Note also KUR.URU (Urusalim), found in Hittite texts, occasionally at Ugarit.

43. For the phonetic changes, cf. Harris, op. cit.

44. Cf. the Causatives *Ia-ú-ṣi* (Bauer, op. cit., p. 31), *Ia-au_x(PI)-ṣi* (*ARM* xv, p. 147; vɪɪ, 189:6; *RA* 49 [1955], p. 26; for *au_x,* see now Kupper, op. cit., p. 73, n. 1, but, in our opinion, he goes beyond the evidence in concluding to *yô*) and possibly *Ia-ú-ḫi* (Bauer, op. cit.). The writer agrees with Bauer, ibid., p. 66, that these are causatives of *Primae-Waw* verbs, and cannot accept Goetze's (op. cit., p. 135, n. 167) *Yūṣi* and *Yūḫi*—nor is *Ia-ṣi/ṣí* a perfect, since it always occupies the initial position in a name.

45. *Skmimi* of the execration texts is probably a dual, but does it stand for *sakmaimi* or *sakmêmi*?

46. See Harris's remarks, op. cit., p. 98. If Noth, *BHT* 16, p. 139, were correct in explaining Mari elements like *Itar* and *Išar* as deriving from *Yitar* and *Yišar,* we would have some evidence for the Barth-Ginsberg law as early as Mari. However, in the writer's opinion, there is so far no clear evidence for a

preformative *yi* in any of the Amorite material. Writings like *Ia-e-im-ṣí, Ia-e-šu-bi, Ia-en-ḫi-mu-um,* etc. (Bauer, op. cit., pp. 25–26) show the existence of *ye,* which is either dialectal for *ya,* or an intermediate stage in the *ya-e* development. Nowhere do we find *Ia-i-* or *Yi-i.*

47. For a fuller discussion and the possible origin of the morpheme, see Speiser, *Israel Exploration Quarterly* 4 (1954), pp. 108–15.

48. Cross and Freedman, *JNES* 14 (1955), p. 245; Huesman, *Biblica* 37 (1956), p. 293.

49. *JCS* 4 (1950), pp. 169–72.

50. Cross and Freedman, op. cit.

51. First properly stressed by Barth, *ZDMG* 53 (1899), p. 593.

52. The participles are *di-ki* (*EA* 131:23), *ḫa-zi-ri* (*EA* 138:80, 130). They are not finite forms, or we should have *di-ka* (cf. *EA* 132:45) and *ḫa-zi-ra.* They can, therefore, only be participles, and probably passive: this is certain for the first, virtually so for the first instance of *ḫa-zi-ri* ('*aṣîri,* "held back, detained"), probable for the second (with same meaning).

53. *ARM* xv, p. 140, p. 144.

54. *JBL* 76 (1957), pp. 87–103.

55. So Driver, op. cit., p. 129, n. 16; p. 130, n. 2.

56. *UH, Krt* 75.

57. *EA* 287:55.

58. Wiseman, *The Alalakh Tablets,* p. 145.

59. *JCS* 8 (1954), p. 21, 267:17 (not indexed in *The Alalakh Tablets*).

60. Wiseman, op. cit., p. 141, and add 455:47 (*JCS* 8 [1954], p. 30). Cf. also *La-ki-in-a-du,* Wiseman, op. cit., p. 141, for *La-kin-ad(d)u,* "Truly trustworthy is Addu."

61. See Nötscher's thorough study in *VT* 3 (1953), pp. 372–80.

62. *Studies in Old Testament Prophecy,* 15, n. u. In *La-aḫ-wi-ma-li-ku* (*ARM* vii, 61:2), *La-aḫ-wi-ba-lu* (*Iraq* 7 [1940], p. 39), *La-[aḫ]-wi-*DINGIR (*RA* 49 [1955], p. 27), *La-aḫ-[wi]-a-du* (Wiseman, op. cit., p. 141, reading *La-ah-[mi?]*), we seem to have *La-yaḫwi* > *Laḫwi* (cf. the verbal preformative *la* of later Aramaic dialects!); note also *La-ḫu-un-*ᵈ*Da-gan* (*ARM* xv, p. 150) and *Ia-ḫu-un-*DINGIR (*ARM* vii, 211:4). However, *E-ki-la-aḫ-wi* of *ARM* vii, 185:3', urges caution; I cannot explain this name. The frequent *Larim* element, however, in view of *Ka-bi-la-ri-im* (*Iraq* 7 [1940], p. 39, and cf. *Ka-bi-*ᵈIM [ibid.; Bauer, op. cit., p. 32; *ARM* vii, 106:10], *Ka-bi-e-ra-ah* [Bauer, op. cit.], *Ka-bi-*ᵈ*Da-gan* [*ARM* vii, 180 iv 24]), seems to be a theophorous element rather than verbal *Larîm* < *La-yarîm.*

63. *HUCA* 23 (1950–51), p. 35.

64. Beegle, *BASOR* 123, p. 28.

65. *UH,* p. 65. See also O'Callaghan, *VT* 4 (1954), p. 175, and Albright, *Mélanges bibliques rédigés en l'honneur de André Robert* (Paris, *n.d.*), pp. 22–26.

66. For references see *UH,* p. 226, 18:602–3.

67. *JCS* 7 (1953), pp. 78–80.

68. *Canaanite Parallels in the Book of the Psalms,* p. 37; cf. also M. Dahood, *CBQ* 16 (1954), p. 16.

69. Finet, op. cit., p. 236, § 84n; 240, § 85g; occasionally in Ugar. Akkadian texts (Nougayrol, op. cit., iii 15.89:12).

70. The writer agrees with Sutcliffe, *VT* 5 (1955), pp. 436–39, that we should not say that these prepositions *mean* "from."

71. *CBQ* 7 (1945), p. 23, n. 64. The form *yᵉqûmun* preserves the old indicative-energic found in Amarna.

72. Cited in *Orientalia*, NS 25 (1956), p. 417.

73. *ARM* xv, p. 159; vii, 217:6, 271:2.

74. *ARM* vii, 227:12'. For the theophorous element *Ḥadu*, cf. also *Su-mu-ḫa-d[u]-ú* in *ARM* vii, 217:1, and in view of these passages we should probably read *Ma-lik-ḫa(!)-du-um* for Bauer's, op. cit., p. 34, *Malik-za-du-um*.

75. *RA* 47 (1953), p. 174. For *Sumum* as a theophorous element, cf. for the present Noth, op. cit., p. 133, and the writer's remarks, *Orientalia*, NS 26 (1957), p. 343, n. 3.

76. *RA* 49 (1955), p. 31. This recalls Biblical *Mᵉtūšā'ēl*, but the *ša*-element is not explained. In *ARM* vii, 232:5, despite the autograph, I would read *Zu(!)-ḫa-am-mu*, "The One of *'Ammu.*"

77. *JCS* 4 (1950), pp. 169–72; ibid., 6 (1952), pp. 76–80. For further Ugaritic material, see A. Jirku, *Jahrbuch für kleinasiatische Forschung* 3 (1954), pp. 111–15. Driver, op. cit., denies that the Karatepe and Ugaritic passages contain infinitives, ignoring the Amarna evidence. Since what we consider infinitives absolute are occasionally found with pronominal suffixes, Driver argues "the form ceases *ipso facto* to be 'absolute' when it is thus qualified." A new term seems the solution of this difficulty.

78. *Biblica* 37 (1956), pp. 271–95, 410–34.

79. *JCS* 4 (1950), p. 172.

80. *UH*, p. 70, § 9:31 and n. 3; ibid., p. 72, § 9:34.

81. *ARM* xv, p. 148.

82. *ARM* vii, 209:4.

83. *ARM* xv, p. 146.

84. *ARM* vi, 79:9.

85. Bauer, op. cit., p. 31.

86. *ARM* xv, p. 147; *ARM* vii, 189:6; *RA* 49 (1955), p. 26.

87. *ARM* vi, 22:14.

88. *JCS* 8 (1954), p. 19, 258:24 (not indexed in Wiseman, *The Alalakh Tablets*), also Wiseman, ibid., p. 136 (*Ia-ši-bi-il-[la]*).

89. Bauer, op. cit., p. 28.

90. *Iraq* 7 (1940), p. 40. The form is a genitive; cf. pl. iv r. 3 (GÌR *Me-mi-hi-im*) and 33 (GÌR *Kab-ka-bi-im*).

91. *ARM* vii, 201 r. 9'.

92. *RA* 49 (1955), p. 28; for the possibility of this element in the execration texts, see *Orientalia*, NS 26 (1957), p. 341.

93. Bauer, op. cit., p. 24 (*Ia-pí-šum*).

94. Wiseman, op. cit., p. 142.

95. *ARM* vii, 185 ii 13'; and cf. also *A-bu-um-e-ki-in*, *ARM* xv, p. 140, and *A-bu-me-ki-[i]n*, *ARM* vi, 18 r. 1'.

96. *Iraq* 7 (1940), p. 40. Gadd does not inform us of the case of the name, so the ending must remain unexplained. With this name cf. Amarna *Ba'al-me-ḫir*, etc. (*EA* ii, pp. 1558–1559) and perhaps Biblical *Jā'îr*.

97. *RA* 47 (1953), p. 173.

98. Ibid., 49 (1955), p. 28.

99. *ARM* xv, p. 152

100. Ibid.

101. Bauer, op. cit., p. 34; for the causative of this stem in personal names, Albright, *JAOS* 74 (1954), p. 227.

102. *JCS* 9 (1955), p. 64, no. 18:18.

103. Ibid., p. 91, no. 57:17.

104. The only evidence for causative participles without *me-*, to the writer's knowledge, is *Maḫšimānum* (Bauer, op. cit., p. 46), and the place name *Mankisum* (*ARM* xv, p. 120). The evidence allows for a *Hif'il* causative, but does not demand it; cf. the divine name *Haddu*, which appears also as *Iandu, Iaddu*, and *Ed(d)a*, intervocalic *h* becoming the "gliding" *y* (see Kupper, op. cit., p. 230, n. 1). Therefore, possibly *muhaqtil* > *muyaqtil* > *muyeqtil* > *meqtil*, but *yahaqtil* > *yayaqtil* > *yaqtil*.

105. *JCS* 5 (1951), pp. 33–35.

106. Most recently *HUCA* 23 (1950–51), p. 17. This is also Driver's explanation for the Ugaritic occurrences (op. cit., p. 130), and he apparently (ibid., n. 6) rejects the writer's arguments for *taqtulû* (cf. above n. 105), accepting only *taqtulûna;* he gives no reasons.

107. *GKC* § 145k.

108. Nah. 1:5, however, might be noted. Albright has clarified the passage (*CBO* 7 [1945], pp. 22–23), but instead of rejecting the *waw* (*tbl W kl*), one may see here an indication that the correct reading is the plural form *têbālû*.

109. For full references and discussion of the Byblian verb, see the writer's forthcoming article on the subject.

110. *EA* 104:17–36.

111. Op. cit., p. 84.

112. Bauer-Leander, p. 273, § 36d.

113. *Grammaire de l'Hébreu biblique²*, p. 315, n. 1.

114. Notice of the construction was taken briefly in *JCS* 2 (1948), p. 245.

115. *EA* 74:25–27.

116. *EA* 103:55–57.

117. *EA* 118:36–38.

118. *EA* 82:16–17.

119. *Orientalia*, NS 5 (1936), p. 177.

120. *UH*, p. 114, § 14:3.

121. For various proposals, J. Aistleitner, *Untersuchungen zur Grammatik des Ugaritischen*, Berlin, 1954, pp. 47 ff.; Goetze, *JAOS* 58 (1938), pp. 266–309; E. Hammershaimb, *Das Verbum im Dialekt von Ras Schamra*, Kopenhagen, 1941. Harris follows Goetze, whereas Albright presents a quite different view (cf. *JAOS* 60 [1940], pp. 418–19). See also Ginsberg's remarks, *Orientalia*, NS 5 (1936), p. 177.

122. *ARM* xv, p. 146; vii, 180 iii' 35'.

123. *ARM* vii, 185 ii 5'; 189:2.

124. *RA* 49 (1955), p. 26.

125. Ibid., p. 26, n. 1.

126. Jean, *RES* 2 (1937), p. 104.

127. *RA* 49 (1955), p. 25; *Iraq* 7 (1940), p. 38.

128. *University of California Publications* 10, no. 89:15.

129. *RA* 49 (1955), p. 26, and n. 4; cf. also *ARM* vii, 180 v' 9'.

130. *RA* 49 (1955), p. 25; *ARM* vi, 14:10.

131. Noth, op. cit., refers only to *Ia-ma-at-ti-*, and without hesitation identifies the form as a *Pi'el*.

132. Finet, op. cit., p. 262, § 91f.

133. Noth, *Die israelitischen Personennamen*, p. 23, and *BHT* 16, p. 140. Posener, *E* 5, cited by Noth, *ZDPV* 65 (1942), p. 24, n. 3, is much more likely to be *'Abi-râpi'* (participle) than *'Abi-rapa'* (perfect), in view of the almost innumerable *râpi'* names in the sources as against one *rapa'* name. The other name, cited

ibid., may be a perfect *'asap* (Posener, *E* 7, *'čphddw*), but it is not certain and the position is against it.

134. *ARM* vii, 263 iii 24'.
135. Wiseman, op. cit., p. 145.
136. *ARM* vii, 210:13.
137. *ARM* vii, 181 r. 3'.

CHAPTER FOUR

The Archaeology
of Palestine

G. ERNEST WRIGHT

THE ARCHAEOLOGY of the Near East may be said to have come of age as a scientific discipline during the period between 1920 and 1940. In Palestine two men in particular may be singled out from among others as of special importance in their influence upon the quality of work done in that country. In the 1920s and early 1930s, C. S. Fisher, professor of archaeology in the American School of Oriental Research in Jerusalem, was either the initial field director or adviser to a majority of the excavations that were undertaken. By training and inclination he was intensely interested in problems of method, particularly in stratigraphical digging of a site, coupled with close observation, careful surveying and mapping, and proper recording of all objects in relation to the stratigraphy. He could not be said to be an archaeological scholar, and because of certain personal factors he was rarely able to remain associated with an excavation for long. Nevertheless, as a result of his activity there was very little careless or unscientific digging in Palestine following the first war. Instead, much more attention was given to method. There were certain exceptions, notably the work of Sellin and Welter at Balatah (Shechem) between 1926 and 1932, but it is of great importance to note that what had been general before World War I now indeed became the exception.

The other name of especial importance is W. F. Albright, who first went to Palestine as Fellow of the American School in 1919 and remained as director from 1920 to 1929 and again from 1933 to 1936. At the outset, his teachers were W. J. Phythian-Adams, who was the first to introduce Aegean methods of trial pits and scarp sections into Palestine, Clarence Fisher, and the great Père H. Vincent of the Dominican École Biblique. He soon went beyond them, however, both in topographical research and in his ability to combine several areas of knowledge with the topic of central interest. His detailed comparative discussions in the publications of his work at Tell Beit Mirsim have made these volumes an indispensable handbook of the present-day Palestinian archaeologist.[1] Perhaps his greatest contribution in this field lay in his work on archaeological chronology. Quickly mastering all that Vincent and Fisher could teach him about Palestinian pottery, he kept adding to his knowledge by the assiduous study of every collection of sherds he encountered. His publication of the pottery of Tell Beit Mirsim in 1932 and 1933 became, as a result, a comparative study of Palestinian ceramics which, for the first time, plotted in writing the typological and stratigraphical evolution of the chief forms, while fixing their chronology within certain well-delimited periods. Before this time ceramic dating was a highly individual matter within broad areas of agreement. The discipline had not been opened in detail to a searching scrutiny in the light of all available knowledge. Its communication was so largely a matter of "oral tradition" that there was inevitably a high degree of subjectivity within it. Albright's Tell Beit Mirsim volumes were the first serious effort to eliminate this subjectivity and to reduce the discipline to writing where others could study it, check the conclusions, and apply the results to old and new excavations. A new era began, and the archaeology of Palestine now became better known and better fixed chronologically than that of any other Near Eastern country, both because of the amount of the work and because that work was placed on a solid comparative basis, with the astronomically fixed Egyptian dynasties serving as the chronological underpinning of the Bronze Age deposits.

Since 1933, when the pottery of the fourth Tell Beit Mirsim campaign was published, a number of important publications of Palestinian digging have assisted in filling in and revising the details of Albright's chronological work. The most important are, of course, the publications of the excavations of the Oriental Institute at the great site of Megiddo.[2] The architectural and other discoveries have made of Megiddo Palestine's best-known archaeological site. The excellence of the mound's stratigraphy has added greatly to our archaeological knowledge. Unfortunately, however, the failure to develop and maintain a staff of first-ranking Palestinian archaeologists at Megiddo and the lack of continuity over the years during which the work was undertaken (1925–39) made it impossible for the maximum results to be obtained with the great sums of Rockefeller money which were initially available for the work. The stratification was fairly well dated in correlation with that of Tell Beit Mirsim, but the detailed ceramic work leaves a great deal to be desired. The dating of the Early Bronze, Late Bronze, and Iron Age strata in part has had to be revised; the deposits of Middle Bronze I (*ca.* 2100–1900 B.C.) were not distinguished as a special occupational phase; and considerable confusion appears to have been introduced when it was not recognized that Stratum V A in the northern gateway area is to be identified with Stratum IV B (and part of V) in the eastern and southern stable areas, and that the two together appear to constitute the Solomonic stratum from approximately the third quarter of the tenth century B.C.[3]

The excavations of Philadelphia's University Museum at Beth-shan between 1921 and 1933 were also exceedingly rich in architecture and small finds, the series of Canaanite temples between the fourteenth and tenth centuries being particularly important. Here again, however, the strata have had to be redated, while the ceramic evidence has never been adequately or completely published.[4] Indeed, the detailed chronological study of the pottery of both this and the Megiddo excavations constitute two important tasks for young archaeologists in the future.

Nearly all excavations, however, add various details to the chronological framework of Palestinian archaeology. Since World War II three pieces of work, in particular, promise, when completed and fully published, to add considerably to the ceramic chronology at points where further clarification is badly needed, particularly in the Iron Age. The small excavation of Hebrew University in 1948–49 at Tell Qasile on the outskirts of Tel Aviv, directed by B. Mazar (Maisler),[5] the large and well-organized expedition under the same auspices and directed by Y. Yadin at Hazor in Galilee, beginning in 1955,[6] and the French work at Tell el-Far'ah, northeast of Nablus, since 1946, directed by Père R. de Vaux[7]—all promise significant new contributions to the chronology, especially of the period between 1200 and 600 B.C., the second half of which (Iron II) has been particularly slow in yielding to close chronological subdivision. It is to be hoped that the Drew-McCormick Archaeological Expedition, jointly with the American Schools of Oriental Research, at Balatah (Shechem) will be able to throw considerable additional light on the chronology of the Hellenistic period (particularly fourth–second centuries B.C.).[8] The work at Tulul Abu el-'Alayiq and at Qumran have so illumined the Herodian and early Roman periods that for the first time they can be clearly distinguished from the Hellenistic Age.[9]

Of particular importance since 1933, however, has been the progress made toward unearthing the prehistory of Palestine before 2000 B.C. On the basis of Albright's pioneering work in the field, the writer was able to present an ordered chronological summary of the evidence in 1937.[10] Much new information has come to light since then which has revised and supplemented the conclusions of this work, though in the main its correlation of archaeological deposits still remains valid. Of especial importance have been the new British excavations at Jericho under the direction of Kathleen Kenyon, beginning in 1952, which have so astonished the archaeological world with their revelation of a great Neolithic town, dating between the seventh and the fifth millennia B.C.[11] Among other excavations of importance we may also mention the French discovery—Jean Perrot directing an important part of the work—of a flourishing fourth-millennium village culture in the Beersheba area,[12] and the excellent necropolis of the late fourth millennium at Tell el-Far'ah unearthed by Père R. de Vaux (cf. note 7).

In the area of prehistory, the new method of radiocarbon dating, developed by Dr. Willard F. Libby at the Institute for Nuclear Studies of the University of Chicago, has been most significant. Carbon 14, as is now generally known, is a special, heavy form of carbon present in all organic matter. It is radioactive and, after the death of an organism, disintegrates at a constant and measurable rate. By means of a special form of the Geiger counter the amount of radioactivity remaining in the pure carbon derived from a burned sample can be computed and its approximate age determined within a calculable margin of error. After some years of testing, it has been discovered that the method cannot be relied on blindly without consideration of a total archaeological context and without more than one test in the general period to which the sample belongs. A sample can be "contaminated," so that the count will not come out right, in a number of ways, either while it is still in its archaeological context or during its removal, shipment, and preparation. The accompanying chart lists pertinent dates of basic importance, however, to prehistorians of the Near East:[13]

It will be noted from this list that the earliest villages known, Jericho and Jarmo, began somewhere in the era between *ca.* 9000 and 7000 B.C. Jarmo continued to be occupied through the first half of the fifth millennium B.C., while Jericho's last pre-pottery age comes down into the first half of the sixth millennium.[14] Judging from this fact and from early pottery-producing village assemblages at Matarrah, Hassuna, and Mersin, pottery vessels must have been first introduced in the sixth millennium, but when the Chalcolithic Age may be said to have begun is unknown, though it was probably before *ca.* 4000 B.C. (see below). The Obeid painted-pottery culture of Iraq, in which the earliest known monumental public buildings (temple installations of considerable size) appear, seems to have begun before 4000 B.C. and continued as late as the 34th century B.C. This would throw the preceding Halaf painted pottery into the second half of the fifth millennium and indicate that the Chalcolithic Age began at that time. On the other hand, the invention of writing in the Iraqi Protoliterate Age (or just before?) must now be dated not before *ca.* 3400–3200 B.C.—in other words, at the dawn of the Early Bronze Age when urbanization was greatly accelerated and the foundations were laid for the dynastic ages which followed in Early Bronze II (beginning between 3000 and 2800 B.C.).

In the remainder of this chapter, instead of presenting a summary of the excavations which have been conducted in Palestine, we will continue to emphasize the central importance of the chronological factor—a subject which has always been one of Albright's major interests—by presenting a series of charts with brief commentary and basic bibliography. The purpose will thus be to present a correlation of most of the Palestinian archaeological deposits within a chronological framework, which basically is that of Albright himself, except for certain adjustments of my own.

Carbon 14 Dates for the Prehistory of the Near East

		B.C. ±
F-40	Jericho, lower Neolithic ("hog-backed brick") phase; two treatments	6765 ± 210 6845 ± 210
GL-28 GL-38 GR-963	Jericho, upper Neolithic ("plastered floor") phase	6250 ± 210 5850 ± 160 6830 ± 100
W-657 W-665 W-607 W-651 W-652 C-113 C-743 F-44 C-742 F-45	Jarmo, Iraq (like Jericho in Palestine, earliest known agricultural village, pottery appearing at the very end of Neolithic stratification).	9285 ± 300 9245 ± 200 7085 ± 250 6875 ± 200 5995 ± 200 4755 ± 320 4740 ± 360 4695 ± 170 4650 ± 330 4615 ± 165
W-623	Matarrah, Iraq (early village)	5615 ± 250
W-660	Hassuna, Iraq (5th level, early village)	5085 ± 200
W-617	Mersin, near Tarsus, Turkey (basal layer)	5995 ± 250
W-627	Byblos, Lebanon (Neolithic A)	4595 ± 200
C-551 C-457 C-550/1	Fayum A, K pits (earliest known Egyptian Neolithic)	4440 ± 180 4145 ± 250 4100 ± 330
C-810 C-811 C-814	Negada, S.D. 34-38 Egyptian Chalcolithic Negada, S.D. 36-46 ("Amratian") Negada, S.D. 34-38	3790 ± 300 3665 ± 280 3625 ± 300
H-138/123	Warka, Iraq (basal Obeid town)	4115 ± 160
C-817	Tepe Gawra, Iraq (levels 17-18, middle Obeid)	3445 ± 325
C-819	Byblos, Lebanon ("First Urban Installation")	3360 ± 300
W-245	Khirbet el-Bitar, Ghassulian (Palestinian Chalcolithic, see Chart 1)	3325 ± 150
GL-24	Jericho, Tomb A94 (Palestinian Early Bronze I, early phase; see Chart 2)	3260 ± 110
C-812 C-813 C-267	Negada II Egyptian 1st Dynasty or end Negada S.D. 58-67 of Predynastic Hemaka, 1st Dynasty	3065 ± 290 2765 ± 310 2930 ± 200

SUMMARY OF PALESTINE'S CULTURAL HISTORY

I. THE FIRST AGRICULTURAL VILLAGES

A. Natufian: within the period ca. *10,000–8000* B.C. *(commonly classed as Mesolithic):* This is the terminal cave-dwelling period, in which the first sickle blades imply at least reaping, if not conscious planting, and in which appears the first hint of the beginnings of animal domestication (evidence for the dog, goat, and perhaps ox and pig?). The era may be regarded as transitional from the food-gathering economy of the Paleolithic Age to the food-producing economy of the first villages, a transition which followed rapidly upon the retreat of the last glaciation in Europe and the arrival of modern climate in the Near East. Since Carbon 14 tests on samples from both America and Europe agree on reducing the date of the end of the last glaciation to around 9000 or 8000 B.C., and the start of the first villages at Jericho and Jarmo to about the same period, we are led to assume that the Natufian probably represents the life of the terminal ice age in its concluding centuries.

Evidence for the culture has been found in a number of Palestinian caves and cave-terraces, having first been described by Dorothy Garrod on evidence preserved with some forty-five skeletons of a long-headed people of small stature (5 feet to 5 feet, 4 inches tall) at Shuqbah in Wadi en-Natuf some ten miles northwest of Jerusalem. The chief deposits of this culture in addition to Shuqbah are el-Wad B and Kebarah B in western valleys of the Mount Carmel range, and el-Khiam C and B in the Judean wilderness.[15] Types of flint implements similar to those in the predominantly microlithic Natufian culture have been found outside Palestine at Yabrud in Syria,[16] and at a station in Sinai.[17]

B. Tahunian and Jerichoan, ca. *8000–5000* B.C. *(commonly classed as Neolithic):* This is the era of the first villages, marking the full introduction of an agrarian economy, though the number of arrowheads discovered suggests that hunting was still a vital part of daily life. Thus far, Jericho in Palestine and Jarmo in northeastern Iraq are the only sites of the first part of this age known in detail. Jericho was a town of some seven or eight acres, surrounded by a massive stone fortification repaired or reconstructed at least twice, and in one place strengthened by a large stone tower, nine meters in diameter, with stairway and tunnel leading down into it from the top. Inside the city some forty-five feet of debris were deposited, comprising most of the tell. The earliest period is characterized by beehive houses made of elongated oval bricks with flat bottoms and ridged tops ("hog-backed"). A second phase has large courtyard houses, the brick walls of which were plastered, painted, and polished. Floors could be covered with large reed mats. Several skulls with the original faces restored by mud plaster appear to be the first attempt at portraiture. Statues in triads (father, mother, child), made of clay on a reed base, have been held by some to be images of deities.

Strata IX–XVII of the Garstang expedition in 1936 were probably the successive floors of a single large building (IX perhaps being an exception) of "megaron" form which was probably a temple. Extensive ruins below this depth have been found by the Kenyon expedition since 1952. Only in the very last stage of this culture did the first pottery appear (Stratum IX).[18]

Jarmo in Iraq is the only other site of the same horizon known, where pottery was introduced at the end of a long period of "Neolithic" village life.[19] In Palestine itself a similar flint industry with a few sherds of comparable pottery has been found in an open site at Abu Ghosh, west of Jerusalem.[20] The one place which appears to prove most clearly that the Tahunian flint industry is later than the "Natufian" is el-Khiam in Judah. El-Khiam A, though probably earlier than Jericho or Abu Ghosh, is a Tahunian deposit lying above el-Khiam B of the Natufian period.[21] Somewhere in the Neolithic horizon, possibly later than Jericho IX and Abu Ghosh, is Level B of the Abu Usba' cave in the Wadi Fallaḥ of the Carmel range, while the upper-terrace deposit of the large cave just across the valley is probably also in the general post-Natufian horizon.[22]

C. *Late Neolithic and Early Chalcolithic:* For the period between about 5000 and 3500 B.C., that is, between the end of earliest Jericho and the Ghassulian culture (see below), Palestinian excavations thus far have produced only hints of what went on. Outside of Palestine we are witness to an extensive agrarian-urban development: Byblos A, Ras Shamra V, Amuq A–B in Lebanon and Syria, and Hassuna, Matarrah, and the earliest assemblage from Nineveh in Mesopotamia,[23] all dating probably from the sixth or the first half of the fifth millennium B.C. They were followed, between 4500 and 4000 B.C., by the beautiful painted-pottery culture named from Tell Halaf, a culture which had a strong effect even in Syria (Amuq C, Ras Shamra IV). This in turn was succeeded by the even more extensive Obeid painted pottery, which marked the first penetration into southern Mesopotamia and the first monumental architecture (temples at Tepe Gawra in the north and at Eridu in the south), and which must have extended well along past the middle of the fourth millennium. The first copper seems to appear in the Halafian, suggesting that at this point the Chalcolithic (copper-stone) Age begins.[24]

In Palestine the Yarmukian–Jericho VIII horizon[25] now appears definitely established as a pre-Ghassulian cultural phase which is pinned through Amuq D to a time approximately between the Halaf and Obeid phases. Consequently, it must be classed as early Chalcolithic.[26] At el-Ghrubba in the Jordan Valley an earlier pottery phase, perhaps very distantly related to the Hassuna-Matarrah horizon of Mesopotamia, has been found, and pieces of comparable pottery were discovered at bedrock level in Megiddo ("Stratum XX").[27] Whether the painted pottery of el-Ghrubba is to be classed as Neolithic or Chalcolithic is a question for which we as yet have no positive evidence. Finally we may mention a small sounding at Sheikh Ali, south of the Sea of Galilee, made recently by M. W. Prausnitz (unpublished). Here Ghassulian pottery (see below) was found near the surface, and immediately below that some bow-rim jars of the Yarmukian-Jericho VIII type, while below them was a new burnished pottery of a type hitherto unnoticed in Palestine. Typical is a bowl with an orange-colored surface, highly polished on the upper exterior and combed or stippled on the lower exterior. This pottery suggests that we do not yet know a great deal about what happened between Jericho IX and the Ghassulian in Palestine; otherwise we would be able to place it.

D. *The Ghassulian Culture (ca. 36th–33rd centuries* B.C.):[28] This is a period of open villages which represent an occupation now known to have been widely scattered in the valleys and plains of Palestine, a time when peasant farming and market towns had reached a stage of comparatively high efficiency. The culture must be reckoned as roughly contemporary with the Obeid painted-pottery period in Mesopotamia (though perhaps allowing for a cultural lag between the two countries), with Phase E of the Syrian Amuq and the Amratian in Egypt (see Chart 1).[29]

Chart 1.   First Agricultural Villages

Period	Economy	Sites	Neighboring Regions		
			Syria-Lebanon	Iraq	Egypt
Ghassulian, c3600-3300 B.C.	Open villages in the Jordan Valley, Esdraelon, Coastal Plain and Beer-sheba basin	Tell Abu Matar Khirbet el-Bitar, and related deposits Teleilat el-Ghassul (Beth-shan XVIII?ᵃ)	Hama L Amuq E Ras Shamra III-IV	Uruk ↑ Obeid	Amratian
Early Chalcolithic, within the period c4300-3600 B.C.	Only fragments, which suggest a number of small country villages	Jericho VIII Yarmukian Elements in Megiddo XX and in Far 'ah "Middle Chalcolithic"	Amuq D Ras Shamra IV Amuq C Hama L	↓ Halaf	Badarian ↑
Transition: Neolithic-Chalcolithic, c5000-4300 B.C.	Not yet well represented in Palestine	⌐ el-Ghrubba └ Elements in Megiddo XX (Sheikh Ali?) (Abu Usba'?)	Amuq A-B Ras Shamra V Byblos A	Nineveh I-II ↑ ↑	Fayum A
"Tahunian" and "Jerichoan," c8000-5000 B.C.	Cave terraces, first towns, first efficient agriculture, first pottery at end of period	Jericho IX, X-XVII and Pre-XVII Abu Ghosh el-Khiam A		⌐ Jarmo Hassuna Matarrah ↓	
"Natufian," within the period between 10,000-8,000 B.C.	Cave dwellers showing evidence of incipient agriculture	Kebara B el-Wad B el-Khiam B-C Shuqbah	Yabrud	Karim Shahir	

ᵃ The position of Beth-shan XVIII and pits is not clear. The clearance was too small in extent and the publication of the pottery too incomplete to enable one to obtain a clear picture of the culture. Until stratigraphical work obtains a clear sequence through the Chalcolithic, we will not know its position in any case. The placing of it between the Ghassulian and Yarmukian is very tentative, based on an oral report of some unpublished discoveries of James Melaart at Tell Abu Habil in the Jordan Valley.

The culture is named from some small tells near the Dead Sea on the eastern side of the Jordan Valley, called Teleilat Ghassul. An expedition of the Pontifical Biblical Institute directed successively by Fathers A. Mallon, S.J., and R. Koeppel, S.J., excavated there between 1928 and 1936 and first identified what appears to be a typical exemplar of this cultural period.[30] In addition to distinctive ceramic and flint styles, fine rectangular houses were uncovered, a few with astonishingly complex wall paintings which evidently possess religious significance. Elsewhere in the Jordan Valley the culture has been reported at Tell el-Mefjar, Tell Abu Habil, Jiftlik, and Tell esh-Shuneh (at Shuneh Mushawah, south of the Sea of Galilee).[31]

Soundings at Tell esh-Shuneh and at 'Affuleh in the Esdraelon[32] appear to fix the position of the Ghassulian pottery as lying directly below the deposits of the following period (see below), thus providing further indication of the relative chronology of the Ghassulian culture against a tendency to date it even later.[33]

Recent years have witnessed a great extension in our knowledge of the spread of this culture along the coastal plain, and especially in the Negeb where it was widely spread. M. Jean Perrot has excavated Tell Abu Matar near Beersheba (1952–54) and found there an exceptionally interesting Ghassulian village. In its first phase, large underground dwellings connected by tunnels were dug in six or seven groups. A second phase of occupation was distinguished by round or oval stone houses, and a fourth phase by rectangular houses on stone foundations, perhaps similar to the better-preserved examples at Ghassul.[34]

In spite of these discoveries, however, we still do not know enough about the fourth millennium to give a connected account of it,[35] though we can now say that the Ghassulian is the first widely spread occupation of Palestine of which we know.

II. URBANIZATION AND THE FIRST CITY STATES

A. Early Bronze I *(ca. 33rd–29th centuries* B.C.*):* The period at the turn of the fourth and third millennia, just preceding the dynastic ages of Egypt and Mesopotamia, marks the first fairly extensive urbanization. Here we have the beginning of the city-state system in Palestine; major cities are fortified with great city walls; and a vigorous material culture is in evidence which lasts, with many variations and brief interruptions, for a period of eight hundred to a thousand years before it is completely and violently destroyed. Furthermore, this is the first period when widespread international trade can be observed on a large scale, influences streaming particularly from the Proto-literate (late Uruk and Jemdet Nasr) period of Mesopotamia through Palestine to Egypt.[36] In Palestine small temples at Megiddo and Jericho make their appearance,[37] though as yet little other significant architecture is known, apart from the city wall of Jericho, and perhaps those of Ai and of Dothan.[38]

A portion of a late predynastic slate palette found at Jericho is the earliest Egyptian object unearthed in the country,[39] though a number of vessels found in Egypt were evidently imported from Palestine.[40]

The relative chronology of the various strata and deposits of this age was first established in the 1930s by Albright and the writer.[41] At that time the feature which was most easily recognizable as a dating clue in the northern sites consisted of gray-black bowls which had been highly "burnished," or better, had been given a highly lustrous effect by polishing. The earliest type was found at Beth-shan; the latest type was found at Megiddo. In the south, around the Jerusalem latitude, the first Early Bronze pottery was a characteristic painted ware first encountered in a group of tomb and cave dwellings at Gezer and in the Ophel water tunnels before the first war.[42] The gray wares do not seem to enter the south[42a] and few of the painted wares invade the north. There was enough evidence to suggest that the Beth-shan gray wares were earlier than the southern painted vessels, with the result that the writer labeled the former the "Esdraelon culture" and considered it Upper, or Late, Chalcolithic, while the latter was considered Early Bronze ia. This analysis has been generally followed to this day, but since 1946 a number of new discoveries, particularly the Upper Chalcolithic tombs, as the excavator calls them, unearthed at Tell el-Far'ah near Nablus,[43] have made a new study of the problem necessary. The southern painted tradition can now be fitted into the gray-ware sequence more securely and it becomes impossible to segregate the two groups into Upper Chalcolithic and Early Bronze i phases. One period is here represented which must be either all Chalcolithic or all Early Bronze,[44] and, in keeping with the general tendency, its chronological spread must be lowered from five centuries to not much more than half that figure. The suggestion that a Uruk bowl from Mesopotamia is present in one of the Far'ah tombs in an early phase of the period[45] rests on a very doubtful identification. If it were true, it would suggest what the writer had previously suspected on the basis of the correlations between Palestinian and Syrian Amuq deposits, namely that not only the Mesopotamian Protoliterate but perhaps Uruk as well is in large measure contemporary with this age in Palestine, while the Obeidian in Iraq is contemporary with Palestine's Ghassulian (see Chart 2).

B. *Early Bronze* II *(ca. 29th–27th centuries) and* III *(ca. 27th–24th centuries):* The next ages in Palestinian archaeology are contemporary with the Egyptian Protodynastic period (Dynasties i–iii) and Old Kingdom (Dynasties iv–vi). Indeed the keystone of Palestinian archaeology before 2000 b.c. is the appearance in Palestinian deposits of certain pottery vessels, especially certain types of pitcher with either a flat or a small stump base, which also appear in tombs of the First Dynasty in Egypt. Direct contacts between Mesopotamia and Egypt seem to dwindle in the First Dynasty, but those between Egypt and Palestine–Syria become common.[46] While most of the foreign pottery of Early Bronze II appears in First Dynasty tombs only, its relative ab-

Chart 2. Early Bronze I (c.33rd–29th cents. B.C.), divided into three phases

Phase	Beth-shan	Megiddo	Jericho	Tell el-Far'ah	Other Sites	Syria	Iraq	Egypt
C	XIV	Tomb 1128 XIX Tombs 903 Lower, 1106	Tomb 24 V	Later deposits in Tombs 5, 12, 14 and 16	Ai, Tombs B, C, and G Dothan, levels 11-10 Ras el-'Ain E.B Tell Asawir Tomb	Byblos "éneolithique" Amuq F ———→ Amuq G Qalat er-Rus 19-16 Qalat er-Rus 16-12	←— Uruk Proto-Literate —→	Early Gerzean S.D. 40-50 Late Gerzean S.D. 50-65 Maadi
B	XV	Elements in xx^a and Stages IV-VII; occupation levels of Tombs 903 Lower, 9, etc.	VI VII Tomb A13 Upper	"Upper Chalcolithic" Tombs	"Upper Chalcolithic" Tell Umm Hamad Sherqi ←— 'Affuleh —→ Beth-yerah I ——→ Beth-yerah II Tell esh-Shuneh ——→			
A	XVI XVII	Tomb A94	Tomb 3	"Middle Chalcolithic"_b	Ai, Tombs B, C and G Gezer, Troglodyte caves Tel en-Nasbeh E.B. Ophel, Tomb 3			

[a] The basal materials at Megiddo are badly mixed, so that "Stratum xx," which has little architecture, cannot be considered a single occupational stratum at all, but a collection of early pottery fragments found on the bedrock which date from the el-Ghrubba and Jericho VIII periods (see Chart 1) and Early Bronze I.

[b] Père de Vaux's Middle Chalcolithic at Tell el-Far'ah near Nablus contains material of the Jericho VIII–Yarmukian time, though the excavator, against present indications to the contrary, continues to date it post-Ghassulian and thus calls it Middle Chalcolithic in agreement with opinions in the late 1930s (see my *Pottery of Palestine . . .*, P. 107). My reason for inserting the stratum here as well as in Chart 1 is that neither the published fragments nor the sherd collection from the 1946 and 1947 seasons, which Père de Vaux generously permitted me to study in the summer of 1956, are homogeneous. The bulk of the material cannot be separated from that in the Upper Chalcolithic, even though undeniably earlier sherds are present. In a letter of November 28, 1956, Père de Vaux affirms that in the 1954 campaign a clear selection of material was found. All one can say, however, is that a mixture of pottery from two different periods in the first excavations certainly suggests that more clearance and complete publication are needed before one can be confident of just what is involved in this stratum. Megiddo "xx" provides a warning as to just how mixed basal materials of a mound can be. In any case, it is quite clear to this writer, on the basis of a study of the comparative material, that de Vaux's Upper Chalcolithic extends well down into Early Bronze I C, while his Early Bronze I is best understood as being more characteristically Early Bronze II (see Chart 3).

sence from tombs of the Second and Third Dynasties may be accidental.[47] Second and Third Dynasty stone vessels have been found in a temple store room at Ai, evidently reused for centuries because they were found in ruins of Early Bronze III.[48] The latter age seems closely tied to the Old Kingdom by several items, and a date between the 27th and 24th centuries cannot be considered far wrong. On the other hand, it must be confessed that thus far the embarrassment of the Palestinian archaeologist is that he does not have enough material to fill the long span of time between the First and Sixth Dynasties. Consequently, the lowest permissible date for the First Dynasty is the one which he most welcomes.[49]

A rather indeterminate correlation between Palestine and Mesopotamia is provided by a number of seal impressions, particularly of cylinder seals with an animal frieze. In Palestine they date mostly from Early Bronze II (or beginning perhaps at the end of Early Bronze I), and are compared with Mesopotamian seals of the first part of the Early Dynastic period.[50]

Among the architectural discoveries of this age, we may mention in particular the following: (1) From the beginning of Early Bronze II, a large stone city wall at Megiddo, originally four to five meters wide, but subsequently doubled to nearly eight meters.[51] (2) From the end of Early Bronze II (or the beginning of III?) an even more tremendous fortification at Tell el-Far'ah near Nablus, made of brick on an earth and stone foundation, which attains a total width of some twelve meters.[52] (3) The complicated series of city walls and wall reconstructions at Jericho is said to reach the number seventeen[53] for the thousand-year period of the Early Bronze Age, but we shall have to await publication for details. (4) A vast public building in Beth-yerah (Khirbet Kerak) near the southwestern corner of the Sea of Galilee, belonging to Early Bronze III. It extended over some 1200 square meters and had walls *ca.* ten meters thick, in which a number of circular pits (eight were found, between seven and nine meters in diameter) were constructed. Comparison with a model Helladic granary from Melos suggests that the building was a great public granary.[54] (5) The beautiful "palace" set in its own walled court found at Ai. The plan of this structure, however, bears no resemblance to the typical palace of ancient times. Instead, as Albright has pointed out, it is a temple, suggesting that during Early Bronze II and III Ai was one of the main holy sites of Palestine. Except for the later temples of Megiddo xv this structure is the finest temple so far known in pre-Roman Palestine.[55]

In the area of ceramic technique Early Bronze II has produced the first pottery furnace so far known in Palestine,[56] though the earliest known potter's wheel was found in Beth-yerah II, dating from the end of Early Bronze I.[57] As for pottery itself, Early Bronze III is noted for the "Khirbet Kerak ware," a beautiful red and black, highly polished pottery, first identified by Albright.[58] It was imported from Syria and imitated in Palestine, though its ultimate source may have been Anatolia.[59] For approximate correlation of related deposits, see Chart 3.

Chart 3. Early Bronze II and III

Period	Megiddo	Beth-shan	Beth-yerah	Tell el-Far'ah	Jericho	Elsewhere	Egypt	Syria	Iraq
Early Bronze III c26th-24th cents. B.C.	XVI XVII-	XI	IV	"Ancient Bronze II: Périodes 3-5"	Tombs A, F2 / III	Tell Beit Mirsim J; Tell ed-Duweir "Early Copper Age"; Ai "Palais" and Niveau III; Dothan, levels 5-6; Gezer, Cave 16 I(?)	Dynasties III-IV-V (c2650-2350)	Amuq H / Amuq I	Early Dynastic III
Early Bronze II c29-27th cents. B.C.	XVIII	XIII XII	III	"Ancient Bronze I: Périodes 1-2" Tomb 2 (later deposit)	IV	Gezer, Cave 6 I(?); Dothan, c levels 9-7; Kinnereth Tomb	Dynasties I-II (c2850-2650 B.C.)	Amuq G	Early Dynastic I-II ——→

III. THE GREAT NOMADIC IRRUPTIONS (CA. 24TH–20TH CENTURIES B.C.)

One of the most striking facts about the Early Bronze civilization is its destruction, one so violent that scarcely a vestige of it survived. Before the end of Early Bronze III this destruction had begun, for both Megiddo and Tell el-Far'ah near Nablus were destroyed before the characteristic Khirbet Kerak ware had become common. Other cities, such as Beth-shan, Beth-yerah, Tell esh-Shuneh, and Jericho in the Jordan Valley, and Ai in the hill country, were destroyed at the end of Early Bronze III. We do not know when the event took place; we only know that there is not an Early Bronze city excavated or explored in all Palestine which does not have a gap in its occupation between Early Bronze III and the Middle Bronze Age. To date this gap, we know that it must be approximately contemporary with a similar period in Egypt, called the "First Intermediate" between Dynasties VI and XI (*ca.* 22nd–21st centuries B.C.), and further that it must occur during the "caliciform" period of Syria, represented by Amuq I–J[60] and Hama J,[61] but before the beginning of the Middle Bronze Age proper in both Syria and Palestine, which falls in the Egyptian Twelfth Dynasty.

Belonging to the first part of the period, roughly about the 24th–22nd centuries, there are a number of small deposits which are not in stratification but which evidently precede a brief settlement of the new invaders. In 1937 the writer gave them the term Early Bronze IV.[62] Yet until what they represent is more clearly defined, it is difficult to classify them. Perhaps Early Bronze III B would be better, inasmuch as some of them are extensions of Early Bronze III. The matter of terminology will not be settled until we know much more about the age in question.

Toward the latter part of this Palestinian dark age, at a time fixed by Albright in roughly the 21st and 20th centuries B.C.,[63] the mist begins to lift enough to allow us to see a few things clearly. A new people have entered the country and are beginning to settle down in unfortified villages, in the hill country, and especially in the Jordan Valley, in southern Transjordan where formerly people were nomadic, and even in the Negeb of southern Palestine.[64] Their pottery seems to have been handmade for the most part, except for the necks and rims of some of the finer jars. They possessed excellent copper implements, evidently in quantity, and as a result the beautiful "Cananean" flint knife, which is so typical of the Early Bronze Age, ceases to be made.[65] Their occupation is thin and could not have lasted long, for very little architecture has survived (see Chart 4).

The most fully illustrated occupational stratum of this age has evidently been found by the Kenyon expedition at Jericho. Over the ruins of the Early Bronze Age there were found walls of green brick, one course in thickness, scattered over the tell. This new architecture, evidently without a serious tradition behind it, is accompanied by a new pottery, new copper weapons, and new burial customs. A great number of tombs (248 in number) of this time have been excavated by Professor Kenyon; instead of the great tombs with multiple burials of the Early and Middle Bronze Ages, these tombs, though sometimes sizable, generally contain only one burial with two to four pottery vessels, and one or two daggers, or a pin and some jewelry.[66]

To Professor Kenyon the evidence definitely suggests an intrusive people with new customs, people who hitherto had been nomads. For this reason she calls the period Intermediate Early Bronze-Middle Bronze. Albright, in

Chart 4. The Period of Nomadic Irruptions (24th-20th cents. b.c.)

Period	Tell Beit Mirsim	Megiddo	Other Deposits	Egypt	Syria	Iraq
Middle Bronze I 21st-20th cents.	H I	Deposits mixed in Stratum xv Tombs 41; 67 A; 217 B, 877 A2, C2; 989 A2, B2, C2, D2; 878; 1098; 891; 922; 1014; 1020; 1120; 911 A2; 912 A2	Ader A Bethel and Beth-shemesh sherds Beit Sahur and 'Ain Karim tombs Various sites found by Glueck in Transjordan, Negeb, and Jordan Valley Jericho stratum and many tombs Beth-shan tomb and deposit on tell mixed with Stratum xi Tell el-Harbaj, Tomb 1 Tell el-'Ajjul, "Copper Age Cemetery" Ma'ayan Barukh Tomb (Israeli Dept. Antiq. Museum) Bab edh-Dra'	Dynasty xii, 1991 b.c.	↑ Amuq J Ras Shamra II.1 Khan Sheikhun Qatna	Third Dynasty of Ur (c2060-1950 b.c.)
Early Bronze IIIB 24th-22nd cents.	X — — — J(?)	Tombs 1101-2 Lower Tomb 16	Ader B Portion of Glueck's Moabite and Edomite Ware Bethel and Beth-shemesh sherds Bab edh-Dra' Ader C Jericho Tomb 351	First Intermediate Dynasty vi	Hama J Amuq I	Empire of Accad (c2360-2180 b.c.)

his pioneer treatment of this phase, named it Middle Bronze i, in order to keep Palestinian terminology in harmony with that in the Greek archaeological world. Miss Kenyon's objection to Albright's term is that the culture has nothing in common with Middle Bronze proper, indeed even less than with the culture preceding it. Hence the following period, Middle Bronze ii A of Albright, is renamed Middle Bronze i. There is a problem, of course, in this unilateral introduction of a new terminology. Confusion of terms is introduced with no attempt made to secure general agreement, while the new term itself is too long and awkward to secure immediate acceptance. Miss Kenyon is certainly correct in her general interpretation of the evidence. Yet I would make this further observation: the new people are those who hitherto have lived along the desert fringes of the Early Bronze culture. When they settled down for a brief time, they imported items from the "caliciform" culture of Syria, but their most common pottery forms are survivals from, and adaptations of, Early Bronze forms, though made in a new way. Consequently, if a new terminology is to be adopted, I should much prefer Early Bronze iv. It is indeed a new pottery, but it is the dying gasp of the last remnant of Early Bronze traditions. To change the terminology unilaterally, however, is simply to introduce confusion. Until an archaeological congress is held to secure a decision on the matter of terminology, it would seem better not to attempt significant changes in terms, if to do so will lead to confusion.

IV. MIDDLE BRONZE II, THE TIME OF PALESTINE'S GREATEST PROSPERITY BEFORE THE PAX ROMANA

A. The "Amorite" Settlement: Middle Bronze II A (Kenyon's Middle Bronze I), ca. 1900–1750/1700 B.C.: A new wave of cultural influence spread over Syria and Palestine during the time of the Egyptian Twelfth Dynasty (ca. 1991–1778 B.C.). It is a fresh and very vigorous culture, with little direct contact with the preceding to be noted in the material remains, except for the cooking pots which seem to be continued from Middle Bronze I. The term "Amorite" is today being used for the nomadic irruptions responsible for Middle Bronze I and II. Middle Bronze II A represents the period when the "Amorite" settlement became so strongly intrenched under the power of fresh cultural influence that it was now able to dominate northern Mesopotamia, Syria, and Palestine.[67] In Syria-Palestine by the end of the twentieth century the Egyptian Twelfth Dynasty was exerting the dominant, perhaps controlling, political influence, as indicated by the discoveries of Egyptian monuments, especially at Ugarit, Qatna, and Byblos to the north, and at Gezer and Megiddo in Palestine.[68]

The pottery which distinguishes this age was first identified and dated by Albright at Tell Beit Mirsim (Strata G–F). Subsequently, it was recognized in a deposit at Ras el-'Ain, discovered during preparations to turn the site into a major source for modern Jerusalem's water supply, in Petrie's "courtyard cemetery" at Tell el-'Ajjul, and especially in the ruins of Megiddo (Strata xv–xiii and Tombs 911–912) where the finest Palestinian city of the age so far unearthed has been found[69] (see Chart 5). Surviving monuments are few in number, but give promise of more as additional city levels are unearthed. Most notable are the stone city wall at Tell Beit Mirsim, ca. 3.25 meters wide between large towers, together with a house of adobe brick;[70] and especially the brick city wall (1.80 meters wide) and gateway, and three beautifully proportioned temples with a great altar, at Megiddo.[71]

B. The Hyksos Period: Middle Bronze II B (ca. ± 1750/1700–1650/ 1625 B.C.), and II C (ca. ± 1650/1625–1550/1500 B.C.): The second phase of Middle Bronze II (II B) is a continuation of the basic material culture of the preceding century (MB II A), but two new and rather spectacular innovations, among other changes of lesser importance, mark the period off from MB II A. The first of these is a series of fragile, beautifully finished bowls, so thin in section and so sharply carinated that it is assumed they are an imitation in ceramics of metal vessels, an imitation which now became very popular. The second is the sudden appearance of a new method of fortification: that is, the surrounding of a city with a great mound of earth, the surface of which was cemented or plastered in place to prevent erosion.

Chart 5. The "Amorite" Settlement: Middle Bronze II A (Kenyon's "Middle Bronze I"), c1900-1750/1700 B.C.

Tell Beit Mirsim	Megiddo	Elsewhere	Egypt	Syria	Iraq
— 1750/1700 B.C. —					
F	XIII	Tell el-'Ajjul, Courtyard Cemetery Jaffa Necropolis (1925) Beth-shan, Burials I-II	Dynasty XIII		Hammurabi (c1728-1686 B.C.)
					Mari Age (Kültepe Ib, c1740-1720 B.C.)
	Tombs 911 A1, D 912 B, D				Khabur Ware
G	XIV	Jericho Tell Kisan Ras el-'Ain Beth-shemesh sherds Gezer sherds and Tombs in III 30			First Dynasty of Babylon (c1830-1530 B.C.)
·	XV		Dynasty XII		Cappadocian Colonies (Kültepe II, c1900-1800 B.C.) Dynasties of Isin and Larsa
— c1900 B.C. —					

Syria column (vertical labels): Ras Shamra II.2 — Byblos, Royal Tombs — Alalakh IX-VIII — Amuq K

This sloping type of earthen (*terre pisée*) construction was first identified by Flinders Petrie at Tell el-Yehudiyeh in lower Egypt[72] and has subsequently been found in nearly every ruined Palestinian city of the period.[73] In addition to this earthen fortification around cities, there have been observed at Hazor and Ascalon in Palestine, at Tell el-Yehudiyeh and Heliopolis in lower Egypt, and at Carchemish and Qatna, among other places in Syria, huge rectangular enclosures surrounded with the great mounds of earth.[74] Y. Yadin has shown that the earthen fortifications should most probably be interpreted as a defense against the newly introduced battering ram. Albright has long supported the view that the most natural interpretation of the vast earth-enclosed camps is the supposition that they were chariot and horse parks for the "Hyksos" chariot warriors, who, during the following century, were able to unite Egypt in its "Second Intermediate" period with Syria-Palestine. In spite of a feudal type of rule, the new overlords were, nevertheless, able to usher in the most prosperous period in Palestine's history before the Roman period.[75]

The new fortifications were built around the outer slopes of the mounds. At Jericho the original installation was rebuilt twice. In the final stage a heavy stone wall around the base of the mound, and erected against the mound's debris, was built to serve as a retaining wall for the plastered earthen slope above it. The most spectacular example of this type of wall is that on the western side of the mound of Shechem, where the cyclopean structure retains its original height of *ca.* ten meters, and had a massive gateway, with the three entryways which were typical of the period, set into it. The Drew-McCormick Expedition in 1957 found that the eastern slope's cyclopean wall was strengthened by the addition, eleven meters up the slope, of a brick wall on a deep stone foundation, *ca.* 3.25–3.75 meters thick. The slope between the two was then filled in and plastered over.[76] A comparable system of outer and inner walls, with the slope between filled in and plastered in place, was found by J. L. Kelso at Bethel in 1957, while at Lachish and Tell Beit Mirsim earthen ramparts are said to have been replaced around the bottom slope of the mounds by large stone walls.[77] At Shechem and at Jericho, in particular, these new fortifications are among the most massive and impregnable structures in Palestinian history. Their date appears to be MB II C.

It is also of interest that three, and probably four, temples of the Palestinian MB II are now known. In Israel, small but well-preserved structures of the age have been unearthed at Nahariyah and at Hazor. In 1957 the massive fortress-temple at Shechem was found to have been originally built in MB II C, carrying with it the implication that the comparable structure at Megiddo is of similar date instead of being first erected in the Late Bronze Age as the excavators thought. Both were probably destroyed during the second half of the 12th century.[77a]

On the basis of Egyptian chronology, when tied to Palestinian stratigraphy, Albright has correlated the earthen fortifications with the "Hyksos" conquest of Egypt and dated them in Palestine about 1700 B.C. or very shortly thereafter. At the same time, it must be noted, however, that evidence from Tell Beit Mirsim, Lachish, and Megiddo seems to prove that the new pottery shapes in imitation of metal were introduced before the earthen embankments were erected.[78] For this reason, MB II B is represented as beginning *ca.* 1750 B.C. or within the decades immediately thereafter.

Other architecture of Middle Bronze II B and C suggests that the city-state system was again in use, with the country divided up into a number of rival provinces, but with over-all control imposed from the outside. This meant that major royal capitals were dominated by royal palaces, around which clustered the huts of a populace composed mostly of very poor serfs.[79] Yet population increased and spread to such an extent that the age is the best known in Palestinian history from the standpoint of material culture, particularly ceramics.[80] Perhaps the most remarkable individual discoveries of the period are the tombs at Jericho, found perfectly sealed with all contents, including food and furniture, intact.[81] Thus far, clear evidence for a sharp separation in ceramic chronology between MB II B and C is lacking. An evolution in forms and the introduction in MB II C of the first examples of a pottery from Cyprus, called "base-ring" ware and known to be common in the Late Bronze Age, has been proved.[82] The period ends during the 16th century when the Egyptian reconquest of the country apparently destroyed every major city. As will be observed from the line drawn for *ca.* 1550 B.C. in Chart 6, the initial Egyptian reconquest was rapid, and the destruction of "Hyksos" cities in Palestine was not a gradual process scattered over a century. Subsequent Pharaohs frequently fought in the country, but their campaigns are probably to be considered as belonging, for the most part, in the Late Bronze Age.

V. THE PERIOD OF EGYPTIAN DOMINATION: THE LATE BRONZE AGE (LATE BRONZE I, CA. 15TH CENTURY; II A, CA. 14TH CENTURY; II B, CA. 13TH CENTURY)

As will be noted from an examination of Charts 6 and 7, the evidence is not yet clear as to precisely when the Middle Bronze Age should be conceived as ending and the Late Bronze beginning. Because of the violence of the Egyptian conquest, it is not certain that we have any deposits that must be dated solely in the second half of the 16th century, following the first and main wave of the conquest in the middle decades of that century. The archaeological evidence certainly suggests that the energy and violence of the Egyptian conquest of Asia was such as to carry the conquerors rapidly through Palestine into Syria with results that cannot be minimized.

Megiddo IX and the corresponding Palace II and Stratum II of Tell el-'Ajjul in southern Palestine belong, for the most part, to the first part of the 15th century. Megiddo IX was destroyed by Thutmose III *ca.* 1468 B.C. and Tell el-'Ajjul was evidently destroyed about the same time.[83] Whether or how far these strata go back into the 16th century is unknown, but it is quite clear that the objects found should be dated for the most part from the last years before the respective cities were destroyed. As a result, these two strata fix chronologically the most characteristic feature of this period: that is, a beautiful bichrome painted pottery, especially characterized by birds and fish drawn in a particularized style within prepared panels. The decoration of the pottery must have originated in a single pottery workshop, one whose influence extended as far away as Egypt, Cyprus, and Cilicia (Tarsus).[84] Hitherto, the ware has been dated between 1550 and 1450 B.C., but, in my judgment, there is thus far no clear evidence which requires that it be dated before 1500 B.C.[85]

For the second half of the 15th century, it is probable that only Phase I of the Fosse Temple at Lachish and Stratum IVA at Beth-shemesh can be

Chart 6. The "Hyksos" Age: Middle Bronze II B (c1750/1700-1650/1600 B.C.) and II C (c1650/1600-1550/1500 B.C.)

Site	Later (II C)	Earlier (II B)
Tell Beit Mirsim	c1500 B.C. — D	c1550 B.C. — E₂ — E₁ — c1750/1700 B.C.
Megiddo	IX(?) — X	XI (Tomb 24) — XII
Beth-shemesh	Tomb 12 — V	Tomb 13 — Tomb 17 — Tomb 9
Gezer	Cave 28 II	Cave 15 I (part) — Tomb 1
Tell el-'Ajjul	City Stratum II — Palace II	City Stratum I — Palace I — "Hyksos" Tombs
Tell el-Far'ah (S)		City occupation — Cemetery 1000 — Cemetery 500 (in part)
Tell el-Far'ah (N)		Niveau 5 — Tombs A — M
Jericho		Watzinger "Red" City — Garstang "City C," "Palace storerooms" — Many Tombs
Hazor Area C	?	Stratum 3
Shechem	?	Wall B — E. Gate — Temple — Wall A — N.W. Gate
Beth-shan	XA(?)	XB(?)
Egypt	Dynasty XVIII	Second Intermediate Age
Syria	Alalakh VII — VI-V	Ras Shamra II.3 — x x x x x x x
Iraq		Babylon destroyed by Hittites — First Dynasty of Babylon

Chart 7. The Period of Egyptian Domination: The Late Bronze Age (LB I, 15th cent. B.C.; LB II A, 14th cent.; LB II B, 13th cent.)

Site	Late Bronze I (15th cent.; c1500–1468 B.C.)	Late Bronze IIA (14th cent.; ±1400 B.C.)	Late Bronze IIB (13th cent.; c1200 B.C.)
Tell Beit Mirsim	(X)	C1	C2
Megiddo	IX — 1468 B.C.	VIII (X)	VIIB
Beth-shan	XA	IX · VIII	VII
Tell el-'Ajjul	Palace II; City Stratum II	Palace III A (Fort) · Palace III B (Fort)	Governor's Tomb and other tombs; Palace IV (Fort)
Beth-shemesh	IVa	← IVb →	Tombs 10, 11
Gezer	City deposits →	Tomb 30	Tombs 7, 9 (early), 252
Hazor Area C	2	1B	1A
Tell el-Far'ah (S)		Cemetery 900	
Tell el-Far'ah (N)	Niveau 4 → Tombs 6, 11 (part), 12 (part), 16 (part)		
Lachish	I	II	III; Fosse Temple
Jericho	(X)	Sherds above Spring; A few vessels in Tombs 4, 5, 13	
Tell Abu Hawam	(X)		V
Egypt	Dynasty XVIII; Amarna Age	Dynasty XVIII; Amarna Age	Dynasty XIX
Syria-Iraq	Ras Shamra i. 1; Alalakh IV; Nuzi Age →	Ras Shamra i. 2 (texts in alphabetic cuneiform, Accadian); Alalakh III-I →	Ras Shamra i. 3

considered as representative among the published Palestinian material.[86] From LB II, however, when quantities of Mycenaean pottery were imported from the mainland of Greece, there is a great deal of information about the period, as the list of chief deposits in Chart 7 makes clear. From Megiddo, Beth-shan, Hazor, and Lachish, there is stratigraphical evidence for the division of the period into at least two parts, the dividing line between them perhaps being the campaigns in Palestine-Syria of Seti I and Ramses II of the Nineteenth Egyptian Dynasty at the turn of the 14th–13th century.[87] The three strata at Beth-shan probably cannot be more precisely dated than they are in Chart 7 until they are better published.

The rich discoveries in city fortifications, palaces, temples, inscriptions, and objects are so well and succinctly described by Albright that we need not duplicate his survey here.[88] Jericho remains even more enigmatic than ever. There seems to be no doubt now that the flourishing 17th-century city there was brought to a violent end in the mid-16th century (see Chart 6) and that the mound was unoccupied during the 15th century. A few sherds on the mound above the spring, dating from the 14th century, preferably the second half of that century, and a few vases of approximately the same date in three tombs, constitute most of what has been found there from the Late Bronze Age.[89] The largest city of the age was probably Hazor in Galilee where the great Hyksos enclosure to the north of the tell was filled, in the places dug, with dwellings. These were destroyed during the course of the 13th century and the enclosure was not again occupied.[90] The Israelite invasion during the second half of the 13th century brought the Bronze Age to a close at a number of the hill-country sites (Tell Beit Mirsim C_2, Beth-shemesh IVb?, Hazor enclosure 1, Lachish Temple III, Bethel LB), whereas the invasion of the Sea Peoples in the early years of the 12th century destroyed a number of other cities, particularly in the plains (including probably Megiddo VII B, Beth-shan VII, Tell Abu Hawam V, and evidently the Tell el-Far'ah (S) residency).[91] At Megiddo and Beth-shan rapid rebuilding meant that Late Bronze traditions lingered longer into the 12th century than at other sites under Israelite control.

VI. THE FIRST ISRAELITE PERIOD: IRON AGE I (IRON I A, EARLY 12TH CENTURY; IRON I B, LATE 12TH AND 11TH CENTURIES, IRON I C, 10TH CENTURY)

The division of the first Iron Age into three phases is that of Albright. He derives these phases from the stratification of Tell Beit Mirsim, where, following the destruction of Late Bronze City C, he found evidence of an intermediate, though crude, reoccupation which he labeled B_1. This was followed by the main period from the mid-12th century through most of the 11th century in which a distinguishing feature was the interesting and characteristic "Philistine" pottery (B_2). Then came the tenth century (B_3), the period of Israel's united monarchy, with its characteristic wares, particularly the hand-burnished red vessels and the first examples of small black oil juglets, both of which represent the beginning of a stable ceramic evolution which lasts into the sixth century B.C.

In dating these phases, Albright worked from Biblical evidence which, at both ends of the period, was roughly pegged by Egyptian evidence. The end of the third phase was interpreted as the destruction of the Pharaoh Shishak, who, in the fifth year of the Judean king Rehoboam (*ca.* 918 B.C.), devastated most of the cities of Palestine (I Kings 14:25–26).[92] The main chronological key was the "Philistine" pottery, the only ware in ancient Palestine that can definitely be ascribed to one people.[93] Since the Sea Peoples invaded Palestine not far from the time when they were defeated on sea and land by Ramses III in Egypt, we can assume that their pottery, made on 13th-century Aegean models, would appear in Palestine by at least the mid-12th century B.C. Furthermore, it is clear that the ware is no longer made by the tenth century, for it does not appear in Tell Beit Mirsim B_3 and related deposits. Hence, Albright is justified in arguing that we must look to the blows which the Philistines received at the hands of Saul and David for the probable dividing line between the second and third phases.

How far this three-phase arrangement will be modified by future work remains to be seen. Iron I A (Tell Beit Mirsim B_1) would appear to represent an Israelite occupation before the Sea Peoples became strong and influential. It would have been of short duration and would be expected only on sites conquered by Israelites during the latter part of the 13th century. Cities like Megiddo and Beth-shan, whose Late Bronze culture continued well into the 12th century, would probably not have it, nor would the Canaanite cities taken over by the Philistines (e.g., Tell Qasile, Tell Abu Hawam, Tell el-Far'ah [S]). Hence, all we can say at present is that the pre-Philistine Iron I A of Tell Beit Mirsim cannot be expected to be an important phase in Palestine's cultural history. If and when found again, it will probably be only at sites occupied by Israel.

On the other hand, Albright's conclusions concerning the Philistine period of Iron I B have been confirmed at all sites where stratigraphy preserves the evidence. The difference between Beth-shemesh III and IIa, for example, is precisely that between Beit Mirsim B_2 and B_3.[94] From Philistine country itself, there are Petrie's discoveries of a fine palace and cemetery of this age at Tell el-Far'ah on the Wadi Ghazzeh. Of particular importance, however, have been the excavations of B. Mazar (Maisler) at Tell Qasile on the northern outskirts of Tel Aviv.[95] There Strata XII–XI contain the best quality of Philistine ware, while Stratum X, which is contemporary with Megiddo VI, Tell Abu Hawam IVb, and Gibeah II, has only a weakened and poorer remnant of the finer traditions of Philistine painted pottery, a state of affairs evidently to be dated in the second half of the 11th century. At the same time, it is to be noted that Philistine power at this time reached its zenith. During the third quarter of the 11th century, after the Battle of Ebenezer *ca.* 1050 B.C., when Shiloh fell (1 Samuel 4), the following destructions can probably be attributed to the Philistines: in addition to Shiloh, Tell Beit Mirsim B₂, Beth-zur, either phase 2 or 3 of Iron Age Bethel (cf. *TBM III,* para. 23), Beth-shemesh III, and Megiddo VI B (?).

The complicated stratigraphy of the post-Philistine period, as exhibited in Chart 8, probably represents the conquests of David (Megiddo V B, Beth-shan V, Tell Qasile X?, Tell Abu Hawam IVb?), on the one hand, and the building of governmental provincial centers by David and Solomon, on the other (e.g. Tell Beit Mirsim B₃, Megiddo V A–IV B, Beth-Shemesh IIa, Lachish V and Hazor X).[96] Then came the Shishak raid from Egypt *ca.* 918 B.C., mentioned above, which seems to have destroyed all the important centers, though many sites were evidently rebuilt on substantially the old plan (e.g. Megiddo IV A and Tell Qasile VIII).[97]

In view of the complexity of the stratification it is, as yet, too early to say whether the division of this age into three periods is permanently established. On the other hand, the ceramic chronology of at least the eleventh and tenth centuries seems now firmly fixed, whatever terms may be evolved for them.

VII. THE SECOND ISRAELITE PERIOD: IRON AGE II (CA. 900—EARLY SIXTH CENTURY B.C.)

The second Iron Age is now generally extended to cover the periods of the divided monarchy of Israel (II A), the kingdom of Judah (II B) after the destruction of the northern kingdom and the division of that territory into Assyrian administrative provinces (732–721 B.C.), and the exilic period (II C) between the Babylonian destruction of Jerusalem in 587 (or 586) and the Persian period after 540 B.C. We shall bring this survey and our charts to a close, however, with Iron II B, ending in Judah in 587 B.C., because at that point the series of coherent and interlacing stratifications of the various excavated sites comes to a close. To be sure, Samaria carries on for centuries, indeed, through the Roman period, but it is the only well-excavated site that so far has been found to do so.[98] And even here, because Hellenistic and Roman building so destroyed the earlier deposits, the stratification is not as instructive as is necessary for the needed knowledge of the periods covered. Megiddo I and Lachish I are strata of the Persian Age, as are also the last cities at Tell en-Nasbeh and Tell Jemmeh, but as surface strata they are not as revealing as one could hope because of erosion and the problem of mixture with lower deposits.[99] Otherwise, for the later periods, only occasional collections of material are available for chronological study, and no comparatively full view of any one period is possible.[100]

The material culture of Iron II, it is interesting to note, was given its basic morphology, within which it was to evolve, in the tenth century (Iron

Chart 8. The First Israelite Period: Iron Age I (I A, early 12th cent. B.C.; I B, late 12th and 11th cents.; I C, 10th cent.)

		Tell Beit Mirsim	Megiddo	Beth-shan	Beth-shemesh	Tell Qasile	Tell Abu Hawam	Gezer Tombs	Tell el-Far'ah (S)	Tell el-Far'ah (N)	Gerar	Lachish	Hazor	Gibeah	Tell en-Nasbeh
c900 B.C.															T. 32 T. 54
c918	A1	A1	IVA	⟶ ?? ⟵	Tomb 1 / IIb	VIII	III	(Some mixture)	"Dyn. XXI-XXII" Level ⟶	Niveau III	Levels 184-187 (or 188)	IV ⟶ / T. 1002 / T. 116 / T. 223 / T. 218 / V / Cave 6024 / T. 521	IX / X (Casemate wall)	⨯	Town Deposits ⟶
IC	B3	B3	V(B)	? / IIa	IX	X		84-85, 96, 138, 142	"Period of Judges" Level					II	
c1000			VIA	V			IVb				Levels c183-176 ⟵		Occupational Deposits		
IB	B2	B2	VA— IVB	V	⟵ III ⟶	XI		58, 59	Residency "Dyn. xx" Level Cemetery 500 (part)					I	
c1150			VIB (c1075)	VI		XII	IVa								
IA	B1	B1	VIIA (c1125)				V								
c1200 B.C.			VIIB												

I C): that is, by the united monarchy of Israel. Mass-production techniques were rapidly developed,[101] perhaps borrowed in part from Phoenicia, so that types of objects were standardized to a high degree, while change was introduced so slowly that Iron II, while a very well-known period, is not an easy time for the archaeologist who would like to date his material closely within a century or less. The most promising site, one which offers hope for detailed improvement in the archaeological chronology of the time, is Hazor. Excavations recently completed at this great Galilean ruin have found that its final major period was in the eighth century, its destruction to be correlated with the campaign of the Assyrian Tiglath-pileser III in 733–32 B.C.[102] Before that, in the ninth–eighth centuries, five building phases have been distinguished, and careful study of the ceramic chronology and of other objects provides fairly precise dating in these centuries.

Megiddo III was also destroyed in 733–32 B.C., but the objects from Megiddo, Strata IV–I, are so schematically published and the strata so mixed that one cannot construct a reliable chronology on its basis alone. Too often one encounters uncertainty with regard to the precise stratum to which single objects belong.

Tell el-Far'ah (N), Dothan,[103] Shechem, and Samaria were all destroyed by the Assyrians in the period 724–21 B.C. At Samaria, Professor Kenyon, in an area east of the royal palace, distinguished six phases, or "periods," between the time when the city was founded (ca. 875 B.C.) and its destruction in 721 B.C. (see Chart 9).[104] Period I is the time of the original fortification and the building of the palace, while II marks a refortification on the summit by the addition on the north and west of a very large and beautifully constructed casemate wall. Kenyon, like Reisner and Fisher before her,[105] dates both these phases to the Omri-Ahab Dynasty (ca. 876–842 B.C.) while III, in which the palace is thought to have been rebuilt, is dated in the second half of the ninth century. Periods IV–VI are minor phases of the eighth century, while VII, with its samples of "Assyrian" pottery, is to be dated after 721 when the Assyrians were in control. Historically, however, it seems rather difficult to suppose that the first two phases should have been constructed by the same dynasty within a twenty-five-year period, especially when the fortifications in each case were of such excellence that they could not have been quickly built.[106] In addition, a study of the pottery and the stratification have led this writer to the conclusion that the pottery periods at Samaria must be separated from the building periods. Because of the extremely difficult stratification problems, Miss Kenyon was led to date the construction of the Samaria periods by debris immediately under the floors instead of by that above them. Such debris, however, can be interpreted as dating the last occupation of the preceding phase, and it cannot be considered as necessarily homogeneous unless all other indications are to the contrary. On present indications from ceramic chronology, the Samaria pottery periods I–II appear mostly to represent a pre-Omri village of the tenth and early ninth centuries. Pottery Period

Chart 9. The Second Israelite Period: Iron Age II (c900—early 6th cent. B.C.)

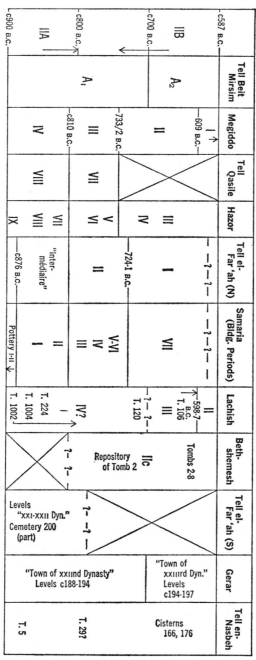

	Tell Beit Mirsim	Megiddo	Tell Qasile	Hazor	Tell el-Far'ah (N)	Samaria (Bldg. Periods)	Lachish	Beth-shemesh	Tell el-Far'ah (S)	Gerar	Tell en-Nasbeh
c587 B.C.	A₂	II		III	I	VII	II / T. 106 / T. 120	Tombs 2-8		"Town of xxiiird Dyn." Levels c194-197	Cisterns 166, 176
c700 B.C.				IV		V-VI / IV / III	III				
IIB		609 B.C.	VII	V / VI	II	II	IV? / T. 224 / T. 1004	IIc / Repository of Tomb 2			T. 29?
733/2 B.C.	A₁	III — c810 B.C.	VIII	VII / VIII		I	T. 1002		Levels "xxi-xxii Dyn." Cemetery 200 (part)	"Town of xxiind Dynasty" Levels c188-194	T. 5
c800 B.C.		IV		IX	"inter-médiaire" — c876 B.C.	Pottery I-II					
IIA											
c900 B.C.											

III, then, for the most part, would appear to date from the time of building periods I and II, while building period VI is to be viewed as being identical with V. The writer's interpretation and redating of the Samaria periods is as follows:[107]

TENTH TO EARLY NINTH CENTURY B.C.		
CA. 875–842 B.C.	BUILDING PERIOD I	POTTERY PERIODS I–II
CA. 842–810 B.C.	BUILDING PERIOD II (?) }	POTTERY PERIOD III
CA. 810–±760 B.C.	BUILDING PERIOD III	POTTERY PERIOD IV
CA. 760–±735 B.C.	BUILDING PERIOD IV	POTTERY PERIOD V
CA. 735–721 B.C.	BUILDING PERIOD V–VI	POTTERY PERIOD VI

An especially characteristic type of pottery has been distinguished at Samaria during the ninth and eighth centuries B.C. It is called "Samaria ware" and is characterized by a high gloss finish on a red to reddish-brown slip. Little of it has been found in Judah, where potters seemed to remain content with their wheel-burnished ("ring-burnished") bowls without the extra hand polishing needed to give the lustrous finish. Heretofore, however, there appears to have been some confusion as to just what it is and is not. As a start toward clarification, this writer has proposed to divide it into Samaria ware A of the ninth century and Samaria ware B of the eighth century, the precise extent of their overlap not as yet being known. Ware B is made of a light, well-cleaned buff paste, with a thick slip of a light red color. Ware A is heavier, less well cleaned, dark in color at the core, and a darker red to reddish-brown slip, as a rule. It is common at Samaria in pottery period III, and at Hazor in Stratum VIII. It first appears earlier, however, in Hazor X–IX and, as Gus Van Beek has observed, in tenth-century Megiddo.[108]

In the territory of ancient Judah, only the seventh and early sixth centuries are well known, particularly from Stratum A_2 at Tell Beit Mirsim, from Strata III and II at Lachish,[109] and from a number of tombs, among them Tombs 2–8 at Beth-shemesh.[110] Indeed, the great abundance of pottery from the last two decades or so of the kingdom of Judah, as published in many photographs and drawings from Tell Beit Mirsim, fixes the ceramic chronology of this age with considerable certainty.[111] We are not as well off for the end of the eighth and the beginning of the seventh century. Surveys of the architecture, inscriptions, and objects of this period have been published elsewhere, and their data need not be repeated here.[112]

From the above survey, it should be clear that a great deal of work remains to be done, for not a single period in ancient Palestinian history is as clear as one would desire it to be. Numerous conclusions here presented, particularly in the charts, may in the future be subject to revision in detail. Yet we are in a position to make one concluding statement with considerable confidence: working outward from the chronological basis which for the most part was fixed by Albright in the 1920s and the 1930s, we are now able to survey the cultural history of ancient Palestine between *ca.* 8000 and 600 B.C. with greater detail than is possible for any other ancient country.[113]

NOTES TO CHAPTER FOUR

1. See W. F. Albright, *The Excavation of Tell Beit Mersim*. Vol. 1. *The Pottery of the First Three Campaigns (AASOR,* Vol. XII, New Haven, 1932); Vol. I A: *The Bronze Age Pottery of the Fourth Campaign* (ibid., Vol. XIII; New Haven, 1933); Vol. II: *The Bronze Age* (ibid., Vol. XVII; New Haven, 1938); and Vol. III: *The Iron Age* (ibid., Vols. XXI–XXII; New Haven, 1943).

2. See especially R. S. Lamon and G. M. Shipton, *Megiddo I: Seasons of 1925–34, Strata I–V* (Chicago, 1939); P. L. O. Guy and R. M. Engberg, *Megiddo Tombs* (Chicago, 1938); R. M. Engberg, and G. M. Shipton, *Notes on the Chalcolithic and Early Bronze Age Pottery of Megiddo* (Chicago, 1934); G. M. Shipton, *Notes on the Megiddo Pottery of Strata VI–XX* (Chicago, 1939); Gordon Loud, *Megiddo II. Seasons of 1935–1939* (Chicago, 1948).

3. For details and revised dating, see the following critical reviews: W. F. Albright, review of *Megiddo I, American Journal of Archaeology,* Vol. 44 (1940), pp. 546–50; review of *Megiddo II,* ibid., Vol. 53 (1949), pp. 213–15; and see his studies in *The Excavation of Tell Beit Mirsim,* Vol. III, pp. 2–3, note 1; p. 18, note 6; pp. 29–30, note 10. See also G. Ernest Wright, review of *Megiddo II, Journal of the American Oriental Society,* Vol. 70 (1950), pp. 56–60; *The Biblical Archaeologist,* Vol. XIII (1950), pp. 28–46; and for a brief listing of the revised dates, *Westminster Historical Atlas to the Bible,* revised ed. (Philadelphia, 1956), p. 113.

4. See Alan Rowe, *The Topography and History of Beth-shan* (Philadelphia, 1930); *The Four Canaanite Temples of Beth-shan,* Part I (Philadelphia, 1940); G. M. Fitzgerald, Part II, *The Pottery* (Philadelphia, 1930); *Beth-shan Excavations, 1921– 1923: The Arab and Byzantine Levels* (Philadelphia, 1931); *A Sixth Century Monastery at Beth-shan (Scythopolis)* (Philadelphia, 1939); *Quarterly Statement of the Palestine Exploration Fund,* 1931, pp. 59–70, and 1932, pp. 138–48; "The Earliest Pottery of Beth-shan," *Museum Journal,* Vol. 24, No. 1 (1935), pp. 5–30. For critical reviews which redate the strata, see W. F. Albright, *The Excavations of Tell Beit Mirsim,* Vol. II, paragraph 86; G. Ernest Wright, review of *The Four Canaanite Temples, American Journal of Archaeology,* Vol. 45 (1941), pp. 483– 85; and for a brief résumé, see *Westminster Historical Atlas to the Bible,* revised ed., p. 114; and B. Mazar (Maisler), *Bulletin of the Israel Exploration Society,* Vol. XVI (1951), pp. 14–19.

5. See his report, *The Excavations of Tell Qasile, Preliminary Report* (Jerusalem, 1951), reprinted from *Israel Exploration Journal,* Vol. 1 (1950–51); and for an application of the results, "The Stratification of Tell Abu Huwam on the Bay of Acre," *BASOR,* No. 124 (Dec. 1951), pp. 21–25.

6. For brief preliminary reports of the first three campaigns (1955–57), see *The Biblical Archaeologist,* Vol. XIX.1 (Feb. 1956), pp. 2–12; Vol. XX.2 (May 1957), pp. 34–47; Vol. XXI.2 (May 1958), pp. 30–48. For the definitive publication of the results of the first season, see Yigael Yadin, et al, *HAZOR I* (Jerusalem, 1958).

7. See the preliminary reports as follows: 1st campaign, *RB,* Vol. LIV (1947), pp. 394–433; 573–89; 2nd campaign, ibid., Vol. LV (1948), pp. 544–80, and Vol. LVI (1949), pp. 102–38; 3rd campaign, ibid., Vol. LVIII (1951), pp. 391–430; 566–90; 4th campaign, ibid., Vol. LIX (1952), pp. 551–83; 5th campaign, ibid., Vol. LXII (1955), pp. 541–89.

8. For preliminary reports of the first two campaigns, see the writer in *BASOR*, No. 144 (Dec. 1956), pp. 9–20; No. 148 (Dec. 1957), pp. 11–28.

9. See the references given in note 100.

10. *The Pottery of Palestine from the Earliest Times to the End of the Early Bronze Age* (New Haven, 1937). The earlier work of Albright on this same question is summarized in his "Palestine in the Earliest Historical Period," *Journal of the Palestine Oriental Society*, Vol. xv, 1935, pp. 193–234. For recent work and the conclusions based upon it, see the articles by Helene J. Kantor, W. F. Albright, and Robert J. Braidwood in Robert W. Ehrich, ed., *Relative Chronologies in Old World Archaeology* (Chicago, 1954); Robert J. and Linda Braidwood, "The Earliest Village Communities of Southwestern Asia," *Journal of World History I* (1953), pp. 278–310; G. Ernest Wright, "Early Bronze I. The Problem of the Transition between the Chalcolithic and Bronze Ages," *Eretz Israel*, Vol. v (1958), pp. 37–45.

11. See especially her articles in *Palestine Exploration Quarterly*, 1952, pp. 62–82; 1953, pp. 81–95; 1954, pp. 45–63; 1955, pp. 106–17; 1956, pp. 67–82; 1957, pp. 101–7; and her book, *Digging Up Jericho* (London and New York, 1957).

12. See J. Perrot, "The Excavations at Tell Abu Matar, near Beersheba," *Israel Exploration Journal*, Vol. 5 (1955), pp. 17–40, 73–88, 167–89.

13. Most of the dates have been published since 1950 in the magazine *Science;* see also J. R. Arnold and W. F. Libby, *Radiocarbon Dates* (Institute for Nuclear Studies, University of Chicago, 1950). The list of dates given below is taken from a selection of Robert J. Braidwood, "Near Eastern Prehistory," *Science,* Vol. 127, No. 3312 (June 20, 1958), pp. 1419–430. The letters before the numbers refer to the laboratories where the tests were made: namely Chicago (c), Washington (w), London (GL), Davy-Faraday (F), Groningen (GR), Heidelberg (H). For a statement of problems connected with sample contamination, see especially F. E. Zeuner, "Radiocarbon Dates," *Eleventh Annual Report,* Institute of Archaeology, University of London (London, 1955), pp. 43–50.

14. Robert J. Braidwood in 1957 was inclined to doubt the reliability of the Jericho dates (see his article in *Antiquity,* No. 122 [June 1957]), but surrendered his doubts when during the winter and spring of 1957–58 new C-14 early dates from Jarmo, Matarrah, and Hassuna provided a setting for the Jericho range. He is still not satisfied, however, with some of the Kenyon terms and interpretations. Note also V. Gordon Childe, "Civilization, Cities, and Towns," ibid., No. 121 (Mar. 1957), pp. 36–38, where he, like Braidwood, criticizes the indiscriminate use of the terms "civilization" and "city" to early Jericho when they have their own generally accepted spheres of usage in anthropology.

15. See especially D. A. E. Garrod, "A New Mesolithic Industry, the Natufian of Palestine," *Journal of the Anthropological Institute*, Vol. LXII (1932), pp. 257–69; D. A. E. Garrod and D. M. A. Bate, *The Stone Age of Mount Carmel*, Vol. I (Oxford, 1937); N. Neuville, et al., *Le Paléolithique et le Mésolithique du Désert de Judée* (Paris, 1951), especially Chapter 10 by J. Perrot, "Le Terrasse d'el Khiam"; Robert J. and Linda Braidwood, op. cit. (see n. 10), pp. 282–86; Jean Perrot, "Les industries lithiques Palestiniennes de la fin du Mésolithique à l'Age du Bronze," *Israel Exploration Journal*, Vol. 2 (1952), pp. 73–81; and "Le Mésolithique de Palestine et les récentes découvertes à Eynan (Ain Mallaha)," *Antiquity and Survival*, Vol. II, No. 2/3 (The Hague, 1957), pp. 91–110.

16. Alfred Rust, *Die Höhlenfunde von Jabrud* (Naumünster, 1950).

17. W. F. Albright, *BASOR*, No. 109, p. 12.

18. See John Garstang, et al, "Jericho: City and Necropolis" (6th and final report), *Annals of Archaeology and Anthropology,* Vol. XXIII (1936), pp. 67 ff.; and Kathleen Kenyon, *Digging Up Jericho*, Chap. v.

19. See Robert J. Braidwood, "From Cave to Village in Prehistoric Iraq," *BASOR*, No. 124 (Dec. 1951), pp. 12–18; *The Near East and the Foundations of Civilization* (Eugene, Oregon, 1952), pp. 23 ff.

20. Jean Perrot, "Le Néolithique d'Abou-Gosh," *Syria* 29 (1952), pp. 119–45.

21. See Perrot, in Neuville, et al, op. cit. (n. 15), Chapter 10.

22. For the *Abu Usba'* cave, see M. Stekelis, "Preliminary Report on Soundings in Prehistoric Caves in Palestine," *BASOR*, No. 86 (Apr. 1942), pp. 2–14 (cf. W. F. Albright, observations, ibid., pp. 10–14); Stekelis, "The Abu Usba Cave," *Israel Exploration Journal*, Vol. 2 (1952), pp. 15–46; and for dating, see Robert J. and Linda Braidwood, op. cit. (n. 10), pp. 284, 288–89. The cave across the valley, *Mugharet Wadi Fallaḥ*, was being excavated in 1956 under the direction of Stekelis.

23. See R. and L. Braidwood, *Excavations in the Plain of Antioch I* (Chicago, shortly to be published)—a study that is basic to early Syrian comparative archaeology and the bridge between Mesopotamia and Palestine. See also Ann Louise Perkins, *The Comparative Archaeology of Early Mesopotamia* (Chicago, 1949).

24. For summary of the evidence, see Ann Louise Perkins, ibid., p. 37.

25. For Jericho VIII see Immanuel Ben-Dor, *Annals of Archaeology and Anthropology*, Vol. XXIII (1936), pp. 84–90; Joan Crowfoot, "Notes on the Flint Implements of Jericho, 1936," ibid., Vol. XXIV (1937), pp. 35–51. Professor Kenyon has not as yet discovered this culture as a separate stratum: see her remarks, *Palestine Exploration Quarterly*, 1955, p. 113; and *Digging Up Jericho*, pp. 85 ff. In the latter, she names the ware "Neolithic B" and relates it to the period of the early pottery at Byblos, Ras Shamra, Judeidah, Mersin, and Hassuna. Chronologically, this would now appear impossible, and to this writer both the title and the comparisons are premature. The Yarmukian-Jericho VIII material is more probably to be dated ±4000 B.C. and thus within the Chalcolithic Age (see below). The flint implements resemble the Tahunian more than they do the Ghassulian, and this was initially the main argument for the decision that the culture is pre-Ghassulian, though see below for what may be stratigraphical evidence at Sheikh Ali. For the Yarmukian, see M. Stekelis, "A New Neolithic Industry: The Yarmukian of Palestine," *Israel Exploration Journal*, Vol. I (1950–51), pp. 1–19—here the author dates his discoveries far too early and fails to equate them with Jericho VIII. The lowest material from bedrock at Megiddo is called "Stratum XX." While mixed and of various periods before *ca.* 3000 B.C., it does contain elements of the Yarmukian-Jericho VIII period (see, for example, Gordon Loud, *Megiddo II*, Pl. 2:37–42). Sherds also appear in de Vaux's "Middle Chalcolithic" at Tell el-Far'ah near Nablus, though in my judgment this stratum is also mixed and in part misdated (cf. especially *RB*, LIV, 1947, p. 407; Fig. 1:18–20, 34, of this stratum and those I have seen in Jerusalem belong to a later period, with the stratum just above it). In 1956 Stekelis found some beautiful stone vessels at Kabri, north of Acre. One of them is a bow-rim jar imitated from pottery (cf. Ben-Dor, op. cit., Pl. XXXIII:18), which presumably dates the deposit to this period.

26. G. Ernest Wright, "An Important Correlation Between the Palestinian and Syrian Chalcolithic," *BASOR,* No. 122 (Apr. 1951), pp. 52–55; and R. and L. Braidwood, op. cit. (note 23). While this correlation may not stand the test of time completely—and a regional cultural lag may be assumed—it appears to be the one bit of concrete evidence, tying Palestine to Syria and to Mesopotamia before Early Bronze I, now available.

27. James Mellaart, "The Neolithic Site of Ghrubba," *Annual of the Department of Antiquities, Jordan*, Vol. III (1956), pp. 24–40; Gordon Loud, *Megiddo II*, Pl. 2:30–36; G. M. Shipton, *Notes on the Megiddo Pottery of Strata VI–XX*, Pl.

18:1–4, and perhaps 12–13; Pl. 20:7–10. Megiddo xx has pottery of three or four periods: el-Ghrubba, Yarmukian-Jericho vIII (Ghassulian?), and Early Bronze I. It is difficult to separate the band-painted Ghrubba pottery from that at Hassuna and Matarrah in Mesopotamia, though not enough information is available other than to suggest that the latter are a millennium earlier: see Seton Lloyd and Fuad Safar, *JNES* Iv (1952), pp. 1 ff. and Figs. 12–14.

28. This dating represents a lowering of the chronology, one which now seems required by a new understanding of Early Bronze I. The latter is now seen immediately to succeed it (see below).

29. In 1937 the writer attempted to see in the Ghassulian a distinct provincial expression of the Mesopotamian Halafian (*Pottery of Palestine . . . ,* pp. 14–41). Since that time, however, the comparative chronology of the early Near East has been considerably clarified and revised.

30. A. Mallon, R. Koeppel, et al, *Teleilat Ghassul,* Vol. I (Rome, 1934) and Vol. II (Rome, 1940).

31. James Mellaart, "Report of the Archaeological Survey in the Yarmuk and Jordan Valleys for the Yarmuk-Jordan Valley Project" (manuscript unpublished, but loaned the writer for study in July 1956 by Mr. G. L. Harding, then Director of Antiquities in Jordan).

32. E. L. Sukenik, *Archaeological Investigations at 'Affula* (Jerusalem, 1948), Pl. I: 1–3. The quantity of stratified material at this site is so slight that it can serve only as a suggestion for dating purposes. The Tell esh-Shuneh evidence is much stronger, but unpublished. Other Chalcolithic sherds at 'Affuleh are unstratified: e.g. Pl. I:4; p. Iv:1–3; p. v:3–4. The stratification at Tell esh-Shuneh, as identified by James Mellaart, and confirmed by Albright, is as follows: unpainted Ghassulian pottery with Ghassulian-like flints, followed by Early Bronze I, and then a great deposit of Khirbet Kerak pottery of Early Bronze III.

33. For a review of the early controversy on the date of the Ghassulian, with Vincent arguing that it did not end until after 2000 B.C., while Albright maintained, correctly, that it was a fourth-millennium culture, see the first two items listed in note 10. A recent suggestion to date the Ghassulian between the mid-fourth and the mid-third millennium B.C. was made by Jean Perrot (*Bulletin of the Israel Exploration Society,* Vol. xvIII, 1954, p. 128), but for the reasons here stated, Perrot's date in the third millennium for the termination of the culture is difficult to accept.

34. See J. Perrot, "The Excavations at Tell Abu Matar, near Beersheba," *Israel Exploration Journal,* Vol. 5 (1955), pp. 17–40, 73–84, 167–89. The last section has a map and full bibliography on the spread of the Ghassulian culture. The author's view, however, that there was a northern and a southern version of the Ghassulian is at this moment hard to follow ceramically. The Beersheba culture may indeed represent a regional survival of an earlier period, but a few decades rather than centuries could give adequate expression to this factor. It is, of course, a truism to suggest that a sharp line drawn in archaeological charts to separate periods is only a rough approximation, since outlying areas do not change as rapidly as those in different geographical circumstances. Yet even when old patterns are retained in new ages, one expects some hint of the new to appear beside the old. While it is true that Tell Abu Matar provides a more extended stratigraphical knowledge than does the work at Ghassul, it nevertheless appears to this writer that there is a peculiar poverty of ceramic forms as compared to the greater richness of forms at Ghassul. W. F. Albright is inclined to consider Matar as, on the whole, later than Ghassul proper. Wealthier Ghassulian villages will sooner or later be excavated in the northern part of the country and in the Jordan Valley.

35. Cf. the range of material found in the Beersheba drainage: e.g. E. Macdonald, et al., *Beth-pelet II* (London, 1932), for a number of sites in the Wadi Ghazzeh. That the earliest occupation of Gezer was Ghassulian has been further indicated by Mrs. Ruth Amiran, "The Cream Ware of Gezer and the Beersheba Late Chalcolithic," *Israel Exploration Journal,* Vol. 5 (1955), pp. 240–45; for earlier views of Albright and the writer, see *The Pottery of Palestine . . . ,* pp. 21–23.

36. "Protoliterate" is a term suggested by the Oriental Institute for materials formerly classed as late Uruk and Jemdet Nasr: see P. Delougaz and Seton Lloyd, *Pre-Sargonid Temples in the Diyala Region* (Chicago, 1942), p. 8, note 10; P. Delougaz, *Pottery from the Diyala Region* (Chicago, 1952). For the international situation, see H. Frankfort, *The Birth of Civilization in the Near East* (Bloomington, Ill., 1952); Helene J. Kantor, "Further Evidence for Early Mesopotamian Relations with Egypt," *JNES,* Vol. XI (1952), pp. 239–50.

37. See Gordon Loud, *Megiddo II,* pp. 61 ff.—a broad-roomed structure; and John Garstang, *Annals of Archaeology and Anthropology,* Vol. 22 (1935), pp. 143 ff. and Pl. 41; *The Story of Jericho* (London, 1940), pp. 71–72. The Jericho temple is a long-roomed structure.

38. For Jericho see now Kathleen Kenyon, *Palestine Exploration Quarterly,* 1952–53, pp. 81–82, where the evidence suggests to the excavator a date in the last phase of Early Bronze I. For Ai, see Madame Judith Marquet-Krause, *Les Fouilles de 'Ay (et-Tell), 1933–35* (Paris, 1949), pp. 21–22, 31–32; the precise date of this fortification is not fixed with certainty. For Dothan see J. P. Free, *BASOR,* No. 131 (Oct. 1953), p. 18 and Fig. 2; the earliest extensive series of pottery here as at Megiddo indicates that though there were occasional settlers there earlier in the fourth millennium, the first extensive settlement came in the last phase of Early Bronze I. Whether the city wall definitely dates from this time or from the next period is not completely certain.

39. Garstang, *Annals of Archaeology and Anthropology,* Vol. 23 (1936), Pl. 36:26.

40. Cf., e.g. the review by Helene J. Kantor in R. W. Ehrich, ed., *Relative Chronologies in Old World Archaeology,* pp. 4–7 and Fig. 1; and "The Early Relations of Egypt with Asia," *JNES* I (1942), pp. 174–213. Cf. earlier G. Ernest Wright, *The Pottery of Palestine from the Earliest Times . . . ,* pp. 47–51.

41. Ibid., pp. 42 ff. and 56 ff.

42. Ibid., pp. 61 ff.; and further G. E. Wright, "The Troglodytes of Gezer," *Palestine Exploration Quarterly,* 1937, pp. 67 ff.

42a. An exception is the appearance of gray wares at Tulul Abu el-Alayiq, near Jericho, just published by J. B. Pritchard, *AASOR,* Vols. XXXII–XXXIII (1958), pp. 14 ff.

43. For references, see note 7.

44. The writer has chosen to call it all Early Bronze I, in order not to separate it too sharply from what follows, because this age inaugurates that city-state political organization and material culture which characterize the third millennium, while separating it radically from the Ghassulian. The latter is certainly true Chalcolithic, but it is thus far known as nothing more than a pastoral and village culture. Bronze, however, cannot be said to be a very satisfactory archaeological term. We do not know when true bronze was first made, and there is no real reason to assume that it was *ca.* 3000 B.C. Copper would be a better term for the period, and perhaps Canaanite would be even better. For a more detailed analysis of the period, see now the writer, "The Problem of the Transition between the Chalcolithic and Bronze Ages," *Eretz Israel,* Vol. 5 (1958; Mazar Volume), pp. 37–45.

45. Cf. de Vaux, *RB,* Vol. LVI (1949), p. 138, Fig. 13:8 and Pl. IX:11.

46. See most recently, Helene J. Kantor in Erich ed., op. cit., pp. 8–10. For an earlier survey see my *Pottery of Palestine* . . . , pp. 70–72; note also M. W. Prausnitz, "Abydos and Combed Ware," *Palestine Exploration Quarterly*, 1954, pp. 91–96.

47. Kantor and Albright in Ehrich ed., op. cit., pp. 9–30.

48. Cf. the writer, op. cit., p. 76; Albright, "Palestine in the Earliest Historical Period," *Journal of the Palestine Oriental Society*, Vol. xv (1935), pp. 209–10; Judith Marquet-Krause, *Les Fouilles de 'Ay (et-Tell)*, p. 19 and Pl. LXVI:1489. The place where these bowls were found is a section of a rather nondescript series of rooms which are called a "sanctuary." However, it now appears better to interpret them as simply temple storerooms, the temple being the great structure called the "palace" by the excavator (see below).

49. That is, the date of Albright, *ca.* 2900, or the 29th century B.C., and that of the Egyptologists Scharff and Stock, which is approximately the same (*ca.* 2850 or 2830 B.C. respectively); see *BASOR* 119, p. 29.

50. See for a list with references, M. W. Prausnitz, "Earliest Palestinian Seal Impressions," *Israel Exploration Journal*, Vol. 5 (1955), pp. 190–93. See also N. Zori, "A Cylinder-Seal Impression from Mount Gilboa," *Palestine Exploration Quarterly*, 1955, pp. 89–90; Barbara Parker, "Cylinder Seals from Palestine," *Iraq* 11 (1949), pp. 1–43; and H. Frankfort, *Cylinder Seals* (London, 1939), pp. 230–32.

51. Loud, *Megiddo II*, pp. 66–70.

52. R. de Vaux, *RB*, Vol. LV (1948), pp. 553–54; Vol. LVIII (1951), pp. 421–22; Vol. LXII (1955), p. 564.

53. See Kathleen Kenyon, *Palestine Exploration Quarterly*, 1953, pp. 88–90; 1955, p. 114; *Digging Up Jericho*, Chapter VII.

54. B. Maisler, B. Stekelis, and M. Avi-Yonah, "The Excavations at Beth Yerah (Khirbet-el-Kerak) 1944–1946," *Israel Exploration Journal*, Vol. 2 (1952), pp. 223–28.

55. See Marquet-Krause, *Les Fouilles de 'Ay*, pp. 14–16; for interpretation cf. W. F. Albright, *The Archaeology of Palestine* (Pelican Books, 1949), p. 76. For a tomb at Taanach which shows resemblances to Egyptian constructions of the Third Dynasty, and dating from Early Bronze II (or Early III), see W. F. Albright, *BASOR*, No. 94 (Apr. 1944), pp. 15–16.

56. Found at Tell el-Far'ah near Nablus: R. de Vaux, op. cit., Vol. LXII (1955), pp. 558–63, where references are given to later furnaces found at Tell el-'Ajjul (M.B.), and at Megiddo and Tell en-Nasbeh (Iron Age). Whether the furnaces from Early Bronze III at Beth-yerah (op. cit., p. 227) and Iron I (11th century) at Tell Qasile (ibid., Vol. 1, 1950–51, pp. 74–75) were for pottery also is uncertain; the later was more probably a smelter.

57. Op. cit. (see n. 54), p. 170. Another complete potter's tournette has been discovered; it is from Hazor and dates from the 13th century B.C. (see *B.A.*, Vol. XX, No. 2 [May 1957], Fig. 9). For the base of a similar tournette, see also Olga Tufnell, *Lachish IV* (London, 1958), Pl. 21:1, dated "MB-LB?".

58. "The Jordan Valley in the Bronze Age," *AASOR*, Vol. VI (New Haven, 1926), pp. 27 ff.

59. See now especially Ruth B. K. Amiran, "Connections between Anatolia and Palestine in the Early Bronze Age," *Israel Exploration Quarterly*, Vol. 2 (1952), pp. 89–103. The main addition which should be made to this author's list of Khirbet Kerak sites in Palestine is Tell esh-Shuneh south of the Sea of Galilee, which soundings in 1953 by James Mellaart (see note 31) have shown to have been a major site of the period. An additional article of importance is Yigael Yadin, "On the Technique of Khirbet Kerak Ware," *BASOR*, No. 106 (Apr. 1947), pp. 9–17.

60. See R. J. Braidwood in Robert W. Ehrich, ed., *Relative Chronologies* . . . , p. 38 and Fig. 1.

61. Cf. Harold Ingholt, *Rapport Préliminaire sur Sept Campagnes de Fouilles à Hama en Syrie* (Copenhagen, 1940), pp. 29–49.

62. *The Pottery of Palestine* . . . , pp. 78 ff.

63. See *Tell Beit Mirsim I*, para. 10 ff.; I A, para. 6 ff. . . ; *Journal of the Palestine Oriental Society*, Vol. 15 (1935), pp. 231 ff.

64. For a summary of the evidence up until 1938, see the writer, "The Chronology of Palestinian Pottery in Middle Bronze I," *BASOR*, No. 71 (Oct. 1938), pp. 27–34. A more recent review is by W. F. Albright, "Early Bronze Pottery from Bab-ed-Dra' in Moab," *BASOR* 95 (Oct. 1944), pp. 3–10. For the Jordan Valley, Transjordan, and the Negeb, see especially the reports of the work of Nelson Glueck, *Explorations in Eastern Palestine I* (*AASOR*, Vol. XIV, 1934); II (ibid., Vol. XV, 1935); III (ibid., Vols. XVIII–XIX, 1939); IV (ibid., Vols. XXV–XXVIII, 1951); *BASOR*, No. 131 (Oct. 1953), pp. 6 ff.; 137 (Feb. 1955), pp. 10 ff.; 138 (Apr. 1955), pp. 7 ff.; 142 (Apr. 1956), pp. 17 ff. For summaries see his *The Other Side of the Jordan* (New Haven, 1940); *The Jordan* (Philadelphia, 1946); "The Age of Abraham in the Negeb," *BA*, XVIII (1955), pp. 2 ff.

65. See the evidence of W. F. Albright from Ader and Bab ed-Dra' in Transjordan, *BASOR* 53 (Feb. 1934), pp. 13–18.

66. See Kathleen Kenyon, *Palestine Exploration Quarterly*, 1952, pp. 65 ff.; 1953, pp. 90, 92–93; 1954, pp. 55–58; 1955, pp. 116–17. Note also her article, "Tombs of the Intermediate Early Bronze-Middle Bronze Age at Tell Ajjul," *Annual of the Department of Antiquities, Jordan*, Vol. III (1956), pp. 41–55; and *Digging Up Jericho*, Chapter 8.

67. Cf. W. F. Albright, *FSAC*, pp. 105 ff. (Anchor ed., pp. 146 ff.); *Archaeology of Palestine*, pp. 80 ff. In central and southern Transjordan, curiously enough, Glueck's discoveries have indicated that people again became nomadic, after the brief period of settlement in Middle Bronze I.

68. For bibliography on this subject, see B. Porter, R. L. B. Moss, and E. W. Burney, *Topographical Bibliography of Egyptian Hieroglyphic Texts, Reliefs, and Paintings*, Vol. VII (Oxford, 1951); John A. Wilson in J. B. Pritchard, ed., *ANET*, pp. 228 ff.; A. Rowe, *A Catalogue of Egyptian Scarabs . . . in the Palestine Archaeological Museum* (Cairo, 1955), pp. xviii–xxii. For the statue of an Egyptian official at Megiddo in the early 19th century, see John A. Wilson, *AJSL*, Vol. LVIII (1941), pp. 235 ff. For the statues of two Egyptians at Gezer during the Twelfth Dynasty, see R. A. S. Macalister, *The Excavation of Gezer*, Vol. II, pp. 311–13. Whether one takes a minimal view of the evidence and holds it to suggest only economic and political relations (cf. Wilson, op. cit.), or a maximum view which believes that the Egyptians were in definite political control, is a subject of debate. For the latter view, see especially W. F. Albright, "The Egyptian Empire in Asia in the Twenty-First Century B.C.," *Journal of the Palestine Oriental Society*, Vol. VIII (1928), pp. 223 ff.; cf. also his discussions of the Berlin and Brussels execration texts in *BASOR*, Nos. 81 and 83 (Feb. and Oct. 1941).

69. For Ras el-'Ain see *Quarterly of the Dept. of Antiquities in Palestine*, Vol. V (1936), pp. 111–26; VI (1937), pp. 99–120; for Tell el-'Ajjul, see Sir Flinders Petrie, et al, *Ancient Gaza*, Vol. II (London, 1932), Pls. 28, 30–32, the forms in question being marked X–XI Dynasties; and for Megiddo see Gordon Loud, *Megiddo II*, pp. 78–87, Strata XV–XIII; and Guy and Engberg, *Megiddo Tombs*, Tombs 911 A 1 and D, 912 B and D. For a tomb found at Jaffa dating from the latter part of this age, see *Bulletin of the Palestine Museum*, No. 2, pp. 2 ff. and Pls. 1–2. For Gezer, see R. A. S. Macalister, *The Excavation of Gezer* (London, 1912), Vol. III, Pls. 32:8, 17–18;

140:4–6; 146:1–3; 147:3; and tombs in Area III 30: Vol. I, pp. 299–300 and Fig. 158. For Beth-shemesh, see Grant and Wright, *Ain Shems Excavations,* Part IV (Haverford, 1938), Pl. XXIV; Part V (Haverford, 1939), pp. 96–99. The Jericho and Tell Kisan sherds of this age are unpublished, as far as I am aware: for Albright's direct observation see *TBM* II, para. 33.

70. See *Tell Beit Mirsim* II, pp. 17 ff., Pls. 49 and 56.

71. *Megiddo* II, pp. 6–8; 78–87. Stratum XV was badly mixed by the excavators, so that MB II A material appears with pottery of MB I. One is thus faced with the problem of precisely when the temples, which are said to belong to XV, were erected. On *a priori* grounds, one would doubt that this architecture could belong to MB I. In checking through the Megiddo loci (or find spots), one discovers that the MB I pottery as published comes mostly from seven places (Loci 5184, S = 4017, S = 5161, NE = 5162, 5192 and E = 5192, S = 5191, E = 5195) in and around the temples. The pottery from these places is MB I, unmixed with MB II A, but we have no idea what the relation was between the walls and floors of the temples and MB I pottery loci. One suspects that the temples were built in MB II A, and that the builders cut into an occupation layer of MB I, leaving pockets of the pottery remaining here and there. In classing Stratum XV as MB II A, therefore, one assumes that the MB I pottery published in it actually does not belong to it.

72. *Hyksos and Israelite Cities* (London, 1906), pp. 3–16.

73. For summaries of the evidence, see Yigael Yadin "Hyksos Fortifications and the Battering-Ram," *BASOR* 137 (Feb. 1955), pp. 23–32; W. F. Albright, *Tell Beit Mirsim* II, pp. 27 ff.; R. M. Engberg, *The Hyksos Reconsidered* (Chicago, 1939)— though this book makes too hasty an identification between new ceramics and a new people. One of the mysteries of Palestinian archaeology is why Megiddo, which was occupied, even though perhaps not a major center at this time, did not possess such an earthen fortification. Was this city an exception? It seems to me more probable that the excavators found it but did not recognize its significance. The wall of Stratum XI seems to have been set on top of, and to have used, an earthen glacis, which may well have had an earlier history before the wall was erected (see Loud, *Megiddo,* II, p. 15 and Fig. 379).

74. See Yadin, loc. cit., for discussion and references, to which we should add his subsequent descriptions of Hazor in *BA* XIX.1 (Feb. 1956); XX.2 (May 1957); XXI.2 (May 1958); and *Hazor* I, Chapter I.

75. See Albright, op. cit. (note 73) and *FSAC,* pp. 151–55 (Anchor ed., 202–6); also T. Säve-Söderbergh, "The Hyksos Rule in Egypt," *Journal of Egyptian Archaeology,* Vol. XXVII (1951), pp. 53 ff.

76. For Jericho, see Kathleen Kenyon, *Palestine Exploration Quarterly,* 1952, pp. 70–71; 1953, p. 90; and *Digging Up Jericho,* Chapter 9. For Shechem, see the writer, *BASOR* 148 (Dec. 1957), pp. 11–28.

77. Albright, *Tell Beit Mirsim* II, p. 28; J. L. Starkey, "Excavations at Tell ed-Duweir," *Quarterly Statement of the Palestine Exploration Fund,* 1934, p. 168; Olga Tufnell, *Lachish IV,* p. 48 (Level VIII).

77a. For the Nahariyah structure, see I. Ben-Dor, *Quarterly of the Department of Antiquities in Palestine,* Vol. XIV (1944), pp. 1–41, and M. Dothan, *Israel Exploration Journal,* Vol. 6 (1956), pp. 14–25; for the Hazor Temple, see Yadin, *BA* XXI.2 (May 1958), pp. 34–39; and for the dating of the Shechem and Megiddo temples, see the writer *BASOR,* No. 148 (Dec. 1957), p. 20 and No. 150 (Apr. 1958), pp. 34–35.

78. For Tell Beit Mirsim E, and some early MB II B tombs at Lachish dating before the "Hyksos" fortification, see Albright loc. cit. and Starkey loc. cit. Megiddo XII

is approximately contemporary with Tell Beit Mirsim E₁, and it evidently precedes the *terre pisée* revetment found in Stratum XI (see note 73).

79. See, e.g., W. F. Albright, *The Archaeology of Palestine*, pp. 90 ff.

80. In addition to the ceramic studies of Albright already referred to above, see also for this period H. Otto, "Studien zur Keramik der mittleren Bronzezeit in Palästina," *ZDPV* 1938, pp. 259 ff.

81. See especially K. Kenyon, *Palestine Exploration Quarterly*, 1953, pp. 90–95 and Pls. XLII–XLV; and *Digging Up Jericho*, Chapter 10.

82. James R. Stewart in an article, "When did Base-Ring Ware First Occur in Palestine," *BASOR* 138 (Apr. 1955), argues that Albright's opinion is wrong to the effect that Cypriote base-ring ware occurred in Tell Beit Mirsim D and was imported into Palestine before 1550 B.C. Stewart's reason is that, according to the relative chronology of Cyprus, ware of the type in question cannot be that early. The debris of the destruction of MB II C at Shechem, however, was found in 1956 and 1957 to contain a sizable number of sherds of this type—whether of Base-Ring I or II must, subsequently, be determined. In any event, Albright's original view on the basis of the Tell Beit Mirsim evidence is confirmed by sealed deposits at Shechem where the Cypriote sherds in the destruction of the East Gate cannot possibly be argued as intrusive.

83. For the latter, see W. F. Albright, "The Chronology of a South Palestinian City, Tell el-'Ajjûl," *American Journal of Semitic Languages and Literatures*, Vol. LV (1938), pp. 337–59. This article straightens out the otherwise hopelessly confused chronology of Sir Flinders Petrie in *Ancient Gaza*, Vols. I–IV (London, 1931–34), the publication of the excavations at Tell el-'Ajjul.

84. The work was individualized as that of "the 'Ajjul Painter" by W. A. Heurtley in his important study of this ware, *Quarterly of the Department of Antiquities in Palestine*, Vol. VIII (1938), pp. 21 ff. The analysis was made on the basis of the methodology used in the study of Greek pottery of the fifth century B.C., and the conclusion was reached that the workshop existed in Palestine, whence the pottery was exported in quantities. That one or more potteries existed in Palestine where the ware was made seems fairly sure, but we shall have to await more evidence before we can be sure these were the sole or even original workshops.

85. The reason for the century spread has been the claim of the Megiddo excavators that the ware appeared in both Megiddo X and IX, though in the latter it was most typical and common. In checking through Gordon Loud's *Megiddo* II, the typical vessels in question are listed in Stratum X from loci T.3070, T.3063, Rm. of T.3056, T. in 3045, Rm. of T.3056. Of these, groups of pottery which can be checked are published only from T.3063 and T.3056, both of which, in my judgment, belong to Stratum IX (as does also locus 2024 with the Cypriote type bowl, Pl. 45:20, and perhaps 4021 with the Cypriote bowl, Pl. 45:21). Consequently, one is inclined to suspect that all of this handful of loci belong to IX and that the bichrome pottery was mistakenly attributed to X by the excavators. Tombs of IX, in other words, were dug down into X debris. Such evidence of faulty workmanship is not uncommon in the Megiddo volumes and indicates that they must be used with caution in detailed study.

86. See Olga Tufnell, Charles H. Inge, and Lankester Harding, *Lachish II. The Fosse Temple* (Oxford Univ. Press, 1940); Grant and Wright, *Ain Shems Excavations*, Part V (Haverford, 1939), pp. 111 ff.

87. For direct Palestinian evidence, note for example the two Seti stelae found at Beth-shan: for the translation of the larger of the two, see John A. Wilson in *ANET*, pp. 253–54; for the smaller, see now W. F. Albright, "The Smaller Beth-shan Stele of Sethos I (1309–1290 B.C.)," *BASOR* 125 (Feb. 1952), pp. 24–32.

88. *The Archaeology of Palestine* (Pelican Books, A199), pp. 96–109.
89. See John Garstang, *Annals of Archaeology and Anthropology,* Vol. xx (1933), pp. 14–38 and tombs 4, 5, and 13; Vol. xxi (1934), pp. 99–136 and accompanying plates where virtually all of the LB sherds found are published; and *Digging Up Jericho,* Chap. 11. For the dating, confirming the earlier published views of Albright and this writer, see now Kathleen Kenyon, *Palestine Exploration Quarterly,* 1951, pp. 101–38.
90. The stratification given in Charts 6 and 7 refers only to the enclosure. As this is written, digging on the Tell has only begun to reach the LB level: see references given in Note 74.
91. The symbol (S) in the charts after Tell el-Far'ah means "south," i.e. Petrie's excavation of the great site on the Wadi Gazzeh. (N) means the Tell el-Far'ah northeast of Nablus being dug by a French expedition under the direction of Père R. de Vaux.
92. There is a disputed question as to whether Shishak actually attacked Judah (so Albright, e.g., *BASOR* 130 [Apr. 1953], p. 7; *Tell Beit Mirsim* iii, p. 38), or whether the tribute of Rehoboam purchased the country's peace (so Martin Noth, *History of Israel,* p. 238; *ZDPV* 61, 1938, pp. 277–304). Recently, B. Mazar (*Supplements to Vetus Testamentum* iv, Leiden, 1957, pp. 57–66) has reconstructed the Shishak list as providing the *route* of the king's raid into Israel and Edom, from the Philistine Plain. Judean territory would have been touched only in Benjaminite territory as the king crossed to the Jordan Valley. This reconstruction, however, does not mean necessarily that the Benjaminite cities and Judean cities along the Philistine Plain were not definitely attacked, as archaeological indications suggest. Certainly the chronicler understands the whole country to have been hit hard, only the capital city, Jerusalem, having been saved by the tribute money (II Chronicles 12:1–12).
93. One partial exception might be the "Assyrian" bowls in seventh-century Gerar, Samaria, Tirzah, and Dothan, a ceramic imported and copied by the Assyrian army and the newly settled peoples from other portions of the empire.
94. See the writer's discussion in Elihu Grant and G. Ernest Wright, *Ain Shems Excavations,* Part v (Haverford, 1939), pp. 127 ff.
95. See his preliminary reports in *Israel Exploration Journal,* Vol. 1 (1950–51), pp. 61–76, 125–40, 194–218; and his comparative treatment of contemporary deposits in "The Stratification of Tell Abu Huwam on the Bay of Acre," *BASOR,* No. 124 (Dec. 1951), pp. 21–25. See further the articles of Gus W. Van Beek, "Cypriote Chronology and the Dating of Iron i Sites in Palestine," ibid., pp. 26–29; "The Date of Tell Abu Huwam, Stratum iii," ibid., No. 138 (Apr. 1955), pp. 34–38. Cf. also W. F. Albright, "Correspondence with Professor Einar Gjerstad on the Chronology of 'Cypriote' Pottery from Early Iron Levels in Palestine," ibid., No. 130 (Apr. 1953), pp. 22–26.
96. Tell Beit Mirsim B$_3$ and Beth-shemesh iia have casemate walls, a new method of city fortification, using two comparatively thin parallel walls with cross walls dividing the space between "casemates." The plans of these two are so identical in measurements that it may be assumed that they were both erected under the same governmental auspices: namely, in this case, the Davidic government (cf. Albright, *Tell Beit Mirsim* iii, para. 6 and 23). In addition, the governmental residency and granary in Beth-shemesh iia are probably contemporary with comparable structures in Lachish v (cf. the writer in *Vetus Testament* v, 1955, pp. 97 ff.; and Cross and Wright, *JBL LXXV,* 1956, pp. 215 f., 224 ff.). In Megiddo v a–iv b at a time before the Solomonic city wall, stables, and residency were erected, a smaller residence in its own walled courtyard was built—probable evidence of initial Davidic provin-

cial construction in what was later to be the Solomonic Fifth Administrative District (I Kings 4:12): see *Megiddo* I, pp. 11 ff. Finally, at Hazor the Rothschild expedition has discovered in Area A a casemate wall which enclosed only the highest part of the mound and, within a short time, was abandoned as a defensive work (cf. *BA* xx.2, Fig. 1). The type of construction and measurements are again so close to those of the casemate walls at Tell Beit Mirsim and Beth-shemesh that one would like to posit contemporary, and therefore Davidic, construction for them all. In 1957, however, a city gate in this wall was found, identical in plan (though not as well constructed) with that of Solomon at Megiddo (see *BA* xxi.2, Fig. 1). Solomonic wall-building at Megiddo and Gezer (see the towers added to the outer wall: Macalister, *Gezer* I, pp. 244 ff.) appears to return to the principle of mass for strength, though employing finely dressed and squared stone blocks for the critical areas. See, however, Y. Yadin, *Israel Exploration Quarterly*, Vol. 8 (1958), pp. 80–86, for casemate construction and a four-entry gate at Gezer which may indeed be Solomonic.

97. At Tell el-Far'ah (N) the tenth-century stratum, Niveau III, is dated by de Vaux "from the end of the 11th to the beginning of the 9th century." This is based upon the supposition that, following Albright, the site is to be identified with Tirzah, which was destroyed by Zimri *ca.* 876 B.C. (I Kings 16:17–18). Yet the pottery found in the stratum would be expected to belong to the last years before the city's destruction, but the forms in this case are clearly tenth century, comparable, as de Vaux himself has pointed out, to other deposits of the Solomonic Age (see *Revue Biblique*, Vol. LXII, 1955, pp. 575 ff.). While awaiting further clarification, we follow de Vaux's dating, though it would be much simpler to assume that Niveau III was brought to an end, like so many other contemporary sites, by Shishak *ca.* 918 B.C.

98. See especially J. W. Crowfoot, K. M. Kenyon, and E. L. Sukenik, *Samaria I. The Buildings* (London, 1942); *III. The Objects* (London, 1957).

99. See Lamon and Shipton, *Megiddo I*, pp. 88 ff.; Olga Tufnell, *Lachish III. The Iron Age* (London, 1953), pp. 71 ff.; C. C. McCown, et al, *Tell en-Nasbeh* (Berkeley and New Haven, 1947), especially pp. 175 ff.; Flinders Petrie, *Gerar* (London, 1928). The last mentioned refers to Petrie's excavation at Tell Jemmeh, which he mistakenly identified with Gerar. This site had an important occupation in the Persian period, with great granaries that must have had something to do with the Persian army. Before that there was a large residency which Petrie dated in the Twenty-sixth Egyptian Dynasty. While it is very difficult to be sure, it would appear to me that both the granary and Twenty-sixth Dynastic levels are to be dated in the Persian periods (city levels roughly 198–204).

100. For this reason, the full publication of the excavations directed by R. de Vaux at Khirbet Qumran, a site of the first centuries B.C. and A.D., will be most important; see the reports in *RB*, Vol. LX (1953), pp. 83–106; Vol. LXI (1954), pp. 206–36; Vol. LXIII (1956), pp. 533–77. Note also James L. Kelso, Dimitri C. Baramki, et al, *Excavations at New Testament Jericho and Khirbet en-Nitla* (*AASOR*, Vols. xxix–xxx, New Haven, 1955); and Paul and Nancy Lapp, "A Comparative Study of a Hellenistic Pottery Group from Beth-zur," *BASOR* 151 (Oct. 1958), pp. 16–27.

101. Note, for example, the technical discussion from a modern ceramist's viewpoint, J. L. Kelso and J. Palin Thorley, "The Potter's Technique at Tell Beit Mirsim, Particularly in Stratum A," in W. F. Albright, *Tell Beit Mirsim* III, Chapter IV.

102. See Y. Yadin, op. cit. (note 74).

103. Cf. J. P. Free, *BASOR*, No. 131 (Oct. 1953), pp. 16–20; No. 135 (Oct. 1954), pp. 14–20; No. 139 (Oct. 1955), pp. 3–9; No. 143 (Oct. 1956), pp. 11–17; No. 153 (Dec. 1958), pp. 10–18.

104. *Samaria I*, pp. 93–112; III, pp. 90 ff.

105. G. A. Reisner, C. S. Fisher, and D. G. Lyon, *Harvard Excavations at Samaria* (Cambridge, Mass., 1924), pp. 93–122.

106. That is, between *ca.* 875 and 850, when Ahab died. It is improbable that his son, Joram, had the strength to plan and construct the huge undertaking involved in Period II. We are inevitably left, therefore, with the dynasty of Jehu after 842 B.C. for the casemate construction.

107. The detailed arguments for this interpretation cannot be given here, but see the writer's article, "Israelite Samaria and Iron Age Chronology," *BASOR* 154 (Apr. 1959), pp. 13–29. For similar observations concerning the pottery of Periods I–II, see Y. Aharoni and R. Amiran, *Israel Exploration Journal*, Vol. 8 (1958), pp. 171–84; and Lawrence A. Sinclair in his treatment of the Gibeah pottery in a forthcoming *AASOR*.

108. See the writer, loc. cit. (n. 107). Cf. Gus Van Beek, *BASOR* 138 (Apr. 1955), pp. 36–37. At Tell Qasile, "Samaria ware" is said to have been found in Strata VIII–VII (*Israel Exploration Journal*, Vol. 1, p. 206). Yet here, as at Hazor, Megiddo, and other sites, the question must be re-examined for purposes of typological differentiation.

109. These and Level I are the only ones that are well known at Lachish, because the excavation had only reached Level III in 1938 when the director, J. L. Starkey, was killed. Olga Tufnell in *Lachish III* dated the destruction of Level III in 701 and II in 587(6) B.C. For critical reviews which make it almost certain that the views of Starkey were correct after all (namely, that Level III was destroyed in 597 and II in 587 B.C.), see the writer in *Vetus Testamentum*, Vol. V (1955), pp. 97–105, *JNES* Vol. XIV (1955), pp. 133–35; B. W. Buchanan, *American Journal of Archaeology*, Vol. 58 (1954), pp. 335–39; and the note by W. F. Albright, *BASOR*, No. 132 (Dec. 1953), p. 46.

110. For the Beth-shemesh tombs see Duncan Mackenzie, *Excavations at Ain Shems* (*Annual of the Palestine Exploration Fund*, Vol. II, 1912–13), pp. 64 ff.; and for dating see the writer in Grant and Wright, *Ain Shems Excavations*, Part IV (Haverford, 1939), pp. 77, 136.

111. See Albright, *Tell Beit Mirsim* I, pp. 76–89; III, pp. 39 ff.

112. See Albright, *Archaeology of Palestine*, pp. 128–42; *TBM* III, Chaps. II–IV, G. E. Wright, *Biblical Archaeology* (London and Philadelphia, 1957), Chaps. IX–XI; Carl Watzinger, *Denkmäler Palästinas* I (Leipzig, 1933), pp. 97–117.

113. Certain periods in a given country may be exceedingly well known, but the point here is based upon the over-all chronological perspective for the whole period of pre-Graeco-Roman civilization.

CHAPTER FIVE

The Textual Criticism of
*the Old Testament**

HARRY M. ORLINSKY

THE PAST SEVERAL DECADES have witnessed a flowering of Old Testament research under the influence largely of archaeological discovery. The Biblical lands, Iraq, Syria, Lebanon, Palestine, and Egypt, coming as they did under the control of England and France, became fertile ground for the rediscovery by excavation of the Fertile Crescent of old. And though the economy and social structure of the various parts of the Near East—as of the European powers—began to change in the twenties, thirties, and forties, so that England and France have been all but replaced by the authority of the United States and the Soviet Union, and such new political groupings as the United Arab Republic, the Hashemite Kingdom of Jordan, and Israel have come into being, with even the immediate end not yet in sight, enough archaeological work is still going on—in Israel more than in Transjordan and Iraq—to satisfy the desires of Biblical scholars, if not the needs of specialists in Biblical archaeology.

At about the same time, however, a new trend began to make itself felt in higher education on both sides of the Atlantic Ocean: the humanities and the social sciences began to give way to the applied sciences. The curricula of high schools and colleges generally became increasingly bereft of Latin and Greek and grammar—shades of the days when a public school was sometimes called Latin school or grammar school!

The consequences for the textual criticism of the Old Testament were soon felt. Here, on the one hand, the written and unwritten documents un-

* The second section of this article was published in *Journal of Biblical Literature* (March 1959), pp. 26–33, under the title of "Qumran and the Present State of Old Testament Text Studies: the Septuagint Text" © 1959, Society of Biblical Literature and Exegesis.

covered by archaeology were attracting the attention of the students of the Biblical world; and there, on the other, students of this same field of research found themselves more and more unable to handle the textual criticism of the Hebrew Bible, for they were entering and leaving their seminaries and Semitics departments with less direct knowledge of Hebrew, Aramaic, Greek, and Latin than the students of earlier decades. We have gone a long way since Ezra Stiles, president of Yale University, himself taught the freshman and other classes Hebrew, and in 1781 delivered his commencement address in Hebrew.[1] To such a low state has our discipline fallen that among the several volumes that have appeared during the past few decades constituting surveys of Old Testament research, virtually the only one that contained a chapter on "The Textual Criticism of the Old Testament" was *The Old Testament and Modern Study* (Oxford, 1951),[2] pp. 238 ff., ably contributed by D. Winton Thomas (with useful bibliography in the footnotes and on pp. 259–63).[3]

There was also a subjective factor that, quite unintentionally, helped to bring down the textual criticism of the Old Testament to its present low level. Back in 1905–6 Rudolf Kittel brought out *Biblia Hebraica*[2], superseding *Textus Hebraici emendationes quibus in Vetere Testamento Neerlandice vertendo,* ed. H. Oort (usi sunt A. Kuenen, I. Hooykaas, W. H. Kosters, H. Oort).[4] The *apparatus criticus* in *BH*[2] was soon recognized, to quote from that great master, S. R. Driver (*Notes on . . . Samuel*[2], 1913, "Introduction," p. xxxv, n. 6), as containing "the best collection both of variants from the versions and of conjectural emendations." Most unfortunately, however, scholars began to regard this apparatus as more sacred and authoritative than the preserved Masoretic text itself: between the preserved reading and its emended form in *BH*[2], students of the Bible tended to accept the latter. They ignored the vigorous *caveat* in Driver (ibid.), "but in the acceptance of both variants and emendations [in *BH*[2]—to which Driver contributed the notes for Deuteronomy], considerable discrimination must be exercised."

For this is the crux of the matter. The convenient collection of notes in *BH*[2] (save Driver's)—and the situation was not substantially improved in *BH*[3] (1937)—in "nearly every line . . . swarms with errors of commission and omission, as regards both the primary and the secondary versions."[5]

I

It took a bit of time for scholarship to express publicly its discontent with *BH*. In 1928 C. C. Torrey made this sweeping attack (*The Second Isaiah,* New York, pp. 214 f.): "The apparatus of Kittel's *Biblia Hebraica* contains very many readings erroneously supposed to be attested by the Greek version, readings gathered blindly from the commentaries. . . ." A sober scholar such as J. A. Montgomery, in working up *The International Critical Commentary on the Book of Daniel* (1927), criticized and bypassed the apparatus in *BH,* and went directly to the manuscripts and editions of the Hebrew text and the versions of it, both the primary and the secondary.[6]

Following up his previous studies, especially the "Specimen of a New Edition of the Greek Joshua,"[7] with his erudite and monumental reconstruction of *The Book of Joshua in Greek* (Paris, 1931—),[8] Max L. Margolis made it clear enough not only that the careful scholar should ignore the data in *BH* but also that he must wherever possible check the readings of the Septuagint in H. B. Swete's editions, and even the apparatus in the Larger Cambridge Septuagint[9]; to rely on the data in *BH* is to seek support from the "bruised reed" made proverbial by Isaiah.

Joseph Ziegler, the expert editor of Septuagint texts, criticized *BH*'s apparatus very severely. In preparing his model edition of the Septuagint of the Minor Prophets in the Göttingen series, Ziegler had occasion to check the use of the Septuagintal material in *BH*[3]. At the end of his "Kritische Bemerkungen zur Verwendung der Septuaginta im Zwölfprophetenbuch der Biblia Hebraica von Kittel,"[10] Ziegler wrote, "Bei einer Neuausgabe der Biblia Hebraica des Dodekapropheton muss das gesamte G-material, wie es die eben erschienene Göttinger Septuaginta-Ausgabe vorlegt, neu bearbeitet werden."

The present writer has long been especially critical of *BH*'s so-called *apparatus criticus.* Ever since he began serious work on his doctoral dissertation, "Studies in the Septuagint of the Book of Job," and published his first article as a result of it,[11] there was scarcely a line in the apparatus, whenever he had occasion to examine it, that he did not find in error, be it in commission or in omission. Thus in 1944, in an extensive article on "The Hebrew Root *ŠKB*" (*JBL* 63, pp. 19–44), he wrote (p. 33), "We note once more how unreliable and inadequate is the *apparatus criticus* for most of the books in Kittel's *BH*[3] . . . Rudolf Kittel, whose forte was not textual criticism. . . ," and in n. 18 (ibid.) he listed seven other articles in which he had taken *BH* to task at numerous points.

Six years later, in the first of a number of articles on the complete Isaiah scroll and some of the Biblical fragments among the Dead Sea scrolls,[12] he wrote, ". . . it has long been my contention that no single publication has had such detrimental effect on the lower textual criticism of the Hebrew Bible as Kittel's *Biblia Hebraica*[2,3]; cf. . . . when M. Burrows' edition of the St. Mark's Isaiah scroll will appear, the chances are that utter confusion will be introduced in the revived study of the Hebrew text of Isaiah by those who will use Kittel's convenient collection of what amounts to *Addenda et Corrigenda.* . . . The careful scholar will distrust these footnotes, and go to the sources whence they are alleged to derive" (p. 153, n. 5). By 1953 it was, unfortunately, possible to state,[13] "There can be little satisfaction in the knowledge that even my worst fears have been exceeded. . . . One doesn't know which is more treacherous for those who do not study critically the data at their source, the text of SM [St. Mark's Isaiah scroll] or the so-called critical apparatus in Kittel. . . ." (pp. 330, 340). At one point, dealing with sing. *yāḳol* in Isaiah 7:1 vs. the plur. *yāḳᵉlū* in the Isaiah scroll, he wrote (p. 332, § 5), "Unbelievable as it may seem . . . Kittel . . . emended the plural *yāḳᵉlū* in II Ki. 16.5 into the singular . . . on the basis of the sing. in MT of Isa. 7.1, having forgotten that he had emended the sing. in the Isaiah passage into the plur., on the basis of the plur. in the Kings passage! Verily the right hand of Kittel in Isaiah did not know what the left hand in Kings was doing." This is how "textual criticism" was made to support the reading in the scroll as the original, as against the reading in the Masoretic text.[14]

In his fine survey of "Septuagintal Studies in the Mid-Century,"[15] Peter Katz wrote *inter alia* of how "Duhm and his school"[16] misused Lagarde's understanding of the textual criticism of the Masoretic and Septuagint texts, so that "One may say with truth: Never was the LXX more used and less studied! Unfortunately much of this misuse survives in *BH³*. I have long given up collecting instances. Ziegler, after ten pages of corrections from the Minor Prophets alone, rightly states that all the references to G must be rechecked. H. M. Orlinsky, who comes back to this point time and again, is not very far from the truth when he says that not a single line in the apparatus of *BH³* in free from mistakes regarding G. . . ."

After all this,[17] it seems unbelievable that instead of scrapping the apparatus in *BH³* and beginning to prepare the groundwork for a new apparatus, one that could claim scholarly respect for reliability and comprehensiveness, the Privilegierte Württembergische Bibelanstalt decided to sponsor a work that would help the student understand and accept the apparatus in *BH³*! In 1951 it published E. Würthwein, *Der Text des alten Testaments, eine Einführung in die Biblia Hebraica von Rudolf Kittel,* and in 1957 an English version of it (translation by P. R. Ackroyd), *The Text of the Old Testament, an Introduction to Kittel-Kahle*[sic!]*'s Biblia Hebraica.* The German version had been criticized severely by a reviewer[18] as follows: "Würthwein furthermore identifies himself so completely with *BH³* that he fails to realize that serious misgivings have been felt about the app. crit. of this edition." Würthwein rejected this devastating criticism ("Foreword to the English Edition," p. XI) as "clearly a misunderstanding," for he had added a special chapter (IV) on "Textual Criticism" which, he claimed, included a criticism of the principles of textual criticism in *BH³* and encouraged "its intelligent and at the same time *critical* use." Yet the simple fact is "that not a single work critical of *BH³* is referred to in Chapter IV, and no one of the three introductory paragraphs (A, B, C) and eight sections warns the student of the misleading and harmful character of the apparatus in *BH³*."[19] The chapter, brief as it is (thirteen pages), can but mislead and harm the unwary student; the scholar certainly does not need to resort to it.

II[20]

The direct effects of the largely uncritical reliance on *BH* can be observed in the study of the Biblical fragments among the Dead Sea scrolls, and these effects, to this writer, are little short of depressing—"depressing" because the average Biblical scholar knows about the textual criticism of the Dead Sea scrolls, and more especially about the relationship between the Septuagint (hereinafter LXX) and the Biblical texts among the scrolls, not what he has learned from a direct study of the Hebrew and LXX texts, nor even for the most part from what other scholars who have published analyses of these texts learned from a direct study, but from what these published analyses derived from the critical apparatus in Kittel's *BH*. Let me cite two illustrations of the point.

In Isaiah 49:17 the Masoretic text (hereinafter MT) of the Hebrew Bible tells us that the prophet assures his fellow Judean exiles in Babylonia that מִהֲרוּ בָּנָיִךְ מְהָרְסַיִךְ וּמַחֲרִיבַיִךְ מִמֵּךְ יֵצֵאוּ, "Your sons will hasten, your destroyers and those who laid you waste will depart from you." Kittel's note urges the reader to emend MT בָּנָיִךְ "your sons" to בֹּנָיִךְ "your builders," with Codex Petropolitanus, the LXX, Vulgate, Targum, and Arabic ("1 c Var^P (G) V T (A) בֹּנָיִךְ"). So when the Isaiah scroll came along with the reading בוניך (=בֹּנָיִךְ) "your builders," it was natural for scholars to accept the scroll's reading, fortified by the data in Kittel, as against the Masoretic reading. Disregarding the relative merits of the two readings in the context,[21] a direct consultation of the sources gave us this picture: (1) Codex Petropolitanus (A.D. 916) does not read בֹּנָיִךְ "your builders" but בָּנָיִךְ "your sons," exactly as MT does. (2) The Arabic evidence for בֹּנָיִךְ "your builders" is no independent evidence whatever; for the Arabic is but a secondary version that helps to prove that the LXX text from which it derived read "your builders." It has no bearing at all on the original Hebrew text. (3) There are, in reality, two traditions in the Targum, not one as claimed by Kittel; one reads "your builders" and the other "your sons." (4) Kittel erred grievously in not telling the reader that two of the Minor Versions, Theodotion and Aquila, read "your builders," whereas a third, Symmachus, read "your sons." These versions are far more important than, say, the Vulgate. Regardless of whether Masoretic "your sons" or the scroll's "your builders" is the original reading, how could scholars decide in favor of the scroll's reading, and of what value was their decision, when the data that they employed consisted of what Kittel offered them?

Or take, as the second case in point, Isaiah 15:9. The prophet, in delivering himself of "The Burden of Moab," enumerates a number of places that will be laid waste, among them "Dimon." But "Dimon" is unknown otherwise, and the Vulgate reads the well-known place name "Dibon." So when the Isaiah scroll exhibited "Dibon" in place of MT "Dimon," some scholars took one look at Kittel's reference to the Vulgate ("al loc דיבון

[V]") and pronounced the scroll's "Dibon" as the original reading, MT "Dimon" being but a corruption of it. But the evidence is not limited to the Vulgate and our scroll. (1) All the earlier witnesses to the LXX (the Chester Beatty Papyrus, Codices Sinaiticus, Vaticanus, Alexandrinus, and the like), translation of the LXX into Bohairic and the Syro-Hexapla, the Targum, all three major Minor Versions (Theodotion, Aquila, Symmachus), the *Hebraios* in Origen's Hexapla—all these early witnesses testify to MT "Dimon." (2) Some time after the turn of the era, "Dibon" came into being alongside "Dimon"; thus such fourth-fifth century sources as Eusebius (*Onomastica Sacra*), the Vulgate, and Codex Venetus, and a number of tenth-eleventh century MSS of the LXX, and the commentary by Basil the Great, read "Dibon." To single out Vulgate "Dibon," as Kittel did, and to ignore all the other textual data and their chronological sequence, is but to make a farce of the textual criticism of the Hebrew Bible and the Isaiah scroll. Yet some scholars did exactly that when the scroll's reading "Dibon" came to light.[22]

But let us get to the Isaiah scroll as a whole, in relation to the LXX text. As is well known, scholars generally tended in the first years after the scroll's appearance to find numerous instances where the reading in the scroll agreed with that found in the LXX, as against the reading preserved in the so-called MT. This was the tenor of the otherwise sober survey article on the scrolls by W. Baumgartner in 1951, in *Theologische Rundschau*. Virtually no scholar bothered to take up these alleged instances in detail, in part because they were blinded by the dazzling antiquity of the scroll, and in part—as mentioned previously—because scholars generally had ceased to work at the discipline of lower textual criticism after World War I and could no longer handle it properly. Your present lecturer was almost the only one who devoted himself to a detailed analysis of a number of these instances. He found most of them lacking all justification, and none convincing. These studies appeared from 1950 to 1954. Interestingly, the tidal wave of scholarly and public opinion, according to which there could be no doubt of both the great antiquity of the scrolls and their superiority to any other existing texts, was such that the scholarly literature on the Isaiah scroll and the LXX largely ignored these caveats, that is to say, it did not attempt to demonstrate the argumentation erroneous, or even to refer to it, but contented itself with making reference to those who had claimed scroll-LXX identification, and let it go at that.[23]

By 1953–54 this attitude had begun to change. Scholars now, at last, were less inclined to identify the Isaiah scroll with the LXX; indeed, the scroll's text was rapidly becoming something of a major disappointment. Thus in October 1954, Professor James Muilenburg published in *BASOR* (No. 135) "Fragments of another Qumran Isaiah Scroll," containing parts of approximately from 12:5 to 13:16 and from 22:13 to 23:6, and he stated flatly (p. 32), ". . . 4Q nowhere diverges in favor of the LXX. This is by no means a unique situation, for many other texts follow the Masoretic tradition. . . ." This was the tenor, too, of Frank M. Cross's article in *The Christian Century*, in August 1955—though I should not have minded it one bit if Muilenburg and Cross had referred specifically to those articles on the scroll and the LXX that had led them to turn their backs on the opinion that had prevailed during the preceding few years.

It was not merely the Isaiah scroll, however, that was involved in this changing attitude. In 1953 Karl Elliger, in the most detailed study of the Biblical text of the Habakkuk scroll (*Studien zum Habakuk-Kommentar vom Toten Meer*), reached the same conclusion. In addition, the new Biblical texts, fragmentary as they were, tended to confirm this conclusion. Thus in 1952, J. T. Milik published in *Revue biblique* "Fragments d'un Midrash de Michée dans les Manuscrits de Qumran," and the editor claimed agreement at two points between the Qumran text and the LXX, as against MT. However, in one instance, at Micah 1:3, he was misled by the critical note in Kittel's *BH*³.²⁴ Had he consulted, say, Ziegler's critical (Göttingen) edition of the LXX of the minor prophets, he would have learned that the LXX did not unequivocally support the scroll's text, but constituted an inner-Greek problem. In the second instance, also in 1:3, involving the scroll's במו[תי האר]ץ and LXX ἐπὶ τὰ ὕψη τῆς γῆς, as against MT בָּמֳתֵי אָרֶץ, without the definite article, the editor overlooked the fact that במתי ארץ is precisely the idiom elsewhere in the Bible (in Deuteronomy, Isaiah, and Amos), analogous to במתי עָב in Isaiah, and to במתי יָם in Job—all without the definite article, as befits ancient Hebrew poetry—and that in every one of these half-dozen instances the LXX employed the definite article—simply because that was Greek idiom, exactly as all our English versions employ the definite article, "the *bamoth* of *the* earth," or "of *the* cloud," or "of *the* sea."²⁵

The same general situation is true also of "A Qoheleth Scroll from Qumran" covering parts of chapters 5–7, published in *BASOR* in October 1954 (No. 135, 20–27). The editor, J. Muilenburg, found a single instance where a reading in the scroll coincided with the LXX against the MT correspondent. I myself found reason to believe that even in this case the LXX did not justify a reading in its Hebrew *Vorlage* that agreed with that of the scroll; perhaps a decision can be reached only after other parts of this scroll should come to light.²⁶

There are other fragments that might be referred to here, e.g., the "Fragment of the 'Song of Moses' (Deuteronomy 32)," published by Father Skehan in *BASOR*, December 1954 (No. 136, 12–15). But since I should like to get on to the most significant Biblical text among the scrolls, that of Samuel, I shall content myself here with quoting from pp. 150–53 of Father Skehan's published paper read at the International Congress for OT Studies at Strasbourg, in 1956.²⁷ "For Isaias, the complete scroll from cave 1 remains textually the most interesting document, and there is nothing among the 13 manuscripts of cave 4 which is recensionally different from the received consonantal text, or yields improved readings in any significant degree. . . . Now, 1QIsa^a and the LXX of Isaias are not recensionally connected, though they have an occasional reading in common; but they are mutually illustrative, because the cave 1 manuscript gives us, for the first time in Hebrew, the kind of glossed and reworked manuscript that the LXX prototype must have been. . . . It has been in conjunction with the text of Isaias that the writer has examined to some extent the likely effects of the extrabiblical documents at Qumran in providing us with text-critical materials for the OT itself . . . the conclusion thus far is largely negative: allusions and *lemmata* in the extrabiblical documents may yield some points of detail, but will not alter our understanding of the textual history of the book. . . ."

It is in dealing with the Samuel text published by Cross in *BASOR,* December 1953 (No. 132, 15–26), that we come to something significant in the *Überlieferungsgeschichte* of the Hebrew text in relation to the LXX. Back in 1871 Julius Wellhausen, in my judgment the most brilliant and penetrating textual critic of the OT, wrote the finest analysis of the Hebrew and Greek texts of Samuel; and several decades later, S. R. Driver wrote the most balanced study, his model commentary, *Notes on the Hebrew Text . . . of Samuel.* These two constitute the best pair of commentaries in our field. That the MT of Samuel is incomplete and difficult has long been recognized. That the LXX text has what might be called "addenda et corrigenda" to the MT has generally been recognized too—as may be seen from Driver's widely used and followed commentary, where so many of Wellhausen's insights were accepted. The new scroll text has so far been published only in small part, so small, as a matter of fact, that I for one have been most hesitant and reluctant to accept it as a basis for any positive statement, or even for a negative conclusion.[28] After all, photostatic reproduction of parts of a total of twenty-three verses in the first two chapters of I Samuel do not yet justify conclusions about the character of the Hebrew text of the scroll of all 1506 verses in I and II Samuel. We all remember the embarrassment of Univac in the national elections a few years ago, when—on the basis of incomplete returns—it elected the "wrong" (or should I say, the "right") man for the presidency. But I have recently made a closer study of these twenty-three verses, and I can but agree with Cross that the scroll's text may well be of considerable importance in the reconstruction of the history of the MT of Samuel, as well as help to determine the character of the LXX translation of Samuel and the kind of Hebrew *Vorlage* from which it derived. If I say "may well be" instead of "will be," it is merely because I have not seen the unpublished Samuel material to which Cross makes reference, most recently in his book on *The Ancient Library of Qumran and Modern Biblical Studies.*

Another Biblical text that may be of great importance for LXX studies is the bit of a fragment of Jeremiah, described by Cross in his book just mentioned. As is well known, the LXX text of Jeremiah and Job are respectively one eighth and one sixth shorter than MT. I first began to work on the problem in Job almost 25 years ago, and I had concluded that the

LXX translator did not curtail a Hebrew text that coincided in length with MT, but had a shorter Hebrew *Vorlage* before him.[29] Whether this shorter Hebrew version is closer to the original than the longer MT, I have as yet not reached any definite conclusion. The problem in Jeremiah has not yet received competent study. I have a student who has just begun to work on the problem; he is currently devoting himself to trying to comprehend the character of the LXX of Jeremiah. Now in the case of Chapter 10, vss. 5–10 of the MT, the LXX lacks vss. 6–8 and 10, and reads vs. 5 after vs. 8. It is precisely this sequence that is present in the Jeremiah fragment. And, finally, Cross has noted that, "The longer recension is also present at Qumran."[30]

A few LXX fragments have been discovered in Qumran, of leather and papyrus, containing parts of verses in Leviticus 2–5 and 26; and in Numbers 3 and 4; and parts of the Minor Prophets.[31] However, since these materials have as yet received but preliminary study it is best not to take them up at this point. But this much may be said: the LXX translation, no less than the MT itself, will have gained very considerable respect as a result of the Qumran discoveries in those circles where it has long—overlong—been necessary. And the LXX translators will no longer be blamed for dealing promiscuously with their Hebrew *Vorlagen;* it is to their *Vorlagen* that we shall have to go, and it is their *Vorlagen* that will have to be compared with the preserved MT. This is true not only of anthropomorphisms and other theological matters, but even of minor and non-tendentious items.[32]

This much, too, may be said. The theory of one original Greek translation of each of the various books of the Hebrew Bible, which in turn gave rise to the various recensions, the theory which has long been associated with Lagarde, Rahlfs, Montgomery, and especially Margolis, has been demonstrated beyond reasonable doubt by the Hebrew and Greek materials from Qumran. Those who have opposed this theory, notably Kahle, have received nothing but opposition from the Dead Sea scrolls.[33]

In fine, it is clear that much work remains to be done by the textual critic of the Hebrew Bible and its LXX version and recensions—although more, and more extensive, Biblical texts from Qumran will first have to be made available to the scholar for a broad enough base to work on. It is something worth looking forward to.

III

While the present essay was being written there appeared an article by P. Wernberg-Møller, "Studies in the Defective Spellings in the Isaiah-Scroll of St. Mark's Monastery."[34] It may be worth-while to analyze this article with special reference to the problem of methodology.

The author begins with the assumption that wherever the scroll failed to use the defective spelling, it may well have been due to a pronunciation that differed from that preserved in the Masoretic text. He then lists some twoscore instances (§ III, pp. 254 ff.) where, in his judgment, the LXX rendering coincided with, and demonstrated, the pronunciation of the word in question in the scroll. We shall deal here with the first two of these instances.

The author has noted (p. 254) that since the MT at 1:29 reads מֵאֵילִים as against the scroll's מאלים, the LXX's ἐπὶ τοῖς εἰδώλοις "shows that מאלים of 1QIsaᵃ means 'of the gods,' and not 'of the terebinths,' as MT has it. Symmachus follows MT." But let us delve into the matter a little more closely.

First of all, it is only a conclusion hastily reached that εἴδωλον "idol; false god" in the LXX of Isaiah, or anywhere else in the Bible, represents אֱל(ים) "god(s)." Indeed, the combination εἴδωλον/אֱלִים occurs only here and in Isaiah 57:5 in the entire LXX.[35] All that one has to do to prove this conclusion wrong is to run down every occurrence of אֱל(ים) "god(s)" in Isaiah (e.g., via Mandelkern's Concordance, pp. 85c–86c) as reproduced in the LXX—and he will find that, whether the Hebrew term is used for "God" or for "god(s), idol(s)," the Greek equivalent is invariably a form of θεός. On the other hand, our אֵילִים is clearly (as elsewhere, e.g., Hosea 4:13) a "terebinth" used in idolatrous worship, i.e., an idol, and it is paralleled by גַּנּוֹת—exactly as in the identical sort of passage, Isaiah 57:5 (not mentioned by our author), אֵלִים//תַּחַת כָּל־עֵץ רַעֲנָן. Accordingly, LXX "idols" represents an excellent interpretation of Masoretic אֵ(י)לִים[36] (so also, e.g., Targum, Symmachus, Aquila, Rashi, Malbim, H. Ewald, Franz Delitzsch, B. Duhm, K. Marti, J. Skinner, G. H. Box, G. B. Gray, O. Procksch, E. J. Kissane; and others)—what else could אֵ(י)לִים mean here? Indeed, our author would scarcely have included 1:29 in his article had he consulted J. F. Schleusner's Novus Thesaurus Philologico-Criticus sive Lexicon in LXX et reliquos Interpretes Graecos ac Scriptores Apocryphos Veteris Testamenti (5 vols., Lipsiae, 1820),[37] s. εἴδωλον (Vol. II, p. 246), אֵילִים:אֵלִים," plur. ex אֵלָה, querceta, in quibus idola colebantur, ut adeo per metonymian etiam ipsa idola significare possit. Ies. I, 29, LVII, 5. Male nonnulli statuunt, LXX utrobique legisse צְלָמִים. . . ."[38] As to the scroll's מאלים, it should teach the student not to rely on the orthography of that idiosyncratic manuscript, to the point where a different pronunciation (and morphology) or a different interpretation is glibly achieved and then readily identified with the LXX's Hebrew Vorlage.[39]

In his second case in point (pp. 254 f.), our author advances the opinion that 1QIsaᵃ (פנים) ונשא and LXX καὶ θαυμαστὸν (σύμβουλον) and καὶ τοὺς (τὰ πρόσωπα) θαυμάζοντας in 3:3 and 9:14 point to (פנים) וְנִשָּׂא for Masoretic (פנים) וּנְשׂוּא—for "In neither of the two parts of 1QIsaᵃ can we imagine a passive participle Qal [נשוא] spelt defectively." However, since no Hebrew form וְנִשָּׂא makes any sense in context, our author has to fall back on the theory that "the Greek translator connected [assumed וְנִשָּׂא] with Aramaic נְפָא 'wonder'. . . ."

1: First of all, our author has failed altogether to note that θαυμαστὸν σύμβουλον in 3:3 (unlike the LXX reading in 9:14) does not correspond to וּנְשׂא פנים; σύμβουλος represents וְיוֹעֵץ immediately following (so already Schleusner, *s.v.* [v, 159]; θαυμ. συμβ. is Aquila's rendering of יוֹעֵץ פֶּלֶא in 9:5, cf. J. Reider *JQR*, 4 [1913–14], p. 592).[40] In his study of *The Septuagint Version of Isaiah* (p. 23 and n. 21), I. L. Seeligmann followed up the discussions and proposed solutions of LXX θαυμάζειν πρόσωπον by G. Bertram (*Theologisches Wörterbuch zum Neuen Testament* 3 [1938], pp. 29 f.), Schleusner (*s.* θαυμαστός/נשׂוא פנים, III, 47), and Ziegler (*Untersuchungen zur Septuaginta des Buches Isaias* [*Alttestamentliche Abhandlungen*, XII, 3; 1934], p. 136), with one of his own.[41]

2: But regardless of σύμβουλον, there is no reason to vocalize וּנְשׂא as anything but the passive participle Qal because of LXX θαυμαστός. Is alleged נְשִׂיא more, or less, "passive" than נָשׂוּא? And would (פנים) נְשֻׂא have to be assumed also in II Kings 5:1 because of LXX τεθαυμασμένος (. . . πρόσωπον)— incidentally also Theodotion's rendering in our 3:3?[42]

3: Furthermore, what is the evidence that Aramaic נְפַּא "wonder" was involved? Indeed, the Targum reproduced (פנים) נְשׂוּא by (אַפִּין) נְסִיב in 3:3; 9:14; II Kings 5:1; סָבִיר in Job 22:8. And where, in Isaiah, is alleged נְפַּא "wonder" used in the Targum even for root פלא?

4: Moreover, our author has erred in restricting LXX θαυμάζω/θαυμαστός to "wonder." One has but to consult the Hebrew equivalents for the various forms of this Greek root (conveniently in Schleusner, III, 45–48; Hatch-Redpath, I, 626–27), or the various translations of this root in the Old Latin and other daughter versions, and he will realize at once that it is quite unnecessary to look for the meaning "wonder" for a root resembling Hebrew נשׂא in some Semitic language. Thus in Leviticus 19:15 (לֹא תִשָּׂא (נָדוֹל) פְּנֵי־דָל) וְלֹא תֶהְדַּר פְּנֵי was reproduced (οὐ λήμψῃ πρόσωπον πτωχοῦ) οὐδὲ θαυμάσεις πρόσωπον (δυνάστου); cf., e.g., ἐθαύμασα (σου τὸ π.) for (פָּנֶיךָ) נָשָׂאתִי in Genesis 19:21. In Job 22:8 ἐθαύμασας (δέ τινων) πρόσωπον (or, ——πα), for נְשׂוּא פָנִים, was translated in the Old Latin (ed. P. de Lagarde, *Mittheilungen*, II [Goettingen, 1897], pp. 189 ff.) (*aut*) *miratus es personam* (*aliquorum*); in 32:22, θαυμάσαι π. (either for אַכֻּנֶּה in v. 22 or [with E. Dhorme, *Le Livre de Job* (Paris, 1926), ad loc.] for [נָשָׂא פְּנֵי אִישׁ] in v. 21) was reproduced (*non enim scio*) *mirari faciem;* and in 34:19 θαυμασθῆναι π. was rendered *admirari facies* (*eorum*). In all these cases, "respect, admire," or the like, suits the context admirably.

5: Last, but very far from least, the Isaiah scroll should not be taken so seriously even in matters of *scriptio defectiva*, at least not until every aspect of it has been studied *per se*, without regard to "superiority" to the Masoretic text, or "identity" with the LXX-*Vorlage;* and the like.[43] This scroll literally cries out for a thorough analysis by a competent textual critic. What should one do with the alternate *plena* and *defectiva* spelling for Pharaoh, פַּרְעֹה . . . פַּרְעֹה, in both 19:11 and 30:2–3 (*plena* in 36:7); should one vocalize the *defectiva* differently from the *plena?* Or again, how would the defective spelling in the scroll at 8:10 change—or more correctly, should it be used for changing—the vocalization of MT וְחָפֵר (עֶצֶּה) עֵצּוּ. Or, getting back to our root, would the scroll's (עֲוֹוֹן) נשׂא at 33:24 for MT נָשֻׂא require the vocalization נָשָׁא? Or would the scroll's כנשׂא at 18:3 for MT כִּנְשֹׂא point to a vowel other than *holem?* If so, what about SM נשׂוא for MT נְלָאֵיתִי (נִלְאֵיתִי) in 1:14? In our very verse (3:3), MT וְיֹעֵץ was written defectively (וייעץ) in our scroll; would that point to a different vocalization or, rather, to the unreliable character of the scroll's scribe as a speller? Or one may note, in the immediate vicinity of (פנים) נשׂא in 9:14, the spelling

ראֹשׁ ... רֹאֹשׁ (9:13–14), where the scribe ignored his frequent *plena* spelling and then "corrected" (i.e., he or another scribe) the second instance alone, by inserting the "missing" *waw* over the *'aleph* of the word. The same thing happened in 9:16, where the scribe's defectively spelled יחמל was later "corrected" by means of an additional *waw* above the *mem*.

   The grammar, as well as the text, of Biblical Hebrew is sometimes revised because of the Isaiah scroll's spelling. Thus, because Masoretic דֻּבַּ/דָּבִּים is written דב/דבים rather than דוב/דובים in 1QIsaᵃ at 11:7 and 59:11, it is assumed to prove that the scribe of the scroll was "preserving a pronunciation found in the cognate languages . . . cf. Syr. *debbā* and Eth. *deb*" (Wernberg-Møller, p. 252). Similarly, 1QIsaᵃ חמר (instead of the *plena* חומר) for MT חֹמֶר at 11:1 recalls Arabic *ḥitrᵘⁿ*. The scroll's חרשׂ (instead of חורשׂ for MT חֹרֶשׂ) at 17:9 coincides with Arabic *ḥiršᵘⁿ*. The spelling צורך (for MT צַוָּארֵךְ) at 52:2 reflects Syriac *ṣaurā*. The spelling קדקד (instead of קדקוד, for MT קָדְקֹד) at 3:17 points to Accadian *qaqqadu*. And so on (pp. 252–53).[44]

   To the writer it would seem that, at best, all that the *scriptio defectiva* in such instances as the above might help to prove is that some of the Jewish "cavemen" of Qumran spoke a dialect of Hebrew that at times coincided with Arabic or Aramaic or Babylonian-Assyrian or Samaritan or Syriac or Ethiopic, etc. However, since such a dialect is *a priori,* shall we say, absurd, it is far more likely that most of these defectively written words in the Isaiah scroll point to nothing more than just that, viz., *scriptio defectiva.* It is one thing to assume for the sake of argument that the above words point to a vocalization different from that preserved in the Masoretic text; but when this line of assumption leads to what is obviously a nonexistent dialect of Hebrew (*reductio ad absurdum* is probably a good technical term for this kind of "reasoning"), then the assumption should be scrapped. If not, then the scroll's קראתי will play havoc with the good sense of MT (אֲנִי) קָרְתִּי (וְשָׁתִיתִי מָיִם) at 37:25.[45]

IV

On the surface, one might not think that the attempted reconstruction of the territorial history of any part of ancient Israel would have much to do with the textual criticism of the Biblical texts involved. That the opposite can be true is evident from Albright's detailed analysis of the archaeological-topographical data in combination with the pertinent documentary sources in the attempt to date the list of Levitic towns in Joshua 21 and I Chronicles 6.[46] His treatment of the Hebrew and Greek forms of the place names (see the commentary on pp. 66 ff.) is something of a tour de force and has gone a long way toward helping to disprove the opinion of Wellhausen and others that the list was essentially unhistorical from the very beginning.[47]

Considerable advance has been made in the textual criticism of the Hebrew Bible as a result of the discovery and sober analysis of the proto-Hebrew Ugaritic texts, along with numerous Aramaic and other Northwest Semitic documents of the Late Bronze and Early Iron periods. These documents have enabled the student of the Old Testament not only to get at the original meaning of the Masoretic text better than ever before, but also to respect its integrity. Here and there in the Bible these Canaanite documents have led to the justified emendation of a reading that has come down to us in corrupted form; far more frequently, however, they have nullified other proposed and sometimes popularly accepted emendations, and have shed light on the preserved text to the point where it often becomes clear and acceptable.

A typical case in point is his analysis of "The Oracles of Balaam" (*JBL* 63 [1944], pp. 207–33). In his brief but detailed introductory statement (pp. 208–11), he noted that the "new text and translation of the poems" (Numbers 23:7–10, 18–24; 24:3–9, 15–24) that he was presenting was

based on cautious use of the versions and especially on full use of the mass of material now available for early Northwest Semitic grammar, lexicography and epigraphy. Since very little of this material has yet been employed by biblical scholars, it is only natural that we are able to progress beyond older commentators in the interpretation of some passages. It is to be noted that our date for the first writing down of these poems depends wholly on the inductive agreement of textual criticism with the spelling of epigraphic documents. In our subsequent sketch of the geographical and historical background of the poems [pp. 227–33] we shall utilize new material from the traditional age of Balaam. . . . Our reconstruction of the consonantal text endeavors to recapture the original orthography with the aid of archaisms in the Masoretic and Samaritan text, hints from the Greek version, and parallels in Northwest Semitic epigraphy. . . .

Albright's study was so well done that his dating of the Oracles ("we must date the first writing down of the Oracles in or about the tenth century B.C. . . . ," p. 210) and his insistence "that there is no reason why they may not be authentic" (p. 233), together with the textual analysis proper, have gained wide acceptance in the scholarly world.[48]

There is much more that remains to be surveyed critically in the field of textual criticism. The renewed study of the Tell el-Amarna tablets—in which Albright has played a prominent role[49]—along with the appearance of the various Northwest Semitic inscriptions,[50] have shed useful light on the grammar and text of Biblical Hebrew. And the Mari tablets that have already appeared indicate clearly that the continued publication and study of these texts will add very considerably to that knowledge.

There is also the matter of the studies and editions of the Septuagint and other versions of the Old Testament. Thus J. Ziegler has been making available a mass of reliable data, much of it well digested in his useful *Einleitungen,* in his editions of *Septuaginta, Vetus Testamentum Graecum* (Auctoritate Societatis Litterarum Gottingensis editum): Isaiah (1939), the minor prophets (1943), Ezekiel (1952), Susannah, Daniel, and Bel and the Dragon (1954), and Jeremiah, Baruch, Lamentations, and the Epistle of Jeremiah (1957).[51] Additional parts of the Larger Cambridge Septuagint have made their appearance, constituting the beginnings of Vol. III in this notable series: Esther, Judith, and Tobit (1940).

There are also the editions of the Old Latin and Vulgate translations of the Old Testament. In 1941 J. Schildenberger published his searching study, *Die altlateinischen Texte des Proverbienbuches untersucht und textgeschichtlich eingegliedert. Erste Teil: Die alter afrikanische Textgestalt*[52]; in 1949 the first fascicle, *Verzeichnis der Sigel,* appeared in connection with *Vetus Latina. Die Reste der altlateinischen Bibel nach Petrus Sabatier neu gesammelt und herausgegeben von der Erzabtei Beuron;* the following four fascicles (1951–54; ed., B. Fischer) constitute the text of Genesis; and this erudite and important work goes on.[53] One cannot leave the Old Latin without at least mentioning two scholarly works by R. Weber, *Les anciennes versions latines du deuxième livre des Paralipomènes* (Rome, 1945) and *Le Psautier Romain et les autres anciens Psautiers latins: Edition critique* (Rome, 1953)—respectively Vols. VIII and X in *Collectanea Biblica.* As for the Vulgate, the monks of St. Jerome's Monastery in Rome have been putting out a critical edition of this landmark in Biblical exegesis, *Biblia Sacra iuxta Latinam Vulgatam versionem ad codicum fidem iussu Pii PP. XI–XII cura et studio monachorum Abbatiae Pontificiae Sancti Hieronymi in urbe Ordinis Sancti Benedicti* (Rome, 1926—). J. O. Smit has written a fine study of *De Vulgaat, Geschiedenis en Herziening van de Latijnse Bijbelvertaling* (Roermond, 1948).

A promising career was cut short when H. C. Gleave died at the age of twenty-eight; C. Rabin helped in getting his manuscript published, *The Ethiopic Version of the Song of Songs* (London, 1951).

As this survey comes to a close, only brief reference can be made to other surveys and reference works. The fine work by D. Winton Thomas, mentioned above, may be recalled here, as well as the writer's survey in *The Study of the Bible,* etc., likewise mentioned above (n. 2). P. Katz's "Septuagintal Studies in the Mid-Century," as well as such other studies of his as *Philo's Bible* and "The Recovery of the Original Septuagint: a Study in the History of Transmission and Textual Criticism"[54] should be noted. Much useful material is available in J. W. Wevers's survey, "Septuaginta-Forschungen," *Theologische Rundschau,* 22 (1954), pp. 85–138, 171–90.[55] And, finally, up-to-date references are available in B. J. Roberts, *The Old Testament Text and Versions* (Cardiff, 1951), *passim* and "Bibliography" (pp. 286–314); and O. Eissfeldt, *Einleitung in das alte Testament*[2] (1956), *passim* and "Der Text" (pp. 822–75; and the "Literaturnachträge" on pp. 876 ff.).

New York; Summer, 1958; revised, January, 1959

NOTES TO CHAPTER FIVE

1. See Orlinsky, "Jewish Scholarship and Christian Translations of the Hebrew Bible," *Yearbook of the Central Conference of American Rabbis* 63 (1953), p. 248.
2. Essays by members of the Society for Old Testament Study, edited by H. H. Rowley. Méntion may be made here of the writer's chapter on "Current Progress and Problems in Septuagint Research," in H. R. Willoughby, ed., *The Study of the Bible Today and Tomorrow* (Chicago, 1947), pp. 141–61.
3. Thus H. H. Rowley, in *Book List* 10 (1955), p. 640, noted that in H. F. Hahn's survey, *The Old Testament in Modern Research* (Philadelphia, 1954), "Philology and textual criticism are left unsurveyed . . ." Or cf. E. C. Colwell's presidential address, "Biblical Criticism: Lower and Higher," *JBL* 67 (1948), pp. 1 ff., "Biblical criticism today is not the most robust of academic disciplines. . . ."
4. Lugduni Batavorum, 1900.
5. See Orlinsky, op. cit. (n. 2 above), p. 151 in the section, "The Use of the LXX and its Daughter-Versions in the Textual Criticism of the Hebrew Bible." Or his discussion of "The Septuagint—Its Use in Textual Criticism," *The Biblical Archaeologist* IX (1946), pp. 21–34.
6. See the valuable section (III) on "Ancient Versions" in the "Introduction" (pp. 24–57); also pp. 3–24 of the "Introduction" to his commentary on *Kings* in the same series (1951; ed. H. S. Gehman). Professor Gehman himself (followed by his student, J. W. Wevers) has frequently objected to *BH*'s collection of emendations; for bibliography, see Wevers, *Theologische Rundschau* 22 (1954), pp. 86, 90.
7. *Jewish Studies in Memory of Israel Abrahams* (New York, 1927), pp. 307–23.
8. Parts I–IV cover Joshua 1:1–19.38. Part V and the all-important introduction are apparently lost forever—a tragedy.
9. Cf. Margolis (*AJSL* 28 [1911–12], p. 3), "For the uncials [of Joshua] I have used the phototypic editions . . . I say this because I have discovered numerous inaccuracies in Swete's edition"; "Corrections in the Apparatus of the Book of Joshua in the Larger Cambridge Septuagint," *JBL* 49 (1930), pp. 234–64. On Margolis' attempt at "The Recovery of the Original Septuagint Text" see Orlinsky, "Current Progress . . . ," (pp. 144 ff.) and "Margolis' Work in the Septuagint," pp. 34–44

in *Max Leopold Margolis: Scholar and Teacher* (Dropsie College Alumni Assoc., Philadelphia, 5712 = 1952).

10. Pp. 107–20 in "Studien zur Verwertung der Septuaginta im Zwölfprophetenbuch," *ZAW* 60 (1944), pp. 107–31.

11. "Job 5.8, a Problem in Greek-Hebrew Methodology," *JQR* 25 (1934–35), pp. 271–78; G. Beer in *BH*[2,3] had failed to note that for Masoretic אלהים the LXX read—only here in the book of Job—τὸν πάντων δεσπότην (G[A] παντοκράτορα; ordinarily = שַׁדַּי), and that Kenn 223 actually read שׁדי. Chapters I ("An Analytical Survey of Previous Studies") and II ("The Character of the Septuagint Translation of the Book of Job") of the dissertation have now appeared: *HUCA* 28 (1957), pp. 53–74; 29 (1958), pp. 229–71.

12. "Studies in the St. Mark's Isaiah Scroll," *JBL* 69 (1950), pp. 149–66.

13. Orlinsky, "Studies in the St. Mark's Isaiah Scroll, IV," *JQR* 43 (1952–53), pp. 329–40.

14. For additional details, and bibliography, on "the footnotes in Kittel's *Biblia Hebraica*—the standard and monotonous source of variants (and conjectural emendations) for those who have no conception or standard of scholarship," see Orlinsky, "Notes on the Present State of the Textual Criticism of the Judean Biblical Cave Scrolls," in *A Stubborn Faith* (the W. A. Irwin *Festschrift*), ed. E. C. Hobbs (Dallas, 1956), pp. 117–31.

15. Subtitled: "Their Links with the Past and their Present Tendencies," in *The Backgrounds of the New Testament and Its Eschatology* (the C. H. Dodd volume), ed. W. D. Davies and D. Daube (Cambridge, 1956), pp. 176–208.

16. Cf. C. C. Torrey, *The Second Isaiah*, pp. 208 ff., for sharp criticism of Duhm, as of those scholars from whom the *Handwörterbuch* of Gesenius-Buhl so freely culled emendations and the like (p. 215 and n.*).

17. One could go on to cite similar opinions by other scholars: e.g., J. B. Payne, "The Relationship of the Chester Beatty Papyri of Ezekiel to Codex Vaticanus," *JBL* 68 (1949), pp. 251 ff., "More care must be employed in the use of the phrase often found in the Kittel Editions of *M*, 'Lege cum Graeco' " (p. 262); A. M. Honeyman, *VT* 5 (1955), p. 223, "Again the reviewer has become increasingly aware of the dangers which Kittel's *Biblia Hebraica*, in spite of its many merits, may constitute for the incautious user, for the *apparatus criticus* is not always as careful or systematic as it should be. . . ."; D. Winton Thomas, op. cit., p. 248, n. 1, "As has already been pointed out (p. 243, n. 1 [*in re* līķᵉhaƚ/γῆρας, Prov. 30.17]), the critical apparatus of *BH*[3] calls for careful use; see Orlinsky's warning . . . and Sperber's criticism, *P. A. A. J. R.* xviii, 1948–49, pp. 303 ff."

18. P. Katz, *VT* 4 (1954), pp. 222–23.

19. From the writer's review of Würthwein, *Journal of Semitic Studies* 4 (1959), pp. 149–51. On the Hebrew text edited by P. Kahle for Kittel's *BH*[3] being no more valuable to the scholar than that of *BH*[2] or of any carefully printed edition of the Bible, see Orlinsky, "The Import of the Kethib-Kere and the Masoretic Note on *Lᵉķāḥ*, Judges 19.13," *JQR* 31 (1940–41), pp. 59–66.

20. This section of the chapter originally appeared as a separate article in *JBL* 78 (1959), pp. 26–33.

21. For the writer's argument in favor of the priority of the MT reading, see "Studies in the St. Mark's Isaiah Scroll, VII" (in Hebrew), *Tarbiz*, XXIV, 1 (Oct. 1954), 4–8 (English summary, pp. I–II).

22. The writer's detailed discussion of Dimon-Dibon constitute "Studies . . . V," *Israel Explor. Jour.*, IV (1954), 5–8.

23. M. Burrows, *The Dead Sea Scrolls* (New York, 1955), and now his *More Light on the Dead Sea Scrolls* (1958), constitute a notable exception; see Chapter XIV

(pp. 301–25) in the former, and Part Three: "Results for Old Testament Studies" (pp. 135 ff.) in the latter.

24. MT reads כִּי־הִנֵּה יהוה יֹצֵא מִמְּקוֹמוֹ וְיָרַד וְדָרַךְ עַל־בָּמֳתֵי־אָרֶץ. O. Procksch in *BH*[3] notes *ad* ודרך: "dl c G V"; and the Micah fragment lacks ודרך; Burrows (*More Light* . . . , pp. 155–56) has suggested that only one of ירד ודרך is original, and that "The reading of the Qumran commentary may indicate which of the two verbs was original." However, in the light of the use of דרך with אֶרֶץ / עָם / אֶרֶץ / עַל־בָּמֳתֵי־עָב in Isaiah 14:1; Amos 4:13; Job 9:8—and cf. וְאַתָּה עַל־בָּמוֹתֵימוֹ תִדְרֹךְ (Deuteronomy 33:29) and וְעַל־בָּמוֹתַי יַדְרִיכֵנִי (Habakkuk 3:10; where Albright would insert יָם if it is not actually to be understood elliptically, "The Psalm of Habakkuk," pp. 12–13 and n. *m'* on p. 18, ad loc., in *Studies in O. T. Prophecy*, ed. H. H. Rowley [Edinburgh, 1950])—and even יַרְכִּבֵהוּ עַל־בָּמוֹתֵי אָרֶץ (Deuteronomy 32:13) וְהִרְכַּבְתִּיךָ/ (Isaiah 58:14) and וְעַל־בָּמוֹ(י)תַי יַעֲמִדֵ(י)נִי (II Samuel 22:34 // Psalms 18:34; where Albright, loc. cit., would restore or understand בְּמֹתַיִם), it would seem more likely that the Micah fragment has preserved the secondary of the two readings; in other words, the fragment derives from the text-tradition that gave rise to the so-called MT.

The verb (עַל במתי) ירד finds a parallel in אֶעֱלֶה עַל־בָּמֳתֵי עָב in Isaiah 14:14 only superficially; the prophet there, in mocking the king of Babylonia, speaks on several occasions of his downfall (e.g., vss. 11–12, אֵיךְ . . . . נָאוֹנָה הוּרַד שְׁאוֹל) after his attempts to rise up against the Lord (e.g., vss. 13–15, וְאַתָּה אָמַרְתָּ בִלְבָבְךָ הַשָּׁמַיִם אֶעֱלֶה . . . אֶעֱלֶה עַל־בָּמֳתֵי־עָב אֶדַּמֶּה לְעֶלְיוֹן אַךְ אֶל־שְׁאוֹל תּוּרָד. Note the pun in עֶלְיוֹן . . . אֶעֱלֶה).

25. Burrows (*More Light* . . . , 156–57) has accepted this argument. The two readings in Micah 1:3 were discussed by the writer on pp. 122–23 of his chapter, "Notes on the Present State of the Textual Criticism of the Judean Biblical Cave Scrolls," in the W. A. Irwin volume, *A Stubborn Faith*, ed. E. C. Hobbs (Dallas, 1956).

26. In 7:9, many scholars, e.g., F. Horst in *BH*[3] (but contrast S. R. Driver in *BH*[2]) held that LXX βοηθήσει derived from a reading תַּעְזֹר חָכָם, as against MT (הֶחָכְמָה) הֵעֹלוּ לָחֶכֶם. This Qoheleth fragment reads תעזור. But a careful study of the root עזז and of LXX βοηθέω (cf. my "Notes on . . . Scrolls," pp. 121–22) shows clearly how frequently a form of the latter is used for the former. Cf. Burrows's discussion (pp. 144–45).

27. "The Qumran Manuscripts and Textual Criticism," *VT Supplement* IV (1957), 148–60.

28. See my "Notes on . . . Scrolls," pp. 124–25.

29. See my "Studies in the Septuagint of the Book of Job," *HUCA*, XXVIII (1957), 53–74; XXIX (1958), 229–71; XXXI (1960); to be continued.

30. *The Ancient Library of Qumran* . . . , p. 139 and nn. 37–38.

31. Cf. P. W. Skehan, "The Qumran Manuscripts . . . ," pp. 155–60 (the Lev and Num fragments from cave 4); D. Barthélemy, "Redécouverte d'un chaînon manquant de l'histoire de la Septante," *RB*, LX (1953), 18–29 (covering parts of verses in Micah, Jonah, Nahum, Habakkuk, Zephaniah, and Zechariah). Some literature on the minor prophets material is cited in Cross, op. cit., p. 21, n. 35; I note also P. Katz, "Justin's Old Testament Quotations and the Greek Dodekaprophreton Scroll," *Studia Patristica*, I (1957), 343–53.

32. Cf. most recently, e.g., M. S. Hurwitz, "The Septuagint of Isaiah 36–39 in relation to that of 1–35, 40–66," *HUCA*, XXVIII (1957), pp. 75–83; A. Soffer, "The Treatment of Anthropomorphisms and Anthropopathisms in the Septuagint of Psalms," pp. 85–107; on these aspects of the LXX of Isaiah see Orlinsky, *HUCA*, XXVII (1956), pp. 193–200; on Job, XXXI (1960).

33. Cf., e.g., Orlinsky, "On the Present State of Proto-Septuagint Studies," *JAOS*, LXI

(1941), pp. 81–92 (= AOS Offprint Series, 13); the chapter on "Margolis' Work in the Septuagint," *Max Leopold Margolis, Scholar and Teacher* (Philadelphia, 1952), 33–44 (note on p. 43 a list of scholars who have accepted the recensional hypothesis of the LXX as against the theory of independent translations, among them Albright, R. Marcus, B. J. Roberts, O. Pretzl, Mercati); Skehan, op. cit., p. 158 (*in re* the Leviticus fragments), "The more general impression with which the writer is left is that we have here one more book of the OT in which a single early Greek rendering seems to have undergone a good deal of what we would today call critical revision, in the period even before Origen"; P. Katz, op. cit. (cf. p. 353, where reference is made to the "wealth of supporting arguments in Kahle's comprehensive paper, among them some which have long been shown to be gravely mistaken. . . . Although there is little hope to convince Kahle, I would conclude by putting right one of his fresh mistakes. . . ."); Cross, op. cit., pp. 124 ff., especially n. 13 (on pp. 125–27) and pp. 128–130 and n. 19; cf. n. 13 (pp. 126–27), ". . . It may be noted that in his article devoted precisely to this new recension, Kahle failed to deal with this point, that the scroll is a Jewish revision, *not* [italics in original] translation, which takes the pre-Christian Septuagint as its base. The failure is most curious, since this is easily the most significant characteristic of the text, as well as most damaging evidence against Kahle's theories of Septuagint origins."

34. *Journal of Semitic Studies* 3 (1958), pp. 234–64. It may be remarked that the Isaiah scroll here referred to, along with the Pesher on Habakkuk, the Manual of Discipline, and the so-called Genesis Apocryphon ceased legally to be the property of the monastery of St. Mark and its archbishop in July 1954, when they were sold to the state of Israel; see the writer's "Notes on the Present State," etc., p. 126, n. 1; Y. Yadin, *The Message of the Scrolls* (New York, 1957), pp. 39–52.

35. Actually, there is at least a third instance. In 41:28 LXX καὶ ἀπὸ τῶν εἰδώλων αὐτῶν represents a form of מֵאֵלִּים for Masoretic (וָאֵרֶא וְאֵין אִישׁ) וּמֵאֵלֶּה (וָאֵרֶא וְאֵין אִישׁ).

36. I. L. Seeligmann, *The Septuagint Version of Isaiah: a Discussion of its Problems* (Leiden, 1948), p. 20, regards Lucianic γλυπτοῖς "as a correction" of LXX εἰδώλοις (in turn, a "misunderstanding" of אֱלִילִים). But apart from the fact that γλυπτοῖς represents εἰδώλοις very well, it may be that γ. constitutes a "correction" of LXX κήποις for גַּנּוֹת (see the apparatus in *Isaias*, ed. Ziegler; Schleusner, II, 29, s. γλυπτός).

37. On the importance of this shamefully neglected scholar, see, e.g., p. 71 of the writer's "Studies in the Septuagint of . . . Job," *HUCA* 28 (1957).

38. At this late date it is only a distortion of the facts to state blandly, "Scholars have already noticed cases of agreement between 1QIsaᵃ and LXX, see. . . ." (Wernberg-Møller, p. 254, n. 1). How many of these alleged instances—usually merely asserted to be so—have been subject to careful analysis? In all fairness to the problem, reference should have been made to the several articles in which the present writer disproved such alleged instances; cf., e.g., O. R. Sellers, *JNES* 7 (1958), p. 219 (in reviewing the W. A. Irwin volume), "Harry M. Orlinsky . . . has been the foremost defender of the Masoretic text against proposed emendations based on the Dead Sea Scrolls . . . or . . . their having a *Vorlage* of the Septuagint or any other ancient version."

39. There can no longer be any doubt that parts of the Isaiah scroll and other Biblical manuscripts among the scrolls were copied from dictation, and probably also from memory—for numerous readings in these texts are due to a *hörfehler*, e.g., in the Psalm fragment (37:20; see Orlinsky, § v, p. 124, of "Notes on the Present State," etc.): "The wicked shall perish//And the lovers of the Lord shall be as thē fat of lambs. . . ." where incongruous וְאוֹהֲבֵי "and the lovers" in the scroll stands for Masoretic וְאֹיְבֵי "and the enemies" (//"the wicked"). Yet our author (p. 254)

makes mention only of "1QIsaᵃ, or the original from which it was copied . . ." without warning the reader that there may frequently not have been any text before the scribe. For some cases in point in Isaiah, cf. Orlinsky, *JBL* 69 (1950), pp. 156–57 and nn. 8–9 (with reference to S. R. Driver and Burrows).

40. It is good to learn that P. Katz and J. Ziegler, an excellent team of Septuagint experts, have "Ein Aquila-Index in Vorbereitung," as described in *VT* 8 (1958), pp. 264–85.

41. The problem is most complicated: cf., e.g., the data at 3:3, 9:5, 14 in the full apparatus in Ziegler's ed. of the LXX. The present writer would tentatively propose as the original LXX reading approximately καὶ θαυμαστὸν (or the like) τὰ πρόσωπα (καὶ) θαυμαστὸν σύμβουλον, deriving from a *Vorlage* (וְ)אֶלָא (וְ)נִשּׂוּא פָנִים (שַׂר־חֲמָשִׁים) (וְחָכַם חֲרָשִׁים וּנְבוֹן לָחַשׁ)—or under the influence of יוֹעֵץ אֶלָא in 9:5. In favor of this are: (1) the original LXX became the present, corrupt text by simple haplography (the scribe's eye going from the end of the first θαυμαστὸν (or the like) to the end of the second; note the accusative ending in the nouns in vv. 1b–3); (2) our verse in the Hebrew would then consist of five two-word expressions, so that וְיוֹעֵץ does not stand out like something of a sore thumb. Note also that in this section the Lord threatens to remove from Judah, *inter alia*, the גִּבּוֹר and the זָקֵן (v. 2), and the שַׂר־חֲמָשִׁים and the יוֹעֵץ [אֶלָא*] (v. 3), and according to 9:5 he will bring restoration through the lad who is to be named: פֶּלֶא יוֹעֵץ אֵל גִּבּוֹר אֲבִי־עַד שַׂר־שָׁלוֹם; and nine verses farther on (9:14) reference is again made to the וּנְשׂוּא־פָנִים זָקֵן.

42. Our author is content with the parenthetic statement, "Aquila follows M.T. in both passages"—whatever that was meant to indicate. Aquila rendered αἰρόμενος (προσωπ[ω]); so Ziegler, but perhaps pl. προσωπ[οις] as in 9:14) in both verses. Symmachus employed αἰδέσιμος in both, Theodotion ἐπηρμένος in 9:14.

43. The Masoretes noted on our word (פָנִים) וּנְשׂוּא at II Kings 5:1: ד'דין חס', i.e., the word ונשא occurs four times in the Bible, and in this instance is written defectively. But with the aid of the Masoretic elaboration in the margin of the Rabbinic Bible and the explanation in *Massora Magna*, ed. S. Frensdorff (Hannover und Leipzig, 1876), Part I, s. נשא (p. 125 and n. 2), it seems clear that what the Masoretes originally meant to convey was this: the word (ו)נשא (פָנִים)—with conj. *waw*—occurs four times in the Bible (II Kings 5:1; Isaiah 3:3; 9:14; Job 22:8), being written *plena* three times, and defectively once (II Kings 5:1); the form נָשָׂא—without conj. *waw*—occurs only once, and is written defectively (Isaiah 33:24). The Masoretic note in Kahle's text in Kittel's *BH*³ reads simply וֹ and gives the reader no idea of what is really involved; see my note 19 above.

44. I do not understand the reference in this section to "M.T.: שִׁבֹּלֶת (twice: xvii.5, xxvii.12), 1QIsaᵃ: defective spelling in both passages, cf. Aram. . . . Syr. . . . Arab. . . . ." (p. 253 and n. 2). Both MT and the scroll read שִׁבֹּלִים twice—not שבלת—in 17:5, and the scroll reads משבל for MT מָשִׁבֹּלֶת in 27:12, and שׁוֹלַיִך for MT שֹׁבֶל in 47:2; in short, 1QIsaᵃ has preserved no form of שִׁבֹּלֶת. As to the discussion in n. 2, how many linguists and textual critics would argue with confidence on the basis of a hapaxlegomenon (שֹׁבֶל) and so meager data otherwise?

The author singled out anomalous צורך in 52:2 (he could have done so, e.g., with MT צִוָּרָם in Neh. 3:5), but he should have told the reader that the word is spelled with the *'āleph* in the other three instances in the Isaiah scroll (8:8; 10:27; 30:28). I suppose that one would assume—on this manner of reasoning—two morphologies for עִוֵּר, because it is spelled as in MT eight times (29:18; 35:5; 42:7, 16, 18, 19; 56:10; 59:10), but עואר in 42:19 (*bis:* עואר ••• עואר ••• עור) and 43:8; or two morphologies for forms of עָוֹן, because it is usually written plene (with two *wāw*s) throughout the scroll (עוון), but with one *wāw* alone in 43:24 and 65:7 (ועונות) for expected ועונות = MT וַעֲוֹנֹת; and right after עוונותיכמה

for MT עוֹלֹתֵיכֶם). In 50:1 שׁלחה (for MT שֻׁלְּחָה) was "corrected" by addition of *wāw* over the *shin* (שׁלּחה). But such inconsistencies should not be made the basis for a new grammar of Biblical Hebrew.

45. The Septuagint and Targum proved most useful in a recent attempt to distinguish in Biblical Hebrew between the Qal inf. const. and the noun used verbally; cf. Orlinsky, "Notes on the Qal Infinitive Construct and the Verbal Noun in Biblical Hebrew," *JAOS* 67 (1947), pp. 107–26 (= No. 22 in the AOS Offprint Series).

46. "The List of Levitic Cities," *Louis Ginzberg Jubilee Volume* (English section; New York, 1945), pp. 49–73.

47. See now M. Haran, "The Levitical Cities: Utopia and Historical Reality" (in Hebrew), *Tarbiz* 27 (1958), pp. 421–39 (with English summary, pp. I–II).

48. Among other poems in the Bible treated by Albright from this angle, cf., e.g., "The Psalm of Habakkuk" (*Studies in Old Testament Prophecy* [the T. H. Robinson volume], ed. H. H. Rowley [Edinburgh, 1950], pp. 1–18) and "A Catalogue of Early Hebrew Lyric Poems (Psalm LXVIII)" (*HUCA* 23, I [1950–51], pp. 1–39).

49. Cf., e.g., his "Amarna Letters" (with G. E. Mendenhall) in *ANET,* pp. 483–90; and articles (with W. L. Moran) in *Journal of Cuneiform Studies* (from 1948 on).

50. See F. Rosenthal, "Canaanite and Aramaic Inscriptions," in *ANET* (2nd, revised edition, 1955), pp. 499–505, with extensive bibliography.

51. Ziegler has offered us also numerous important studies, some of monographic proportions, arising from his work on these editions of the LXX; most of these are listed in J. W. Wevers, op. cit., pp. 90–91.

52. In the series, *Texte und Arbeiten herausgegeben durch die Erzabtei Beuron,* I. Abteilung, pp. 32–33.

53. See H. Kusch, "Die Beuroner Vetus Latina und ihre Bedeutung für die Altertumswissenschaft," *Forschungen und Forschritte* 29 (1955), pp. 46–57.

54. *Philo's Bible: the Aberrant Text of Bible Quotations in some Philonic Writings and its Place in the Textual History of the Greek Bible* (Cambridge, 1950); "The Recovery," etc., in *Actes du Ier Congrès de la Fédération Internationale des Associations d'Etudes Classiques* (Paris, 1951), pp. 165–82 (cf. "Das Problem des Urtextes der Septuaginta," *Theologische Zeitschrift* 5 [1949], pp. 1–24).

55. Mention should be made of I. Soisalon-Soininen, *Die Textformen der Septuaginta-Übersetzung der Richterbuches* (*Annales Academiae Scientiarum Fennicae,* LXXII, 1; Helsinki, 1951), and his *Vanhan Testamentin alkuteksti* (Helsinki, 1953). G. Zuntz has been adding to our scholarly understanding of things Septuagintal; cf., e.g., "Die Antinoe Papyrus der Proverbia und das Prophetologion" (*ZAW* 68 [1956], pp. 124–84) and "Das Byzantinische Septuaginta-Lektionar 'Prophetologion'" (*Classica et Mediaevalia* 17 [1956], pp. 183–98).

CHAPTER SIX

The Development of the Jewish Scripts[1]

FRANK MOORE CROSS, Jr.

IN THE PAST DECADE the field of early Jewish palaeography has grown rich in materials for typological analysis. The caves of the Wâdī Qumran have yielded nearly six hundred[2] documents on skin and papyrus (and in one instance copper) ranging in date from the mid-third century B.C.[3] to the third quarter of the first century of the Christian era. These manuscripts and manuscript fragments exhibit a variety of scripts: Palaeo-Hebrew;[4] Early Jewish,[5] including formal and cursive hands; and, sporadically, Greek. Hardly less important for Jewish palaeography are the documents from the Wâdī Murabba'ât and the undesignated caves farther south in the Judaean desert, dating in large part to the first and second centuries of the Christian era. Included are materials in the Jewish formal scripts and, more significant perhaps, in the true cursive, as well as in Greek, Latin, and Nabataean.

While these discoveries have occupied the center of the stage, lesser finds have steadily pyramided which extend our knowledge of the typology of the Jewish hands. Several significant series of funerary inscriptions have been discovered in newly excavated tombs in and about Jerusalem. The most important of these, perhaps, are the graffiti on some fifteen ossuaries of the tomb of Jebel Ḥallet eṭ-Ṭûrī[6] which include one of the longest of the inscriptions of this genre yet found, and the thirty-three inscribed ossuaries of the tombs of Dominus Flevit.[7] Both groups[8] contain a number of graffiti in cursive script alongside the more usual inscriptions in formal characters.

In addition to such materials now becoming available for typology, there has been a rapid accumulation of discoveries which provide additional data for fixing absolute dates within the relative dating systems provided by typological analysis.

Most striking are the documents of Murabba'ât containing date formulae of the first century A.D. (in cursive script) and of the second century A.D. (both in formal and in cursive scripts), thus *overlapping with,* as well as extending beyond, the Qumran series.

As a matter of fact, the dating of documents and inscriptions of the Herodian Age (30 B.C.–A.D. 70) is capable of considerable refinement. The limits of the period are marked by materials either bearing date formulae or otherwise absolutely dated within narrow limits by archaeological or historical context. From the excavations at Ḥirbet Qumran has come a small but useful group of inscriptions closely dated by their stratigraphic context. For example, among the Qumran inscriptions so far published is an ostracon bearing a practice alphabet from (the end of) Level I (before 31 B.C.), in a crude, but advanced script providing another check point for the transition between the Hasmonaean and Herodian series.[9] Again, excavations at Masada have produced an ostracon and papyrus deposited before the destruction of the bastion in A.D. 73, which, however slight in content, nevertheless add to the corpus of closely dated materials at the terminus of the Herodian Age.[10] New and old funerary inscriptions from Jerusalem and its environs in several styles of script can now be dated more precisely within the Herodian era. On the basis of both archaeological and historical evidence, the Benê Ḥēzîr inscription (end of the first century B.C.) and the Queen Helena inscription (*ca.* A.D. 50) have long been dated securely.[11] The ossuary inscriptions regularly have been attributed to the last century before the destruction of the Temple, on historical and archaeological as well as typological grounds,[12] and this dating is not only confirmed but the ossuary scripts may now be used boldly in setting up typological series of formal, semicursive, and cursive scripts of the Herodian era. We can demonstrate now that the scripts of these funerary inscriptions, at the present just short of three hundred fifty in number, whether engravings,[13] dipinti, or graffiti, belong precisely to formal or cursive styles used in leather and papyrus documents.[14] Less important, no doubt, but worthy of notation, is the fact that in newer ossuary finds, careful descriptions of associated finds of pottery have been published,[15] even as our knowledge of common Roman pottery has been made more precise by the large and narrowly dated ceramic series from the strata of Ḥirbet Qumran. Thus older indices for the absolute dating of Herodian hands are confirmed and extended in usefulness by a variety of archaeological and palaeographic advances independent of the discovery of contemporary and later documents bearing date formulae. In the present state of palaeographical study, therefore, we are enabled to draw a typological line of development of several script types, each appearing in scores if not hundreds of documents inscribed on a variety of materials, the evolution pegged by a series of absolute datings at intervals throughout the Herodian Age and the subsequent era between the two Jewish Revolts against Rome.

The dating of documents in the Archaic or proto-Jewish period (*ca.* 250–150 B.C.) is less precise, still being largely based on typological sequence. Qumran, however, has produced two series, a formal hand stemming from the Persian Aramaic of the fourth century B.C., and a protocursive series influenced by the formal hand but more directly connected with the Aramaic vulgar scripts of the third century B.C. Of some use in dating the Archaic Qumran hands in absolute terms are the Palmyrene and Nabataean hands. Thanks to the publication of new inscriptions, especially the early group from Palmyra,[16] we can reconstruct more precisely the time when the prototypic Palmyrene and Nabataean broke away from their mother Aramaic scripts and began their independent evolution.[17] It must be emphasized most strongly, however, that these sister scripts to the Jewish hand are useful *only* for placing a single peg in the typological development, the date of their separation and the beginning of their independent development.

The dating of documents of the intermediate, Hasmonaean period (*ca.* 150–30 B.C.) is, as one would expect, less dependent on pure typology and other indirect means of fixing absolute dates than the proto-Jewish scripts, but more difficult to fix with precision than Herodian hands. The appearance of early Herodian script types serves, of course, as a terminus *ad quem* toward 30 B.C. Fortunately, a disproportionate number of Qumran manuscripts, Biblical and sectarian, fall into this era, furnishing a great variety of hands with which to establish the precise lines of typological evolution. It may be observed also that specifically sectarian works make their first appearance fairly early in the Hasmonaean period, to judge purely on palaeographical grounds.[18] Apparently it was the heyday of sectarian composition. At all events, the upper limit of this period, the lower limit of the Archaic period, is marked by the emergence from the slowly evolving Archaic book hand of a characteristic and rapidly developing style, which may be associated naturally with the decline (or suppression) of Greek, the resurgence of Aramaic and especially Hebrew as the official languages of Judaea in the era of Maccabaean nationalism.

These recent discoveries have done much to advance the study of late Aramaic and Early Jewish scripts. It must be noted, however, that the programmatic study which organized the basic typological outlines of the late Aramaic and the Early Jewish formal hand was published before the most important of these discoveries: W. F. Albright's exemplary analysis of the Nash Papyrus written in 1937.[19] The publication of the scrolls from Cave I, Qumran, brought a spate of articles and monographs of which only a few are of permanent value.[20] A major contribution of this period, still in progress of publication, is Birnbaum's *The Hebrew Scripts,*[21] a monumental attempt to deal with all periods of Hebrew writing. It is a work which will remain for many years a standard handbook for student and scholar alike. The publication of documents from Cave IV, Qumran, and from Murabba'ât have prompted new attacks on palaeographical problems. The late Aramaic cursive and the earliest Qumran scripts in the formal character were studied by the writer in 1955.[22] N. Avigad, in an excellent survey of the palaeography of the Qumran scrolls, has made contributions of the first importance, especially to the study of the late Jewish book hand and cursive.[23] Most recently J. T. Milik has enormously expanded our knowledge of the late Jewish cursive, both in his studies of ossuaries and in his brilliant decipherment of documents from Murabbaʻât.[24]

In the present study the writer proposes to summarize the present state of the study of Early Jewish scripts and at the same time to attempt a contribution to a number of remaining problems, especially problems of the origin and development of the protocursive and semicursive scribal traditions. The formal hand is now well established[25] in its three major phases: the Archaic (*ca.* 250–150 B.C.), the Hasmonaean (*ca.* 150–30 B.C.), and the Herodian (*ca.* 30 B.C. to A.D. 70).[26] Each of these phases is marked by general typological shifts,[27] though, of course, there is steady evolutionary change within each period, and many manuscripts may be dated to phases within the major periods, especially within the Hasmonaean and Herodian eras (see Fig. 1 and especially Fig. 2). Indeed it is not too much to say that, thanks to the rapid evolution of the script in this era, the palaeographer can often fix a characteristic book hand within fifty years in terms of absolute dates,[28] or even to a generation in terms of relative (typological) relationships.[29]

We shall deal in turn with (I) the standard Aramaic cursive and the rise of the national scripts, (II) the development of the formal Jewish hand, and (III) with the evolution of scripts in cursive traditions.

I. THE ARAMAIC SCRIPT OF THE LATE PERSIAN EMPIRE AND THE RISE OF THE NATIONAL SCRIPTS

1: The starting point for the study of Early Jewish palaeography is the Persian chancellery hand of the fourth century B.C., that is, at the end of the empire. The official Persian hand finds its origin in an elegant cursive which took form in the late sixth century and evolved into what may be called its classical tradition in the early fifth century. Thereafter, the development of the hand slows perceptibly, especially in leather documents, persisting with only minor evolutionary shifts into the mid-fourth century.

This standard Aramaic character was in regular use throughout the empire, from Asia Minor to North Arabia and Upper Egypt, and from Palestine to the eastern reaches of Iran; to judge from contemporary and later inscriptional evidence, it remained relatively undifferentiated by local peculiarities in the western reaches of the empire until the fall of the Persian power. So powerful was its sway that old formal or lapidary styles fell into disuse,[30] and the chancellery hand, while cursive in its inspiration, was used not only for commercial and diplomatic correspondence but as a fully formal script.[31]

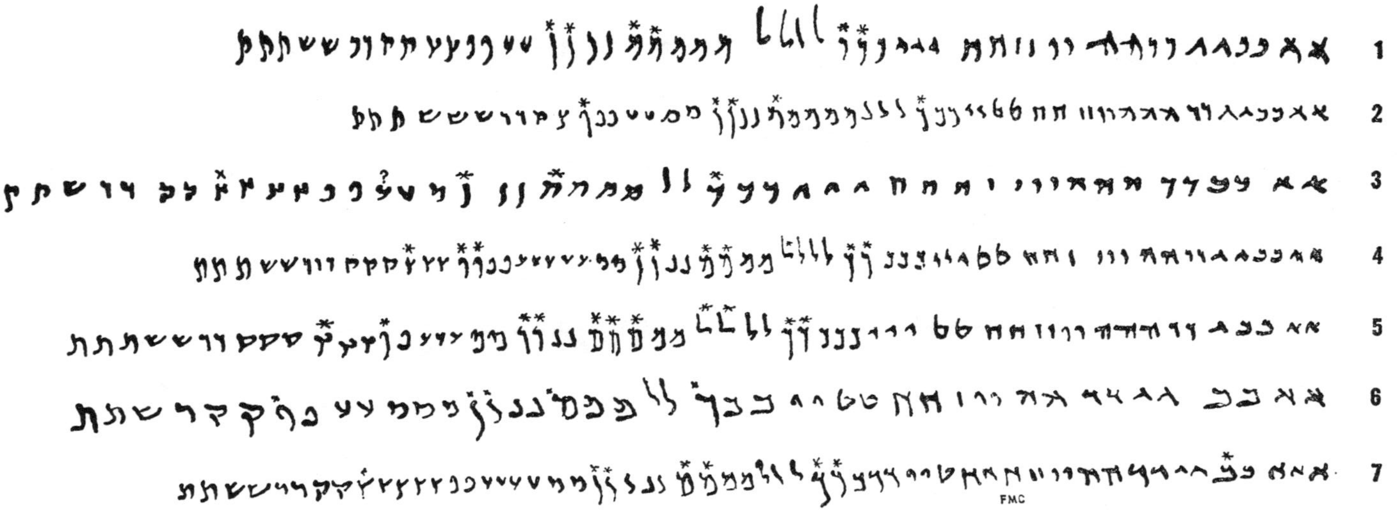

FIGURE 1. EARLY ARAMAIC AND PROTO-JEWISH SCRIPTS

Line 1. The classical Aramaic cursive of the late Persian Empire. From Papyrus Luparensis, *CIS* (*pars secunda*) I:1, 146 A, B, Tab. XVII. *Ca.* 375–350 B.C. A script of this character was the proto-type of the formal Jewish hand.

Line 2. An Aramaic vulgar cursive of the early third century B.C. from Egypt. From the Edfū Papyrus published by Sayce-Cowley, *PSBA* 29 (1907), Pls. I, II.

Line 3. An Archaic proto-Jewish hand of the mid-third century B.C. From an unpublished manuscript of Exodus from Qumrân (4QEx[f]). The script includes letter forms which ultimately evolve into the early Jewish cursive character.

Line 4. The proto-Jewish formal hand of the late third century

B.C. From a manuscript of Samuel (4QSam[b]) published by the writer in *OMQ*, pp. 147–72, esp. Fig. 6 and Fig. 2, 1.2.

Line 5. The proto-Jewish formal hand of *ca.* 200–175 B.C. From an unpublished manuscript of Jeremiah from Qumrân (4QJer[a]).

Line 6. An Archaic or early Hasmonaean semiformal script of *ca.* 175–125 B.C. From a manuscript of Qohelet from Qumrân (4QQoh[a]) published by J. Muilenburg, *BASOR* 135 (Oct. 1954), pp. 20–28.

Line 7. An Archaic or early Hasmonaean semiformal script of *ca.* 175–125 B.C. From a manuscript of an unknown work from Qumrân (4Q Prières liturgiques A) to be published by J. Starcky.

All scripts were traced from photographs of natural size with the exception of line 2, traced from a reduced photograph.

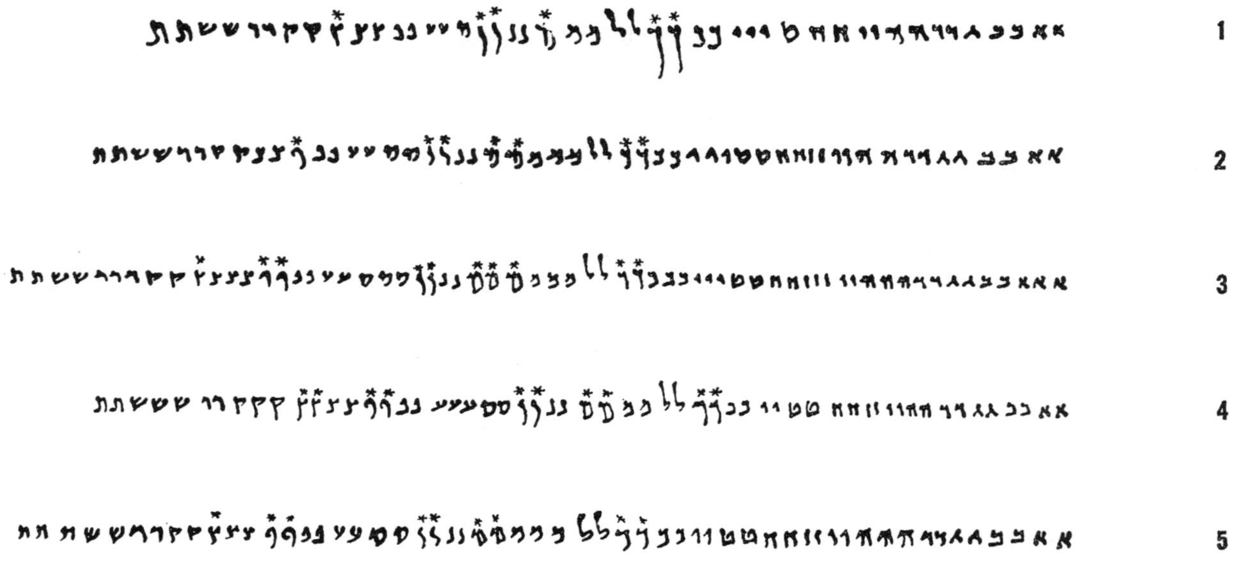

1

2

3

4

5

FIGURE 2.   THE EVOLUTION OF THE FORMAL HAND IN THE HASMONAEAN AND IN THE HERODIAN PERIODS

Line 1. A script transitional between the Archaic (proto-Jewish) and Hasmonaean periods (*ca.* 175–150 B.C.). From an unpublished exemplar of Deuteronomy from Qumrân (4QDeut*).

Line 2. A typical Hasmonaean script (*ca.* 125–100 B.C.). From an unpublished manuscript of Deuteronomy (4QDeut*). Cf. the hand of the great Isaiah scroll (1QIsa*) of about the same date.

Line 3. A late Hasmonaean or early Herodian book hand (*ca.*

50–25 B.C.). From a manuscript of Samuel (4QSam*) published in part by the writer in *BASOR* 132 (1953), pp. 15–26. Cf. the hand of 1QIsa* of roughly the same date.

Line 4. A typical early Herodian formal script (*ca.* 30–1 B.C.). From a manuscript of the Order of the War (1QM).

Line 5. An early Herodian "Round" semiformal hand (*ca.* 30 B.C.–A.D. 20). From an unpublished exemplar of Numbers (4QNum*).

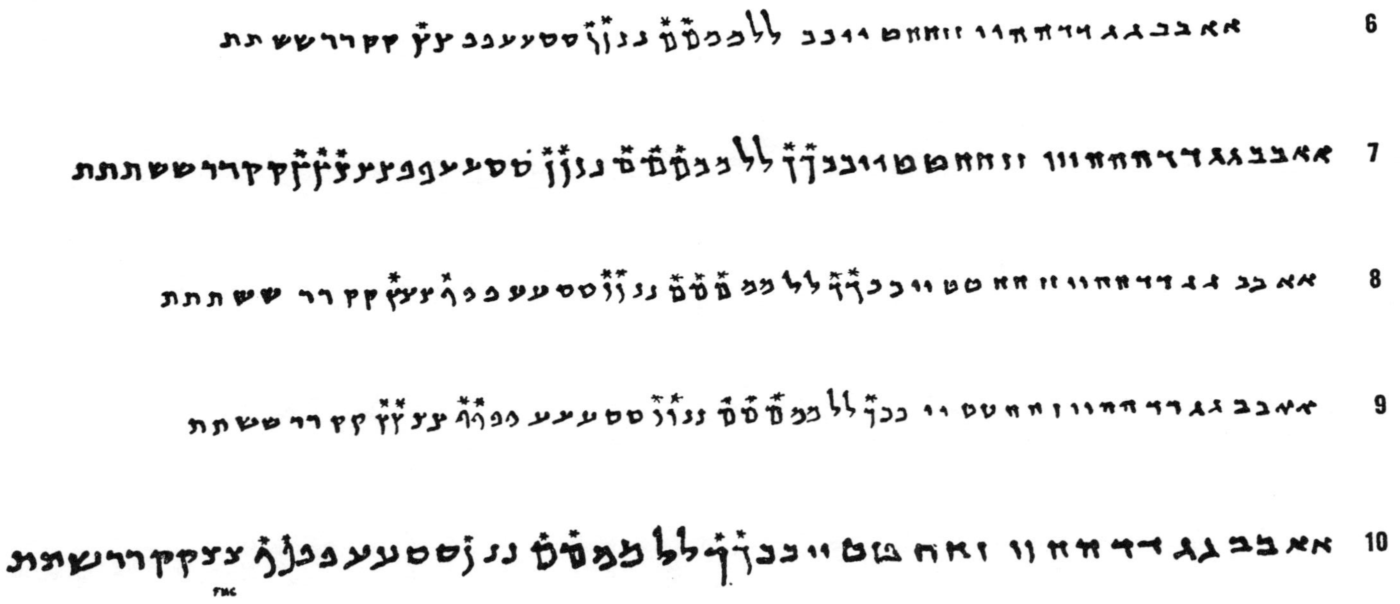

FIGURE 2. THE EVOLUTION OF THE FORMAL HAND IN THE HASMONAEAN AND IN THE HERODIAN PERIODS (*Continued*)

Line 6. A developed Herodian formal script (*ca.* A.D. 20–50). From an unpublished manuscript of Daniel (4QDan[b]).

Line 7. A late Herodian formal book hand (*ca.* A.D. 50). From an unpublished exemplar of Deuteronomy (4QDeut[t]).

Line 8. A late Herodian formal script (*ca.* A.D. 50 [–68]). From a manuscript of Psalms from Qumrân to be published by P. W. Skehan. This script represents the classic book hand of the First Jewish Revolt, the prototype of the post-Herodian Biblical hand.

Line 9. A post-Herodian Biblical hand (*ca.* A.D. 75–100). From fragments of a Biblical scroll preserved by members of a camp of Bar Kokhba (from an undesignated cave south of Murabbaʿât: Unid. Ps).

Line 10. A formal Jewish script from a Hebrew contract dated A.D. 133, published by J. T. Milik, *DJD* II, Pls. XXV–XXVI.

All scripts are traced from infrared photographs of natural size.

The immediate ancestor of the earliest *formal* book hands of Qumran has proved to be the standard Aramaic hand of the late Persian Empire. Apparently the proto-Jewish book hand of the late third century B.C. was little influenced by the vulgar Aramaic cursives which developed at the end of the fourth century and in the early third century B.C. when Greek replaced Aramaic for official purposes.[32] On the other hand, the earliest Qumran scripts exhibit a rare example or two of a protocursive tradition alongside the formal hand, and it is evident that the Early Jewish cursive derives from the vulgar Aramaic cursives of the early Greek period.

Texts in the chancellery hand of the fourth century B.C. are few in number, and the historical palaeographer has given them insufficient attention. Among the most developed hands from the texts from Elephantine[33] are two papyri from the first two years of the fourth century, Sachau Papyrus 18 (400 B.C.)[34] and Brooklyn Museum Papyrus 13 (399 B.C.).[35] In them we recognize cursive tendencies which became the standard forms of the later fourth-century texts. From the first half of the fourth century come the texts published by Aimé-Giron in 1931,[36] including one indirectly dated to the years 393–381.[37] Most important of the fourth-century texts is the Papyrus Luparensis[38] to be dated in the second quarter of the fourth century and perhaps as late as 350 B.C. The script of Papyrus Luparensis is slightly more formal in tendency than Aimé-Giron texts, but is at least as highly developed typologically. As we shall see, it is our nearest prototype[39] to the earliest formal hands from Qumran.[40] Finally, there is a single ostracon published by Sachau[41] which can safely be dated to the end of the fourth century B.C., presumably from the era immediately before the penetration of Greek names southward in Egypt at the beginning of the third century B.C.[42]

Two groups of documents from the third century B.C. preserve scripts derived from the standard Aramaic character: a small corpus of papyri and ostraca from Egypt, and two, perhaps three, manuscripts from Cave IV, Qumran. The latter group will be treated in more detail in the discussion of the Archaic period of the early Jewish script. It consists of 4QEx[f],[43] 4QSam[b],[44] and (at the turn of the third-second centuries) 4QJer[a].[45] The group from Egypt includes the Edfū papyri published by Sayce and Cowley,[46] the ostracon from Zâwiyet el-Meitîn published by Weill,[47] and the ostraca, from Elephantine when of known provenience, published by Lidzbarski and Sachau.[48] The hands of these papyri and ostraca from Egypt must all be dated in the first decades of the third century.[49] The forms are only slightly advanced over those of the early fourth century, and very slightly beyond those of the Sachau ostracon of the late fourth century. Historical circumstances, namely the rapid decline of Aramaic for business or public purposes in Egypt, support such a conclusion, confirming the palaeographic evidence. The hand of these early third-century documents tends to be an irregular cursive and manifests certain aberrancies which probably are to be attributed to local differentiation upon the breakdown of the controlling Persian chancellery tradition.

There are several general characteristics which mark the development of the Aramaic hand in the course of the fourth and early third centuries. The elegant shading of the classical fifth-century hand survives in the more formal hand (P. Luparensis) but tends late in the century to give way to a monotonous stroke, or, alternately, shading is used in an idiosyncratic fashion. This tendency is fully realized in the monotonous line of the third-century cursives.

The extreme difference in the length of various letters below the ceiling line,[50] characteristic of the fifth century, persists throughout the first half of the fourth century. In the third century the formal hand preserves the long and slim letters of the classical tradition; in the cursive, forms become squat, more regular in size.

One very important development which was destined to modify radically the size and form of letters first appears as a cursive trait in the late fifth century and gathers speed in the fourth. This is the trend to create what may be called semiligatures, a tendency of the scribe to bend the final stroke of a letter in the direction of writing; that is, to the position for forming the next letter. Especially affected were the long downstrokes of such letters as *kaf nun, pe,* and frequently *ṣade.* However, other letters were affected by the tendency, notably *mem,* whose left oblique stroke tends to curve upward to the left, and *lamed,* whose broad sweep to the right tends to narrow, and in the course of the fourth century, straightens and begins the development of a tick on the right. Naturally, this tendency was felt most strongly in the case of letters in non-final positions, so that we see here the commencement of the development of "medial" letters. So-called "final" letters, actually the older letter forms, were preserved where the tendency toward creating semiligatures was not so strong. By the third century B.C., the distinction between final letters and medial letters was full blown, though different script traditions froze different sets of medial and final forms.[51] And in the course of time, certain forms were lost (e.g., final *lamed*),[52] and secondary distinctions between final and medial forms elaborated (e.g., the artificial distinction between final and medial *he* in certain cursive scripts).[53]

A sketch of some of the detailed typological changes in the fourth- and early third-century Aramaic script follows; and it is suggested that the reader follow the description by frequent reference to Fig. 1.

'Alef remains small, as in fifth-century forms. Its left leg is no longer a high, straight, very short line; it becomes crescent shaped in the early fourth century, tending to lengthen somewhat, usually cutting the diagonal at the base of the lower side, as well as protruding in a high curved point on the upper left of the diagonal. This form is found in both *A.-G.* P. 87 and P. Luparensis. The "crescent-legged" form dies away in the late fourth- and early third-century cursives in favor of a "high-kicking" but rounded left

leg; it survives in the formal hand, however, as is patent from its appearance in late third-century texts from Qumran.[54]

Bet remains small and relatively narrow. Its right stroke is drawn downward, almost diagonally, in a gentle curve. By the third century the right stroke tends increasingly to the vertical, is strongly curved. The entire form broadens, especially the ticked head.

Gimel in the fourth century is in process of becoming smaller. The left leg, long and gently curved earlier, straightens, shortens, and begins to lower its point of junction with the right downstroke below the latter's top, a shift which is to continue to develop in later centuries.

Dalet remains long and narrow in the fourth century. Its stance, unstable in the fifth century, tends at the end of the century and in the early fourth to be right to left (the downstroke from top to bottom). In the late fourth and third century the stance again reverses and becomes left to right. *Resh* is only slightly distinguished from *dalet* in the mind of the scribe, and frequently only context permits one to distinguish the forms in a document. Often the right shoulder of *resh* is slightly more rounded, but the head is narrow and sharply ticked. Also, in some scripts *resh* tends to be shorter than *dalet*.

He[55] throughout the fourth century is made in classical fashion, that is, with three strokes as follows: the right downstroke runs obliquely down to the right, is shaded to a point at the top, tapers at the bottom; the second stroke is drawn horizontally (sometimes, in archaic fashion, sloping down to the left) from just below the peak of the right downstroke, from *right* to *left*, the pen spreading at the end of the stroke; the left downstroke is made from near the junction of the other two strokes. In the cursive of the third century there is the beginning of a new tendency to make the horizontal stroke from left to right, then continuing, without lifting the pen, into the downstroke; in the formal character the old style of penning the *he* is preserved, but the left downstroke begins its shift leftward along the horizontal bar.

Waw changes little in this period; its thick curved head and short tapering downstroke simplify slightly, with less shading, in the third-century Egyptian texts.

Zayn is a single, vertical stroke, shaded to a point at the top, tapering in characteristic fashion at the bottom. Like *waw,* its tapered, pointed form simplifies with loss of shading as early as the fourth century.

Ḥet at the beginning of the fourth century consists of two shaded downstrokes, tapering downward, often in slight, parallel curves leftward; they are joined by a very short crossbar, which angles downward from the broad head of the shaded, right downstroke to the left downstroke. In the fourth century there is a major change: scribes increasingly began the crossbar lower on the right downstroke, thereby often creating a bulge upward before the crossbar meets the left downstroke; also the right downstroke, or later both downstrokes, tend toward the vertical.

Tet is relatively stable in the formal scripts of the fourth–third centuries; its left downstroke reaches above the ceiling line, descends to a strongly curved base. The left upstroke ends in an acute angle with a slanting crossbar.

Yod is made with a triple movement: down, then to the left, then curving up and down strongly again to the right. In the fourth century this movement often creates a figure-two form (Brooklyn Museum P. 13; P. Luparensis), or a "proto-Nabataean" form. Double movement *yods* appear at the end of the fourth century, presumably developed from the older *"lambda"* forms,[55a] shifting to the "inverted-v" shape, especially in the third and early second centuries.

Kaf in the early fourth century has already gained its narrow, ticked head. Medial (with curved base) and final forms are sporadically distinguished; this distinction becomes more regular in the fourth century in formal hands. The major shift in *kaf* is in its stance; earlier fourth-century forms slant downward right to left; by the end of the century, and in the third century in most hands, the downstroke characteristically is vertical, or in *medial* forms tends to be concave, the beginning of later figure-three types.

Lamed, as described above, narrows, lengthens, begins the development of a tick downward on the right. Formal hands in the third century often preserve the broad archaic form in the final position.

Mem in the fourth and third centuries develops several new forms. In the formal script, the right downstroke curves leftward, especially in medial forms. The left diagonal downstroke similarly tends to curve to the left in medial forms, while in final forms the diagonal is most frequently a straight stroke. In the formal hand, the left diagonal (as early as P. Luparensis) tends to drop, often not breaking cleanly through the bowed top of *mem*. The *mem* is very long and narrow in both fourth- and third-century formal hands; in the cursive it broadens slightly and becomes squat. The cursive develops a variety of forms in the third century. Two may be singled out. One is the "medial" form of earlier times with the diagonal breaking through at the top, a form normal in the Egyptian cursive. It survives also at Qumran.[56] Another type, broad, rounded, with a long diagonal, appears in 4QEx[t],[57] the ancestor of the later elliptical forms of the true cursive.[58] As will be gathered from the length of our discussion, *mem* in the fourth–third centuries, as in earlier and later eras, is extremely useful to the palaeographer by reason of its complex and rapid evolution.

In the early fourth century medial *nun* sporadically is simplified into a straight downstroke, or a downstroke only slightly bent at the top, and a base rounded to the left. It is, of course, quite long still. By the mid-fourth century (P. Luparensis), final *nun* is also simplified, and the distinction between medial and final forms firmly set.[59]

Samekh in the fourth century loses its characteristic, complicated head in certain scripts.[60] The latest fifth-century forms are long and narrow, curving at the bottom only slightly. The extant fourth-century forms consist of a small hook followed by a large hook, emerging out of the center of the first. The lower stroke curls more tightly to the left than in the fifth century. In the third century formal script, *samekh* is more primitive than even extant fourth-century forms (*A.-G.* 87). In 4QJer[a61] the *samekh* is of "double-hook" type, but the right shoulder is angular in archaic fashion and the form long and narrow. In 4QSam[b], the angular shoulder and (relatively) narrow form is normal, but the type is intermediate between older and cursive third-century styles. The third-century *samekh* at Edfū is aberrant, a side development of the cursive *samekh,* which was later to invade the Early Jewish character as well as to appear in earliest Palmyrene.[62]

'*Ayn* in the fifth and fourth centuries is small and narrow. The left stroke is heavy (shaded); the left is thin and less curved than the right. In the third century, two types of '*ayn* diverge. One remains small and narrow; shading persists. The right, thin stroke tends to become a straight diagonal and breaks through at the bottom to create a "lower-case *y*" form. The other '*ayn* tends to broaden, retain its curved sides, and withstands longer the tendency to break through at the bottom. It is difficult to decide which is the formal, which the cursive. The Egyptian scripts of the early third century, normally an ancestral cursive, use the latter (as well as early Qumran semiformal and protocursive scripts). The most formal Archaic hands at Qumran[63] use the former "*y*" type '*ayn*. However, in the later course of the development of the Early Jewish scripts, the "*y*" form survives only in certain semicursive hands. For áll this, it appears best to label the "*y*" form formal, the broad form cursive. The crossing of formal and cursive traditions is not infrequent, though normally cursive forms invade formal traditions. Actually the terms "formal" and "cursive" are often arbitrary, applying at best to the origin or destiny of a style or tradition.

Pe in the fourth century develops in the medial position a shorter form; the base curls more tightly, and by the mid-fourth century (P. Luparensis), the stance of the downstroke has shifted to the vertical. The shift which forms a square corner at the right side of the base is still wholly in the future.

Ṣade in the fifth century has three forms, each defined by the treatment of the right arm. One, probably the oldest typologically, bends the arm at a right angle downward; a second forms the right arm with two strokes, often forming a horizontal "T." The third type is simplified and no doubt latest typologically: a straight or slightly curved stroke forms the arm. All three are used through most of the century, and all three survive (in evolved types) in the national scripts: the first in Nabataean, the second in Palmyrene, the third in the Early Jewish character. In the fourth century, the third type shortens. In the medial position, the left downstroke sometimes bends leftward at the bottom, but not consistently. The right arm curves back toward the left downstroke. By the end of the fourth- and in the third-century cursives, the curve may become a right angle, the horizontal stroke looping or tending to loop into the downstroke.[64]

Qof in the fifth century exhibits two forms, a more archaic with a relatively long tail, and a short-tailed form. Both appear in the fourth and third centuries. In the early second century the tails of both cursive and formal hands lengthen beyond those of either of the earlier types.

[65]*Shin* in the fourth- and third-century formal hand is made with a shaded left stroke, and clean, straight, oblique strokes. In the cursive of the third century the upper oblique tends to rise along the left downstroke, and a slight, but significant, tendency to curve the oblique strokes sets in.

Taw is of special typological interest. It is very long in the fourth and third centuries. The earliest fourth-century forms already exhibit a cursive bend at the bottom of the left downstroke; in P. Luparensis and the third-century forms, the left downstroke is doubly curved, at the top and at the bottom. The left curved arm steadily lengthens in the fourth, third, and second centuries. But, beginning in the third century, the over-all length of *taw* steadily reduces, ultimately to conform with that of other letters.

2: The Archaic or proto-Jewish period includes manuscripts of the second half of the third century and the first half of the second century. This is the era of the rise of the national scripts of Palmyra and Nabataea as well as Judaea. The development appears from our evidence to have proceeded in two stages: (1) the era following the fall of Persia and the introduction of Greek when local scripts tended to differentiate (the formal hand in the third century held to the late Persian style, evolving very slowly, no doubt owing to its restricted use; at the same time, a vulgar cursive marked by local peculiarities tended to spring up); and (2) the era late in the third and especially in the early second centuries when the crossing of formal and cursive styles gave rise to the local scripts: the classical Palmyrene, Nabataean, and Hasmonaean styles.

Four categories of scripts may be isolated, tentatively, for purposes of classification. These categories persist in usefulness into later periods, and, while suppressing, perhaps, the full complexity of the typological evolution even in the Archaic period, will be utilized as a descriptive language.

(1) The formal character: this script in the Archaic period is essentially the successor of the late Persian chancellery hand, hence bypassing many developments in the third-century local cursives. The early type scripts are 4QSam[b] and 4QJer[a] (see Fig. 1, lines 4 and 5 respectively).

(2) The semiformal character: this is a subtype of the formal hand, formed by the influence of a third-century cursive on the formal character.[66] Early examples are 4QQoh[a] and 4QPrières lit. A,[67] both probably from the second quarter of the second century (Fig. 1, lines 6 and 7). The Palmyrene hand develops from a similar prototype.[68]

(3) The cursive hand: this script is the successor of early third-century cursives, and the ultimate prototype of the extreme, late Jewish cursive of the ossuaries and Murabba'ât as well as a rare contract or two from Qumran,

Cave IV. By and large it is absent from the literary texts of Qumran in pure form, but strongly influences other hands.

(4) The semicursive: this is an intermediate script formed by the crossing of formal script types and the developed cursives, especially those of the second century B.C. and later. It is an unstable type, in which much mixing of traditions occurs, and hence a source of "infection" of both formal and cursive styles. While unstable, it is not merely a mixed script. Often it maintains common traits over considerable periods of time despite its great variety in individual styles (Figs. 3 and 4).[69]

The Archaic formal hand can best be described, perhaps, by using 4QSam[b] (Fig. 1, line 4) for reference as a type script.[70] It is the earliest of the formal hands from Qumran, dating to the third century B.C., no doubt late in the century. Occasional reference will be made to 4QJer[a] (Fig. 1, line 5); the latter, however, is a less typical exemplar of the Archaic formal style.

'Alef in 4QSam[b] is very small compared with Hasmonaean types, or even with most of those of the early third-century cursives. Its left leg is crescent shaped, breaking back from the diagonal at the bottom. The closest parallel forms are early fourth century, and even P. Luparensis, which has the crescent-legged form, preserves a later type slightly enlarged and sprawling. In fact, the 'alef of 4QSam[b] is prior typologically to any known Aramaic hand extant, after the fourth century. This applies to its size and shaded, calligraphic technique (both shared with 4QJer[a]) as well as the treatment of the left leg.[71]

Bet is small, rounded at bottom right, though the downstroke is moving to the vertical. In 4QJer[a] the downstroke has become vertical or even bulges slightly to the right. In neither 4QSam[b] nor 4QJer[a] has it approached the larger, square-cornered Hasmonaean bet. The top is short with sharp ticks, unlike the broader, cursive forms with a rounded right shoulder. The "square-cornered" base stroke develops in the cursives, appearing in the earliest semiformal hands. As early as the late second century in the cursive and semicursive, this latter form shifts to the style in which the base is drawn from left to right.

Gimel: the left leg has shortened slightly and lost its curve. Sometimes in 4QSam[b] it branches off very near the top of the right leg in the fashion of the fourth-century scripts; sometimes it has shifted slightly down and tends to kick up as in the third-century cursives and early semiformal hands. The right leg is a straight, shaded stroke; it exhibits no tendency to bow in, a trait characteristic of early (and later) Hasmonaean hands.

The dalet of 4QSam[b] finds its closest parallels in the long, narrow forms of the fourth century. Actually the extreme narrowness of the heads of dalet and resh in 4QSam[b] with their sharp ticks go beyond the fourth- and fifth-century forms, perhaps in a formal counter-tendency to the broadening of the forms, and the softening of the ticks in the cursive of the third century.

The downstroke of *dalet* and *resh* is vertical, unlike the usual right-to-left slant of the early fourth, and the left-to-right stance in the third- and early second-century scripts of cursive or semiformal type.[72] *Dalet* and *resh* in third-century formal scripts, as in fourth-century hands, are little distinguished, a feature of typological importance. In the early second-century semiformal scripts, and in the Hasmonaean formal script, the broad, deep-cornered crossbar of *dalet* appears together with the shallow, round-shouldered crossbar of *resh*.

He in the third-century formal script of Qumran is made with three strokes. The right downstroke shows the calligraphic technique of older times: shaded, pointed at the top. The stroke leans, its top to the left, although it is already shifting to the vertical. The crossbar is drawn right to left in formal hands and normally is drawn upward to the left in 4QSam[b]; 4QJer[a] occasionally exhibits a crossbar which is horizontal or slopes down to the left. While both 4QSam[b] and 4QJer[a] here show development beyond fifth- and early fourth-century forms, it is to be noted that the slant (up or down to left) of the cross stroke is in itself not a decisive typological feature. On the one hand, cross strokes sloping upward to the left may appear (rarely) in the fifth century; on the other hand, and more important, the cross stroke slanting downward to the left survives in the cursive into late times.[73] However, the short, upslanting cross stroke is important taken with other features: the direction in which the stroke is made and the formation of the left leg. In the formal hand, the left leg tends to move outward along the crossbar, the scribe even looping slightly from the end of the leftward motion into the downstroke. In the cursive series, the scribe draws the leg from close to the junction of the right leg and cross stroke, that is, from near the end of a cross stroke drawn left to right. Thus the formal script preserves the technique of earlier times, the cursive the outward appearance of the earlier form, but not the technique. The semiformal *he* (Fig. 1, lines 5 and 6) is made in cursive fashion, but in form resembles the formal *he*. It is, therefore, secondary to the third-century forms of both formal and cursive type.

Waw in 4QSam[b] and Jer[a] is a gently bowed downstroke. It continues fifth–fourth century modes; later, by the early second century, the downstroke straightens. However, the *waw* of 4QJer[a] (very rarely 4QSam[b]) on occasion shows a tendency to tighten the curve at the head, anticipating the later hook-headed, straight *waw*.

Zayn in the third-century formal scripts is often shaded, as in the fifth and early fourth centuries; often it is a simple vertical line as in the fourth through the early second centuries. In early Hasmonaean times *zayn* is sometimes bent rightward at top (or the whole stroke is bowed), sometimes thickened on the top right. This may be a distorted "memory" of the shaded *zayn* since the simple stroke dominates in the cursive hands; on the other hand, the thickening on the right may be secondary to the bent form.

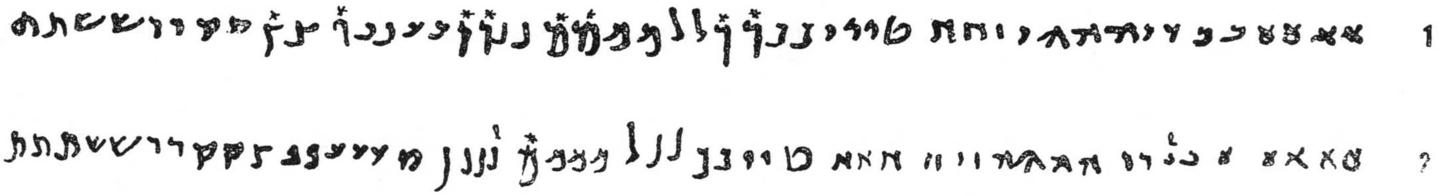

FIGURE 3. EARLY SEMICURSIVE SCRIPTS

Line 1. An early Jewish semicursive, or mixed, hand from Egypt (*ca.* 150 B.C.). From the Nash Papyrus, published by Cook, *PSBA* 25 (1903), pp. 34–56; the best reproduction of the papyrus is that of J. Trever, *Annual Report, Smithsonian Institution*, 1953, Pl. 7 (opp. p. 430).

Line 2. A Jewish semicursive script from the Judaean wilderness (*ca.* 125–100 B.C.). From a Murabba'ât ostracon published by J. T. Milik, *DJD* II, Pl. LII.

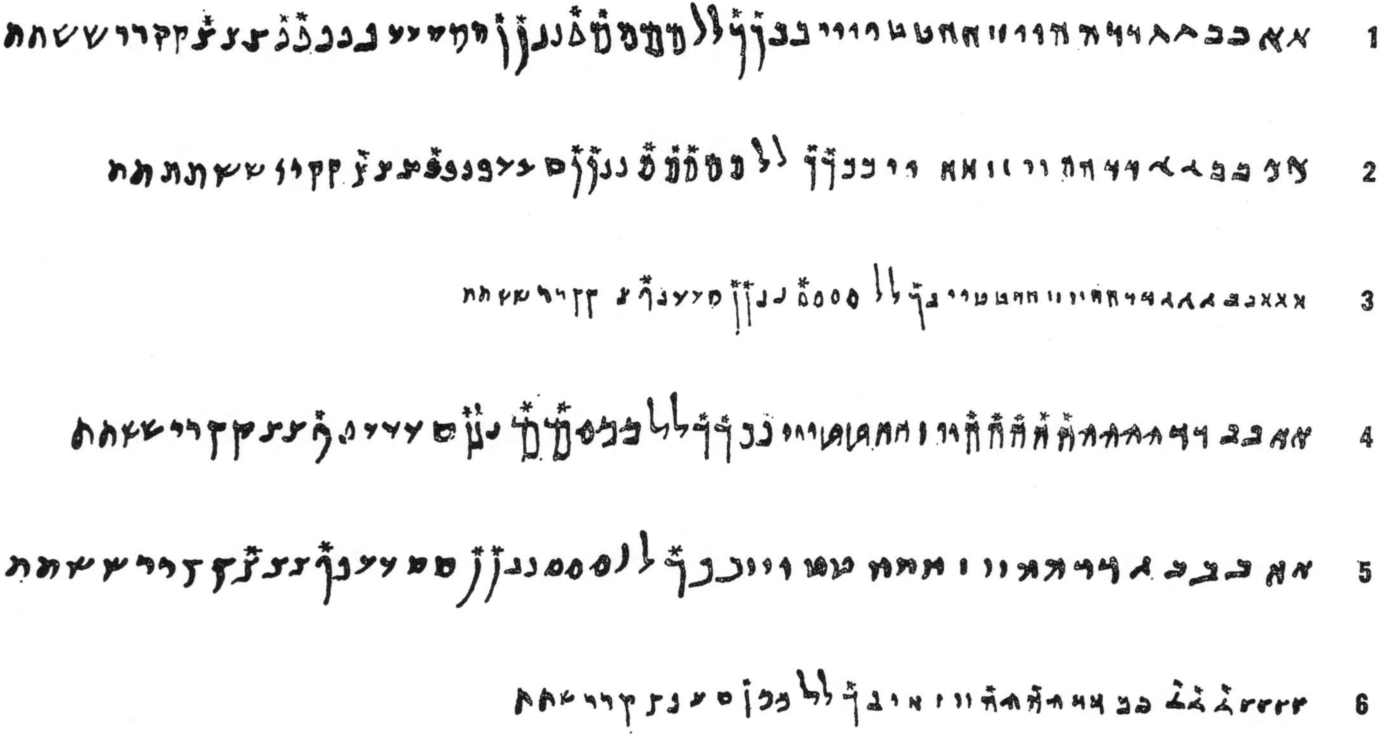

FIGURE 4. SEMICURSIVE SCRIPTS FROM QUMRAN

Line 1. A semicursive hand from an unpublished manuscript of the Twelve Minor Prophets (4QXII^c). *Ca.* 150–100 B.C.

Line 2. A semicursive script from an unpublished manuscript of Daniel (4QDan^c). *Ca.* 100–50 B.C.

Line 3. An unusual semicursive from a non-Biblical Aramaic work of Cave IV, provisionally designated pseudo-Enoch (4Q ps.-Enoch^a). *Ca.* 100–50 B.C. To be edited by J. Starcky.

Line 4. A late Hasmonaean semicursive script from an unknown work in Hebrew to be edited by J. Strugnell. *Ca.* 50–25 B.C.

Line 5. A hand from a manuscript containing the so-called Apocalypse of Weeks, to be edited by J. T. Milik (4QEnoch V). *Ca.* 50–1 B.C.

Line 6. A script used in an Aramaic papyrus from Cave VI (6Qp8), to be edited by M. Baillet. *Ca.* 50–1 B.C.

Het in 4QSam[b] exhibits the characteristic treatment of the crossbar which develops in the fourth century, dies in the early second (except where preserved in the sister scripts, Palmyrene and Nabataean). The crossbar has dropped slightly on the right, bulges upward before dropping to meet the left leg; or, sometimes, the bar is almost horizontal. Often the left leg is shaded, and tapers, bending to the left (cf. P. Luparensis); but generally *het* is becoming straight-legged. The dropping of the crossbar on the right continues in the cursive tradition, ultimately producing the "N" form.[74]

The *tet* of 4QJer[a] shows little development from fifth–fourth century forms. The *tet* of 4QSam[a] is slightly more evolved. The final cross stroke is rounded, rather than angular at the right; on the other hand, it retains the high left arm and round base of Archaic forms.[75] Abrupt changes enter in the late third-century cursive, to judge from the indirect evidence of early second-century, semiformal hands: the left arm shortens, angling (rather than curving) into a straight oblique which in turn bends back into a curled crossbar (4QQoh[a]; 4QPrières lit. A; cf. P. Nash). This latter form invades the formal hand in the Hasmonaean period.

Yod in 4QSam[b] is regularly drawn in three motions. Sometimes there is a slight simplification; the left stroke is barely suggested, the stroke up and down to the right (normally producing a shaded triangle) becoming a motion to the right and down. This produces a *yod* common in the early third-century cursives, normative in Nabataean. It also survives in certain second-century semicursives.[76] An occasional "figure-two" *yod* appears in 4QSam[b]. The *yod* of 4QJer[a] appears to be a form of the two-movement *yod*.[77] In the late fourth century and in 4QEx[f] the archaic two-stroke (*lambda*-shaped) *yod* survived in developed form. This latter archaic *yod* is made from the top, first a right oblique downstroke, then a left stroke *down* from near the top or (later) the top of the right downstroke, forming a *"lambda."*[78] In 4QJer[a], and probably in isolated Egyptian third-century forms, the left stroke is penned upward to a peak, then down, forming the late inverted "v" *yod*. This is the type found in the semiformal hands of 4QQoh[a], 4QPrières lit. A, and other early hands of this tradition,[79] including Palmyrene. Probably it invades the formal hand from the prototype of the semiformal hands.

Medial and final forms of *kaf* are distinguished in 4QSam[b] and 4QJer[a]. In both, final *kaf* is very long, its head quite narrow. Medial *kaf* is similarly narrow and relatively long (especially in Jer[a]). In these traits the Archaic formal hand stands closest to fifth–fourth century scripts. On the other hand, the stance of *kaf* has moved closer to the vertical, a shift becoming apparent in the late fourth- and early third-century cursives. The base of medial *kaf* is gently curved in archaic style. The broad, flattened base drawn horizontally and later diagonally begins its development in the Egyptian cursive[80] and is found first in the semiformal hands of the early second century (Fig. 1, lines 6 and 7). It invades the formal script in the Hasmonaean era. In 4QSam[a], and to a lesser degree in 4QJer[a], the downstroke of medial *kaf* bends inward to the left, creating a rudimentary "figure-three" *kaf*. The rudimentary form appears also in the Egyptian cursives, the developed form in Palmyrene, sporadically in Nabataean, and in early semicursives from Qumran.[81]

Final *lamed* is always distinguished from medial *lamed* in 4QJer[a]. The scribe of 4QSam[b] also knew the form, but used it rarely. It is, of course, a form descended ultimately from fifth-century broad *lamed*. In the formal hands of Qumran, however, the curved downstroke has straightened, angling sharply at the ceiling line into the broad horizontal stroke, ending in an almost imperceptible hook. Its closest parallels are the *lameds* of P. Luparensis. Presumably the distinction between the medial and final *lamed* in systematic fashion developed in the formal hands of the late fourth century. The cursives of the late fourth and early third century normally do not distinguish two forms of *lamed*, and the archaic final form disappears from the formal Qumran character in the third century. Its only survival appears to be a sporadic occurrence in early Palmyrene and Nabataean inscriptions.[82] One early third-century letter published by Lidzbarski is perhaps the earliest example of the systematic distinction between medial and final *lameds*,[83] but its forms are cursive, the final forms more advanced than the *Qumran* examples.

Medial *lamed* in 4QSam[b] and 4QJer[a] is short and straight. Its hook is narrow, made with a thin, short, and uncurved downstroke. In the latter feature it stands in contrast to the casually curved hooks of the third-century cursives and early second-century semiformal scripts. Once again, we see the closest typological ties of the formal hand with early fourth-century scripts, requiring the reconstruction of a late fourth–early third-century formal tradition not extant in our documents.

Final *mem* in 4QSam[b] is extraordinarily archaic. There is nothing like it in extant texts after the fifth–fourth centuries. It is long and narrow, open at the bottom. The diagonal stroke is straight. Medial *mem* in 4QSam[b] is little developed beyond that of P. Luparensis. Like it, the diagonal no longer regularly cuts through the topstroke, and the letter as a whole is exceedingly long below the ceiling line, and narrow. The *mems* of 4QSam[b] are not to be reckoned in the series of cursive types, neither the protocursive form of 4QEx[f] nor the alternate cursive *mem* of the Edfū and early Qumran semicursives (e.g., 4QXII[a], Fig. 4, line 1). The latter retains certain archaic features: the left downstroke slices through the topstroke; often the left downstroke (diagonal) is straight or nearly straight. It is, however, a frozen form leveled through the semicursive tradition, and the distinction between medial and final *mem* is rarely observed. *Mem* is another instance of a letter in which certain archaic features persist in the cursive, certain others in the formal hand;[84] we are again warned thereby that there is no simple developmental relationship between the cursive and formal scripts.[85]

Medial *nun* in 4QSam[b] is still very large and long and sometimes bends right at the top, in archaic fashion. The latter feature often survives, also, of course, in later scripts. Final *nun* is often simplified, a feature without typological significance since it develops in the fourth century, and more archaic forms survive into Hasmonaean times. 4QJer[a] shows the first signs of the rapid shrinking of the length of medial *nun,* a shift beginning in earnest at Qumran in the semiformal scripts.

Samekh in the third-century formal scripts of Qumran has been described sufficiently above. Both 4QSam[b] and 4QJer[a] exhibit complicated, hooked heads with typological features most nearly related to fourth-century cursive styles.

'Ayn: both 4QSam[b] and 4QJer[a] exhibit the "lower-case y"-shaped *'ayn.* Normally, though not always, the right arm breaks well below the junction with the left, curved arm. This development of the form, without parallel[86] in extant cursives of the fourth–third centuries, must be attributed to a putative formal style of the late fourth and early third centuries.

Medial *pe* in 4QSam[b] is gently rounded at both top and bottom as in the fourth–third century scripts. The later pointed top and rectangular base develop first in the semiformal and semicursive scripts of the second century, entering the formal character in Hasmonaean times. Final *pe* in 4QJer[a] is typologically identical with fourth–third century forms. In 4QSam[b], there appears to be a slight shift to a vertical stance, but the head is gently rounded, neither pointed nor tightly curled.

Ṣade in the formal scripts belongs to the third type described above. 4QSam[b] and 4QJer[a] preserve rather different but strikingly archaic forms of this type. There is no distinction in medial and final forms of *ṣade* in Sam[b]. The letter is the small, simplified *ṣade* of the fifth century. The slight bending in of the right arm which characterizes *ṣade* in P. Luparensis and certain later fourth- and third-century forms appears—in exaggerated fashion —in Jer[a]. It is striking that the *ṣade* of 4QSam[b] shows no tendency to bend leftward at the bottom even in medial forms. There are ample parallels of the reverse, the systematic use of *medial* forms in the *final* position; the present usage is certainly an archaic element of the formal hand of the late Persian Empire.

The *qof* of 4QSam[b] is distinguished by its relatively short tail and its fairly narrow head; its closest parallel is the early fourth-century specimens of P. Luparensis. 4QJer[a] uses a *qof* with virtually no tail. The latter develops as early as Sachau P. 18 and persists as late as P. Nash (*ca.* 150 B.C.). The narrow, open head of *qof* (4QSam[b]) is also indicative of relative antiquity (in this period!).

Shin is drawn in both 4QSam[b] and Jer[a] with clean, straight oblique strokes, intersecting the shaded downstroke. The tendency to curve one or both right oblique strokes, which appears already in the early third-century cursive, does not influence either script; however, 4QJer[a], but not 4QSam[b], reveals a slight tendency to shift the upper oblique toward the top of the left downstroke, a characteristic of third-century cursives and second-century hands of several traditions.

Taw in 4QSamᵇ is extraordinarily large with a short right leg. Its closest parallels are again Sachau P. 18 and P. Luparensis; however, the third-century forms are quite similar, except in calligraphic technique. In 4QJerᵃ, the right leg is lengthened, but the letter is still very large. Beginning in the third century, the relative size of *taw* is steadily reduced to conform to that of other letters.

The result of this analysis is to show that 4QSamᵇ, especially, but also 4QJerᵃ, belongs to a formal third-century tradition derived from the Persian chancellery script of the fourth century B.C. This tradition is distinguished by its shading techniques in penning letters, and in the size of letters: their length below the ceiling line and their narrowness. Certain letters, *'alef* (4QSamᵇ), *dalet, ṭet* (4QJerᵃ), final *mem* (4QSamᵇ), *samekh, ṣade, resh,* and *shin* (4QSamᵇ), have their closest parallels with fourth-century types but must be explained as belonging to a formal line of evolution, distinct from the cursive tradition of the third century, but contemporary with it: *bet* (4QSamᵇ), *he, kaf* (final), *lamed* (medial and final), *mem* (medial, 4QSamᵇ), and *'ayn. Waw, bet, yod, nun* (medial and final), *qof, shin* (4QJerᵃ), and *taw* have equally good parallels in the fourth and third centuries. *Bet* (4QJerᵃ), *gimel, ṭet* (4QSamᵃ), *kaf* (medial), and *pe* (medial and final) stand closest to early third-century letters.

It is evident from these data that the Archaic Jewish book hand of 4QSamᵇ and 4QJerᵃ belongs to a formal tradition which parallels the extant cursives of the third century B.C., and that this formal tradition has evolved very slowly after the end of the Persian period. This was to be expected with the disuse of Aramaic for official purposes during the period of Hellenization.[87]

The manuscript 4QExᶠ (Fig. 1, line 3) raises certain special palaeographical problems.[88] While it belongs clearly to the third-century hands in the Archaic series, it does not belong to the formal tradition and at many points diverges from the cursive tradition of the early third century as known from the Egyptian papyri and ostraca.

Its general character may be described as protocursive. Letter forms are broad and squat. Some letters are obvious precursors of later cursive forms. Slight or no distinction is made between medial and final letters. On the other hand, some of the script's traits are dismayingly archaic, and the combination of cursive and archaic features suggests that 4QExᶠ belongs to a line of cursive development which branched off from an Aramaic archetype of the fourth century and developed independently of the line of cursive development revealed in the late fourth- and early third-century Egyptian cursive texts.

The *'alef* of 4QExᶠ is relatively large; the left leg protrudes in a high arc not unlike fourth–third century forms. The central, oblique downstroke of the *'alef* frequently curves upward at the base, reminding one vaguely of early Nabataean *'alef*.[89] At the same time, the stroke is often straight or even curved downward. The closest parallels to the *'alef* of 4QExᶠ are found in the

Sachau ostracon (62:2, late fourth century). Occasionally 4QEx^f uses the precise form found in the painted epitaph of 'Aqabyah, an archaizing inscription from the end of the fourth century or the beginning of the third century B.C.[90] The latter comparison, in itself not especially striking, becomes significant in view of a series of points of contact between the script type of the 'Aqabyah Dipinto and 4QEx^f,

Bet combines archaic and developed elements. The head has broadened in the fashion of the third-century cursives, but the downstroke is strongly curved, normally from the head downward. A few forms (Fig. 1, line 3, second specimen of *bet*) lengthen the downstroke into a rudimentary base. Both forms can be found in fourth- and early third-century cursive hands.

Dalet is unusually long in 4QEx^f; the head is ticked, but of the relative breadth found in the late fourth- and early third-century cursives, broader than the formal hands of the late third century (4QSam^b). The most important feature typologically of the *dalet* of 4QEx^f is the slant of the downstroke, which is consistently right to left. While vertical and even left-to-right slants of *dalet* (and especially *resh*) appear in the fifth and fourth centuries, the usual stance of the late fifth and early fourth century is right to left. On the other hand, in the third and second centuries the shift to a vertical or left-to-right stance is universal in cursive and semiformal scripts.[91] In the later hands, the only example of *dalet* with right-to-left stance is to be found in the Nash Papyrus (*ca.* 150 B.C.). The form here, however, derives from the narrow formal series. 4QSam^b also sporadically exhibits a gently curved or right-to-left downstroke. Like Nash, however, the form is formal in origin, and hence in this instance probably archaic.

Resh is usually distinguished from *dalet* in 4QEx^f by its shorter downstroke. While it frequently is penned with the right-to-left stance of *dalet*, more commonly the downstroke approaches the vertical.

He is small, drawn in formal style, with the horizontal thick, often looping into an oblique left leg. It has no close parallel in the fourth–third century scripts of cursive derivation. The *he* of 4QSam^b is a close parallel, and the *he* of the 'Aqabyah Dipinto, while more formal in ductus, is similar.

Waw is a "thick-headed," gently curved stroke, identical with fourth–third century cursive forms. It shows no tendency to form the hooked head and straight downstroke that first appears in the third century and becomes general in the scripts of the early second century.

Zayn in 4QEx^f is a simple vertical stroke, usually shaded.

Het tends to be squat in accord with the general tendency of the script. Otherwise its significant typological features are those of the early and late fourth-century scripts. The two legs normally curve downward to the left. The crossbar usually is drawn from the top of the right leg, either horizontally or downward to the left leg. Rarely the crossbar bulges slightly at midstroke, a tendency beginning in the fourth century, dying out in the first half of the second century B.C. in the Jewish script.

Yod in 4QEx^t is the *"lambda* form," not the "inverted-v" type which developed from it in the early third century. *Yod* in 4QEx^t is large, on occasion as large as *'alef* or *he*. It is made with a right downstroke forming the right leg; the left leg is begun from the top or near the top of the right downstroke, moves, usually in a slight curve, away from the right leg and then downward, often below the base of the right stroke. The closest parallels may be found in Sachau Pl. 62:2 (late fourth century B.C.) and especially in the 'Aqabyah Dipinto.

Kaf has a single form used in both medial and final positions. As in the case of *nun* and *sade* it is the archaic (i.e., the later final) form which is utilized in all positions. The form is short, broad, but the stance is slanted like the *kaf* in fourth-century and earlier scripts.

Lamed is protocursive in style regularly in 4QEx^t. Its hook is slight and rounded. The letter is short and vertical. The form is common in the third-century texts from Egypt and persists later in cursive and early semiformal Jewish hands.

Mem in 4QEx^t is unique. The head is thick and broad, the right downstroke usually curved to the left in medial forms, often virtually a straight line in final forms. The right downstroke is exceptionally short even for a cursive *mem;* the left downstroke is singularly long, usually extending below the right stroke, especially in forms where the right stroke is curled. The left diagonal almost never breaks through the "head." The final, or "open" *mem* type of 4QEx^t is evidently derived from *mem* of the style found in P. Luparensis. In the latter case, medial and final forms are little distinguished. The left diagonal rarely breaks through the head, but has "dropped"; at the same time it is very long. However, the *mems* of P. Luparensis are long and narrow-headed. *Mem* in 4QEx^t is obviously much developed beyond such forms, but not in the direction in which the formal script moved (4QSam^b). The tradition of 4QEx^t is simply absent from the Egyptian cursives, as well as from the third- and early second-century scripts from Qumran. There is some evidence, however, that the form of *mem* represented in 4QEx^t was not a local aberration which died out; it belonged no doubt to a local tradition, but probably is the distant precursor of the *mem* of the pure cursive scripts.[92] The latter invades the semicursive scripts of Qumran in the early first century B.C. (cf. Fig. 4, lines 3, 4, 5).

The *nun* of 4QEx^t belongs typologically with fifth- and early fourth-century scripts which make little distinction between final and medial forms. The *nun*, whether used medially or finally, is regularly a long downstroke, slightly bent to the right at the top, to the left at the bottom. *Nun* in medial positions is bent leftward no more than *nun* in final positions, and in neither position is there an example of the typologically more developed medial *nun*. The latter develops as early as the fifth century in many scripts. However, scripts as late as the late fourth century use the archaic *nun* in all positions.

The 'Aqabyah Dipinto is perhaps the latest published text using a fully archaic *nun* in a medial position.[93]

The *samekh* of 4QEx[f] is more archaic than any form in the cursive Egyptian texts of the late fourth and third centuries. It stands typologically between the simplified forms of *BM* P. 13 or Sachau P. 18 (respectively 399 and 400 B.C.) and *A.-G.* P. 87 (early fourth century B.C.). It is typologically less advanced than the formal *samekh* of 4QJer[a] or 4QSam[b], though the former has a few traits in common. The head is heavy and slightly rounded, and the stroke forming the right shoulder emerges from the bottom of the head. The right downstroke bends leftward at the bottom only slightly. The form is relatively long and narrow.

'Ayn has two forms in 4QEx[f], though one, the more developed of the two, appears only in damaged, nearly illegible contexts and cannot be reconstructed with certainty. One form (Fig. 1, line 3, first specimen) is the standard Persian "v"-shaped *'ayn,* slightly broadened, which continues in regular use in the third-century cursive in Egypt and survives with only a slight break-through of the right leg into the proto-Nabataean inscription from Khalaṣah (*ca.* 170 B.C.),[94] and the earliest semiformal scripts of Qumran (e.g., 4QQoh[a]; 4QPrières lit. A). The other form, if our decipherment is correct, is very like the cursive *'ayn* of a much later date (cf. Fig. 4, line 5), a modified "y"-shaped form.

Pe appears in decipherable contexts only in the medial position. Normally, the downstroke slants right to left. The head is small, rounded rather than peaked, and the base is gently rounded, not abruptly bent leftward. The form has shortened, but is otherwise best compared with fourth-century medial forms of *pe.*

Ṣade in 4QEx[f] is probably a much shortened derivative of the second fifth-century type of *ṣade* described above. Its right arm is usually made with two strokes, frequently forming a "T" turned on its side. Sometimes the arm seems to be made in the fashion of the *ṣade* of 4QJer[a]. While the tail of *ṣade* in 4QEx[f] not infrequently is bent leftward in a semiligature, medial and final forms are not systematically distinguished.

Qof is made with a sharply ticked, broad head and a short, stumpy leg which normally fails to join the cross stroke of the head. The form has no precise parallels between the beginning of the fourth century (cf. Sachau P. 18) and the semiformal scripts of the early second century B.C. The latter are particularly close to 4QEx[f]. The 'Aqabyah Dipinto shares some characteristics.

The *shin* of 4QEx[f] is undistinguishable from the form developed in early third-century Egyptian cursives. The upper oblique has moved up, joining the left downstroke near the top; it is normally straight. The lower oblique often curves slightly upward. The form appears in slightly developed form in the early semiformal hands and in P. Nash.

Taw in relation to the other letters of 4QEx^f is extremely long. The right arm is very short. The relative proportion of the left leg and right arm, an important typological criterion, points to the excessively archaic character of this form. The comparable forms typologically come from fifth- and early fourth-century texts. At one point the *taw* of 4QEx^f seems to show development. The right arm stems from near the top of the left leg. However, this trait does not survive elsewhere in extant texts.

The detailed study of the unusual script of 4QEx^f above can be recapitulated as follows: *dalet, ḥet, nun,* and *samekh* have their best parallels in fourth-century scripts; *'alef, bet, waw, yod,* and *pe* have equally good parallels in fourth- and early third-century scripts; *shin, lamed,* and *he* belong typologically with third-century styles; *qof, zayn,* and *'ayn* may fit naturally into any period between the fourth and early second century B.C. Special problems exist in the case of *kaf, mem, ṣade,* and *taw.* Each combines extremely early features, having parallels in extant texts no later than the fourth century, with developed, but unique features.

The broad, squat character of the script suggests that it has developed some distance from the elegant Persian chancellery hand. On the other hand, the script preserves an archaic style which does not use the semiligatured ("medial") forms. *Nun* is an especially striking instance. However, there is some evidence of a local style of script which maintains single forms of letters well into the third century: the Marisa graffito and the 'Aqabyah Dipinto.[95] Moreover, Palmyrene and the Qumran cursives bear witness to such a tradition. Palmyrene distinguishes only between final and medial forms of *nun* regularly, and the early semicursives usually distinguish slightly, if at all, between medial and final *mem, ṣade,* and *pe.* However, in the latter scripts it is the semiligatured forms for the most part (*mem* is an exception) which are used. In the case of 4QEx^f it is the *non-ligatured* forms, or forms intermediate between the archaic and the semiligatured forms, which survive in its script.

The script of 4QEx^f is to be described, on the basis of our evidence, as a protocursive script, developed in a locality, presumably Syria-Palestine, where a set of archaic features survived, and a series of changes evolved, which were not altogether paralleled in the evolution of the fourth- and third-century cursives in Egypt. The contacts between the script of 4QEx^f and the later semiformal hands of Qumran, the Jewish cursives, and, remotely, Palmyrene, are made intelligible if this description is accurate. The several parallels between the 'Aqabyah Dipinto and the hand of 4QEx^f are probably to be explained in a similar fashion. It is most likely on historical grounds that the scribe who painted the 'Aqabyah epitaph was a Jew lately come to Alexandria in the influx of Jews to Alexandria in the days of Ptolemy I. The uniqueness of the style of the epitaph among Egyptian documents of roughly contemporary date suggests an outlandish tradition; and, finally, it is not without significance that the typological parallels between the 'Aqabyah epitaph and 4QEx[f] exist despite the radical difference in style: the cursive ductus of 4QEx[f], the archaizing, formal character of the epitaph.

These general considerations warn against attributing 4QEx[f] to the highest date permitted by a letter-by-letter analysis. The manuscript is probably contemporary with or even slightly later in date than the early third-century Egyptian cursives which furnish parallels to the latest, typologically, of the letter forms of 4QEx[f].

We shall return to the problem of the absolute dating of the earliest Qumran manuscripts, after taking up two special problems of the Archaic hand: the semiformal scripts of the Archaic period; and the development of the Palmyrene and the Nabataean scripts.

3: Alongside the formal scripts of the late third and early second century B.C. from Qumran appears a special style which we have labeled the early semiformal character. It has been defined above as a script formed by the influence of the third-century cursive upon the formal character. This is a loose definition which describes origin but which does not adequately indicate that the hand in question, when it appears at Qumran, is a fully formed style which maintains its integrity and special traits for more than a century, until it disintegrates and can no longer be traced toward the end of the Hasmonaean period or slightly later. The primary specimens of the script with which we shall be dealing are 4QQoh[a] and 4QPr[a].[96] In the same tradition are the scripts of 4QPsa[a] (unpublished) from the Archaic period and an unidentified document to be published by Abbé Jean Starcky, 4QSy48 (Hasmonaean period). Two common hands of the Hasmonaean period are strongly influenced by the semiformal tradition: the hand of the scribe of the Rule of the Community (1QS),[97] 4QSam[c] (unpublished), and the testimonia list published by J. Allegro,[98] et al.; and a hand commonly appearing in papyri, for example in pM34 recto (unpublished).

The scripts of the early semiformal manuscripts 4QQoh[a] and 4QPr[a] are in general effect strikingly different from the formal hands of the Archaic period (see Fig. 1, line 6): letters are broad; the stroke is simple (unshaded) and free; often flourishes ornament the script. In each instance we recognize traits stemming from the third-century cursive. The semiformal character, however, is also closely allied with the formal tradition. Medial and final letters are normally distinguished, and while individual letter forms are influenced by third-century cursive developments, the semiformal hand is not the archetype of the semicursive and cursive hands.

'Alef has a semilooped left leg. The form of 4QQoh[a] is less developed, but anticipates the *'alef* of early Nabataean. 4QPr[a] tends to bend the central oblique stroke to the left on occasion, so that the letter approaches the (contemporary) fully looped cursive *'alef. Bet* is broad. The head is more or less ticked, and the downstroke is drawn vertically or slanting slightly to the right, then bends sharply back into a long base stroke. This form originates in the third-century cursive, appears in early Palmyrene and Nabataean, and

early infects the formal character. *Gimel* in both manuscripts is archaic. The right leg is unbent; the left leg is high. *Dalet* is a new emergent. Formal and cursive traits are combined. The head broadens in cursive fashion; the slant of the leg has shifted to its extreme left-to-right position (the point at which the Palmyrene *dalet* began its development) and later moderates. The head of *dalet*, while broad, preserves the formal tradition in its deep ticked, rectangular form. *He* is drawn in cursive style, the horizontal arm drawn from left to right. On the other hand, it maintains a formal "shape," unlike the true cursive[99] and Palmyrene. *Waw* is sometimes archaic, sometimes tends to develop a curling head as in early Nabataean. The *ḥet* is straight-legged, its bar drawn upward to the left, creating a bulge at the mid-point of the stroke (cf. early Nabataean and Palmyrene) or creating a rudimentary "N"-shaped *ḥet* which develops fully in the cursive.[100] Both treatments of the crossbar are to be found first in early third-century cursives (e.g., Sachau Pl. 68:1). As we have noted above in the analysis of the formal hands, the semiformal scripts introduce abruptly a developed form of *ṭet*. The left arm is shortened radically; the base is straight rather than curved, and curled back into a looped "crossbar." The "inverted-v" *yod* is introduced in the semiformal scripts. Often in the early exemplars (4QQohᵃ and 4QPrᵃ) there is a small flourish at the beginning of the stroke, giving the form something of the appearance of a small Syriac *taw*.

Kaf, like *bet*, is exceedingly broad in 4QQohᵃ. It has developed a true base. The head is bowed, rather than ticked, a cursive trait not found in 4QPrᵃ. The latter often uses final forms in a medial position. The true medial form of 4QPrᵃ is a significant form. Its head is narrow, but otherwise resembles the "rectangular" head of *dalet;* the downstroke slants left to right and bends into a sloping, straight base. This form is characteristic of the semiformal hands and later invaded the formal scripts. *Lamed* derives from the cursive tradition of the third century, only slightly influenced by the formal *lamed* in the Archaic period, more strongly in Hasmonaean semiformal scripts. Medial *mem* in 4QQohᵃ is an idiosyncratic form. It is essentially a formal *mem*, simplified in stroke, closely paralleled in the earliest Nabataean *mem* (Aṣlaḥ). The curved downstroke of archaic formal *mems* has now become a straight base stroke. Final *mem* in 4QQohᵃ is also abnormal; the head is broad like the cursive *mem* (e.g., 4QXIIᵃ; Fig. 4, line 1), not narrow in formal style. 4QPrᵃ presents the usual semiformal types of medial and final *mem*, both more closely bound to the formal tradition of the late third century. *Nun* in both manuscripts is in the formal tradition of 4QJerᵃ.

In 4QQohᵃ and 4QPrᵃ the cursive *samekh* makes its first appearance in Qumran scripts. The form may be compared with Edfū cursive forms (Fig. 1, line 2). It is more easily derived by collateral development from an archetype of the Egyptian cursive. The Palmyrene *samekh* also derives from the same tradition as the Qumran semiformal. *'Ayn* is broad, the left arm breaking through only slightly. The closest parallels are found in the script of 4QExᶠ, the Khalaṣah Inscription, and Palmyrene. *Pe* is developing a true base. *Ṣade* in 4QPr^a is formal in type, developing from the style found in 4QSam^a. Unfortunately, 4QQoh^a in the extant fragments has no examples of *ṣade*. In later semiformal hands, the early cursive *ṣade,* derived from a prototype much like 4QEx^t, frequently is used. *Qof* is developed from a protocursive form similar to that of 4QEx^t. The head is broad, the leg normally not joining the top stroke of the head. The leg is beginning to lengthen after its extremely short phase. *Resh,* like *dalet* and *kaf,* reflects the introduction of a new style. The top is broad, the right shoulder rounded. *Dalet* and *resh* are easily distinguished, as in the protocursive of 4QEx^t. *Shin* has also taken on cursive breadth; the lower arm is slightly curved upward, the upper arm is straight but connects high on the left downstroke. *Taw* is a new form. The right leg has become as long as the left. The slight curve of the bottom of the left leg found in earlier formal and cursive scripts has become now a separate, distinct part of the letter.

The Archaic semiformal script merges formal and early cursive elements into a hand of calligraphic beauty and simplicity. It is not surprising that it created a style which continued in vogue for several generations. The importance of the script, however, lies in its position as a transitional script. The national scripts of Palmyra, Judaea, and Nabataea became fully independent and began their rapid evolution into their later classical styles at a time not distant from the introduction of the semiformal character. It is the latest of the script styles we know which has affected each of the national scripts. Palmyrene may be properly described as a derivative of a semiformal script. To be sure, the archetype of the Palmyrene hand was not identical with the Archaic semiformal hands of Qumran and was no doubt marked by local peculiarities. But it belongs typologically in the semiformal tradition and stems from the same era. Both the Hasmonaean hand of Judaea and the Nabataean character stem from the formal tradition of the Archaic period. The Hasmonaean hand, however, is influenced strongly by the semiformal script. The development of the Nabataean is more complex but in its earliest stages has certain traits which are to be attributed to the influence of a semiformal tradition.

4: The sister scripts, Palmyrene and Nabataean (Figs. 6 and 7), have a very limited usefulness in the study of Early Jewish palaeography. By establishing the dates of the branching apart of the three national scripts from the common stream of a more or less undifferentiated Aramaic script, the typological sequence of the Jewish scripts, in the interval between dated documents of the fourth and third centuries and the Hasmonaean documents of established date, are furnished with additional "pegs" for absolute dating. The earliest Nabataean and Palmyrene texts in their classical styles are, of course, much later than the divergence of the two sister scripts from the line of Jewish development. If the typologist is to make use of the Nabataean and Palmyrene scripts, therefore, he must project backward in time along the line of the special evolution of each, to the point at which the line of Jewish development and one of the related scripts converge. This is not as complicated as it sounds. Each script in isolation evolves in its peculiar fashion, preserving certain archaic traits, producing certain novelties; inevitably these archaic and novel elements are different in each national script;[101] moreover, the period of specialization of the three scripts is roughly the same as is now established both on typological and historical grounds.

The earliest of the Nabataean materials are the Khalaṣah Inscription from the reign of Ḥaretat I (*ca.* 170 B.C.),[102] the inscription of Aṣlaḥ (*ca.* 95 B.C.),[103] the Wâdī Tumīlât inscription dedicated to 'El-Kutbā'[104] (*ca.* 77 B.C.),[105] and the Rabb'el Inscription (*ca.* 66 B.C.).[106] The Khalaṣah script is actually a pre-Nabataean script of semiformal affinities; the main line of development of the Nabataean character proper stems out of the formal hand of the late third and early second centuries; the earliest extant specimen of this tradition is the Aṣlaḥ text (Fig. 6, line 1).

The script of Aṣlaḥ preserves the narrow, long, and irregularly sized letters of the formal script. Indeed, contrary to the trend toward uniformity in script operating in semiformal hands, and especially in Hasmonaean and Herodian Jewish scripts, Nabataean develops and exaggerates this element of the old, formal Aramaic hands. The Aṣlaḥ script, however, has only begun this secondary development.

The "archetype" of the Aṣlaḥ script, to judge from archaic elements, fits into the typological series of Qumran hands late in the Archaic period. The left leg of *gimel* is high; *het* has a domed crossbar (cf. 4QSam^a; 4QDt^a [Fig. 2, line 1]); *yod* is developed from a three-movement formal *yod; mem* and *nun* remain very long; but *mem* has a short left diagonal and *nun* no tendency to bend right at the top; *'ayn* seems to be developed from the "y" form and is very small (4QJer^a; 4QDt^a); *ṣade* perpetuates a much developed form of the "T"-arm type.[107] *Shin* is a derivative of pre-Hasmonaean types. *Taw* is later than third-century *taws;* it stands close to 4QJer^a and 4QDt^a.

Bet, he, waw, ṭet, and *kaf* have late traits, that is, traits which appear not in the earliest Archaic scripts (4QSam^b) but in formal and semiformal scripts immediately prior to or transitional to the Hasmonaean character. Some of these developed characteristics may be explained by supposing parallel evolution in proto-Nabataean and proto-Jewish script. This is probably the best explanation for early Nabataean *'alef* (not taken into account above). It may have been derived independently from a protocursive form like that of 4QEx^f or the cursive type of Edfū texts, quite as well as from the later forms of semiformal or semicursive type.[108] Such an explanation is more difficult in the case of the letters listed above: *bet* with its broad top, square lower right corner, and base line;[109] *he* with its perpendicular left leg, attached far left on a horizontal or slightly sloping crossbar; *waw* with curved head and downstroke; *ṭet* with its pointed base; *kaf* with broad head and developed,

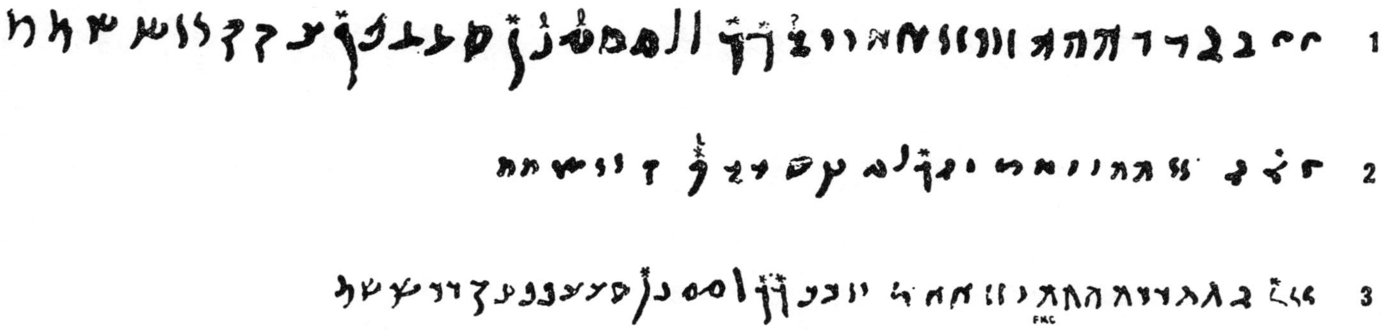

1

2

3

FIGURE 5. HERODIAN AND POST-HERODIAN CURSIVE SCRIPTS

Line 1. A cursive hand from an Aramaic contract found at Murabbaʿât dated in the second year of Nero (A.D. 55/56). The papyrus was published by J. T. Milik, *DJD* II, No. 18, Pl. XXIX. Cf. *SDF* I, Fig. 24, p. 102.

Line 2. A cursive hand from an Aramaic marriage contract, probably dating in the year A.D. 117 (Mur 117). *DJD* II, No. 20, Pl. XXX.

Line 3. A semicursive hand from an Aramaic contract of sale, found in an undesignated cave of the Judaean desert (Unid. 134). It is dated in A.D. 134. Published by J. T. Milik, *RB* 61 (1954), pp. 182–92, Pl. IV; cf. *Biblica* 38 (1957), pp. 264–68, Pl. IV.

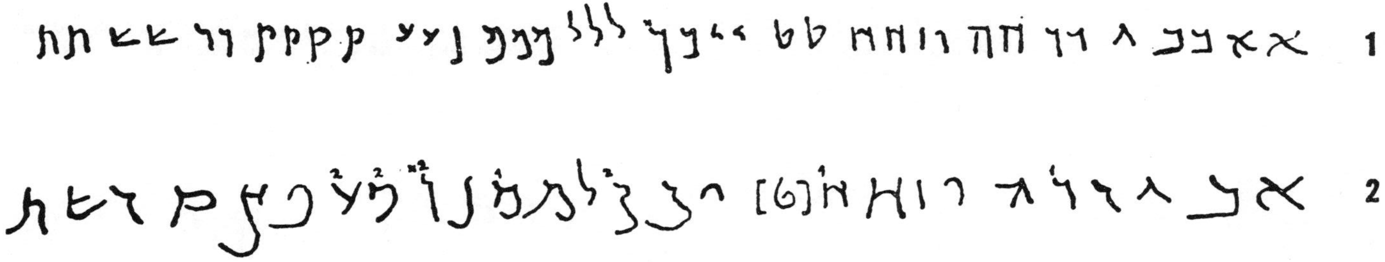

FIGURE 6. EARLY NABATAEAN AND PALMYRENE SCRIPTS

Line 1. The script of the Aslaḥ Inscription (*ca.* 95 B.C.), published by G. Dalman, *Neue Petra-Forschungen, usw.* (Leipzig, 1912), Abb. 68, No. 90 (p. 99).

Line 2. The script of the earliest dated Palmyrene inscription (44 B.C.), published by J. Starcky, *IAP*, p. 510, Pl. I. The siglum[1]

refers to letters taken from a contemporary inscription dedicated to *Bêl, Bêlḥammân,* and *Manawāt* (ibid.); the siglum[2] refers to the inscription published by du Mesnil du Buisson (*Inventaire des inscriptions palmyréniennes de Doura-Europos* [Paris, 1939]), dated 33 B.C.

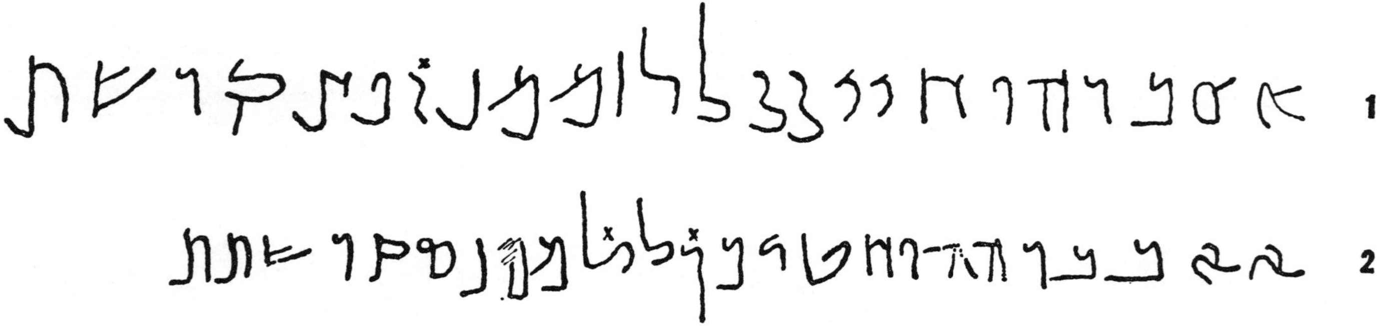

FIGURE 7. EARLY NABATAEAN SCRIPTS

Line 1. The script of the El-Kutbā' Inscription published by Clermont-Ganneau, *RAO* VIII, Pl. VII. It may be dated provisionally in 77 B.C.

Line 2. The script of the Rabb'el Inscription (*CIS* II, Tab. XLV, No. 349) from *ca.* 66 B.C.

angular base.[110] Each of these peculiarities appears first in the semiformal script of Qumran.

Early Nabataean is to be explained, therefore, as going back to a script with many traits characteristic of the Archaic formal hand, with a number of traits stemming from an Archaic semiformal tradition. It does not, however, combine formal and semiformal characteristics in the fashion in which they combine and develop in the Hasmonaean hand. Finally it is to be noted that in the first century B.C. the Nabataean lapidary style is influenced by a parallel cursive tradition,[111] and secondary final letters begin development.

The earliest of the Palmyrene inscriptions are three texts recently published by J. Starcky.[112] One of these, the inscription of the priests of Bêl, is dated in the year 44 B.C.; the other two are roughly contemporary.[112a] After this little group of texts comes the inscription published by Du Mesnil du Buisson dated in 33 B.C.[113]

Palmyrene has achieved a strongly individual style when our series of inscriptions begins. However, it gives clear-cut evidence of descending from an archetype closely allied to the Archaic semiformal character (see Fig. 6, line 2). The letters are broad and simplified. *'Alef, bet, gimel, waw, yod, lamed, mem, 'ayn, shin,* and *taw* stem from forms virtually identical with the Archaic semiformal of Qumran (4QQoh[a]; 4QPr[a]). *He* derives from a more cursive tradition; *het* (domed crossbar), *kaf* (figure-three), *qof* (formal, short-legged type), and *ṣade* (with the "T"-shaped arm) belong to different traditions, but with parallels in the same period. *Dalet* has assumed its extreme (semiformal) stance.

These data on the Nabataean and Palmyrene scripts all point to the conclusion that the national scripts had their origin in the first half of the second century B.C. and became wholly independent in the main lines of their special development by about 150 B.C. On typological grounds we have already attempted to place the transition between the two scripts which we have called proto-Jewish Archaic and Hasmonaean into precisely the same era. Indeed, since the typological sequence of the Archaic and Hasmonaean scripts is tied down at either end by closely dated documents, an absolute date for the transition to the new Hasmonaean style in the mid-second century has seemed inevitable. The discovery that the transitional periods of the sister scripts fall precisely in the same general period, diverging at the same stage in the development of the Aramaic character, tends to confirm the chronology of the Jewish scripts on independent palaeographical grounds.

At the same time, the common date of the rise of the national scripts demands historical explanation. We should expect that the national scripts would make their appearance in a time of nationalistic expansion and resurgent Orientalism. It is not by chance, therefore, that it is precisely in the same era, the second and third quarters of the second century B.C., that we witness the decline of the Hellenistic empires, following the death of Antiochus Epiphanes (163 B.C.), and the rise of autonomous states in Judaea, Nabataea, and Palmyra. By 140 B.C., Judaea had completed her war of independence and Simon had established the Hasmonaean dynasty. The Nabataean dynasty of Ḥaretat I was founded in Maccabean times and had sufficiently consolidated its power by the late second century, so that Ḥaretat II and ʿObodat I were enabled to proceed to conquests abroad. Palmyra no doubt exercised considerable autonomy during the Seleucid civil wars and became free of any sustained control from Antioch after the fall of Seleucia in 141 B.C.

5: The later Archaic hands, both formal and semiformal, now can be given absolute dates within fairly narrow limits with no little assurance. The transition from the Archaic to the formal Hasmonaean hand begins in a script of the type of 4QDeut[a], which must be dated *ca.* 175–150 B.C. (Fig. 2, line 1). The semiformal character develops immediately before the rise of the national scripts and must be attributed, in all likelihood, to the first half of the second century B.C. 4QQoh[a] may be dated between 175 and 125 B.C.; 4QPr[a] is scarcely later. The mixed or semicursive hand of the Nash Papyrus also belongs within this transitional era, preferably toward 150 B.C. At the upper end of the Archaic formal series is the pure formal hand of 4QSam[b]. We have seen that its affinities are with fourth-century documents, and that it must be judged a formal third-century script paralleling the third-century cursive. It stands at a considerable distance, typologically, from the formal hands of the second century B.C. and can be safely attributed to the last half of the third century, and probably toward the end of the century. 4QJer[a] is only slightly more developed; it probably falls within the limits 225–175 B.C.

Most difficult to date with precision is the strange protocursive script of 4QEx[f]. In our analysis above we underlined its primitive characteristics, but also argued that the manuscript is probably copied in a script whose tradition is more conservative than that of the better-known cursives from Egypt. The manuscript may be given extreme limits of 275–200 B.C., and a date in the third quarter of the third century seems quite suitable. In this case, 4QEx[f] is the earliest of the manuscripts of Qumran.

II. THE DEVELOPMENT OF THE FORMAL JEWISH HAND

1: Out of the many scores of exemplars of the formal Hasmonaean script from Qumran, we have selected three typical specimens, the first from the transitional period at the beginning of the Hasmonaean development, 4QDeut[a] (Fig. 2, line 1), the second a typical Hasmonaean book hand from the middle of the period, 4QDeut[c] (Fig. 2, line 2), and the third a late transitional script from the end of the Hasmonaean period or the beginning of the Herodian epoch, 4QSam[a] (Fig. 2, line 3). These will be used to furnish the framework of the historical typology of the Hasmonaean hand. The absolute dates for the Hasmonaean series are established between 150 B.C., as we have shown in the preceding section, and *ca.* 30 B.C., as required by the well-fixed chronology of the Herodian formal hands. The practice alphabet from Qumran, from a stratum sealed in 31 B.C., exhibits the mixture of developed and undeveloped letters characteristic of the transitional period at the beginning of the Herodian series[114] and, except for its crudity, could have been substituted for 4QSam[a]. The better-known script of 1QIsa[a][115] might have been used in place of 4QDeut[c]; both must be dated toward 100 B.C.; the script of the published scroll, however, includes several idiosyncratic forms; 4QDeut[c] was copied by a more conventional scribe.[116]

'Alef in 4QDeut[a] sometimes is very small, almost identical with the *'alef* of 4QJer[a]. Its left leg in such forms is extremely short and made low on the diagonal axis of the *'alef*. In other forms, the Hasmonaean tendency to enlarge *'alef* (by attraction to semiformal or cursive styles) makes itself felt. In these forms the left leg is strongly bowed, but never crescent shaped. The axis is straight, the right arm thin and short. The fully developed Hasmonaean *'alef* (4QDeut[c]; 1QIsa[a]) has become a letter of "standard" size. This tendency to uniformity in the size of letters, arising especially in the early semiformal hand, is felt throughout the Hasmonaean alphabet. By the end of the Hasmonaean period, there is a feeling for a base line as well as a ceiling line, and in late Herodian manuscripts the scribe occasionally lines in a base line. The *'alef* of 4QDeut[c] has a lengthened and only slightly bowed left leg, which reaches as low as the bottom of the axis stroke. The top of the left leg is moving toward the top of the axis (on its way to the Herodian inverted-"v" form). The right arm has become larger and, as early as 4QDeut[c] and 1QIsa[a], has a slight tendency to bow (cf. the early semiformal *'alef*). In the late Hasmonaean and early Herodian *'alef* these tendencies become fully evolved. The bowed right arm thickens at the top; the left leg straightens further and has moved to the top of the downstroke of the axis. At the beginning of the Herodian period, the axis and left leg begin to be made without lifting the pen (the inverted-"v" form).

Bet in 4QDeut[a] is still narrow, and the downstroke curves into a short horizontal base; the form is not influenced by semiformal styles. In 4QDeut[c], however, the Hasmonaean form is fully developed. The letter has broadened; the right downstroke is vertical or even bowed back before turning into a horizontal base stroke. The angular corner of the downstroke and base stroke is characteristic. *Bet* is still, however, made without lifting the pen; the base is made from right to left. At the end of the Hasmonaean era and the beginning of the Herodian period two forms of *bet* are used: one which continues the earlier Hasmonaean treatment of *bet,* but frequently exaggerates the bending back of the downstroke, so that instead of a right angle an acute angle (or a slight overlapping of strokes) is made when the scribe reverses the direction of his pen to draw the base;[117] the other form abandons the older formal technique and draws the base stroke in a separate, left-to-right stroke normally breaking through the vertical slightly at the "corner." Often it is difficult in individual instances to differentiate the two forms without minute examination of the pen stroke. The latter *bet* develops early in the

Hasmonaean period in the cursive and semicursive scripts. It invades the formal hand in the transition between the Hasmonaean and Herodian scripts, but does not wholly oust the early type until late Herodian times.

The *gimel* of 4QDeut[a] is a full-fledged Hasmonaean type found in none of the formal (or semiformal) proto-Jewish hands. The right leg is no longer straight but singly or doubly curved; the left leg joins, not at or near the top of the right leg but at the point where the right leg bends inward to the left. The lowering of the left leg and the curving of the right result from a cursive tendency which continues to operate until the left leg joins near the base of the right leg. In the cursive, indeed, the *gimel* is often made without lifting the pen after the right downstroke. The late Hasmonaean *gimel* (4QSam[a]) is often made with a singly curved right leg; the left leg is now often below the mid-point of the right; sometimes there is a slight thickening at the top of the right leg, a rudimentary tick.

Dalet in 4QDeut[a] is relatively narrow, its head sharply ticked; it is not until we reach the scripts toward the end of the second century that the semiformal *dalet* replaces the formal *dalet* (4QDeut[c]; 1QIsa[a]). In the typical Hasmonaean form the head is made without lifting the pen. In certain late Hasmonaean hands, and especially in the Herodian period, the right downstroke is made separately, after lifting the pen. The head of the Hasmonaean *dalet* no longer should be described as "ticked"; it is made with a left, distinct downstroke, slightly slanting, turning in an acute angle to the horizontal line of the crossbar. Then the pen moves up sharply (contrary to *resh*), and then down in the slanted (to the right) right leg (4QQoh[a]; 4QPr[a]; 4QDeut[c]).

The *he* of 4QDeut[a] retains a number of Archaic traits not typical of standard Hasmonaean types. It is relatively large, not of "standard" size. The right leg is slanted down to the right; the left leg is usually slanted down to the left; the crossbar is drawn in formal style, from the right to the left, and is straight, long, and heavily shaded. Toward the end of the second century, a tendency to loop slightly back into the left leg develops. It is invisible in the heavily shaded crossbars of early *he*s;[118] in the simplified stroke of 4QDeut[c] (cf. 1QIsa[a]), the form becomes transparent. The crossbar is drawn right to left; at the end of the stroke on the left, the crossbar tends to drop preparatory to retracing and turning down to the left leg. Sometimes the pen is lifted, sometimes not; in either case, the curving down of the crossbar on the left is normal. In its next stage (4QSam[a]) the left side of *he* is regularly made without lifting the pen, often giving a triangular shape to the left end of the crossbar.[119]

The Archaic semiformal hand introduces a *waw* with a curled head and more or less straight downstroke. In 4QDeut[a] the older formal *waw* is frequent, but an influence from the semiformal type has shaped the direction of development. Some *waws* have a small, curled (but still shaded) head and straight downstroke. The latter form is regular in 4QDeut[a] and 1QIsa[a]. In the late Hasmonaean script, the curled head becomes an angular hook, often shaded so that a triangular effect is given. The latter development of the head of *waw* parallels the development of *yod* so that the heads of *waw* and *yod* become virtually identical in some (but not all) scripts of the early Herodian period. The ligaturing of *waw* and especially *yod* with the preceding letter becomes increasingly frequent in the late Hasmonaean era, continuing on, of course, into the Herodian scripts.

Zayn does not appear in 4QDeut[a], but in other very early formal Hasmonaean hands it is a simple vertical stroke or, rarely, a stroke slightly and evenly shaded at the top (cf. 4QJer[a]). In 4QDeut[c] the simple form is normal; in 1QIsa[a] and less often in 4QDeut[c] the shaded form is found. Rarely, but significantly, the shading is slightly heavier on the right side of the top or, with much the same effect, the stroke is slightly bent at the top. This trait develops and becomes a standard element of *zayn* at the end of the Hasmonaean era and in the early Herodian script. Sometimes the form is a downstroke with a triangular bulge to the right at the top; often a "head" is created by bending the stroke to the right near the top.

The *ḥet* of 4QDeut[a] is somewhat unstable. Sometimes its crossbar curves up at mid-stroke reminiscent of the domed *ḥet;* sometimes it slants upward from the right to left in semiformal fashion. The legs are more or less straight. The semiformal treatment of the crossbar is dominant in the standard Hasmonaean scripts (4QDeut[c]; 1QIsa[a]). Sometimes, however, the crossbar tends to loop slightly or form a continuous stroke with the left leg. This produces a new effect. The crossbar drops at its point of juncture with the left leg, "lowering" the crossbar.

The form becomes frequent after the turn of the second century (e.g., IQS). It continues to evolve in the late Hasmonaean period; the crossbar becomes short, almost straight, or bent downward in the center. In the transitional scripts the *ḥet* is often made without lifting the pen, the right leg now also "looping" slightly into the crossbar. This produces the neat *ḥet* of 4QSam[a].

Tet in 4QDeut[c] is Archaic in style, only slightly evolved beyond 4QSam[b]. Other early Hasmonaean hands (e.g., 4QGen[a]) already show the influence of the semiformal development; in 4QDeut[c] the semiformal *ṭet* with its angular base and shortened left arm has become standard. In the late Hasmonaean forms the left arm shortens to the ceiling line; the base flattens and becomes broad. A major shift takes place in the transitional and early Herodian hands in the fashion in which *ṭet* is drawn. The left arm and base line are drawn first; but then the pen is lifted and the right, curled portion is made separately, ending in a downstroke into the base line. This technique appears first in the Hasmonaean semicursive and spreads to the formal character as early as 4QSam[a].[120]

Yod at the beginning of the Hasmonaean era may be made in the style of 4QSam[b] (with three movements) or in the semiformal style. In 4QDeut[a], *yod* is small, a shaded triangle with a short right leg actually drawn in three movements. The semiformal, inverted "v"-shaped *yod* shortly becomes the standard form (4QDeut^c; 1QIsa^a). Toward the end of the Hasmonaean era the older *yod* has become a short stroke with a triangular tick; the semiformal has lengthened the right leg and rotated its stance slightly to form a hooked, *waw*-like form. The *yod* regularly is attached by ligatures to the preceding letter; this creates a lengthened right leg in ligatured forms, and often the ligatured form influences the independent form, so that *yod* and *waw* become easily confused, each having a fairly long right leg. In the scribe's mind, however, though often not reflected in his pen, the head or left leg (as the case may be) of *yod* extends farther to the left than in the case of *waw*.

The medial *kaf* of 4QDeut^a is long, narrow, and often inclined to a figure-three form. The base is rounded in Archaic fashion. The form persists in slightly shortened form in early Hasmonaean scripts, surviving in 4QDeut^c. However, in Deut^c, and especially in 1QIsa^a, a new form, derived from the semiformal style, makes its appearance. In this form the downstroke straightens and turns in a right angle into a straight, slightly slanting base line. In 4QSam^a, at the end of the era, this form is regular. Final *kaf* in the early Hasmonaean script is made with a small, tightly ticked head and excessively long tail. The head broadens and the tail shortens toward the end of the second century (4QDeut^c),[121] but otherwise it changes only slightly (cf. 4QSam^a) until the early Herodian period when the head abruptly broadens.

Lamed is a relatively static letter form in the Hasmonaean era. The arm above the ceiling line tends to lengthen in formal hands early in the period, to remain short in hands influenced more strongly by semiformal traditions (4QDeut^c). Late in the period (4QSam^a) the long-armed variety becomes dominant. A major change in the formal *lamed,* the enlargement of the hook, does not take place until Herodian times.

The medial *mem* of 4QDeut^a preserves the formal, long, and slim lines of Archaic scripts. The head is narrow, ticked; the right downstroke plunges deep below the ceiling line; the left diagonal is long, sometimes gently curved up, especially in ligatures with following letters. In early Hasmonaean scripts (4QGen^a) and *a fortiori* in mid-Hasmonaean hands (4QDeut^c) the semiformal broad *mem* (cf. 4QPr^a) ousts the older formal style. The right downstroke shortens radically in the mid- and late-Hasmonaean period. It straightens and angles (rather than curves) into a slightly slanting, straight base line. The development follows a pattern of the Hasmonaean script: the base of medial *kaf,* final *mem,* and often that of *pe* and *ṣade* (cf. *bet*) shift in the same sequence from gently curved to angular bases of much the same stroke. The left diagonal shortens in the Hasmonaean script, but even in transitional scripts (4QSam^a) continues to be drawn downward to the left (contrary to developed Herodian forms, on which see below), as may be ascertained in forms where ligatures occur.

Final *mem* is extremely long and narrow in 4QDeut^a (cf. 4QJer^a), and often the letter is "open" at the lower right. The right downstroke is curved at the base. The form shortens and broadens in the course of the Hasmonaean period. The right downstroke becomes vertical, turns at an angle into a slanting straight base toward the turn of the century (see above). The formal, final *mem* is under the influence of the semiformal hand; however, the left diagonal "breaks through" at the top in formal hands; in the semiformal it normally does not (4QPr^a; IQS). In the late Hasmonaean period, at least in some hands (4QSam^a), the left diagonal of final *mem* is drawn downward at an angle to the cross stroke of the head and then turns into a vertical direction at the crossbar. The form becomes regular in early Herodian times.

Nun in non-final positions steadily shortens in the Hasmonaean period in line with the trend toward uniform letter size. In the elegant formal hand the downstroke bends to the right at the top, a vestigial element which becomes active and develops anew at the end of the Hasmonaean, and especially in the Herodian hand, into a bent or shaded head, much like the development of the head of *zayn*. Aside from a tendency to grow short, final *nun* remains fairly static in the Hasmonaean era.

Samekh in the Archaic formal hand was drawn in a double-hooking motion, beginning at the top of the upper left "hook." The semiformal hand introduces a new form in which the upper left hook is simplified and some-times the left stroke is drawn downward in Archaic style (4QPr^a), sometimes upward (4QQoh^a). The *samekh* of 4QDeut^a, in the transitional period, is Archaic, both in the fashion it is penned and in its narrow, long shape (cf. 4QJer^a; 4QEx^f). However, the left downstroke has lengthened. In early Hasmonaean hands a developed form of the semiformal *samekh* is introduced. It is penned beginning at the lower left in an upward motion, looping back into the shoulder (4QGen^a; 4QDeut^c). The left upstroke is normally too short for the right curving downstroke to close the form (1QIsa^a), or the right downstroke does not curve sufficiently to form a junction; in any case, it is "open" at the bottom. The *samekh* closes at the bottom in the middle phase of the Hasmonaean epoch in the semicursive scripts; the closing of the *samekh* in the formal hand begins sporadically in late Hasmonaean scripts,[122] becoming the standard form in early Herodian hands.[123]

'Ayn in 4QDeut^a is very small, like the Archaic formal *'ayn,* but rounded, the right arm breaking through below only slightly. The right arm lengthens in subsequent scripts, and in late Hasmonaean scripts the letter has become generally larger. In transitional scripts, in elegant formal hands, the right arm develops a sharp curve at the top or a slightly thickened tip, and the arm below the top tends to straighten, the beginning of the clockwise rotation of *'ayn* in formal Herodian scripts.

Medial *pe* in the early Hasmonaean script develops an angular peak; the right downstroke straightens and curves into a horizontal base. By the beginning of the first century the curve is lost, and the right downstroke turns at a right angle into a slightly slanting, straight base following a general Hasmonaean trend (1QIsa^a). The form persists until the end of the period.

Meanwhile, in the cursive and semicursive hands, the technique of penning the base of *pe* shifts (as in the case of *bet* and *kaf*) so that the stroke is drawn from left to right rather than the reverse. Only rarely, however, does this technique invade the formal style.

Final *pe,* when it is used in Hasmonaean scripts, retains the Archaic curved head (4QDeut^c), but, especially in the early Hasmonaean period, tends to shift its stance counterclockwise from the vertical (cf. 4QQoh^a; 4QDeut^c). However, the latter trait is not universal, and by the end of the Hasmonaean era final *pe* usually has a vertical stance. As is to be expected, the long tail of Archaic formal final *pe* is shortened in semiformal manner in the early, and especially in developed, Hasmonaean hands.

Medial *ṣade* in 4QDeut^a retains the gently curved or oblique right arm of older forms. Medial and final forms are distinguished by the long, straight tail of the final form, by the slightly bent tail of the medial form. In the developed Hasmonaean hand (1QIsa^a; cf. 4QDeut^c), the right arm is sharply bent, and the bend of the tail develops into a typical Hasmonaean base stroke. Toward the end of the Hasmonaean era, and in the transitional scripts (4QSam^a), two types evolve: a cursive *ṣade,* made without lifting the pen (cf. 4QDan^c; Fig. 4, line 2), which sometimes invades the formal script; and a formal style in which the right arm is thickened at the top instead of bent. Often the types are conflated (4QSam^a; 4QDan^c) in the transitional period, less often in the Herodian scripts.

Qof in 4QDeut^a and the later Hasmonaean hands is unstable in length. The *qof* with virtually no tail, which had its vogue in certain of the Archaic scripts, does not survive. While some Hasmonaean scripts use a fairly short *qof* (4QDeut^c), most are influenced by the semiformal and semicursive scripts of the Hasmonaean period in which the tail of *qof* is steadily lengthening. More significant typologically is the treatment of the head. The early Hasmonaean *qof* shows a tendency to move the tail leftward along the head so it joins, not to the right of the downward tick at the beginning of the "s"-shaped head, but with the tick (4QGen^a; 4QDeut^c). In the late Hasmonaean script this tendency has turned into a characteristic trait (4QSam^a), giving rise to new techniques of penning *qof.* The flaring, heavy tick of *qof* thus begins to atrophy in scripts of late Hasmonaean date.

The *resh* of 4QDeut^a retains the narrow Archaic form; the right shoulder, if not ticked, is sharp. The early Hasmonaean *resh* normally remains narrow, but the right shoulder is increasingly rounded, and the stance of the downstroke becomes increasingly oblique, two tendencies originating in the Archaic semiformal. They are fully developed in the late Hasmonaean *resh* (4QSam^a).

Shin in early Hasmonaean formal scripts also perpetuates semiformal traditions. The lower left arm is gently curved, or bent back *slightly* at the beginning of the stroke. The upper arm also tends to curve in certain hands, and in some is looped into the left downstroke (4QDeut^c). At the end of the period, both right arms are normally bent back, or alternately are slightly thickened at the ends. The development follows the pattern of the right leg of *'ayn,* and the right arm of *ṣade,* in some degree.[124] In certain late Hasmonaean scripts of semiformal derivation, the left downstroke is also curved and "breaks through" at the bottom.

Taw in 4QDeut[a] is archaic both in its excessive size and doubly curved left leg. The right leg has lengthened to equal the left. In 4QDeut[c] and 1QIsa[a] the Hasmonaean form has fully emerged. The *taw* has been reduced in size radically, though it normally is slightly larger than the standard letter size. The left leg ends no longer in a curved flourish, but in an angular base. The gentle leftward curve at the top of the left leg straightens in the course of the Hasmonaean development and becomes short, so that by the end of the period *taw* is no longer a "kerned" letter[125] (4QSam[a]). Actually, this "shortening" of the upper part of the left leg is better described as a lifting and straightening of the beginning of the right leg.[126]

2: The term *Herodian* is used here and throughout our paper to apply to the era 30 B.C. to A.D. 70, that is, to the last century before the fall of Jerusalem to Titus, which is roughly equivalent to Period II at Qumran (31 B.C. to A.D. 68).[127] At the same time, it applies fittingly to a stage of the formal script, which, owing to the emergence of a complex of new characteristics at the end of the Hasmonaean era, has its own style and integrity. In the Herodian era the formal script finally achieves full uniformity of letter size; only the final letters, *qof* and *lamed,* are "kerned." There is a conscious feeling for a base line. Ligatures become increasingly frequent in the early Herodian formal scripts.[128] The Herodian scripts are marked also by the development of *keraiai,*[129] or ceriphs. These are rudimentary in the thickened, bent, or ticked elements of strokes in transitional and early Herodian scripts, become fully evolved in later Herodian hands, and develop into a baroque phase in the formal book hands of the First Jewish Revolt and the Bar Kokhba period (A.D. 70–135).

The evolution of the scripts in the Herodian period is very swift. An early Herodian formal script and a late formal script are easily distinguished. Our analysis will deal chiefly with these formal hands. There are also at least two semiformal script types. One is an elegant, but free and rounded character, the other a vulgar version of the formal character. The former, or rounded semiformal (hereafter *Round* semiformal) is not descended directly from the early semiformal script discussed above, though it serves a similar function and has a number of traits in common.[130] One is tempted to call it a *Rustic* semiformal as opposed to a *Square* formal, borrowing the two (rather misleading) terms applied to the elegant styles of Roman capital script in contemporary and later documents. The Vulgar semiformal is more difficult to describe since its tradition is loose, often mixed, with little integrity. Certain early Herodian specimens show some traits which may stem from the late, more or less degenerate Hasmonaean phase of the early semiformal script.[131] It may be that with further study the term "Vulgar semiformal" will prove to be the label of a genus rather than a species. At all events, the script is a crude, simplified form of the Herodian formal script which, by and large, replaces, together with the Round semiformal, Hasmonaean semiformal and semicursive traditions and which survives in the post-Herodian era in the so-called "chancellery" hand of Murabba'ât.[132]

We have chosen seven scripts to represent the Herodian era (Fig. 2, lines 4–10). The first two are early Herodian, one formal (1QM), one a Round, or Rustic semiformal (1QNum[b]). The Vulgar semiformal will be drawn into the analysis only at special points where it aids our understanding of the evolution of the elegant book hands.[132a] The script of 1QM (Fig. 2, line 4) is an excellent example of the delicate, usually minuscule, formal script which evolved directly from transitional hands of the type of 4QSam[a] (Fig. 2, line 3). Its lapidary equivalent is found in the Běnê Ḥezîr Inscription from about the turn of the Christian era.[133] Similarly, 4QNum[b] is a typical exemplar of the extremely popular Round semiformal style.[134] Five scripts have been chosen to represent the complex evolution of the late Herodian formal character. 4QDan[b] (Fig. 2, line 6) and 4QDeut[j] (Fig. 2, line 7),[135] especially the latter, exhibit the characteristic thick ductus and squat configuration of the late formal scripts of Qumran.[136] Perhaps the latest formal hand of Qumran is to be found in 4QPs [Sn 38] (Fig. 2, line 8). Its script is very nearly as highly evolved as the hand of another manuscript of Psalms from the unidentified provenience south of Murabba'ât (*Unid Ps;* Fig. 2, line 9), dating to the end of the first century of the Christian era.[136a] From a comparison of the idiosyncrasies of the two scripts, it is easily shown that the stylized, formal hand of 4QPs and its congeners is the precursor, or archetype of the official Biblical book hand of the post-Herodian, Bar Kokhba era (A.D. 70–135).

In discussing the latest scripts of Qumran, i.e., the last phase of the Early Jewish script, we shall refer to the book hands of Murabba'ât: Mur Gen-Ex,[137] and Mur XII.[138] In Fig. 2, line 10, we have chosen a closely related script to terminate our series taken from a contract dated in the year A.D. 133.[139] Our concern here, however, is with the Early Jewish character, and reference will be made to hands later than A.D. 70 only as they are useful in fixing the direction of evolution of the earlier scripts and in adding precisely dated termini to the Early Jewish typological series.

'Alef in the early Herodian formal script (1QM) is characterized by rudimentary *keraiai*. The right arm is thickened frequently at the top; the left leg is bent to the right in a tick. The *'alef* of the contemporary, early Herodian 4QNum[b] is similar, though the *keraia* of the left leg is merely a rightward bulge, the right arm more often simple (cf. 4QSam[a]). The *'alef* of 1QM is always made with the oblique axis drawn upward, the left leg downward in a continuous stroke either overlapped at the peak or in the developed inverted-"v" configuration.[140] The tick of the left leg develops

as a vestige of the older curled leg, but also as part of a movement toward the final stroke, the right arm. The *'alef* of 4QNum[b] is drawn in identical fashion, but with a free, "s"-shaped axis, developed in anticipation of the overlapping movement into the left leg. The late Herodian *'alef* is characterized by highly evolved *keraiai,* the advanced inverted-"v" style of penning the oblique axis and left leg, and a heavy-lined, squat form.[141] In the latest Qumran hands (4QDeut[j] and 4QPs) the oblique axis is doubly curved, and the trait characterizes the Murabba'ât book hand (Mur XII). The tick at the base of the left leg is not always found in *'alefs* of Murabba'ât or the late Herodian of Qumran (4QDeut[j]), but the element is not vestigial as is clearly evidenced by the baroque *keraia* used in Mur XII and Mur Gen-Ex. The *keraia* of the right arm of *'alef* is particularly characteristic in the late Herodian scripts; it is on its way to becoming the bar or crown of the Murabba'ât book hand.

Bet in the early Herodian scripts is in process of two shifts. The right, upper shoulder is losing its tick, and the direction of the base stroke is shifting from right to left to left to right. The first shift is not systematically carried through the scripts until late Herodian and post-Herodian times.[141a] The second begins in the transitional scripts, stemming ultimately from the Hasmonaean semicursive. It is difficult to be sure always if the change has taken place in careful hands (1QM); it is normal in the semiformal (4QNum[b]). This change in the method of penning *bet* soon creates the *bet* whose base line extends beyond the vertical right downstroke. The new form is sporadic in early Herodian scripts, systematic in late Herodian scripts.

Gimel in 1QM continues traits already visible in late Hasmonaean hands. The left leg is low on the right downstroke. The right downstroke is in process of change from a simple, curved or doubly curved, oblique stroke to a stroke thickened at the top and either gently curved or straight (1QM). In the Herodian semiformal, the curved form becomes exaggerated (4QNum[b]). The late Herodian *gimel* is distinguished by the *keraia* at the top of the right downstroke, now fully developed from the thickened or bent top of earlier hands.

Dalet in 1QM and most of the early Herodian formal hands is made, not with a continuous stroke as in the Hasmonaean hands, but in two motions, the pen being lifted on completion of the horizontal part of the head, the right downstroke being penned independently. The semiformal hand, to the contrary, often conserves the Hasmonaean technique, but evolves in its own direction by tending to form a semiloop, or characteristic "s"-shaped right leg. The late Herodian *dalet* shows the effects of the change of stroke in the early Herodian script. The horizontal often breaks through the vertical leg (4QDan[b]; 4QDeut[j]; Mur Gen-Ex; etc.), or the right leg drops so that it begins flush with the horizontal stroke (4QDeut[j]; Mur 133[142]). The latter form is sporadic.

He in 1QM and the early Herodian formal scripts is little evolved beyond 4QSam[a]. The cross stroke is drawn to the left, "drops" slightly before doubling back or looping slightly into the left leg. The Round semiformal hands of the early Herodian period present a variety of letter forms. All share the continuous stroke of the Herodian *he,* but the crossbar of the semi-formal script is heavily shaded. The movement of the pen into the left leg is frequently triangular as in 4QSam[a] (e.g., 4QEx[a]), or a distorted triangle caused by a downward movement of the pen before doubling back into the loop or triangle (4QNum[b]). One new rudimentary element of the early Herodian formal *he* betrays the direction of the evolution: at the top of the *right* leg above the crossbar a small projection to the right of the right leg begins to appear. This projection is caused by the scribe doubling back or looping in, moving from the top of the right leg (an upstroke) into the horizontal bar. In the late Herodian script of 4QDan[b] the new technique is fully revealed. The *he* of 4QDeut[j] is more evolved. The scribe now "lowers" the loop by using a triangular movement, precisely the equivalent triangular movement to that used on the left side of the crossbar. The *he* of the type of 4QDeut[j] continues with little change into the post-Herodian scripts (cf. especially Mur XII).[143] An interesting lapidary version of the late Herodian *he,* a form with unshaded triangles, is found in the 3Q copper document as well as in late funerary inscriptions.[144]

Waw and *yod* evolve very slightly in the Herodian period. In the early Herodian formal hands the heads of *waw* and *yod* are usually shaded; in the Round semiformal they are normally simple angular heads. While theoretically the head of *yod* is larger than that of *waw,* the tail shorter, ligatured forms tend to minimize these distinctions. In the late Herodian hands, the extreme use of ligatures moderates, and *waw* and *yod* are increasingly distinguished, *waw* becoming slightly longer, *yod* tending to shrink.[145]

Zayn in the early Herodian hands takes two forms, a simple stroke thickened or slightly bent to the right at the top, or a doubly curved down-stroke, strongly bent to the right at the top, gently curved leftward at the base. The curved forms dominate in the Round semiformal scripts, the simple, shaded stroke in the formal character. Characteristically in the late Herodian hands the thickened or bent element develops into a *keraia,* a sharp tick angled upward to the peak of the downstroke. In 4QDeut[j] and post-Herodian hands, the base of the downstroke of *zayn* often curves slightly to the left.

Het in 1QM is made without lifting the pen in the fashion of late Hasmonaean forms. However, the letter is more developed in the treatment of the right shoulder. While the *ḥet* of 4QSam[a], for example, neatly moves from the right upstroke, dipping with only a slight overlapping into the crossbar, early Herodian *ḥets* are doubled back in the movement to the cross-bar, creating a characteristic projection to the right. The pattern is similar to that in the evolution of *he.* The semiformal *ḥet* of 4QNum[b] achieves a similar effect by curving the right leg inward before looping into the crossbar.

In late Herodian scripts the shoulder is made with a triangular stroke, again following the pattern of the evolution of the right shoulder of *he*. In the post-Herodian scripts, especially *Unid Ps* and Mur Gen-Ex (cf. 4QPs), the "projection" on the right of the right leg of *he* and *ḥet* drops very low; 4QDeut[j] occasionally anticipates this form of *ḥet*. The treatment of the left shoulder and leg of *ḥet* is not altered significantly in the Herodian period.

Ṭet in the Herodian era, early and late, continues to be made by drawing the left arm and base in one movement, the curled head and right downstroke in a second movement. The *ṭet* continues to grow broad and squat through the Herodian period. One new feature appears sporadically in the early Herodian semiformal and late Herodian hands, especially, a thickening or bending of the tip of the left arm. In the post-Herodian formal hands (*Unid Ps,* Mur xii, Mur 133), the feature, which we may call a *keraia*, is standard.

Medial *kaf* evolves only slightly beyond the transitional forms described above. The depth of the ticks of the head, especially of the right shoulder, becomes shallower in the early Hasmonaean formal scripts. In the Round semiformal *kaf,* the squarish head of the Hasmonaean semiformal (not formal) survives in evolved form. The right downstroke is straight or even curved outward (to the right), rather than curved inward in "figure-three" fashion. Medial *kaf* in the late Herodian and post-Herodian scripts becomes shorter and broader; sometimes this tendency sporadically appears in the early Herodian period (1QM), leading to an easy confusion of *kaf* and *bet* for a short period before *bet* develops its late Herodian base.

The final *kaf* of 1QM is a new form in the formal script, taken over from the semicursive script of the Hasmonaean period.[145a] The head is very broad, shaded, often without a tick at the beginning of the stroke. The right leg in the early Herodian scripts is often made as an isolated downstroke. The Round semiformal *kaf* retains its initial tick, but broadens and often loops or doubles back into the tail. In the late Herodian script of 4QDeut[j] the final *kaf* is drawn with a flat, broad crossbar which begins either with a slight tick or shading. The right shoulder is typologically significant, being made by doubling or looping back into the tail. The loop is flat (4QDeut[j]), or protrudes upward and to the right very slightly (4QPs). The "looped" form persists in post-Herodian scripts, sometimes forming a "low" triangle.

Lamed in the early Herodian period begins slowly to evolve a larger hook. Often a tendency to round as well as lengthen the final stroke may be seen in the formal hand, regularly and in exaggerated style in the semiformal (4QNum[b]). In the late Herodian hand the hook is fully enlarged (4QDan[b]; 4QDeut[j]). The thickened top of the upper arm of *lamed* is idiosyncratic in the Herodian era; however, in the post-Herodian period in the literary scripts a neat flaglike *keraia* comes into consistent use (cf. 4QPs).

Medial *mem* in 1QM and most of the earlier Herodian formal and elegant semiformal scripts (4QNum[b]; 4QEx[a]) are made in the late Hasmonaean technique, the left oblique stroke being penned last. However, the oblique often joins the ticked head in a fashion which makes difficult a determination of the order and direction in which the oblique is made. A new method of drawing medial *mem* is introduced in some early Herodian hands, especially Vulgar semiformals, and makes its way into the formal character. The left oblique is made first, upward into the shoulder of the letter and then down to form the right downstroke and base. A short, straight stroke or tick, added on the top of the oblique, completes the letter. In the late Herodian scripts (4QDan[b], 4QDeut[j]; 4QPs) and in the post-Herodian scripts the new technique dominates.

Final *mem* in the early Herodian script takes two forms, a relatively slender, long *mem* preserving Hasmonaean lines, used regularly in the formal script, and a broad squat form in the Round and Vulgar semiformals. In the formal final *mem,* especially, one particularly noteworthy development begins early in the Herodian period. In the late Hasmonaean formal hand, as we have noted above, the left downstroke begins above the crossbar in an oblique direction, turns at an angle at the crossbar into a vertical direction. In the early Herodian period the technique alters in some scripts: the downstroke begins flush with the crossbar, or even below it,[146] and a tick or short stroke is added above the bar.[147]

The new technique does not immediately oust the old. Typologically contemporary scripts may make use of either the older type (1QM) or the later type (1QGen Apoc).[148] In some scripts the types are mixed. Especially in the Round semiformal the older type persists late, sometimes invading the formal script of the late Herodian period.

In the late Herodian hand, the "ticked" *mem* is dominant (4QDan[b]) and continues in some post-Herodian hands (*Unid Ps*).[148a] However, in certain very late hands, the semiformal *mem* is taken over into the formal script; sometimes in such scripts an independent tick appears, sometimes not.[149] A third method of penning the left downstroke enters the formal script for the first time in the late Herodian period: a simplified *mem* with neither an independent tick nor an extension of the oblique above the crossbar.[150] Actually, a *mem* of this type is frequent in the early Herodian, Vulgar semiformal,[151] as well as in advanced Vulgar semiformal scripts.[152] It may be that this is the source of the new formal type. On the other hand, it may evolve from forms where the tick has moved to the right shoulder, merging with it. Such a possibility is suggested by the existence of manuscripts in which the simplified *mem* is frequent, but is mixed with an occasional *mem* "ticked" on the right shoulder (4QGen[b]; 4QPs), or a combination of the tendency of the formal evolution and the influence of the Vulgar semiformal may account for the appearance of the type in formal scripts. At all events, the simplified *mem* comes into consistent use first in the post-Herodian scripts.

Medial *nun,* by the early Herodian period, has reached "standard" height, except in certain ligatured forms where the archaic, long *nun* survives.[153] The vestigial bend at the beginning of the downstroke of *nun* becomes in effect a rudimentary *keraia* in late Hasmonaean and transitional scripts (4QSam[a]; 1QIsa[b]), sometimes a "bend," sometimes a thickening on the right of the downstroke. In the Round semiformal, the "bend" deepens (4QNum[b]); in the formal script, the thickening develops into a triangular *keraia* (1QM), and in the late Herodian scripts into a sharp *keraia,* either triangular or hooked downward (4QDan[b]). The post-Herodian letter is the expected baroque version of the latest Herodian type (4QDeut[j]).

It will be noted that the evolution of the heads of *gimel* and *zayn* are parallel to that of *nun.* As a matter of fact, the *nun,* the only letter of the three which "legitimately" has a curved head, leads in the evolution.

Final *nun* in the Herodian period continues in the late Hasmonaean tradition. In the late Herodian period a tendency develops to conform the head of the final *nun* to the *medial* pattern, that is, to transform the initial short, bent stroke into a *keraia.* The development is not completed fully, however, until post-Herodian times (Mur XII, Mur Gen-Ex).

Samekh in the early Herodian script (1QM) is drawn in the formal mode. The left leg is drawn upward, looping into the crossbar. However, *samekh* is now fully closed,[154] imitating in form, if not in technique, the Hasmonaean semicursive *samekh.*[155] Often in the semiformal scripts the loop is made in a heavy triangular motion (4QNum[b]); this form appears sometimes in the late Herodian formal, sometimes in the post-Herodian script (Mur XII).[156]

'Ayn in the early Herodian period develops its characteristic late form. In 1QM, for example, the left leg is initially bent to form a *keraia,* the lower part shifted clockwise in stance. The left arm has a slight tendency to thicken at the tip. The early-Herodian Round semiformal retains essentially the older, Hasmonaean semiformal *'ayn,* though often the beginning of the right and especially the left downstroke are thickened. The late Herodian *'ayn* shows little change from the formal early Herodian type. The chief development is in the further thickening of the tip of the left arm.

Medial *pe* in 1QM and early Herodian formal hands shows little change from late Hasmonaean forms. In the Round semiformal a slight tendency to curl the head under toward the right downstroke may be discerned; a similar tendency is found in the formal as well as semiformal final *pe.*

In the late Herodian scripts the head of *pe,* medial and final, becomes even more complex in some scripts (4QDeut[j]; 4QPs). The "curl" becomes angled before reaching the peak of the head. This doubly angled head does not wholly replace the simpler form in all late Herodian forms of *pe;* in the post-Herodian literary script, however, the form becomes dominant.[157]

Medial and final *ṣade* in the early Herodian scripts, both formal and semiformal, continue late Hasmonaean advanced forms. The right arm is bent up and thickened at the tip. In the semiformal scripts, especially, the thickening is often triangular, a *keraia* in effect, rather than a "bent arm."

The latter trait invades the formal character in many late Herodian scripts and is normal in post-Herodian hands. In the early Herodian Round semi-formal, another characteristic is significant, a curving of the top of the left arm of *ṣade* inward to the right. This trait also invades the late Herodian formal hand, usually appearing as a "bend," or thickening of the tip of the left arm. In the latest Herodian scripts, the thickening is transformed into a triangular *keraia* (pointing leftward), so that each arm of *ṣade* is ornamented. This baroque form becomes standard throughout the post-Herodian scripts.

Qof in the early Hasmonaean formal hands ceases to be made with two independent strokes. Rather, a new mode of penning this letter is introduced: the tailstroke is drawn upward, the pen moving continuously into the head, usually with a slight loop or doubling back. This form is not universal in early Herodian hands. The "atrophied," or small-"p"-form, developed in the late Hasmonaean period, survives, especially in the semiformal hands (4QNum[b]; 4QEx[a]). Under the influence of the Hasmonaean semicursive *qof,* presumably, the early Hasmonaean *qof* begins to plunge deep below the base line. Incidentally, this is the first evolutionary trend in operation in the late Hasmonaean and early Herodian period to run counter to the powerful impetus toward conformity to a uniform letter size.

In the late Herodian and post-Herodian formal hands the loop into the head grows in size, being made with a triangular motion in some late Herodian (4QDeut[j]) and post-Herodian hands (*Unid Ps;* Mur Gen-Ex; Mur XII).

Resh develops very little beyond late Hasmonaean forms in the Herodian period; the breadth of the head widens slightly; the tick at the beginning is penned in the style of the era in question, following the technique of *bet* and *dalet.*

Shin in 1QM is virtually identical with 4QSam[a] and the late Hasmonaean *shins.* An increased tendency for the left downstroke to break through below the right lower arm can be seen, especially in semiformal hands (4QNum[b]). However, the tendency, arising in the semicursive tradition, does not develop in Herodian hands and, indeed, is reversed in the late Herodian style. The bent or thickened right lower arm found in certain late Hasmonaean scripts is found regularly in early Herodian formal hands. In the late Herodian and post-Herodian periods, it follows the evolution of the right leg of *'ayn.* The upper right arm of *shin* is an especially sensitive typological indication. At the end of the Hasmonaean era, it is gently curved, or slightly thickened at the tip. This trait continues to be characteristic in most early Herodian scripts. In the middle and late Herodian period, the thickened, or curved tip develops into a *keraia,* and often the stroke stops, or thins out just short of the left downstroke (1QH [first hand]; 4QDan[b]). In the latest Herodian and post-Herodian scripts, the stroke develops a baroque (often triangular) *keraia;* the "stem" of the stroke, however, firmly joins the left downstroke. The right downstroke changes little in the Herodian period until immediately before the end of the period when in some scripts it begins to develop a *keraia* at the tip of the stroke. However, the ornament does not become general until the Second Jewish Revolt, that is, in the most developed of post-Herodian scripts.

The formal *taw* in the early Herodian era tends to be made in a continuous stroke. The shortening of the left leg and/or rise of the initial part of the right leg in the late Hasmonaean period initiates the shift. The left leg is now drawn upward and looped slightly into the right leg (1QM; 4QNum[b]). However, under the force of the cursive tradition, some scripts preserve the older mode of penning. New forms develop; for example, in the Vulgar semiformal a *taw* which is intermediate between the formal and looped cursive is frequent (cf. the 3Q Copper Document). In the late Herodian period *taw* becomes increasingly squat and broad.

III. THE DEVELOPMENT OF SCRIPTS IN SEMICURSIVE AND CURSIVE TRADITIONS

The Jewish cursive script in the post-Herodian period is now well known, thanks to the rich dated corpus of commercial and legal documents from Murabba'ât and elsewhere in the wilderness of Judah.[158] Two specimens of such script, one a true cursive (Mur 117[159]) and one related to the older semicursive tradition from A.D. 134[160] are given in Figure 5, lines 2–3. They serve as an "anchor" to Early Jewish typology. However, our interest here will be directed almost entirely to the earlier scripts in cursive traditions, especially to the Hasmonaean semicursive hands, which have never been studied systematically and which bristle with problems for the historical palaeographer.

The Herodian cursive is not adequately represented in the monuments and documents at our disposal. Certain ossuary groups contain cursive graffiti.[161] Cave IV, Qumran, has preserved a couple of fragmentary non-literary texts in the true cursive, one early Herodian.[162] The Bethphage Lid is an important witness to the cursive script of the late first century B.C., but has never been adequately published.[163] Recent work at Masada has produced an ostracon and fragment of a papyrus.[164] Most important is the Murabba'ât contract dated in the second year of Nero, 55/56.[165]

The cursive of the post-Herodian and Herodian periods, notably the Nero Papyrus, is a highly evolved, sophisticated script. Unfortunately for the palaeographer, it was not used as a literary hand, so that the long prehistory of its tradition can be reconstructed only indirectly from the Hasmonaean semicursive scripts, from occasional mixed scripts, cursive corrections in formal manuscripts, and, even more indirectly, from its influence upon semiformal and formal scripts.

The semicursive script springs from the crossing of two traditions, the early formal character and the cursive scripts of the second century B.C. From this combination toward the beginning of the Hasmonaean era, it gains its integrity as a script type. On the other hand, it is a script quite sensitive to the cursive development, and its evolution is never wholly independent of the cursive. For this reason, it exhibits a considerable variety even in scripts of the same date; one exemplar may stand very close to the cursive tradition, another quite close to the formal script.

The semicursive script at Qumran is represented largely in documents of the Hasmonaean Age. In the Herodian period, the semiformal scripts, especially the Vulgar semiformal, seem largely to replace the semicursive script in literary documents. The reappearance of the semicursive at Murabba'ât and elsewhere, however, guarantees its continued use for some purposes, at least in certain scribal circles. Its rarity in extant documents of the Herodian period is not especially surprising since it must have served chiefly as a "chancellery" hand, that is, for non-literary documents, and even in the Hasmonaean period at Qumran, it is a rare hand, especially rare in carefully prepared Biblical manuscripts.

The semicursive scripts, since they mix cursive and formal typological elements, provide extra, if interwoven and complex, criteria for dating. Since the script has a certain integrity in its tradition, an inner typology can be constructed; this is no simple task, owing, as we have noted, to the variety within the tradition. The formal attributes, or wholly formal letter forms can be fitted into the type series of the formal scripts; this task, too, is complicated since at times formal letter forms persist in the semiformal after their demise in formal scripts. Finally, the cursive features of the script can be related to the cursive development. Once again, this procedure is not easy; dated cursive scripts of the Herodian period are at a great distance, typologically, from even the most evolved cursive elements of the Hasmonaean semicursive scripts. The early cursive typology is a projection backward from the Herodian cursive, dependent in no small part on the semicursive tradition itself for elucidation and concreteness.

In Figure 3 we have given two specimen scripts of an early mixed script, combining, in unstable fashion, formal and cursive traits: the Nash Papyrus (line 1) and the Murabba'ât Ostracon (line 2). They form a group apart. In Figure 4 a type series of characteristic semicursive scripts is presented: an early Hasmonaean Biblical hand (4QXII[a], line 1); two developed Hasmonaean hands, one Biblical (4QDan[c], line 2), one from an unknown Aramaic work (line 3);[166] and three late Hasmonaean hands, the last two of which may be as late as the beginning of the Herodian period (lines 4–6).[167]

1: The script of the Nash Papyrus and the Murabba'ât Ostracon will not be studied in detail here. The Nash Papyrus (Fig. 3, line 1) stands very close to the formal tradition and can be fitted without difficulty into the formal typology in the transition between the Archaic and Hasmonaean eras, toward 150 B.C.[168] It is roughly contemporary with the (more formal) hand of 4QDeut[a] (Fig. 2, line 1). It mixes with its formal characters, cursive forms of *'alef, he, lamed, 'ayn, ṣade,* and *taw.* The Murabba'ât Ostracon uses cursive forms more extensively, but its remaining formal traits prohibit lowering its date below *ca.* 100 B.C.[169] The cursive features of these manuscripts will be taken up when appropriate in the discussion of the detailed characteristics of the Qumran semiformal scripts.

2: The *'alef* of the early Hasmonaean semicursive is normally little differentiated from the contemporary formal, or rather semiformal *'alef.* In 4QXII[a], for example, *'alef* has become large, unlike most specimens in 4QDeut[a]; its form, however, with its bowed left leg, is that of the Archaic semiformal and the early Hasmonaean formal scripts.

The looped cursive *'alef* which appears in the Nash Papyrus[170] rarely appears in the semicursive hands of the Hasmonaean period. Its influence is felt, however, in the curious form of 4QDan[c] and later, in a simplified form, it reappears.

The late Hasmonaean *'alef* requires little comment. It develops directly from the early semicursive type, little influenced by the development in the formal scripts of the inverted-"v" *'alef.* Even in the latest scripts (4QEnoch V), the semicursive *'alef* is drawn with three separate strokes, unlike contemporary and later (Herodian) formal styles.

The medial and final cursive forms of *'alef* in the Cave VI Papyrus (Fig. 4, line 6) require special comment. The looped, medial form stands intermediate between the older looped style of the Nash Papyrus and the Murabba'ât Ostracon and the *gamma*-shaped[171] form of the Herodian and post-Herodian cursive (Nero Papyrus; Mur 117). Already the loop is closing in 6Qp8 forms. But it is never wholly simplified as it appears in the Herodian and later examples of cursive *'alef.*[172] The final cursive *'alef* (6Qp8, Mur 117, etc.) is not a parallel development from the looped cursive *'alef.* It derives, as is normally the tendency in cursive scripts, from the older formal *'alef,* preserved in the final position. The form in the 6Q Papyrus is remarkably developed. However, the intermediate stage between the older final *'alef* and the full cursive final *'alef* used in the 6Q Papyrus and later documents is to be found in the final *'alef* of the Bethphage Lid and an occasional ossuary text,[173] an *'alef* which has lost its left leg. The cursive final *'alef* evolves from this form by being made with a single cursive movement of the pen.[174]

The dating of the shifts of forms of semicursive and cursive *'alefs* is not wholly clear. It is probable that the old looped *'alef* with an oblique axis (Nash Papyrus, Murabba'ât Ostracon) does not long survive after *ca.* 100 B.C.; the looped form with a single right arm probably lasts until early Herodian times (6Qp8), being simplified in Herodian times to the *gamma* form (Nero Papyrus). The true semicursive *'alef* changes almost imperceptibly in the Hasmonaean period.

Bet undergoes a major change at the beginning of the Hasmonaean period. Even in the earliest semicursives of this period (4QXII[a]), *bet* has begun to be made in two non-continuous strokes, the base an independent, shaded stroke made from left to right.[175] As we have observed, this style influences the formal hand only in the late period, at the beginning of the Herodian formal development. After its initial shift, *bet* remains fairly static in the semicursive. In the Herodian cursive, however, a new form appears, developed from the Hasmonaean semicursive, the "figure-2" *bet*, made in a continuous motion, but with the base drawn from left to right in semicursive style (Nero Papyrus).

Gimel in 4QXII[a] is undifferentiated from the Archaic series. As early as 4QDan[c], the right downstroke begins to bow in the fashion of Hasmonaean formal *gimels* (4QDeut[c]) and in the late first century B.C. shifts to a form drawn in a continuous stroke (Bethphage Lid, 4QEnoch V). Properly the latter form is cursive, however, and the older two-stroke semicursive *gimel* survives, even into the post-Herodian period (Mur 134).

Dalet in the early and late Hasmonaean semicursives retains the Archaic semiformal style, almost without change. The cursive *dalet*, made either with a simple head (Nero Papyrus; cf. Mur Ostracon) or with a head similar to cursive *resh* (Mur 117), belongs to a quite distinct tradition.

He in the early Hasmonaean semicursive manuscripts (4QXII[a]) is undifferentiated from the earliest Hasmonaean formal *he* (4QDeut[a]). In the developed hands (4QDan[c]), it tends to narrow; the crossbar usually slanting up to the left, contrary to the formal development. Normally, the crossbar is heavily shaded. In the late Hasmonaean and early Herodian period, two forms of *he* are used, one formal in origin, one cursive. In 4QS135[b] (Fig. 4, line 4), the cursive form, retaining a most archaic shape,[176] is used as medial *he*; the formal *he* is used in the final position. A similar distinction obtains in the 6Q Papyrus and often in late Hasmonaean semicursives.

In the late Hasmonaean and early Herodian period the cursive and semi-cursive develop at least two new forms of *he*. From the formal *he* develops the cursive form found in the Nero Papyrus; later this *he* is made almost in the fashion of a modern cursive *he*, the crossbar and right leg formed in a single curved stroke, the left leg separately, often not touching the crossbar or right leg.[177] The other *he*, cursive in origin, takes on a characteristic "reversed-'k' form," commonly made with the crossbar and left leg in a continuous angular stroke, meeting the right leg at the apex of the angle (Bethphage Lid, 4QEnoch V).[178]

Waw and *yod*,[179] in the Hasmonaean semicursive hands, follow the pattern of development of the formal scripts. The broad, inverted-"v" *yod* does not appear, however, and in some hands, especially in cursive or late scripts, *waw* is simplified into a slightly curved, headless stroke.

Zayn, throughout the Hasmonaean semicursive scripts, was made with a straight, simple stroke.[180] At the end of the period, and in the developed Herodian scripts, *zayn* has a head (6Qp8) or is bent to the right at the top (Nero Papyrus).

Het in 4QXII[a] is little differentiated from early Hasmonaean formal types. A cursive tendency appears strongly in 4QDan[c], the crossbar slanting up to the left. The latter form, however, is still distant from the "N"-form *het* (Bethphage Lid; Nero Papyrus). The *het* of 4QEnoch V is quite primitive also, warning against too late a date for its script. On the other hand, it may be that the cursive tendency that produced the cursive "N"-shaped *het* was reversed in the late Hasmonaean semicursive under the influence of the formal hand.

The *tet* in the earliest semicursive scripts combines early and novel features. The left arm is quite high; at the same time the base is flat (4QXII[a]) and the right side is made independently, downward, joining the base line at the right lower corner. It will be recognized that the latter trait is introduced into the formal script at the end of the Hasmonaean period. In certain late semicursive scripts this type is preserved in an evolved form: the left arm shortens, the base broadens (4QEnoch V). However, other semicursives follow rather the cursive trend (4QS135[b]). The base of *tet* becomes yet broader, and characteristically the right stroke begins flush with the base line, curls upward and down below the base line on the right. In the true cursive scripts, by the beginning of the Herodian period this form begins to be made with a continuous stroke, giving rise to a new "S"-curved *tet,* comparable to the cursive Nabataean *tet.* The most primitive examples are found in the Bethphage Lid.[181] One damaged specimen appears in the Nero Papyrus.[182] The even more evolved "S"-curved *tet* is standard, of course, in the post-Herodian cursives of Murabba'ât.

Medial *kaf* in 4QXII[a] is early in type: its head is normally narrow and ticked; a slight tendency to the figure-three shape persists. On the other hand, often the base is straight rather than curved, sometimes giving the impression that it is drawn from left to right in the fashion of semicursive *bet* and *pe* (4QPs.-Enoch[a]). The final *kaf* of 4QXII[a] maintains wholly the old formal tradition (cf. 4QDeut[a]).

In 4QDan[c], both medial and final *kaf* are drawn with a new technique. The "head" is drawn in a single shaded stroke, the right leg separately, beginning above the left stroke of the head. The medial form is, apparently, a transitory Hasmonaean type. The final form becomes popular, however, continuing into the later scripts (4QS135[b], 4QEnoch V, 6Qp8) and in the early Herodian period replaces the proper formal final *kaf* in the formal scripts (1QM).

Medial *kaf* in the later semicursives is unstable in type. In 4QPs.-Enoch[a], a cursive form is used, the base stroke shaded and drawn from left to right. This form appears sporadically in the semicursive scripts (6Qp8) and is regular in the Herodian and post-Herodian pure cursives (Nero Papyrus, Mur 117, etc.). 4QS135[b] preserves a developed formal type; 4QEnoch V exhibits the developed semicursive *kaf* which influences the early Herodian formal hand and persists in post-Herodian semicursives (Mur 134).

Lamed, as usual, is without special interest to the typologist. 4QXII[a] normally uses a form derived from the old protocursive (4QEx[f]), used also in Archaic and early Hasmonaean semiformal scripts (4QQoh[a]; 4QPr[a]). 4QDan[c] continues in the same tradition. In the late scripts, *lamed* is strongly influenced by formal styles (4QPs.-Enoch[a]; 4QS135[b]; 6Qp8); 4QEnoch V mixes formal and pure cursive forms (cf. the Nero and post-Herodian papyri).

The development of medial and final *mem* in the semicursive scripts is both important for typological dating and most interesting. A variety of forms, many conserving old traditions lost in the other scripts, persist in the Hasmonaean semicursive. 4QXII[a] preserves a medial form of *mem* which resembles superficially final *mem*. Actually, both the *medial* and final forms derive from the third-century cursive types which survive elsewhere, neither in the formal nor cursive series. The medial form is usually open at the bottom left. The left downstroke always cuts sharply through the crossbar. The medial and final forms are normally clearly distinguished. The final *mem* is longer and thinner, like the formal final *mem* (cf. 4QDeut[a]); however, normally the final form is closed at the bottom left.[183]

In 4QDan[c], the old cursive medial *mem* and the final *mem* have fallen together. In later scripts, under the influence of the formal hand, this older semicursive form appears only in final positions (4QS135[b]).

As early as 4QPs.-Enoch[a], the "ovoid," cursive *mem* intrudes itself into semicursive scripts. In the early scripts it is often a simple elongated circle, usually with only the slightest projection to the left. However, the form no doubt arises in the Archaic protocursive *mems* of the type of 4QEx[f] and is highly developed in the cursive script before its first appearance in our extant literary texts. The more typical form is probably that of 4QS135[b], which has a fairly developed projecting arm.[184] In the earlier semicursives this *mem* is made beginning with the projection, the pen moving clockwise. In later cursives the ovoid *mem* begins to be ligatured to following letters, so that the projection left is made last, often causing the top to open (cf. the Nero Papyrus).

In the late Hasmonaean and early Herodian semicursives, a medial semicursive version of the formal medial *mem* is often used (4QS135[b], 6Qp8). The form is very like the Round semiformal *mem* of the early Herodian period. In some forms (6Qp8), the left oblique stroke appears to be made first, as is the case in certain Herodian semiformal and (later) formal scripts.

Nun in non-final positions follows for the most part the development of its Hasmonaean formal counterpart. In the earlier scripts it is long, in the later script shortens, except in ligature with final *nun* (cf. 4QS135[b]). The Archaic curved downstroke and the Herodian bent, or ticked *nun* do not appear. Final *nun* usually follows the cursive pattern: a straight or slightly curved line extending far below the (theoretical) base line.

Samekh in the Hasmonaean semicursives normally follows a special cursive development. The form of 4QXII[a] is exceptional, following the pattern of the Archaic *semiformal samekh* (from which early *Hasmonaean* formal *samekh* stems). The latter form is open, the left stroke drawn upward, looping into the crossbar. The form in 4QXII[a] is, however, exceptionally long and narrow in the Archaic formal pattern. The standard semicursive *samekh* only superficially resembles the form of 4QXII[a] and later formal *samekh*s. Actually, it is drawn like the *Archaic formal samekh,* the left stroke downward, but without the characteristic Archaic hook.[185] The right portion is drawn clockwise, often in a simple curve producing a "D"-shaped *samekh* (4QDan[c]; 4QPs.-Enoch[a] [open at base]). In some forms, usually of a later date, the right shoulder becomes angular (4QS135[b]), and often in late Hasmonaean and Herodian semicursive and cursive scripts the left downstroke breaks downward below the curving base line (4QEnoch V; Nero Papyrus). This latter tendency does not develop systematically, however, and is rare in post-Herodian scripts.

The *'ayn* of 4QXII[a] is small, made with curved strokes in the fashion of early Hasmonaean formal *'ayns*. In the later scripts, two forms emerge, the older, small-"*y*" form (4QDan[c]; 4QPs.-Enoch[a]; 4QS135[b]) and a cursive-"*y*" form made in a continuous stroke. A development of this latter form, shifted clockwise, appears in the Nero Papyrus. The post-Herodian semicursive of the type of Mur 134 develops still another version of the "*y*" form.

The evolution of *pe* in the semicursive scripts offers little of special typological interest. We have already noted above the tendency in certain scripts to draw the base line from left to right in the fashion of *bet* and *kaf* (4QPs.-Enoch[a]). The looped *pe* of 4QDan[c] is worthy of note. The form is ephemeral.[186]

Sade early in Hasmonaean times develops its characteristic semicursive form, being drawn without lifting the pen. The form persists throughout the Hasmonaean semicursives with insignificant changes. A distinct final form of *sade* is rarely used in the semicursive scripts.

Qof in the early Hasmonaean semicursive hands develops from earlier protocursive and semiformal styles. The tail is long and often separated from the head (4QXII[a]), in considerable contrast to the usual Hasmonaean formal *qof*. Sporadically, the head is simplified, the heavy, shaded stroke failing to loop back (4QPs.-Enoch[a]; 4QS135[b]). In very late forms, the tail is made continuously with the loop of the head (4QEnoch V). This latter style ultimately gives rise to the open *qofs* of the Herodian and later cursives (Nero Papyrus; Mur 117; Mur 134; etc.).

The *resh* of 4QXII[a] is narrow, sharply ticked on the left, but "round-shouldered" in the style of the Archaic and early Hasmonaean semiformal scripts. Both traits persist and, indeed, are often exaggerated in later semicursive scripts (4QDan[c]; 4QS135[b]). In the Herodian and post-Herodian cursives (but not in the late semicursive), this form further evolves into a narrow "S"-curved *resh* (Nero Papyrus; Mur 117).

Shin in 4QXII[a], and sporadically in later semicursives (4QS135[b]), exhibits an excessively archaic form. The right arms are uncurved. Sometimes the upper right arm is high in the fashion of the third-century cursives. As early as 4QDanᶜ, the cursive *shin* invades the semicursive script. In the early exemplars of this *shin,* the form is made with a shaded, slightly curved, left downstroke. The right arms are made in one continuous stroke, the point of the angle joining at about the mid-point of the left downstroke. The lower, left arm, especially, is gently curved in shape. In the semicursive hands this form persists until the Herodian period.

The Hasmonaean semicursive scripts normally use the looped, cursive *taw* familiar from the Nash Papyrus. It shows little development in the Qumran scripts. In Herodian and post-Herodian cursives the loop is often simplified and the right leg sometimes lengthens. 4QDanᵇ mixes the cursive *taw* and a relatively archaic formal *taw*. Typologically, the latter is closest to the formal *taw* of the earliest Hasmonaean period.

In the legend to Figure 4, tentative dates have been assigned to the semicursive scripts described above. In general the typological sequence of the earlier Hasmonaean hands is clear: 4QXIIᵃ, 4QDanᶜ, 4QPs.-Enochᵃ; and the absolute dating in century between 150 and 50 B.C. can hardly be far wrong. The later semicursive hands are more difficult to date and to place in typological sequence: 4QS135ᵇ, 4QEnoch V, and 6Qp8. On the one hand, their letters, especially the cursive forms, preserve archaic characteristics remote from the Herodian cursive; on the other hand, the letter forms with formal traits often anticipate the (later) formal evolution. Again, the scripts in question combine different sets of cursive and formal elements in letter forms, making precise typological comparison difficult. It is quite possible that the order of the last three scripts as given in Figure 4 is wrong. But in any case, all three belong to the late Hasmonaean period or, at latest, to the beginning of the early Herodian era. A gap of considerable length must be posited between the latest of the semicursives of Qumran and the extant Herodian cursives and post-Herodian semicursives.

Jerusalem, Jordan, Summer, 1959

NOTES TO CHAPTER SIX

1. The following abbreviations are used in the text of this chapter, in addition to those listed in the table of abbreviations for the volume as a whole:

ADSS: N. Avigad, "The Palaeography of the Dead Sea Scrolls and Related Documents," *Scripta Heirosolymitana* IV (1957), pp. 56–87.

AG: N. Aimé-Giron, *Textes araméens d'Égypte* (Cairo, 1931).

ALQ: F. M. Cross, *The Ancient Library of Qumrân* (New York-London, 1958).

ANASH: W. F. Albright, "A Biblical Fragment from the Maccabaean Age: The Nash Papyrus," *JBL* 56 (1937), pp. 145–76.

BHS: S. Birnbaum, *The Hebrew Scripts* II (London, 1954–57).

CIS: *Corpus inscriptionum semiticarum.*

DJD: *Discoveries in the Judaean Desert* (Oxford, 1955—).

DSS: Burrows, Trever, and Brownlee, *The Dead Sea Scrolls of St. Mark's Monastery,* 2 volumes (New Haven, 1950–51).

IAP: J. Starcky, "Inscriptions archäiques de Palmyre," *Studi Orientalistici in onore di Giorgio Levi della Vida* II (Rome, 1956), pp. 509–28.

IEJ: *Israel Exploration Journal.*

MG: E. L. Sukenik, *'Ôṣar mĕgillôt gĕnūzôt* (Jerusalem, 1954).

OMQ: F. M. Cross, "The Oldest Manuscripts from Qumrân," *JBL* 74 (1955), pp. 147–72.

PEQ: *Palestine Exploration Quarterly.*

PSBA: *Proceedings of the Society of Biblical Archaeology.*

RAO: C. Clermont-Ganneau, *Recueil d'archéologie orientale.*

SACHAU: E. Sachau, *Aramäische Papyrus und Ostraka* II (Leipzig, 1911).

SDF: *Gli scavi del "Dominus Flevit,"* parte I, ed., Bagatti and Milik (Jerusalem, 1958).

SS: *Supplementary Studies* to *BASOR.*

Sigla and abbreviations not listed here or explained in the text are those regularly used in *DJD,* to which the reader is referred.

2. The precise number of documents from the eleven caves of Qumran is not yet known. Two purchases of Cave IV materials in the summer of 1958 (the cave was discovered six years earlier) appear to have exhausted the resources of clandestine diggers; but there is every reason to believe that a considerable portion of the manuscripts of Cave XI, found in 1956, remain in Bedouin hands.

3. 4QExᶠ; see Fig. 1, line 3.

4. The Palaeo-Hebrew script of Qumran is properly described as an archaistic survival from the book hand of Israelite times. It shows little development in the interval between the epigraphs of the seventh–fifth centuries B.C. and manuscripts of Maccabaean or Hasmonaean date. Evidently the script was taken up anew in the era of nationalistic revival of the second century B.C., to judge from its use as a monumental script by the Hasmonaeans on their coinage, as well as its resurgence as a Biblical hand. It is in the Hasmonaean era also that the Samaritan Pentateuchal text separates from the main stream of Jewish tradition, preserving in its special hand the Palaeo-Hebrew tradition (cf. the writer's remarks and references in *ALQ,* pp. 127 ff.). Moreover, in the second century B.C., Palaeo-Hebrew forms, dormant for some four centuries, begin afresh to evolve at a fairly steady pace. This new development is reflected in the series of MSS at Qumran, as well as in the coinage of the First and Second Jewish Revolts, and in the earliest Samaritan epigraphs. On the other hand, the earliest exemplars of the Palaeo-Hebrew hand at Qumran exhibit a remarkable fidelity of form and stance, when compared with archaic scripts, and were penned with fluid grace and speed. One can best explain these characteristics of the Qumran Palaeo-Hebrew hand by assuming that though relatively static, the old script was preserved alive in some narrow circle, presumably by a coterie of erudite scribes, as a Biblical book hand. When the first of the Palaeo-Hebrew fragments were found in Cave I, an alternate explanation was proposed, that the fragments were in fact archaic, from the fourth or fifth century B.C. But later finds, including manuscripts in which there is extensive mixture of Palaeo-Hebrew and Jewish scripts (and in one instance a mixture of Palaeo-Hebrew, Jewish, and Greek scripts), have rendered this proposal inadmissible.

5. The term "Early Jewish" is used here and throughout to designate the scripts developed in Judaea and used by Jews beginning in the Maccabean period and

continuing to the time of the First Jewish Revolt. It stands in contrast to Palaeo-Hebrew (see n. 4 above) and to the Aramaic cursive of the late Persian and early Greek periods from which Jewish, Nabataean, Palmyrene, et al., were derived. The traditional designations, "Assyrian," "Aramaic," "square" do not apply accurately to the several Early Jewish script types and cannot be used in scientific palaeographical discussion. The last-mentioned term, "square," applies at best to the formal hand of the First Jewish Revolt (and later), or less happily to the Herodian book hands, and should be abandoned.

We have chosen the designation "Early Jewish"; it could be argued plausibly that "Judaean" would be even more precise. However, the broader term seems a happier alternative since the Early Jewish script was in use by Jews outside Judaea (cf. the Nash Papyrus), and it permits us to speak of the scripts of the late Roman and Byzantine eras from Palestine, Egypt, and Mesopotamia (e.g., from Dura), which are continuous with the early series, as "Late Jewish."

6. Published by J. T. Milik, "Trois tombeaux juifs," *Studii Biblici Franciscani Liber Annuus* VII (1956–57), pp. 232–67.

7. Preliminary publication of these ossuaries may be found in the following: P. B. Bagatti, "Scoperta di un cimitero giudeo-cristiano al 'Dominus Flevit'," and Bagatti and Milik, "Nuovi scavi al 'Dominus Flevit'." The principal report on the ossuaries with an excellent discussion of their scripts has now appeared, *SDF* I, pp. 70–109.

8. Slightly later than the period of our chief interest are the new funerary inscriptions of Beth-she'arim (late second–early fourth centuries A.D.) published by N. Avigad, "Excavations at Beth-she'arim, 1955," *IEJ* 7 (1957), pp. 73–92; 239–55.

9. R. de Vaux, "Fouilles au Khirbet Qumrân," *RB* 61 (1954), Pl. X a; cf. p. 229; an analysis of the script is given in the writer's paper, "The Oldest Manuscripts from Qumrân," *JBL* 74 (1955), p. 147, n. 2.

A graffito on a bowl from locus 86/89, reading *'l'zr,* has already been a subject of some dispute although the piece is unpublished. According to de Vaux, the piece comes from the destruction of Qumran at the end of Period I a; Milik has argued both on archaeological grounds and on palaeographical that the bowl belongs to Period II (*ca.* A.D. 1–68). The writer, unlike de Vaux and Milik, was not present when the deposit was excavated, but for palaeographical reasons has sided with Milik (*ALQ*, p. 48, n. 21). In the summer of 1958, however, Père de Vaux kindly reviewed the archaeological data and went over the pottery associated with the inscribed bowl with the writer. De Vaux's case is strong, and it appears that the graffito, despite its Herodian tendencies (inverted-"v" *'alef;* large-based *lamed;* large *'ayn,* lying on its right leg; curved *zayn,* with distinct suggestion of extension of the head to the right; and broad *resh*), must be placed tentatively at the end of Period I b (*ca.* 31 B.C.), rather than in the first century of the Christian era. A final decision on the context of the graffito must await full publication of the excavations at Ḥirbet Qumran. Meanwhile, the possibility should be borne in mind that the minimal dates in our absolute chronology on shifts of certain letter forms (notably *zayn*) to full-blown Herodian styles may be slightly low.

A third important, small inscription from a dated context is the dipinto on a jar published by de Vaux, op. cit., Pl. XII, also belonging to Period I b (*locus* 34).

10. *Masada, Survey and Excavations, 1955–1956,* by M. Avi-yonah, N. Avigad, et al. (Jerusalem, 1957), pp. 59 f. and Pl. 16 C, D.

11. On the other hand, the Gezer Boundary Inscriptions have been dated too early on indirect archaeological arguments. Probably they were inscribed in the era

of the First Revolt; the script is certainly Herodian: *taw* is very late; *zayn* in one of the inscriptions (cf. *JPOS* X [1930] Pl. II, D) is heavily ticked; *gimel* has a *keraia*. Cf. *OMQ*, p. 163, note 34.

12. See the discussions of W. F. Albright, *ANash*, pp. 157–63, and references cited; N. Avigad, *ADSS*, pp. 77–81. J. T. Milik [*SDF* I, pp. 100–9] has attempted to show that the latest, especially the extremely cursive graffiti of the Dominus Flevit ossuaries may date in the interval between the Jewish revolts. His evidence does not appear decisive, and I remain unconvinced. The question will be decided, however, when analysis of the late cursive is further advanced. Meanwhile, the Herodian dating of the great mass of ossuary inscriptions is certain, as Milik himself would insist.

13. The Jewish book hand and the semi-formal hand used in deeply engraved inscriptions (Běnê Ḥēzîr, Uzziah Plaque, Helena Inscription) show no significant or systematic differences which would permit us to speak of a lapidary style over against the formal hand. The engravers appear to have imitated the usual formal and semi-formal styles as closely as their material would permit. The old Aramaic lapidary, already ousted as an official hand as early as the fifth century B.C., dies in the fourth century. Its last traces may be detected in certain isolated forms in the Demanhur coin graffiti (325–318 B.C.) and in the Tobiah Inscription (late fourth or early third century B.C.).

14. Hitherto there has been some confusion produced by the extreme cursive script sometimes used on ossuaries, especially those of relatively late date. Some of the strange forms were attributed to the crudeness or ignorance of the scribe (always a dangerous procedure methodologically) rather than to the script tradition he had chosen. Similarly, the formal and Vulgar semiformal styles (see below) which dominate in the funerary inscriptions were sometimes called lapidary, sometimes cursive by scholars, not on the basis of an inductive knowledge of the development of the scripts, but apparently on intuitive grounds. There are still unsolved problems, to be sure, in tracing the influence of the cursive upon the formal tradition and vice versa, especially in the rise of what we shall term here semicursives; but the basic script types are now easily defined.

15. Cf., for example, the pottery associated with the ossuary groups listed in note 7 and the older synthetic studies of P. Kahane, "Pottery Types from the Ossuary-Tombs around Jerusalem," *IEJ* II (1952), pp. 125–39; 176–82; III (1953), pp. 48–54; and references, to which should also be added P. and N. Lapp, "A Comparative Study of a Hellenistic Pottery Group from Beth-zur," *BASOR* 151 (1958), pp. 16–27.

16. See *IAP*, pp. 509–28.

17. Cf. *OMQ*, pp. 159–65, and J. Starcky, op. cit.

18. Cf. *ALQ*, pp. 88–90.

19. *ANash.*

20. Among the few are, e.g., the articles of S. A. Birnbaum and his polemical summary, *The Qumran (Dead Sea) Scrolls and Palaeography* [*BASOR SS* 13–14] (New Haven, 1952). The latter monograph is a useful guide to both the beginner in palaeography and to the history of the controversy over the palaeographical dating of the Qumran manuscripts. The polemical tone of this otherwise excellent study is to be regretted; at the same time, it should be remembered that it was written by a professional palaeographer tried to the limit by the Lilliputian attacks of non-specialists.

The useful pioneering work of John C. Trever also deserves mention; see his summary article and references in "The Problem of Dating the Dead Sea Scrolls," *Smithsonian Report,* 1953, pp. 425–35.

M. Martin's two-volume work, *The Scribal Character of the Dead Sea Scrolls* (Louvain, 1958) presents useful data on Qumran scribal practices; he makes no serious attempt, however, to deal with problems of historical palaeography.

21. *Part Two, The Plates* (London, 1954–57); Part One is in press.

22. *OMQ*, pp. 147–65.

23. *ADSS*, pp. 56–87.

24. See the studies listed in notes 6 and 7 and *DJD* II, *passim*. Special note should be taken of his drawing of the Bethphage script, *SDF* I, p. 102, Fig. 24, col. 1, which is based on a re-examination of the Bethphage Lid itself. Earlier studies and photographs of the lid are almost useless for palaeographical study.

25. Even the formal script, however, has several substyles in the various periods, which, while sharing major typological features, have individual traits which persist for longer or shorter periods and hence cannot be considered the peculiarities of an individual scribe. These substyles (semiformal scripts) require more leisurely study when the great Qumran corpus is fully published.

26. Cf. the writer's remarks, *OMQ*, p. 164.

27. We may illustrate these general shifts to be discussed below in detail with one or two of the more obvious traits of each period. The Archaic book hand is marked by two characteristics surviving from the end of the Persian era: the widely differing sizes of letters and the preservation of variety in the width of strokes ("shading") according to fixed fashions. The Hasmonaean hand preserves in part the tradition of large and small letters with letters "hung from line." But the tendency to uniformity of size, begun in the Aramaic cursive scripts of the third century, here "infects" the formal character. Shading is idiosyncratic. The Herodian hand sharply breaks with tradition of variety in size and tends to standardize letter height. Letters continue to be hung from the line, but a feeling for a base line sets in. "Tittles" (*not tāgîn!*), archaic survivals or idiosyncratic in the Hasmonaean script, develop and multiply, becoming standard parts of letters. In elegant hands new techniques of shading are often used.

28. On the speed of the evolution of the early Jewish hands, see my remarks in *ALQ*, p. 88, n. 15. The task of dating archaizing scripts, for example the Palaeo-Hebrew hand of the fifth–second centuries B.C. and medieval Biblical scripts, is far more complicated and, because of their extremely slow rate of evolution, can be dated only within much broader time spans. On occasion, scholars accustomed to dealing with medieval manuscripts (though with the exception of Birnbaum's work almost no fully scientific palaeographical analysis has been carried on in the medieval field) have expressed skepticism concerning the precision of datings claimed by workers in the Early Jewish field. This skepticism is based on a fallacious transfer of problems occasioned by experience with a surpassingly conservative script to scripts of a radically different tradition. Actually, the precision of typological dating is a simple reflex of the speed of a script's evolution. Absolute dating is, of course, a different matter and depends on the number of absolute dating "pegs" established in the typological series.

29. The dating of a script of Qumran to a single generation on typological grounds, in the case of individual manuscripts, cannot, of course, be converted into absolute dating. Despite the speed of evolution in this period, allowance must be made always for the extension of the professional life of a conservative scribe beyond his generation, or for an individualistic hand which holds out against the powerful current of scribal styles and fashions. However, in the case of a group of scripts belonging typologically to a certain generation, we can assume methodologically that the majority of the group were copied in the normal span of a generation.

30. See above, note 13; for bibliographical references to the latest of the lapidary forms, cf. *ANash*, pp. 155–56.
31. This is clear from its use in stone and metal inscriptions; e.g., in the Carpentras stele, *CIS* II, 141; Tab. XIII; the inscribed silver bowls published by I. Rabinowitz, "Aramaic Inscriptions of the Fifth Century B.C.E. from a North-Arab Shrine in Egypt," *JNES* 15 (1956), pp. 1–9; "Another Aramaic Record of the North Arabian Goddess han-'ilat," *JNES* 18 (1959), pp. 154–55; etc.
32. Cf. my discussion of the origin of the early Jewish book hand in *OMQ*, pp. 149–59.
33. Full bibliographical notices of publications before 1939 relating to the Elephantine finds may be found in F. Rosenthal, *Die aramaistische Forschung* (Leiden, 1939), pp. 289–301; among the important recent publications of texts are G. R. Driver, *Aramaic Documents*, etc. (Oxford, 1954; abridged edition, Oxford, 1957); and E. G. Kraeling, *The Brooklyn Museum Aramaic Papyri* (New Haven, 1953).
34. The date of this papyrus (= Cowley, No. 22) has been disputed but most scholars have taken the "fifth year" to apply to Darius II, hence 419 B.C. In *OMQ* (p. 149, n. 4; Fig. 1, line 1), while recognizing that its script was typologically the most developed of the Elephantine scripts, and using it for comparison with fourth-century forms, the writer failed to follow his convictions and lower its date. With the publication of the Brooklyn Museum Papyri, however, it has become clear that the "fifth year" is 400 B.C., i.e., the fifth year of Amyrtaeus. It is not impossible that the scribe avoids naming his suzerain in the papyrus because both Amyrtaeus and Artaxerxes II, whose regnal years coincide, claim control of Elephantine (Artaxerxes appears to have exercised nominal control as late as 401 B.C.). Against the latter possibility is the existence of Sachau P. 35, dated in the same month and year (June 400 B.C.) but in the name of Amyrtaeus. On the lower date of Sachau P. 18, cf. Kraeling, op. cit., p. 283.
35. Kraeling, op. cit., pp. 283–90, and Pl. XIII.
36. N. Aimé-Giron, *Textes araméens d'Égypte* (Cairo, 1931). Most useful is P. 87, Pl. X; cf. also Ostracon 4 *bis,* Pl. I; and P. 86 *bis;* 88; 89. A table of the script of P. 87 together with Sachau P. 18 is given in *OMQ,* Fig. 1 lines 1, 2.
37. Aimé-Giron, op. cit., p. 68. (P. 86 *bis*).
38. *CIS* II, 146 A, B; Tab. XVII.
39. That is to say, nearest in tradition, not in date.
40. See Fig. 1, line 1.
41. Sachau, op. cit., Tafel 62:2; *OMQ,* Fig. 1, line 3.
42. The evidence for this dating is marshaled in *OMQ*, p. 151, note 9.
43. That is, Exodus MS, exemplar f, from Cave IV, Qumran. The MS is unpublished, but the characteristic letters of its script may be found in Fig. 1, line 3.
44. Samuel, exemplar b, from Cave IV, Qumran. A preliminary publication of fragments of the MS may be found in *OMQ*. A detailed discussion of its script is found on pp. 155–59. In *OMQ*, Fig. 2, one set of forms is given; a new set based on unpublished fragments is given in our present paper, Fig. 1, line 4.
45. Jeremiah, exemplar a, from Cave IV, Qumran. Its script is given in *OMQ*, Fig. 2, line 3. Its date is discussed on pp. 155–59 of the same paper. Here in Fig. 1, line 5, an alternate set of letter forms has been drawn.
46. *PSBA* 29 (1907), Pls. I, II; 37 (1915), Pl. II (cf. G. R. Driver, *The Hebrew Scrolls* [London, 1951], Pl. II).
47. "Un document araméen de la moyenne Égypte," *Revue des études juives* 65 (1913), pp. 16–23.

48. Lidzbarski, *Ephemeris für semitische Epigraphik* III (1915), Taf. II, III (opposite p. 36); Sachau, *Aramäische Papyrus und Ostraka* II (Leipzig, 1911), Taf. 62:1; 68:1, 2.
49. Cf. *ANash,* pp. 154–55.
50. There is, of course, no feeling for a base line.
51. Cf. the medial and final letters in the formal hands, Fig. 2, and in the semicursive and cursive hands, Fig. 4.
52. Certain formal hands at Qumran still distinguish final and medial *lamed.* 4QJer[a] (Fig. 1, line 5) is perhaps the best example. Final *lamed* also ·survives rarely in very early Palmyrene and Nabataean inscriptions. Cf. Starcky, *IAP,* Figs. 1 and 2, pp. 521–22.
53. See Fig. 4. *'Alef* is similarly treated in the Jewish cursive; the fullest development of secondary final forms occurs in Nabataean, among the sister national scripts, where as many as ten or twelve letters may be so distinguished. Cf. J. Starcky, "Un contrat nabatéen sur papyrus," *RB* 61 (1954), pp. 161–81.
54. Cf. 4QSam[b], Fig. 1, line 4.
55. In *OMQ,* Fig. 3, p. 154, the development of *he* is diagrammed in detail. It is a complicated development and in the diagram is oversimplified, especially the cursive development as may be seen from a perusal of Fig. 4 in the present paper.
55a. On the *yod* shaped like minuscule *lambda,* see below in the analysis of 4QEx[f].
56. Cf. Fig. 4, lines 1 and 2.
57. Cf. Fig. 1, line 3.
58. For example, Fig. 4, line 3.
59. Cf. *A.-G.* P. 87, where the distinction is still ill-defined.
60. Two forms are preserved in *A.-G.* P. 87 (cf. *OMQ,* Fig. 1, line 2); unfortunately, the one possible *samekh* in P. Luparensis is too badly damaged to be utilized. At all events, the aberrant Edfū *samekh* is enough to guarantee a general, rapid fourth-century evolution.
61. Fig. 1, line 5. Cf. 4QEx[f], Fig. 1, line 3.
62. Fig. 6, line 2.
63. 4QSam[b], 4QJer[a], and several unpublished hands.
64. This form is especially clear in (formal) 4QJer[a].
65. For *resh,* see above under *dalet.*
66. This definition serves only for the early semiformal script; on the Round semiformal and Vulgar semiformal scripts of the Herodian Age, see below.
67. Fig. 1, lines 6 and 7.
68. It is not impossible that the semiformal hand is a style of local (Syrian?) origin which made its way into the scribal schools of Judaea; it is, in any case, a style at Qumran, not a script belonging to a few imported manuscripts or to an imported scribe or two (see below).
69. Cf. Fig. 4, especially, and Fig. 3. The Nash Papyrus and the Murabba'ât Ostracon (Fig. 3, lines 1 and 2) may deserve a special classification. Both stand close to the formal tradition with inconsistent use of a few cursive forms. In some sense they resemble Nabataean, a script arising in the formal character, later invaded by isolated cursive forms in the first century B.C.
70. The following is a slightly revised version of my first palaeographical analysis of 4QSam[b] found in *OMQ,* pp. 155–59.
71. In *OMQ,* p. 155, the looped *'alef* of Nash, etc., is derived from the crescent form. This is true if the qualification is made that the looped form probably arises not directly from the third-century formal *'alef,* but from a third-century semiformal type which invaded the cursive.

72. The forms of *dalet* in the Nash Papyrus are strikingly formal, or Archaic; the *dalet* of 4QEx[f] also betrays, if our dating is correct, the normal development and preserves a most archaic stance.

73. In the Nash Papyrus, Fig. 3, line 1; and in later semicursives, Fig. 4, lines 4, 6, etc.

74. See the discussion of the cursive and semiformal *ḥet* below.

75. The form is virtually identical with the most common *ṭet* of Edfū (Fig. 1, line 2, first specimen). It appears also in the archaizing inscription of Tobiah of 'Arâq el-'Emîr (early third century B.C.). Cf. *BHS,* No. 80.

76. Notably in P. Nash, Fig. 4, line 1.

77. After close examination of the large new fragment of 4QSam[a], I suspect that the scribe began all his *yods* at the top; that is, that none was made in inverted-"v" style.

78. Cf. Sachau ostracon 62:2; *OMQ,* Fig. 1, line 3.

79. 4QPs[a] (unpublished); 4QSy48 (unpublished), etc.

80. A notable example is the *kaf* of Sachau 68:1.

81. Cf. Fig. 3, lines 1, 2.

82. Cf. note 52.

83. *Ephemeris* III, Pl. II (to p. 23). In the short text *lamed* appears six times in the medial position, twice in the final. Both final forms are archaic; all medial the usual narrow, cursive forms.

84. We have found the same to be true in the case of *he, yod* (above), and *'ayn* (below).

85. An illustration of this complex relationship is found in the trait of ligaturing. Normally, we expect a cursive script to develop ligatures. However, the actual development of the Early Jewish scripts is not so simple. The tendency in the Aramaic script toward the creation of ligatures, or better semiligatures, ceased earlier in the cursive script than in the formal hand, with an attendant trend toward the standardization of forms (non-observance of distinctions between medial and final letters). Examples are 4QEx[f] which has no hard and fast distinctions between semiligatured (medial) and non-ligatured (final) forms, and Palmyrene which distinguishes only medial and final *nun.* Later in the history of the scripts, the formal hand develops an abhorrence of ligatures, while the pure cursive develops into a running hand, featuring an abundance of full ligatures. Cf. *OMQ,* p. 151, n. 11.

86. But see the discussion of 4QEx[f] below.

87. On the absolute dates of 4QSam[b] and 4QJer[a], see below in the summary of this section. Perhaps it is worth-while here to indicate typological relations of these two MSS to each other. 4QJer[a] exhibits a number of forms typologically secondary to letter forms of 4QSam[b]: *'alef, bet, dalet, mem* (medial and final), *nun* (medial), *ṣade, shin,* and *taw.* Of these, medial and final *mem,* and final *taw,* are especially striking. On the other hand, 4QJer[a] preserves strikingly archaic forms, typologically less advanced than 4QSam[b], in two, perhaps three cases: *ṭet, samekh,* and *he.* 4QJer[a] is thus in the general horizon of 4QSam[b] in date, but slightly later.

88. The MS is unpublished. It was studied for the first time in the summer of 1956, after the publication of my paper on the earliest scripts from Qumran (*OMQ*). Its condition was such that decipherment was successful only after special preparation, and then only with the aid of both infrared and ultraviolet photographs, and by *étude par transparence.*

89. Especially the *'alef* of the Aṣlaḥ Inscription (Fig. 6, line 1).

90. *RAO* VIII, Pl. II, and pp. 59–65. On the date of the inscription in the reign of Ptolemy I, and the archaizing character of its script, see *ANash,* pp. 155 f.

91. This does not mean that one cannot discover isolated instances of *dalet* in a right-to-left stance in third-century crude cursives. These are aberrant forms, however, in the documents in which they appear. I know of no third-century cursive in which such forms are frequent, much less consistent. 4QEx^t exclusively uses the right-to-left stance.

92. The pure cursive does not appear, as is to be expected, in the literary documents of Qumran. A few scraps of contracts (unpublished) have turned up in Cave IV. They are in a cursive script but of relatively late date. For the pure cursive, cf. Fig. 5 and *SDF* I, Fig. 24, p. 102.

93. W. F. Albright has written that an unpublished graffito from the Marisa tombs, probably of the end of the third century B.C., uses "the older elongated ('final')" forms, including *nun,* and compares the 'Aqabyah forms of *'alef, bet, he, waw, yod,* and *nun* (*ANash,* pp. 165 f.).

94. On the date, cf. *OMQ,* p. 160, n. 25, and the literature there cited, to which is to be added Starcky's study (cited in n. 16).

95. Cf. note 93.

96. That is, 4QPrières lit. A.

97. The same hand continues in 1QSa and 1QSb (*DJD* I, Pls. XXII–XXIX). M. Martin's analysis of the hands of the 1QSab complex is badly confused.

98. "Further Messianic References in Qumran Literature," *JBL* 75 (1956), pp. 174–87.

99. Preserved, for example, in the medial *he* of the script in Fig. 4, line 4.

100. Cf. Fig. 5; earlier examples may be found in the Bethphage Lid (*SDF I,* Fig. 24, line 1).

101. Certain qualifications should be made. In rare instances, a letter may evolve in parallel fashion in isolated scripts. But when dealing with an entire alphabet, such coincidences are, methodologically speaking, of no real effect upon the analysis. Again there is some evidence that the formal styles of Nabataean and Jewish scripts diverged sooner than the early cursive. Once again, this problem may be eliminated from our main task in which we deal with the formal scripts. Finally, it is to be noted that in using such terms as "branching apart" or "convergence," we may seem to imply that the scripts arise in one or two common archetypes. This is not the case, unless we move backward a great distance to an archetype to be found in the late Persian hand. The development of the local scripts can be understood by visualizing three lines in three-dimensional space, each parallel for a considerable distance (the mainstream of Aramaic script traditions moving slowly, with some few local peculiarities sufficient to distinguish the stream, into three or more "lines," insufficient to separate into local scripts), then each in turn diverging, at first slowly, then in flaring curves (the accelerating evolution in the interval between the rise of the national scripts and the establishment of their classical styles).

102. The text was edited by Cowley (*Palestine Exploration Fund Annual* [1914–15], p. 146; Fig. 59). On the script and date, cf. *OMQ,* p. 160, n. 25, and the citations therein; and *IAP,* p. 523.

103. The inscription is precisely dated to the first year of 'Obodat son of Ḥaretat who ascended the throne sometime after 100, before 93 B.C. (*IAP,* p. 523). A squeeze of the inscription is published by G. Dalman, *Neue Petra-Forschungen, usw.* (Leipzig, 1912), *Abb.* 68, No. 90 (p. 99). Cf. Fig. 6, line 1.

104. *RAO* VIII, Pl. VII. On the goddess 'El-Kutbā', see the forthcoming paper of J. Strugnell in *BASOR.*

105. The inscription is dated in the fourth year of Ptolemy, probably either Ptolemy Auletes, or his successor, the first coregent of Cleopatra, thus either *ca.* 77 B.C. or 48 B.C. (cf. *IAP,* p. 524, n. 1). The choice between a date in the seventies and

a date in the forties rests on the typological relationship of its script to Aṣlaḥ (95 B.C.) on the one hand, and, on the other hand, to the script of the Rabb'el Inscription which is contemporary with the 'El-Kutbā' hand. Both Rabb'el and 'El-Kutbā' must be placed at a maximum distance below the Aṣlaḥ Inscription. On the other hand, the date of the 'El-Kutbā' text prohibits an attempt to lower the date of Rabb'el into the reign of Ḥaretat IV and requires that we date Rabb'el in the reign of Ḥaretat III, *ca.* 66 B.C. The problem, then, is whether the 'El-Kutbā' Inscription is to be placed immediately before or immediately after the Inscription of Rabb'el.

No little confusion has been introduced into the discussion by bad facsimiles of the Rabb'el script, notably that of J. Cantineau [*Le Nabatéen* II, p. 2]. The squeeze of the inscription (*CIS* II, *Tab.* XLV, Text 349) has been interpreted in light of later Nabataean developments. There is no clear evidence in the squeeze of either final *he* or cursive *het*. And the *'alef* of Cantineau's drawing exists nowhere; it is clear that he has attempted to read a *final 'alef* of the type of the later 'El-Ḥijr texts into Rabb'el where a single *'alef* form appears (in both medial and final positions). Unfortunately, later scholars have repeated the error of Cantineau (and his predecessors!). The *'alef* of Rabb'el is developed from a semilooped form like that of 'El-Kutbā'. The final *'alef* of later Nabataean is developed from the *'alef* of 'Aṣlaḥ, that is, formal *'alef*.

In general, the 'El-Kutbā' text is slightly earlier, typologically, than Rabb'el. But this cannot be turned necessarily into absolute dates in such a narrow span of time. 'El-Kutbā' has broader forms; Rabb'el tends toward the elegant long forms of the late classical style. *Yod, pe,* and *ṣade* are remarkably archaic in 'El-Kutbā'. The distinctions between the forms of *qof* and *kaf* in the two inscriptions are based on slightly differing traditions but are all archaic and no doubt contemporary letter forms. Both Rabb'el and 'El-Kutbā' retain a final form of *lamed* (line 1 of each). In one feature (of negligible importance in this period), Rabb'el is less developed: *shin.* The left downstroke of the 'El-Kutbā' *shin* shows a slight tendency to lengthen. The looped *'alef* of the 'El-Kutbā' inscription need not indicate late date. It is a cursive or semicursive form which invades the formal script in the first century B.C. A developed form appears in the early Ḥawrān text, *CIS* II, 162 (published by De Vogüé, *Inscriptions sémitique* [Paris, 1868] Pl. 13:1), from the first century B.C. and, more important, in a semicursive hand of Qumran in the first half of the first century (4QXII^d). This indicates an archetype of looped *'alef* and semilooped *'alef* which precedes the divergence of the Jewish and Nabataean scripts, and indeed we find precursors in the earlier type of looped *'alef* in the Nash Papyrus and other second-century texts (cf. Fig. 3). Actually, the earliest appearance of a looped or semilooped *'alef,* so far as I am able to ascertain, is in an early Seleucid sealing published by M. Rostovtzeff, *Yale Classical Studies* III (1932), pp. 19, 94–97 [Excursus by R. P. Dougherty]; Pl. III, 4. (The reference was first called to my attention by Abbé J. T. Milik.) The little inscription belongs to the late third or early second century B.C. The problem, then, is not the "availability" of looped *'alef,* but the date of its introduction into Nabataean formal scripts within the first century B.C. In terms of typological relationship, then, the semilooped *'alef* of Rabb'el is more developed than the semilooped form of 'El-Kutbā'; but the looped *'alef* of 'El-Kutbā' is not significant for comparison *in this period.*

In short, we may provisionally date the 'El-Kutbā' text toward 77 B.C., the Rabb'el text slightly later, but still distant from the fully Nabataean ductus of such a text as *CIS* II, 198 from El-Ḥijr. Cf. J. Starcky's discussion and charts, *IAP,* pp. 522 (Fig. 2) and 524 f.

106. See preceding note.

107. The 'El-Kutbā' text preserves an archaic specimen (Fig. 7, line 1).

108. In point of fact, the closest parallel to the larger sprawled Nabataean *'alef*, with its semilooped left leg, is the *'alef* of the Murraba'āt Ostracon (*DJD* II, Pl. LII; Fig. 3, line 2). But it also resembles the types of 4QPr* and Palmyrene.

109. Cf. the forms of 'El-Kutbā' and Rabb'el texts, Fig. 7.

110. The figure-three form of *kaf* in the 'El-Kutbā' inscription is a further development of the earlier figure-three form of the Nash Papyrus (Fig. 3, line 1).

111. The cursive forms include looped *'alef*, headless *bet*, the "s"-curved *ṭet*. The *shin* with tail and late *samekh* probably also arise first in the cursive to judge from Early Jewish parallels.

112. *IAP*, Pl. I, p. 510.

112a. *IAP*, p. 519; cf. *OMQ*, p. 159, note 22.

113. *Inventaire des Inscriptions Palmyréniennes de Doura-Europos* (Paris, 1939), No. 1; cf. *IAP*, Pl. IC.

114. Cf. note 9.

115. For a table of the script, cf. *BHS*, No. 85.

116. The Rule of the Community (IQS) and the other documents copied by the same scribe (4QSamᶜ; 4QTestimonia, et al.) are properly left out of this sequence of typical formal documents. Their script stems from the semiformal tradition of the Archaic period, influenced at a number of points by the standard Hasmonaean style. This complicates the problem of dating the script. However, it is roughly contemporary with 4QDeutᶜ (and 1QIsaᵃ) and may be assigned provisionally to ca. 100–75 B.C. For tables of the script of 1QS, see *BHS*, No. 86.

117. This is the technique used in 4QSamᵇ. Contrast *ADSS*, p. 76, n. 31.

118. For example, in the unpublished MSS (not shown in Fig. 2), 4QDeutᵈ; 4QLev-Numᵃ, et al.; cf. the forms of *he* in *OMQ*, Fig. 3, p. 154 (key in note 15, p. 153).

119. The latter trait is very frequent in Herodian hands. Cf. the early Herodian hands, IQM (Fig. 2, line 4) and 1QpHab (edited in *DSS I*).

120. The *ṭets* of the Qumran practice alphabet are made with the new technique, as well as the *ṭet* of the Yoḥanan Dipinto (before 31 B.C.). Cf. note 9.

121. 1QIsaᵃ and 1QS follow a semiformal tendency (cf. 4QPrᵃ) in failing to distinguish systematically between medial and final *kaf;* the trait is ephemeral in the formal scripts.

122. Cf. 4QSamᵃ where closed forms occasionally appear; 1QIsaᵇ, where *samekh* is normally closed; the Qumran practice alphabet where *samekh* (one example) is closed; and the Běnê Ḥēzîr Inscription (*ca.* A.D. 1) where *samekh* is closed.

123. An exception is the early Herodian hand of 1QpHab (edited in *DSS II:* 2), where *samekh* is commonly open. Cf. *ADSS*, p. 74. Avigad is certainly correct in placing 1QpHab after 1QIsaᵇ.

124. This is another illustration of the tendency toward homogeneity of stroke in a given era of the script. We noted above the treatment of the bases of (*bet*), *kaf, mem, pe,* and *ṣade,* and in the Herodian hand will note below the development of letters with "ceriphs" or tittles.

125. I.e., having projections beyond the ceiling and/or (theoretical) base line. The semiformal script (e.g., 1QS) retains the doubly curved left leg somewhat longer than the formal script and sometimes exaggerates it (e.g., 4QSᵉ [unpublished]).

126. In the Archaic *taw,* and some early Hasmonaean hands, the curved stroke of the right arm moves upward first, creating a deep curve (4QSamᵇ); in the late Hasmonaean hand the stroke moves straight to the right in a horizontal direction, then down in a curved right shoulder (4QSamᵃ).

127. This is to ignore the period of abandonment of Qumran during a small or large part of Herod's reign. The era of abandonment, whatever its length, does not produce an equivalent lacuna in the typological sequence of manuscripts.

128. Cf. *ADSS*, p. 73 f.

129. The *keraia* of the New Testament (Mt. 5:18 = Lk. 16:17), normally translated "tittle," no doubt refers to an ornamentation of the Herodian book hand. The term *tittle*, however, and the Rabbinic terms *qôṣ*, *tāgā*, etc., are usually taken in older literature to apply to an ornamentation which developed only in medieval times. Confusion is best avoided, perhaps, by choosing alternate terms: *keraiai*, or from printer's cant, *ceriphs*.

130. Unlike the earlier semiformal hand, it is virtually uninfluenced by the cursive hand. It is properly a flourished, readily written variety of the formal book hand.

131. An unpublished exemplar is 4QJer^c. Despite a number of Hasmonaean features of this script, presumably derived from the older semiformal, it has a number of remarkably advanced traits. For instance, in medial *mem* the oblique left arm is drawn first (see below); *zayn* has the *keraia*. The final *mem* is notable; it continues the Hasmonaean semiformal tradition in which the left downstroke begins flush with the crossbar; no tick is added above the crossbar (cf. 1QS; 4QpM34 *recto* [unpublished]; etc.).

132. Cf. Milik, "Une lettre de Siméon bar Kokheba," *RB* 60 (1953), p. 276, n. 1; and *DJD* II, Pls. 45–47 (Nos. 42–45). I should prefer to call this Murabbaʿât script a semiformal in view of its derivation.

Examples of the Vulgar semiformal script from Qumran include the second hand of IQH (*MG*, especially Pls. 45, 46, and 52–55), and especially 4QCant^b and the Copper Document of 3Q. It is an exceedingly common style also in the ossuary texts.

132a. For a detailed analysis of the Vulgar semiformal together with comparative typological tables, see the writer's excursus on the date of the Copper Scroll in *DJD* III (in press).

133. See *OMQ*, Fig. 2, line 5. It should be noted that the Běnê Ḥēzîr Inscription reflects the early Herodian tendency to use ligatures despite its lapidary medium.

134. Cave IV has a great many documents in this style, but relatively few are Biblical. Published exemplars of this script include 1Q26 (*DJD* I, Pl. x); 4QpPs37 (Allegro, *PEQ* 1954, pp. 69–75; *JBL* 75 (1956), pp. 89–95, Pls. 3, 4); and 4QEx^a (*ALQ*, Pl. opp. p. 77).

135. Another specimen of the script of 4QDeut^j is given in *OMQ*, Fig. 2, line 6, opposite p. 150.

136. The formal scripts of the final phase of the Herodian era are poorly represented in Cave I, Qumran, but are not excessively rare in Cave IV. The first hand of 1QH (*MG*, Pls. 35–58) is a developed Herodian formal script, but it does not belong to the latest stage of the Qumran formal character. On the other hand, 1Q30 (*DJD* I, Pl. xxx) probably does, though it is too badly preserved to permit a full typological analysis.

136a. The manuscript is the earliest of the Biblical documents found in the caches left by adherents of Bar Kokhba. However, since the dated non-literary texts include documents of both the late first and early second centuries, there is no reason to lower its date as late as the Second Revolt proper.

137. *DJD* II, Pls. XIX–XX.

138. I.e., the Minor Prophets Scroll, *DJD* II, Pls. LVI–LXXIII.

139. *DJD* II, XXV–XXVI.

140. The simplified inverted-"v" *'alef* appears in the Běnê Ḥēzîr Inscription, the Qumran Jar Dipinto (before 31 B.C.), the Qumran Bowl Graffito (cf. note 9), to mention

only documents dated on non-typological grounds. Cf. the 3Q Copper Document *DJD* III (in press), Pls. 48–71.

141. The size of letters and thickness/thinness and "monotony"/shading of the pen stroke vary considerably within the scripts of one phase of a period. But they are useful typological elements if judiciously analyzed and if a sufficient number of hands are available. For example, the elegant formal hand of the early Herodian period "inclines" to minuscule, thin-lined forms; the "Round" semiformal to majuscule forms and moderately thick-pointed pens. The elegant formal letters of the latest Herodian phase are normally large and drawn with thick, even strokes, and this ductus becomes normal in the Murabba'ât literary hands.

141a. Post-Herodian herein will always refer to the era, A.D. 70–135.

142. That is, the contract of A.D. 133, Fig. 2, line 10.

143. The same *he* is found also in the Uzziah Plaque (cf. *MG*, Fig. 26, opp. p. 25; E. L. Sukenik, *Tarbiṣ* II, No. 3 (1931), Pl. I, opp. p. 288). Indeed the Uzziah Plaque and the Dositheus Ossuary (E. L. Sukenik, *JPOS* VIII [1928] Pl. 2:4) are lapidary versions of the late Herodian character, very close to the style of 4QDeut[j]. Note the *'alefs* with two *keraiai* (in stone!); the curled head of *pe*, etc.

144. Cf. *ADSS*, Col. XXVII, opp. p. 80; and the writer's excursus on 3Q Copper Document in *DJD* III.

145. One trait, sporadic in the latest Herodian hands, frequent in post-Herodian, should be underlined. *Yod,* especially, is made in a three-movement stroke, reminiscent of Archaic proto-Jewish and Nabataean *yod;* in some manuscripts the movement is quite consistent (4QGen[b], Mur Gen-Ex).

145a. Cf. Fig. 4, lines 4–6.

146. The "open" *mem,* familiar from the ossuaries, is not used as a regular form in any of the Herodian hands of Cave I. It is rare in Cave IV, but does appear (e.g., in the early Herodian manuscript, 4QWisd[b] [unpublished]), and sporadically in the late Herodian 4QPsalms.

147. This type is found already in the Běnê Ḥēzîr Inscription (line 3), though the short, independent stroke above the crossbar is partly obscured by damage and has been generally overlooked in facsimiles.

148. Published by N. Avigad and Y. Yadin, *A Genesis Apocryphon* (Jerusalem, 1956).

148a. Cf. *DJD* II, Pl. XXI, 1.

149. 4QDeut[j] uses a semiformal final *mem;* sometimes the tick is independently drawn; sometimes it appears to be continuous with the lower downstroke, but probably is drawn as a separate stroke to judge from a close examination of the ink.

150. The form is especially frequent in the ossuary scripts.

151. Cf. note 131.

152. For example, in the second hand of 1QH.

153. The long ligatured *nun* appears also in the Hasmonaean semicursive (Fig. 4, line 4) and, indeed, in an early Herodian cursive contract from Qumran (sic!).

154. Sporadically open *samekhs* appear in some of the early Herodian hands, but the major shift of form is in the transitional period.

155. On the Hasmonaean "D"-shaped semicursive *samekh,* and contemporary or older closed cursive *samekhs*, see below.

156. In Mur Gen-Ex a new type of *samekh* appears. It is made in the pattern of final *mem,* but flattened and rounded, the left side being made with an independent downstroke.

157. The *pes* of Mur. 133 are atypical. Cf. Mur XII, and Mur Gen-Ex, as well as *Unid Ps.*

158. *DJD* II, *passim;* cf. *SDF* I, pp. 100–5; Milik, "Deux documents inédits du Désert de Juda," *Biblica* 38 (1957), pp. 255–64; Pls. II–III. The edition of texts from the

unidentified site, which includes another lot of first- and second-century cursive documents, is scheduled in a forthcoming volume of *DJD*.

159. *DJD* II, No. 20; Pl. xxx.
160. Hereafter Unid[entified] 134. Published by J. T. Milik in *RB* 61 (1954), pp. 182–92; Pl. IV; cf. *Biblica* 38 (1957), pp. 264–68; Pl. IV.
161. Among the most important are the group from Dominus Flevit (cf. note 7); Ḥallet eṭ-Ṭûrî (cf. note 6); a group from the Kedron Valley published by Savignac, *RB* 34 (1925), pp. 253–66; Pls. x–xi; the inscription published by Lidzbarski *Ephemeris* II, p. 196; and the Kallon group published by H. Hänsler, *Das Heilige Land* 57 (1913), pp. 85–95; 129–44.
162. To be published by J. T. Milik in a forthcoming volume of *DJD*.
163. R. Dussaud, *Syria* IV (1923), pp. 241–49, Fig. 1; and E. L. Sukenik, *Tarbiṣ* 7 (1936), pp. 102–9. Cf. note 24; and *ANash*, pp. 160 f.
164. Cf. note 10.
165. *DJD* II, No. 18; Pl. xxix; cf. *SDF* I, Fig. 24, p. 102; and our Fig. 5, line 1.
166. The latter is among the Cave IV documents being edited by J. Starcky and is used here with his permission. Here we shall use the siglum, 4QPs.-Enoch[a] to designate it.
167. All three are unpublished; the first (line 4) is an unknown work in Hebrew from Cave IV to be edited by J. Strugnell; the second (line 5) from Cave IV (4QEnoch V) to be edited by J. T. Milik; the third (line 6) a manuscript from Cave VI (6Qp8) to be edited by M. Baillet.
168. Elsewhere the writer has discussed the date and character of the Nash Papyrus and referred to the relevant literature: *OMQ,* p. 148, note 3.
169. The dating of the Murabba'ât Ostracon by Starcky and Milik (*DJD* II, ad loc.) is too late. Comparison has been made *directly* with first century B.C. Palmyrene and Nabataean inscriptions, an inadmissible procedure as we have stressed above. The traits observed in the sister scripts are elements which persisted after the separation of the national scripts, but which died out early in the Jewish tradition. Actually, the Nash Papyrus furnishes by far the best parallels to the Murabba'ât Ostracon. The *'alef* of the Mur Ostracon is not to be compared with the Nabataean, Wâdî Tumîlât ('El-Kutbā') *'alef;* it is actually a form developed only slightly beyond the Nash form. It retains the axis stroke (breaking above the loop on the left) unlike later Nabataean *'alef* (Fig. 7, line 1) or the Jewish cursive form of 4QXII[d] (unpublished; first half of first century B.C.) and the 6Q Papyrus (Fig. 4, line 6). Moreover, the looped Nabataean *'alef* is, as we have shown above (note 105), a cursive form invading the formal Nabataean lapidary script. It does not develop first in the first century B.C. in Nabataean, but belongs to the older pre-Nabataean cursive. Thus the *'alef* of the Mur Ostracon is properly an indicator of the early character of the script in a *Jewish* context; and this fact is immediately confirmed by the form of the formal *'alef* which appears sporadically, especially in the final position.

Again, *he, mem,* and *qof* have their proper parallels in the Jewish series, especially with Nash, and the fact that similar traits survive in Palmyrene at a much later date is evidence not of the late date of the Mur Ostracon, but of the date of the divergence of the Palmyrene and Jewish scribal traditions. *Lamed,* similarly, is not to be compared with Nabataean forms, but with Archaic forms (4QEx[f]) and Nash. *Samekh* belongs to the early cursive tradition and will be discussed below.

The formal letters in Mur Ostracon, *kaf* (long, figure-three shaped), medial and final *mem, shin,* and *taw,* are all quite early in type. The most developed letters are the ligatured cursive *bet* (used alongside very early formal types), the "N"-shaped cursive *ḥet,* and especially the short-armed *ṭet* (made in two separate movements). In general, the script stands far closer to the relatively unknown cursive tradition than does Nash. But no feature of the script requires a date later than *ca.* 100 B.C., and the ostracon may be considerably earlier.

170. On its early development, cf. notes 105 and 169.

171. In the Nero Papyrus, the form is curved; the proper Herodian form, however, is angular, much like the capital *gamma*.

172. On the ossuary examples of cursive *'alef,* see J. T. Milik, "Nuovi Scavi al 'Dominus Flevit'," p. 263 and references.

The cursive contract from Cave IV contains an extremely interesting form of *'alef,* midway between the 6Q type and that of the Nero Papyrus.

173. For example, *SDF* No. 3, Fig. 19:1 (p. 75). The photograph of the inscription is published in "Scoperta di un cimitero giudo-cristiano al 'Dominus Flevit,' " p. 156, Fig. 7. This final form of cursive *'alef* also appears rarely in the medial position; e.g., *SDF,* No. 25, fot. 90; Fig. 20:3 (p. 80).

174. In the era of the Second Revolt (pMur 134), medial (*gamma* form) and final *'alef* evolve toward each other and tend to coalesce. In origin, however, they are quite distinct, one arising from a simplified looped *'alef,* the other from a simplified formal (final) *'alef.*

175. An exception is the headless, ligatured *bet* which properly is a cursive form. It develops early (Mur Ostracon) and persists late, especially in the *ben* or *bar* element of personal names.

176. Regularly, the crossbar slopes down from right to left, and the peak of the right leg stands high above the crossbar.

177. Cf. the papyrus published by J. T. Milik, *Biblica* 38 (1957), Pls. II and III (opp. p. 252); and *DJD* II, Pl. XLVIII, No. 48.

178. Cf. *OMQ,* Fig. 3, Nos. 3–7.

179. Occasionally 4QXII[a] preserves a three-stroke *yod* of Archaic type.

180. 4QDan[c] exhibits the slightly curved *zayn* of the Hasmonaean formal hands (4QDeut[c]).

181. Cf. *SDF,* Fig. 24, col. 1 (p. 102). In older facsimiles of the Bethphage script, the form has gone unrecognized.

182. *DJD* II, Pl. XXIX, No. 18, line 7. The form is not given in Fig. 5, line 1, owing to its damaged condition.

183. Once in the extant fragments of 4QXII[a], which are quite extensive, a novel triangular *mem* is used in the final position. Evidently, it derives from an obscure cursive tradition. It appears again, not infrequently, in ossuary inscriptions, especially those in cursive traditions. Possibly it derives from a cursive by-form of the Archaic semiformal final *mem* whose shoulder often is narrowed to a point (cf. 4QPr[a]); alternately, it may derive from the protocursive *mem* from which the ovoid cursive *mem* develops (cf. 4QEx[f]; 4QPs.-Enoch[a]).

184. Actually the form is excessively rare in 4QS135[b], appearing only once certainly.

185. One or two cursive *samekh*s from Cave IV Qumran, though relatively late in date, actually preserve the hook.

186. The form is vaguely reminiscent of the cursive Nabataean *pe*. It is more than doubtful, however, that there is any connection between the forms.

CHAPTER SEVEN

The Chronology of Israel and
the Ancient Near East

SECTION A. OLD TESTAMENT CHRONOLOGY

DAVID NOEL FREEDMAN

PROFESSOR W. F. ALBRIGHT has contributed more to the clarification of the problems of Near Eastern and Biblical chronology than any other scholar in this century. The present survey of Old Testament chronology, in the light of recent discovery and analysis, is therefore in large part a tribute to Dr. Albright's labors. In general his approach, conservative but critically informed, characterizes acceptable scholarship today and is in line with a common trend in Biblical studies. Dismissal of or radical shifts from the Biblical chronology itself have not commended themselves. At the same time no comprehensive chronological system has proved convincing in detail. The laborious efforts of older scholars to harmonize and classify the Biblical data have all passed into limbo with Archbishop Ussher's famous tabulation. No modern reconstruction of Biblical chronology can ignore the fixed dates provided by extra-Biblical sources; and the Biblical dates must be modified in accordance with the pattern of Near Eastern chronology now firmly established for the second and first millennia B.C., within limits that decrease from a generation in the earlier periods to a few years in the central section to certainty in the latter part. A number of synchronisms with Biblical events are fixed within the narrowest range, thus forming a framework around which the superstructure of Old Testament chronology must be erected. Near Eastern chronology for the Biblical period has now been worked out both vertically, for Egypt on one side and Assyro-Babylonia on the other in great detail, and horizontally across the Near Eastern nations with numerous synchronisms, thus forming a substantial grid upon which to plot the chronology of the smaller nations and their dynasties.[1]

The subject of Biblical chronology may be divided into four sections: the Patriarchal Age; Exodus, Conquest, and Settlement; the monarchy (with several subdivisions); and the postexilic period. We expect to deal briefly with each of these and follow with a general appraisal.

I. THE PATRIARCHAL AGE[2]

Considerable progress has been made in developing the chronological co-ordinates of the Patriarchal Age, though efforts to pinpoint events and their dates have been repeatedly frustrated. For the most part, the Patriarchal stories of Genesis can be attributed with confidence to the Middle Bronze Age (ca. 2100–1550) for their origin and initial oral formulation. Aside from a scattering of anachronistic revisions and interpolations (e.g., the references to camels and the Philistines), the narratives reflect validly the customs and manners of MB, roughly the first half of the second millennium. The pattern of the age has been illuminated by recent excavations, especially those at Mari and Nuzi, while the many Egyptian texts of the Middle Kingdom, including particularly the Tale of Sinuhe and the execration tablets, have contributed to an understanding of the prevailing conditions in Palestine. The tradition of a Patriarchal migration from Harran roughly contemporary with the Amorite eruption into the civilized areas of the Near East is entirely plausible; while a subsequent movement into Egypt in loose association with the Hyksos penetration seems similarly acceptable. Further efforts at organizing the chronology of the Patriarchal Age, or even the relative sequence of Patriarchs and their experiences, cannot at present be controlled by extra-Biblical data. Thoroughgoing skepticism is hardly justified in dealing with the material; at the same time, the artificial character of the Biblical chronology and its genealogical scheme needs also to be recognized, to say nothing of the extraordinary longevity of the Patriarchs themselves. Genesis 14 remains enigmatic.[3] While its original formulation was doubtless poetic, and we have now the end product of a long process of oral transmission, there is no reason to doubt the nuclear validity of this Patriarchal tradition. Unfortunately, from the chronologer's point of view, it has thus far proved impossible to date the episode satisfactorily in the context of second-millennium Near Eastern history. On the whole, scholars lean toward a date later in MB (ca. 17th–16th century), rather than earlier (ca. 20th–19th century). Part of the dating difficulty may be due to the process of transmission whereby details of name and place (and therefore of date) have been changed or added in the course of centuries, thus creating a composite or mosaic which has chronological connections with more than one period. It is the present writer's impression that the original tradition of Abram's military exploit is among the oldest in our collection, but that it has undergone considerable adjustment in detail, so that it cannot now be referred with confidence to any particular moment in the history of Mesopotamia.

Several recent discussions and revisions of the date of the Patriarchs have centered on the large gap between them and the generation of the

Exodus, according to the tradition some 400 years.[4] The Bible treats this period as a kind of vacuum in which nothing happened, or at least nothing is recorded (cf. Genesis 50 and Exodus 1). But the Biblical pattern is too rigid and too simple. It is quite possible that some of the Patriarchal traditions reflect circumstances and experiences during the so-called sojourn in Egypt, even though they are placed in Canaan, because it is virtually certain (and the common assumption of scholars) that not all the ancestors of Israel went down to Egypt, or came out of it. On the other hand, attempts to eliminate the gap entirely, and to bring the Patriarchs and their traditions into the Late Bronze Age (*ca.* 1500–1200), have not proved successful. Comparison of the Biblical material with data from Nuzi and Ugarit has led some scholars to lower the date of the Patriarchs to the 15th–14th centuries.[5] The Nuzi data, which come from the 15th century, offer striking parallels to the Patriarchal accounts, thus confirming the Mesopotamian origin of the Fathers but implying a possibly later date than we have followed. The conclusion to be drawn is rather that the MB pattern of social custom and practice survived basically unchanged for centuries in certain localities in the Near East; and Nuzi, at least, cannot be used as determinative for dating. Caution must be exercised in using cultural and social patterns for dating purposes; since these are our principal clues in the case of the Patriarchal Age, considerable flexibility in fixing the chronology is advisable.

The case of Ugarit is quite different. Here the chief points of contact are with the mythopoetic texts, not the legal and economic documents. These so-called epics are themselves the final surviving product of a long process of oral (and possibly written) composition and transmission covering many centuries. They are not in any case the creation of 14th-century Ugaritic civilization, though doubtless they constitute a major part of Ugarit's religio-literary tradition. The traditions which make up the Keret and Dan'el epics go back several centuries behind the present texts, while the Baal materials may be older still. If, therefore, the correspondence in various themes between the Ugaritic poems and the Patriarchal stories suggests a common era of composition, or occurrence, then the period is not the 14th century, but the first half of the second millennium. One clue that emerges from a comparative study of the Biblical and Ugaritic materials concerns the relationship between El and Baal, the principal gods of the Canaanite pantheon. In the Canaanite epics, Baal has already displaced El as the most prominent deity in the pantheon. El has been relegated to a passive status; he has retired, as it were, from active exercise of his former sovereignty.[6] In the Biblical traditions, however, the God of the Fathers is regularly identified with El, the head of the pantheon, never with Baal, who is not even mentioned. It is true that the Genesis narratives have been edited from the point of view of orthodox Israelite monotheism and have doubtless been affected by the bitter struggle between the forces of Yahweh and Baal of the period after the settlement in the land. The omission of Baal in Genesis, therefore, can be understood on internal grounds. But the positive identification with El suggests a period for the Patriarchal traditions when El was the dominant figure in the Canaanite religious pattern. This would take us back to an earlier stage of Canaanite religion for the background of the Patriarchal narratives than that reflected in the Ugaritic poems.

Other attempts to fix Patriarchal chronology have centered on Joseph and the Pharaoh who elevated him to power.[7] Unfortunately, precise information is wanting either on the Biblical or the Egyptian side, and the data are insufficient to select definitely from among various possibilities between the 17th and 14th centuries. There are numerous candidates for the honor but none can be said to have gained the field. A complicating factor here, as in the case of Genesis 14, is that the Joseph story has been modified and modernized in the course of transmission, not reaching the form underlying the present JE accounts until perhaps the 11th century. At present, the Joseph story can be used to confirm the fact of the Israelite sojourn in Egypt and the existence of an important Egyptian strand in the Israelite background, but hardly to fix chronological details.

Then there is the question of the genealogies.[8] The several genealogies connecting the age of the Patriarchs with that of the Exodus average out at about four generations. This has led some scholars to the conclusion that the period between the two amounted to 100 years or so, certainly not 400. The argument from the genealogies has an inherent weakness in that, properly speaking, these are not genealogies at all. The standard Patriarchal pattern of four generations (Abraham, Isaac, Jacob, and the Twelve) is itself an artificial construction which can hardly carry the weight of historical, much less chronological, evidence.[9] Nevertheless, it forms the foundation for the entire Israelite genealogical structure, for all Israelites are inevitably tied into the Patriarchal pattern by the addition of these generations to whatever genealogy was originally assigned. For the Exodus-Numbers cycle, however, we do not have ordinary genealogies in the sense of tracing a man's lineage through several generations, but simply an identification according to a standard Biblical pattern, i.e., the man's name, that of his father, then the clan (sometimes omitted), and finally the tribe. This is not a genealogy; though, for the period of the Exodus, it may be taken as such if we equate the clan and tribe with the eponymous ancestors. In short, the identifying data have been interpreted as a genealogy not alone by modern scholars but by the ancient editors as well; the genealogical pattern is a familiar characteristic of the priestly framework of the Pentateuch.

Except for special individuals like Samuel, Saul, and David, there are no true genealogies for the early period. For the Exodus generation we have in general only the name, the father's name, and then direct linkage to the Patriarchal pattern. The absence of an extended genealogy of Moses can be explained on the grounds that the intermediate names have been lost or were simply not known; on the other hand, it can be argued that no names are missing and that Moses belongs either to the third or fourth generation from Levi, taken here as the Patriarch himself, not as the tribe.[10] The latter alternative involves a significant assumption about the accuracy and character of the Patriarchal genealogies; it is straining the evidence to use them, and those of the Mosaic Age, as evidence for the duration of the sojourn. The principal questions are (1) whether they were originally intended as genealogies; and (2) even if they were so construed (as they were later), whether they can be regarded as authentic and complete.

II. THE EXODUS, CONQUEST, AND SETTLEMENT

For the chronology of the Exodus, Conquest, and Settlement, we are on much firmer ground. The 13th century is now all but unanimously agreed upon as the date of the Exodus; both earlier and later centuries have been discarded, and it alone remains as both plausible and inevitable.[11] Greater precision, while desirable, is not easily gained. The Conquest, for those who accept substantially the Biblical tradition in Joshua, is commonly dated in the last quarter of the 13th century (or *ca.* 1200),[12] but there is some variation as to the date of the Exodus, i.e., in the first or second half of the century.[13] Much depends upon whether we assign a full forty years to the wilderness wandering and settlement in Transjordan or reduce this figure. A general date in the period 1280–1230 would seem appropriate, with somewhat greater probability for the earlier rather than the later figure.[14]

For the following period we have a variety of chronological traditions, including the schematic reconstruction of the Deuteronomic editor, who apparently reckoned twelve forty-year generations from the Exodus to the building of the Temple, as well as archival information about the minor judges. There is an incomplete pattern of such generations scattered through the books of Judges and Samuel, with periods of forty, eighty, and twenty years assigned to various oppressors and deliverers of Israel.[15] For chronological purposes it is important to distinguish between artificial and actual figures; it is clear that the forty-year pattern is both artificial and inaccurate, since the most that can be allowed for the period from Joshua to David is 200 years (*ca.* 1200–1000), while the Biblical pattern apparently requires 360 (i.e., subtracting the forty-year periods of Moses, Joshua, and David from the 480 total).[16] We can perhaps detect an extension of the pattern of Judges in Samuel and I Kings as far as the reign of Solomon. Beginning with Eli we have a record of five rulers of united Israel. A rule of forty years is attributed to three of the five: Eli, David, and Solomon.[17] No figure is given for Samuel, but the general description of his career would imply a rule of forty years rather than anything less.[18] The figure for Saul has been dropped from the Masoretic text, but Josephus and Acts preserve the tradition that his reign also was forty years.[19] Such a sequence can hardly be accidental; at the same time it can hardly accord with the facts. While forty may be probable as a round number for one, two, or even three of the men involved, it can hardly apply to all of them and, in any case, is not likely to be exact. This is especially interesting in the case of David and Solomon, for whom precise figures must have been available. The force of tradition must have superseded the official record, though we cannot rule out the possibility of an exact reign of forty years for both men. Apparently, then, the chronology of Israel was reckoned according to generations (i.e., forty-year periods) down to the time of the divided kingdom, when a regular dynastic chronology was followed. Traditions of a more exact nature existed, and some details have survived, but for the period in question the comprehensive Deuteronomic pattern of forty-year generations has taken precedence. In the reconstruction of Israelite chronology in the pre-monarchic and early monarchic age we must reckon with the common use of round and approximate figures.

III. THE MONARCHY

With the period of the monarchy, or more particularly the dual monarchy in Israel and Judah, we are dealing with exact numbers, based ultimately on official records and comparable in principle with the great king-lists of Egypt and Mesopotamia, while perhaps more closely akin to the Babylonian synchronistic chronicle.[20] Since the Biblical records have passed through a long process of transmission, and our earliest documents are many centuries removed from the original archives, we cannot expect to find the same degree of accuracy that we have in the ancient dynastic lists of the Near Eastern empires. While we must not undervalue the fidelity and care of the Israelite scribes, there are nevertheless numerous inconsistencies in the recorded figures; no system has yet been devised to accommodate all of them, despite an occasional claim to the contrary. These figures include not only the standard regnal years for the kings of Judah and Israel but a considerable number of synchronisms between the two nations, as well as an occasional synchronistic dating with foreign kings and events. Minor inconsistencies may well be due to diversity in the method of reckoning regnal years and calendrical overlapping. As is well known, Israel employed two calendars (at least) during most of its history: one (the familiar Nisan-Nisan year) commencing in the spring and the other six months later in the fall (the Tishri-Tishri year).[21] In spite of the fall New Year, months are always counted from Nisan. The year could be reckoned either way, or probably both ways, for different purposes. The spring year was doubtless the more original and is attested in the earliest sources;[22] it unquestionably survived the introduction of the fall calendar, so that both persisted throughout the period of the monarchy and beyond.[23]

In addition there were two different ways of counting regnal years.[24] In one (the so-called antedating system), the accession year was reckoned twice, as the last year of the deceased king and as the first year of the new king; while in the other (the so-called postdating system), the accession year was reckoned only as the final year of the deceased king, and the new king's reign was regarded as formally beginning with the following new year. Antedating was the vogue in Egypt, while postdating was the regular practice in Assyro-Babylonia, at least during the period of the Israelite monarchy. It appears that the Tishri-Tishri calendar, along with the antedating method, was introduced with the monarchy in Israel; thus we should normally expect the chronological data to fall into this scheme. The persistence of the Nisan-Nisan calendar in the religious traditions, however, and the possible shift to a postdating pattern (under the influence of Assyrian domination and conquest), indicate that some of the figures may belong to a different pattern.[25] We do not know whether the Deuteronomist compiled his own figures on the basis of a single scheme from various sources or whether he simply incorporated the information from tables already prepared. The net effect in any reconstruction is to leave a margin of adjustment of at least a year or two in reconciling the figures in the Israel-Judah dynastic chronology. Greater precision is largely illusory, except where we have confirmed extra-Biblical dates to control the Biblical figures. Under the circumstances, we must expect different scholarly reconstructions of Israelite chronology, which will legitimately vary by a few years. A greater degree of agreement is not likely to be achieved until new extra-Biblical data bearing specifically on chronological matters turn up.

For the monarchical period there are four dates fixed by synchronisms with extra-Biblical records; these form the framework within which the Israelite king lists must be worked out.

(1) The accession of Solomon, ca. 961 B.C.: This date is based upon a synchronism recorded in Josephus between the 11th (or 12th) year of Hiram and the fourth year of Solomon, the year work began on the construction of the Jerusalem Temple.[26] Working from the Tyrian king list given by Josephus and known synchronisms with Assyrian rulers, M. B. Rowton has arrived at the year 959 for this event, or an accession date for Solomon of 962.[27] We prefer 958 to Rowton's 959, but the argument is not affected by this slight shift. The resulting chronology for Hiram of Tyre, and David and Solomon of Israel, is entirely in keeping with the incidental Biblical information about their relationships and overlapping reigns, i.e., David must have been on the throne for several years after the accession of Hiram 969 (or 968). We may then calculate David's reign as extending from 1000 to 961; this must be roughly correct, though perhaps we should not regard the figures as precise. Similarly Solomon's reign covers the years 961–922, if we allow him the full forty years assigned in the Bible. The latest specific regnal year recorded is the 20th; how much longer Solomon reigned cannot be settled with certainty.[28] The limits set by contemporary scholars for the beginning of the dual monarchy (not earlier than 931, not later than 922)

fit well with our fixed date for Solomon's accession, as well as the round figure for the length of his reign. The later we set the date, the better it fits.[29]

(2) *The accession of Jehu, 842/1 B.C.:* On the basis of the records of Shalmaneser III of Assyria, it is certain that 841 is the latest possible date for the accession of Jehu.[30] Scholarly opinion is virtually unanimous that 842 is the earliest feasible date for his accession, which makes 842/1 a key date for any reconstruction of Israelite chronology.[31] In addition there is the fortunate circumstance (for the chronologer) that Jehu was an efficient butcher; by killing both Joram of Israel and Ahaziah of Judah at the same time, he provided us with a firm synchronism for Israelite-Judahite chronology. Thus we have a fixed period of 120 years from the accession of Solomon to that of Jehu within which to fit the regnal years of the kings of Israel and Judah. For this period we have, in addition to Solomon's forty years, ninety-eight for Israel and ninety-five for Judah. By making use of the antedating system presumably operative at this period, the numbers for Judah and Israel can be reduced to ninety and thus reconciled with each other.[32] Beyond this point, scholars are pretty much on their own. The figures can be reduced by reference to certain synchronisms, co-regencies can be inferred from excessive or overlapping numbers, and apparent or supposed errors can be corrected on the basis of necessity, probability, or conjecture. Two extra-Biblical dates have been brought to bear on the problem, but without decisive effect. It is known that Ahab was king of Israel in 853, when he fought in a coalition against Shalmaneser III.[33] The question is how much more time must be allowed for the campaign against Aram (Israel's ally in 853) in which Ahab was killed.[34] 853 is the earliest possible date for the end of his reign, but a later date is more likely, with 850 as a terminus.

Another important synchronism is recorded in I Kings 14:25, where Shishak's invasion of Judah is dated to the fifth year of Rehoboam. Unfortunately, the corresponding year of Shishak's reign is not given in the Bible, and the evidence of the Egyptian records is likewise not definitive. Albright, however, has recently shown that the invasion must have taken place late in Shishak's reign, which is to be dated approximately 935–915.[35] This makes probable a date *ca.* 918 for·the invasion, which would establish an accession year for Rehoboam in 922, the latest date (cf. above) for the death of Solomon.

In the light of this dating, we must then reduce the presumed Deuteronomic chronology of ninety years to about eighty. Some compression and reshuffling of the dates are required to attain this end, and some variation in the assignment of the intermediate regnal years is therefore possible. Such a reduction is not in itself improbable when we reckon with the normal tendency for figures to increase in the course of transmission, and the absence of critical historical techniques in antiquity for the determination of specific dates. If, however, we are to reckon with ninety years as the proper figure, then we must reduce Solomon's reign accordingly and assign the Shishak synchronism to the 15th rather than the fifth year of Rehoboam. His accession year would then be 931.[36]

(3) *The Fall of Samaria in 722/1 B.C.*: This date is certified by the annals of Sargon II of Assyria; in spite of recent efforts to undermine it, there is no reason to question its accuracy.[37] We are not provided, however, with a solid Judahite synchronism, which is all the more deplorable since the chronological material in the Bible for this period is in a state of confusion, with at least two conflicting patterns of synchronisms between Israel and Judah.[38] The divergent totals of both north and south for the period from Jehu to the fall of Samaria must be compressed or otherwise resolved into a sum of 120 years. The difficulty with the northern figures centers around the turmoil of the last years, during which there were frequent changes of rulers and overlapping claims of authority. In the south the total number of years is even higher, and considerable juggling is required to bring the figures into line with the established limits. Co-regencies may be involved here, since we have the attested regency of Jotham during the later years of Uzziah's reign.[39] The question may be raised whether Athaliah's regency was officially reckoned to Joash's forty-year reign, since the queen could hardly have exercised royal power in her own name (but presumably only in behalf of the heir apparent).[40] This view may be held in spite of the fact that the Deuteronomic editor has calculated the synchronisms on the basis of an independent reign for the queen. The synchronisms for this period are in notorious disarray and can hardly be relied upon for a reconstruction of the chronology.

(4) *The First Capture of Jerusalem, March 15/16, 597 B.C.*: For the remaining period of the monarchy we are concerned only with the chronology of Judah. Here there is one certain date, the capture of Jerusalem by Nebuchadrezzar in March 597, along with other synchronisms which make the reconstruction of this era relatively more precise than the others. The first of these synchronisms concerns Sennacherib's invasion of Judah in 701, which is dated in the 14th year of Hezekiah.[41] Thus Hezekiah's twenty-nine-year reign is to be dated from 715/14 to 687/86, a figure now widely accepted by scholars in preference to earlier dates formerly proposed.[42] This chronology fits better with the two-campaign hypothesis, cumulative evidence for which is now quite impressive. Analysis of the material in II Kings and Isaiah, along with consideration of new data on Egyptian dynastic chronology for this period, strengthens the case for a second Assyrian campaign against Hezekiah between ca. 689 and 686.[43] Reckoning from Hezekiah's dates to the fixed chronology of the last years of Judah, there is an excess of ten years in the recorded regnal totals. Since the figures for the kings from Amon to the end are either reasonable in themselves (e.g., thirty-one years for Josiah) or well attested otherwise, the only possible reduction is in the case of Manasseh, who is assigned the longest reign (fifty-five years) in the entire king list. It is clear that he cannot have enjoyed a sole reign of more than forty-five years,

presuming that the other regnal totals are correct. There are two possible ways of dealing with the ten-year excess: either assign it to a co-regency of Manasseh with his father Hezekiah or regard 55 as a scribal error (of one kind or another) for an original 45.[44] It is easy enough to account for this change on the basis of the general tendency for numbers to increase in the course of transmission, and the error involved in the change from forty-five to fifty-five is a simple one. At the same time we must reckon with the general reliability of the figures for this period and the consistency of the textual tradition; and this might reasonably incline us to the co-regency theory as the simplest way out of the dilemma. The point to be considered is that resort to the co-regency is occasioned by the numerical problem and does not arise from any certain knowledge of normative (rather than exceptional) Israelite or Judahite practice. If indeed the overlapping figures are a hitherto unrecognized clue to a widespread institution in Israel, the implications for understanding the operation of the monarchy in Israel will be far-reaching. At present the evidence is too slender to draw a firm conclusion about the prevalence of co-regencies in Israel. Following out either method here, the major conclusion is the same: an independent reign of forty-five years for Manasseh. Beyond that, we cannot now go with confidence.

For the final years of the Judahite monarchy we have exact dates not only for the initial capture of the city of Jerusalem but also for the accession of Nebuchadrezzar and the battle of Carchemish.[45] Since, however, we are handicapped by uncertainty about the calendar and system of counting regnal years in use in Judah at this time, or according to which the historian made his calculations, there is still a permissible leeway of a year in fixing certain dates (and this margin is reflected in the conflicting synchronisms in the Biblical materials). We may summarize the situation as follows: beginning with March 597 for the capture of Jerusalem, we can date the three-month reign of Jehoiachin from December 598. The 11th and final year of Jehoiakim, therefore, began either in Nisan or Tishri of 598, and his first year must therefore have been 608, though he may have come to the throne as early as 609 (after the three-month reign of Jehoahaz which falls somewhere in the period 609/8). The death of Josiah, at the battle of Megiddo, must be placed in 609, or at the latest, early in 608. His first regnal year must have been 639, though he may have come to power in 640.[46] The synchronism between Jehoiakim's fourth year and the battle of Carchemish, dated in May–June 605, confirms this reconstruction.

Working forward from March 597, the first year of Zedekiah must be 597 and the 11th, 587. If we suppose that he was actually regarded as a regent for the captive Jehoiachin (who is reckoned as the king of Judah in Babylonian records), then his regnal years would be calculated on the same basis as those of Jehoiachin (and Ezekiel's years of the captivity).[47] If the official reign was reckoned from Nisan 597, then the end of his rule and the fall of Jerusalem are to be dated in the summer of 587. If it was reckoned from Tishri 597,[48] then the proper date for the destruction of the city would be 586. An absolute decision between the two dates is not yet possible, and the discrepancy corresponds to the two different sets of synchronisms between Judahite and Babylonian records, namely the eighth and 19th years of Nebuchadrezzar for the successive captures of the city, and the seventh and 18th years.[49] Since the Babylonian Chronicle places the first captivity explicitly in the seventh year, it would appear that the advocates of the 18th year, namely 587, for the second capture have the stronger case. The discrepancy in the Biblical accounts might lie ultimately in the fact that the first capture took place at the turn of the year,[50] i.e., the last month of Nebuchadrezzar's seventh year, and doubtless mopping-up operations continued on into the next year. However we explain the conflicting data, a final solution must await discovery of further confirmatory evidence.

IV. EZRA–NEHEMIAH

The chronological problems connected with the era of Ezra–Nehemiah remain unsolved, though there is a growing scholarly consensus in favor of reversing the traditional order (which placed Ezra in the seventh year of Artaxerxes I, i.e., 458, and Nehemiah in the 20th year, or 445).[51] Van Hoonacker was the chief exponent of the view that Ezra followed Nehemiah and was therefore to be dated in the reign of Artaxerxes II (seventh year = 398).[52] While in most respects this hypothesis has provided an eminently satisfactory reordering of the events of the late fifth and early fourth centuries, it has nevertheless resulted in the complete sundering of the careers of Ezra and Nehemiah. Since the Biblical record explicitly couples them on more than one occasion, and otherwise links their ministries, it is too drastic a solution to separate them entirely.[53] A third hypothesis has been supported by Albright, among others, which attempts to do justice both to the persuasive arguments in favor of the sequence Nehemiah–Ezra, and to the Biblical tradition that their ministries overlapped.[54] The date arrived at for the commencement of Ezra's work is the 37th year of Artaxerxes I (428), regarding the 7 of the Masoretic text as an error for the larger number. A date for Ezra about this time fits best with all the available evidence in the Biblical sources, as well as the collateral evidence about the Jerusalem situation toward the end of the fifth century in the Elephantine Papyri.[55] Nevertheless, the number itself has no textual warrant and ought not to be pressed.

During the last forty years, or approximately the span of Dr. Albright's career, ancient Near Eastern and Biblical chronology have been solidly grounded on the basis of archaeological data. In the process of fixing the limits for chronological reconstruction, he has been the prime mover. With regard to the Biblical picture, the general lines are not likely to be changed drastically in the future, though, as is to be expected, the further back we go, the greater the margin of error and uncertainty.

The Patriarchal Age can be dated with confidence in the Middle Bronze period (*ca.* 2000–1550). Beyond this, caution is necessary, though it is the present writer's judgment that the central nucleus of tradition, and specifically the Abrahamic stories, go back to the earliest part of this era (i.e., the 20th and 19th centuries), with inevitable modifications and adaptations in the course of a long and complex process of transmission.

The chronological limits for the period from Moses to the monarchy are now firmly fixed: the Exodus in the 13th century and the kingdom of David at the beginning of the tenth. Within these limits, all dates are necessarily approximate, though there are definite correlations between Biblical tradition and archaeological data.

Beginning with the monarchy, a much greater degree of precision is possible; several absolute dates, fixed by extra-Biblical evidence, offer both a framework and control points in the reconstruction of the chronology. A maximum variation of ten to twenty years is possible in the case of certain kings, but for the most part the limits are narrower; for the final century and a half of Judah's history there is general agreement practically to the year. Almost all possible combinations and permutations of the Biblical figures have been worked out by scholars; in many cases the detailed reconstruction outruns the evidence. No final decision among the competing systems is likely until new evidence has been introduced into the picture. As this becomes available with new synchronisms and fixed dates, we can expect further progress in settling outstanding problems.[56]

Jerusalem, Israel; July 1, 1959

SECTION B.   THE ANCIENT NEAR EAST: CHRONOLOGICAL BIBLIOGRAPHY AND CHARTS

EDWARD F. CAMPBELL, JR.

The chronological lists here presented seek to summarize the so-called "low" chronology held by a significant group of American and continental scholars, among whom W. F. Albright has been, and is, a pioneer. A complete defense and documentation of the presentation has not been given, but the general bibliographical suggestions point to key studies which have been used in the preparation of the lists.

The "low" chronology takes its name from the chronological position assigned both to the early dynasties of Egypt and to the First Dynasty of Babylon, with the arrangement which results from the study of synchronisms with these two foci. Two separate bibliographical sections here included cite the major scholarly presentations defending the various conflicting positions. A further relatively minor problem is the chronology of the Eighteenth Egyptian dynasty; here again the important studies are cited.

It goes without saying that these lists are provisional. The more one studies the intricacies of the chronological problems in the ancient Near East, the less he is inclined to think of any presentation as final. For this reason, the term *circa* could be used even more liberally than it is. It is used in these lists only where the date given is fairly certain but may be off the actual date by a matter of just a few years. Numbers in parentheses after the name of a king refer to the duration of a co-regency with his predecessor.

GENERAL DOCUMENTATION:

ALBRIGHT, W. F., *From the Stone Age to Christianity.* 2nd ed. New York, 1957 (1940).

BORCHARDT, L., *Die Mittel zur zeitlichen Festlegung von Punkten der ägyptische Geschichten und ihre Anwendung.* Cairo, 1935.

GELB, I. J., "Two Assyrian King Lists," *JNES* XIII (1954), pp. 209–30.

GURNEY, O. R., *The Hittites.* Harmondsworth, 1954.

HELCK, H. W., *Untersuchungen zu Manethō und den ägyptischen Königslisten. Untersuchungen zur Geschichte und Altertumskunde Aegyptens,* XVIII, ed. H. Kees. Berlin, 1956.

HELCK, H. W., and OTTO, E., *Kleines Wörterbuch der Aegyptologie.* Wiesbaden, 1956.

JACOBSEN, T., *The Sumerian King List. Assyriological Studies* 11. Chicago, 1939.

MEER, P. VAN DER, *The Chronology of Ancient Western Asia and Egypt.* Leiden, 1955.

PARKER, R. A., *The Calendars of Ancient Egypt. Studies in Ancient Oriental Civilization,* no. 26. Chicago, 1950.

PARKER, R. A., "Chronology" in the article "Egypt." *Encyclopedia Americana,* 1955 ed., pp. 14b–14e.

PARKER, R. A., "The Lunar Dates of Thutmose III and Ramesses II," *JNES* XVI (1957), pp. 39–43.

POEBEL, A., "The Assyrian King List from Khorsabad," *JNES* I (1942), pp. 247–306, 460–92; *JNES* II (1943), pp. 56–90.

POEBEL, A., *The Second Dynasty of Isin, according to a New King List Tablet. Assyriological Studies* 15. Chicago, 1955.

ROWTON, M. B., "Mesopotamian Chronology and the 'Era of Menophres,' " *Iraq* VIII (1946), pp. 94–110.

ROWTON, M. B., "Ṭuppu in the Assyrian King Lists," *JNES* XVIII (1959), pp. 213–21.

SCHARFF, A., and MOORTGAT, A., *Ägypten und Vorderasien im Altertum.* Munich, 1950.

TADMOR, H., "Historical Implications of the Correct Rendering of Akkadian *dâku*," *JNES* XVII (1958), pp. 129–41.

WISEMAN, D. J., *Chronicles of Chaldean Kings (626–556 B.C.) in the British Museum.* London, 1956.

WRIGHT, G. E., "The Problem of the Transition between the Chalcolithic and Bronze Ages," *Eretz-Israel* V (1958), pp. 37–45.

For bibliography on the subject of Old Testament chronology, see the notes to the article, "Old Testament Chronology," by David Noel Freedman in this chapter.

BIBLIOGRAPHY FOR THE DATING OF THE EARLY EGYPTIAN DYNASTIES:

ALBRIGHT, W. F., "Some Recent Publications Received by the Editor: Egyptology," *BASOR* 119 (Oct., 1950), pp. 29 f.

ALBRIGHT, W. F., "A Survey of the Archaeological Chronology of Palestine from Neolithic to Middle Bronze," *Relative Chronologies in Old World Archaeology*, ed. R. W. Ehrich. Chicago, 1954, pp. 28–33.

DRIOTON, E., and VANDIER, J., *Les peuples de l'Orient Méditerranéen*, II: *L'Égypte.* Paris, 1952.

HAYES, W. C., *The Scepter of Egypt.* Part I: *From the Earliest Times to the End of the Middle Kingdom.* New York, 1953, esp. pp. 34 ff.

KANTOR, H. J., "The Chronology of Egypt and Its Correlation with That of Other Parts of the Near East in the Periods before the Late Bronze Age," *Relative Chronologies in Old World Archaeology*, ed. R. W. Ehrich. Chicago, 1954, pp. 1–27, esp. 7–10.

PARKER, R. A., "Chronology" in the article "Egypt," *Encyclopedia Americana*, 1955 ed., esp. p. 14b.

SCHARFF, A. and MOORTGAT, A., *Ägypten und Vorderasien im Altertum.* Munich, 1950, esp. pp. 34–37.

STOCK, H., *Die erste Zwischenzeit Ägyptens: Untergang der Pyramidenzeit, Zwischenreiche von Abydos und Herakleopolis, Aufstieg Thebens.* Rome, 1949.

BIBLIOGRAPHY FOR THE DATING OF THE FIRST DYNASTY OF BABYLON:

The works here cited are listed according to the position which the author takes on the chronological placement of the reign of Hammurapi. Many of the early studies are not cited because the positions defended in them are universally recognized as no longer possible.

ca. 1900: The "ultra-high" chronology:

LANDSBERGER, B., "Assyrische Königsliste und 'dunkles Zeitalter,'" *JCS* VIII (1954), pp. 31–45, 47–73, 106–33.

1848–1806: The "high" chronology:

GOETZE, A., "The Problem of Chronology and Early Hittite History," *BASOR* 122 (Apr. 1951), pp. 18–25.

GOETZE, A., "The Date of the Hittite Raid on Babylon," *BASOR* 127 (Oct. 1952), pp. 21–26.

GOETZE, A., "Alalaḫ and Hittite Chronology," *BASOR* 146 (Apr. 1957), pp. 20–26.

SIDERSKY, P., "Nouvelle étude sur la chronologie de la dynastie Ḫammurapienne," *RA* XXXVII (1940), pp. 45–54.

THUREAU-DANGIN, F., *La chronologie de la première dynastie Babylonienne. Mémoires de l'Academie,* XLIII, 2ᵉ partie. Paris, 1942.

1792–1750: The "middle" chronology:

ALBRIGHT, W. F., "New Light on the History of Western Asia in the Second Millennium B.C.," *BASOR* 77 (Feb. 1940), pp. 20–32.

ROWTON, M. B., "The Date of Hammurabi," *JNES* XVII (1958), pp. 97–111.

SMITH, S., *Alalakh and Chronology.* London, 1940.

SMITH, S., "Middle Minoan I–II and Babylonian Chronology," *American Jour. of Archaeology* XLIX (1945), pp. 1–24.

UNGNAD, A., *Die Venustafeln und das neunte Jahr Samsuilunas (1741 v. Chr.). Mitteilungen der altorientalischen Gesellschaft,* XIII/3. Leipzig, 1940.

1728–1686: The "low" chronology:

ALBRIGHT, W. F., "A Third Revision of the Early Chronology of Western Asia," *BASOR* 88 (Dec. 1942), pp. 28–36.

ALBRIGHT, W. F., Review of S. Smith, *Alalakh and Chronology, American Jour. of Archaeology* XLVII (1943), pp. 491–92.

ALBRIGHT, W. F., "An Indirect Synchronism between Egypt and Mesopotamia, cir. 1730 B.C.," *BASOR* 99 (Oct. 1945), pp. 9–18.

ALBRIGHT, W. F., "A Note on the Chronology of the Second Millennium B.C.," *BASOR* 126 (Apr. 1952), pp. 24–26.

ALBRIGHT, W. F., "Further Observations on the Chronology of the Early Second Millennium B.C.," *BASOR* 127 (Oct. 1952), pp. 27–30.

ALBRIGHT, W. F., "Stratigraphic Confirmation of the Low Mesopotamian Chronology," *BASOR* 144 (Dec. 1956), pp. 26–30.

ALBRIGHT, W. F., "Further Observations on the Chronology of Alalakh," *BASOR* 146 (Apr. 1957), pp. 26–34.

CORNELIUS, F., "Die Chronologie des Vorderen Orients im 2. Jahrtausend v. Chr.," *AfO* XVII (1954–56), pp. 294–309.

OTTEN, H., "Die hethitischen 'Königslisten' und die altorientalische Chronologie," *Mitteilungen d. Deut. Or. Gesellschaft* 83 (1951), pp. 47–71.

ROWTON, M. B., "Mesopotamian Chronology and the 'Era of Menophres,'" *Iraq* VIII (1946), pp. 94–110.

ROWTON, M. B., "Manetho's Date for Ramesses II," *JEA* XXXIV (1948), pp. 57–74.

ROWTON, M. B., "*Tuppu* and the Date of Hammurabi," *JNES* X (1951), pp. 184–204.

ROWTON, M. B., "The Date of the Hittite Capture of Babylon," *BASOR* 126 (Apr. 1952), pp. 20–24.

WAERDEN, B. L. van der, "On Babylonian Astronomy I: The Venus Tablets of Ammiṣaduqa," *Jaarbericht No. 10 van het vooraziatisch-egyptisch Genootschap "Ex Oriente Lux"* (1945–48), pp. 414–24.

ca. 1704–1662: The "ultra-low" chronology:

BÖHL, F. M. TH., "King Hammurabi of Babylon in the Setting of His Time (about 1700 B.C.)," *Mededeelingen der Koninklijke Nederlandsche Akademie van Wetenschappen, Afd.* Letterkunde, Nieuwe Reeks, Deel 9, No. 10 (1946), pp. 341–68.

SCHUBERT, K., "Die altorientalischen Dynastien zur Zeit Hammurapis von Babylon," *Wiener Zeitschrift für die Kunde des Morgenlandes* LI (1948/52), pp. 21–33.

WEIDNER, E., "Bemerkungen zur Königsliste aus Chorsābād," *AfO* XV (1945–51), pp. 85–102.

BIBLIOGRAPHY FOR THE EIGHTEENTH EGYPTIAN DYNASTY:

The chronology of the Eighteenth Dynasty depends upon the position taken on six problems: (1) the length of Amenophis II's reign; (2) the assumed co-regency of Amenophis III and Amenophis IV (Akhenaten); (3) the length of Tutankhamun's reign; (4) the length of Haremhab's reign; (5) the length of Seti I's reign; and (6) the date of Ramses II's accession. The following studies give a picture of the various solutions available.

ALBRIGHT, W. F., *From the Stone Age to Christianity*. 2nd ed. New York, 1957. Chronological table on pp. 404–9.

ALDRED, C., "The End of the El-'Amārna Period," *JEA* XLIII (1957), · pp. 30–42.

ALDRED, C., "Two Theban Notables During the Later Reign of Amenophis III," *JNES* XVIII (1959), pp. 113–20.

ALDRED, C., "Year 12 at El-'Amārna," *JEA* XLIII (1957), pp. 114 ff.

CAMPBELL, E. F., *The Hypothetical Coregency of Amenophis III and Akhenaten with Special Reference to the Amarna Letters*. Unpublished Ph.D. dissertation at Johns Hopkins University. Baltimore, 1959.

ENGELBACH, R., "Material for a Revision of the History of the Heresy Period of the XVIII Dynasty," *Annales du Service des Antiquités de l'Égypte* XL (1940), pp. 133–84.

GARDINER, A. H., "The So-called Tomb of Queen Teye," *JEA* XLIII (1957), pp. 10–25.

HAYES, W. C., "Inscriptions from the Palace of Amenhotep III," *JNES* X (1951), pp. 35–56, 82–112, 156–83, 231–42.

HELCK, H. W., "Die Sinai-Inschrift des Amenmose," *Mitteilungen des Instituts für Orientforschung* II (1954), pp. 189–207.

HELCK, H. W., "Eine Stele des Vizekönigs *Wśr-St.t*," *JNES* XIV (1955), pp. 22–31.

HELCK, H. W. and OTTO, E., *Kleines Wörterbuch der Aegyptologie*. Wiesbaden, 1958. See the entries under the various kings' names.

PARKER, R. A., "The Lunar Dates of Thutmose III and Ramesses II," *JNES* XVI (1957), pp. 39–43.

PENDLEBURY, J. D. S., et al., *The City of Akhenaten*, III. *44th Memoir of the Egyptian Exploration Society*. London, 1951. H. Fairman's summary of chronological information is on pp. 152 ff.

ROWTON, M. B., "Manetho's Date for Ramesses II," *JEA* XXXIV (1948), pp. 57–74.

SEELE, K., "King Ay and the Close of the Amarna Age," *JNES* XIV (1955), pp. 168–80.

Chicago; July 1, 1959

CIRCA	EGYPT	PALESTINE	SYRIA-ASIA MINOR	ASSYRIA	BABYLON
3800	Badarian	Yarmukian Jericho VIII and "Neolithic B"	Amuq D		Obeidian
3700				Obeidian	
3500	Amratian	Ghassulian	Amuq E		
3200	Gerzean	Early Bronze I	Amuq F		Warka Period
3000					Jemdet Nasr Period
2850	I Dynasty & II Dynasty c2850-2615	Early Bronze II	Amuq G		Early Dynastic I
2600	III Dynasty c2615-2565	Early Bronze III	Amuq H		Early Dynastic II
2500	IV Dynasty c2565-2440				Early Dynastic III
2400	V Dynasty c2440-2315		Amuq I-J		Dynasty of Accad Sargon I 2360-2305 Rimush 2304-2296 Manishtushu 2295-2281 Naram-Sin 2280-2244 Sharkalisharri 2243-2219 Dudu 2215-2195 Shu-durul 2194-2180 Gutians 2180-2082
2300	VI Dynasty c2315-2175 Pepi II c2270-2180	Early Bronze IV (IIIB)			
2100	VII Dynasty 2175 VIII Dynasty 2175-2160 IX & X Dynasties 2160-2040 XI Dynasty 2133-1992	Middle Bronze I			III Dynasty of Ur c2060-1950 Ur-nammu c2060-2043 Shulgi c2042-1995 (Gudea in Lagash c2000) Bur-Sin c1994-1986 Shu-Sin c1985-1977 Ibi-Sin c1976-1952
2000	XII Dynasty 1991-1786 Amenemhet I 1991-1962 Sesostris I (10) 1971-1928				

	Egypt	Palestine	Syria / Anatolia	Assyria	Babylonia
					Isin Dynasty c1958-1733 **Larsa Dynasty** c1961-1699
1900	Amenemhet II (2) 1929-1895 Sesostris II (3) 1897-1879 Sesostris III 1878-1843 Amenemhet III 1842-1797 Amenemhet IV (2) 1798-1790 Sebeknefrure 1789-1786	Middle Bronze IIA		Erishu I	I Dynasty of Babylon 1830-1531 Shumu-abum 1830-1817 Shumu-alim 1816-1781
1800	XIII & XVI Dynasties c1785-1647 XIV Dynasty c1785-1603 XV Dynasty c1678-1570	Middle Bronze IIB	Mari Aleppo Hittites Anitta Alalakh VII	Ikunu Sharru-kin I Puzur-Asshur II Naram-Sin Erishu II Shamshi-Adad I 1748-1716 Ishme-Dagan I c1715-1676 (Several kings vie for throne) Asshur-dugul c1675-1670 (Several kings vie for throne) Belu-bani c1669-1660 Libaya c1659-1643	Zabum 1780-1767 Apil-Sin 1766-1749 Sin-muballit 1748-1729 Hammurapi 1728-1686 Shamshi-iluna 1685-1648
1600	XVII Dynasty c1600-1570 Kamosis c1580	Middle Bronze IIC	Tudhaliya I Labarna Hattusili c1580	Sharma-Adad I c1642-1631 IP-tar-Sin c1630-1619 Bazaya c1618-1591 Lullaya c1590-1585 Kidin-Ninua c1584-1571 Sharma-Adad II c1570-1568	Abi-eshu' 1647-1620 Ammi-ditana 1619-1583 Cossean Dynasty c1600-1150 Ammi-saduqa 1582-1562 Shamshu-ditana 1561-1531
	XVIII Dynasty 1570-c1304 Amosis c1570-1545 Amenophis I c1545-1525	Late Bronze I	Mursili c1550-1530 Hantili Zidanta Ammuna Huzziya Telipinu Alluwamna	Erishu III c1567-1555 Shamshi-Adad II c1554-1549 Ishme-Dagan II c1548-1533 Shamshi-Adad III c1532-1517 Asshur-nirari I c1516-1491	Agum II Burnaburiash I
1500	Tuthmosis I 1525-1508 Tuthmosis II 1508-1490 Tuthmosis III 1490-1436 Hatshepsut 1484-1469 Amenophis II c1436-1410		Tudhaliya II Arnuwanda I Hattusili II	Puzur-Asshur III c1490-1467 Enlil-nasir I c1466-1454 Nur-il c1453-1442 Asshur-rabi I Asshur-nadin-ahhe I } c1441-1424(?) Enlil-nasir II 1423-1418 Asshur-nirari II 1417-1411	
1400	Tuthmosis IV c1410-1402 Amenophis III c1402-1364	Late Bronze IIA	Tudhaliya III Suppiluliuma c1380-1342	Asshur-bel-nisheshu 1410-1402 Asshur-rim-nisheshu 1401-1394 Asshur-nadin-ahhe II 1393-1384 Eriba-Adad I 1383-1357	Karaindash I Kadashman-Enlil I Burnaburiash II

CIRCA	EGYPT	PALESTINE	SYRIA-ASIA MINOR	ASSYRIA	BABYLON
					Karaindash II
	Amenophis IV c1364-1347			Asshur-uballiṭ 1356-1321	Kadashman-Harbe I
	Semenkhkere c1347-1346 (?)				Kurigalzu (reigned 22
	Tutankhamun c1346-1337		Arnuwanda II		or 25 years)
	Ay c1337-1333			Enlil-nirari 1320-1311	
	Haremhab c1333-1304		Mursili II	Arik-den-ili 1310-1299	
	XIX Dynasty c1304-1200		Muwatilli		Nazimaruttash (26 years)
1300	Ramses I c1304-1303	Late Bronze IIB	Urhi-Teshup (Mursili III)	Adad-nirari I 1298-1266	Kadashmanturgu (17 or 18)
	Seti I c1303-1290	Moses **The Exodus**			Kadashman-Enlil II (15)
	Ramses II 1290-1224	c1280-1230	Hattusili III	Shalmaneser I 1265-1236	Kudur-Enlil (9)
			Tudhaliya IV		Shagaraktishuriash (13)
					Kashtiliash (8)
		Conquest			(Interregnum?)
		Joshua			Enlil-nadin-shumi (1½)
			Arnuwanda III	Tukulti-Ninurta I 1233-1199	Kadashman-Harbe II (1½)
		Iron Age I		Asshur-nadin-apli 1198-1195	Adad-shum-iddina (6)
			Suppiluliuma II	Asshur-nirari III 1194-1189	Adad-shum-uṣur (30)
				Enlil-kudur-uṣur 1188-1184	
				Ninurta-apil-Ekur 1183-1181	Meli-Shipak (15)
1200	Merneptah 1223-1211				Marduk-apla-iddina (13)
	XX Dynasty c1200-1065			Asshur-dan I 1180-1135	Zababa-shum-iddina (1)
	(Interregnum c1200-1175)			Ninurta-tukulti-Asshur	Enlil-nadin-ahhe (3)
	Ramses III c1175-1144	Period of the Judges		Mutakkil-Nushku	(Interregnum?)
					II Dynasty of Isin
	Ramses IV				Marduk-kabit-ahheshu (18)
	← to →				Itti-Marduk-balatu (8)
				Asshur-resh-ishi I 1134-1117	Ninurta-nadin-shumi (6)
					Nabu-kudurri-usur (22)
					Enlil-nadin-apli (4)
1100	Ramses XI			Tiglathpileser I 1116-1078	Marduk-nadin-ahhe (18)
	XXI Dynasty 1065-935			Asharid-apil-Ekur 1077-1076	Marduk-shapik-zeri (13)
	Smendes 1065-			Asshur-bel-kala 1075-1056	Adad-apla-iddina (22)
				Eriba-Adad II 1057-1056	Marduk- ? (1)
				Shamshi-Adad IV 1055-1052	Marduk- ? (12)

		Saul c1020			**Nabu-shum-libur (3)**
		David c1000-961			Dynasty of Sealands

Assyria

Asshur-naṣir-apli I 1051-1033
Shalmaneser II 1032-1021
Asshur-nirari IV 1020-1015
Asshur-rabi II 1014-974
Asshur-resh-ishi II 973-969
Tiglathpileser II 968-936

Asshur-dan II 935-913

Adad-nirari II 912-892
Tukulti-ninurta II 891-885

Asshur-naṣir-apli II 884-860
Shalmaneser III 859-825

Shamshi-Adad V 824-812
Adad-nirari III 811-784

Shalmaneser IV 783-774
Asshur-dan III 773-756
Asshur-nirari V 755-746
Tiglath-pileser III 745-728   Nabonassar 747-728

Shalmaneser V 727-723
Sargon II 722-706
Sennacherib 705-682
Esarhaddon 681-670

Asshur-ban-apli 669-633
Chaldeans
Nabopolassar 626-605
Fall of Nineveh 612
Nebuchadrezzar II 605-561

Solomon c961-922

Judah	**Israel**
Rehoboam c922-915	Jeroboam c922-901
Abijah c915-913	Nadab c901-900
Asa c913-873	Baasha c900-877
	Elah c877-876
	Zimri c876
Jehoshaphat c873-849	Omri c876-869
	Ahab c869-850
Jehoram c849-842	Ahaziah c850-849
Ahaziah c842	Joram c849-842
Athaliah c842-837	Jehu c842-815
Jehoash c837-800	Joahaz c815-801
Amaziah c800-783	Joash c801-786
Uzziah c783-742	Jeroboam II c786-746
Jotham (?) c750-735	Zechariah c746-745
	Shallum c745
	Menahem c745-738
	Pekahiah c738-737
Jehoahaz c735-715	Pekah c737-732
	Hoshea c732-724
Hezekiah c715-687	Fall of Samaria 722/1
Manasseh c687-642	
Amon c642-640	
Josiah c640-609	
Jehoahaz 609	
Jehoiakim 609-598	
Jehoiachin 597	
Zedekiah 597-587	
Fall of Jerusalem 587	

Egypt

1000

XXII Dynasty c935-725
Shishak I c935-914
Osorkon I c914-874

Takelot I (?) c874-860

Osorkon II c860-832 (?)
(Shishak II)
Takelot II c837/6-823
Shishak III c822-770(?)
Pami c770-765
Shishak IV c765-725(?)
XXIII Dynasty c759-715(?)
Petubastis c759-735
Osorkon IV   -715   XXV Dynasty 751-656
                        P'eakhi 751-710
XXIV Dynasty c725-709   Invades Egypt 716/5
Tefnakht c725-715
Bocchoris c715-709   Shabako c710-696
                        Shebteko c696-685
                        Taharqo c685-663
                        Assyrian Conquest 671
XXVI Dynasty 663-525   Tanutamun 663-656
Psammetichus I 663-609

800

700

Necho 609-594

600

Psammetichus II 594-588

CIRCA	EGYPT	PALESTINE	SYRIA-ASIA MINOR	ASSYRIA	BABYLON
	Apries 588-568				Amel-Marduk 561-559
	Amasis 568-526				Neriglassar 559-556
					Labashi-Marduk 556-555
					Nabonidus 555-539
		Edict of Cyrus 538			Cyrus conquers Babylon 539
	Psammetichus III 526-525				Cyrus -530
	Cambyses conquers Egypt 525	Persian Conquest			Cambyses 530-522
					Darius I (Hystaspes) 522-486
					Xerxes I 486-464
		Nehemiah in Jerusalem 445			Artaxerxes I 464-423
		Ezra in Jerusalem c428 (?)			
400	XXVIII Dynasty				Darius II 423-404
	Amyrtaios 404-398				Artaxerxes II 404-360
	XXIX Dynasty 398-378				
	XXX Dynasty 378-341				Artaxerxes III 359-338
	Second Persian Period (Dynasty XXXI) 341-332				Arses 338-335
					Darius III 335-

ALEXANDER THE GREAT CONQUERS EGYPT AND ASIA BETWEEN 334 AND 323

NOTES TO CHAPTER SEVEN, SECTION A

1. See Albright's synchronistic chart, prepared for the 2nd edition of his *Recent Discoveries in Bible Lands,* supplement to *Young's Concordance* (2nd ed., 1955), and reprinted separately by the Biblical Colloquium (1956). For bibliography on chronological data presently available, see the notes to the chronological tables in this volume.

2. The most comprehensive studies of the Patriarchal Age in recent years are by R. de Vaux in "Les patriarches hébreux et les découvertes modernes," *Revue biblique,* LIII (1946), pp. 321–48; LV (1948), pp. 321–47; LVI (1949), pp. 5–36; and H. H. Rowley in "Recent Discovery and the Patriarchal Age," *Bulletin of the John Rylands Library,* XXXII (1949–50), pp. 44–79, and *From Joseph to Joshua* (1950). See also G. E. Wright's *Biblical Archaeology* (1957), pp. 40–52, and *The Westminster Historical Atlas* (2nd ed.; 1956), chap. ii, "The World of the Patriarchs." Cf. C. H. Gordon, *Introduction to Old Testament Times* (1953), pp. 100–19.

3. Rowley, *From Joseph to Joshua* (hereafter *FJJ*), pp. 61–67; cf. Albright, "A Third Revision of the Early Chronology of Western Asia," *BASOR,* No. 88 (1942), pp. 33–36.

4. Rowley, *FJJ*, pp. 70–73, and Gordon, op. cit., pp. 103–4.

5. Cf. Gordon, op. cit., pp. 100–19.

6. Cf. M. H. Pope, *El in the Ugaritic Texts, Supplement to Vetus Testamentum* II (1955), pp. 82–104. "The El of the patriarchs was the god at the height of his power and prestige, and this was the god with whom YHWH was identified" (p. 104). Also A. Kapelrud, *Baal in the Ras Shamra Texts* (1952).

7. Cf. Albright, *From the Stone Age to Christianity* (hereafter *FSAC;* 2nd ed., 1946), pp. 83–85; Rowley, *FJJ*, pp. 116 ff.

8. Rowley, *FJJ*, pp. 70–73; Gordon, op. cit., pp. 103–4.

9. M. Noth, *Das System der zwölf Stämme Israels* (1930), pp. 12, 122–23.

10. The narrative of Moses's birth in Exodus 2 is entirely lacking in genealogical details; even the names of the parents are omitted, unlike similar birth stories (e.g., Samson, Samuel). In the Samuel story (I Sam. 1:1 ff.) extensive information is supplied. The implication is clearly that the data were simply lacking in the case of Moses; this deficiency is made up in the P material, but aside from the parents' names, which may be accepted without question, the other names are drawn from the common pool of tradition. In Exodus 2:1 *bat Lēvī* can only mean a member of the clan or tribe of Levi, rather than Levi's daughter, as it was construed by P in Numbers 26:59, cf. Exodus 6:18, 20.

11. Cf. Rowley, *FJJ*, chaps. i & iii. The recent excavations at Hazor by Y. Yadin have established a 13th-century date for the destruction of the last Canaanite city, in conformity with the Biblical account in Joshua 11:10–11; see Yadin's reports in the *Biblical Archaeologist* XIX (1956), pp. 2–11; XX (1957), pp. 34–47; XXI (1958), pp. 30–47; XXII (1959), pp. 2–20; and the first volume of the formal publication by Y. Yadin, et al., *Hazor I, An Account of the First Season of Excavations, 1955* (1958).

12. Albright, *FSAC,* pp. 208 ff.; Wright, *Biblical Archaeology,* pp. 69–84; Rowley, *FJJ, passim.*

13. For the earlier date, see Albright, *FSAC,* pp. 193 ff., and references; for the later date, see Rowley, *FJJ,* pp. 138 ff., who develops a rather intricate scheme to accommodate both the Biblical and the archaeological evidence.

14. There must be a chronological factor in the Biblical tradition of a new generation growing to manhood in the wilderness; other elements which favor a stay of some duration are the Transjordan tradition, the persistence of the wilderness motif in the religious and especially the prophetic literature of Israel, the significant increase in population between Exodus and Conquest, and the image of a new national identity reflected in the Oracles of Balaam, itself an ancient poem coming from this period (cf. Albright, "The Oracles of Balaam," *JBL* LXIII [1944], pp. 207–33).

15. Rowley, *FJJ*, pp. 86–98. Noth deals with the question of the Deuteronomic chronology of Judges in his *Überlieferungsgeschichtliche Studien* (1943), pp. 47–61.

16. No figure is given for Joshua, but it is a reasonable assumption that his period of leadership was reckoned at a full generation (note his advanced age at death: 110 years, Joshua 24:29). Rowley gives a number of different schemes in *FJJ*, pp. 86–98; the approach indicated on p. 98 is doubtless correct: the generations were reckoned in terms of outstanding individuals. After Moses and Joshua, we can list Othniel (forty years, Judges 3:11), Ehud (eighty years, 3:30), Deborah and Barak (forty, 5:31), Gideon (forty, 8:28), Samson and the Philistines (Samson is accorded twenty years in 16:31, the Philistines forty in 13:1; the two are probably to be combined as forty, unless Samson is to be grouped with Eli who is credited with only twenty years in LXX, against forty in MT), Eli (forty, I Samuel 4:18), Samuel (probably forty, though only twenty is given for part of his career, I Samuel 7:2, 15), Saul (MT is confused in I Samuel 13:1, but both Josephus and Acts reckon his reign at forty years), David (forty, II Samuel 5:4 and I Kings 2:11), and Solomon (forty, I Kings 11:42).

17. See n. 16.

18. Cf. I Samuel 7:15, and I Samuel 8 & 12.

19. Acts 13:21 and Josephus, *Jewish Antiquities* VI.XIV.9; a variant tradition in Josephus gives Saul only twenty years.

20. Albright, "The Chronology of the Divided Monarchy of Israel," *BASOR,* No. 100 (1945), pp. 16–22, in which he discusses the character of Biblical regnal and synchronistic tables.

21. See Albright's discussion of the calendar in *BASOR,* No. 100, p. 18, and more recently in his review of R. North's *The Sociology of the Biblical Jubilee* in *Biblica,* XXXVII (1957), pp. 488–90. Cf. E. R. Thiele, *The Mysterious Numbers of the Hebrew Kings* (1951), pp. 14 ff.

22. Cf. Albright, *Biblica* XXXVII, p. 489; Biblical references are Exodus 13:4, 23:15, and 34:18; also 12:2.

23. The uniform reckoning of the months from Nisan alone demonstrates the survival of the spring calendar, while the celebration of the New Year in Tishri shows that the fall calendar also continued in use after the monarchy. The Gezer calendar is evidence for the introduction of the Tishri year at an early date, probably under the sponsorship of David, certainly not later than Solomon. Instead of supposing that one calendar displaced the other, we must reckon with a pattern of dual usage extending over the larger part of Israelite history; a modern illustration would be the overlapping civil and fiscal calendars of the U. S. Government. In practice, a dual calendar poses no particular difficulties; the problem for the scholar is to determine the calendrical basis of the preserved figures.

24. See Thiele's lucid presentation of the relevant data, op. cit., pp. 14–42.

25. Shifting the basis of computation between north and south, as well as assuming alterations within each kingdom, will accommodate discrepancies up to a year or two, but such efforts at precision are hardly warranted in view of the material involved.

26. Josephus, *Jewish Antiquities* VIII.iii.1 (11th year); *Against Apion* I.126 (12th year).
27. "The Date of the Founding of Solomon's Temple," *BASOR,* No. 119 (1950), pp. 20–22.
28. I Kings 9:10.
29. How to reckon the Biblical "forty years" in the context of early chronology remains a difficult problem. In the instances from the Exodus to the monarchy, the Israelites doubtless had in mind the effective working life of an adult (i.e., from twenty to sixty, or thirty to seventy); this is the way in which the duration of the wilderness generation was calculated: until all the adults died off, which would be a rough way of measuring forty years. In the case of any individual, this period could be much shorter or somewhat longer; so far as the chronology of the Judges is concerned, we must reckon also with overlapping careers. Nevertheless, forty must represent a substantial period of time, and it would be dangerous to reduce it below thirty, or even close to that number. The Mesha Stone, which uses round numbers consistently, lists the duration of the Israelite oppression as forty years, comparable in this respect to the forty-year Philistine oppression of Israel; since this oppression ended with Mesha's revolt, it is clear that accurate and exact figures were available to the king. That the round number was preferred accords with the usage in the case of David and Solomon. It is of interest, however, that Mesha also records the length of his father's reign as thirty, not forty years. While thirty is also a round number, a distinction is made between it and forty. Unless we suppose that the numbers are merely symbolic, we must recognize that the use of round numbers does not allow license in translating them into precise figures. When the figure forty is used in the historical period, it is a round number certainly, but it can hardly signify a period less than thirty years, and probably closer to forty than thirty (but of this we cannot be sure; in the Bible the next lower round number seems to be twenty); cf. F. M. Cross and D. N. Freedman, *Early Hebrew Orthography* (1952), pp. 39–40, n. 13.
30. Cf. J. B. Pritchard (ed.), *Ancient Near Eastern Texts* (hereafter *ANET;* 1950), pp. 280–81.
31. Albright, *BASOR,* No. 100, pp. 19, 21; Thiele, op. cit., p. 62.
32. Cf. Thiele, op. cit., pp. 20 ff. and 55 ff., who, however, complicates the calculation with changes in the method of computation.
33. *ANET,* pp. 278–79.
34. Cf. I Kings 22. The three-year datum in vss. 1 and 2 must include the battle of Qarqar and the period of alliance between Israel and Aram before it. Thus Ahab's reign cannot have extended beyond 850, and 851 or possibly 852 may be a more feasible date.
35. "New Light from Egypt on the Chronology and History of Israel and Judah," *BASOR,* No. 130 (1953), pp. 4–8, and "Further Light on Synchronisms between Egypt and Asia in the Period 935–685 B.C.," *BASOR,* No. 141 (1956), pp. 23–27.
36. This is Thiele's date, op. cit., pp. 54 f.
37. *ANET,* pp. 284–85.
38. See Thiele's exhaustive study of this period, pp. 99–152, especially pp. 136–52.
39. II Kings 15:5.
40. There is no instance of a queen exercising royal authority in her own name in either kingdom, though the position and power of the queen, or more properly the queen mother, are familiar features in an oriental monarchy. In all likelihood, Athaliah was officially acting in behalf of the rightful king, though she may well have usurped that post and, in any case, abused the authority she gained. This point was made by Dr. H. L. Ginsberg in a paper read at a recent meeting of the Society of Biblical Literature and Exegesis, but I have not seen it in print.

41. II Kings 18:13 = Isaiah 36:1.
42. Albright, *BASOR*, No. 100, p. 22, n. 28. Thiele, op. cit., pp. 101, etc.
43. Albright, *BASOR*, No. 130, pp. 8–9; also No. 141, pp. 23–26.
44. Cf. Thiele, op. cit., pp. 155–57, and Albright, *BASOR*, No. 100, p. 22, n. 30.
45. Cf. D. J. Wiseman, *Chronicles of Chaldaean Kings* (1956). The material is presented and discussed in a number of articles: e.g., J. P. Hyatt, "New Light on Nebuchadrezzar and Judean History," *JBL* LXXV (1956), pp. 277–84; H. Tadmor, "Chronology of the Last Kings of Judah," *JNES* XV (1956), pp. 226–30; Thiele, "New Evidence on the Chronology of the Last Kings of Judah," *BASOR*, No. 143 (1956), pp. 22–27; Albright, "The Nebuchadnezzar and Neriglissar Chronicles," *BASOR*, No. 143 (1956), pp. 27–33; D. N. Freedman, "The Babylonian Chronicle," *BA* XIX (1956), pp. 50–60.
46. Cf. Freedman, *BA* XIX, p. 55; Tadmor, *JNES* XV, pp. 229–30; Albright, *BASOR*, No. 100, p. 22, and No. 143, pp. 31–32.
47. Cf. Albright, "King Joiachin in Exile," *BA* V (1942), pp. 49–55.
48. Or Nisan 596 (so Tadmor), which seems improbable in view of the statement in the Babylonian Chronicle that Zedekiah was placed on the throne during the seventh year of Nebuchadrezzar, i.e., before Nisan 597. Thiele similarly assumes that the exile of Jehoiachin took place after Nisan (*BASOR*, No. 143, pp. 26–27).
49. Freedman, *BA* XIX, pp. 56 ff.
50. Cf. Thiele, *BASOR*, No. 143, pp. 26–27.
51. H. H. Rowley has dealt with this subject at length in "The Chronological Order of Ezra and Nehemiah," *Goldziher Memorial*, I (1948), pp. 117–49, reprinted in *The Servant of the Lord and Other Essays on the Old Testament* (1952), pp. 131–59. See also "Nehemiah's Mission and Its Background," *Bulletin of the John Rylands Library* XXXVII (1954–55), pp. 528–61. R. A. Bowman's survey of the chronological problem in his commentary on Ezra-Nehemiah, *The Interpreter's Bible* III (1954), pp. 561–63, is also useful.
52. A. van Hoonacker, "La succession chronologique Néhémie-Esdras," *Revue Biblique* XXXII (1923), pp. 481–94; XXXIII (1924), pp. 33–64.
53. Cf. Nehemiah 8:9 and 12:26, 36; also 10:1. Nehemiah is mentioned only once in Ezra, at 2:2.
54. Albright's original view is stated in *FSAC*, p. 248; it was subsequently modified as indicated in the text, cf. *The Biblical Period* (1950), pp. 45–55, 62–65. On the view that Ezra's ministry belongs between Nehemiah's two visits, see W. Rudolph, *Esra und Nehemia (Handbuch zum Alten Testament;* 1949), pp. 70–71.
55. A. Cowley, *Aramaic Papyri of the Fifth Century B.C.* (1923); letters No. 21 and 30 are particularly important. For a general reconstruction of the Elephantine community and its life, see E. G. Kraeling, *The Brooklyn Museum Aramaic Papyri* (1953).
56. I wish to express my thanks to the Pontifical Biblical Institute in Jerusalem for permission to use its library in the preparation of this paper; and my deep appreciation to Dr. Edward F. Campbell of McCormick Theological Seminary for his assistance in completing it.

CHAPTER EIGHT

South Arabian History
and Archaeology

GUS W. VAN BEEK

I

THIRTY–FIVE YEARS AGO, South Arabia was one of the least-known areas of the ancient world. Since that time many explorers and several archaeological expeditions have brought to light enough new data to place South Arabian studies on a firm footing. If we are to see these advances in their proper perspective, it is necessary to sketch the sources available in 1920 and to summarize the status of South Arabian studies at that time.

The sources upon which knowledge of South Arabia was based thirty-five years ago included: some accounts in ancient literature, descriptions of the area by travelers of the late 18th and 19th centuries, a number of South Arabian inscriptions copied in the course of these journeys, and some objects acquired for Western museums and private collections. The literary sources were spread in time over a millennium and a half and, except for classical writings, supplied little information. The Bible contains several references to South Arabia,[1] but their authenticity was frequently doubted and they were often considered secondary; even when taken at face value, they told us little. The only recognizable South Arabian state names were Sheba (Saba') and Hazarmaveth (Ḥadhramaut), both of which were believed to be related to Israel. The former is pictured as a distant land, ruled by a queen or by kings, engaged in caravan trade in frankincense, spices, gold, and precious stones. Assyrian sources yield much the same picture, but contain in addition some important chronological information. In particular, the names of two Sabaean kings appear: Iti'amra [Yithi''amara] in the annals of Sargon,[2] and Karibi-ilu [Karib'il] on a foundation stele of the *bît akîti* commemorating Sennacherib's restoration of the building.[3] These synchronisms indicated that Saba' and the neo-Assyrian Empire were contemporary, but, since several Sabaean rulers bore these names, precise identification was impossible.

The best ancient sources are the classical writers Theophrastus, Strabo, the author of *The Periplus of the Erythraean Sea,* Pliny, and Claudius Ptolemy.[4] Although their reports occasionally conflict and contain mistakes, the area of agreement among them is surprisingly large, and they provide a generally reliable picture of South Arabia between the late fourth century B.C. and the second century A.D. They contain valuable geographical data, describe the location of the major South Arabian states and principal cities, and trace in part the changing political alignments of the period. They attribute the wealth of the area to agriculture and traffic in myrrh and frankincense. It was with incense, the primary and most valuable export of the region, that the classical writers were principally concerned, and they devote pages to all aspects of incense, from a description of the trees to the prices of various grades in the world market. They also throw light on the government, social organization, and customs of the area, and furnish important chronological data by supplying the names of several kings.

Arabic literature supplies little information owing to the fact that Islam reacted sharply against pagan pre-Islamic culture.[5] Much of this material is legendary, although some of it contains an historical nucleus, particularly for the two or three centuries preceding the rise of Islam. Nevertheless, some important historical and geographical material is preserved, for which al-Hamdânî is the best source.

These literary sources formed the basis for the historical reconstruction of ancient South Arabia in 1920. But they were of less value than they might have been, since virtually every detail was questioned by one or more scholars, and there was wide disagreement as to their interpretation.[6]

Supplementing the literary sources were the descriptions of South Arabia by scholars and travelers of the late 18th and 19th centuries.[7] Yemen was the best-known area, having been explored by Carsten Niebuhr and his ill-fated Danish expedition in 1763; Seetzen, who copied inscriptions around Ẓafâr in 1810 and gave the Western world its first glimpse of ancient South Arabian inscriptions; Arnaud, the first European to visit Mârib (1843); Halévy, who traveled through Nejrân and the Jauf (ancient Ma'în) in 1869; and E. Glaser, who made four journeys, copying more than 2000 inscriptions and describing many sites including Mârib, in 1882–84, 1885–86, 1887–88, and 1892–94. Other sections of South Arabia were also being explored. In 1834–35, Wellsted discovered and described Ḥuṣn el-Ghurâb (Bîr 'Ali) and Naqab el-Hajar on the south coast; the Bents traveled through the Ḥadhramaut in 1893–94 and, in 1895, along the Dhofâr coast, noting ancient sites; Landberg described little-known areas of South Arabia, using native informants in Aden, in 1895–97; G. Bury, with the South Arabian expedition of the Vienna Academy (1898–99), made squeezes and photographs of inscriptions at Hajar Koḥlân (in Wadi Beiḥân).

Virtually all of these travelers copied inscriptions wherever they went, with the result that several thousand texts were available to scholars by 1920.

Unhappily, as is the case with most South Arabian inscriptions, this corpus of material consisted for the most part of personal and clan names, and included only a few long historical texts. Much of this material had been published by 1920, but some, particularly parts of the Glaser *Nachlass*, appeared after the beginning of the period with which we are concerned, and a considerable part still remains to be published. A series dedicated to the publication of the South Arabian texts began to appear in 1889 as Part IV of the *Corpus Inscriptionum Semiticarum* and by 1920 Vols. I and II were in print.

By 1920 no South Arabian site had been excavated. Nevertheless, some objects, which had been dug by natives and purchased by Glaser, government officials, and dealers, were brought out and deposited in public and private collections. Included in this group were bronze plaques and lamps, architectural fragments, sculpture, reliefs, amulets, incense burners, and coins. The number of pieces was not great and included some fakes. But even the genuine objects provided little information since their archaeological contexts were wholly unknown.

These sources, then, were the foundation of South Arabian studies thirty-five years ago. Risking the danger of oversimplification, we may briefly summarize what was known of the antiquity of the region as follows:[8] The language was known, having been deciphered by Gesenius and Roediger in 1841, and the different dialects had been distinguished. The names of a great number of rulers of the various ancient states were known from texts and had been arranged in lists by means of filiation but not palaeography, since the latter could not be used successfully until photographs were available and basic problems of chronology had been solved. The names of the ancient kingdoms, their capitals, and some important cities were also known; but the boundaries of the states and the location of the cities were generally disputed. Several important sites, e.g., Ṣirwâḥ, Mârib, Ma'în, Hajar Koḥlân, Naqab el-Hajar, and Bîr 'Ali, had been roughly described, but none excavated. Little progress had been made in the study of the organization of the states, their systems of law, religion, and social structure. Little was known about art and architecture, and virtually nothing of the influence exerted on them by other cultures. Pottery was wholly unknown. The details of the economic life of the region were the subject of conjecture, although it was generally held that agriculture and trade in incense formed the foundation of the economy, in view of the known irrigation remains and the discussions of incense in the classical sources.[9] Contacts with the north, particularly Palestine and Assyria, were assumed, based on the requirements of trade and the information contained in the Bible and Assyrian texts. The nature of the climate in ancient times was disputed; some held that desiccation was less advanced, owing to greater rainfall at that time.[10] By far the most vexing problem was that of chronology. The general chronological position of Saba' was known from the Assyrian and classical synchronisms. But the relationship of the three states Maʻîn, Qatabân, and Ḥadhramaut, which were known to be partially contemporary with one another from South Arabian texts, to Saba' was the subject of bitter controversy, with the foremost scholars ranging themselves in two camps, those who supported a high chronology holding that Maʻîn preceded Saba', and those who advocated a low chronology holding that Saba' was earlier than Maʻîn.[11] Generally, scholars had gone as far as they could in reconstructing ancient South Arabian history and culture with the limited sources available. What was needed to fill the enormous gaps and to solve the most pressing problems was more information. Further exploration and particularly archaeological excavation were the only means by which knowledge of the area could be advanced.

II

Between 1920 and the end of World War II, great strides were made on all fronts of South Arabian studies. Here we must limit ourselves to non-epigraphic developments.

During the first decade or so of our period, a number of handbooks appeared, but most of them were syntheses of the material available in 1920, and they contributed little or nothing new; we will mention only one in passing: J. A. Montgomery's Haskell Lectures at Oberlin, *Arabia and the Bible*.[12] These lectures covered the whole field of South Arabian studies, with particular reference to ethnic, linguistic, political, and commercial contacts between South Arabia and the remainder of the Semitic world. As is the case with the other historical and cultural studies of this period, it is now largely antiquated; however, it contains useful observations and is still of value.

The archaeological recovery of pre-Islamic South Arabia began in 1928 when C. Rathjens and H. von Wissmann conducted a brief campaign at Ḥuqqa, a small site twenty-three kilometers north of Ṣanʻâ. In spite of the fact that they were unprepared to dig, having planned their trip to Yemen for other purposes, they seized the opportunity to excavate a small area of the site. They cleared a temple with a square open court surrounded on three sides by a peristyle hall, which was supported by eight-sided columns crowned with capitals, and on the fourth side by the chief building of the complex, access to which was gained from the open court. Fragments of wall panels, some imitating marginally drafted, pecked masonry, others simulating recessed windows, and still others with a vine motif in relief were recovered from the debris. A number of pieces of plaster painted with stylized rosettes which presumably covered the ceilings and walls were also found. In all, thirteen pottery types were recovered; although they are not well drawn, the descriptions, sketches, and photographs are useful for comparative study. Fragments of stone and bronze vessels, including the tripod base and neck of a large inscribed bronze jug, a bronze lion head, and numerous small iron objects complete the finds. Basing themselves on the inscriptions and the architectural evidence, Rathjens and von Wissmann suggested that the temple was built in the third century B.C. and destroyed in the third century A.D.

Although the Ḥuqqa excavation was neither planned nor carried out by trained field archaeologists, it provided a body of extremely useful material. At long last there was a reasonably clear plan and a plausible reconstruction of a South Arabian building, even though it had been destroyed nearly to floor level. The excavation also added greatly to our knowledge of architectural forms and elements. While the uses of some of the fragments were successfully explained, the purpose of others could only be conjectured, owing to the fact that they were not found *in situ*. Finally it brought to light a small group of objects which were contemporary with the temple and the inscriptions. Even though no imported objects were found to fix the dating, the correlation of artifacts with architectural and epigraphic material was a distinct gain.

After completing their excavations, Rathjens and von Wissmann journeyed to Ḥaz and el-Gherâs in the Ṣanʿâ area, studying geology and describing ancient remains. Noteworthy among the latter were architectural fragments, sculpture, and small objects such as rings, seals, and beads. The acquisition of many of these objects permitted Rathjens and von Wissmann to study them in greater detail than would have been possible in the field. Attention was also devoted to various types of cisterns, aqueducts, caves, and rock drawings seen in the course of their journey. The excavations and the material collected were subsequently published[13] with drawings, photographs, and comparative material; their publication is still extremely valuable.

Essential to the opening of South Arabia for exploration and excavation was the active interest taken in the area by the British. From the colony of Aden they extended their influence into the Aden Protectorate, negotiating treaties between the various tribes and bringing a new security to that region. This work was accomplished by a group of political officers, many of whom recorded ancient sites, described the area, and collected artifacts and inscriptions in their spare moments. Among this group were the Ingrams, S. Perowne, and R. A. B. Hamilton (Master of Belhaven). In 1934 H. Ingrams traveled in the Ṣeiʿar country, to the north and west of Wadi Ḥadhramaut, where he noted the existence of cairns at ʿUrum, and in Wadi Masîla, the southeastward extension of Wadi Ḥadhramaut, where he recorded for the first time the sites Ḥuṣn el-ʿUrr, Ḥuṣn ʿÂd, Qara, and Maqrat.[14] On a journey from Bîr ʿAli to Ḥuṣn el-ʿAbr by way of Wadi Hajar and Shabwa in 1939, he discovered a number of graffiti and inscriptions, and called attention to the existence of ancient remains at Maʿber and Sheʿb Derbesh.[15] That same year, Doreen (Mrs. H.) Ingrams traveled through the Hajar province between Bîr ʿAli and Mukalla, in the course of which she described and photographed the ancient boundary wall at Bana, previously seen only by von Wrede.[16] S. Perowne (in 1937) studied the ruins at Imʿâdîya, a site about ninety miles north of Aden and west of Mukeiras, where he found the remains of buildings constructed of well-dressed Ashlar and a few inscriptions.[17] In 1938, he visited Hajar Koḥlân (in Wadi Beiḥân), describing the site and acquiring antiquities which are now in the Aden Museum.[18] Later that year, J. Duncan also examined Hajar Koḥlân and located the neighboring cemetery at Ḥeid bin 'Aqîl. R. A. B. Hamilton made important contributions to our knowledge of the region by describing a number of sites in the Western Aden Protectorate.[19] In the Aden area, he noted the causeway joining Aden with the mainland, the mounds in the Wadi Tiban delta near the village of Ṣubur between Laḥej and Aden, the reservoirs on Little Aden, and similar remains at Khôr el-Umeira and in the extinct volcano Jebel Kharas. He also called attention to the hill aqueducts at Ḥeid Dhujan near Niṣâb, to an-Nâb in the Markha district, the second largest site in the Western Aden Protectorate, to the ruins of Mariaba near 'Ain ar-Raṣâṣ (south of Niṣâb), and to ruins at the mouth of Wadi Jirdân and in Wadi 'Irma and Wadi Ḥarîb. For his work at Shabwa, see below.

The increasing security and gradual opening of the Aden Protectorate made it possible for others to explore this area also. Two journeys were made to the Ḥadhramaut by van der Meulen and von Wissmann in 1931[20] and 1939.[21] The major contributions of their work lay in mapping their routes and in describing, photographing, and making sketch plans of a number of sites. The latter included Gheibûn, Ḥureidha, Ḥuṣn el-'Urr, Mekeinûn, el-Bureyira, Qâriet as-Senahîya, el-Qaru, together with cairn fields and cisterns at a number of places. Freya Stark also journeyed to the Ḥadhramaut twice in this period. In 1935, she visited the sites of Gheibûn, 'Andal (a medieval site), and mentioned the ruins near Ḥureidha.[22] She returned two years later as a member of the first South Arabian archaeological expedition (to Ḥureidha) and, after the brief campaign, traveled to the coast by way of Wadi 'Amd and Wadi Maifa'. En route she studied several important sites: Ṣuwaidât, Naqab el-Hajar, and Ḥuṣn el-Ghurâb (Bîr 'Ali, the site of Qana).[23]

Although the major sites of the coastal plain of Dhofâr had been noted by Bent in 1895, B. Thomas discovered a number of fields of triliths during several exploratory journeys in the late twenties and early thirties. These monuments are located between Wadi Sarab (longitude 58°) and Dhofâr,[24] as well as inland from the Dhofâr coast as far north as Aiyun in Wadi Ghudun and between Hamra Miskad and Qarn Shaiba in Wadi Dauka.[25]

In 1936, H. St.John B. Philby, who had ranged far and wide exploring central Arabia, successfully crossed southwestern Arabia from Nejrân to the coastal port of Shiḥr and returned by automobile. In addition to mapping the area, he visited a number of important sites which he described in detail.[26] Of special interest to us are his descriptions of Shabwa, Bîr Ḥamad (near the entrance to Wadi Ḥadhramaut), Asâḥil, Khirbet Sa'ûd, and Duraib (the last three are located in the Raghwân oasis). His study of Shabwa, together with that of Hamilton (see below), yields most of our information for this site.

Philby also called attention to irrigation remains in the Shabwa area, near Bîr Ḥamad, in Wadi Anṣâṣ and Wadi Markha, and to cairn fields at Radm el-Amîr, Ruwaiq, on the 'Alam ridges, and in Nejrân.

Meanwhile C. Rathjens continued his studies in Yemen, making three additional journeys (1931, 1934, and 1937–38) in the course of which he purchased antiquities and visited important sites, including 'Amrân, Ghaimân, Shibâm el-Kaukabân, and Sila'. He described, photographed, and made sketch plans of the exposed remains of fortresses, buildings, and cisterns, devoting special attention to architectural elements such as columns, capitals, moldings, and wall panels. This material, including the objects purchased, has recently been published[27] and is extremely useful for technical and comparative study of South Arabian material culture. It also contains a wealth of information on the topography and geology of the region. Unhappily, because he follows the now discredited high chronology, much of the general outline and many details of his historical reconstruction are wrong.

The importance of the work of these political officers and explorers for the historical and archaeological recovery of South Arabia can hardly be overstated. Their descriptions of the land and the people, gained always with difficulty and occasionally at the risk of their lives, have added greatly to our knowledge of the area; they are indispensable background material for those planning archaeological work in this region. To them we are also indebted for the present maps of the region. Some are excellent in quality; others are little more than sketch maps; but all have made contributions to our knowledge of the topography of South Arabia. But for our purposes, their major contribution lay in the discovery and description of sites. While their visits to sites do not obviate the need of an archaeological survey, they have given us a nucleus with which to work and an over-all picture of what we can expect to find. In short, they have paved the way for the controlled archaeological excavations to which we will now turn.

The most important development during this period was the first excavation in South Arabia by a trained archaeologist. Gertrude Caton Thompson, accompanied by geologist Elinor Gardner and explorer Freya Stark, conducted one campaign at Ḥureidha (ancient Maḍâbum) in Wadi 'Amd, a lateral wadi feeding Wadi Ḥadhramaut, during the winter of 1937–38. Miss Gardner studied the ancient irrigation system of the area from the single deflector dam and the main take-off channel sixteen kilometers upstream, to the secondary and tertiary channels which distributed water over the fields. Miss Caton Thompson cleared a small temple, rectangular in plan, which had been destroyed to floor level. Three phases of construction were observed, the last two of which consisted of additions to the original structure. Based on the evidence found, she tentatively dated the first two phases (A and B) between the middle of the fifth and the fourth centuries B.C., and the third phase (C and post-C) to the Seleucid period. Some extra-mural shrines were also excavated and assigned to the post-C phase. She partially cleared a small

mud-brick "farmhouse" near the temple and two hewn circular cave tombs
in the scree slopes of the cliffs on the north side of the wadi. Both the "farmhouse" and the tombs are dated to the same general period as the temple by
typological similarities in the objects found. In her publication of the site,[28]
the material is carefully presented and the conclusions are cautiously advanced.
It is an excellent example of the contribution that can be made to human
knowledge by a small but competently staffed excavation.

The Ḥureidha excavation added greatly to our knowledge of ancient
South Arabia. Of special importance was the measure of chronological control
provided by the discovery of objects reflecting foreign influence. A number of
beads having affinities with Syrian beads of the seventh–fifth centuries B.C.
and seals influenced by the Achaemenian style of the sixth–fourth centuries B.C. were discovered in the tombs with pottery similar in style to that
found at the temple and "farmhouse." This discovery established the con-
temporaneity of the different areas excavated and provided an upper chronological limit for the structures cleared. Equally important, the excavation
brought to light a small datable corpus of South Arabian pottery, properly
described, drawn, and photographed. The technical study made of some of
the pottery sets a high standard for archaeologists not only of this area but
also of other areas in the Near East. On the architectural side, it yielded
another temple, wholly different in plan and construction from the one at
Ḥuqqa (see above). Valuable information was provided for the study of
South Arabian building techniques and architectural elements. Without going
too far afield, we must note that it also furnished a limited basis for the study
of palaeography. Since the phases of the temple were dated by non-epigraphic
evidence, the inscriptions, though generally reused, received an *ante quem*
dating according to the phase of reconstruction in which they were found.
Finally, it yielded the best anthropological evidence we have so far on ancient
South Arabian types of man. Although the skeletal finds were meager, they
exceed those recovered by all other excavations in the area; evidence of this
type appears to be unusually rare in South Arabia.

Later that same year (1938) R. A. B. Hamilton conducted a trial
excavation at Shabwa,[29] during the course of a visit to the area in connection
with his political work in the Western Aden Protectorate. There he cleared a
small building which may have been a mausoleum, in view of the bones and
sherds found in the chambers, and partially excavated an adjoining structure
which was apparently a temple. A number of objects were recovered, including
inscriptions, fragments of reliefs, and an incense burner.[30] All of these objects,
with the exception of the inscriptions, can be assigned to about the first
century A.D. or a little later. One surprising result of his excavation was the
discovery that the ruins of Shabwa are comparatively shallow; the foundations
of the excavated building reach a depth of only twelve feet and rest on rock
salt. This suggests that the site was first occupied comparatively late in South
Arabian history. The shallowness of the ruins, together with their relatively

small area as described by both Philby and Hamilton, places Shabwa in proper perspective, making it something less than it has been to most students of ancient South Arabia.

With Hamilton's work at Shabwa we bring to a close our brief survey of the historical and archaeological developments of the period between 1920 and World War II. Enormous contributions had been made during the period; it is not too much to say that it had been the most fruitful period in the recovery of ancient South Arabia since Glaser's epoch-making journeys in Yemen during the late 19th century.

III

World War II brought a halt to South Arabian archaeology, except for two journeys to the Jauf in northern Yemen by M. Tawfik in 1944–45. Although he was primarily engaged in entomological research, Tawfik devoted his spare time to the study of the surface remains at Ma'în. His descriptions, sketch plans, and photographs are the best we have of this site.[31]

With the end of World War II South Arabian studies were intensified. In 1947 another Egyptian scholar, A. Fakhry, traveled through northern Yemen and visited a number of sites, including, Ṣirwâḥ, Mârib, Berâqish, Khirbet Sa'ûd, Ma'în, el-Ḥazm, Kamna, and es-Saudâ. He described, photographed, and made rough sketches of the major structures, architectural elements, sculpture, and small objects exposed at each site. He also copied and photographed a great number of inscriptions; some were already known, but many others were new to South Arabian epigraphy. This material, which has been published in three volumes,[32] is particularly valuable for epigraphy and for comparative study of South Arabian architecture and art, as well as in recording objects which have since been destroyed by the continuing depredation of antiquities in this area.

Dhofâr and 'Omân were also explored during this period by W. Thesiger, who made several trips through eastern and southeastern Arabia in the course of his locust-control activities. Besides mapping the area, he noted a number of trilith monuments, similar to those described by B. Thomas (see above), and the remains of an ancient building near Andhur.[33]

Although it is somewhat outside the range of our survey, we mention in passing the journey from Ṭâif, through Nejrân, and northward to Riyâdh made by G. and J. Ryckmans, Philby, and P. Lippens in the winter of 1951–52.[34] On this trip they studied the irrigation remains at Ṭâif and the ruins of Ukhdûd (ancient Negrân). A considerable number of Sabaean inscriptions and graffiti, some of great historical value, were found.

Meanwhile, a number of studies appeared, which attests to the growing interest in South Arabia. The first of these, *The Background of Islam,* by Philby, appeared in 1947.[35] Based on the knowledge gained through his explorations, on his study of the material available to him, and on the writings of early Arab historians, Philby reconstructed the chronology, political history, and interrelations of the various South Arabian states. Unhappily he followed Hommel's long chronology which has been superseded by the low chronology as a result of subsequent discoveries.

Among important recent contributions to our knowledge is J. Ryckmans' book, *L'institution monarchique en Arabie méridionale avant L'Islam.*[36] Although it is based solely on epigraphic evidence and is thus outside the scope of this article, it must be mentioned here because it contains much valuable material bearing on the history and chronology of Ma'în and Saba'. Particularly useful for the South Arabian archaeologist and historian is the author's well-documented summary of the information contained in inscriptions regarding the political, military, and building activities of the various kings of these states. In general his chronology follows the low chronology; but many details will have to be corrected in the light of still more recent archaeological and palaeographic research.[37]

During this period, the distinguished South Arabian geographer, H. von Wissmann, collaborated with a leading epigraphist, Maria Höfner, in producing the first comprehensive historical geography of South Arabia.[38] This work is indispensable to all students of the area. From the Jauf in the west as far as Wadi Masîla in the east, they discuss the topography and history of each area, locating and describing in a general way the exposed remains of virtually every known site, bringing together the classical and Arabic sources, travelers' accounts, epigraphic evidence, and summaries of the results of archaeological excavations prior to 1951. Particularly useful are the excellent bibliography and the most complete archaeological map of central South Arabia yet produced.

An unusual reconstruction of South Arabian history was published in 1955 by Jacqueline Pirenne,[39] a pupil of G. Ryckmans. In this study she develops the thesis that South Arabian culture came into being in the fifth century B.C. as the result of strong Greco-Persian influence.[40] To support this view she argues that the monumental South Arabic script, which is characteristic of the *mukarrib* period, was adopted from Greek script at the beginning of the fifth century B.C.,[41] and that the origin of South Arabian material culture, especially architecture and sculpture, must be attributed to Greco-Persian influence.[42] She asserts that the origins of the people and language of South Arabia ought to be separated from the historical problem of the origin of their civilization,[43] and in effect denies the influence of all ancient Near Eastern cultures before the Greco-Persian period on South Arabia.

In general this theory is supported by arbitrarily selected facts, many of which have been culled from preliminary archaeological reports. Her inadequate understanding of modern methods of stratigraphy and typology leads to inevitable error in her use of archaeological material.[44] We cannot enter into a detailed evaluation of her point of view. As we shall see below, recent study has shown that South Arabian civilization did not emerge fully mature, like Athena from the head of Zeus, as a result of Greco-Persian influence in the fifth century, but rather developed over a long period of time, in part indigenously but chiefly under the influence of Egypt and the cultures of the Fertile Crescent.

Meanwhile, a young American explorer, Wendell Phillips, who had led the University of California African expedition, joined forces with W. F. Albright to organize the American Foundation for the Study of Man, which turned its attention in 1950 to South Arabia. The four expeditions sponsored by the foundation were the largest and best-equipped expeditions ever to work in this area. Limits of space prohibit a detailed treatment of the sites excavated and the objects recovered during these campaigns. Several final reports, as well as a number of monographs and papers, have already appeared[45] and others are in preparation. The best general survey of the expeditions is found in Wendell Phillips' *Qataban and Sheba*,[46] and more detailed preliminary reports have been published by W. F. Albright, A. Jamme, F. P. Albright, and the writer.[47] Here we will only list the sites excavated, concentrating instead on some of the contributions made by the new material to our knowledge of the history and culture of ancient South Arabia.

In 1950–51 the expedition excavated a number of sites in Wadi Beiḫân, the heart of the ancient state of Qatabân, about 155 miles in a straight line north-norfheast of Aden. At Hajar Koḥlân, the site of ancient Timna' (Pliny's Thomna), several areas of the topmost stratum, containing the remains of the final occupation of the site, were cleared: the south gate of the city and the open square just inside, parts of two streets and four of the adjoining houses; the temple of 'Athtar near the center of the site; and a few houses at the extreme north end of the mound. At the cemetery of Timna', Ḥeid bin 'Aqîl, located a short distance north of the mound, a series of three mortuary chapels, a larger temple, and a number of stone-built tomb structures were excavated, yielding a mass of funerary objects. About nine miles south of Timna' is Hajar bin Ḥumeid, a mound small in extent but with about fifty feet of stratified occupational debris. Here a section was dug from the top to the bottom of the mound in order to obtain sufficient stratified pottery for a typological sequence and chronology. In the Hajar bin Ḥumeid area, a great number of installations of the ancient irrigation system were cleared and the silt deposits marking the ancient fields were intensively studied. Many other silted areas and irrigation systems in the wadi were also examined, but time did not permit the clearance of the remains. Finally a complete archaeological survey of Wadi Beiḫân was made, in which all visible ancient remains were recorded.

In 1951–52 the expedition moved to Mârib, the capital of the ancient Sabaean kingdom, where F. P. Albright undertook important excavations at the 'Awwâm temple (Ḥaram Bilqîs). There he cleared the interior of the entrance hall of the temple and a complex contiguous to the entrance hall on the north. He also examined the oval wall of the temple in detail and made a small sounding against it in order to study its foundations. A small mausoleum adjoining the oval wall and a few tombs to the south of 'Awwâm were also excavated. When circumstances forced the abandonment of excavations at Mârib after a campaign of only two months, the expedition moved to the Dhofâr province of 'Omân on the southeast coast. In 1952 and early in 1953, F. P. Albright conducted preliminary excavations in the fortress at Khôr Rôri (ancient SMRM), in an ancient temple at Khôr Maghseil, and in the walled medieval city at el-Balîd. He also investigated the site of ancient Mirbâṭ.

These campaigns of the American Foundation, together with other explorations and excavations of the past thirty-five years, have vastly increased our knowledge of the history and archaeology of the area. We will now sketch briefly the present status of South Arabian studies in the light of these developments.

With regard to chronology, the controversy that raged over the high and low dating has now been definitely decided in favor of the latter, thanks to several archaeological finds. Foremost among these was the discovery of two bronze lions and infant riders with identically inscribed bases, buried in the debris of the final destruction of Timna'. The typically late Hellenistic style of the lions and riders was immediately recognized by W. F. Albright[48] and has since been fully treated by Berta Segall.[49] The relief inscription on the bases contains two names which also appear with the name of a well-known Qatabanian king, Shahr Yagil Yuhargib, in inscriptions on the building at the foot of which the lions were found. The association of this king with Hellenistic lions and riders proved that he belonged to the period when Hellenistic influence was strong (in this instance the first century B.C.), rather than to ca. 825 B.C. according to the latest high chronology. The limits of the date of the final destruction of Timna' were narrowed even more by the discovery of imported pottery, including in particular Arretine ware, which can be dated with some precision. On the basis of the study of this material by Howard Comfort,[50] we can now place the fall of Timna' after about A.D. 10, but within the first quarter of the first century A.D.

The recently published radiocarbon date of one of the wooden beams from the stratified debris of Hajar bin Ḥumeid provides a fixed point for the earlier period.[51] The radiocarbon analysis indicated that the beam dates ca. 852 B.C. ±160 years. Since it was found 3.34 meters above the bed of irrigation silt upon which the first town was built, the first settlement here probably belongs to the tenth century with limits in the twelfth and ninth centuries B.C. This radiocarbon date provides a peg for dating the typological sequence of the pottery and thus aids materially in establishing its absolute chronology. In this connection we must note that Miss Pirenne's suggestion that the symmetry of the South Arabian alphabet can be attributed to the influence of the Greek alphabet of the early fifth century B.C.[52] is wholly untenable, since we now have an inscription written in the earliest known monumental script on a large jar from stratified debris found *below* the carbonized wood in question; it thus goes back at least to the eighth and probably to the ninth century B.C., if not earlier.

Of great value for the control of chronology is the first typological sequence of South Arabian pottery being established by the writer ɛ ˙d based on the pottery recovered from Hajar bin Ḥumeid.[53] Although complete pieces are comparatively rare in this material, a number of forms now represented only in sherds will become clear with the publication of the pottery from Timnaʻ and Ḥeid bin ʻAqîl, and our knowledge of South Arabian pottery will thus be immeasurably advanced. Since the occupation of Hajar bin Ḥumeid seems to have been continuous through the first millennium B.C., the sequence will provide secure footing for the study of comparative stratigraphy in South Arabia and will furnish a basis for determining the date of occupational periods in other sites when a thorough archaeological survey is made. Of course some revision of this sequence may be necessary when more material is brought to light by the excavation of other sites. But the basic framework is being fixed and the enormous benefits of pottery chronology, demonstrated time and time again in other regions, are now at hand for South Arabia.

Our knowledge of the history of the area has been pushed back even farther by Bowen's research on the origins of irrigation in Beihân.[54] By reckoning the rate of silt accumulation on ancient fields, known to date between the beginning of the first millennium B.C. and the third century A.D., he has shown that the deposition of the bed of silt beneath the first settlement of Hajar bin Ḥumeid must have required about half a millennium. This proves that the practice of irrigation in Wadi Beiḥân goes back to the middle centuries of the second millennium B.C., and possibly earlier, and shows that there was sedentary occupation in the wadi by that period at the latest.

In this connection, we must mention a limestone piriform macehead found near Shabwa and given to a member of the American Foundation expedition. W. F. Albright has identified it as a northern type which disappeared at the beginning of the Late Bronze Age. Its appearance in South Arabia points either to a period before about 1500 B.C. or to a late survival of the type in this area. In view of the evidence for occupation of this region in the second millennium, the former alternative seems probable.

For the history of earlier times, little data is as yet available. Implements of neolithic type have been reported from camp sites on the southern fringe of the Rubʻ el-Khâli, but these may have been used well into the historical period, just as obsidian microliths, which would be indicators of mesolithic or neolithic occupation in most areas, abound on some comparatively late historical sites. The palaeolithic period is represented by flaked implements of Levalloisian type which have been found by Caton Thompson and Gardner near Mukalla, in Wadies ʻAmd and Ḥadhramaut, and on the Jôl overlooking Wadi Ḥadhramaut.[55] But until thoroughgoing archaeological surveys have been made and excavations of early sites have been undertaken, the prehistory of South Arabia will remain sketchy.

Although minor adjustments in our over-all South Arabian chronology will doubtless be necessary, the later archaeological periods can be considered as fixed. The implication for the history of the region is far-reaching. Hitherto, the structure of South Arabian chronology has been based solely on the arrangement of South Arabian kings, whose order was determined by filiation, and on a few synchronisms between kings. With the newly discovered chronological pegs, the inscriptions found in association with stratified objects can be dated with a measure of precision. In turn they permit epigraphers to assign approximate dates to the various stages of palaeographic development. Once we know the chronological limits of different forms of palaeography, we shall be able to arrange many texts lacking archaeological context in reliable (though not infallible) palaeographic sequence. It will then be possible to re-examine the traditional arrangement of South Arabian kings. W. F. Albright has pioneered in this field and has already provided us with new lists of the kings of Qatabân, Ḥadhramaut, Maʿîn, and Saba';[56] both he and A. Jamme continue this important task.

With a firmer chronological footing, we can now describe our increasing knowledge of South Arabian culture. It is the current fashion in some quarters to ascribe the origin of South Arabian art, particularly sculpture, to classical Greek or Greco-Persian influence; this point of view is strongly advocated by Jacqueline Pirenne (see above). A priori the thesis is suspect because, in seeking to explain South Arabian art in terms of a single foreign influence, it proposes a simplified solution unparalleled elsewhere in ancient Near Eastern and classical art. No matter how isolated by barriers of geography or by attitudes of insularity and isolationism, every ancient Near Eastern culture displays a mixture of traits in its art which are in part indigenous and in part foreign. The foreign traits themselves are usually derived not from one but from several sources, as the influences of different civilizations rise and wane. The art of South Arabia is no exception; it is a complex of native and foreign elements. While there are certain similarities between South Arabian and Greek art, Berta Segall has correctly emphasized that they are superficial and that they . . . "exist because certain features of both styles evolved under similar circumstances and from similar sources."[57]

During the past five years, Berta Segall has made notable progress in distinguishing characteristic elements of native and syncretistic origin in South Arabian art, and has successfully defined many of the sources of the non-Arabic influence apparent in the syncretistic style. She has shown that the sources of foreign influence largely depend on the historical period: during the last centuries B.C., Hellenistic influence is apparent in many objects;[58] in the second quarter of the first millennium B.C., and especially in the late seventh and the early sixth century, elements of Aramaic syncretism stemming from Syro-Hittite art are prominent;[59] for the still earlier period, we have adaptations of Syrian and Phoenician art which go back either directly or indirectly to prototypes belonging to the tenth–eighth centuries B.C. and possibly even earlier.[60] The isolation of these elements and the study of the motifs embodied in them will enable us to describe the impact of foreign cultural forces on native South Arabian culture, and to deduce historical and economic connections between various ancient states in the first millennium B.C.

Turning to South Arabian pottery, we see at once that it is basically native, as functional objects in this medium usually are. But discernible elements of foreign influence are present in certain forms and decorative styles which can be traced to Mesopotamia and Syro-Palestine at different periods, as shown by the writer.[61] The earliest pottery at Hajar bin Ḥumeid can be tentatively traced to the north, and with some degree of probability to Syria or Mesopotamia. An analysis of typology suggests that these pottery forms were derived from northern pottery forms of Middle Bronze or early Late Bronze, about the middle of the second millennium B.C. The time gap between that period and the first occupation at Hajar bin Ḥumeid about the beginning of the first millennium B.C. precludes certainty at this time. But if we assume a slow development of South Arabian pottery in isolation during that period, the time lag is not insurmountable; it would account for both similarities and differences apparent in ceramic typology.

Thanks to the excavations of the last thirty-five years, our knowledge of South Arabian architecture has increased enormously. We now have examples of religious architecture in the temples at Ḥuqqa, Mârib, Timna', Ḥureidha, and Khôr Rôri. Domestic structures are represented at Ḥureidha, Timna', and Hajar bin Ḥumeid; with regard to the latter, however, further excavation in an adjoining section will be necessary before the present plans are architecturally very instructive. Funerary architecture is illustrated at the Timna' cemetery, and in the mausoleum and south tombs at Mârib. When all of the architectural material has been published, detailed comparisons between plans, construction techniques, and special features of the various structures (particularly the temples) can be made, and the function of many architectural elements and forms can be explained. Such studies will indicate the source or sources of many of the styles and elements found in South Arabian architecture and will enable us to date some of the structures for which other chronological evidence is not available. Here we will limit ourselves to one example. Among the types of masonry used in South Arabian construction, the most distinctive is marginally drafted, pecked masonry. The writer has recently shown[62] that this style was probably borrowed from Assyria about the middle of the seventh century B.C., where it developed from "rusticated" masonry whose origin can in turn be traced to Phoenicia in the late second millennium B.C. In South Arabia, the style underwent a series of typological developments which we can date with some confidence. The implications of this study for South Arabian chronology and cultural interrelations are obvious. Similar research will doubtless add immensely to our knowledge of the history and culture of the region.

The economy of ancient South Arabia is also better known than ever before. There can be no doubt that it was based on both trade and agriculture. The question of their relative importance is hardly relevant, since both were necessary to produce the high level of prosperity enjoyed by the region.

That agriculture in South Arabia was highly developed is shown by the remains of ancient irrigation works in virtually every wadi. The principles of irrigation and the mechanics of the systems used have now been worked out in detail by Bowen (see above). He has shown that *seil* (flash flood) irrigation was used throughout the area, and that dams functioned not to store but to divert the fast-moving water into channels from which it was distributed by means of sluices and both secondary and tertiary channels to various fields. As silt was deposited the height of the fields gradually increased, and the distribution systems of channels and sluices had to be correspondingly raised. In his excavation of the Hajar bin Ḥumeid system, he was able to distinguish three construction phases in the sluices, which can be dated approximately by several lines of evidence. Using the information gathered in Beiḥân, Bowen has convincingly described the operation of the Mârib and Ḥureidha systems and has provided us with a valuable summary of all known irrigation remains in South Arabia. Thanks to his careful study, the principles and mechanics of South Arabian irrigation are far better known than those of any other area in the ancient Near East.

The routes and extent of South Arabian trade have become clearer during recent years. Thanks to the work of the various explorers (see above), A. Grohmann,[63] Bowen,[64] and the writer,[65] we now know the areas in which frankincense and myrrh were grown, and some of the routes over which these commodities were transported. That the South Arabians traded far and wide and enjoyed a high level of prosperity is indicated by the discoveries of Arretine ware[66] from Italy in the west and the bronze statuette of a dancing girl[67] from India in the east. With further excavation, we can expect to find many more examples illustrating the range of South Arabian commerce.

We have seen a few examples of the growth of our knowledge of ancient South Arabia; there are many others which cannot be described in this brief survey. When all of the material at hand has been studied and published, we shall be able to fill in many of the remaining gaps. Considering the status of South Arabian studies thirty-five years ago, the strides recently made are almost overwhelming. Although the study of the history and archaeology of the region is still in its infancy, when compared to that of other areas of the ancient Near East, the field is growing each year. It is already taking its proper place among Near Eastern studies and making its own contribution to the archaeology and history of the ancient Near East.

Washington, D.C.; Spring, 1957; revised Fall, 1958

NOTES TO CHAPTER EIGHT

1. Especially Genesis 10, 25:3; I Kings 10:1–10, 13; II Chronicles 21:16; Job 1:15, 6:19; Psalms 72:10, 15; Isaiah 60:6; Jeremiah 6:20; Ezekiel 27:22 f., 38:13; Joel 3:8.
2. Luckenbill, *Ancient Records of Assyria and Babylonia* II (Chicago, 1927), pp. 7 f.
3. Ibid., pp. 185 f.
4. See Theophrastus, *Enquiry into Plants,* tr. by Arthur Hort (*Loeb Classical Library,* London, 1916), IX.iv; *The Geography of Strabo,* tr. by H. L. Jones (*Loeb Classical Library,* London, 1930), XVI.iv.2–4, 19, 22–25; *The Periplus of the Erythraean Sea,* tr. and annotated by W. H. Schoff (New York, 1912), para. 21–32; Pliny, *Natural History,* tr. by H. Rackham (*Loeb Classical Library,* London, 1952), VI.xxvi.104; xxxii.153–55, 160–62; XII.xxx–xxxv, xli.
5. See H. St.J. B. Philby's essay, "Arab Historians and Ancient History," in his *Background of Islam* (Alexandria, 1947), pp. 127–40; also J. Tkatsch, "Saba'," *Encyclopedia of Islam,* IV (London, 1934), pp. 15 f.
6. For convenient summaries of the areas of controversy, see Tkatsch, ibid., pp. 4–10; and "Ḳatabān," *Encyclopedia of Islam,* II (London, 1927), pp. 809–12.
7. For the published accounts of their work, we refer the reader to the excellent bibliography in H. von Wissmann and Maria Höfner, *Beiträge zur historischen Geographie des vorislamischen Südarabien, Mainz Akademie der Wissenschaften und der Literatur. Abhandlungen der geistes- und sozialwissenschaftlichen Klasse,* 1952, no. 4 (Wiesbaden), pp. 364–70; and Tkatsch, "Saba'," pp. 17 f.
8. The best summary of the status of South Arabian studies for this period is the series of essays edited by D. Nielsen and published under the title, *Handbuch der altarabischen Altertumskunde* I (Copenhagen, 1927). The contributors included some of the foremost specialists of that time: D. Nielsen, F. Hommel, N. Rhodokanakis, and A. Grohmann.
9. The most complete study of frankincense and myrrh published to date is A. Grohmann's, *Südarabien als Wirtschaftsgebiet* I in *Osten und Orient* (Vienna, 1922), pp. 122–56. Although some details must be corrected in the light of recent research, it remains the standard work on South Arabian incense.
10. See the discussion by J. A. Montgomery, *Arabia and the Bible* (Philadelphia, 1934), pp. 90–106.
11. See the brief summary by W. F. Albright, "The Chronology of Ancient South Arabia in the Light of the First Campaign of Excavation in Qataban," *BASOR* 119 (1950), pp. 5 f. For a more detailed treatment, see J. Tkatsch, "Saba'," pp. 12–15.
12. See reference in note 10.
13. C. Rathjens and H. von Wissmann, *Vorislamische Altertümer* (Hamburg, 1932).
14. W. H. Ingrams, "Hadhramaut: A Journey to the Sei'ar Country and through the Wadi Maseila," *Geographical Journal* 88 (1936), pp. 524–51.
15. H. and D. Ingrams, "The Hadhramaut in Time of War," *Geographical Journal* 105 (1945), pp. 1–29.
16. Mrs. H. Ingrams, "Excursion into the Hajr Province of Hadhramaut," ibid., 98 (1941), pp. 131 ff.
17. S. Perowne, " 'Im'adiya and Beihan, Aden Protectorate," *Antiquity* 13 (1939), pp. 133 ff.
18. Ibid., pp. 135 ff.

19. R. A. B. Hamilton, "Archaeological Sites in the Western Aden Protectorate," *Geographical Journal* 101 (1943), pp. 110–17.
20. D. van der Meulen and H. von Wissmann, *Ḥaḍramaut: Some of Its Mysteries Unveiled* (Leyden, 1932).
21. D. van der Meulen, *Aden to the Hadhramaut, A Journey in South Arabia* (London, 1947).
22. Freya Stark, *The Southern Gates of Arabia* (New York, 1936), especially pp. 166 ff., 233, 253.
23. Freya Stark, "Some Pre-Islamic Inscriptions on the Frankincense Route in Southern Arabia," *Journal of the Royal Asiatic Society*, 1939, pp. 479–98; "An Exploration in the Hadhramaut and the Journey to the Coast," *Geographical Journal* 93 (1939), pp. 1–17; *A Winter in Arabia* (London, 1940).
24. B. Thomas, "The South-Eastern Borderlands of Rubʿ al-Khali," *Geographical Journal* 73 (1929), pp. 193–212.
25. B. Thomas, "A Journey into Rubʿ al-Khali—The Southern Desert," ibid., 77 (1931), pp. 1–31.
26. H. St.J. B. Philby, *Sheba's Daughters* (London, 1939).
27. C. Rathjens, *Sabaeica, Mitteilungen aus dem Museum für Völkerkunde in Hamburg*, xxiv, i *Der Reisebericht* (Hamburg, 1953); ii *Die unlokalisierten Funde* (Hamburg, 1955).
28. G. Caton Thompson, *The Tombs and Moon Temple of Hureidha (Hadhramaut)*, *Reports of the Research Committee of the Society of Antiquaries of London* xiii (Oxford, 1944).
29. R. A. B. Hamilton, "Six Weeks in Shabwa," *Geographical Journal* 100 (1942), pp. 107–23.
30. W. L. Brown and A. F. L. Beeston, "Sculptures and Inscriptions from Shabwa," *Journal of the Royal Asiatic Society*, 1954, pp. 43–62.
31. M. Tawfik, *Les Monuments de Maʿîn (Yemen)*, *Publications de l'Institut Français d'Archéologie Orientale du Caire, Études sud-Arabiques:* Tome i (Cairo, 1951).
32. A. Fakhry, *An Archaeological Journey to Yemen* i (Cairo, 1952) contains the account of his journey plus descriptions and plans; ii (Cairo, 1952), the publication of the inscriptions by G. Ryckmans; iii (Cairo, 1951), plates.
33. W. Thesiger, "A New Journey in Southern Arabia," *Geographical Journal* 108 (1946), pp. 129–45; "Desert Borderlands of Oman," ibid., 116 (1950), pp. 137–68.
34. G. Ryckmans, "Through Sheba's Kingdom," *Geographical Magazine* 27. 3 (1954), pp. 129–37.
35. See note 5.
36. J. Ryckmans, *L'institution monarchique en Arabie méridionale avant L'Islam (Maʿîn et Saba)*, *Bibliothèque du Muséon* 28 (Louvain, 1951).
37. See the review by W. F. Albright in *JAOS* 73 (1953), pp. 36–40.
38. See note 7.
39. Jacqueline Pirenne, *La Grèce et Saba, Extrait des Mémoires présentés par divers savants à l'académie des inscriptions et belles-lettres* xv (Paris, 1955).
40. Ibid., pp. 12, 101 ff.
41. Ibid., p. 35.
42. Ibid., pp. 59 ff.
43. Ibid., pp. 20 f.
44. One example will suffice. Recognizing that a seventh-century date for the oval wall of the 'Awwâm temple at Mârib cannot be reconciled with her theory of the Greco-Persian origin of South Arabian architecture and her chronological scheme, she proposes to date this structure in the fifth century, making it contemporary with the entrance hall (p. 23), and supports this suggestion by asserting that similar

masonry was used in both structures and that the end of the oval wall overhangs the wall of the entrance hall. Concerning the masonry, see now the writer's detailed study in F. P. Albright, R. LeBaron Bowen, and others, *Archaeological Discoveries in South Arabia, Publications of the American Foundation for the Study of Man,* II (Baltimore, 1958), Appendix V, pp. 287–95. Here we will only note that there are several phases of construction in the oval wall; the masonry of the second phase of the oval wall is typologically similar to that of the entrance hall, while that of the first phase is typologically earlier and goes back to the seventh century B.C. It must also be observed that the ends of the oval wall do *not* overhang the entrance hall as she has suggested. At present they are preserved to a greater height than the walls of the entrance hall, which were certainly one story higher originally, and possibly reached the height of the oval wall. In any case the relative heights of preserved sections of a monumental structure have no chronological significance apart from other clear-cut evidence.

45. Especially *Archaeological Discoveries in South Arabia,* see note 44. Bibliography on other studies will appear in succeeding notes.

46. This book, published in 1955, is now available in American, English, and German editions.

47. W. F. Albright, "The Chronology of Ancient South Arabia in the Light of the First Campaign of Excavation in Qataban," *BASOR* 119 (1950), pp. 5–15; A. Jamme, "Les expéditions archéologiques américaines en Arabie du Sud (1950–1953)," *Oriente Moderno* 33 (1953), pp. 133–57; F. P. Albright, "Explorations in Dhofar, Oman," *Antiquity* 113 (1955), pp. 37–39; Gus W. Van Beek, "Recovering the Ancient Civilization of Arabia," *The Biblical Archaeologist* 15 (1952), pp. 2–18.

48. W. F. Albright, op. cit., p. 9.

49. Berta Segall, "Sculpture from Arabia Felix: The Hellenistic Period," *American Journal of Archaeology* 59 (1955), pp. 207–14; and more recently, "The Lion Riders from Timna'," in *Archaeological Discoveries in South Arabia,* pp. 155–64.

50. H. Comfort, "Imported Pottery and Glass from Timna'," *Archaeological Discoveries in South Arabia,* pp. 199–207.

51. G. W. Van Beek, "A Radiocarbon Date for Early South Arabia," *BASOR* 143 (1956), pp. 6–9.

52. See note 41.

53. To appear in 1962.

54. R. LeBaron Bowen, "Irrigation in Ancient Qatabân," *Archaeological Discoveries in South Arabia,* pp. 43–88.

55. On recent neolithic finds, see F. E. Zeuner, " 'Neolithic' Sites from the Rub-al-Khali, Southern Arabia," *Man* LIV (1954), 209. For summaries of the status of prehistory in this region, see Henry Field, *Ancient and Modern Man in Southwestern Asia* (Coral Gables, 1956), pp. 112–24; and C. S. Coon, "Southern Arabia, A Problem for the Future," *Annual Report Smithsonian Institution,* 1944, pp. 388 ff.

56. W. F. Albright, op. cit., pp. 10 ff.; "The Chronology of the Minaean Kings of Arabia," *BASOR* 129 (1953), pp. 20–24; "A Note on Early Sabaean Chronology," *BASOR* 143 (1956), pp. 9 f.

57. Berta Segall, "Sculpture from Arabia Felix: The Earliest Phase," *Ars Orientalis* II (1957), p. 37.

58. See note 49.

59. Berta Segall, "Problems of Copy and Adaptation in the Second Quarter of the First Millennium B.C.," *American Journal of Archaeology* 60 (1956), pp. 165–70.

60. Berta Segall, "Sculpture from Arabia Felix: The Earliest Phase," *Ars Orientalis* II (1957), pp. 38 ff.

61. See note 53.

62. Gus W. Van Beek, "Marginally Drafted, Pecked Masonry," *Archaeological Discoveries in South Arabia,* Appendix v, pp. 287–95.
63. A Grohmann, *Südarabien als Wirtschaftsgebiet* II, *Schriften der Philosophischen Fakultät der Deutschen Universität in Prag,* XIII (Brünn, 1933), pp. 101–31. An excellent study of South Arabian sea and land trade routes in the light of ancient and modern sources.
64. R. LeBaron Bowen, "Ancient Trade Routes in South Arabia," *Archaeological Discoveries in South Arabia,* pp. 35–42.
65. Gus W. Van Beek, "Ancient Frankincense-Producing Areas," *Archaeological Discoveries in South Arabia,* Appendix II, pp. 139–42.
66. See note 50.
67. F. P. Albright, "From South Arabia," *Archaeology* 7. 4 (1954), p. 254.

CHAPTER NINE

Sumerian Literature,
A General Survey

SAMUEL NOAH KRAMER

DURING THE PAST THREE DECADES, research in the field of Sumerian literature has made no little progress. Quite a number of new texts and translations have become available in one form or another, and these have made possible a clearer understanding of the form and content, the nature and background, of the Sumerian literary documents. The present paper aims to present to the scholarly world—particularly to those scholars who are not cuneiform specialists—a brief survey of the extant Sumerian literary material in the light of these fuller data and surer insights. It is a privilege and a pleasure to dedicate this study to William Foxwell Albright, who has been deeply interested in Sumerian literature *u₄-tur-ra-ni-ta* "from the days of his youth," and has been instrumental directly and indirectly in advancing the researches related to it.

One of the most significant achievements of Near East archaeology in the course of the past hundred years consists of the uncovering of the Sumerians and their civilization. Certainly it was one of the least expected. For what the archaeologists who first began excavating in Mesopotamia were looking for was not the Sumerians, but the Assyrians and Babylonians. For these peoples and their civilizations they had at their disposal considerable Biblical, classical, and post-classical sources which spurred their search and intensified their efforts. But of Sumer and the Sumerians they had not an inkling. There was no recognizable trace either of the land or of its people in the entire literature available to the modern scholar; the very name Sumer had been erased from the mind and memory of man for over two thousand years. Yet today, the Sumerians are one of the best-known peoples of the ancient Near East. Thus, we know to some extent what the ancient Sumerians looked like from their own statues and steles, scattered throughout several museums in Asia, Europe, and America. There, too, will be found an excellent representative cross section of their material culture—the columns and bricks with which they built their temples and palaces; their tools and weapons, their pots and vases, their harps and lyres, their jewels and ornaments. Moreover, Sumerian clay tablets by the tens of thousands—literally so—inscribed with their business, legal, and administrative documents, crowd the tablet collections of these same museums; their contents help to reveal the ethnic layers, the social structure, and administrative organization of this ancient people. Indeed—and this is where archaeology, because of its mute and static character, is usually least productive—we can even penetrate to a certain extent into their hearts and souls. For we actually have now at our disposal a large number of Sumerian clay documents on which are inscribed the Sumerian literary creations revealing their religious, moral, and philosophical concepts. For the Sumerians were one of the very few peoples who not only probably invented a system of writing but who also developed it into a vital and effective instrument of communication.

The identification and decipherment of the Sumerian language came about rather unexpectedly and at first evoked considerable skepticism. The first major excavations in Mesopotamia were conducted in the north, in such Assyrian sites as Nineveh, Khorsabad, and Nimrud. The thousands of tablets and inscriptions there uncovered date from the first millennium B.C. and are nearly all written in Semitic Akkadian (also known as Assyrian or Babylonian). Since the existence of a Sumerian people and language was entirely unknown at the time, it was naturally assumed that all the Mesopotamian cuneiform inscriptions were in the Akkadian language. Further study, however, showed that some of the tablets found at Nineveh were inscribed in part with a language other than Akkadian, one which was not Semitic in character. In 1869, the French scholar Jules Oppert, basing his view on the royal title "king of Sumer and Akkad," which was found in some of the Akkadian inscriptions, first suggested the name "Sumerian" for the language. The suggestion was not taken very seriously, however, until toward the end of the 19th century when excavations began in southern Mesopotamia. There tablets were unearthed by the thousands, particularly at the sites of Lagash and Nippur; these dated from about 2400 B.C. and later, and were inscribed in the Sumerian language only. Since then archaeologists have excavated, at least to some extent, such important sites as Shuruppak, Adab, Kish, Jemdet Nasr, Tell el-Ubeid, Ur, Erech, Eshnunna, Tutub, Mari, and Eridu, and have amassed a vast amount of source material for the study of Sumerian history, culture, language, and literature.

It was probably early in the third millennium B.C., almost five thousand years ago, that the Sumerians, as a result of their economic and administrative needs, came upon the idea of writing on clay. Their first attempts were crude and pictographic and could be used only for the simplest administrative notations. But during the centuries that followed, the Sumerian scribes and teachers gradually so modified and molded their script that it lost completely its pictographic character and became a highly conventionalized and purely phonetic system of writing. During the course of the *second* half of the third millennium B.C. the Sumerian writing technique had become sufficiently plastic and flexible to express without difficulty the most complicated of their historical and literary compositions. And there is little doubt that sometime before the end of the third millennium B.C. the Sumerian men of letters actually wrote down on clay tablets, prisms, and cylinders many of their creations which until then were current in oral form only.

For one reason or another, however, only a few literary documents from this earlier period have as yet been excavated, although the same period has yielded tens of thousands of economic and administrative tablets, and hundreds of votive inscriptions. It is not until we come to the first half of the *second* millennium B.C. that we find a group of approximately five thousand clay documents inscribed with the Sumerian *literary* compositions. These range in size from large twelve-column tablets inscribed with hundreds of compactly written lines of text to tiny fragments containing no more than a few broken lines. As for the literary works inscribed on these tablets and fragments, they run into the hundreds and vary in length from hymns of less than fifty lines to myths of close to a thousand lines. And from the point of view of form as well as of content, they display a variety of type and genre, which, considering their age, is both impressive and instructive. Here in Sumer, a good millennium before the Hebrews wrote down their Bible and the Greeks their Iliad and Odyssey, we find a rich and mature literature; literature, be it noted, in the restricted sense of *belles lettres,* consisting of myths and epic tales, hymns, lamentations, and historiographic documents, as well as a many-sided group of wisdom compositions including proverbs, fables, and sundry didactic types. It is not too much to predict that, once achieved, the recovery and restoration of this ancient and long-forgotten literature will turn out to be a major contribution of our century to the humanities.

The full accomplishment of this task, however, is no simple matter; it will entail the devoted efforts of more than one cuneiform scholar over the coming years. While most of the documents were excavated more than half a century ago, the piecing together and translation of the compositions inscribed on them made relatively little progress over the ensuing decades. In the first place, the great majority of the tablets came out of the ground broken and fragmentary, so that only a small part of their original contents was preserved on each. Offsetting this disadvantage is the fact that the ancient scribes themselves prepared more than one copy of any given composition. The breaks and lacunae in one tablet or fragment may therefore be frequently restored from duplicating pieces which may themselves be in a most fragmentary condition. To take full advantage of these duplications and the resulting restorations, however, it is essential to have available as much as possible of the source material in published form. This frequently entails copying by hand hundreds and hundreds of minutely inscribed tablets and fragments—a tedious, wearisome, and time-consuming task. No wonder that as late as 1935 only a portion of the Sumerian literary documents had been made available, in spite of the devoted efforts of numerous cuneiformists: Hermann Hilprecht, Hugo Radau, Stephen Langdon, L. W. King, Heinrich Zimmern, Cyril Gadd, Henri de Genouillac, Arno Poebel,—and, especially, Edward Chiera.

To help remedy this situation, at least to some extent, I have devoted much of the past two decades to the studying and copying of this unpublished Sumerian literary material scattered in museums the world over. But with the passage of the years, it has become more and more apparent that this is not a "one-man" task. Fortunately, in the past several years a number of other scholars have shown no little eagerness to collaborate in the work: Edmund Gordon, whose work on the Sumerian proverbs and fables has opened up new vistas in the comparative study of world "wisdom" literature; Muazzez Çiğ and Hatice Kizilyay, the two curators of the Tablet Archives of the Museum of the Ancient Orient in Istanbul; Dr. Inez Bernhardt, assistant keeper of the "Hilprecht Sammlung" of the Friedrich Schiller University in Jena; Dr. Eugen Bergmann of the Pontificio Istituto Biblico in Rome; and George Castellino, of the University of Rome. At the same time, J. A. van Dijk, a former student of de Liagre Böhl and Adam Falkenstein, has been copying and publishing Sumerian literary texts from the Iraq Museum in Baghdad, and the Böhl collection in Leiden. And most important, several hundred Sumerian literary tablets, excavated between 1923 and 1934 at Ur, have been copied over the years by Cyril Gadd and are to be published in the near future. All in all, therefore, there is every reason to hope that the coming decade will witness the publication of a very considerable part of the Sumerian literary tablets and fragments which have been lying about for years in the museum cupboards.

As experience has shown, however, and as more than one Sumerologist will testify, even given the complete text of a Sumerian literary work, its translation and interpretation present a difficult and at times even heart-rending task. To be sure, the Sumerian grammatical problems are no longer as acute as in earlier days. The gratifying progress in this field is due largely to the past efforts of such eminent cuneiformists as Delitzsch and Thureau-Dangin, Zimmern and Landsberger, and particularly Arno Poebel; it is the latter's *Grundzüge der Summerischen Grammatik,* published about a quarter of a century ago, which has placed Sumerian grammar on a scientific basis. But, sad to say, no comparable advance has as yet been made in Sumerian lexicology although the contributions of such scholars as Adam Falkenstein, Thorkild Jacobsen, and Benno Landsberger—to name only the "giants"— show promise of surmounting at least some of the more frustrating obstacles. Our major Sumerian lexical sources consist of ancient bilinguals where the Sumerian words are translated into *Semitic* Akkadian. But unfortunately a large number of the words found in the Sumerian literary texts have no Akkadian equivalents; not infrequently, therefore, the meaning of a word has to be guessed from the surrounding context, the interpretation of which may of itself be far from assured. On the other hand, many a Sumerian word has, or at least seems to have, more than one Akkadian counterpart. In these cases the difficulties involved in the selection of the appropriate equation are at times disastrous, for a wrong choice may color falsely an entire context. Nevertheless, in spite of all these perplexities, textual, grammatical, and lexical, it is not unlikely that as a result of the cumulative and co-operative contributions of cuneiformists the world over, the coming decade will see relatively trustworthy translations of quite a number of the more significant literary compositions. Be that as it may, we are now in a position to take a "new look" at Sumerian literature as a whole, and this is what the following general survey aims to do.

Sumerian literature, as the term is used in this article, is restricted to myths and epic tales, hymns, lamentations, and historiographic documents, essays large and small, precepts and proverbs.[1] The Sumerians probably first began to write down their literary works sometime about 2500 B.C., although the earliest literary documents as yet recovered date from about 2400 B.C.[2] Their literary output, there is every reason to believe, increased with the centuries, and no doubt became quite prolific toward the end of the third millennium,[3] when the Sumerian academy known as the *Edubba* (literally, "house of tablets") came to be an important center of education and learning. Sumerian literary activity continued unabated through the first half of the second millennium, in spite of the fact that the Sumerian language was gradually being replaced by the Semitic Akkadian as the spoken language of Sumer. In the *Edubbas* which functioned throughout this, the first post-Sumerian, period, the earlier literary works were studied, copied, and redacted with zest and zeal, with care and understanding; almost all the literary works which have come down to us are known only from copies and redactions prepared in these post-Sumerian *Edubbas*. The presumably Akkadian-speaking teachers, poets, and writers who comprised the *Edubba* personnel even created new Sumerian literary works,[4] although naturally enough these followed closely the form and content, the style and pattern of the earlier documents.

It has often been assumed that the Sumerian literary works were all religious in character and that they were composed and redacted by priests for use in the temple cult. However, with the possible exception of the hymns and lamentations, this view is hardly tenable. To begin with the most clear-cut cases, it is absurd to assume that the Sumerian proverbs and precepts, or the essays dealing with the *Edubba* (see below), were written either by priests or for priests, or that they had any connection whatever with the temple cult. Nor is there any valid ground for assuming that the epic tales revolving about the heroes Enmerkar, Lugalbanda, and Gilgameš[5] were composed by priests and recited in the temple.[6] Even in the case of the myths, there is no indication that they were recited during temple services and religious festivals, at least not for the Sumerian and early post-Sumerian periods. Only in the case of the hymns and lamentations does it seem reasonable to suppose that they were composed and redacted for use in the temple cult.[7] But since the tablets inscribed with the hymns and lamentations, like those inscribed with the other types of literary works, were found not in the temples but in the Scribal Quarters,[8] these too must have been composed in the *Edubba* and by the members of its staff rather than by priests.[9]

Except for the "historiographic" compositions, proverbs, precepts, and essays,[10] the Sumerian literary works are all written in poetic form. The use of meter and rhyme was entirely unknown, but practically all other poetic devices and techniques were utilized with no little skill, imagination, and effect: repetition and parallelism, metaphor and simile, chorus and refrain. Sumerian narrative poetry, the myths and epic tales, for example, abounds in static epithets, lengthy repetitions, recurrent formulae, leisurely detailed descriptions, and long speeches. By and large, the Sumerian writers show little feeling for closely knit plot structure; their narratives tend to ramble on rather disconnectedly and monotonously, with but little variation in emphasis and tone. Above all, the Sumerian poets seemed to lack a sense of climax; they did not appreciate the effectiveness of bringing their stories to a climactic head. The myths and epic tales show little intensification of emotion and suspense as the story progresses, and often the last episode is no more moving or stirring than the first.[11] Nor is there any attempt at characterization and psychological delineation; the gods and heroes of the Sumerian narratives tend to be broad types rather than recognizable flesh and blood individuals.

The Sumerian myths[12] now recovered, wholly or in large part, are as follows: two in which the god Enlil plays the major role ("Enlil and Ninlil: The Birth of the Moon-god"[13] and "The Creation of the Pickaxe"[14]); four in which the god Enki is the leading protagonist ("Enki and the World Order: The Organization of the Earth and Its Cultural Processes,"[15] "Enki and Ninhursag: A Sumerian 'Paradise' Myth,"[16] "Enki and Ninmah: The Creation of Man,"[17] and "Enki and Eridu"[18]); one concerning the moon-god Nanna-Sin ("The Journey of Nanna-Sin to Nippur"[19]); two Ninurta myths ("The Deeds and Exploits of Ninurta"[20] and "The Return of Ninurta to Nippur"[21]); five in which the goddess Inanna plays the major role ("Inanna and Enki: The Transfer of the Arts of Civilization from Eridu to Erech,"[22] "Inanna and the Subjugation of Mt. Ebih,"[23] "Inanna and Šukallituda: The Gardener's Mortal Sin,"[24] "Inanna's Descent to the Nether World,"[25] and "Inanna and Bilulu"[26]); four in which the god Dumuzi plays the major role ("Dumuzi and Enkimdu: The Wooing of Inanna,"[27] "The Marriage of Dumuzi and Inanna,"[28] "Dumuzi and His Sister Geštinanna,"[29] and "Dumuzi and the *Gallê*"[30]); one myth concerned with the god of Martu, the Semitic

Bedu living west of Sumer ("The Marriage of Martu"[31]); the "Flood" myth in which the identity of the deity (or deities) who was the chief protagonist is still uncertain;[32] and seven "disputation" myths ("Summer and Winter,"[33] "Cattle and Grain,"[34] "Bird and Fish,"[35] "Tree and Reed,"[36] "Silver and Copper,"[37] "Pickaxe and Plough,"[38] and "The Mill and the *Gulgul*-stone"[39]).

The Sumerian epic tales[40] now restorable, wholly or in large part, are nine in number and vary in length from a little over one hundred to more than six hundred lines.[41] Two of them revolve about the hero Enmerkar ("Enmerkar and the Lord of Aratta"[42] and "Enmerkar and Ensukušsir-anna"[43]); two center about the hero Lugalbanda, although Enmerkar also plays a role in both of them ("Lugalbanda and Enmerkar"[44] and "Lugalbanda and Mt. Ḫurrum"[45]); five revolve about the best known of Mesopotamian heroes, Gilgameš[46] ("Gilgameš and the Land of the Living,"[47] "Gilgameš, Enkidu and the Nether World,"[48] "Gilgameš and Agga of Kiš,"[49] "Gilgameš and the Bull of Heaven,"[50] and "The Death of Gilgameš"[51]).

Turning to the hymns, it is to be noted first of all that hymnography was a carefully cultivated, highly sophisticated art in Sumer. Scores of hymns, varying in length from less than fifty to well-nigh four hundred lines, have come down to us, and there is every reason to believe that this is only a fraction of the hymns composed in Sumer throughout the centuries.[52] To judge from their contents, the extant Sumerian hymns may be divided into four major categories: (1) hymns extolling the gods; (2) hymns extolling kings; (3) hymnal prayers in which paeans of praise to the gods are interspersed with blessings and prayers for kings; and (4) hymns glorifying Sumerian temples.[53]

The divine hymns are either in the form of an address by the poet to the deity, or they may glorify the deity and his achievements in the third person. Among the longer and more important are the following: (1) a hymn to Enlil noteworthy for its poetic summary of civilization's debt to his beneficence;[54] (2) a hymn to the god Ninurta addressed to him not only under that name but under the names Pagibilsag and Ningirsu as well;[55] (3) a hymn to the goddess Inanna by Enḫeduanna, who may be identical with the high priestess Enḫeduanna, long known as the daughter of Sargon the Great;[56] (4) a hymn to Inanna as the Venus planet, noteworthy for its description of the hieros-gamos ceremony celebrating the union of the goddess and the king Iddin-Dagan of Isin on New Year's Day;[57] (5) a hymn to Inanna as the goddess of war and wrath;[58] (6) a hymn to Utu as the god of justice who regulates and supervises the world order;[59] (7) a hymn to the goddess Nanše[60] as the guardian of man's ethics and morals;[61] (8) a hymn to the goddess Ninisinna as the "great physician of the 'black-heads,' " the patron deity of the art of medicine and healing;[62] (9) a hymn to Ninkasi as the goddess of intoxicating drink;[63] (10) a hymn to Nidaba as the goddess of writing, accounting, and wisdom;[64] and (11) a hymn to the god Sumugan as "the lord of the palace" and as judge and protector of the "black-heads."[65]

Of the hymns exalting kings, the most important group belongs to Šulgi, the second ruler of the Third Dynasty of Ur; five of these are now restorable wholly or in large part.[66] Two hymns sing the praises of Šulgi's father, Ur-Nammu.[67] There are quite a number of hymns celebrating the rulers of the Isin Dynasty (which followed the Ur III rulers), particularly Iddin-Dagan, Išme-Dagan, and Lipit-Ištar.[68] Most of the royal hymns are extravagantly self-laudatory; the king himself is purported to have uttered grandiloquent, inflated, and vain-sounding paeans of self-glorification without hesitation and inhibition. This unusual and, from our point of view, rather unworthy kingly behavior is not without psychological significance; it fits in with the drive for prestige and superiority characteristic of Sumerian behavior in general.[69]

A high favorite with the Sumerian hymnographers was the type of composition in which paeans to the gods are interlarded with blessings and prayers for the kings. Except, rather unexpectedly, for the mother goddess Ninhursag, practically all the major deities are represented in this hymnal category: An, Enlil, Enki, Nanna, Utu, Ninurta, Nergal, Inanna, Bau, and Ninisinna. As for the kings blessed and prayed for, all the rulers of the Third Dynasty of Ur, as well as the first six rulers of the First Dynasty of Isin, are represented. One of these hymns is addressed to the goddess Bau as the friend and supporter of Eannatum of Lagash, which indicates rather conclusively that this hymnal type was current in Sumer already in pre-Sargonic days.[70]

The temple hymns, finally, are represented by a song of praise to the Ekur, Enlil's temple in Nippur;[71] by the well-known hymn to the temple of the goddess Ninhursag at Keš;[72] and best of all by a composition of over four hundred lines containing brief hymns to all the more important temples of Sumer and Akkad.[73] One of the most noteworthy of all extant temple hymns is that inscribed on the long-known Gudea cylinders, which consists of more than 1300 lines of text and celebrates the rebuilding of the Eninnu temple in Lagash.[74]

Turning to the formal aspects of Sumerian hymnography, it is worth noting that hymn writing had become so sophisticated a literary art in Sumer that it was subdivided into various categories by the ancient poets themselves, and many of the extant hymns are ascribed to their appropriate categories by a special subscription at the end of the composition. The common Sumerian word for hymns is *sìr*, which may or may not have anything to do with the Hebrew *šîr*. Some of the categories of *sìr* are: *sìr-ḫamun*, perhaps "harmony hymns," *sìr-nam-nar*, "musical hymns," *sìr-nam-gala*, "hymns of gala-ship," *sìr-nam-šub-ba* (meaning uncertain), *sìr-gíd-da* (meaning uncertain), *sìr-nam-ur-sag-gá*, "hymns of heroship," and *sìr-nam-sipad-ᵈinanna-ka*, "Inanna's hymns of shepherdship (that is, hymns to the god Dumuzi)." Hymnal categories which seem to be named from the musical instruments accompanying them are *tigi*, probably a lyre-accompanied hymn; *ir-šèm-ma*, perhaps a drum-accompanied hymn;[75] and *adab*, a hymn accompanied by some still unidentified stringed instrument. The *tigi* and *adab* hymns are broken up by the ancient poets into sections bearing the notations *sa-gar-ra* and *sa-gíd-da,* which seem to mean literally "the set string(s)" and "the long string(s)" respectively, further proof that these hymns were accompanied by musical instruments. The *adab* hymns also include special sections bearing the notations *bar-sud* and *šà-ba-tuku,* the meanings of which are still unknown; they usually end with a three-line prayer for the king designated as an *uru-en-bi-im,* "he is the city's lord." Both the *adab* and *tigi* categories also make use of an antiphon consisting of from one to four lines, something like a choral refrain, bearing the still obscure notation GIŠ-*gi₄*-IG. Finally there are a number of hymns which are divided into stanzas with the notation *ki*-RU-*gú,* a phrase which may perhaps mean "genuflection"; following the notation *ki*-RU-*gú,* there is often found the refrainlike passage designated GIŠ-*gi₄*-IG.[76]

The Sumerian lamentations are primarily of two kinds: those bewailing the destruction of Sumerian cities and city-states, and those lamenting the death of the god Dumuzi or one of his counterparts.[77] Of the former, two of the best preserved concern the destruction of Ur.[78] A third concerns the destruction of Nippur; it begins as a lament, but ends on a note of joy with the restoration of the city by Išme-Dagan of Isin.[79] A fourth lamentation, as yet restorable only in part, concerns the destruction of Sumer and Akkad as a whole.[80] As for the Dumuzi laments, they range in size from long compositions of over two hundred lines to brief laments of less than fifty lines. Quite a few of these Dumuzi texts have been published to date. But there is still no trustworthy translation available for many of them, especially those written in a phonetic rather than in the historical orthography, which makes even the word division uncertain, let alone the meaning and interpretation.[81]

The longest Sumerian "historiographic" text[82] as yet known is "The Curse of Agade," an excellently preserved composition which attempts to explain the catastrophic destruction of the city of Agade by the barbaric Guti.[83] Another well-preserved historiographic document revolves about the defeat of the Guti by a Sumerian ruler of Erech, Utuḫegal.[84] A third and rather brief "historiographic" document concerns the successive restorations of the Tummal, the goddess Ninlil's shrine in the city of Nippur.[85] Finally, there are indications that there had existed a series of legendary tales clustering about Sargon the Great and his contemporaries, Lugalzaggesi of Erech and Ur-Zababa of Kiš.[86]

The last group of Sumerian literary documents to be considered in this article are the "wisdom" compositions,[87] consisting of essays large and small, and collections of precepts and of proverbs. Except for the "Job"-like poetic essay concerned with human suffering and submission,[88] the longer Sumerian essays all deal, in one way or another, with the Sumerian academy, the *Edubba,* and its faculty and student body. At present five of these are restorable wholly or in large part: (1) "Schooldays," a composition consisting, in the main, of a schoolboy's version of his early school life;[89] (2) "A Scribe and His Perverse Son," a composition of about two hundred lines consisting largely of a bitter harangue by a disappointed father to his ungrateful and disobedient son;[90] (3) "The 'Supervisor' and the Scribe," a brief composition of about seventy-five lines consisting of a battle of words between these two professionals;[91] (4) "Enki-mansi and Girini-išag," a composition consisting in large part of a bitter debate between two *Edubba* worthies couched in insulting and vituperative language;[92] and (5) an essay devoted to the *Edubba* as the "house of learning."[93] As for the miniature essays, they may vary in length from four or five to some fifty lines and, in a number of cases, end with what seems to be an ironic phrase; their contents, however, are not too intelligible at the present time.[94]

Three Sumerian collections of precepts are now known: "The Farmer's Almanac," which contains the instructions of a farmer to his son;[95] "The Instructions of King Šuruppak to His Son Ziusudra,"[96] which seems to consist of practical admonitions for wise and effective behavior; and a third, which also consists of admonitions but is too fragmentary for closer identification.[97] As for the Sumerian proverbs, they run into the hundreds and include all types of maxims, sayings, apothegms, and even short Aesop-like fables. At least ten to twelve collections of these proverbs, compiled by the ancient scribes themselves and used as textbooks in the schools both at Nippur and Ur, have now been identified. In at least four of these collections[98] the proverbs were arranged in groups according to their initial signs, while in others no such basis for the arrangement is apparent.[99]

So much for our general survey of Sumerian literature as a whole. As for its significance for the history of literature and thought, it goes without saying that a written literature so varied, comprehensive, and time honored left a deep impress on the literary products of the ancient Near East, including the Bible. This is particularly so, since at one time or another practically all the peoples of western Asia—Akkadians, Assyrians, Babylonians, Hittites, Hurrians, Canaanites, and Elamites—to name only those for which positive and direct evidence is available at the moment—had found it to their interest to borrow the cuneiform script in order to inscribe their own records and writings. For the adoption and adaptation of this syllabic and logographic system of writing, which had been developed by the Sumerians to write their own agglutinative and largely monosyllabic tongue, demanded a thorough training in the Sumerian language and literature. To this end, no doubt, learned teachers and scribes were imported from Sumer to the schools of the neighboring lands, while the native scribes traveled to Sumer for special instruction in its more famous academies. All of this resulted in the spreading abroad of Sumerian culture and literature. The ideas and ideals of the Sumerians—their cosmology, theology, ethics, and system of education—permeated, to a greater or lesser extent, the thoughts and writings of all the peoples of the ancient Near East. So, too, did the Sumerian literary forms and themes—their plots, motifs, stylistic devices, and aesthetic techniques. To all of which, Palestine, the land where the books of the Bible were composed, redacted, and edited by the Hebrew men of letters, was no exception. As I hope to show in a forthcoming study (to appear in a volume dedicated to the fiftieth anniversary of the founding of the Pontificio Istituto Biblico), there are quite a number of Biblical parallels from Sumerian literature revolving about such themes as the creation of the universe, the creation of man, paradise, the flood, the Cain-Abel type of rivalry, the earth and its organization, the "personal" god and the "covenant" relationship, law, ethics and morals, divine retribution, suffering and submission, death and the nether world. And this list only "skims the cream" and "scratches the surface." There is little doubt that in the coming years, as more and more of the Sumerian literary documents become available, the number of Sumerian parallels to the Bible will grow and multiply, particularly for such books as Psalms, Proverbs, Lamentations, and Song of Songs.

Philadelphia; Fall, 1957; revised, October, 1959

NOTES TO CHAPTER NINE

1. Excluded are the votive inscriptions, some of which have no little literary value (cf., for example, the Entemena historical document and the Urukagina "reform" text treated in chapters 5 and 6 of the writer's *From the Tablets of Sumer* [*FTS*]); the political letters, some of which have a distinct literary flavor (cf., for example, the Ibbi-Sin letter translated in *ANET*, pp. 480 f.); the letters to deities or deified rulers (cf., for example, Falkenstein in *ZA* XLIV [1938], pp. 1–25, and Van Dijk in *La Sagesse suméro-accadienne* [*SSA*], pp. 15 f.); and the incantations. References to *FTS* can now also be found in the corresponding chapters of *HBS* (*History Begins at Sumer*, Doubleday Anchor Books, 1959, a revised edition of *FTS*).

2. Cf., for example, the Enlil-Ninḫursag myth inscribed on a solid clay cylinder now in the University Museum (for details, see the writer's *Sumerian Mythology* [*SM*], pl. III and p. 18, and *FTS*, p. 280, note to Pl. 6), and the Istanbul fragment Ni 12501 cf. *FTS*, pp. 106 and 280, Pl. 6a). The plot of the former is still largely unintelligible, but the individual words, phrases, and incidents show a structure and style quite similar to those of the myths of a much later date; even the initial words (u₄-rí-a) are the same as those of two other compositions (cf. now *Wissenschaftliche Zeitschrift der Friedrich-Schiller-Universität Jena* [*WZJ*], Jahrgang 6 [1956/57], Gesellschafts– und Sprachwissenschaftliche Reihe, p. 393, note 2, reference to title no. 5). As for the Istanbul fragment, the text as far as it is preserved seems to contain a mythological motif revolving about the disappearance of Enlil's son Iškur to the nether world; its most intelligible lines (col. iv) contain the words: "My son has disappeared (?) in the nether world, who will bring him back? Iškur has disappeared (?) in the nether world, who will bring him back?" The following space contains the word for "fox," and it is not unlikely, therefore, that the fox offers to bring Iškur back to Enlil, a mythological motif identical with one in the Enki-Ninḫursag myth of a much later day (cf. now *FTS*, pp. 170 f.). Strangely enough, no literary documents have been found at Fara, although the numerous god lists and other school tablets recovered there point to their existence.

3. This is quite clear from the large number of hymns composed for the rulers of the Third Dynasty of Ur. To be sure, these have all come down to us in copies made in the early post-Sumerian period, but there is no reason to doubt that they are copies of contemporary Ur III documents. Note, too, that in the case of at least two compositions which are not hymns, there is reasonably conclusive evidence that they were first composed in Ur III days: the "Tree and Reed" disputation (see note 36 below) which mentions Šulgi, and the "Summer and Winter" disputation (see note 33 below) which mentions Ibbi-Sin. However, very few literary documents actually inscribed during the last quarter of the third millennium have as yet been uncovered; the most significant of these are the long-known Gudea cylinders from Lagash (see note 73 below). But there is little doubt that this is due to archaeological accident; the excavators have simply failed to uncover the sites of the scribal quarters of these earlier centuries.

4. Notably the hymns of the rulers of the dynasties of Isin, Larsa, and Babylon, as well as the lamentations over the destruction of Ur, of Nippur, and of Sumer and Akkad as a whole (see notes 67, 69, 76, 77, and 78).

5. Cf. *FTS*, pp. 227–38.

6. It would be much more likely to assume that, if at all, the epic tales were recited in the palaces on the occasion of royal feasts and banquets.

7. The hymns and lamentations are usually divided into stanzas and often contain rubrics which seem to be of a liturgical nature, all of which points to their use in the temple services.

8. Cf. especially the relevant data in McCown's contribution to the forthcoming monograph on the first two campaigns of the Joint Nippur Expedition of the Oriental Institute and the University Museum.

9. For the *Edubba,* cf. now Falkenstein, *Die Welt des Orients* I/3 (1948), pp. 172–86; Gadd, *Teachers and Students in the Oldest Schools* (London, 1956); Kramer, in Mylonas, *ed., Studies Presented to David Moore Robinson* (St. Louis, 1951), Vol. I, pp. 238–45; and Van Dijk, *SSA,* pp. 21–27. Nowhere in the extant material are priests mentioned as part of the *Edubba* personnel. The *nar,* that is, the musician and singer, the minstrel, does appear side by side with the scribe several times, but his connection with the *Edubba* is not clear. It is not impossible, of course, that some of the graduates of the *Edubba* specialized in religious compositions, such as hymns and lamentations, and went into the service of the temple to teach them to its singers and musicians and to supervise and help conduct the cult liturgies, while others, specializing in myths and epic tales, went into the service of the palace to train and instruct the court singers and entertainers. As yet, however, we have practically no data on these and similar details. Nor do we know anything about the audience or the reading public for whom the Sumerian literary compositions were prepared. It is clear that only the *Edubba* graduates could read and write, and it seems hardly likely that even these men of letters made it a practice to collect *private* libraries for their own personal entertainment and instruction. Only the *Edubba* probably had such libraries, although the temple and the palace may also have possessed copies of those compositions which were relevant to their needs. In any case, it seems incredible that the Sumerian literary works should have stayed on the *Edubba* "shelves" for teaching purposes only, and that they should not have been used, in one way or another, in public gatherings, whether these took place in the temple, the court, or the market place.

10. An exception is the "Job"-like essay concerned with human suffering and submission, which is written in poetic form throughout (cf. *FTS,* pp. 147–51). The "historiographic" compositions, moreover, are written in a highly poetic prose which in some ways is hardly distinguishable from poetry, except that it does not resort quite as much to the repetition pattern for rhythmic effect.

11. The sense of climax is a Semitic psychological characteristic; cf. the comment to the Akkadian epic of Gilgameš and its Sumerian forerunners in Chapter 21 of *FTS*. This psychological contrast between Sumerian and Akkadian narrative style is also apparent in art—the well-known stele of Narâm-Sin, for example, with its strong climactic unity, is a Semitic, not a Sumerian, creation—as well as in the languages themselves (note, for example, the absence of emphatic consonants and strong tonal accent in Sumerian as contrasted with Akkadian).

12. The category "myth" is restricted in this article to those poetic narratives in which the gods are the major protagonists, although, in the case of some, mortals may play a not insignificant role—for example, Ziusudra in the "Flood" myth (cf. *FTS*, pp. 176–81) and Šukallituda in "The Gardener's Mortal Sin" (ibid., pp. 66–70). Included among the myths are the "disputations" between deified or personified protagonists (except for the "disputation" poem "Enmerkar and Ensukušširanna" which is treated as an epic tale). Although in one sense these literary debates may be classified as a "wisdom" genre, since the arguments concern cultural evaluation, they qualify as myths as well, particularly since they usually begin and end with mythological passages.

13. Cf. now *FTS*, pp. 79–82.

14. Cf. *SM*, pp. 51 ff., and Jacobsen, *JNES* v (1946), pp. 134–37.

15. Cf. now *FTS*, pp. 89–91, and *WZJ*, Jahrgang 5 (1955/56), pp. 756–58. A definitive edition of the myth has now been prepared jointly with Dr. Inez Bernhardt of the "Hilprecht-Semmlung" of the Friedrich-Schiller University and will appear in a forthcoming issue of *WJZ*.

16. Cf. *FTS*, pp. 170–75, as well as Gadd, *JAOS* 66 (1946), pp. 266 f. A discussion of the contents of an important duplicate from Ur will be found in my paper "Magan and Meluḫḫa" read before the Huitième Rencontre Assyriologique Internationale in Heidelberg and to appear in its *Proceedings*.

17. Cf. *FTS*, pp. 101 f. and 143 f., and Jacobsen, *JNES* v (1946), p. 143.

18. Cf. *SM*, pp. 62–63, and Falkenstein, *Sumer* vii (1951), pp. 119–25.

19. Cf. *SM*, pp. 47–49.

20. Cf., for the present, *FTS*, pp. 198–200. A definitive study of this myth (as restored from close to a hundred published and unpublished pieces) is now being prepared by Dr. Eugen Bergmann of the Pontifical Biblical Institute, to appear as a volume of *Analecta Orientalia*.

21. Cf., for the present, *Proceedings of the American Philosophical Society* 85 (1942), p. 321; this myth, too, will be prepared for definitive publication by Dr. Bergmann. Two additional Ninurta myths should also be mentioned here, although as yet they are known only partially: one in which the god Enki, too, plays a considerable role (this myth is inscribed on a tablet from Ur, copied by C. J. Gadd and to be published in a forthcoming volume devoted primarily to Sumerian literary texts from Ur), and another which narrates Ninurta's journey to Eridu to obtain Enki's blessing and the *me*'s essential to Sumer's welfare (*STVC* 34; note that the scribe designated this poem as a *sìr-gíd-da*, that is, a type of hymn, and indeed the second half of the composition is entirely hymnal in character). For an excellent translation of the Ninurta composition *STVC* 34, cf. now Falkenstein, *Sumerische Götterlieder* (Abhandlungen der Heidelberger Akademie der Wissenschaften, Philosophisch-historische Klasse, Jahrgang 1959. 1. Abhandlung), pp. 80–106.

22. Cf. *FTS*, pp. 91–96.

23. Cf. *SM*, pp. 82 f.

24. Cf. *FTS*, pp. 66–70.

25. Cf. now *FTS*, pp. 183–95. For new material to "Inanna's Descent to the Nether World" see my "Death and the Nether World according to the Sumerian Literary Texts" to appear in the forthcoming *Woolley Festschrift*.

26. Cf. Jacobsen and Kramer, *JNES* xii (1953), pp. 160–88.
27. Cf. *FTS*, pp. 164–68.
28. Cf. Kramer, *Sumerian Literary Texts from Nippur in the Museum of the Ancient Orient at Istanbul* (*AASOR*, Vol. 23, New Haven, 1944; hereafter *SLTN* no. 35), and comment in the Introduction, pp. 18 f. There are three other Sumerian poems concerned with the Dumuzi-Inanna affairs of the heart; cf. my article "Love, Hate and Fear: Psychological Aspects of Sumerian Culture" in *Eretz-Israel,* Vol. v (1958; the Mazar *Festschrift*), pp. 66–74.
29. Cf., for the present, Jacobsen, *JNES* xii (1953), p. 165 and note 19, as well as my comment to *SLTN,* no. 36, on pp. 18 f. of that work. A new study of the myth "Dumuzi and His Sister Geštinanna," which might be better entitled "The Death of Dumuzi" (also known as "Dumuzi's Dream," see now Jacobsen *apud* Oppenheim, *Dreams and Their Interpretation,* p. 246) is now in preparation; for details see note 24 of my forthcoming "Death and the Nether World According to the Sumerian Literary Texts."
30. Cf., for the present, my summary of this myth in *JCS* iv (1950), p. 207, note 50; cf. also Witzel, *Analecta Orientalia* 10, pp. 88 ff., and Falkenstein, *ZA* xlv (1939), pp. 175–78, no. 4. For a modification of this summary see note 24 of my forthcoming "Death and the Nether World According to the Sumerian Literary Texts."
31. Cf. *SM,* pp. 98–101.
32. Cf. *FTS,* pp. 176–81.
33. Cf. *FTS,* pp. 161–64.
34. Cf. *FTS,* pp. 144–46.
35. Cf., for the present, *Vorderasiatische Schriftdenkmäler der Königlichen Museen zu Berlin* x, no. 204; in addition, quite a number of fragments of this composition will be published in the forthcoming volume of literary texts from Ur (cf. note 21 above), and these, together with the still unpublished pieces from the University Museum and the Istanbul Museum of the Ancient Orient, will provide us with a well-nigh complete text of the composition.
36. Still largely unpublished; cf., for the present, H. de Genouillac, *Textes religieux sumériens* (Musée du Louvre, *Textes cunéiformes,* Tomes xv–xvi, Paris, 1930; hereafter *TRS*) ii, 53 and *Publications of the Babylonian Section, University Museum, University of Pennsylvania* (hereafter *PBS*), xiii, 42.
37. To appear in a forthcoming issue of the *Proceedings of the American Philosophical Society* as a joint article of the writer and Dr. Inez Bernhardt, curator of the "Hilprecht-Sammlung" of the Friedrich-Schiller Universität Jena.
38. To be published by Thorkild Jacobsen in a volume devoted to Sumerian agricultural techniques.
39. Only one fragmentary text has as yet been identified: *SLTN* 131, obv., columns i and ii (lines 1–3).
40. The category "epic tale" is restricted in this article to those narrative poems in which mortal heroic figures play the major roles, although deities may also participate in the action in one way or another (actually there is only one epic tale in which the deities play no role at all: "Gilgameš and Agga of Kiš," for which cf. note 49 below).
41. The Sumerian epic poems, therefore, consist of individual disconnected tales, each of which is restricted to a single episode in the life of the hero; the Sumerian poets seem to have made no attempt to articulate and integrate a whole series of such episodes into a larger unit such as the Babylonian epic of Gilgameš or the Greek *Iliad* and *Odyssey.*
42. Cf. now *FTS,* pp. 15–25 and 259–62.
43. Cf. op. cit., pp. 232–34.
44. Cf. op. cit., pp. 235–37.

45. Cf. op. cit., pp. 237 f., as modified in *WZJ*, Jahrgang 5 (1955/56), pp. 756 and 758 f.
46. For a discussion of the etymology of the name Gilgameš, cf. *JAOS* 64 (1944), p. 11, note 15.
47. Cf. *FTS*, pp. 200–7. For new material to the Gilgameš epic tales see my "Gilgameš: Some New Sumerian Data" in the *Proceedings of the Septième Rencontre Assyriologique Internationale* (now in press).
48. Cf. op. cit., pp. 222–26.
49. Cf. op. cit., pp. 27–31.
50. Cf. op. cit., pp. 217 f.
51. Cf. op. cit., p. 219.
52. Cf., for example, the two hymnal catalogues published in *WZJ*, Jahrgang 6 (1956/57), pp. 389–95, which between them contain the titles of eighty-five hymns; only a very few of these hymns have actually been recovered to date.
53. For a fairly representative cross section of the Sumerian hymnal material, cf. now Falkenstein's contribution to *Sumerische und Akkadische Hymnen und Gebete* (*SAHG*) (Zurich/Stuttgart, 1953), pp. 7–37 and 57–182; see also the writer's review of this work in *Bibliotheca Orientalis* XI (1954), pp. 170–76. The first fascicle of a new publication called *Sumerische Götterlieder* under the editorship of Adam Falkenstein has now appeared (see note 21 above).
54. Cf. *FTS*, pp. 85–88.
55. Cf. *SLTN*, no. 61 and no. 62, and the comment in the Introduction, p. 22. For a new edition of the Enlil hymn see now Falkenstein, *Sumerische Götterlieder*, pp. 5–79.
56. This hymn may also be classed as a prayer to Inanna to look with favor upon Enḫeduanna, and the last passage actually contains the statement that Inanna accepted her prayer. Cf., for the present, Van Dijk, *Sumer* XIII (1957), p. 65.
57. Cf. now Falkenstein, *SAHG*, pp. 90–99 (no. 18).
58. Cf., for the present, *Orientalia*, n.s., 22 (1953), p. 193 (comment to Ni. 4202).
59. Cf., for the present, *TRS* II 79 and its duplicates in *PBS* I/2 (note that the latter pieces seem to be copies dating from the Kassite period rather than from the early post-Sumerian period). The Utu hymn is now being prepared for publication by G. Castellino.
60. The name of the goddess hitherto known as Nanše is probably Nazi, cf. Stephens *apud* Hackman, *Sumerian and Akkadian Administrative Texts* (1958), p. 13.
61. Cf., for the present, *FTS*, pp. 98–100.
62. Cf. Chiera, *Sumerian Religious Texts* (Upland, Pa., 1924), no. 6 = no. 7; cf. also Ebeling, *Tod und Leben*, pp. 156 f. Note that this hymn ends with a self-laudatory paean of praise by the goddess, in which she describes herself as an heroic savior of Sumer from some unnamed inimical land.
63. Cf. Edward Chiera, *Sumerian Texts of Varied Contents* (Chicago, 1934; hereafter *STVC*), Introduction, p. 3 (comment to no. 38), as well as *Orientalia*, n.s., 21 (1952), p. 249.
64. Cf. Falkenstein, *SAHG*, pp. 65–67 (no. 6), and Kramer, *Bibliotheca Orientalis* XI (1954), p. 172.
65. Cf., for the present, *SLTN*, Introduction, pp. 23 f. (comment to no. 70), where the description *"Hymn to a goddess"* is to be corrected to *"Hymn to the deity Sumugan"* in accordance with some still unpublished material from Nippur; note, however, that Sumugan is actually designated as *nin* (not *en* or *lugal*) throughout the composition.
66. Cf. Chiera, *Sumerian Religious Texts*, Introduction, p. 24 (comment to nos. 13–15 incl.), *STVC*, Introduction, p. 4 (nos. 50–60), and *SLTN*, Introduction, pp. 24–28 (nos. 73–83); for a translation of one of these hymns, see now Falkenstein, *SAHG*,

pp. 115–19 (no. 24). Two of the five Šulgi hymns referred to have now been prepared for publication by G. Castellino.

67. Cf. Chiera, ibid., no. 11, translated in *SAHG*, pp. 87–90, no. 17 (note, too, the comment on this hymn in *Bibliotheca Orientalis* XI (1954), pp. 173 f.), as well as *TRS* II, 12 (a self-laudatory hymn). One of the Ur-Nammu hymns has now been published by G. Castellino in *ZA* 52, pp. 1–57, and the other, by the same author, in *ZA* 53, pp. 106–32.

68. For details concerning the Isin Dynasty hymns, cf. the Introduction to *STVC*, pp. 4–6 (comments to nos. 61–79), and to *SLTN*, pp. 28 f. (comment to nos. 84–87); see also Falkenstein, *SAHG*, pp. 120–30 (nos. 26, 27, and 28), for translations of three of these hymns.

69. Cf. my article "Rivalry and Superiority: Two Dominant Features of the Sumerian Culture Pattern" in the forthcoming *Proceedings* of the Fifth International Congress of Anthropological and Ethnological Sciences.

70. Cf. now Falkenstein, *SAHG,* pp. 70–73 (no. 9), pp. 85–90 (nos. 16–17), and pp. 99–114 (nos. 19–23 incl.), as well as the relevant comments in *Bibliotheca Orientalis* XI (1954), pp. 172–75 (!), and especially note 19 on p. 172.

71. The hymn to the Ekur has now appeared in *Rivista degli Studi Orientalni* XXXII (Furlani Festschrift), pp. 95–102.

72. Cf., for the present, the "David Prism," published by Langdon in *Oxford Editions of Cuneiform Texts* I, pp. 48–59, and Pls. 42–45.

73. Cf., for the present, *SLTN*, Introduction, pp. 29–31 (comment to nos. 88–89). A definitive edition of this hymn collection is now being prepared by Drs. Bergmann and Moran of the Pontifical Biblical Institute.

74. Although the ancient scribe himself designated the compositions inscribed on these two cylinders as hymns, they actually consist of a heterogeneous conglomeration of narrative and descriptive, as well as hymnal, passages. These two Gudea compositions are in a sense *sui generis* and have no counterparts in the known Sumerian literary documents; the composition resembling them most closely is the myth "Enki and Eridu" (see note 18 above). Actually they are loosely organized, long-winded, and rambling, and the author seems to have been feeling his way with some difficulty in an experimental literary style. For a translation of these two hymns, see now Falkenstein, *SAHG*, pp. 137–82 (no. 32).

75. The word *ir* of the term *ír-šèm-ma* indicates that these compositions should be laments rather than hymns, and the majority of them actually are laments of one type or another.

76. For an excellent discussion of the various hymnal categories and their stylistic features, see Falkenstein, *ZA* 49 (1949), pp. 84–105, and *SAHG*, Introduction, pp. 18–37; cf. also the writer in *WZJ*, Jahrgang 6 (1956/57), pp. 389–95. For the reading and meaning of *uru-en-bi-im,* see now the detailed discussion by Falkenstein in *ZA* 52, pp. 69–72.

77. Under lamentations might also be included two funerary dirges inscribed on a tablet in the Pushkin Museum in Moscow which I studied in the course of two months' visit to the USSR in the fall of 1957 and which, as far as I know, are the only examples thus far uncovered of the elegiac literary genre. A definitive edition of the two compositions is now in the hands of the Pushkin Museum authorities and will be published under the auspices of the Academy of Science of the USSR.

78. An edition of one of these has been published by the writer as *Assyriological Studies* (Oriental Institute, Univ. of Chicago) 12 (cf. now also *ANET,* pp. 455–63, as well as Falkenstein, *SAHG,* pp. 192–213, no. 38); the other can be pieced together to a large extent from the literary material from Ur to be published by C. J. Gadd and the writer in the near future (for the initial fifty-nine lines of this composition, cf. the "Ibbi-Sin Klage" in Falkenstein, *SAHG,* pp. 189–92, no. 37).

79. Cf., for the present, *SLTN*, Introduction, p. 33 (comment to nos. 101–2), and *WZJ*, Jahrgang 5 (1955/56), p. 763 (no. 142). Note, too, that the two Ur lamentations as well as the Nippur lamentation are divided into stanzas with the rubric *ki*-RU-*gú* and include antiphons designated by the rubric GIŠ-*gi₄*-IG.

80. Cf. *SLTN*, Introduction, pp. 32 f. (comment to no. 100).

81. For bibliographical purposes, the reader will find M. Witzel's "Tammuz-liturgien und Verwandtes" (*Analecta Orientalia* 10) useful; the translations there offered are, however, not to be taken seriously.

82. The term "historiographic" is here used of compositions which utilize historical events for literary purposes of one kind or another and is not to be taken in its usual meaning.

83. Cf. *FTS*, pp. 267–71.

84. Cf. Thureau-Dangin, *RA* IX (1912), pp. 111–20, and *RA* X (1913), pp. 98 ff.

85. Two new pieces belonging to this text are in the "Hilprecht-Sammlung" of the Friedrich-Schiller Universität Jena and will be published in the near future by the writer in *BASOR*. For a translation of the new data furnished by the new pieces, cf. my "Gilgameš: Some New Sumerian Data" (see note 47 above).

86. Cf. the Lugalzaggesi—Sargon fragment published in *TRS* II 73, and an as yet unpublished Sargon—Ur-Zababa tablet from the recent excavations of the Joint Nippur Expedition. Perhaps, too, the Nintu "hymn" (*Babylonian Expedition of the University of Pennsylvania* VI/2, no. 130 = *PBS* V 75; cf. Poebel, *PBS* IV, p. 135, notes 8 and 9, and Güterbock's translation in *ZA* XLII [1934], pp. 40–46) and the Ur-Nammu text *PBS* X/2, no. 6 (cf. my note in *BASOR* 94 [1944], p. 6, note 11), should also be classed as "historiographic" compositions.

87. The Sumerian "wisdom" literature, consisting of proverbs, fables, essays large and small, riddles, disputations, precepts, etc., has been sketched in considerable detail and with complete bibliographical annotation by E. I. Gordon in his study "A New Look at the Wisdom of Sumer and Akkad" to appear in a forthcoming issue of *BiOr*.

88. Cf. now *FTS*, pp. 147–51.

89. Cf. *JAOS* 69 (1949), pp. 199–215.

90. Cf., for the present, the writer's "A Father and His Perverse Son: The First Example of Juvenile Delinquency in the Recorded History of Man" (*National Probation and Parole Association Journal*, Vol. 3 [1957], pp. 169–73).

91. The "supervisor" (Sumerian *ugula*) is also mentioned in the composition "A Scribe and His Perverse Son," and seems therefore to refer to someone connected with the *Edubba* in one way or another. For the published texts belonging to this composition, cf., for the present, the comment in *SLTN*, Introduction, pp. 37 f., nos. 115 and 117; there are also a number of unpublished pieces available which will make the text of this composition practically complete.

92. Cf., for the present, Gadd, *Teachers and Students in the Oldest Schools* (London, 1956), pp. 29–36.

93. Still unpublished.

94. Cf., for the present, Kramer, *BASOR* 122 (1951), pp. 29 f. and notes 12 f. there, as well as Van Dijk, *SSA*, pp. 89–99.

95. Cf., for the present, *FTS*, pp. 61–65.

96. Cf., for the present, Kramer, *BASOR* 122 (1951), p. 30. Among the literary tablets from Ur, there are two fairly well-preserved pieces which will help considerably in the restoration of this text; there is also a piece in the Hermitage in Leningrad according to information provided by Diakonov.

97. Cf. Van Dijk, *SSA*, pp. 102–12.

98. Proverb Collections One, Two, Five, and at least one other (the numbers given to these ancient collections by their editor, Edmund I. Gordon, are purely a modern

convenience for identifying them in publication). Proverb Collection One, with 202 proverbs, is largely arranged in groups according to the initial signs of the individual proverbs: the sign GAR (= *níg*, "thing," or *ninda*, "bread/food"); *uru*, "city"; *áš*, "curse"; *gišmá*, "boat"; *šà*, "heart/inside"; then some groups with initial signs of uncertain meaning, and finally a long section consisting of proverbs either dealing with women and household affairs or else written in the *Emesal*, or female dialect of Sumerian. Proverb Collection Two, with 154 proverbs, after an opening passage, arranges its proverbs also by their initial signs: *nam-tar*, "fate"; *ukú*, "a poor man"; *dub-sar*, "scribe"; and *nar*, "singer"; *ka₅-a*, "fox"; *lul*, "liar"; *anše*, "ass"; *gud*, "ox"; *gala*, "the *kalûm*-priest"; *ur* and *ur-ger₍ₓ₎*, "dog"; then a group of proverbs containing antithetical terms in pairs; and finally a group with the initial sign *é*, "house." Proverb Collection Five, the 125 proverbs of which include a large number of "Aesopic" animal fables, is entirely arranged into groups by the initial words: *am-si*, "elephant"; *am*, "the wild-ox"; *gud*, "ox"; *áb*, "cow"; *amar*, "calf"; *anše-kur*, "horse"; *anše*, "ass"; *anše-ŠÚ.AN*, "mule"; *ur-maḫ*, "lion"; *ur-bar-ra*, "wolf"; *ur-deb(?)*, "the cheetah(?)"; *ur* and *ur-ger₍ₓ₎*, "dog"; and finally *nig*, "the bitch." Still another unpublished collection contains proverbs with the initial words *uzu*, "flesh," and *lú-inim*, "witness"; to this collection may also belong several pieces with proverbs opening with the words *lú*, "man," and *lugal*, "king." Another collection, tentatively named Collection Six by Gordon, includes groups of proverbs beginning with the initial signs *é*, "house," and *é-gal*, "palace," *mušen*, "bird" (published pieces belonging to this collection are *SLTN* 145 and 147, Chiera, *Sumerian Lexical Texts* (Chicago, 1934) 189, and *Mémoires de la Mission archéologique de Perse* XXVII, 206). For Proverb Collections One and Two, see, for the present, Gordon's doctoral dissertation *Sumerian Proverbs and Their Cultural Significance* (Univ. of Pennsylvania, 1955; University Microfilms, Ann Arbor); a fuller edition of both these collections, with revisions and additional material, together with contributions by the writer and Thorkild Jacobsen, will appear in the near future as a University Museum Monograph entitled *Sumerian Proverbs: Glimpses of Everyday Life in Ancient Mesopotamia*. For Proverb Collection Five, see Gordon's "Sumerian Animal Proverbs and Fables: Collection Five" in *JCS* XII (1958).

99. Proverb Collection Three, with nearly 200 proverbs, in process of being prepared for publication by Gordon, is the best preserved of all the Sumerian proverb collections (thanks to two large six-column tablets in nearly perfect condition excavated at Nippur in 1951 by the Joint University Museum—Oriental Institute Expedition; published fragments belonging to this collection include *SLTN* 153 and *PBS* I/2, no. 136). Collection Four (a single unduplicated tablet containing the texts of approximately forty-two proverbs and fables) has just recently been published by Gordon (*JAOS* 77 [1957], pp. 67–79). Another collection, Collection Seven (the large broken six-column tablet published as *STVC* 3 + 4) contains, according to Gordon, scattered proverbs excerpted from Collections One, Two, Three, and Six, and seems to be the forerunner of a later bilingual proverb collection represented by several pieces in the Library of Ashurbanipal at Nineveh. Another of the collections, as yet only partly reconstructed by Gordon, is represented by the following published pieces: *PBS* I/2, no. 117, *SLTN* 128 and 149, and *Mémoires de la Mission . . . Perse* XXVII, 216. Still another collection is inscribed on a twelve-column tablet joined together by Gordon from four fragments, two of which were published as *PBS* XII, 29 and *PBS* XIII, 50. Another partial collection is represented by several pieces, of which the only published piece is *PBS* XIII, 38. Finally, two or three other collections are represented only by unpublished pieces, while a number of smaller published fragments have as yet to be "placed" into their proper proverb collections.

CHAPTER TEN

Formative Tendencies in
Sumerian Religion

THORKILD JACOBSEN

1. RELIGION AS RESPONSE

BASIC TO ALL RELIGION, formal or otherwise, is a unique experience which, with a term coined by Rudolph Otto, is usually called the "numinous" experience. Otto has analyzed it as the experience of a *Mysterium Tremendum et Fascinans,* a confrontation with the "Wholly Other," outside normal experience and indescribable in terms of normal experience; terrifying, ranging from sheer demonic dread through awe to sublime majesty; and fascinating, with irresistible attraction demanding unconditional allegiance. It is the human response to this experience in thought (mythology and theology) and action (cult) which constitutes religion, and it is with the manifold forms which the response takes that the study of religion properly concerns itself. The aim of such study must be, beyond all, to understand and to interpret the varied religious forms as response, as ultimately meaningful in relation to the underlying numinous experience only.[1]

To the student of Sumerian religion such understanding is not readily come by. Remoteness in time and great differences of culture separate him, and the forms of religious response meaningful to him, from those of the ancients; imperfect knowledge of the language closes his ear to overtones; different habits of thought and differences in values tend to leave him uncomprehending or mistaken. He must wonder at every step whether his interpretation is leaving the ancient forms dry, empty of content, or whether he is unconsciously filling them with his own new wine only to shatter them. But no way is open to him in his dilemma other than to persevere in attempts to understand with continued attention to inner consistency in his results.

The following pages are part of such a preliminary attempt. They seek to point up the two major psychological tendencies which seem to us to structure the Sumerian response: namely, (1) an early spontaneous reliance upon features and values of the situations in which man experienced the numinous for guidance to its nature and approachability, and (2) a later similarly spontaneous reliance upon social forms and attitudes taken from the developing human society as vehicles for further understanding and approach.

Inasmuch as we are dealing in these pages with viewpoints for materials generally familiar and readily adduced by the reader, documentation has been held at a minimum.[2]

2. ATTRIBUTION OF FORM

It is characteristic for Sumerian religion, especially in its older phases, that the human reaction to the experience of the numinous remained singularly bound by the situation in which the numinous was encountered, and by some central phenomenon or group of phenomena in it particularly. The numinous appears to be immediately and unreflectingly apprehended as a power in, underlying, and willing the phenomenon, as a power within it for it to come into being, to unfold in this its particular and distinctive form. In consequence the phenomenon largely circumscribes the power, for the numinous will and direction appear as fulfilled in the phenomenon and do not significantly transgress it.

This boundness to a phenomenon one might describe with a grammatical metaphor as intransitivity; it is found typically in such figures of the Mesopotamian pantheon as Nissaba, the goddess of the reeds; Sumukan, god of the wildlife in the desert; Nintu, goddess of birth; Ninkasi, goddess of beer; and many others. These deities are little more than active principles underlying certain specific forms, numinous powers for certain things to be, reeds, animals, births, beer; they act not, they suffer not, they appear, are, and vanish only.

It may be confidently assumed that such intransitivity is a general and an old feature, for an unmistakable intransitive core is traceable in all figures of the Sumerian pantheon. In figures where transcendence is met with, involving concerns beyond the being of some phenomenon, active intervention in human affairs—these aspects of the god are always connected with, and expressed under, inherently late anthropomorphic forms borrowed from human society and its human dignitaries.

The boundness of the numinous will as a will to a phenomenon makes it natural to attribute to it as its external form the form for which it strives, in which it fulfills its aspirations. We find that the earliest expressions of the nature of the gods, their names, and their earliest external forms are like those of the phenomena in which they were seen to reveal themselves. Utu is the numinous power that comes into being as the sun, the sun-god, and the visible form which that power takes is the flaming sun disk; the language allows no distinction between the two. Nanna is the power in the moon and the moon itself, the form that power wills and takes. An is heaven and the god of heaven. Ezinu is the power in the grain and the grain itself in all its forms. The single seed corn dropped by the farmer in the furrow is Ezinu dropped. The green stalks coming up are also Ezinu "standing in the furrow like an attractive young girl."

These early forms of the gods, the forms of the phenomena in which they reveal themselves, survive to the latest times as divine emblems: the sun disk of Utu, the moon sickle of Nanna/Enzu, the gate symbol of the goddess of the storehouse, Inannak, the lion-headed bird of the god of the thunderstorm, Ningirsuk/Ninurta, and many others. That the emblems are but variant forms of the gods to whom they belong may be seen clearly from the fact that when these gods follow the armies into battle, or when they are present at oath ceremonies, they go in their emblem form.

The anthropomorphic forms of the gods, which eventually came to rule supreme, were imposed relatively late and supplanted the older forms slowly and only with difficulty. To the latest time, the divine will to other, non-human form is alive under the human exterior and threatens it: rays pierce through the human body of the sun-god; ears of corn grow out through the human shoulders of the grain goddess; serpent heads look at the beholder each side of Ningishzida's human head in reminder of the true nature of the power within.

At times the long struggle to bring the gods closer to man and to human understanding under the human form resulted in open hostility toward the older forbidding shape. An example may be seen in the case of the god of the thundercloud, whose early shape, after becoming his emblem, ended up as his enemy. The numinous power in the thundershowers, which in the early spring clothe the bare desert with green and transform it into pastureland overnight, was named from the phenomenon Imdugud, "shower." It took external form from the floating cloud as an enormous bird with outstretched wings; its head, to account for the lionlike roar of the thunder, that of a lion. In this form Lugalbanda met the god in the Lugalbanda epic. The earliest evidence of tendencies to humanize the bird shape dates from the Second Early Dynastic period. On seal cylinders of this period the bird shape is shown with the legs and lower parts of a human body draped in a kilt. Completely humanized, the god appears in the cult statue from Tell Asmar, where the bird shape occurs only as an emblem carved on the base of the statue. The advent of the human form seems to have been accompanied by a tendency to designate the god under his new form by some epithet other than the old name Imdugud, so closely associated was the latter with the earlier shape. In Girsu the god was known as Ningirsuk "the lord of Girsu"; in Nippur as Ninurta, and in Eshnunnak as Aba-ú, "Old Man Pasture." The victory for the human shape was not easily won. In Girsu, as late as Enannatum I, a macehead dedicated to Ningirsuk still shows the ruler adoring him under his bird shape; and later still, when Gudea sees the god in a dream in partially human shape, he still retains the outspread wings of the Imdugud shape. After the time of Gudea, as the human form comes to reign more and more supreme, a growing hostility toward the older form begins to show itself. In the Nippur versions of *Lugal-e,* Imdugud is included in the list of Ninurta's conquered enemies. In Akkadian mythology, as the evil Zû-bird, it becomes his archfoe. On Assyrian reliefs, finally, Ninurta, still with the wings of his original bird shape, is shown fighting and routing the thunderstorm, his own former self, the lion bird.[3] The hostility toward the older non-human form which here changed it into an enemy is, it may be added, probably part of a general and growing tendency, as anthropomorphism became more and more established. A very similar instance is found in Mummu and Apsû, both old forms of the god Enkik/Ea, who in Enuma-elish, the creation epic, are depicted as enemies of the god, captured and slain by him.

3. SITUATIONAL VALUES: GOOD AND EVIL

As the immediate apprehension of numinous power as power and will to a given phenomenon became determining for the inner and outer form under which the power was envisaged, so under this immediate apprehension were human values inherent in the phenomenon unhesitatingly accepted as incentives or deterrents to the ever present human urge to seek security and salvation by establishing ties of allegiance to the numinous power.

A clear case is that of the "evil god" (*dingir hul*). The term *dingir* "god" was used generally by the Sumerians to designate any numinous power known to them, but specifically it applied to the protective genius of an individual and his family, a "personal god." The situation of numinous experience which underlies this latter concept is reasonably clear from the use of the term "to acquire a god" (*dingir tuku*), used to denote unbelievable and conspicuous good fortune. The "uncanny" feeling of some outside supernatural agency at work which may accompany extraordinary luck or success is well known. In Sumerian religion the power whose presence was felt in such experiences was given form from the situation and was envisaged as a benevolent father or mother figure concerned with the individual in question and bent on furthering his fortunes. Inviting spontaneous allegiance as "good," the personal god was made the object of a permanent cult in the house of his or her protégée.

But a very similar numinous experience may accompany instances of spectacular misfortune, which may equally be felt as uncanny. The numinous power recognized in such cases was also a "god" (*dingir*), but the very different situation in which this power was encountered determined it as evil, bent on destruction, and the human response was one of avoidance and defense through incantations and other magical means. No allegiance was invited or offered, no cult developed. The "evil god" took its place among the innumerable other destructive numinous powers, demons, and evil spirits who are inimical to man and for whom it is characteristic and very particularly terrifying that they are altogether inhuman, have nothing in common with us, are purely a dread unreachable wholly other:

> *Neither males are they, nor females,*
> *They are winds ever sweeping along,*
> *They have not wives, engender not children,*
> *Know not how to show mercy,*
> *Hear not prayer and supplication.*

As indicated by their various names, these demons are forms given to the numinous power experienced in sudden illness and pain, or other situations of uniformly terrifying nature. They are the supernatural wills and power which come into being in evil things.

4. SITUATIONAL VALUES: OUR DAILY BREAD

The tendency for the human response to take color as negative or positive from the human values inherent in the situation in which the numinous power was encountered could not but act to single out for special attention certain situations and certain powers which were recognized as good and approachable. Human allegiance and the establishment of regular cult naturally centered on those numinous powers which from the situations in which they revealed themselves were recognizable as approachable and friendly toward man. To some such process of natural selection we may ascribe the marked uniformity with which the major deities of the older Mesopotamian pantheon prove, on closer inspection, to be powers in phenomena or activities of primary economic importance to their worshipers. On the more primitive economic levels, with their terrible uncertainties and ever present threat of famine and slow, horrible death from hunger, the all-important security sought by man is economic security: "Give us today our daily bread." The powers confronting him in the sources of his food supply, in numinous experience on the hunt, with his cattle, in his fields, commanded an allegiance born of values in the situation, forced by the anguish of his deepest anxieties, and irresistibly invited by the element of fascination in the numinous.

That the major deities of the Sumerian pantheon are powers in phenomena and activities of primary economic importance also means, of course, that they differ in character from region to region, as natural conditions give prominence now to one, now to another type of economy. From the marshlands of the hunter and fisherman in the south, over the grasslands in the center, to the farms in the north and east, each had its own pantheon determined by its particular economy.

Beginning with the south and the chief deities of the ancient cities of the marshlands we find ourselves in the world of the hunter and fisherman.

In Eridug resides Enkik, the "Ibex of the Deep" (*Dara-abzuk*), the numinous inner will to form in the Deep, visualized as a gigantic hart or ibex, the antlers of which showed above the water as reeds. As a will to the ibex form this power, the "ibex-fashioner" (*Dara-dím*), provided the hunter with his game, as a will to reeds the "Lord Reedbundle" (*En-uru*) it provided him his reed hut for protection. As numinous will in the Deep to the form of the reed bundle and imbued with the cleansing power of water, Enkik is also the power behind all purification magic.

If Enkik may be seen as the power behind the game of the marshes, his daughter Nanshe in Nina is the numinous will that produces the teeming schools of fish moving under the surface and gives the fisherman his livelihood. Fish are everywhere around her; a scepter fish is the scepter in her hand; sandal fish are the sandals on her feet. South of Nina, in Kinirsha, finally, is the home of Dumuzid-abzuk, the "quickener of the child (in mother's womb)" of the Deep. Under the form of a goddess we meet here the mysterious numinous power that brings new life into being, lets life multiply and thrive in the marshlands.

Through the marshlands along the Euphrates from Ki-abrig over Ur up to Uruk runs the country of the ox herdsman, and here the numinous powers behind the bovine form are supreme. In Ki-abrig resides the bull god Nin-EZEN + LA and his consort Nin-é-ì-garak, "The Lady of the Creamery." In Ur we find Nanna, the moon-god, envisaged by the herdsman as a frisky young bull with gleaming horns grazing in the heavenly pastures. In Uruk lastly are Nin-sún, "Lady Wild Cow," and her bull-god husband, Lugal-banda.

In Uruk the cow country borders upon the sheep country, the broad grassy steppe in the center of southern Babylonia which the ancients called the *edin*. Here cult cities of the gods of the shepherds, Dumu-zid, the "quickener of the young one (in mother's womb)" and his young wife Inannak, personification of the storehouse in which the produce of the flocks was kept, ring the *edin* around: Uruk, Bad-tibira, Umma, Zabalam. From these cities, when lambing time is over and Dumuzid, the numinous power which miraculously gave life to the lambs and filled their mothers' udders with milk, has ceased to be, there issued each year the sorrowful processions to lament in the desert the dead god, killed by invaders from the mountains, the land of death, as happened so often to the human young shepherds in the *edin*. Two other important cult centers on the borders of the *edin* should also be mentioned. In the north lies IM^{ki}, the city of Ishkur, god of thunder and rain who yearly makes the desert green with grass for the flocks to feed on. In the south lies Larsa, the city of the sun-god Utu and his son Sumukan, god of goats and of all four-legged wild creatures of the plain, providing herdsman and hunter alike with their means of existence.

North and east of the *edin*, finally, lie the plowlands with cities dedicated to the cereal and chtonic deities which dominate the pantheon of the tiller of the soil. In Shuruppak we find Sud, goddess of the ear of corn, daughter of Ninshebargunu, the "mottled barley," and bride of Enlil, the numinous power in the wind which pollenizes the grain. Further north is Nippur with Enlil and his wife Ninlil, who is identical with the grain goddess Sud. Here also is Enlil's divine store, Dukug, "the pure mound" in which grain, wool, and milk were kept in the morning of time before men were given a share in them. Nippur is also the home of Enlil's son Ninurta, god of the thunder-showers and god of the plow. Under the name of Pabilsag he is worshiped as husband of the city goddess of nearby Isin, and as Ningirsuk he is the chief god of Girsu in the fertile regions southeast of the *edin*. Further north, in Kutha, resides Nergal, the death- and life-giving will in the soil, a power to receive and hold the dead, the dark will of the grave, but also a power to life and growth from which the roots of grain, plants, and trees draw strength, a will to fertility and plenty. In Babylon we find Marduk, also an agricultural deity, originally the powers in the spade (*mar*), the chief tool of the irrigator and orchardman. In the northeast, finally, resides Ninazu, like Nergal a chtonic god combining death- and life-giving powers. His city, Eshnunnak, is the capital of the fertile lands of the Diyala region.

5. ACTS OF ALLEGIANCE

With numinous power apprehended directly as will in specific phe-nomena, and with attention tending to focus on those powers which informed and willed phenomena of crucial economical importance, it is but natural that the early response in action to the numinous experience should direct itself to assisting these favorable powers in their will to be and to assuring their presence in the community. Two means were available to these ends, the cult drama and the temple. In the cult drama[4] man takes on the identity of a numinous power and, thus identified, activates it by letting its will to be in its appropriate form realize itself externally in the cult act. The cult act makes it present, and once present it will manifest itself everywhere. The most important of the Sumerian cult dramas were: (1) the *hieros gamos* in which the king took the identity of the god Dumu-zid, the "quickener of the little ones (in mother's womb)" and through a ritual act of coitus ensured magically that the power of fertility, which was the god, became present to pervade all nature and ensure plenty in the new year; (2) the battle drama at new year in Babylon, where the king in symbolic action fought and won as embodiment of Marduk the battle against chaos which established the ordered cosmos for the new year as it had done primevally; and (3) lastly— slightly differently oriented—the dramatic lament for the dead god Dumuzi which, in its vivid expression of grief and longing, served to strengthen the community's ties with the lost power of engendering new life and to give it such succor against oblivion and total extinction as mention of its name and maintaining it in living memory could provide.

As man in the cult drama endeavored to bring into being and give reality to the numinous powers of his allegiance, so he sought by creation of the visual tangible form of the power, the divine image, and by providing the power with a dwelling among the houses of the community, a temple, to keep the power present and with him always. The purpose of the temple as a dwelling for the god is clear from the fact that Sumerian had no special word for temple. The structure was but a house (é) among other houses, differing only by having a god rather than a human magnate as owner. Further confirmation is offered by its plan, which, as one follows it back in time, proves to be the simple plan of a dwelling house.

6. ANTHROPOMORPHISM: NEW SOCIO-POLITICAL PATTERNS

The strong urge to tender allegiance and therein to achieve security and salvation, which characterizes the human response to the numinous experience, contains in it a temptation to remodel the image of the numinous ever closer to the heart's desire, to see it more and more under human forms, to soften estrangement in its stark otherness by seeing it under familiar images taken from human society and human interrelations, so as to broaden the basis for community and contact.

In ancient Mesopotamia this tendency early led to the development of a finely spun, closely interwoven, and complete pattern. This guided the human response to the numinous into channels parallel to those developed for relations of dependence in human society. Thus in a progressively more differentiated, stratified, and complex society, the image of the numinous powers, individually and as a functioning group, was subtly molded into the likeness of an earthly landed aristocracy. In blunt fact the gods came to be part of society, the ruling caste exercising all basic economic and political functions of the country.

Central in this new view stands the temple, the god's mighty house, the center of a great estate with extensive holdings of land. At its head, as owner and administrator, is the great god himself, and with him his divine consort and children, who may themselves own similar estates. The house is run by the god's wife, who directs a staff of divine servants. These in turn guide and lend their divine efficacy to a corps of human servants, the priests. There are chamberlains, who make the divine bed, see to the bathing and anointing of the god, keep his rooms clean and swept. There are cooks who prepare his daily meals, carvers and cupbearers, who serve at table, singers and musicians, who entertain the god and his guests, and also singers of elegies who soothe his darker moods. In the administration of his estates and in looking after his far-flung interests, the god has the aid of a divine vizier, a sukkal, who announces visitors and states their business, and who also goes on errands for his lord. Divine and human stablemen care for the god's donkey teams and keep his war chariot in good order. Overseers of fields, canals, forests, and fisheries look after the running of the estate according to the god's orders, all assisted by human personnel guided in ordinary matters by their knowledge of the job, in all exceptional matters by direct orders from the god given in omens and extispicy. As a great and influential personage, the god participates in the political councils of his peers, the divine assemblies, in which all major decisions affecting the country are taken, laws passed, and political offices assigned. Here the god may have been chosen "king" (*lugal*) to lead the country in war through his human representative, or "lord" (*en*) to guide as administrator the internal affairs of the country. He may also hold traditional office by virtue of his special talents and abilities. Thus, for example, Utu, the sun-god, is judge; Enkik, god of the subsoil waters, through his organizing abilities, rises to a position comparable to that of a secretary of the interior, planning and directing the whole of the economic life of the country. In these offices (*me*) of the god, held traditionally or by appointment, we find in slightly reinterpreted form most of the old relation between numinous power and features of the situation in which that power was experienced. But the earlier immediate apprehension of the numinous as direction and will in and to the phenomenon in which it was seen revealed is now yielding to a more reflected mode: the numinous has receded from the visible phenomenon, is no longer one with it as mind with body but appears as a power in charge of it, administering, owning it. Thus countless individual phenomena and processes of nature and human life, both once alive with numinous will and power, have become works, the outcome of conscious, organized, dutifully carried out tasks of numerous divine functionaries, tasks which in their planned interrelated totality structure world order and maintain the universe as a cosmos.

7. RELATION TO EARLIER VIEWS

The form of a divine aristocracy on earth, dividing the cosmic tasks between its members, living the life of human landed gentry on big estates, can obviously have been neither as cleanly set off from earlier very different forms, nor as barren and empty of real religious content as it must appear on brief modern restatement. It is easy to sense that the old immediate apprehension of the numinous as awesome inner will in a phenomenon of the universe still lives under the anthropomorphic image of the human lords and rulers. What at first seems metaphor will on occasion spring to sudden life as the true reality, a terrifying non-human form taking the place of the familiar human image. In Gudea's dream the man who reaches from heaven to earth does not have arms, but instead the outstretched black wings of the thundercloud, while his body below becomes a raging flood wave. And even where the older form does not break the human image, that form still pulses under it as a deeper truth, endowing the metaphors and similes applied with almost uncanny life and making it capable of carrying rather more numinous content than we are at first likely to allow to it. Gudea's humanizing terms "master" and "lord" convey in his prayer to Ningirsuk his profound awe before a mysterium tremendum, the wholly other terrifying power in the flood wave sweeping down from the mountains:

O my master Ningirsuk, lord, fiercely eroding (flood-) water,
good lord, (seminal) water emitted by the great mountain (Enlil),
hero without challenger,
Ningirsuk, I am to build you your house,
but I have nothing to go by.
Warrior, you have called for the things that are proper,
But, son of Enlil, lord Ningirsuk,
I cannot know what that means.
Your heart, rising as (rise the waves in) mid-ocean,
Crashing down as (does the falling) ushu tree,
Roaring like the waters pouring out (through a breach in a dike),
Destroying cities like the flood wave,
Rushing at the enemy country like a storm,
O my master, your heart, an outpouring (from a breached dike) not to be
* stemmed,*
Warrior, your heart, remote (and unapproachable) like the far-off heavens,
How can I know it?

8. THE TEMPLE AS CENTRAL SYMBOL

Particularly powerful and concrete in the new anthropomorphic view was the symbol of the temple, the god's house. Towering over the flat roofs of the surrounding town, it gave the townsmen visible assurance that the god was present among them. The vast expanses of temple fields and orchards were unspoken testimony that his ties were the strong ties of a landowner to his land, and the numerous ways in which man served him as house servant and worker in the fields gave man status: needed by the god, belonging to him as a servant belongs to his master, bound to absolute obedience in unquestioning loyalty, unprotected against arbitrary moods and unjust punishment, but always belonging, never under any circumstances to be abandoned.

In this strong human tie between master and servant, transferred to man's relation with the numinous powers which ruled the universe, lay Mesopotamian religion's warrant of human salvation, its answer to the human need for security. It was a limited security that it offered. Sonship man had only to his personal god, who was usually a minor power able at most to intercede for him with other greater gods, not to save him on its own. It was, furthermore, security in life only. Outside the kingdom of the gods was a foreign power in the eastern mountains. Death's kingdom raided the land of the living and carried its people away to eternal servitude in regions where the gods of the living were powerless.

And even in life, security was not so absolute as might have been thought. The power of even the strongest gods could not prevail against the combined will of the divine assembly; and the assembly, swayed by inscrutable motives, might order death and destruction of its own. At such times the gods flee their city, flutter like terrified doves before the terrible enemy who enters their sanctuaries contemptuously with shod feet. The city is sacked and plundered, its people killed or carried off into captivity. In the ruins around the destroyed temple the survivors face the utter collapse of their world, the terrible reality of being abandoned by their gods. Only one means is still at hand—the lament.

The lament is rightly central to Sumerian ritual and to Sumerian religious poetry, for it alone plumbs the depths of utmost despair without giving in to it. In magical emphasis the emotional ties to god and temple are strengthened, the god and goddess are implored, are called back into existence, the turbulent dark despairing mind of the god is soothed by music of harps and drums that it may once more regain strength to act, strength to rebuild what is lost:

My Lady, your city cries for you as for its mother,
Ur seeks you as were it a child lost in the streets.
Your house reaches forth its hand for you, as does one who has lost something,
Your bricks in the good house, as were they mortals, say: Where is she?

9. CONCLUSIONS

We have sought in the preceding pages to point up two successive attitudes to the numinous in Sumerian religion. An older attitude which attempted to understand the numinous power directly from the situation in which it revealed itself as a power willing that situation or some specific phenomenon central to it. The numinous power was seen as intransitive, its relation to man lay essentially in a community of interest when the numinous will and man both desired the phenomenon informed by the power to manifest itself. The younger attitude, gaining ground slowly but eventually emerging victorious, was born of a growing conviction that the numinous power was primarily to be understood in human terms, even in terms of known social and political power. The numinous was given form as master and ruler; man became a concern to it in so far as he was a needed and useful servant. Therein man found a limited security.

After Sumerian times, a span of the development not of direct concern here, the application of the human social and political forms of the ruler to the numinous drew into the form of the divine a growing emphasis on the ruler's duty to dispense justice. Also the old political forms of a primitive democracy applied to the gods tended to lose meaning and to yield subtly to monocratic attitudes, which mostly took henotheistic forms.

To the end, however, the polarity of human and non-human essence in the numinous continued to give Mesopotamian religious expression its peculiar vibrant tension, and both modes of viewing the numinous contributed to it valid and profound insights.

Chicago; January, 1958

NOTES TO CHAPTER TEN

1. On religion and the study of religion generally, see Rudolph Otto, *The Idea of the Holy* (London, 1943); G. van der Leeuw, *Religion in Essence and Manifestation* (New York, 1938); Ernst Cassirer, *Philosophie der symbolischen Formen* II: *Das mythische Denken* (Berlin, 1925).
2. For general orientation, see, e.g., E. Dhorme, *Les Religions de Babylonie et d'Assyrie* (Paris, 1945).
3. Cf. *JNES* XII (1953), p. 167, note 27.
4. The credit for first recognizing the true nature of the Mesopotamian cult drama belongs to Sv. Aa. Pallis, *The Babylonian Akîtu Festival* (Copenhagen, 1926). On the nature of the identity involved, see the work of Cassirer cited above in note 1.

CHAPTER ELEVEN

*Egypt: Its Language
and Literature*

THOMAS O. LAMBDIN

BECAUSE OUR PRESENT TASK is to survey in some detail the most significant contributions made during the past thirty or forty years to the vast field of Egyptology, we must perforce pass over completely the formative period of the science, the brilliant achievements of decipherment, and the untiring diligence of the scholars who during the last century devoted their talents exclusively to the recovery of a forgotten language and a nearly forgotten civilization. From the virtually endless array of specialized studies which characterize this sphere of scholarly research, we have chosen to discuss in order the following three: (1) the science of grammar and lexicography, (2) the history of the Egyptian language, and (3) selected topics on the study of Egyptian literature. Needless to say, restrictions in space have forced us to omit even the mention of innumerable important works, but we hope that the interested reader will find here a guide sufficient to allow him to pursue more thoroughly the fascinating and rewarding results of scholarship in this area of study.

I

The Pyramid Texts, which are of incalculable value for the understanding of Egyptian religion, prehistory, and general cultural activity, form the largest single body of texts surviving from the Old Kingdom (Dynasties III–VIII), and it is from them that the grammar of Old Egyptian as a distinct phase is constructed.[1] To the publication and elucidation of these difficult and obscure guides for the deceased in the afterworld, the German Egyptologist Kurt Sethe devoted the major portion of his highly productive life. The results of this research, published in four large volumes after his death,[2] contain the nucleus of a grammar of Old Egyptian, but because this work is incomplete and is essentially a commentary on individual texts, a comprehensive treatment of the language alone remained a desideratum until the appearance of Elmar Edel's *Altägyptische Grammatik* (Rome, 1955). With the publication of this work, a second volume of which is promised, Edel has reaffirmed his position as an Egyptologist of the first rank. In addition to exhaustive treatment of the grammatical material itself, the compiler has distinguished his work as the first major Egyptian grammar to give careful consideration to the problems of vocalization and word structure, thus superseding Sethe's *Verbum* in this respect.[3] The remaining material from the Old Kingdom covered by this grammar includes an array of miscellaneous funerary inscriptions and biographies, the texts of most of which were published by Sethe in 1932–33,[4] a group of remarks and songs which accompany scenes from everyday life found in the tombs of the late Fifth Dynasty,[5] and the extraordinary letters to the dead, several of which are assignable to the Old Kingdom.[6] The few texts surviving from the First and Second Dynasties are too obscure orthographically and too unrewarding linguistically to warrant inclusion in a study of Old Egyptian grammar.

Middle Egyptian, properly the written language of the Middle Kingdom (Dynasties IX–XIII), is generally regarded as the classical form of Egyptian because of its comparatively consistent orthography and the plene (full) writing of its verbal forms. The grammar, which in the case of a language whose vowels are not represented in the script reduces primarily to a study of syntax, has been most completely set forth by Sir Alan Gardiner in his *Egyptian Grammar* (2nd ed., London, 1950), the first edition of which appeared in 1927. There is no exaggeration in stating that Egyptian grammar was canonized by this superb work and that all present and future students of the language can only benefit from Gardiner's concern as a teacher in designing a text which is unequaled in the entire Near Eastern field as a felicitous combination of an exhaustive reference grammar and a graduated lesson book to guide the student from his first hieroglyphs onward. Other noteworthy treatments of Middle Egyptian are those of Adolf Erman (German),[7] Gustave Lefebvre (French),[8] and Adriaan De Buck (Dutch and French);[9] all of these are reference works only, that of Lefebvre being the most detailed. De Buck's treatment is the briefest and may appeal to beginning students for that reason; it is also accompanied by a useful reader, *An Egyptian Readingbook I* (Leiden, 1948), which is currently the best available chrestomathy for Middle Egyptian. A second volume containing commentary and vocabulary has been promised but has not yet appeared.

A comparison of the first and second editions of Gardiner's *Grammar* provides a convenient measure of the major contributions and alterations made in the intervening time. Truly important adjustments have been few and, as to be expected, are concerned mainly with certain verbal forms, specifically those designated as the prospective relative and the geminating *sḏm.f.*[10] The prospective relative and the prospective participle on which it is presumably based were isolated and so classified by Battiscombe Gunn in 1924.[11] Gardiner subsequently accepted the forms as correctly analyzed and included them in the first edition of his grammar. In the second edition, however, he has abandoned the name and has reclassified the forms as the perfective relative. In support of this change he adduces further examples to show that in early Middle Egyptian the form is used with past as well as prospective meaning, whereby an aspectual (i.e., perfective) designation is preferable to a temporal one. Lefebvre[12] prefers to follow Gunn in this respect, but Edel[13] finds no clear evidence for such a category of forms in Old Egyptian and consequently rejects their independent existence. He also cites several passages in which the form in question is replaced in parallel texts by the *sḏmwnf* relative; this correspondence weighs heavily in Gardiner's favor. The problem centering about the geminating *sḏm.f* is more difficult: on the basis of his studies in Coptic syntax,[14] to which we shall return below, H. J. Polotsky seeks to set up a distinctive category "relativ abstrait" in which the geminating *sḏm.f* and its immediate adjuncts are taken as a clausal unit which functions as an element of a non-verbal sentence. The details of this argument are too lengthy for discussion here, and even the serious student of Egyptian will have difficulty in deciding whether or not a difference in terminology and point of view is not creating *ex nihilo* a formal distinction not warranted by the morphology of the language itself. Polotsky's suggestion[15] is nevertheless of great interest and merits careful attention because the significance of this form as opposed to that of the regular *sḏm.f* is otherwise rather uncertain. Edel[16] admits that the theory clarifies many passages, previously difficult, but claims that it does not apply to all instances of the form.

From the Eighteenth Dynasty onward it becomes virtually impossible to speak of a single language in our surviving texts. The many official inscriptions from the first half of this dynasty are written in a language which must be classified as Middle Egyptian, whereas the bulk of letters, business documents, and literary works, dating from the time of Akhenaten onward, exhibit what is properly termed New Egyptian. The most compendious grammar of these texts is Adolf Erman's *Neuägyptische Grammatik* (2nd ed., 1933), equal in scope to the above-mentioned grammar of Gardiner, but designed as a reference work only. An invaluable supplementary study, the *Untersuchungen zu Stil und Sprache neuägyptischer Erzählungen* (Berlin, 1950–52) by Fritz Hintze, provides an exhaustive analysis of nearly all the syntactic and stylistic features of the major literary texts. In addition to clarifying many difficult problems on the logical connection implied by the use of the various forms and sentence types, Hintze has also provided a careful tabulation of the forms as used in the individual texts, a procedure from which some concrete notions of the chronological as well as the stylistic development of the language can be safely derived. Certainly such intensive studies of small groups of texts, or even of single texts, are an essential prerequisite for a permanently authoritative grammar of a linguistic situation as complex as that now subsumed under the name of New Egyptian.

Demotic is properly the name of a style of writing evolved from hieratic and used in a wide variety of texts from about 700 B.C. to 450 A.D., but the term serves to designate the language of those texts as well. The great studies[17] of Demotic belong to our present century, beginning with the masterful *Catalog of the Demotic Papyri in the Johns Rylands Library I–III* (London, 1909) of F. Ll. Griffith. These texts and commentaries along with K. Sethe's *Demotische Urkunden zum ägyptischen Bürgerschaftsrechte* (Leipzig, 1920) and the innumerable collections of texts published by the indefatigable Wilhelm Spiegelberg served until recently as the standard introduction for the Egyptologist who was courageous enough to venture into this complex and trying field. The only systematic treatment of the grammar was W. Spiegelberg's *Demotische Grammatik* (Heidelberg, 1925), which, though a dependable work, suffered from progressive incompleteness. The initial difficulties of the potential Demoticist have now been lessened, however, by several important publications, the most remarkable of which is the *Grammaire démotique* of František Lexa (Prague, 1947–51) in seven volumes totaling over twelve hundred pages. A more complete study is difficult to envisage and although some criticism of Lexa's handling of past scholarly opinion on the origin of certain forms and the classification of others is justified,[18] the work will undoubtedly retain a permanent value for many years to come as an exhaustive and carefully copied repertory of citations, grammatically categorized and handsomely indexed. Of even greater pedagogical value are the two chrestomathies prepared by W. Erichsen, *Demotische Lesestücke* (Leipzig, 1937) and *Auswahl frühdemotischer Texte* (Copenhagen, 1950), both of which contain helpful transliterations of the included texts in addition to an indispensable sign list and glossary. Equipped with these reliable aids for study, scholarship in this fascinating and hitherto too restricted field should make rapid and rewarding progress.

The written form of Egyptian known as Coptic owes its existence to the zeal of the early Church Fathers, centered in Alexandria, who recognized the necessity of translating the Bible into the local vernaculars of Egypt. The reduction of the spoken language to writing was in no wise haphazard but was done with careful regard for matters of orthography and grammar.[19] The alphabet employed was the Greek with the addition of several characters adapted from Demotic, which was still current at this period. The standardization of the grammar, at least so far as translated works are concerned, proceeded along lines set down by the Greek grammarians of the day, and the vocabulary itself was supplemented generously with Greek words from the very beginning. The language thus created, which at its inception must have been tolerably representative of the actual spoken language, became rapidly a standard literary vehicle and was consequently arrested in its development. Although Coptic continued as the official language of the Church in Egypt, it disappeared as a spoken language after the Moslem conquest, at which time it was replaced by Arabic. Vestiges of the language appear to have survived into the present century according to investigations made by Worrell and Vycichl, but the precise status of this continuous tradition is a difficult one to define.[20]

The extraordinary importance of Coptic both as a language of extremely valuable early Christian documents and as the only fully understood and vocalized form of Egyptian has promoted its study among Western scholars. The first extensive grammar was compiled by L. Stern during the last century, but the complete exploitation of Coptic for Egyptological studies was realized by Georg Steindorff, whose *Koptische Grammatik* (Berlin, 1894) was the first detailed treatment of the sounds and forms of Coptic in relationship with those of Egyptian of an earlier period. The undisputed worth of the language as well as its accessibility have resulted in a wealth of grammars. True to his school and his specialty, Steindorff's final endeavor, the *Lehrbuch der koptischen Grammatik* (Chicago, 1951), remains the best available synthesis of Egyptian and Coptic, but many of the details of vocalization proposed in that work are now antiquated and the book must be used with some caution.[21] The absence of a chrestomathy and glossary, which made his earlier work so valuable for the beginning student of Coptic, greatly lessens the utility of this otherwise resourceful study. Perhaps the best of the grammars of Sahidic presently available is that of Walter Till, *Koptische Grammatik* (*Saidischer Dialekt*) (Leipzig, 1955), which, though rather expensive, is destined to replace the above-mentioned works of Steindorff on the basis of both its excellent scholarship and its useful appendages, including bibliographies, a chrestomathy, and a glossary.[22] Among the more impressive studies on the various dialects we must mention the same writer's *Achmimisch-koptische Grammatik* (Leipzig, 1928) and the *Koptische Dialektgrammatik* (Munich, 1931); also valuable is M. Chaine, *Éléments de grammaire dialectale copte* (Paris, 1933).

The two dominant problems of Coptic grammar which have received noteworthy treatment in recent years are (1) the interrelationships of the various dialects and (2) the origin and use of the second tenses. The dialect problem was attacked by W. Worrell in his now standard work, *The Sounds of Coptic* (Ann Arbor, 1934). After establishing the phonetic content of Coptic by careful investigation of the historical phonology of Egyptian and a mass of other data, Worrell was able to define clearly for the first time the principles underlying the more intricate relationships between the various dialects and, as a consequence of certain geographically imposed restrictions, to present an eminently acceptable hypothesis on the original position of the different dialects in the Nile Valley. Worrell's work is marked by a rigorous logic and constant attention to phonetic potentialities in the interpretation of the available and often conflicting data. Thus the older and less precise notions on the dialect relationship were replaced by an exact and well-demonstrated pattern which has already gained general acceptance. In the realm of Coptic syntax, new light was shed on an intricate problem by H. J. Polotsky in his *Études de syntaxe copte* (Cairo, 1944). By comparing the various Coptic translated texts with their Greek originals, he was able to reach the fundamental principles which govern the use of the second tenses in Coptic and thus bring order to what had previously been a virtual hodgepodge of seemingly unrelated grammarbook rules. Only further research can determine the validity of Polotsky's extension of this particular classification to the older stages of the language; we have discussed one of these results above in our paragraphs on Middle Egyptian grammar.

In 1897 the immense task of compiling a dictionary of the Egyptian language was undertaken under the auspices of the German academies;[23] it is debatable whether the project has yet reached a satisfactory conclusion. While aware of the enormous labor involved, the editors of the work could not anticipate the obstacles which constantly confronted them in this arduous and seemingly infinite enterprise, not the least of which were two world wars and intermittent depressions. The collecting, transcribing, and interpreting of the texts as well as the preparation of the reference slips on which the dictionary was to be based were done by a large number of Egyptologists throughout the scholarly world, but the final writing of the individual articles, a Herculean task in view of the one and a half million slips thus acquired, rested with the editors in Berlin: Adolf Erman, Kurt Sethe, and Hermann Grapow. Circumstances finally decreed that Grapow alone be responsible for the editing and publication of this work, and in spite of any imperfections the Berlin dictionary may have, Egyptology will be forever indebted to him for accomplishing the virtually impossible: the five principle volumes of the *Wörterbuch der ägyptischen Sprache* appeared from 1926 to 1931, and the publication of the *Belegstellen* (references) was completed only in 1953.

The overwhelming importance of lexicography both as a summary of and a check on the progress being made toward an ideal understanding of Egyptian makes criticism more essential than praise in connection with a project like the above. Sir Alan Gardiner, who was closely associated with the Berlin dictionary in its early stages and with its editors, has offered the most valuable critique of its merits and defects.[24] The latter arise from two sources: (1) the method of compilation and (2) the method of publication. Concerning the former, Gardiner points out the practical impossibility of one or two scholars' digesting one and a half million slips satisfactorily; this difficulty lies thus with the planning of the project and does not at all reflect on the scholarly ability of the individual editors involved. Gardiner offers a suggestion which would place the final editing on a more reasonable level, namely that separate complete dictionaries be compiled by specialists in various phases of Egyptology and that after these lesser works have been used and corrected by other scholars they be compiled into a single work.[25] The separation of the references from the main body of the dictionary has proved also to be a source of chronic complaint; in addition to the inconvenience caused by such an arrangement, the long period of time separating the publication of the main entry and that of the references allows for a great deal of disparity between the two in some cases. One can only agree wholeheartedly with Gardiner when he insists that the references be published with the relevant entry. The references should include a carefully selected bibliography on the discussion of the word in periodicals and books; this type of reference to scholarly opinion and the basis for the meanings assigned is almost entirely absent from the *Wörterbuch*. Regardless of the need for the supplementing and correcting of future editions, the Berlin dictionary as it stands is of immeasurable value and a truly impressive monument to the industry and brilliance of those who participated in its making.

A similar project was envisioned in the less extensive field of Coptic lexicography. The British scholar, W. E. Crum, who had already begun independently to accumulate material for a Coptic dictionary, was offered funds necessary for the task by the Berlin Academy in 1914. World War I put an end to this subsidization, but Crum continued unsupported, with the assistance of many scholars, and was able to publish his *A Coptic Dictionary* in 1931 with the generous aid of the Clarendon Press. Few examples of devotion to scholarship exist to match the quality and completeness of this work, which, though concise to the point of being cryptic, provides a firm and authoritative basis for the future translation of Coptic texts. However, because Crum has omitted from his dictionary all but passing reference to etymology, W. Spiegelberg's *Koptisches Handwörterbuch* (Heidelberg, 1921) remains as the standard work on this aspect of Coptic and indeed retains a lexical value by virtue of its brevity and handiness.

The most recent addition to Egyptian lexicography is the *Demotisches Glossar* (Cophenhagen, 1954) by W. Erichsen. As the only dictionary for existing Demotic texts, the work, which its compiler describes as "ein kurzes und bequemes Nachschlagewerk," is extensive in its coverage and deals honestly with the many words of doubtful form and meaning. The numerous references throughout add much to the value of the work, which should indeed, as Erichsen wishes, win new friends for Demotic studies by relieving them of much tedious and unrewarded searching.

II

The descriptive treatises discussed in the preceding paragraphs are but one part of the study of the Egyptian language. Scholars must also concern themselves with investigating the more extensive problems raised by such questions as: (1) What unity, if any, underlies and connects the five separate phases of the language as represented by Old, Middle, and New Egyptian, Demotic, and Coptic? (2) Is this unity itself amenable to the traditional treatment of historical linguistics? And if so, what are the results of this study?

(3) Is Egyptian isolated from the languages which border it, or does it have recognizable affinities with other known language groups? None of these questions is easily answered, but considerable progress has been made within recent years toward unraveling the complex relationships involved in these categories of research. We shall treat briefly the questions in the order given above.

The first question, dealing with the underlying linguistic unity of Egyptian, has been studied thoroughly by B. H. Stricker, *De Indeeling der Egyptische Taalgeschiedenis* (Leiden, 1945), and we shall base our remarks on the results of that work. Both the evidence at hand and linguistic common sense force us to conclude that one language dominated the Nile Valley in Egypt from prehistoric times until the Moslem conquest so far as the popular language is concerned. Successive invasions by the Hyksos, the Assyrians, the Persians, the Greeks, and the Romans did of course leave their mark on the language, nor can we deny that the language was differentiated dialectally through all the historical period, but these are not of basic significance for the investigation of the language we shall term Spoken Egyptian to distinguish it from the various written forms which have survived. Once this unbroken spoken tradition is established, then our problem becomes one of determining the relationship of the written forms of the language with it at particular points in Egyptian history.

In 1925 Sethe contended that a significant difference existed between the language of the Pyramid Texts, which he designated as the "oldest language," and that of the other documents from the Old Kingdom.[26] Stricker re-examined the evidence carefully and finds no real justification for this position, but Edel[27] sides with Sethe and suggests similarly that the older material of the Pyramid Texts antedates linguistically other texts of a contemporary date. While this differentiation of Old Egyptian itself is thus in dispute, the nature of the relationship between Old and Middle Egyptian seems more clearly understood, although some disagreement exists. Both Sethe and Batiscombe Gunn[28] regarded Middle Egyptian as a return to the spoken language with the rise of the Middle Kingdom, but Stricker and Edel are of the opinion that the relationship between the two phases is simply a consecutive one. All scholars are agreed, however, that from the beginning of the Middle Kingdom the divergence between the spoken and written language became greater and greater; the subsequent adoption of Middle Egyptian as the classical written language is attested throughout the remainder of Egyptian history. A rather unique situation developed near the close of the Middle Kingdom when a modified form of the written language appeared; the best source for this poorly documented form of the language at this date is the Westcar Papyrus, so ably studied by A. Erman.[29] Stricker seconds Erman's contention that herein lies the genesis of New Egyptian, which emerged finally as a literary language under the rule of Akhenaten, though it is attested sporadically before that time. At some time between the New

Kingdom and the Graeco-Roman period, this second literary tradition, which underwent constant modification on the basis of the spoken language, became more or less standardized and is known in this altered form as Demotic. A detailed account of the relationships between Demotic and Coptic may be found in the above-mentioned article of Sethe; more recent details have been added by H. Grapow.[30] Because Coptic was at the beginning very close to the actual spoken language, these differences are marked, but are quite expected in the light of the foregoing theory. Simply stated, then, the relative status of the various phases of Egyptian must be considered in reference to (1) the spoken language, (2) the written language as represented by Old Egyptian and classical Middle Egyptian, (3) the written language of the Vulgar Middle Egyptian—Literary New Egyptian—Demotic tradition, and (4) the Coptic tradition. Nor must account be lost of the fact that the latter three were at one time or another in relatively close contact with the first.

The historical phonology of Egyptian as presented in the exemplary study of J. Vergote, *Phonétique historique de l'Égyptien, Les consonnes* (Louvain, 1945), is now fairly well understood in regard to the consonants.[31] One of the best-trained linguists working in the field of Egyptology, Vergote has been able to reconstruct the major sound shifts which have characterized the development of the Egyptian language and, by judicious use of external sources, to fix within reasonable limits their actual phonetic content at the different stages of the language. Recovery of the vocalization, however, is another problem, and because of the particular interest this study holds we shall recount briefly the progress which has been made.

Because the normal Egyptian orthography of all but the later two phases of the language provides no clue whatever to the vocalization of a particular word or form, the problem of reconstructing the vocalization of the language is a particularly difficult and treacherous one. With the exception of data provided by Coptic, most of the information has had to be gleaned from sources external to the written text itself. The use of a fully vocalized modification of Greek script in writing Coptic enables us to gain some insight into the vowel structure of the earlier stages of the language and indeed was fully utilized by Steindorff and Sethe, as we have mentioned above. While the work of these two scholars laid the foundation for future research, it was evident that from Coptic alone, where many of the principal verbal forms of the earlier language no longer survived, or were present in an extremely reduced and hence uninformative state, only a general theory of syllabification and word structure could be deduced and that possible variations in vocalic quality, as must have taken place in the course of the language's development, could only be guessed. Whereas the structural features isolated by Sethe and Steindorff remain valid at the present time, they were only recently treated in detail as a related unity by W. F. Edgerton, in whose study the reader will find a careful and critical discussion of the subject.[32]

In 1910 Hermann Ranke published the first extensive collection of Egyptian names as found transcribed in the cuneiform tablets of Tell el-Amarna and Boğazköy during the period of New Egyptian and in the annalistic texts of the late Assyrian and Babylonian periods.[33] For the first time Egyptologists were in possession of material showing with very little ambiguity the actual pronunciation of Egyptian at two distinct periods prior to Coptic. Because Egyptian proper names consist to a large extent of short sentences and epithets, scholars were able to obtain from these transcriptions important details on the quality of the vowels whose positions and quantities had already been inferred from Coptic. Two summary articles based on this new evidence appeared in 1923, one by K. Sethe[34] and the other by W. F. Albright.[35] The former is rich in detail and aims at being compendious while the latter is typified by boldness and seeks to examine the pertinent data in a much wider frame of reference.

It is perhaps appropriate here to mention one of the more interesting results of Albright's study, namely the relationship between the vowel *u* of New Egyptian and that represented in Coptic by *eta*. This rather unexpected correspondence was treated in greater detail by W. F. Albright in his monograph on the syllabic orthography, to which we shall return below, but even the wealth of examples marshaled there did not convince all scholars of its validity. When Worrell and Vycichl published in 1936 their reports on an old Coptic tradition at Zeniya,[36] it became clear from the texts transcribed by them that Albright's thesis was correct, since entire groups of words specified earlier by Albright, on the basis of the cuneiform transcriptions and the syllabic orthography, to have contained an original *u* in New Egyptian turned up here with sufficiently distinguishing pronunciation. The correspondence is thus generally accepted.

Further cuneiform material has been added to the existing corpus by Ranke,[37] Albright,[38] and Edel,[39] but the over-all picture has not been materially altered. A convenient summary of recent date is that of Edel,[40] but the reader should keep in mind that the problem is still far from a consistent and demonstrable solution. Other sources of less importance are the collections of Egyptian words and names in other languages where vocalized texts are present. The writer has made a study of Egyptian words in the Old Testament[41] and miscellaneous pre-Greek sources, but the abundance of transcriptions to be found in the Greek papyri of the Ptolemaic and post-Christian periods have yet to be fully utilized.

Sometime before the middle of the Twelfth Dynasty a special system of writing was devised by the Egyptian scribes. This new orthography differed from the traditional by the novel indication of vowels in the script itself, and its invention was undoubtedly due to the pressing need for an unambiguous mode of writing the numerous foreign personal and place names finding their way into Egyptian official records at that time. The orthography itself is based entirely on traditional hieroglyphs but expresses the vocalism in two distinct ways: first in importance is the use of monosyllabic Egyptian words of the type consonant-vowel-(consonant), of which the final consonant, ordinarily a weak laryngeal or *w,* is ignored for the purpose; second is the use of the consonants *y* and *w* to indicate the vowels *i* and *u* respectively, a practice which has counterparts in several Semitic systems of writing. Because the syllable, and not the individual constituents, appears to be the most convenient unit, the system of writing is referred to as the syllabic orthography. For the solution of the problems concerning the nature and origin of this orthography, we are indebted to W. F. Albright, whose monograph *The Vocalization of the Egyptian Syllabic Orthography* (New Haven, 1934) is the standard text on the subject. The success of this work, in contrast to the earlier attempts of Müller[42] and Burchardt,[43] lies not only in the larger amount of data available but also in Albright's profound knowledge of the Canaanite languages whose names lay at the source of most of the syllabic writings. Although some skepticism has been expressed by certain scholars as to the validity of Albright's results, publication of recent additional material by Albright and the present writer more than confirms his original thesis.[44]

Because the language of a people is often more informative as to their earlier relationships with other ethnic groups than is the evidence afforded by anthropological, archaeological, and historical studies, the determination of the ancestral relationships between Egyptian and other language families is of great significance. Even though scholars realized from the very beginning of the decipherment of Egyptian that the language unfolding before them had many morphological and lexical features in common with those of Semitic, little progress was made in the scientific investigation of these affinities during the last century. This lack of progress is readily understandable in view of the amount and quality of the data then available. On the Egyptian side, innumerable early and important texts lay undiscovered and unstudied, lexicography as represented by the great dictionary of Brugsch was only tentative and uncertain, and countless details of grammar remained to be correctly analyzed. Whereas more progress had been made in the Semitic field, it is none the less true that most of the major works, both descriptive and comparative, are the products of the present century.

The first major effort to collect and evaluate the known material bearing on the Egypto-Semitic problem was A. Erman's "Das Verhältnis des ägyptischen zu den semitischen Sprachen," *ZDMG* 46 (1892), pp. 93 ff., in which are brought together many pages of grammatical and lexical comparisons. The linguist who is accustomed to the high degree of regularity in comparable disciplines like that of Indo-European will stand aghast at the apparent incongruities displayed by these lists, even when such troublesome details as loan words have been weeded out. This irregularity remains today, though somewhat lessened, but as a philological fact has led to a general consideration of the relationship involved. Important etymological studies have been made since Erman's investigation by A. Ember,[45] W. F. Albright,[46] and others, all the results of which were collected together in a critical essay by Franz Calice in 1936.[47]

To just what conclusion the evidence is leading is still uncertain. Opinions vary from one extreme to another, that is, from regarding Egyptian as a purely Semitic language whose vocabulary has been obscured by phonetic change and shifts in meaning, to regarding it as an African language whose vocabulary has been Semiticized by one or more invasions. For Calice the answer is more complex and, for the present writer, more in keeping with the evidence: that Egyptian consists of an early level of Hamitic, itself related to Semitic, to which has been added at several distinct periods a large amount of Semitic speech material as a result both of actual invasion and of commercial contact. While such a thesis is far from being proven, it explains why one group of etymologies tallies so regularly with Semitic and another group appears to be related in a more remote and less easily discerned way. As may be inferred from the above remarks, the Egypto-Semitic problem is simply part of the larger one which deals with Hamito-Semitic relationships. Recent studies by Rössler,[48] in which the intimate relationship between Berber and Semitic was rather convincingly demonstrated, have seriously disturbed the classification "Hamitic," which now appears to be more a geographical designation than a linguistic one. Clearly then, the work which must first be done is a restudy of the classifications such as Cushitic, Nilotic, "African," and Hamitic to determine what basis there is for assigning various languages to these subgroups and then to attack the larger historical problem. The remote date of the connecting forms of the language in the case of Egypto-Semitic and the total lack of material before about 3000 B.C. make these studies highly conjectural ones in which an acceptable thesis must be an extraordinarily convincing one.

III

As Max Pieper observes, the classification of literature into distinct formal types is possible only in those cultures which possessed an aesthetic theory of literature.[49] Since this is not the case in ancient Egypt, the widely varied species of texts which have survived and form the subject matter of Egyptology defy rigid categorization to some extent, but groupings on the basis of structure, content, or purpose of composition serve as a convenient guide for discussion. Even if we reject as literature proper those texts which deal with technical matters, such as astronomy, mathematics, or medicinal treatments, or those which are mainly historical records, or those which contain countless spells and incantations for religious purposes, the remainder is of a scope and quality sufficient to engender admiration for the civilization of which this literature constituted an important part. The best glimpse into this literary wealth is afforded by the catalogue compiled by G. Posener, where not only surviving works but also those known only by title are considered.[50]

Two collections of translations of representative works from nearly all types of Egyptian literature are available: Adolf Erman's *Die Literatur der Ägypter* (Leipzig, 1923) and those prepared for *Ancient Near Eastern Texts* (Princeton, 1950) by John A. Wilson of the Oriental Institute. The latter are of course more up-to-date, and in addition are supplied with useful bibliographies of the more important scholarly work dealing with the individual texts. So far as treatments of the literature from the point of view of development, style, structure, and composition are concerned, only two again may be mentioned. The first is that prepared by Max Pieper in 1928, where the reader will find a sensitive and interesting discussion of the principle texts arranged chronologically.[51] The second is Volume I, 2 of the *Handbuch der Orientalistik* (Leiden, 1952), where essays on the various types of texts are presented by such noted specialists as Hellmut Brunner, Hermann Grapow, Hermann Kees, Siegfried Morenz, Eberhard Otto, Siegfried Schott, and Joachim Spiegel. Because this latter work fills a long-felt need and is an authoritative summary of the results of Egyptology to which every person interested in Egyptian literature must refer immediately, we shall devote the brief space remaining for us here to a discussion of only three types of texts and the major contributions made toward their elucidation; (1) stories, tales, and myths, (2) the so-called wisdom literature, and (3) the (auto)-biographical texts.

The texts which belong to the species of stories, tales, and myths have enjoyed great popularity among Egyptologists, who find in them much more than grammatic interest. While an enumeration of all the recent studies devoted to these texts is not possible here, the importance of many requires at least a passing notice. The tales of Sinuhe and the Shipwrecked Sailor, both belonging to the Middle Kingdom, are available in hieroglyphic transcription in A. M. Blackman's *Middle-Egyptian Stories* (*Bibliotheca Aegyptiaca* II; Brussels, 1932); the text of Sinuhe is an indispensable collation of the chief manuscripts and ostraca, to which must now be added the text of the Ashmolean ostracon, published by J. W. B. Barns in 1952.[52] This ostracon contains a virtually complete Ramesside copy of the story and constitutes a valuable addition to the known texts. W. F. Albright and others have emphasized the importance of the tale of Sinuhe and that of Wenamun from much later times for our understanding of the political and religious attitudes of the respective periods. Most important of the remaining Middle Egyptian literary texts, the Eloquent Peasant has been restudied by Émile Suys,[53] whose work is a fine supplement to the earlier studies of Gardiner and Vogelsang on this difficult composition.

The Legend of Astarte, oldest of the New Kingdom tales, was newly published and translated by Gardiner in 1933.[54] The extremely fragmentary condition of this papyrus renders interpretation difficult, but obvious comparisons between what is legible and the Canaanite texts discovered at Ugarit have prompted careful study of the remains. The most penetrating investigation of the story and its background was made by G. Posener,[55] who finds the basic elements of the legend to be entirely Egyptian, with points of contact with the teachings of Merikarê (First Intermediate Period), and sees in it a modification of an Egyptian prototype on the basis of a Canaanite myth. The stories of the Doomed Prince and the Taking of Joppa were treated in critical studies last by Peet[56] and Blok[57] in 1925; most recent articles on the Doomed Prince concern themselves with the missing finale of the tale, which need not detain us here.

During the thirties A. H. Gardiner published for the first time two papyri from the library of A. Chester Beatty of enormous value for the study of Egyptian literature. The first of these contains the now well-known story of the Contendings of Horus and Seth,[58] which he typified as "a broadly conceived and logically developed description of the legal conflict between Horus and Seth, culminating in the triumph of the former." In view of the paucity of mythological texts from ancient Egypt, this lengthy tale, which is unusual in having only gods as characters, was rightly entrusted to the most able of all living Egyptologists, whose initial edition in this case approaches the definitive. Joachim Spiegel, an outstanding interpreter of the cultural history of Egypt, has devoted an entire monograph to a thorough study of this text;[59] in it he considers the story as a literary work, giving much room to the questions of form, motivation, and construction. The second papyrus[60] contains the story of the Blinding of Truth, a didactic work characterized by the use of personifications of abstract concepts. Also included on the first-mentioned papyrus is a rich collection of love songs which greatly increases our repertory of this genre in Egyptian.[61]

The story as a literary type in ancient Egypt has been studied by Max Pieper, who has also attempted to define its place in world literature;[62] the validity of his suggestions, which are perhaps a little premature, must of course await future confirmation. Superb translations, commentaries, and bibliographical notes on the entire groups of Egyptian stories may be found in Gustave Lefebvre's *Romans et contes égyptiens de l'époque pharaonique* (Paris, 1949), which we recommend without reservation to both student and general reader.

Egyptian wisdom literature, as it is commonly called, is attested from all periods of the country's history, beginning with the teachings of Imhotep, Djedefhor, and other sages of the Old Kingdom and ending with the Demotic Papyrus Insinger. Actually the earliest texts of which we possess any significant portion are the teachings of Kagemni and of Ptahhotep, the style of which is fairly standard for all texts of the same type. In a highly perceptive study[63] of these texts and the attitudes presented by the instructions they offer, Rudolf Anthes discerns three stages, wherein the "confident affirmation in belief in the worldly order" of the Old Kingdom is replaced by a period of doubt and searching for a new way and finally by one in which trust in a resourceful and gracious divine power dominates. The relationship between these changes in perspective and the upheavals in the political and religious life of the Egyptians is reasonably discussed. Anthes also stresses the fact, as does Hellmut Brunner,[64] that these works are to be regarded as instructions, the object of which was to transmit a set of rules of conduct based on very practical experience and that wisdom *per se* is a by-product. The obvious importance of these texts and the difficulty in translation that their concise utterances occasion demand their constant restudy and reinterpretation in the light of our progressing knowledge of the language. A highly commendable summary of the recent work done on these manuscripts by H. Brunner may be found in the above-mentioned volume of the *Handbuch der Orientalistik.*

A somewhat new and stimulating interpretation of several Middle Kingdom texts of the above two genres has been made by G. Posener in his *Littérature et politique dans l'Egypte de la XIIe dynastie* (Paris, 1956). Following observations made earlier by A. De Buck and C. Kuentz on the significance of certain wisdom texts in the light of the political situation prevalent during the Middle Kingdom, Posener has reanalyzed a large part of the literary remains of this period and has established a finely detailed and coherent relationship between this literature and the gradual rise of pharaonic power during the Twelfth Dynasty. In short, he demonstrates quite convincingly (although perhaps a bit too neatly) the probable propagandistic origins of The Prophecy of Neferty, The Instructions of Amenemhet, the Adventures of Sinuhe, and two further texts of instructions. This work is one of the most important analyses yet made of a phase of Egyptian literature and will undoubtedly have considerable influence on the future interpretation of these texts and others of the same type.

Sharing in the didactic nature of the instructions, but not intended primarily as such, the biographical inscriptions provide one of the best sources for our understanding of the Egyptian character, the social order, and the ideals, both religious and communal, which motivated the life and ambitions of the individual. The biographies are attested from the Fourth Dynasty onward and show a development in form and content which was conditioned by contemporary changes in religious and political attitudes. Two excellent studies of these inscriptions are now available: Jozef Janssen, *De traditioneele Egyptische Autobiografie vóór het Nieuwe Rijk* (Leiden, 1946) and Eberhard Otto, *Die biographischen Inschriften der ägyptischen Spatzeit* (Leiden, 1954). Janssen's work is essentially a catalogue of words and phrases which serve to characterize the individual deceased; it is regrettable that more space is not devoted to a summarizing of the results, which must instead be gleaned by the reader from the numerous technical discussions. The study of Otto, on the other hand, foregoes this minute analysis and deals with the basic concepts involved, but a useful translation of the more important inscriptions is included.

In concluding this brief section on the literature of ancient Egypt, we must mention a series of manuscript finds which have been termed by some as sensational and equated in importance by others to the discovery of the Dead Sea scrolls. We refer first to the discovery around 1930 of seven volumes of Manichaean documents from the Fayum written in the Subakh-mimic dialect of Coptic; these texts, an outstanding contribution to our knowledge of this branch of Gnosticism, have been studied and edited by a number of specialists. In particular we note the work of C. Schmidt and H. J. Polotsky,[65] H.-Ch. Puech,[66] C. R. C. Allberry,[67] A. Bohlig,[68] and Säve-Söderberg.[69] Of even greater significance, however, was the recovery in 1945 of the library of Gnostic manuscripts near Nag Hammadi on the site of Chenoboskion in Upper Egypt. The details of this find and the subsequent history of the manuscripts are shrouded in the mystery which seems *de rigeur* for sensational discoveries at the present time,[70] but one of the manuscripts is now in the possession of the Jung Institute at Zurich, while the remainder have found their way to the Coptic Museum in Cairo. Dating from the third and fourth centuries of the Christian era, the codices contain, complete or in part, a total of forty-eight Gnostic works in various dialects of Coptic; most of them, however, are in the Upper Egyptian dialect of Sahidic. While we cannot elaborate on the rich contents of these codices, the pre-liminary reports make it sufficiently clear that they will reopen the study of Christian Gnosticism, and that their discovery must be reckoned as one of the most important of our century. The portion of the Jung Codex known as the Gospel of Truth has been published in a scholarly edition, somewhat lavishly, by M. Malinine, H.-Ch. Puech, and G. Quispel.[71] Under the editor-ship of Pahor Labib, the first volume of the Cairo texts has appeared;[72] of the works therein, The Gospel According to Thomas will soon appear in a scholarly edition by A. Guillaumont, Puech, Quispel, W. Till, and Yassah 'Abd Al Masīḥ. In the meantime, a short, inexpensive edition of text and translation is available.[73] Certainly no further delay should be tolerated in laying these valuable documents before the scholarly world, where their real worth can be determined and the data they contain be utilized.

Baltimore; May, 1957

NOTES TO CHAPTER ELEVEN

1. For the texts themselves, see K. Sethe, *Die altägyptische Pyramidentexte* I–IV (Leipzig, 1908–22). Supplementary texts are to be found in the following works of G. Jéquier: *Le monument funéraire de Pepi II* (Cairo, 1936); *Les pyramides des*

reines Neit et Apouit (Cairo, 1933); *La pyramide d'Oudjebten* (Cairo, 1928); and *La pyramide d'Aba* (Cairo, 1935).

2. K. Sethe, *Übersetzung und Kommentar zu den altägyptischen Pyramidentexten,* 4 volumes (Glückstadt, 1935).

3. Among the many interesting results of this study is Edel's newly proposed verbal form *sḏmwf* (pp. 238–47). While final judgment must of course await the opinion of specialists, the present writer finds the arguments contained there inconclusive. The close parallelism in usage between the presumed *sḏmwf* and the regular *sḏmf* suggests that an insistence here on differentiation because of a terminal *w* necessitates a corresponding one between the relatives *sḏmf* and *sḏmwf*, between the relatives *sḏmnf* and *sḏmwnf*, and between the perfective passive participles with and without a written *w*, on which these verbal forms are presumably based. Perhaps these latter distinctions should also be made.

4. K. Sethe, *Urkunden des Alten Reiches*, 1–4 (Leipzig, 1932–33).

5. A. Erman, *Reden, Rufe, und Lieder auf Gräberbildern des Alten Reiches* in *Abhandlungen der Preuss. Akademie der Wissenschaften* (Berlin, 1919). See also P. Montet, *Scènes de la vie privée dans les tombeaux égyptiens de l'ancien empire* (Strasbourg, 1925).

6. A. H. Gardiner and K. Sethe, *Egyptian Letters to the Dead* (London, 1928).

7. A. Erman, *Ägyptische Grammatik*, 4th ed. (Berlin, 1928).

8. Gustave Lefebvre, *Grammaire de l'Égyptien classique* (Cairo, 1940).

9. A. de Buck, *Egyptische Grammatica* (Leiden, 1944).

10. For the reader who is not familiar with the terminology of Egyptian grammar we note the following points. The majority of narrative verbal forms in Middle Egyptian have evolved from an extended use of the passive participles, of which there are two varieties, a perfective and an imperfective; the latter is distinguished in certain verbal classes by a reduplication of the second root consonant and is called also the geminating form. The individual conjugations are referred to by simply quoting the third-person masculine singular form, the mark of which is a suffixed *f*. The paradigm verb commonly employed is *sḏm*, "to hear." As opposed to the narrative forms, the relative form is a rather unusual construction wherein the verbal form itself introduces the relative clause and no relative pronoun is expressed. The actual origin and use of the form is quite complicated and the simplified definition given here will suffice for what follows.

11. Battiscombe Gunn, *Studies in Egyptian Syntax* (Paris, 1924), pp. 1–44.

12. Op. cit., pp. 219 and 237.

13. Op. cit., §§ 652–53, 672, 674.

14. H. J. Polotsky, *Études de syntaxe copte* (Cairo, 1944).

15. Acceptance of Polotsky's classification will have far-reaching effects on our concept of Egyptian grammar. An equally interesting new approach is presented, for the Old Perfective form, by the study of J. Vergote entitled *La fonction du pseudoparticipe*, in *Ägyptologische Studien* (Berlin, 1955), pp. 338–61, where he classifies the use of that form on the basis of a new category of relationship "nexus," developed by O. Jespersen. See for details J. Vergote, "Onderzoek naar de grondslagen van de algemene grammatica," *Mededelingen van de Vlaamse Academie* XIII, 2 (Brussels, 1951).

16. Op. cit., § 493.

17. For a general survey, see W. Erichsen, "Demotische Urkundenstudien," *JNES* XII (1953), pp. 197–200.

18. Cf. W. F. Edgerton's review, *JNES* XII (1953), pp. 287–89.

19. See G. Steindorff, "Bemerkungen über die Anfänge der koptischen Sprache und Literatur" in *Coptic Studies in Honor of Walter Ewing Crum* (Boston, 1950), pp. 189–214.

20. Cf. W. Vycichl, "Pi-Solsel, ein Dorf mit koptischen Überlieferungen," *Mitteilungen des Instituts für ägyptische Altertumskunde* 6 (1936), pp. 169–74; W. Worrell and W. Vycichl, "Popular Traditions of the Coptic Language," in Worrell, *Coptic Texts* (Ann Arbor, 1942), pp. 297–354.

21. See the long review by W. Till, *Orientalia* 23 (1954), pp. 152–69.

22. Also to be recommended is J. M. Plumley, *An Introductory Coptic Grammar* (London, 1948), and the extremely useful chrestomathy of M. A. Murray and D. Pilcher, *A Coptic Reading Book (with Glossary)* (London, 1933).

23. For a detailed account of the history of the project, see the introduction of the first volume of *Wörterbuch der ägyptischen Sprache* (Leipzig, 1926).

24. A. H. Gardiner, *Ancient Egyptian Onomastica* (Oxford, 1947) I, pp. ix–xxi.

25. An outstanding example of what is needed is the translation, commentary, and glossary of *Late-Egyptian Miscellanies* (London, 1954), prepared by Ricardo A. Caminos under the supervision of A. H. Gardiner.

26. K. Sethe, "Das Verhältnis zwischen Demotisch und Koptisch und seine Lehren für die Geschichte der ägyptischen Sprache," *ZDMG* 79 (1925), pp. 290–316.

27. E. Edel, *Altägyptische Grammatik* (Rome, 1955), § 14.

28. B. Gunn, *Studies in Egyptian Syntax* (Paris, 1924), p. 9. Note, however, that Gunn does not insist on the identity of the written language and the spoken at this juncture in the history of the language.

29. A. Erman, *Die Sprache des Papyrus Westcar* (Göttingen, 1889).

30. H. Grapow, "Vom Hieroglyphisch-demotischen zum Koptischen," *Sitzungsberichte der Preuss. Akademie der Wissenschaften* (Berlin, 1938), pp. 322–49.

31. Note also W. Czermak, *Die Laute der ägyptischen Sprache* (Vienna, 1931).

32. W. F. Edgerton, "Stress, Vowel Quantity, and Syllable Division in Egyptian," *JNES* VI (1947), pp. 1–17.

33. H. Ranke, "Keilschriftliches Material zur altägyptischen Vokalisation," *Abh. kon. preuss. Akad. Wissen., Phil.-hist. Classe* (Berlin, 1910), Anh., Abh. II.

34. K. Sethe, "Die Vokalisation des Ägyptischen," *ZDMG* 77 (1923), pp. 145–207.

35. W. F. Albright, "The Principles of Egyptian Phonological Development," *Recueil de Travaux* 40 (1923), pp. 64–70.

36. See note 20 above.

37. H. Ranke, "Keilschriftliches," *Zeitschrift für ägyptischer Sprache* 58 (1923), pp. 132–38; 73 (1937) pp. 90–93; 56 (1920), pp. 69–75; 48 (1910), p. 112.

38. See especially W. F. Albright, "Cuneiform Material for Egyptian Prosopography," *JNES* V (1946), pp. 7–25.

39. E. Edel, "Neue keilschriftliche Umschreibungen ägyptischer Namen aus den Boğazköytexten," *JNES* VII (1948), pp. 30–43.

40. E. Edel, "Zur Vokalisation des Neuägyptischen," *Mitteilungen des Instituts für Orientforschung* II (1954), pp. 30–43.

41. T. O. Lambdin, "Egyptian Loan Words in the Old Testament," *JAOS* 73 (1953), pp. 145–55.

42. W. Max Müller, *Asien und Europa nach altägyptischen Denkmälern* (Leipzig, 1893).

43. Max Burchardt, *Die altkanaanäischen Fremdworte und Eigennamen im Ägyptischen* (Leipzig, 1909).

44. W. F. Albright and T. O. Lambdin, "New Material for the Egyptian Syllabic Orthography," *Journal of Semitic Studies* II (1957), pp. 113–27.

45. See chiefly Aaron Ember, *Egypto-Semitic Studies* (Leipzig, 1930), edited by Frida Behnk.

46. W. F. Albright, "Notes on Egypto-Semitic Etymology," *AJSL* 34 (1917), pp. 81–98 and 215–55; and a third installment in *JAOS* 47 (1927), pp. 198–237.

47. Franz Calice, *Grundlagen der ägyptisch-semitischen Wortvergleichung* (Vienna, 1936).

48. Otto Rössler, "Der semitische Character der libyschen Sprache," *ZA* 16 (1952), pp. 121–50; "Verbalbau und Verbalflexion in den semitohamitischen Sprachen," *ZDMG* 100 (1950), pp. 461–514.

49. Max Pieper, "Das ägyptische Märchen," *Morgenland* 27 (1935), p. 5.

50. G. Posener, "Les richesses inconnues de la litterature égyptienne," *Revue d'Égyptologie* 6 (1951), pp. 27–48.

51. Max Pieper, *Die ägyptische Literatur* (Wildpark-Potsdam, 1928).

52. J. W. B. Barns, *The Ashmolean Ostracon of Sinuhe* (London, 1952).

53. Émile Suys, *Étude sur le conte du fellah plaideur, Analecta Orientalia* 5 (Rome, 1933).

54. A. H. Gardiner, "The Legend of Astarte," *Studies Presented to F. Ll. Griffith* (London, 1932), pp. 74–85.

55. G. Posener, "La légende égyptienne de la mer insatiable," *Annuaire de l'Institut de Philologie et d'Histoire Orientale et Slave* 13 (1953), pp. 461–78.

56. T. E. Peet, "The Foredoomed Prince," *Journal of Egyptian Archaeology* 11 (1925), pp. 225–29.

57. H. P. Blok, *De beide Volksverhalen van Papyrus Harris 500 verso* (Leiden, 1925).

58. A. H. Gardiner, *The Library of A. Chester Beatty; Description of a Hieratic Papyrus with a Mythological Story, Love Songs, and other Miscellaneous Texts—the Chester Beatty Papyrus No. 1* (London, 1931).

59. J. Spiegel, *Die Erzählung vom Streite des Horus and Seth* (Glückstadt, 1937).

60. A. H. Gardiner, *Hieratic Papyri in the British Museum, Third series, Chester Beatty Gift* (London, 1935).

61. For a recent study on this type of Egyptian poetry, see Siegfried Schott, *Altägyptische Liebeslieder* (Zürich, 1950), especially noteworthy for its translations.

62. Work cited in note 49 above.

63. Rudolf Anthes, *Lebensregeln und Lebensweisheit der alten Ägypter. Der alte Orient* 32 (1933).

64. *Handbuch der Orientalistik I,* 2, p. 90.

65. C. Schmidt and H. J. Polotsky, *Ein Mani-Fund in Ägypten. Sitzungsberichte der Preuss. Akademie der Wissenschaften* (Berlin, 1933), 1. H. J. Polotsky, *Manichäische Homilien* (Stuttgart, 1934).

66. H.-Ch. Puech, *Le Manichéisme. Son fondateur, sa doctrine* (Paris, 1949).

67. C. R. C. Allberry, *A Manichaean Psalm-Book, Part II* (Stuttgart, 1938).

68. A. Bohlig, *Kephalaia,* Part I (Stuttgart, 1940).

69. T. Säve-Söderbergh, *Studies in the Manichaean Psalm-Book* (Uppsala, 1949).

70. For details and bibliography see H.-Ch. Puech, G. Quispel, and W. C. van Unnik, *The Jung Codex* (London, 1955).

71. M. Malinine, H.-Ch. Puech, Gilles Quispel, *Evangelium Veritatis* (Zürich, 1956).

72. Pahor Labib, ed., *Coptic Gnostic Papyri in the Coptic Museum at Old Cairo,* Vol. 1 (Cairo, 1956).

73. A. Guillaumont, H.-Ch. Puech, G. Quispel, W. Till, and Yassah 'Abd Al Masīḥ, *The Gospel According to Thomas* (Leiden and New York, 1959).

CHAPTER TWELVE

Egyptian Culture
and Religion

JOHN A. WILSON

THE STUDY of ancient Egyptian spiritual life and material culture, over the past thirty-five years, has produced a paradox to which all maturing fields are subject: the increase in known material makes understanding more difficult.

On the one hand, there has been great amplification of data, both from Egypt and her neighboring countries, while more exacting methods of technique and analysis have been trained on the data. The result is more relevant detail in every phase; knowledge of factors and of interrelations is present.

On the other hand, the increased complexity of the field and the greater awareness of the nature of the problems have made the interpreter's task narrower and more cautious, so that the resulting statement is no longer confidently magisterial. Egyptian culture cannot now be treated as though it were purely self-generating, insulated from outside influence, and yet dominating neighbors and successors. Further, the terms which characterize spiritual and social manifestations in our own day cannot longer be directly applied to ancient Egypt. The scholar who tries to understand Egypt in her own terms cannot easily describe her in modern terms. He tries to study her development in relation to other cultures, parallel in time or in development. Since a more complex mass of factors, assessed in ancient values, is not so easy to present with simple lucidity, the result is not satisfactory to the lay public.

This situation holds challenge and opportunity. The very necessity of clarification may produce some latter-day Erman or Breasted, who will again present ancient Egypt in luminous comprehension. Egyptology, after a career of more than a century, has a full and responsible future.

Ancient Egypt used to be presented as a detached and benign uncle to the neighboring cultures, or as the well-endowed great-uncle who left a major legacy to later cultures. Egypt and Mesopotamia now appear as the two elder brothers to the other cultures of their day. The later cultures, such as the Hebrews and the Greeks, earned their own high standings; their inheritance from the Egyptians was chiefly the inspiration of a vast, imperfectly understood, and already obsolete accomplishment. For a new appreciation of ancient Egypt, with interrelations but also discontinuities, the credit belongs to a whole generation of working scholars. The contributions of William F. Albright, particularly in the Asiatic relations of Egypt, are important and gratefully acknowledged.

The landmarks of the past thirty-five years should be presented with the simplicity of a sketch map. If our critical comment sometimes becomes so subjective as to magnify heights or depths along the way, the reader is here warned to take his own bearings as he goes.

EGYPTIAN HISTORY

By the end of the nineteenth century, the Bible and the classical writers were no longer the essential foundations for the general history of ancient Egypt. A large body of writings in Egyptian was known, and there was a closer grammatical control of these texts. Flinders Petrie in particular had shown the critical value of material objects derived from controlled and recorded excavation. Thus Egyptian materials were speaking with an independent voice. The first two decades of the twentieth century lay under several magisterial influences: Gaston Maspero of France, Eduard Meyer and Adolf Erman of Germany, and James H. Breasted of the United States.[1] Here and there an independent figure cast its own intensified shadow, such as the highly personalized histories of Budge and Petrie.[2] Soon after World War I, two works appeared as standard authorities to permit a fresh assessment of the field: a new Erman's *Aegypten* and the successive volumes of the *Cambridge Ancient History*.[3] The former of these dealt with the several phases of Egyptian culture with a comprehensiveness which has not yet been surpassed.[4] The Cambridge history, by using specialists to write individual chapters, gained authority by a loss of continuity. Because the 1920s witnessed a spate of new results, many of the Cambridge chapters were out of date almost as soon as they were published. It is regrettable that the second edition has not yet appeared. In particular, those contributions dealing with the prehistoric, with the culture of the Old Kingdom, and with Egyptian foreign relations appear seriously outdated. Meanwhile, the one sound and handy history of ancient Egypt is in French, the little volume by Drioton and Vandier.[5] In English there is nothing new which tries to be specifically a history.[6]

Two recent compilations are of great utility in assembling materials for reference or research, the selections of texts and of pictures having some relation to the Old Testament.[7] Even though the purpose here is not Egyptological, the generous space allocated in the *Texts* volume to translations from the Egyptian is valuable, because there is no recent publication gathering together significant texts from ancient Egypt.

This account would become too prolix if it attempted to itemize the many specialized works and articles on Egyptian cultural history. Many of them employ already known materials in a more disciplined way to advance our understanding. One example may be permitted. G. Posener, *Littérature et politique dans l'Égypte de la XIIe Dynastie* (Paris, 1956), demonstrates convincingly how the kings of the Twelfth Dynasty used popular literature as propaganda to support the throne. It is a formidable task to keep abreast of the current literature. As Alice learned, in *Through the Looking Glass,* "It takes all the running you can do, to keep in the same place." However, despite the magnitude of the task, it is clear that we need a cultural history of ancient Egypt, a study which will take account of all the new work and will present it with clarity and integrity.

ARCHAEOLOGY

As of 1921 it might have seemed that the cream had been skimmed in the excavation of significant sites in Egypt. Mariette had started work seventy years earlier. For more than thirty years Petrie's genius in selecting productive sites had greatly augmented knowledge, from the prehistoric into the Roman periods. The obvious temples and cemeteries and the city of Tell el-Amarna had been exploited to the point where there seemed to be either exhaustion or greatly diminishing returns.

Yet the 1920s now appear as a kind of golden age of Egyptian archaeology. At the beginning, political conditions were hospitable. In Egypt and the neighboring countries there was a time of hopeful good will, and many of the services of antiquities were organized under Western administration. Finances were favorable, with low field costs and nearly adequate assets. Within these external factors, archaeology had reached a new maturity and was aware of professional standards and responsibilities. The wealthy dilettante or the exploiter for showy treasures was no longer in place. Better standards were expressed in antiquities laws which demanded responsible agency, controlled operation, and publication of results.

In 1922, at the beginning of this fortunate period, the tomb of Tut-ankh-Amon was discovered.[8] The spectacular nature of the finds, the fascination of the Amarna personalities, and the speed and assurance of modern communications combined to make the discovery a sensation. However, the consciousness of vast treasure and a controversy over the legal rights of the discoverer brought political factors into the antiquities situation, at a time when nationalism was otherwise becoming aggressive. The Egyptians felt it necessary to protect their national assets against dispersal and exploitation. They began to use the law more jealously to control the work of foreign expeditions.[9] The era of good will and open opportunity was not destined to last very long.

Anti-foreign feeling in the Near East, the drying up of available finances in the depression, and even a glut of materials and a responsibility for publication slowed up excavation in Egypt from 1930 on. As foreign expeditions went home and stayed home, Egypt began to increase her own field activity, through the *Service des Antiquités* and through the national universities. Egyptian archaeologists, who had been constrained to conservation of already discovered sites and materials, increasingly gave responsible attention to developing new problems. If an outsider may venture criticism, an effective obstacle to full scholarly activity lies in the responsibilities of government position, which demands new discoveries each season, rather than the drudgery of definitive publication. Egypt can now boast many experienced Egyptologists, and most of the future exploitation of archaeological materials will lie in their hands. One hopes that their mature self-confidence will welcome co-operation with foreign scholars.[10]

This account, however, has leaped ahead from the clearance of the tomb of Tut-ankh-Amon, as though that discovery had been the only notable activity of the 1920s. There was a great deal of other admirable work, that of Hermann Junker at Gizeh, of Gustave Jéquier at south Sakkarah, of the Metropolitan Museum of Art at Thebes and Lisht, and of the Egypt Exploration Society at Abydos, Armant, and Tell el-Amarna.[11] It will not be invidious to these and others to praise the work of Reisner at the Pyramids, for exacting methodology and careful recording. The recovery of the burial furniture of Queen Hetep-heres near the Great Pyramid was a classic of meticulous observation, patient removal, and sound reconstruction under difficult physical circumstances. Since this furniture could be fitted into a gap in our knowledge, it should be prized as highly as any discovery in Egypt in the 1920s and 1930s.[12]

At the turn of the century, the genius of Petrie had sorted out the predynastic periods which preceded the historical age in Egypt.[13] Although his system of "sequence dating" was subject to criticism and modification, it remained generally normative.[14] In 1924–25 Petrie's expedition extended the predynastic horizon by the discovery of a still older culture at al-Badari in Middle Egypt.[15] Subsequently our knowledge of other phases of the prehistoric was enlarged by the work of Miss Caton-Thompson in the Faiyum and the Khargah Oasis and the work of Sandford in the Nile Valley and the Red Sea Coast.[16]

A revelation for the period was the architectural complex of the Stepped Pyramid at Sakkarah. The sudden explosion of monumental stone architecture, the ingenuity with which a new medium was used for old purposes, and the aesthetic glory which was attained without previous models were all exciting and revised our appreciation of early Egyptian culture.[17] Also at Sakkarah, the work of Emery over the past twenty years has brought a far clearer understanding of the monumental burials of the first two dynasties and the interplay of southern and northern forces in the *mastaba* structures. In this early cemetery Emery found that servants had been buried at the same time as their lords, apparently an older severe practice surviving into the earliest historic times.[18]

As the predynastic and early dynastic times in Mesopotamia have also become better known, it has become possible to gain an appreciation of the interrelations between Mesopotamian and Egyptian cultures around the beginning of history. Thanks particularly to the work of Scharff and Frankfort, we now see that there were influential borrowings by Egypt from Mesopotamia, clearly in such factors as cylinder seals, artistic motifs, and monumental architecture in brick with recessed paneling, perhaps also in so effective a factor as the idea of writing. Equivalent Egyptian elements in Mesopotamian context are lacking.[19]

Although the discoveries in Egypt were important, the really significant advances were made in the knowledge of Egypt's foreign relations, particularly with Asia. Some of the new understanding came out of Egypt itself, as in the execration texts, the Wisdom of Amen-em-Opet, or newly published Aramaic documents. Some came from Egyptian-held Sinai. But most of it came from excavations in Palestine, Syria, and Anatolia. Even the work in Iraq made its negative statement in showing how Egyptian cultural dominance could not cross the Syrian desert or the Euphrates. The story in Palestine-Syria had been present for the digger. The opening up of the region under Western mandates permitted more excavation and—generally speaking—more responsible excavation. Further, as Egyptian nationalism was deemed to be restrictive, some agencies, such as Petrie's British School of Archaeology in Egypt, moved out, to study "Egypt across the border."[20] New excavations on Asiatic soil illustrated the cultural penetration of Egypt under the Old and Middle Kingdoms and the political control of the New Kingdom. Work at such places as Tell el-'Ajjul, Lachish, Megiddo, Beisan, Byblos, Ugarit, Kadesh on the Orontes, and Qatna unearthed some Egyptian structures, Egyptian steles, exports or gifts, locally Egyptianizing objects, or evidence on the difficult Hyksos problem.[21] At the same time, the contents of the Hittite archives were becoming known, to set beside the Amarna Letters and illustrate more clearly the struggle of empires for Asia.[22]

Four of the sites listed above deserve further comment. Petrie's excavations at Tell el-'Ajjul (in southern Palestine) did show the dual Canaanite-Egyptian nature of the place in the second millennium B.C.[23] Then Albright used Petrie's observations to straighten out the chronology, put the Hyksos in their proper perspective, and show the administrative importance of Gaza for the Egyptian empire.[24]

In terms of major Egyptian influence, Megiddo was somewhat disappointing. To be sure, there were Middle Kingdom statuettes, many scarabs, Egyptian pieces among the ivories, a bronze statuette base of Ramses VI, and a fragment of a Shishak stele. But the town retained a certain stubborn Canaanite independence; it was not a nucleus of Egyptian influence in the same sense that Gaza, Beisan, and Byblos were. In particular, the evidences of Thut-mose III's siege of Megiddo were negative.[25] We shall revert to this negativity later.

Byblos, on the other hand, proved to be much more under Egyptian influence, from the early Old Kingdom until the fall of the empire. Better-controlled excavations in the 1920s would have sharpened this picture, but the evidence is clear from an "Egyptian temple," a treasure with Egyptian objects, gifts from the Egyptian kings of the Old and Middle Kingdoms to the princes of Byblos, and hieroglyphic inscriptions in which the local Asiatic rulers carried the Egyptian title, "Count (*haty-a*) of Byblos."[26]

Another northern city, Ugarit, produced evidence of strong ties to Egypt, such as the statuette of a Middle Kingdom vizier and the stele of a New Kingdom scribe worshiping the local Baal. Ugarit's commercial bonds to Egypt may not have been as strong as those of Byblos, but since Ugarit lay more to the north, its Egyptian and Egyptianizing materials are significant.[27]

The evidence suggests that Egyptian influence may have been largely coastal and may have leapfrogged central Palestine to concentrate on Phoenicia. We realize how little we know about maritime trade in the eastern Mediterranean, about the sea power of the Egyptian state, and the effective clearing power of port cities in the Delta.[28]

It seems clear that the Egyptian weight in hither Asia under the Old and Middle Kingdoms was economic and cultural, not political and military in an imperialistic sense. In this respect Nubia forms a contrast, since it was seized and held by the Twelfth Dynasty.[29] In the New Kingdom, Egypt did extend power domination over Asia. The area of political claim ran north to the Euphrates and east as far as there was a sedentary population. Egypt's major interests, however, lay in the coastal towns, particularly those of Phoenicia, and along a road which followed the Philistine coast, cut through the Carmel Range into the Plain of Esdraelon, touched the Jordan at Beisan, cut through the hills of Galilee, and followed the Orontes River north to the disputed city of Kadesh. The concentration of interests seems moderately clear from excavations, which have confirmation from textual material, as we shall now argue.

FOREIGN RELATIONS FROM WRITTEN SOURCES

Egyptian texts which have become known in the past thirty-five years have strengthened our knowledge of Egypt's foreign relations and have helped greatly in the identification of the population of hither Asia in the second millennium B.C. In these problems Albright has been particularly penetrating.

In 1923 Budge published the British Museum papyrus which contained the Wisdom of Amen-em-Opet, and in the following year Erman was able to relate this late text to the Hebrew Book of Proverbs, particularly 22:17–24:22. This was the closest demonstrable interlocking of Egyptian and Hebrew literature, no matter how one may phrase the factor of "borrowing."[30]

The first series of execration texts was published by Sethe in 1926, and Posener added parallel and additional texts some years later.[31] These texts, which cursed actual or potential enemies of the Egyptian king, were written on pottery bowls or clay figurines, which were ceremonially smashed, to effect the execration. Their date was set as running somewhere between the mid-nineteenth and the mid-eighteenth century B.C. The Asiatic countries and rulers known to Egypt at that time were of great interest and importance. Albright's work on these identifications has been of major weight.[32]

Hayes recently published a Brooklyn papyrus, which included names of Asiatic slaves in Egypt, thus supplementing the material from the execration texts. Here again the authority of Albright was of critical value.[33]

Re-examination of the inscriptions found at the Egyptian mines in Sinai was also helpful on the problems of Asiatics and Semites. For Middle Kingdom times, Černý pointed out the character and standing of the Asiatics who dealt with the Egyptians at that site.[34] Then a more careful sifting of the evidence on the proto-Sinaitic writing enabled Albright to lower its dating to about 1500 B.C. and to effect a transliteration and translation.[35] Thus, one of the early phases of the Semitic alphabet—and of our own—was placed in firmer control.

A publication and a discovery also belong to this account. Sir Alan Gardiner has published those curious catalogues—"heaven with its affairs, earth and what is in it"—which were used in the late New Kingdom and thereafter for the training of scribes. In addition to clarifying what the Egyptian thought important, including the geography of his own countries, these texts carry more than fifty names of foreign peoples or places.[36] In 1954 in the temple of Karnak, Labib Habachi discovered a stele of Ka-mose, which continues the account known from Carnarvon Table I, with valuable reference to the war of expulsion of the Hyksos from Egypt.[37]

More than thirty years of work in Phoenicia, Cilicia, and Anatolia has permitted fuller consideration of the Sea Peoples, with whom Egypt came into conflict from the 14th to the 12th centuries B.C. A fundamental article by Albright trained a closer perspective upon these peoples and their relations to the oriental and classical worlds.[38] Meanwhile, the Egyptian use of one of these peoples, the *Sherden,* as mercenaries and their location on Egyptian soil have emerged from various documents.[39]

Finally, turning to the lands south of Egypt, Reisner's work in the Sudan brought into chronological order the Kushite (formerly called "Ethopian") rulers, who were important factors in the history of the Sudan and of Egypt from the eighth to the fourth centuries B.C.[40] F. Ll. Griffith's excavations at

Kawa near the Third Cataract produced texts which made the nature of the Kushite culture clearer and which focused upon the Biblical Tirhakah.[41]

SCIENCE AND TECHNOLOGY

The period under consideration witnessed no revolution in the general knowledge of scientific lore nor of technology, with the possible exception of the monumental architecture before the Fourth Dynasty. However, new publications put the mathematical and medical papyri into firmer control and more favorable light.[42]

There were no new texts to permit a tightening up of Egyptian chronology. The general trend of the past thirty-five years has been toward lower dates for the beginning of the dynastic period. In the absence of conclusive data, there is no agreement between the conservatives, who begin the First Dynasty about 3200 B.C., and the revisionists, who press down to about 2850, conforming to the downward trends in Mesopotamian chronology. The objective process of testing organic material for radioactive carbon has proved to be a disciplinary blessing for prehistory, but its inherent margin of error is too great to settle the problems on historic periods.[43] Perhaps the long-run (and expensive) testing of many separate pieces from the same reign would cut down on the margin of error usefully, but we have not been in a position to lay such a clear-cut proposition before the physicists.

Parker's *Calendars,* the first member of a series of calendrical, astronomical, and chronological studies, exorcised many chimeras of previous research. It also served warning that these problems are dangerous for the scholar who is not so well armed as Parker.[44]

Fortunately, there is a host of good little books on craftsmanship, technology, materials, and Egyptian archeology.[45]

ART

We are today in a much better position to study and understand ancient Egyptian art. For one thing, the camera is a more flexible instrument than it used to be, so that reproductions are more faithful and more widely distributed. Modern processes are even spreading color prints within the reach of smaller libraries and interested laymen.[46] For another thing, there has been a deliberate attempt to get inside of Egyptian art and to try to understand it in setting, purposes, and psychology. The influence of the German scholar Heinrich Schäfer was fundamental.[47] Even those who found the technical German difficult or those who rejected some of Schäfer's dicta were influenced by him. It is a great loss that the sensitive Henri Frankfort did not live to present a study on Egyptian art for the Penguin Press. Fortunately, the proposed volume is now in the good hands of William Stevenson Smith, author of a solid and detailed analysis of Old Kingdom art.[48] Mrs. Frankfort has argued that earlier Egyptian art was normally timeless and spaceless, in its emphasis on eternal life, whereas the art of the Amarna movement abruptly accepted the here and now.[49] Egyptian art is no longer exotic and esoteric. In the past thirty years its fundamental principles have been recognized.

Of course the copying of scenes and texts has improved since Napoleon's expedition began epigraphy. A better knowledge of subject matter, a scientific conscience, and the competition of the camera guarantee a more exact product. In 1924 the Oriental Institute of the University of Chicago sent an Epigraphic Expedition to Luxor to combine the mechanical fidelity of the camera, the trained eye and wrist of the artist, and the collating skill of the Egyptologist. Eight exacting volumes on Theban temples have appeared.[50] The Chicago method has been criticized as laborious and expensive, but, since it approaches an ideal, it has strongly influenced other epigraphic work.

The handsomest publication of the period came from the gifted and experienced brush of Mrs. Davies: an anthology of painting, which showed Egyptian art at its liveliest and at its most serene.[51]

GOVERNMENT AND LAW

As in the case of art, the authority and function of Egyptian rule came to be treated in its own terms, rather than through a facile use of modern concepts. In contrast to Mesopotamia, there has appeared no body of ancient Egyptian law, which might be referred to as a "code," and even reference to such law in other documents is lacking. It appears that the dogma that the king was a god, functionally resident upon earth to articulate his divine will, could not tolerate the competition of impersonal, written law. Of course a system of law was known and practiced in ancient Egypt, but this must have been traditional law—or laws—asserting its binding sanctions as the word of the god-king.[52]

Two German scholars advanced our knowledge of the practice of law and government. Erwin Seidl worked on the evidence of legal documents and references to legal procedure.[53] Hermann Kees clarified both the relationship of the central government to provincial administration and the relationship of the priesthood to the civil government.[54]

Several legal or administrative documents came into effective play. A Nineteenth Dynasty decree, found at Nauri in the Sudan, regulated the activities of civil officials in relation to temple personnel and property.[55] It was a useful parallel to the Old Kingdom decrees of temple privilege, even though it did not go as far as they in offering the temples special immunities.[56] Work on the Hittite archives made possible a closer parallel between the Egyptian and Hittite versions of the treaty between Ramses II and Hattusilis about 1270 B.C.[57]

The most important new document was a Ramesside tax record on a long papyrus of the Brooklyn Museum. The masterly publication by the dean of Egyptologists is unexceptionable, but the form in which the record was set down did not permit the clarification of two essential problems: the exact nature of the data given and the consequent tax rates, and the specific liabilities of temples and priests toward the civil government.[58]

RELIGION—GENERAL

It is a confession of defeat and of challenge to say that the central expression of ancient Egyptian culture, its religion, continues to be somewhat baffling to the modern analyst. A dogma was insistently proclaimed over two thousand years, but there is evidence that practice within that dogma showed change with the passing of time. In a theocratic state, which controls communication, only the official religion shows a clear face. We may catalogue and categorize the gods, but deity and divinity remain fluid concepts. Gods blend and re-emerge and blend again. The king was a god, but some kings enjoyed exceptional worship in their own lifetimes. Viziers and wise men were recognized as gods after death. A system of mortuary religion was formulated for the god-king, was taken over for his queens, and then was appropriated by the nobles of the land, while continuing to assert the king's rule as the god Osiris. The great emphasis is on eternal life after death, and yet the Egyptians were not morbidly preoccupied with thoughts of death, but scrambled eagerly for the fruits of this life. A cynic might suggest that a people who defined the highest good as "truth" had given themselves over to a series of paradoxes or contradictions.

This states the situation at its most difficult, which means only that understanding has to rest on carefully prepared ground. Because of these complexities, one of the best books remains Erman's *Religion,* simply because it is descriptive and historical, rather than valuative.[59] The facts are there, and we are free to play our personal prejudices upon them. When Breasted attempted a high appreciation of Egyptian religion and asserted, "The sources of our inheritance of moral teaching . . . include . . . especially Egypt, where the earliest transcendental vision of social idealism arose,"[60] he evoked protest. Jewish and Christian theologians felt that he was claiming for Egypt that which rightly belonged to later visions. Pessimists observed that Egypt herself had scarcely realized the high vision which Breasted credited to her and that Breasted's melioristic view of history permitted him to see only the triumphant mountaintops and never the foggy swamps. The focus, they said, is too concentrated to do Egypt justice by appreciating her in her own time and scene. Egypt was neither dormantly primitive nor presciently modern.

About ten years ago scholars at the University of Chicago attempted to set up guideposts for the ancient Near East in a series of lectures on the basic spiritual backgrounds.[61] This was an effort to find common ground for the world outlooks of the Egyptians, Mesopotamians, and Hebrews. The search for such understanding found both commonality and contrast within these cultures. The attempt to understand ancient man confronting his universe and thinking about it was a starting point for further effort along these lines.

That further effort was achieved only in part. One of the Chicago lecturers, Frankfort, followed one line with his *Kingship,* in which the Egyptian concept of divine rule was studied with a great deal of patient detail.[62] This book has also the merit of pointing a firm finger at an African element in Egyptian religion to place beside those elements which had already been recognized as Asiatic.

Frankfort followed this with a little series of lectures on the general subject of Egyptian religion.[63] In this, he reiterated a viewpoint in the two preceding works, that ancient "myth-making" man approached his world from a multiplicity of approaches, each of which he believed to be simultaneously valid and therefore not demanding reconciliation within an apparent contradiction. This is a correct working hypothesis, but in lesser hands it might permit mere descriptive analysis, without an attempt to grapple with apparent heterodoxies. In his preface, Frankfort insisted that his search for unity in Egyptian religion must not be distracted by "local and temporal differences." This was honest, but it is not so easy for others to ignore the erosive force of two thousand years of historical process.

There is—and probably will continue to be—disagreement arising out of the analysts' various approaches and attitudes. For the beginner, it is still safer to consult less tendentious works, but books which modestly confine themselves to exposition.[64]

Mention should be made of Sethe's brave attempt to trace the political history of predynastic and earliest dynastic times, chiefly from the mythology as interpreted by him from the Pyramid Texts.[65] He separated out seven or eight predynastic phases, including a predynastic union about a thousand years before the dynastic union and centered at Heliopolis. Sethe argued that mythology was the creature of political process, that the earliest theological assertions by political units had survived unimpaired into dynastic texts, and that it was possible to dig such chronological strata out of these later texts and to arrange them in sequence. The study was relatively innocent of any recognition of the evidence from physical archaeology. Although Sethe's philological competence was supreme and although he emphasized that his study was "ein persönliches Vorstellungsbild," there has been vigorous dissent. Other scholars cannot so easily recognize chronological evidence in these mortuary texts, and they are uneasy about accepting a mythology visible in texts of the Fifth and Sixth Dynasties as creations of and vestiges of political and geographic power.[66]

RELIGION—SOURCE MATERIALS

Many new texts appeared in the past thirty-five years, serving both to elucidate and to complicate the problem of understanding. Jéquier's excavations in south Sakkarah brought to light structures having old and new Pyramid Texts. The unfinished work of the lamented Kurt Sethe serves as our main basis for the understanding of the Pyramid Texts.[67] In the fourth volume of an otherwise secondary study, there are important contributions by Drioton, Schott, Kees, Lacau, and others, dealing with phases of this earliest body of Egyptian mortuary texts.[68]

In 1922 Breasted, Gardiner, and Lacau began a major copying task, the neglected Coffin Texts, a mortuary link between the Pyramid Texts and the Book of the Dead. This project was soon turned over to de Buck's capable hands, and at this writing five volumes of copies have appeared.[69]

An article by de Buck discussing one of the Coffin Texts shows both his mastery of the field and the complexity of the subject.[70] Meanwhile, advance in the study of the Book of the Dead has been lagging, but a real contribution to this field should be made by T. George Allen within a short time.

In 1928 Gardiner and Sethe brought out a series of letters in which living Egyptians continued relation to their dead relatives.[71] Gardiner pondered this problem of the living and the dead and later gave an important lecture at the University of Cambridge, in which he emphasized that there was no fear of the dead or worship of the dead, but that the continuing concern for life after death was based almost completely upon the known factors of this life.[72]

About the same time Sethe put out his *Dramatische Texte,* a characteristically mature analysis of two mystery plays of Egyptian religion, in which priestly actors assumed the roles of the gods.[73] Although there are still many unsolved problems about the presentation of such dramas, it is clear that they were a normal factor in the religion from very early times.[74] It is distinctly possible that a great deal of temple and funerary ritual was "acted out" to illustrate the vicarious participation of the gods. We now know a great deal more about the daily ritual in the temples, with emphasis upon the awakening, bathing, annointing, clothing, and feeding of the image of the god in his shrine.[75]

Similarly, several different scholars have gathered the scattered evidence on the important role of a god's image in oracular response and command. This was a phenomenon which appeared most clearly in the late New Kingdom, although there is evidence that the oracle of the great gods was consulted on behalf of the state somewhat earlier.[76]

The most sumptuous find of new documents having to do with ancient Egyptian religion was the Chester Beatty Papyri from Thebes, most of which are now in the British Museum.[77] These include nineteen hieratic papyri of the 13th and 12th centuries B.C., apparently a uniform lot. Chester Beatty I turned a familiar mythological story, the contest of the gods Horus and Seth for rule, into a tale "frankly farcical" in its treatment of the great gods of the land. Although such an irreverent attitude could be paralleled elsewhere, this was the most outspoken *vulgarization* of the pantheon and must be assigned to secular literature, rather than to the mythology which was formally sponsored by the clergy.

Two other items in this collection were also novel. An allegory, the Blinding of Truth by Falsehood, treated the protagonists of the familiar Osiris-Seth-Horus myth through the metaphorical figures of Truth, Falsehood, and the son of Truth. Explicit in the tale is the irony that Truth was finally vindicated because his son told a bigger lie than did Falsehood. Thus this allegory may also fit into the secular category, despite its general conformance to accepted theology.

A manuscript for the interpretation of dreams provided a parallel to the Joseph story, although this type of omenology is more familiar from Mesopotamia than from Egypt. It is true that the Egyptians regarded sleep as entry into the next world and therefore a realm of the gods,[78] but this papyrus was the first known document in which they related the manifestations in dreams to good or evil results to come.

The Beatty Papyri also include materials for the daily temple ritual of the deified king Amen-hotep I, a eulogy of the ancient wise men who achieved their immortality through the writings which they left behind, and some hymns which the editor unhesitatingly calls "monotheistic." Perhaps this term needs clearer definition for the modern mind, to eliminate the alternative words "henotheistic" or "syncretistic," but Gardiner believes that these and other hymns "reflect a genuinely monotheistic outlook conditioned by and, as far as might be, reconciled with the traditional polytheism of Egypt,"[79] and he appropriately notes the prior influence of the Amarna religion. Perhaps we need some abominable jargon like "protomonotheistic" to characterize texts of this kind.

The religious items in the Beatty collection definitely do belong to the current of religion of the late New Kingdom. Since the collection seems to be a unity and since other texts in these papyri are definitely of the type used for the instruction of government clerks in the scribal schools, we may assign the collection to the secular world, rather than to the orthodox temple literature. These papyri are thus valuable in illustrating that slow and incomplete secularization which was forced by a government in need of a large bureaucracy. In part, that demand took writing, the medium of communication and indoctrination, out of the hands of the priests.

This study began *penseroso,* with the somber thought that the materials of Egyptology may have exceeded our grasp. After reviewing the rewards and achievements of the past thirty-five years, we are moved to end it *allegro.* The temper of scholarship in this field is more detached and objective in dealing with the materials than in any previous period. That temper has the stimulus of more data and a wider variety of data to work upon. The future looks very attractive.

Like the ancient Egyptians, we have the faith that Truth, even though he may be occasionally blinded, will be vindicated by a loyal son.

Chicago; January 4, 1957

NOTES TO CHAPTER TWELVE

1. Maspero's little *Histoire ancienne des peuples de l'Orient* (Paris, 1875) developed into a three-volume work, of which the English translations were *The Dawn of Civilization* (London, 1894), *The Struggle of the Nations* (London, 1896), and *The Passing of the Empires* (New York, 1900). Meyer's five-volume *Geschichte des Altertums* (Stuttgart, 1884–1902) is still current in a third edition (ed. by H. E. Stier, 1928–1956). Erman's *Aegypten und ägyptisches Leben im Altertum* (Tübingen, 1885) was translated into English by H. M. Tirard as *Life in Ancient Egypt* (London, 1894). Breasted based *A History of Egypt* (Scribners, New York, 1905; 2nd ed., 1912) on a five-volume set of translations, *Ancient Records of Egypt* (University of Chicago Press, 1906–7).

2. E. A. Wallis Budge's *A History of Egypt from the End of the Neolithic Period to the Death of Cleopatra VII, B.C. 30* (London) came out in 1902. W. M. Flinders Petrie was constantly revising his *A History of Egypt* (London): *I. From the Earliest Times to the XVIth Dynasty* (1894; 10th ed., 1923); *II. During the XVIIth and XVIIIth Dynasties* (1896; 7th ed., 1924); *III. From the XIXth to the XXXth Dynasties* (1905; 3rd ed., 1925).

3. Adolf Erman, *Aegypten und ägyptisches Leben im Altertum, neu bearbeitet von Hermann Ranke* (Tübingen, 1923); *The Cambridge Ancient History*, ed. by J. B. Bury et al.; 12 vols. (Cambridge, 1923–39).

4. There is, however, admirable quality in Hermann Kees, *Aegypten* (*Kulturgeschichte des alten Orients*, I; München, 1933). For social-economic history, the most rewarding products come from Jaroslav Černý's study of prices, wages, and social conditions among the Theban necropolis workers in the late New Kingdom, e.g., his article, "Prices and Wages in Egypt in the Ramesside Period," in *Cahiers d'Histoire Mondiale* (*Commission Internationale pour une Histoire du Développement Scientifique et Culturel de l'Humanité*), I (1954), pp. 903–21, with the antecedent literature there cited.

5. É. Drioton et J. Vandier, *L'Égypte*, in the series, *Clio I: Les Peuples de l'Orient méditerranéen, 2* (Paris, 1938; 3rd ed., 1952).

6. W. S. Smith, *Ancient Egypt as Represented in the Museum of Fine Arts* (Boston Museum of Fine Arts, 1942; 3rd ed., 1952); William C. Hayes, *The Scepter of Egypt. A Background for the Study of the Egyptian Antiquities in the Metropolitan Museum of Art. I. From the Earliest Times to the End of the Middle Kingdom* (Harper & Bros., New York, 1953); and John A. Wilson, *The Burden of Egypt. An Interpretation of ancient Egyptian Culture* (University of Chicago Press, 1951), are too heavily indebted to some special interest to serve as general histories.

7. *Ancient Near Eastern Texts Relating to the Old Testament*, ed. by James B. Pritchard (Princeton University Press, 1950; 2nd ed., 1955); James B. Pritchard, *The Ancient Near East in Pictures Relating to the Old Testament* (Princeton University Press, 1954).

8. Howard Carter, *The Tomb of Tut-ankh-Amen*, 3 vols. (London, 1923–33).

9. The Oriental's instinctive distrust of the westerner was not allayed by the publication of E. A. W. Budge, *By Nile and Tigris*, 2 vols. (London, 1920), in which the author told of his ingenuity in acquiring antiquities for the British Museum.

10. This was written at a time of tragic crisis centered upon the Suez Canal. Scholarly exchange of ideas, purposes, and courtesies will be damaged by political tensions, but we fervently hope that official and personal colleagueship will be resumed. For a warm appreciation of some of the Egyptian Egyptologists, see the words by Albright in *BASOR* 109 (Feb. 1948), p. 7.

11. As a partial record of publications: Hermann Junker, *Giza*, 12 vols. (Wien und Leipzig, 1929–55); Gustave Jéquier, *Fouilles à Saqqarah*, 9 vols. (Le Caire, 1928–40); Herbert E. Winlock, *Excavations at Deir el Bahri*, 1911–31 (New York, 1942); Henri Frankfort, *The Cenotaph of Seti I at Abydos*, 2 vols. (London, 1933); Sir Robert Mond and Oliver H. Myers, *The Bucheum*, 3 vols. (London, 1934); *Cemeteries of Armant I*, 2 vols. (London, 1937); and *Temples of Armant*, 2 vols. (London, 1940); J. D. S. Pendlebury, *Tell el-Amarna* (London, 1935).

12. George A. Reisner, *The Development of the Egyptian Tomb down to the Accession of Cheops* (Cambridge [Mass.], 1936); *A History of the Giza Necropolis*, 2 vols. (Cambridge [Mass.], 1942–55). The second volume of the latter, completed by W. S. Smith, reports the work on the tomb of Hetep-heres.

13. W. M. F. Petrie, *Diospolis Parva* (London, 1901); *Corpus of Prehistoric Pottery and Palettes* (London, 1921).

14. Helene J. Kantor, in *JNES* III (1944), pp. 110–36, synchronized Petrie's third and final predynastic period (Semainean) with the later phases of his second (Gerzean).

15. Guy Brunton and Gertrude Caton-Thompson, *The Badarian Civilization and Predynastic Remains near Badari* (London, 1928).

16. Gertrude Caton-Thompson and E. W. Gardner, *The Desert Fayum*, 2 vols. (London, 1934); *Kharga Oasis in Prehistory* (London, 1952); Kenneth S. Sandford and W. J. Arkell, *Prehistoric Survey of Egypt and Western Asia*, 4 vols. (Chicago, 1929–39).

17. Especially J.-P. Lauer, *Fouilles à Saqqarah, La pyramide à degrés. L'architecture*, 3 vols. (Le Caire, 1936–39).

18. Walter B. Emery, *Excavations at Saqqara*, appearing as *The Tomb of Hemaka* (Cairo, 1938); *Hor-aha* (Cairo, 1939); and *Great Tombs of the First Dynasty*, 2 vols. (Cairo, 1949–54). A mass burial was found by Reisner at Kerma in the Sudan, datable to the Middle Kingdom: G. A. Reisner, *Excavations at Kerma* (*Harvard African Studies*, V–VI; Cambridge [Mass.], 1923).

19. Alexander Scharff in *Zeitschrift für ägyptische Sprache*, LXXI (1935), pp. 89–106; Henri Frankfort, in *AJSL*, LVIII (1941), pp. 329–58; and *The Birth of Civilization in the Near East* (Bloomington, Ill., 1951), pp. 100–11.

20. Petrie announced his decision to leave Egypt in his journal, *Ancient Egypt*, 1926, p. 96.

21. In order not to multiply references, only William F. Albright, *The Archaeology of Palestine* (Penguin Books, 1949), will be cited here.

22. O. R. Gurney, *The Hittites* (Penguin Books, 2nd ed., 1954).

23. W. M. F. Petrie, *Ancient Gaza*, 5 vols. (London, 1931–52).

24. In *AJSL* LV (1938), pp. 337–59.

25. For the present terms, two reviews by Albright of the publications by the Oriental Institute, in *American Journal of Archaeology* XLIV (1940), pp. 546–50; LIII (1949), pp. 213–15, are most pertinent. See also G. E. Wright in this volume, p. 91 and Chart 7, where the violent destructions visited upon Megiddo IX and City Stratum II of Tell el-'Ajjul are attributed to Thutmose III.

26. Pierre Montet, *Byblos et l'Égypte*, 2 vols. (Paris, 1928–29); Maurice Dunand, *Fouilles de Byblos*, 2 vols. (Paris, 1937–54); P. E. Newberry, in *Journal of Egyptian Archaeology*, XIV (1928), p. 109.

27. Claude F.-A. Schaeffer, *Les fouilles de Ras Shamra-Ugarit*, 17 vols. (Paris, 1929–55); *Ugaritica*, 2 vols. (Paris, 1939–49).

28. Even the admirable little study by T. Säve-Söderbergh, *The Navy of the Eighteenth Egyptian Dynasty* (Uppsala, 1946), can find only spotty material for that important period.

29. T. Säve-Söderbergh, *Aegypten und Nubien, ein Beitrag zur Geschichte altägyptischer Aussenpolitik* (Lund, 1941), esp. pp. 63–116.

30. The most pertinent references are cited in *ANET*, p. 421.

31. Kurt Sethe, *Die Aechtung feindlicher Fürsten, Völker und Dinge auf altägyptischen Tongefässcherben des Mittleren Reiches* (*Abhandl. d. preuss. Akad. d. Wiss.*, Jahrgang 1926, phil.-hist. Kl. Nr. 5; Berlin, 1926); G. Posener, *Princes et pays d'Asie et de Nubie* (Bruxelles, 1940).

32. See *Journal of the Palestine Oriental Society* VIII (1928), pp. 223–56; *BASOR* 81 (Feb. 1941), pp. 16–21; 83 (Oct. 1941), pp. 30–36.

33. *A Papyrus of the Late Middle Kingdom in the Brooklyn Museum*, edited by William C. Hayes (Brooklyn, N.Y., 1955); W. F. Albright, "Northwest-Semitic Names in a List of Egyptian Slaves from the Eighteenth Century B.C.," *JAOS* LXXIV (1954), pp. 222–33.

34. Jaroslav Černý, "Semites in Egyptian Mining Expeditions to Sinai," *Archiv Orientální*, VII (1935), pp. 384–89.

35. *BASOR* 109 (Feb. 1948), pp. 5–20; 110 (Apr. 1948), pp. 6–22; see also 118 (Apr. 1950), pp. 12–14.

36. Alan H. Gardiner, *Ancient Egyptian Onomastica*, 3 vols. (London, 1947).

37. L. Habachi, *Annales du Service des Antiquités de l'Égypte*, LIII (1955), pp. 195–202. At this writing, a definitive publication is still to come.

38. W. F. Albright, "Some Oriental Glosses on the Homeric Problem," *American Journal of Archaeology*, LIV (1950), pp. 162–76.

39. Cf. Alan H. Gardiner, *The Wilbour Papyrus II. Commentary* (London, 1948), p. 80.

40. Cf. Dows Dunham and M. F. L. Macadam, in *Journal of Egyptian Archaeology*, XXXV (1949), pp. 139–49.

41. M. F. L. Macadam, *The Temples of Kawa. I. The Inscriptions*, 2 vols. (Oxford University Press, 1949).

42. T. Eric Peet, *The Rhind Mathematical Papyrus* (Liverpool, 1923); V. V. Struve, *Mathematischer Papyrus des Staatlichen Museums der Schönen Kunste in Moskau* (Berlin, 1930); James H. Breasted, *The Edwin Smith Surgical Papyrus*, 2 vols. (Chicago, 1930).

43. See Helene J. Kantor's contribution to R. W. Ehrich, *Relative Chronologies in Old World Archeology* (Chicago, 1954).

44. Richard A. Parker, *The Calendars of ancient Egypt* (Chicago, 1950).

45. A. Lucas, *Ancient Egyptian Materials and Industries*, 3rd ed. (London, 1948); Somers Clarke and R. Engelbach, *Ancient Egyptian Masonry, The Building Craft* (London, 1930); R. Engelbach, *Introduction to Egyptian Archaeology with special Reference to the Egyptian Museum, Cairo* (Cairo, 1946); and Jacques Vandier, *Manuel d'archéologie égyptienne*, 2 vols. (Paris, 1952–55).

46. E.g., Arpag Mekhitarian, *Egyptian Painting* (Skira, New York, 1954); Albert Champdor, ed., *La peinture égyptienne ancienne, peintures choisies, copiées et décrites par Nina M. Davies, avec la collaboration de Alan H. Gardiner*, 5 vols. (Guillot, Paris, 1953–54).

47. H. Schäfer, *Von ägyptischer Kunst* (Leipzig, 1919; 3rd ed., 1930).

48. W. S. Smith, *A History of Egyptian Sculpture and Painting in the Old Kingdom* (New York, Toronto, London, 2nd ed., 1949).

49. H. A. Groenewegen Frankfort, *Arrest and Movement. An Essay on Space and Time in the Representational Art of the ancient Near East* (Chicago, 1951).

50. The Epigraphic Expedition, *Medinet Habu*, i–iv (1939–40); *Reliefs and Inscriptions at Karnak*, i–iii (1936–55); Harold H. Nelson, *Key Plans Showing Locations of Theban Temple Decorations* (1941); all University of Chicago Press.

51. Nina M. Davies and Alan H. Gardiner, *Ancient Egyptian Paintings*, 2 vols. containing 104 plates, 1 vol. of text (Chicago, 1936).

52. Cf. my chapter in *Authority and Law in the Ancient Orient* (Supplement No. 17 to the *JAOS*, July-Sept., 1954, pp. 1–7).

53. His chapter in *The Legacy of Egypt*, edited by S. R. K. Glanville (London, 1942); A. Scharff und E. Seidl, *Einführung in die ägyptische Rechtsgeschichte bis zum Ende des neuen Reiches*, i (*Aegyptologische Forschungen*, Heft 10; Glückstadt, 1939).

54. H. Kees, *Beiträge zur altägyptischen Provinzialverwaltung und der Geschichte des Feudalismus* (Göttingen Nachrichten, 1932–33); *Herihor und die Aufrichtung des thebanischen Gottesstaates* (Göttingen Nachrichten, 1936); *Das Priestertum im ägyptischen Staat vom Neuen Reich bis zur Spätzeit* (Leyden, 1953).

55. Most recently studied by W. F. Edgerton in *JNES* vi (1947), pp. 219–30.

56. Cf. William C. Hayes, in *Journal of Egyptian Archaeology*, xxxii (1946), pp. 3–23.

57. *Ancient Near Eastern Texts*, op. cit., 199–203.

58. *The Wilbour Papyrus*, edited by Alan H. Gardiner, 3 vols. (London, 1948), conclusions in Vol. ii. *Commentary*, pp. 197–210.

59. Adolf Erman, *Die Religion der Aegypter. Ihr Werden und Vergehen in vier Jahrtausenden* (Berlin und Leipzig, 1934).

60. James H. Breasted, *The Dawn of Conscience* (New York, 1933), p. 401.

61. H. and H. A. Frankfort, John A. Wilson, Thorkild Jacobsen, and William A. Irwin, *The Intellectual Adventure of Ancient Man* (University of Chicago Press, 1946); abridged, by the elimination of the chapters on the Hebrews, as *Before Philosophy* (Penguin Books, 1949).

62. Henri Frankfort, *Kingship and the Gods* (Chicago, 1948).

63. Henri Frankfort, *Ancient Egyptian Religion, An Interpretation* (New York, 1948).

64. E.g., Jacques Vandier, *La religion égyptienne* ("Mana." *Introduction à l'histoire des religions*, 1, i; 2nd ed., Paris, 1949); Jaroslav Černý, *Ancient Egyptian Religion* (London, 1952).

65. Kurt Sethe, *Urgeschichte und älteste Religion der Aegypter* (Leipzig, 1930).

66. See Frankfort's remarks in *Kingship*, op. cit., p. 349, and the literature he cites there.

67. His *Uebersetzung und Kommentar zu den altägyptischen Pyramidentexten*, 4 vols. (Glückstadt, 1935–39), covers a little more than half of the then published texts.

68. In S. A. B. Mercer, *The Pyramid Texts*, 4 vols. (New York, 1952).

69. Adriaan de Buck, *The Egyptian Coffin Texts* i–v (Chicago, 1935–54).

70. "The Earliest Version of Book of the Dead 78," *Journal of Egyptian Archaeology*, xxxv (1949), pp. 87–97.

71. Alan H. Gardiner and Kurt Sethe, *Egyptian Letters to the Dead Mainly from the Old and Middle Kingdoms* (London, 1928).

72. Alan H. Gardiner, *The Attitude of the Ancient Egyptians to Death and the Dead* (Cambridge, 1935).

73. Kurt Sethe, *Dramatische Texte zu altägyptischen Mysterienspielen* (*Untersuchungen zur Geschichte und Altertumskunde Aegyptens*, Bd. 10; Leipzig, 1928).

74. Cf. also B. H. Stricker, "The Origin of the Greek Theatre," *Journal of Egyptian Archaeology*, xli (1955), pp. 34–47.

75. *Hieratic Papyri in the British Museum. Third Series. Chester Beatty Gift,* edited by Alan H. Gardiner (London, 1935), Vol. I. *Text,* pp. 79–106; Harold H. Nelson, *JNES* VIII (1949), pp. 201–32, 310–45.

76. A. M. Blackman, *Journal of Egyptian Archaeology,* XI (1925), pp. 249–55; XII (1926), pp. 176–85; XXVII (1941), pp. 83–95; W. R. Dawson, ibid., XI (1925), pp. 247–48; A. H. Gardiner, ibid., XIX (1933), pp. 19–30; XXXII (1946), p. 55; J. Černý, in *Bulletin de l'Institut Français d'Archéologie Orientale,* XXX (1930), pp. 491–96; XXXV (1935), pp. 41–58; XL (1941), pp. 135–41; C. F. Nims, *JNES* XII (1948), pp. 157–62.

77. Alan H. Gardiner, *The Library of A. Chester Beatty. Description of a Hieratic Papyrus with a Mythological Story, Love-Songs, and other Miscellaneous Texts* (London, 1931); *Hieratic Papyri in the British Museum. Third Series. Chester Beatty Gift,* edited by A. H. Gardiner, 2 vols. (London, 1935).

78. A. de Buck, "De godsdienstige Opvatting van den Slaap inzonderheid in het oude Egypte," *Ex Oriente Lux,* No. 4, 1939.

79. *Hieratic Papyri in the British Museum,* op. cit., p. 36.

CHAPTER THIRTEEN

Hittite and

Anatolian Studies

ALBRECHT GOETZE

DURING THE LAST TWO DECADES our knowledge of ancient Anatolia has vastly increased.[1] Not only have the foreign nations, to whom early research owed so much,[2] continued their endeavors,[3] still more important is the fact that the Turks themselves have become highly conscious of their national past[4] and are contributing vigorously to the further elucidation of the early Anatolian civilizations.[5]

The archaeological exploration of the country is far advanced, and we can today draw an archaeological map of large parts of the peninsula. After a beginning—unfortunately as good as unpublished—by E. O. Forrer in the twenties and thirties,[6] the task has been resumed on a comprehensive scale by Şevket Aziz Kansu and I. Kiliç Kökten on the one hand[7] and by the British Institute of Archaeology at Ankara on the other.[8] All periods profit by these undertakings.

For the sake of convenience the Anatolian past up to the Greek colonization can be divided into the following main parts:

1. *Palaeolithicum*
2. *Chalcolithicum and Early Bronze Age*
3. *The Hittite Periods (Middle and Late Bronze Age)*
4. *The post-Hittite Period (Early Iron Age)*

Each period presents its special problems which, in the light of new discoveries, must be reconsidered again and again.

1. PALAEOLITHICUM

The last comprehensive surveys of the present stage of our knowledge are those by M. Pfannenstiel, *Die altsteinzeitlichen Kulturen Anatoliens*

(*Istanbuler Forschungen* 15, 1941), by K. Bittel in *Grundzüge* . . . (see n. 1; 2nd ed. [1950], pp. 11–15), and by A. Goetze in *Kleinasien* (see n. 1; 2nd ed. [1957], pp. 13–17). The picture, still spotty, has been filled in considerably. The most important undertaking is Kiliç Kökten's research in the Karain cave near Antalya;[9] it began in 1946 and has been continued ever since. Its significance rests on the stratification which it has revealed. After some remnants of the Early Bronze Age, the Chalcolithicum and the Neolithicum (Level I), it furnishes no less than seven Palaeolithic levels (II–VIII), the oldest of which rests on the original floor of the cave. The classical sequence of the west is roughly repeated. Level II can be described as Aurignacian and Level III as Mousterian. Level IV is similar to the Acheulean in its Levalloisian variant, but by no means identical with it. Kökten thinks now in terms of a special and characteristically Anatolian form of the Lower Palaeolithic Age. The climate was then in part tropical. Level V is sterile, but VI gives us an early Anatolian blade culture, the beginnings of which can be seen in the finds from VII. The lowest Level VIII reveals a still older culture with small blades. The Karain cave will no doubt become basic for Palaeolithic research in Anatolia. Only the discovery of additional caves in other parts of the country can show to what extent the results already obtained are valid for the peninsula as a whole.

Caves near the Mediterranean in the southern foothills of Musa-Dağ (Vil. Hatay) likewise reveal finds from the Aurignacian superimposed on those from the Levalloiso-Mousterian.[10]

2. CHALCOLITHICUM AND EARLY BRONZE AGE

Until recently the Chalcolithic period, richly documented in Cilicia[11] and adequately represented on the central plateau,[12] was missing in the vast western part of Turkey. Only in the extreme northwestern corner, in the vicinity of Troy, a few early sites could be quoted.[13] To them, Fikirtepe, in the village of Kadiköy across the Bosporus from Istanbul, has recently been added.[14] Together with Erenköy and Pendik, both on the north shore of the Gulf of Izmit, it exemplifies an early pre-Troy civilization of still unknown connections. On the south shore Menteşe is another station of this civilization.[15]

The apparent lack of Chalcolithic finds in southwestern Anatolia resulted in theories like those advanced by F. Schachermeyr, purporting that the earliest civilization of Thessaly, that of the Neolithic Sesklo, be related to the "Halaf" civilization of which Mersin in Cilicia is the westernmost outpost.[16] Today, there are increasing indications that the southwestern part of Turkey and Pisidia as well as the Konya plain will eventually furnish Chalcolithic remains. Even painted pottery exists there.[17] Excavations penetrating into deep layers, if possible to the virgin soil, are badly needed in all these areas. Before the sequence which the numerous mounds will eventually provide is firmly established, it is better to abstain from speculations.

The Early Bronze Age is relatively well known already.[18] In Cilicia it is best attested in Tarsus[19]—in Mersin the stratification is disturbed at the transition from the Chalcolithic to the Early Bronze Age[20]—on the plateau it is dramatically revealed by Alaca Hüyük and its royal tombs,[21] and less dramatically by Alişar I.[22] In the northwest this is the great time of Troy II and its successors, Troy III–V.[23] We now possess it also in the southwest, thanks to the work of the British Institute at Beycesultan near Denizli in the valley of the upper Maeander.[24] Discoveries of the Early Bronze Age were made there in 1955 and 1956 and have brought significant results. To this age belong the levels from VII on downward to XV; examples of red-cross bowls and of depata show this convincingly. There is a break in the development between XIII and XII; the older layers yield an inventory that resembles that from farther south. In other words, starting out from the foundations laid at the beginning of the Early Bronze Age and exemplified by Kusura[25] and the finds from Pisidia,[26] the western reaches of Anatolia develop along separate lines; only later on, in the Hittite period, a new convergence can be observed.

3. THE HITTITE PERIOD

The definition of the term "Hittite" still proves to be controversial;[27] trouble exists on both ends of the scale. Everybody agrees that the great Hittite Empire, old (period of Hattušiliš and of Muršiliš, the conqueror of Babylon) and new (dynasty of Šuppiluliumaš), must be included. But the question is: how far can we go back into the past, and must the late "Hittites" of Malatya and of northern Syria also be included? Even the pre-Boğazköy definition of the term[28] has been revived, particularly when applied to art. It states that "Hittite" art is not the art of a certain people, called the Hittites, but belongs to that vast cultural complex which is an integral part of the geographical unit comprising the Persian province of Luristan, Upper Mesopotamia, Armenia, Central Anatolia, and North Syria.[29] Let us assume for the sake of the argument that the civilization, and hence also the art, of all these areas form indeed a unit; then it must be said that in any case the term "Hittite," applied to it, is a misnomer. It is, in my opinion, an illegitimate procedure to extend an historical term from the periphery of the area, of which we have learned more or less by chance, to the heterogeneous whole. Moreover, the assumption of such a unit is a mere stopgap device. Today, our knowledge of history, both political and cultural, is quite sufficient to show that such a unit never existed.

Boğazköy has taught us to distinguish between Ḫattic and Hittite. Quite true, had we known about Ḫattic when Hittite, the language in which the records of the Hittite Empire has come down to us, was discovered and deciphered, we would probably have created a different terminology. As it is, we have to live with that terminology, and, historically speaking, it has everything to recommend it. Changing it at this late stage can result only in utter confusion. There is hardly any doubt that in the realm of archaeology the Early Bronze finds from Alaca must be paralleled with the Ḫattic past of Anatolia and called Ḫattic. This includes in particular the tombs of Early Anatolian princes excavated there. Hence the term "Hittite" must not be applied to them.

Alaca Hüyük ended in a catastrophe, and this catastrophe has left its mark wherever excavations have been conducted. It is this break, ushering in the Middle Bronze Age, with which the Hittite period begins.[30] Much as it took over from the preceding period—in fact, it is so much that the ethnic change would hardly be recognizable to the archaeologist—nevertheless, the texts which fortunately begin to become available at this point—first in Kültepe and then in Boğazköy—teach us that the Hittites, or at least close relatives of the Hittites, were present in Anatolia at the beginning of the Middle Bronze Age.[31]

The development runs more or less uninterruptedly through Middle and Late Bronze. The next caesura comes with the beginning of the Early Iron Age, around 1200 B.C. We know from written sources, as well as from archaeological evidence, that at that time a new catastrophe fell upon the Near East, and that in this catastrophe the Hittite Empire which centered in Ḫattuša (Boğazköy) came to an end. Hittite tradition survived only farther east, in the region around Malatya and south of the Taurus ranges in northern Syria. This territory in which the Assyrians since Aššur-uballiṭ had intermittently clashed with the Hittites and which was gradually absorbed into the Assyrian Empire continued to be known as Ḫatti land. But there is little that connects this period with the past empire.[32] Its civilization, still little known, must be seen in a Syrian context. The century which had tied these states politically to Anatolia had been far too short to obscure this basic connection. Its art, the link most striking to the casual investigator, derives from Mesopotamian roots and springs from the same source that had also inspired the art of the great kings of the empire, perhaps newcomers from farther south.[33] Its script is different; it uses the hieroglyphs commonly called "Hittite" (occasionally employed also in Anatolia by the Šuppiluliumaš dynasty). The language behind this script is not Hittite but a related language akin to (or more or less identical with) Luwian, the tongue spoken during the empire in southern Asia Minor. And the Phoenician-Aramaic infiltration at the beginning of the first millennium could only serve to restrengthen the Syrian ties, so prominent with the late "Hittites" from the beginning. Hence the term "Hittite" should not be used for these states, at least not without the absolutely necessary qualifications. It should be reserved for Anatolia from about 2000 to 1200 B.C.

Thanks to the excavations at Kaniš (Kültepe), directed by Tahsin and Nimet Özgüç,[34] we know quite a good deal about the beginnings of the Hittite period. The site outside the town proper where the Assyrian merchants resided, the so-called Kārum Kaniš, furnishes four levels before virgin soil is reached. What may be called the classical period—the one that yields the Old Assyrian tablets of the period of Šarrumkēn of Assur[35]—is the second of them. The tablets provide us with the earliest historical date in ancient Anatolia. Below it are two more levels, the lowest one (IV) containing the painted ware known as "Cappadocian," which in Ališar comes between the Early Bronze wares (Ališar I) and the Hittite ones (Ališar II).

Of great importance is the refinement of Kültepe chronology, which we owe to the diligence of Kemal Balkan.[36] He was able to isolate among the many thousands of tablets a younger group which must be assigned to I b and chronologically to the reign of Šamši-Adad of Assur. It is significant that to this younger group of texts belong the tablets from both Ališar and Boğazköy. This group of tablets testifies to a resumption of the Assyrian trade in Anatolia after the Assyrians had overcome the effects of a dynastic change. The observation also affects Anatolian chronology in so far as it requires a somewhat younger date for the respective layers at these sites.[37]

The work of the Özgüç's on the city mound of Kaniš is about to tie in the Kārum with the over-all picture at the other end. Early in 1956 the situation was essentially as follows (proceeding from the younger to the earlier):

0: The palace (temple?) excavated by Hrozný (with remains of sculptured orthostats).[38]

I: The Hittite "megaron."[39]

II: Underneath it the building in which the dagger of Anitta was found.[40] Roughly contemporaneous is the building in which the tablets of 1955 were discovered,[41] the most important one a letter of Anum-Ḫirbi, king of Mama, to Waršama, son of Inar, king of Kaniš.[42]

III: Little known so far.[43]

IV: = Kārum Kaniš IV.

V: Containing Cappadocian pottery.

VI: Containing Cappadocian and "intermediate" ware.

VII: Containing Ališar I b ware (including depata).

It is clear that with VII we are in the Early Bronze Age; Level II is contemporaneous with Kārum Kaniš I b, which in terms of Mesopotamian chronology means with the time of Šamši-Adad of Assur (Mari Age).[44] Level I, and what is above it, brings us into the Hittite period.

The other site of paramount importance for Hittite archaeology and Hittite early history is Boğazköy, where K. Bittel resumed in 1952 his yearly campaigns for the German Archaeological Institute and the Deutsche Orient-Gesellschaft.[45] He has by now completely cleared the Büyükkale (acropolis) and begun important research in the "Unterstadt" where deeper layers are being opened up.

The chief result consists in establishing an archaeological chronology which makes it now possible to subdivide the Old Hittite layers antedating the Hittite Empire (Šuppiluliumaš dynasty, beginning *ca.* 1500 B.C.).[46] The stratification is as follows:

iva: Period of rather poor building. Pottery: "Hittite," the forms are those that dominate in Level III of the Büyükkale. Pieces of a large animal figure; a "Hittite" relief in secondary use.[47]

ivb: Large-scale architecture; fortifications. Pottery: "Hittite," like iva and different only by degrees from that of ivc.[48]

THICK LAYER OF ASHES

ivc: Monumental buildings several times repaired and renovated. Pottery: like Kārum Kaniš I; examples of "Wellen-Keramik."[49]

DESTRUCTION

ivd: Houses with small rooms. Pottery: "Early Hittite" corresponding with Boğazköy "Unterstadt" and Kültepe Kārum Kaniš II; little Ališar IIIb ("Cappadocian" painted), also some Ališar I b (Early Bronze).[50]

With ivd the link-up with the late layer of the Assyrian colonies is reached. The Cappadocian tablets excavated in Boğazköy—one (Bo 30/a) on Büyükkale immediately upon the rock, most of them in the "Unterstadt" —all prove to belong to the Kārum Kaniš I b variety (time of Šamši-Adad of Assur).[51]

In terms of Mesopotamian history the sublevels of iv bridge archaeologically the period from Šarrumkēn (= Sargon I) of Assur to the beginning of the Amarna Age.

More specifically the following historical interpretation seems to me necessary:

iva: End of the Hittite "Middle Kingdom."
ivb: From Telepinuš to Zidantaš II.
ivc: From Anittaš to Ḫantiliš.
ivd: Final phase of the Assyrian colonies.

I do not assign here to these sublevels specific dates. This would necessitate a discussion of the chronological problem which is beyond the scope of this paper.[52]

4. THE POST-HITTITE PERIOD

1. The West: With the violent end of the Hittite Empire about 1200 B.C., our historical sources cease, and a dark period begins about which we are ill informed. As far as the west is concerned, it is usually called "Phrygian." But the legitimacy of this term has rightly been doubted.[53] The presence of Phrygians (in the linguistic sense of the term) is primarily attested in the west of Anatolia and even there not before the eighth century. On the other hand, the painted pottery termed "Phrygian" is a phenomenon at home east of the Halys; it extends far toward the east, e.g. Malatya, into territory to which Phrygians never penetrated.

The "Phrygian" painted ware has been extensively studied by Ekrem Akurgal in his *Phrygische Kunst.*[54] Measuring it on Greek geometric art, he reaches the conclusion that there is no Phrygian ware before 800 B.C. He states that we therefore cannot know anything about the cultural development in Anatolia between 1200 B.C. and 800 B.C. However, one might question the justification of Akurgal's procedure and, at any rate, his results are hardly reconcilable with the evidence obtained by the excavations at Boğazköy and at Alişar.

The early Phrygian style of vase painting, characterized in particular by silhouettes of animals, especially stags,[55] is well represented in Boğazköy Büyükkale II, the layer that overlies the ruins of the Hittite Empire. To be sure, there is a hiatus between the great catastrophe and the re-establishment of local rulers in this Anatolian center. But the new buildings avail themselves in many cases of the foundations of the old, and Bittel, the excavator, allows only a moderate time lag.[56] Hence, four hundred years of abandonment is certainly too much. Placing the end of the Level II in the seventh century,[57] Bittel lets it begin at the end of the second millennium. In the meantime, new discoveries have been made on Büyükkaya (Boğazköy). Here a brown ware with simple geometric ornaments has come to light which stratigraphically, as well as typologically, marks the beginning of the "Phrygian" series.[58] This is one more reason to make the gap between the end of the empire and the resettlement of the capital not too long.

When the citadel of Alişar was rebuilt in Level 4c M, use was likewise made of the Hittite foundations.[59] The early Phrygian ware with stag design, etc., is here associated with button seals inscribed with Hittite hieroglyphs, and impressions of such seals.[60] Their date should lie before *ca.* 700 at the latest,[61] shortly after the date at which Akurgal allows this ware to begin. According to Bittel, Level 4c M covers "about" the "11th–9th centuries."[62]

I conclude that there is every reason to believe that the early Phrygian ware existed, or at least began to exist, around 1000 B.C.

2. The Southeast: In the southeast, Hittite political traditions survived. North of the Taurus, Malatya, and, south of the mountains, the region of

Mar'ash and particularly the town of Kargamish are important centers. Malatya[63] was for Tiglath-Pileser I (*ca.* 1100 B.C.) the capital of the "great Hatti land"; Kargamish[64] was considered by the Assyrians as the most important city of the Hittites before its conquest in 717 B.C.

But it would be rash to see, on the basis of the continuity in terminology, in these late "Hittites" the descendants of the Hittites of the empire, as has been done much too frequently. They are in many respects quite different, as has already been remarked. It is to this period that most of the monuments belong, which, since Wright and Sayce, have been called "Hittite," but which we gradually have learned to distinguish from the monuments of the empire. With the monuments go inscriptions in a hieroglyphic script likewise called "Hittite." This script, long one of the riddles of the ancient Near East, can now be read. Decipherment[65] was well on its way when H. Th. Bossert discovered bilingual inscriptions (Phoenician and "Hittite") at Karatepe.[66] In the meantime in Ras Shamra bilingual seals have been discovered[67] which give us further aid. Thus we are provided with a new and broader basis for the interpretation of all hieroglyphic inscriptions. In consequence one can now judge their language with greater confidence. It proves to be related to, if not identical with, Luwian, a language spoken in the south of Asia Minor and also represented among the clay tablets from Boğazköy.[68]

Hence one must assume that Luwians—the people from which local rulers like Kantuzili, Lubarna, Mutalli, Sapalulmi stem—had penetrated the regions concerned and became there the ruling class. This most likely happened during the upheaval around 1200 B.C.,[69] although it may have had antecedents.

The history and the civilization of these late "Hittites" (or rather Luwians) will become known as soon as their inscriptions are available in a final reading and interpretation. It is clear already that in the Taurus and south of it these Anatolians had entered a decidedly Syrian milieu which makes it imperative to deal with them in conjunction with the complicated history of that area.

Great as the advances of Anatolian research have been in recent years, there remains much to be done. The main periods: Early Bronze Age, Hittite period, Early Iron Age begin to stand out more or less clearly before our eyes. The problems rather lie at the points where they join. No doubt future research will concentrate on these obscure spots.

For the East one may expect further results from continued work in Kültepe and in the deeper layers of the "Unterstadt" of Boğazköy. It also is desirable to investigate the post-Hittite levels at a site south of the Taurus where Hittite tradition survived the break of 1200 B.C., preferably in Kargamish. The West is still badly known. Beycesultan has yielded important results, but the hope of finding written documents has not been realized; the search must continue elsewhere. In Gordion deeper layers might profitably be opened up.[70] And the host of problems presented by the northwest should be attacked at a fresh site. Sardis has now been reopened and activities there will expand in the years to come. Let us hope that the next *Festschrift* dedicated to the scholar we honor today can report on the results of such future undertakings. They will certainly solve some old problems, but no doubt pose as many new ones.

[*First submitted Jan. 1957; brought up-to-date Sept. 1958. Later revision proved impossible.*]

NOTES TO CHAPTER THIRTEEN

1. The latest comprehensive presentations are the following: A Goetze, *Kleinasien* (*Kulturgeschichte des Alten Orients* in *Handbuch der Altertumswissenschaft* III 1, e, 1933), zweite neubearbeitete Auflage, 1957; K. Bittel, *Grundzüge der Vor- und Frühgeschichte Kleinasiens*, 1945, 2nd ed., 1950; H. Th. Bossert, *Altanatolien, Kunst und Handwerk in Kleinasien von den Anfängen bis zum völligen Aufgehen in der griechischen Kultur*, 1942 (important because of the vast store of illustrations it contains); S. Lloyd, *Early Anatolia. The Archaeology of Asia Minor before the Greeks* (Pelican Books, 1956) (discusses the various sites and the results there obtained). The numerous popular accounts can here remain unmentioned.
2. The Germans at Troy, Zencirli, and Boğazköy; the British at Kusura, Mersin, and Kargamish; the French in Malatya and in Phrygia; the Americans in Alişar, Troy, Tarsus, and Gordion.
3. Main current undertakings: Boğazköy (German), Beycesultan (British), Gordion (American).
4. Much of the work is organized and sponsored by the Türk Tarih Kurumu (Turkish Historical Society)—in the following abbreviated TTK—which has been endowed under the will of Kemal Atatürk, the founder of modern Turkey. The Society also sees to it that the results of the research are made known either through its *Belleten* (since 1937) or through its series of publications (*Türk Tarih Kurumu Yayinlari*).
5. See also the general reports on "Archaeology in Asia Minor" by M. J. Mellink in *AJA* 59 (1955), pp. 231–40; 60 (1956), pp. 369–84; 61 (1957), pp. 91–104.
6. See *MDOG* 65 (1926), pp. 27–43; furthermore, the map added by the same author to his article on Arzawa in *Klio* 30 (1937), pp. 135–86.
7. The latest articles by I. Kiliç Kökten known to me are found in *DTCF Derg.* 10 (1952), pp. 167–207, and 11 (1953), pp. 177–209; they contain detailed bibliographies and are illustrated by maps. See also the map presented to the 4th Turkish Historical Congress (Nov. 1948) repeated in *Orientalia*, NS 18 (1949), Pl. 36; compare l.c. pp. 364 ff.
8. M. V. Seton-Williams, "Cilician Survey," *Anat. Stud.* 4 (1954), pp. 121–74; J. Mellaart, "Preliminary Report on a Survey of Preclassical Remains in Southern Turkey," ibid., pp. 175–240; "Iron Age Pottery from Southern Anatolia," *TTK Bell.* 19 (1955), pp. 115–36; "Some Pre-historic Sites in North-Western Anatolia," in *Istanbuler Mitteilungen* 6 (1955), pp. 53–88; C. A. Burney, "Northern Anatolia before Classical Times," *Anat. Stud.* 6 (1956), pp. 179–203. Cf. also W. Lamb, "The Culture of North-East Anatolia and its Neighbours," *Anat. Stud.* 4 (1954), pp. 21–32.

9. A summary has been presented by I. Kiliç Kökten in *TTK Bell.* 19 (1955), pp. 271–93 (Turkish and German).

10. M. Şenyürek and E. Bostanci, *Anatolia* I (1956), pp. 81–83; *TTK Bell.* 86 (1958), pp. 158 f., 205–7 (not seen by me); M. Şenyürek, *Anatolia* 3 (1958), pp. 64–70; *TTK Bell.* 87 (1958) (not seen by me).

11. Mersin: J. Garstang, *Prehistoric Mersin* (1953), pp. 45–180; Tarsus: H. Goldman, *Excavations at Gözlü Kule, Tarsus* II (1956), pp. 5–8, 72–91.

12. Alişar: H. H. von der Osten, *Oriental Institute Publications,* Vol. XXVIII (1937), pp. 28–109; Büyük Güllücek: Hamit Z. Koşay and Mahmut Akok, *TTK Bell.* 12 (1948), pp. 479–85; Alaca Höyük: Hamit Z. Koşay, *Alaca Höyük Hafriyati* (= *TTK Yayinlarindan* V/2, 1938, German edition 1940), Level IV.

13. Beşik Tepe: H. Schliemann, *Ilios* (1881), pp. 739–44; W. Lamb, *Prähistorische Zeitschrift* 23 (1932), pp. 124–29; Kumtepe: Hamit Koşay and Jerome Sperling, *Troad'da dört Yerleşme Yeri* (1936), pp. 24–52.

14. Excavations by K. Bittel and Halet Çambel on behalf of the TTK (unpublished).

15. J. Mellaart, *Istanbuler Mitteilungen* 6 (1955), p. 56.

16. *Nouvelle Clio* 1–2 (1949/50), pp. 567–601. See also F. Schachermeyr, *Die ältesten Kulturen Griechenlands* (1955), pp. 51 ff. Cf. now A. Perkins and S. S. Weinberg, *AJA* 62 (1958), p. 225.

17. J. Mellaart, *Anat. Stud.* 4 (1954), pp. 179 ff. If Schachermeyr's thesis is to be substantiated, comparisons of Sesklo forms and wares would have to be made with this early pottery.

18. For a comprehensive comparative treatment see J. Mellaart, "Anatolian Chronology in the Early and Middle Bronze Age," *Anat. Stud.* 7 (1957), pp. 55–88.

19. H. Goldman, *Excavations at Gözlü Kule, Tarsus* II (1956), pp. 9–39, 92–163.

20. J. Garstang, *Mersin* (1953), p. 192.

21. Remzi Oğuz Arik, *Les fouilles d'Alaca Höyük* (*TTK Yayinlarindan* V/1, 1937); Hamit Z. Koşay, *Alaca Höyük Hafriyati* (ibid. V/2, 1938); *Alaca Höyük Kazisi 1937–39* (ibid. V/5, 1951). See also M. J. Mellink in *The Aegean and the Near East, Studies presented to Hetty Goldman* (1956), pp. 39–58. For related finds see T. Özgüç and M. Akok, *TTK Bell.* 82 (1957), pp. 201–9, 211–19.

22. H. H. von der Osten, op. cit. (n. 12), pp. 110–207.

23. Troy II: C. Blegen (et al.), *Troy I* (1950), pp. 201–378; Troy II–V: C. Blegen (et al.), *Troy II* (1951).

24. Seton Lloyd and J. Mellaart, *Anat. Stud.* 5 (1955), pp. 39–92; 6 (1956), pp. 101–35; 7 (1957), pp. 27–36; cf. also 7 (1957), p. 74.

25. W. Lamb, "Excavations at Kusura near Afyon Karahisar," *Archaeologia* 86 (1937), pp. 1–64; 87 (1938), pp. 217–73.

26. H. A. Ormerod, *Annual of the British School at Athens* 18 (1911/12), pp. 80–94; K. Bittel, *Kleinasiatische Studien* (1942), pp. 176–86; J. Mellaart, *Anat. Stud.* 4 (1954), p. 192, Map 3.

27. See most recently H. G. Güterbock, *Oriens* 10 (1957), pp. 233–39.

28. It was propagated especially by E. Herzfeld; see his article "Der Tell Halaf und das Problem der Hethitischen Kunst," *Archaeologische Mitteilungen aus Iran* VI 3/4 (1934), pp. 111–223.

29. M. Vieyra, *Hittite Art* (1955), p. 15.

30. The article by J. Mellaart, "The End of the Early Bronze Age in Anatolia and the Aegean," *AJA* 62 (1958), pp. 9–33, is a daring and imaginative attempt at correlating archaeological results and history. I feel it is a little premature. I still see no real evidence for the Hittites coming across the Caucasus (quite some feat!) and cutting a destructive swath from Karaz to Central Anatolia with repercussions far beyond.

31. Compare K. Bittel, *Historia* I (1950), pp. 267–86; M. Mellink, *A Hittite Cemetery at Gordion* (1956), 52 f.

32. It is the basic fault of the book of M. Riemschneider, *Die Welt der Hethiter* (1954), that it does not differentiate between the Hittites of the empire and the "Hittites" of the late period. The author even goes one step further and, reversing the orthodox point of view, makes the late "Hittites" the real Hittites. With C. W. Ceram, Enge Schlucht and Schwarzer Berg (1955) the identification is naïve, but with Riemschneider it is conviction. Cf. A. Goetze, *Gnomon* (1957), pp. 301–4.

33. The monuments and the hieroglyphic inscriptions on the high plateau begin with the dynasty of Šuppiluliumaš. It is quite possible that the *interpretatio hurritica* of the divine world, as exemplified in Yazilikaya, is due to this dynasty. On the Hurrians in the Hittite Empire cf. most recently H. G. Güterbock in *Journal of World History* 2 (1954), pp. 383–94.

34. Tahsin Özgüç, "Kültepe Kazisi Raporu 1948," *TTK Yayinlarindan* v/10 (1950); Tahsin and Nimet Özgüç, "Kültepe Kazisi Raporu 1949," ibid. v/12 (1953); in addition current reports in *TTK Belleten*.

35. Since the bibliography presented in *Kleinasien*, pp. 67 f., was completed, a new volume of "Cappadocian" texts has been added: Sidney Smith and D. J. Wiseman, *Cuneiform Texts from Cappadocian Tablets in the British Museum* v (1956), for which the abbreviation is CCT v. Indices listing the personal names, the place names, etc., contained in this volume were given by K. Deller, *Orientalia* 27 (1958), pp. 184–98.

36. Kemal Balkan, "Observations on the Chronological Problems of the Kārum Kaniš," *TTK Yayinlarindan* VII/28 (1955). The views there expressed were subjected to a rather sharp attack by Julius Lewy, *Orientalia* 26 (1957), pp. 12–36. Lewy admits the existence of late tablets (Kārum I b); he maintains, however, that neither the Ališar tablets nor those from Boğazköy are later than the large majority of the tablets from Kārum Kaniš II. Lewy's views were rejected by H. Otten, *MDOG* 89 (Juni 1957), pp. 68–79, and thereby his criticisms shown to be unjustified.

37. Anittaš and his conquests, as related in the famous text (newest translation by H. Otten in *MDOG* 83, 1951, pp. 40 ff.), would fall after Šamši-Adad of Assur whose empire disintegrated after his death. The gap between Anittaš and Labarnaš, the founder of the old Hittite Empire, thereby grows rather narrow. Labarnaš, Hattušiliš I, and Muršiliš I fill the first half of the 17th century and probably more.

38. B. Hrozný, *Syria* 8 (1927), pp. 1–12.

39. Tahsin Özgüç, *TTK Bell.* 77 (1956), p. 33; *Anat. Stud.* 4 (1954), p. 19.

40. Tahsin Özgüç, *TTK Bell.* 77 (1956); *Anat. Stud.* 5 (1955), p. 19. For the dagger see Tahsin Özgüç, *TTK Bell.* 77 (1956), pp. 33–36, and Kemal Balkan, *Observations on the Chronological Problems of the Kārum Kaniš* (1955), pp. 78 f.

41. Tahsin Özgüç, *Anat. Stud.* 6 (1950), p. 25.

42. Kemal Balkan, "Letter of King Anum-Hirbi of Mama to King Warshama of Kanish," *TTK Yayinlarindan* VII Seri, No. 31a (1957).

43. What follows is based on information with which the excavator, Professor Tahsin Özgüç, graciously furnished me during my visit in July 1956. Since then, work has continued on the city mound as well as in the Kārum.

44. As was shown by Kemal Balkan. For the whole sequence, compare also J. Mellaart, *Anat. Stud.* 7 (1957), p. 62 f.

45. Compare the preliminary reports in *MDOG* 86 (Dez. 1953), 87 (Feb. 1955), 88 (Juli 1955), and 89 (Juni 1957). See also K. Bittel, R. Naumann (and others), *Boğazköy* III. *Funde aus den Grabungen 1952–1955* (*Abh. der Deutschen Orient-Gesellschaft*, Nr. 2, 1957).

46. Bittel discussed with me these problems during my stay in Istanbul in July of 1956, and subsequently I was able to enjoy the hospitality of the expedition in Boğazköy itself. I wish to thank him publicly for all his kindnesses.

47. R. Naumann, *MDOG* 86 (1953), pp. 13 ff.; K. Bittel, *MDOG* 88 (1955), pp. 22 ff.

48. R. Naumann, *MDOG* 86 (1953), pp. 15–19; K. Bittel, *MDOG* 88 (1955), p. 22.

49. R. Naumann, *MDOG* 86 (1953), pp. 19 f.; K. Bittel, *MDOG* 88 (1955), pp. 20 ff.

50. R. Naumann, *MDOG* 86 (1953), p. 20; K. Bittel, *MDOG* 88 (1955), p. 20.

51. This identification is due to Kemal Balkan; he made it as soon as he was shown autographs of some of the earlier tablets (Leitperson *Da-a-a*). The texts have now been published by H. Otten in *Keilschrifttexte aus Boghazköi* (KBo) IX, pp. 1–41.

52. It is well known that Albright and myself adhere to different chronological systems. See most recently *Journal of Cuneiform Studies* 11 (1957), pp. 53–61, 63–78.

53. Particularly by K. Bittel; see his *Kleinasiatische Studien* (*Istanbuler Mitteilungen* 5, 1942), pp. 66 ff.; *Grundzüge der Vor- und Frühgeschichte Kleinasiens* (2nd. ed., 1950), pp. 82 ff.

54. *Ankara Üniversitesi, Dil ve Tarih Coğrafya Fakültesi Yayimlari*, No. 95, *Arkeoloji Enstitüsü*, No. 5, 1955.

55. E. Akurgal, l.c., pp. 1 ff.

56. K. Bittel, *Boğazköy* (*Abhandlungen der Preussischen Akademie der Wissenschaften* 1935, phil.-hist. Klasse 1) 25; *Grundzüge* . . . (2nd ed., 1950), p. 81: "mindestens ein Jahrhundert."

57. K. Bittel, ibid., p. 26.

58. K. Bittel, *MDOG* 86 (1953), p. 50; *MDOG* 88 (1955), p. 24.

59. *Oriental Institute Publications*, Vol. XXIX (1937), p. 287.

60. Ibid., pp. 414 ff.

61. H. Th. Bossert, *Die Welt des Orients* 1 (1952), pp. 480–84. In this argument I disregard the fact that in 4b M a sherd with incised hieroglyphs was found on the floor (*Oriental Institute Publications*, Vol. XXIX, Fig. 472).

62. K. Bittel, ibid., p. 339. The same author dates Level 4b M tentatively to the ninth or eighth century (p. 312), and Level 4a M still prior to the middle or the end of the sixth century B.C. (pp. 325, 339).

63. L. Delaporte, *Malatya* I (1940): *La Porte des Lions*.

64. C. L. Woolley (et al.), *Carchemish, Report on the Excavations at Djerabis on behalf of the British Museum* I (1914); II (1921); III (1952).

65. For details see J. Friedrich, *Entzifferungsgeschichte der hethitischen Hieroglyphenschrift* (1939); R. D. Barnett, "Karatepe, The Key to the Hittite Hieroglyphs," *Anat. Stud.* 3 (1953), pp. 53–95.

66. On the state of the publication see H. Th. Bossert, *TTK Bell.* 17 (1953), pp. 143–49; 18 (1954), pp. 27–34. Add H. Th. Bossert, *MNHMHS XAPIN Gedenkschrift für P. Kretschmer* (1956), pp. 40–57.

67. E. Laroche in C. F. A. Schaeffer, *Ugaritica* III (1956), pp. 97–160.

68. For literature see *Kleinasien* (1957), pp. 47 ff.

69. B. Landsberger, *Sam'al* (*Veröffentl. der Türkischen Hist. Gesellschaft* VII/16, 1948), pp. 12 ff.

70. Tests on the city mound have revealed the existence of archaeological layers belonging to the second millennium. For tombs see M. J. Mellink, *A Hittite Cemetery at Gordion* (University of Pennsylvania, Museum Monograph, 1956).

The Role of the Canaanites in the History of Civilization*

W. F. ALBRIGHT

AS OUR TITLE STANDS, it may seem rather restricted in scope, since the Canaanites are known to most people only as the unhappy precursors of Israel in Palestine. However, if we remember that the word "Canaanite" is historically, geographically, and culturally synonymous with "Phoenician,"[1] the title immediately becomes more impressive, since it also deals with the role of the Phoenicians in the history of civilization. For convenience we shall employ "Canaanite" below to designate the Northwest Semitic people and culture of western Syria and Palestine before the 12th century B.C. and the term "Phoenician" to indicate the same people and culture after this date.

First and last the Canaanites played a very important part in the history of civilization. In the third and second millennia they bridged the gap between Egypt and Mesopotamia and to them we undoubtedly owe much of the slow, but constant, transfusion of culture which we find in the ancient Near East. Across the Canaanite bridge went innumerable techniques and motifs, to say nothing of countless ideas and ways of expressing them. Through the conquest of Palestine by Israel and of Syria by the Aramaeans, these two peoples became in large measure the heirs of Canaanite culture. The subsequent history of Israel, with all its significance for the world, would have been very different without this initial Canaanite influence. Forced out of Palestine and most of Syria in the 13th and 12th centuries, the Phoenicians turned their energies seaward and became the greatest mariners and traders of all time, if we may relate their accomplishments to the extent of the known

---

* This paper is a revised edition of an article which originally appeared in *Studies in the History of Culture* (the Waldo H. Leland Volume), Menasha, Wis., the George Banta Publishing Company (1942), pp. 11–50. Copyright, 1942, Modern Language Association of America.

world. It is true that there has been a strong tendency in the last half century to belittle the classical traditions of early Phoenician expansion and influence on the Greeks. Just why the Hellenes should have been so eager to attribute their achievements in the arts of peace to the Phoenicians, unless the tradition was very strong, remains unclear. Recent discoveries, a number of which will be presented for the first time in this paper, prove that the reaction against classical tradition is not warranted by the facts, though the reaction against exaggerated modern deductions from classical tradition is indeed justified.

I. THE REDISCOVERY OF THE CANAANITES

In the late 16th and 17th centuries Phoenician coins and inscriptions began to be collected and published, but no progress worth mentioning was made in their interpretation. After the discovery of several Greco-Phoenician bilinguals in Malta and Cyprus, more successful efforts at decipherment were made almost simultaneously by Swinton and Barthélemy (1750–58); the work of the French scholar was much more methodical and successful than that of his English colleague. On the whole, little progress was made by their successors, except in increasing the number of available inscriptions and in publishing more accurate copies, until the brilliant work of Gesenius, *Scriptura linguaeque Phoeniciae monumenta quotquot supersunt* (Leipzig, 1837), appeared.[2] In this epochal book he collected all accessible documents in accurate copies and interpreted them on the basis of sound epigraphical method, profound grammatical knowledge, and balanced judgment.

Gesenius's decipherment and publication of all known texts was followed closely by Movers's four-volume work, *Das phönizische Alterthum* (1841–56), which collected everything then known about the Phoenicians and their colonies, utilizing the results of his great predecessor's research. Movers has been unduly criticized in some quarters for his hazardous conjectures and especially for his wild etymologies. However, he was in these respects only a child of a generation which was so dazzled by the rapidity of philological and archaeological discovery that it followed mirages with as much confidence as it did solid horizons. We still draw freely from the vast reservoir of information which Movers brought together and sifted, mainly from classical sources. During the fifteen years which elapsed between the first and the fourth volume of his work, such remarkable epigraphic progress was made that much of his work was speedily antiquated. Among the many new inscriptions which came to light were the Sacrificial Tariff of Marseilles (1845), the funerary text of Eshmunazar (1855), and several new inscriptions from Phoenicia which had been recovered by the expedition of Renan in 1860–61. The wealth of new documentation naturally antiquated Gesenius's grammatical sketch and made possible a sound new study by Schröder (*Die phönizische Sprache,* 1869), which remained standard up to the appearance of Z. S. Harris's *Grammar of the Phoenician Language* in 1936. In 1881 the first part of the great *Corpus Inscriptionum Semiticarum* was issued, entirely as a result of the enthusiasm and organizing capacity of Renan; this work is still in progress, though greatly slowed down since the First World War and now far behind the progress of epigraphic discovery. Seventeen years later appeared Lidzbarski's solid *Handbuch der nordsemitischen Epigraphik* (1898), which was speedily followed by Cooke's *Text-book of North-Semitic Inscriptions* (1903); Phoenician epigraphy was now established on a solid basis, which has had to be extended, but seldom reconstructed, during the past half century. We now have a first-class historical and descriptive grammar of the Phoenician and Punic inscriptions in Johannes Friedrich's *Phönizisch-punische Grammatik* (1951).

Meanwhile, excavators were engaged in the archaeological recovery of the Phoenician past. Renan's pioneering expedition of 1860–61 was followed rapidly by its publication in *Mission en Phénicie* (1864). Numerous minor excavations were undertaken between 1887 and 1914 by Turkish, French, and American archaeologists. The end of the world war found the French ready to undertake systematic excavations in Syria. Of the many archaeological enterprises which they carried out between 1921 and 1939 we may mention in particular the work at Byblos under Montet and Dunand (1921———), at Ugarit under Schaeffer (1929———), at Khadattu (Arslan Tash) under Thureau-Dangin (1928), at Hamath on the Orontes under Ingholt (1931–38), at three mounds in the Plain of Antioch under McEwan (1932–37), at Mari under Parrot (1933———), and at Alalakh under Woolley (1936–39). Other major and minor excavations have contributed their quota to the recovery of ancient Syria; we have mentioned only those which have been of most value for our knowledge of Canaanite history and civilization. Curiously enough, excavations in Syria have thrown most light on the Bronze Age and the Hellenistic-Roman period; the earlier Iron Age, from the 12th to the 4th centuries B.C., has been something of a stepchild in Syrian archaeology. In Phoenicia itself scarcely any intact remains of the pre-Hellenistic Iron Age have been discovered, and even Byblos has yielded almost no fresh information of importance bearing on the Iron Age except for the tomb of Ahiram. The Phoenician strata of Tyre, Sidon, and other great cities lie so deeply buried under later accumulations that it will probably be long before they are explored. Our knowledge of Phoenician culture must, therefore, still come mainly from discoveries made outside Phoenician soil. The Canaanite background of Phoenician civilization has been enormously broadened, as we shall see, by the discoveries of C. F. A. Schaeffer at Ugarit. The alphabetic cuneiform script, which came to light during his work there, was quickly deciphered by H. Bauer, E. Dhorme, and especially by Ch. Virolleaud. The latter has now published the overwhelming majority of the alphabetic tablets, which are written in a script strongly influenced by the linear "Phoenician" alphabet and in a dialect closely related to the ancestral Canaanite of Phoenicia and Palestine. We now have a good basic handbook for the study of Ugaritic in the successive editions of C. H. Gordon's *Ugaritic Grammar* (1940), *Ugaritic Handbook* (1947), and *Ugaritic Manual* (1955).

The task of synthesizing the monumental data and writing a history of Phoenician art and architecture, etc., was first seriously undertaken by Perrot and Chipiez as part of their monumental history of ancient art. Vol. III, dealing with Phoenicia and Cyprus, came out in 1885 in both a French and an English edition and still remains the most complete and best-illustrated treatment of the subject. While the massive volume by the two French historians of art cannot be considered as a critical history of Phoenician art in the modern sense, it must always hold a high place in the history of the subject, in spite of its mistakes and it *naïvetés*. In 1912 it was to a considerable extent antiquated by Poulsen's important book, *Der Orient und die frühgriechische Kunst,* which still remains standard, in spite of the tremendous influx of new material from Arslan Tash, Samaria, Megiddo, and elsewhere. We shall discuss the curious oscillations of scholarly opinion on Phoenician art and its originality relative to Aegean art below, in Part V of our study.

While archaeological research in Syria was dormant and while Phoenician epigraphy was developing slowly toward scientific status, archaeologists began excavations in Palestine which were to prove of very great importance for our knowledge of the Canaanite prehistory of the Phoenicians. In 1890 Flinders Petrie began the epochal excavation at Tell el-Hesi; his initial six-week campaign at that site was followed by stratigraphic excavations at many Bronze Age sites, such as Gezer, Taanach, Megiddo, and Jericho. After the First World War, excavations were resumed with increasing momentum and a vast body of archaeological data was gathered and analyzed, until the chronology of ordinary Bronze Age artifacts is better established in Palestine than in any other country of the Near East except Egypt, in spite of the paucity of datable inscriptions. Sites like Megiddo, Beth-shan, and Jericho, like Lachish and Tell el-'Ajjul, like Tell Beit Mirsim and Beth-shemesh, like Bethel and Ai, Beth-yerah, Hazor, and Shechem, have yielded many of their secrets and have enabled us to write a history of the evolution of Canaanite material culture. We shall not enter into a detailed discussion of this topic, since it has often been undertaken elsewhere[3] and is only incidental to the theme of the present paper.

II. THE CANAANITES BEFORE THE 17TH CENTURY B.C.

There is no object in dealing in this paper with the origin of the Phoenicians. The time is past when we need discuss the Erythraean theory of Herodotus, or the derived speculations of Lieblein and other Egyptologists of the 19th century who connected "Phoenician, Punic" with Egyptian Punt (probably Eritrea and Somaliland),[4] or the more recent hypotheses of Virolleaud, Dussaud, and others, who brought both Canaanites and Israelites from the dry Negeb, south of Palestine.[5] Nor need we stop to consider the prehistoric state of Phoenicia and Palestine[6] or the question of the home of the Semites. The Canaanites may well have been settled in Palestine and southern Syria as early as the fourth millennium, and we now know that their predecessors in the land were not appreciably dissimilar in race, judging from skeletal remains. The oldest towns in this region, whose foundation is dated by clear archaeological evidence before 3000 B.C. at the latest, already bear such excellent Canaanite names as "Jericho," "Beth-shean," "Beth-yerah," "Megiddo."[7] The Phoenician cities, such as Accho, Tyre, Sidon, Sarepta, Byblos, Arce,[8] Simyra, virtually all have good Semitic names, often names which may be called specifically Canaanite. Even in the extreme north of Canaan, Ugarit, Gabala,[9] and many smaller towns bear names which are certainly or probably Canaanite. On the other hand, non-Semitic names like "Arvad" (Arwada), Wallazi (Ullazi)[10] appear in northern Phoenicia in the 15th and 14th centuries B.C., and may be much older.

While we still lack any direct monumental evidence from Mesopotamia bearing on Syria south of Mount Amanus until the Ur documents of the 21st century B.C.,[11] our Egyptian material is now relatively rich. The excavations at Byblos have yielded dated Egyptian inscriptions extending as far back as Nebka (Khasekhemwi), the last king of the Second Dynasty, and a number of characteristically Thinite objects have been found in the debris of an early temple. Early Egyptian remains at Byblos belong mostly to the Fifth and Sixth Dynasties, when the cedar trade was most active and Byblos had practically become a colony of Egypt. At least as early as the Sixth Dynasty we find ships used for Mediterranean traffic called "Byblos (ships)," *kbnyt.* In Palestine, excavations are also yielding an increasing number of objects imported in early times from Egypt; the royal Canaanite acropolis at Ai, for instance, has furnished a considerable number of Egyptian stone bowls of the Third Dynasty, found in a sanctuary belonging to about the middle of the third millennium.[12] Canaanite pottery and other objects occur in the royal tombs of the First Dynasty, and more such material will unquestionably be discovered as excavations proceed.[13] At least two Canaanite loan words are known in early Egyptian: one, *ka(r)mu,* "vineyard," appears in hieroglyphic texts of the Second Dynasty while the other, *qamḥu,* is found in the Fifth Dynasty.[14]

There can no longer be any doubt that the Egyptians actually claimed political suzerainty over most of Canaanite Palestine and Syria in the Old Kingdom. As we have seen above, Byblos was virtually an Egyptian colony from the re-establishment of the Thinite Empire by the Memphite king Nebka, Zoser's predecessor, to the collapse of the Memphite Empire under the long-lived but weak Phiops II. According to the minimum Egyptian chronology which we follow here,[15] this period lasted over four centuries, from *ca.* 2600 to after 2200 B.C. Several Egyptian invasions of Canaan are attested during the Fifth and the Sixth Dynasties. Under Phiops I of the Sixth Dynasty no less than five rebellions against Egyptian rule are said to have taken place and a force of several myriads was required to crush one of the rebellions in question.

Between 2100 and 1900 B.C. we find a rapid decline in the density of sedentary occupation in Palestine, both east and west of the Jordan.[16] This decline, which reached its lowest point about the end of the third millennium, cannot be separated from the contemporary Babylonian reports of aggression on the part of the nomadic western Semites, whom they call "Amorites" (i.e., westerners).[17] Before the end of the Third Dynasty of Ur, the movement of Semitic nomads into Babylonia had become sufficiently significant to be mentioned in year names and documents, and the Larsa Dynasty, which arose in southern Babylonia immediately after the fall of Ur III (*ca.* 1950 B.C.) was founded by Amorites. Between 1850 and 1750 we find Amorite dynasties replacing native Accadian rulers at Babylon, at Eshnunna in northeastern Babylonia, and at Mari on the Middle Euphrates. The Mari documents, from the late 18th century, illustrate the Amorite occupation of most of Mesopotamia with a wealth of detail.[18] In them we find that practically all the region between the Taurus and the Zagros, between the coastland of Syria and the highlands of Elam, is dominated by princes with Amorite names. The region of Mari, which was still Accadian in the 20th century, to judge from proper names, had become overwhelmingly Amorite. Amorite dynasties were likewise installed in such Syrian cities as Aleppo and Qatna (el-Mishrifeh northeast of Emesa).

The evidence of the Egyptian execration texts from the Twelfth Dynasty (*ca.* 1991–1786 B.C.), which have been greatly increased in number and importance by Posener's publication, shows that Palestine was still dominantly in the hands of nomads with characteristic Amorite names about 1900 B.C., and that it became rapidly urbanized during the following two centuries, strictly in accord with the results of excavation.[19] The execration texts, combined with the data from Mari and from Byblos itself, make it possible for us to draw some extremely interesting conclusions about the political history of Byblos at this time. In sharp contrast to virtually all of the Palestinian and Phoenician towns mentioned in these documents, no princes or chieftains of Byblos are named, only its Asiatics and its clans. Since the execration texts may be dated (*JAOS* 74 [1954], pp. 222 f.) in the century between *ca.* 1925 and 1825, it would seem that Byblos was then ruled by a council of elders rather than by princes, as we know was the case later and probably earlier.[19a] It is very interesting to note that some, at least, of the cities of the Egyptian delta were, at a slightly earlier time, also governed by their own magistrates and enjoyed fiscal autonomy.[20] It is hard to avoid seeing some connection between the gerontocratic organization of the cities of the delta in the early 21st century B.C. and the similar political structure of Byblos in the late 20th century, especially since the same word *whyt,* "clan," is employed with reference to both. The "republican" constitution of the cities of the delta may safely be regarded as a result of the civil wars and Asiatic raids which reduced Egypt to a state of anarchy in the 22nd century, when the cities had to protect themselves as best they could. Since Byblos had previously formed part of the Egyptian Empire, it was natural enough that it should follow the example set by the ports of the delta, with which it was so closely bound by ties of commerce.

Before the end of the third millennium, perhaps even before the close of the Sixth Dynasty in Egypt, the Canaanites had invented a syllabary of their own, clearly modeled to some extent after the Egyptian hieroglyphic system and containing at least eighty characters.[21] A considerable number of inscriptions in this script, all on stone or copper, have been discovered by Dunand at Byblos; the finding of one inscription on copper in the ruins of the Egyptianizing temple of the Old Empire is decisive for the general date of the script. The writer is inclined to consider the weathered inscription on a reused stele from northern Moab as an example of the same script; reasons for dating the original stele in the late third millennium have been given elsewhere[22] and there is no denying the fact that the traces do remind one strongly of the Byblian syllabary of the same age. It is quite possible that this script would have become standard in Canaanite and Amorite territory if it had not been for the conquering march of Accadian cuneiform in the first centuries of the second millennium.

There can be no doubt that the Canaanites were physically enriched by the afflux of fresh blood from the east and we may perhaps suppose that they would have built up a civilization of their own in the next two or three centuries if it had not been for the pressure of Egypt from the south and of Mesopotamia from the east. The execration texts have demonstrated conclusively that the Egyptian Pharaohs of the Twelfth Dynasty claimed suzerainty over Palestine and Phoenicia. That they not only claimed it but also exercised it has been shown by the discoveries at such sites as Byblos, Ugarit, and Qatna in Syria, to say nothing of previous discoveries in Palestine, recently increased in number by finds at Megiddo.[23] We now know that political pressure from Babylonia did not begin until the early 18th century, in the time of the weak Pharaohs of the Thirteenth Dynasty. However, owing in large part evidently to the occupation of nearly all Mesopotamia by the Amorites between 1900 and 1700 B.C., cultural contacts between Syria and Mesopotamia were so close as to produce a virtually identical culture from the Orontes Valley to the Zagros Mountains. This has been proved beyond cavil by recent excavations at Mari and Alalakh.

The collapse of Egyptian power in the early 18th century gave the Canaanites freedom to develop the cultural influences which had been streaming from Egypt and Mesopotamia during the preceding two or three centuries. The new culture of the Middle Bronze II was surprisingly rich in many respects, but it remained too syncretistic to possess a really independent artistic life, in this respect foreshadowing the cultural history of Iron Age Phoenicia. The royal tombs of the late 19th century at Byblos still exhibit slavish cultural dependence on Egypt; it was not until about the middle of the 18th century that the Canaanites finally broke away, as shown especially by the ceramic and glyptic arts, which reached an extraordinary level of excellence at this time.[24] Our data nearly all come from Palestine; Syrian sites hitherto excavated show a very remarkable lacuna, for reasons on which we shall presently touch. Sporadic finds in Phoenicia (especially at Ugarit) show that the focus of the new Canaanite civilization was really there and that Palestine was in general only an outlying district of it. It would seem that the ruling princes of Byblos in the 18th century were of Amorite, not Canaanite stock, but this point is of comparatively little significance, since the racial and linguistic difference between the two peoples can scarcely have been appreciable.[25] Their difference in culture was mainly due to the simple geographical fact that the Amorites were strongly influenced by Mesopotamian civilization, while the Canaanites were almost equally affected by Mediterranean and by Egyptian material culture.[26]

III. THE CANAANITES FROM THE 17TH TO THE 12TH CENTURY B.C.

The elusive problem of the racial origin of the Hyksos conquerors of Egypt has now been substantially solved by the new data from Mari and Ugarit. Contrary to general opinion, it turns out that most of the Hyksos names now known are certainly or probably Canaanite or Amorite.[27] Manetho was, accordingly, right in designating the Hyksos as "Phoenicians,"[28] and the Egyptians of the New Empire were essentially correct in calling them '*A3mu,* a name otherwise applied only to nomadic or semi-nomadic Semites. The hypotheses of recent writers, including the author of this paper, who would make them dominantly Hittite or Hurrian or Indo-European, thus prove to be unfounded, though it would be rash indeed to insist that there were no non-Semitic groups among the foreign conquerors of Egypt.[29]

Three dynastic groups of Syrian rulers of Egypt in the Second Intermediate Age are known. The first group consists of an obscure succession of "rulers of foreign lands" named '*Anat-har* (probably the '*Anata* of the Turin Papyrus), *Ya'qob-har,*[30] *Samuqena,*[31] *Bablimma,*[32] etc. That this group preceded the Fifteenth Dynasty is certain from the evidence of stratigraphy,[33] glyptic style,[34] and the Turin Papyrus.[35] The six kings of the Fifteenth Dynasty form the second group, but only the names of the last three are preserved in hieroglyphic form.[36] Under them was established an ephemeral Hyksos Empire, ruled by such kings as Apophis I and Khayana, monuments of whom are found scattered over the Near East from Crete to Babylonia; this dynasty may now be dated *ca.* 1675–1575 B.C.[37] The third group consisted at least of two Apophids and a king named *Shurk,*[38] or the like; it lasted not over thirty years, until the expulsion of the Hyksos in the latter part of

the reign of Amosis I. It is scarcely accidental that our knowledge of the
relative chronology and the material culture of the Hyksos Age comes mainly
from Palestine, since the focus of their power must have remained in their
native land.

There is both archaeological and documentary evidence pointing to a
great migratory movement or movements from the northeast into Syria in
the 18th century B.C.[39] As a result of this movement, Hurrian and Indo-
Iranian tribes flooded the country. By the 15th century we find most of
eastern and northern Syria occupied predominantly by Hurrians and Indo-
Iranians. Even as far as southern Palestine non-Semitic groups are in the
ascendancy. Megiddo, Jerusalem, and Ascalon are all ruled by princes with
Anatolian or Indo-Iranian names. The cranial type at Megiddo, which was
previously Mediterranean in character, now becomes brachycephalic Alpine.[40]
In the 17th century great rectangular earthworks, after the model of older
earthworks from Europe and Central Asia, were built in different parts of
Syria, Palestine, and Lower Egypt; their chronological association with the
Hyksos is certain and their connection with horse-drawn chariotry is obvious.[41]
Horses and chariots were introduced into western Asiatic warfare by the
Hittites between the 20th and the 18th centuries, but the strong and speedy
chariots which became so universal in the Late Bronze Age seem to have
been introduced by the Indo-Iranians slightly later.[42] The first emergence of
the latter in our available sources must be dated in the 16th century, when
several "Hurrian" kings bear clear Indo-Iranian names.[43]

It would, therefore, appear that the Canaanites of the Late Bronze Age
were a much more mixed people than their ancestors of the Middle Bronze
Age had been and that they were influenced by even more complex cultural
trends. The extraordinary development of Aegean civilization inevitably led
to the corresponding expansion of sea trade, which already plays a respectable
role in the Mari archives,[44] whereas there is no clear trace of it in the business
documents of the Assyrian merchant colonies in Asia Minor in the 19th to
18th centuries B.C. Objects of import are found increasingly in Egypt, Syria,
and the Aegean after the 20th century. During the following centuries trade
expanded more or less steadily, reaching a climax in the 14th century B.C. and
falling off notably in the 13th and especially in the 12th, as we shall see.
Thanks to the new wealth brought by trade, the Canaanites were able to
develop a very high degree of material civilization, best known to us from
Ugarit. Canaanite sculpture was at its height in the 16th century and the art
of the goldsmith attained its peak in the following two centuries. The excavations in Cyprus, especially at Enkomi, have vividly illustrated the distribution
of Canaanite works of art there. In northern Mesopotamia, too, Canaanite
art was in demand, as we know from the excavations at Assur and Kar-
Tukulti-Ninurta,[45] etc.

During these centuries Phoenicia became the center of the manufacture
of purple dye and embroidered textiles. The murex shellfish was doubtless

native to the Syrian coast as well as to the coasts of Asia Minor and the Aegean, but the earliest evidence for the existence of the purple industry comes from the 15th century and is found in the Nuzi documents from eastern Mesopotamia.[46] At Ugarit it became highly developed in the next two centuries, as we know from Schaeffer's excavations at Minet el-Beida,[47] as well as from two tablets, one in Accadian and the other in Canaanite cuneiform.[48] Speiser has recently shown that the Greek name "Phoenicia" must refer to the purple industry ($\phi o\iota\nu\acute{o}s$ = "purple"),[49] and the writer believes the name "Canaan" itself is a West Semitic expression meaning "belonging to [the land of] Purple."[50] The purple industry must then have been dominant in Phoenicia when the Hurrians came into close contact with the coast before the 16th century; we may perhaps date its rise to a place of economic importance in the 18th century, after the Mari documents. The only other valuable natural resources possessed by the Canaanites were the coniferous woods of Lebanon and Casius, exported to Egypt (the Mesopotamians can scarcely have come into direct contact with the Canaanites on the eastern slopes of Amanus, from which the former drew most of their coniferous timber), so their foreign trade may well have been dominated at that time by the purple-garment industry.

It is still quite impossible to outline the reciprocal relationship between Minoan, Mycenaean, and Phoenician sea power and commerce. In spite of the artistic and intellectual superiority of Minoan culture, the Cretans seem to have been lacking in enterprise, if we may judge from the fact that Asiatic and Egyptian imports into Crete seem to be more numerous from *ca.* 1600 to *ca.* 1400 B.C. than Minoan imports into Egypt and Canaan. Whether the piratic activities of the Lycians (who were doubtless not alone), known to us from the Amarna tablets, had anything to do with the comparative slackness of trade, we cannot say. In any event, it is certain that an unparalleled period of Mycenaean trade expansion eastward began with the fall of Cnossus and continued until the irruption of the Sea Peoples toward the end of the 13th century. For a century and a half, from *ca.* 1375 B.C. to *ca.* 1225 B.C.,[51] enormous quantities of Mycenaean vases were imported into all parts of Canaan, from Ugarit and Qatna in the north to the Negeb of Palestine in the south.[52] In these vases were brought mainly perfumes and cosmetic products.[53] Since few Syrian vases of this age have been found in the Aegean area, we must resort to guessing the nature of the Syrian merchandise received in exchange. A fair guess would be that manufactured goods such as purple garments and furniture (see above) and natural products such as grain and spices (e.g., myrrh and balsam, both mentioned in the Amarna tablets) formed a large part of the bartered Syrian merchandise. What other manufactured goods and natural products were imported into Canaan from the Aegean at that time is not yet clear.[54]

All branches of Canaanite art and craftsmanship which we can follow from century to century through Palestinian excavations show pronounced—

often catastrophic—decline between their height about the 16th century and their lowest point about the end of the 13th.[55] This fact becomes particularly clear when we examine successive groups of pottery made in Canaan and not imported from outside, when we compare the sculpture and glyptic art of the period 1600–1400 with that from the 13th century, when we compare tomb groups and patrician houses or fortifications from earlier and later phases. Ugarit shows the same general picture in this respect as Beth-shan and Tell Beit Mirsim. Explanations for this general situation are not hard to find, though each must remain strictly limited in its validity and there may be additional causes which we cannot control. The oppressive weight of heavy Egyptian taxation and often corrupt administration during the long period of the New Empire, from *ca.* 1550 to *ca.* 1220, must be placed first in any catalogue, since it is only too well attested by Egyptian sources, vividly illustrated by the Amarna tablets.[56] Hittite rule in the north from *ca.* 1370 to *ca.* 1220 was much less centralized, local administration being largely in the hands of several hereditary kings belonging to the Hittite imperial family. Nor is there any evidence that Hittite officialdom was organized on anything like the bureaucratic plan which the Egyptians had inherited from the Pyramid Age. Canaanite social organization did not lend itself to the development of independent crafts and guilds, since it combined an aristocracy of "chariot warriors," partly non-Semitic in origin,[57] with a lower class composed partly of half-free serfs or coloni (*khupshu*)[58] and partly of slaves.[58a] A true middle class seems to have been wanting. In other words, there was apparently no class or stratum of the population which was in a position to undertake enterprises on its own initiative or which could be fired with ambition to change its ways and develop along new lines. A third reason, which must not be discounted because of its relative intangibility, was probably the extremely low level of Canaanite religion, which inherited a relatively very primitive mythology and had adopted some of the most demoralizing cultic practices then existing in the Near East. Among these practices were human sacrifice, long given up by the Egyptians and Babylonians, sacred prostitution of both sexes, apparently not known in native Egyptian religion though widely disseminated through Mesopotamia and Asia Minor, the vogue of eunuch priests (*kumru, komer*),[59] who were much less popular in Mesopotamia and were not found in Egypt, serpent worship to an extent unknown in other lands of antiquity. The brutality of Canaanite mythology, both in the tablets of Ugarit and in the later epitome of Philo Byblius, passes belief; to find even partial parallels in Egypt and Mesopotamia one must go back to the third millennium B.C. The reasons adduced to explain Canaanite decline in the Late Bronze Age may at least be called impressive, and their cumulative force cannot be disregarded.

Canaanite literature has been partly recovered by the excavations of Schaeffer at Ugarit and the publication of many tablets by Virolleaud. Three mythological epics, Baal and Anath, Danel and Aqhat, and Keret, contained a number of tablets each, over half of the extant remains of which have been published. All other literary remains are religious, including abstracts of myths, rituals, and hymns. Verbally and stylistically these specimens of Canaanite literature show striking similarity to Hebrew poetry, especially to such early poems as the Song of Miriam (Exodus 15), the Song of Deborah (Judges 5), the Blessing of Moses (Deuteronomy 33), the 29th and 68th Psalms.[60] There is somewhat less influence on many other early poems, in the Psalter and outside of it. There is also a great deal of less direct influence on didactic literature, as well as some striking direct influence on archaistic compositions such as the first two thirds of the Psalm of Habakkuk. This influence is particularly clear in the early repetitive style as first isolated by C. F. Burney, as compared directly with Ugaritic style by H. L. Ginsberg, and as first utilized for the chronology of literary style by the writer and his pupils.[61] There can be no doubt whatever that Hebrew poetic literature was under immeasurable obligation to Canaanite poets of the Bronze Age, who fashioned the vehicle and cultivated the style which have given Biblical verse most of its formal appeal. There are striking parallels between the prosody and the style of Canaanite and of early Accadian poetry, especially Accadian poetry of the so-called hymnal-epic category, which clearly goes back to pre-Sumerian times for its roots. The bulk of Accadian verse arose, however, as translation or adaptation of Sumerian originals and, even when the language shows strong stylistic influence from hymnal-epic sources, the result bears little similarity to Canaanite or to Biblical Hebrew poetry. On the other hand, Canaanite poetry was strongly influenced by Hurrian models[62] and by Hurrian poetic devices,[63] as might have been expected, in view of the symbiotic relation in which many Canaanite and Hurrian groups lived in the late Middle and the Late Bronze Ages. There is increasing evidence for influence of some kind from Canaanite literature on early Greek, presumably exerted through South Anatolian intermediation, but our data is still isolated and subject to eventual reinterpretation.

In the Late Bronze Age there were at least two consonantal alphabetic scripts which had been devised by Canaanites for their own use. The cuneiform alphabet is still known only from Ugarit and Beth-shemesh, but there can be little doubt that it was more widely used at one time—perhaps in the 16th and 15th centuries. There is no adequate reason to suppose that it was anything but an original Canaanite invention, the work of a man who was acquainted with the idea of writing on clay in wedges, as well as with the hieroglyphiform alphabet of Canaan in the late Middle Bronze, which employed only consonants.[64] We may perhaps suppose that he knew little or nothing about the details of either script, since he would otherwise presumably have modeled his new script more directly after cuneiform or have devised only one *aleph* sign instead of three, each with a different vowel.[65] The other alphabetic script was the direct progenitor of later Phoenician, but there is little reason to believe that it was directly influenced by the earlier syllabic script of Byblos.[66] We now possess a number of short inscriptions in this script from the Late Bronze Age, all datable to the period 1400–1200 B.C. and all partly, if not wholly, decipherable.[67] We also possess at least three inscriptions in the same script from Middle Bronze Palestine, between 1700 and 1500 B.C.,[68] as well as a considerable number of more cursive graffiti and inscriptions from Sinai, which can now be dated between *ca.* 1550 and 1450 B.C.—mainly in the early 15th century. The writer published a new essay at decipherment in 1948 (*BASOR*, No. 110, pp. 6–22), which was correct in essentials but needed further development. In the autumn of 1957 the writer renewed his work, with very successful results, to be published in the near future. Aided by a valuable suggestion of F. M. Cross, Jr., and greatly heartened by striking confirmation of his results from recent archaeological discovery and publication, he has cleared up the awkward places in his 1948 translations. The dialect proves to be fully consistent with a date about 1500 and a location in the northeastern delta. It is a remarkable commentary on the versatility of the Canaanites of the Middle Bronze Age that they should have invented at least two original alphabets in which to record their transactions, in spite of the fact that they were already familiar with at least three more complex scripts: Accadian cuneiform, Egyptian hieroglyphics, and Byblian syllabic characters. It is an equally striking commentary on their imitative propensities that in the Late Bronze Age they failed to employ either alphabet generally, but preferred the complicated Accadian cuneiform system, even for ordinary business transactions.

IV. THE CANAANITES IN THE TRANSITION FROM BRONZE TO IRON

In the 13th century the decadent Canaanites were rudely disturbed by the movements which brought the Israelites into Palestine and the Aramaean tribesmen into Syria. The Israelite invasion seems to have begun about the middle of the century and to have reached its climax about 1230 B.C.[69] By the end of the 12th century, at the latest, the Israelites had established themselves firmly in the hill country of Palestine, from Laish and Abel, due east of Tyre, to the extreme south. Closely following the Israelites came the irruption of the Sea Peoples, who swept over the eastern Mediterranean basin like a flood in the half century which began *ca.* 1225 B.C.[70] After devastating the Hittite Empire, as well as the coast of Syria and Palestine, they were defeated by Ramses III in a great land and naval battle on the Egyptian coast (*ca.* 1175 B.C.). However, the Egyptians were quite unable to dislodge the invaders from the occupied territory, and the Philistines took permanent possession of the Canaanite territory in the south, from Gaza to south of Joppa, while the Tsikar settled farther north at Dor. Ugarit was certainly destroyed at this time and Tyre was probably destroyed soon afterward, since it was just as much exposed to a sufficiently powerful attack by sea as it was protected by its insular situation from land invasion. Shortly after these two formidable invasions, the Aramaean[71] tribesmen from the Syrian desert occupied much of the Canaanite hinterland of Phoenicia, from Hauran to the Eleutherus Valley, but details escape us entirely; we know only that the Aramaean movement reached its climax in the 11th century.

These invasions reduced the extent of Canaan along the coast by about three fifths, from over 500 kilometers in a straight line to less than 200. In the south the Canaanite border was pushed north from Raphia to the Ladder of Tyre; in the north it was pushed south from the northern boundary of Ugarit (Mons Casius) to just north of Arvad. In later times the Phoenicians regained the coast of Palestine as far south as Joppa, but they never recovered any appreciable part of the hinterland, which was lost for good. At a conservative estimate they lost *nine tenths* of the region over which Canaanite culture had once prevailed. What a terrific shock this must have been cannot easily be appreciated today. On the other hand, they were forced by circumstances and enabled by the march of civilization to exploit their mountainous hinterland of Lebanon to an extent not previously possible. Thanks to the then recent discovery of the uses to which plaster made with slaked lime could be put, they were able to dig cisterns everywhere and to line them with true lime plaster, impervious to water.[72] As in Israelite Palestine, this made it possible not only to develop intensive cultivation of the rich coastal lands of the Libanese Riviera but also to build villages in the mountains, as well as to provide for a much larger population on such islands as Tyre and Arvad. In coming centuries it would similarly make it possible for the Phoenicians to colonize waterless islands all over the Mediterranean, thus giving them well-protected stations for their expanding commerce. The vast forests of Mount Lebanon made it possible to build great navies, and the discovery of iron there[73] enabled the Phoenicians to build their ships and arm their sailors without interference from outside.

Another factor of importance for the new colonizing activity of the Phoenicians was the invigoration of the decadent Canaanite stock by fresh blood, especially from the hardy mountaineers of Syria and the equally hardy peasants of northern Israel, who were drawn into Phoenician service by its tempting emoluments. We need not go so far as Slousch[74] and Rosen[75] to recognize the great significance of these sources of man power.

The destruction of Ugarit in the north and apparently of Tyre in the south made Sidon and Byblos the leading—perhaps the only autonomous—states of Phoenicia. In the Bible the Phoenicians were thenceforth called "Sidonians," and "Sidonian" appears in the Homeric poems as a synonym of "Phoenician." Both in the Bible and in Phoenician and Assyrian inscriptions, kings of Tyre (e.g., Ittoba'al I, Hiram II, and Elulaeus) are designated as "kings of the Sidonians." Eduard Meyer has explained this as due to a great expansion of Tyre at the expense of its sister city, Sidon, after the reign of Hiram I (*ca.* 969–936 B.C.),[76] but this is quite an unnecessary supposition. Justin, probably quoting Timaeus, tells us that the Sidonians founded Tyre after a defeat at the hands of the king of Ascalon.[77] Moreover, Sidonian coins of the Seleucid Age call Sidon "mother of Kambe [Carthage], Hippo, Citium [in Cyprus], and Tyre." Since Carthage and Citium (also called "Carthage," i.e., New Town, Qart-ḥadasht) were both Tyrian colonies, their mention proves clearly enough that the Tyre of this list is none other than the Phoenician city itself. It follows that sometime after the reoccupation of Tyre as a Sidonian settlement in the early 12th century (the traditional era of Tyre was 1198–1197 B.C.) it became the official seat of Sidonian government, the capital of the Sidonians. During these centuries, then, the terms Tyrian and Sidonian are merely synonyms. Between 950 and 850 B.C. the territory controlled by the Sidonian state was extended southward as far as Carmel and northward as far as Tripolis; this period saw the climax of Sidonian power, as far as Phoenicia proper was concerned.

Owing mainly to the lack of deep excavations at Sidon, as well as to the virtual impossibility of carrying out effective work at Tyre, we know nothing about early Sidonian history from inscriptions. On the other hand, a whole series of inscriptions, discovered at Byblos by Montet and Dunand (including two previously discovered but misinterpreted for lack of parallel material), enable us to reconstruct a partial list of Byblian kings in the tenth century. The two latest rulers in this list, Abiba'al and Eliba'al, are dated by the reigns of their Egyptian suzerains Shishak I and Osorkon I to the second half of the tenth century. The inscriptions of Ittoba'al (on behalf of his father Ahiram) and Yehimilk have been erroneously dated back to the 13th or the 12th centuries B.C., whereas they cannot be earlier than the beginning of the tenth.[78] These inscriptions show a most striking progress toward flowing cursive on the part of the Canaanite alphabet; such examples as the *mem* of Yehimilk and the *aleph* of Ittoba'al show that the scribes not only imitated cursive script successfully on stone but also sometimes employed extreme cursive forms which failed to obtain general vogue and rapidly went out of use. It is evident that writing was intensively cultivated by the Phoenicians of that day, as vividly illustrated by Zekarba'al's receipt of 500 papyrus rolls from Egypt as part payment for cedar wood (*ca.* 1060 B.C.).

We can state with considerable confidence that Phoenician commercial expansion in the Mediterranean did not seriously begin until after the time of Zekarba'al, as we may infer from the data found in the report of Wenamun, special envoy from Egypt to Byblos, about 1060 B.C.[79] In the first place, piratic activity on the part of the Sea Peoples was still acute. In the second place, Cyprus appears as a land quite outside the political spheres of both the Egyptians and the Phoenicians. Thirdly, we find an explicit statement about the mercantile organization prevailing in Wenamun's time. In the harbor of Byblos were twenty ships (not all there at once) which were in *khubûr* relationship with Smendes, prince of Tanis. At Sidon there were fifty ships in a similar relation to a man with the non-Semitic name *Wrktr,* or *Wlktr.* From the context and from the meaning of the word *khubûru* in Accadian and Ugaritic (and of the derived *shbêr* in Coptic), we must suppose that it has some such meaning as "trading company."[80] Thanks to the *khubûr* it was possible to find the necessary capital with which to build and outfit trading fleets, as well as to protect them after they were built. These merchant fleets were still employed mainly in trade between Egypt and Phoenicia; there is no hint of a developed commerce with more distant lands, such as the Aegean. In fact, we may very probably assume that trade between Syria and the Aegean was still mainly in the hands of the Sea Peoples and their congeners.

V. THE PHOENICIAN PROBLEM

Attentive study of Greek and Latin historical sources, in the absence of archaeological or epigraphic check, could only result in the attribution to the Phoenicians of a dominant role in the early history of the Mediterranean before the beginning of Greek colonization, and even to some extent after it. Such solidly established historical facts as the Phoenician origin of the Carthaginians, who controlled the western Mediterranean for more than three hundred years, and as the Phoenician origin of the letters of the Greek alphabet, seemed to authenticate the sweeping statements of ancient writers. After the decipherment of Phoenician there was a strong tendency to go even further than classical sources in making claims for the Phoenician origin of Mediterranean civilizations. Men like Movers, followed by third-rate etymologizers, filled the Mediterranean with Phoenician colonies and geographical names. All Greek art and culture were derived from Phoenician sources.

The discovery of the Mycenaean civilization which began with Schliemann's excavations at Mycenae in 1874 was not long in effecting a complete *volte-face.* After a brief period during which the astonishing new finds were naïvely attributed to the Phoenicians, such savants as Milchhöfer and Salomon Reinach came out strongly (both in 1883) in favor of their autochthonous character. In 1893 Reinach published his famous brochure, *Le mirage oriental,* and though he was opposed by Helbig (1896) and others, the sensational finds at Cnossus after 1900 carried the day completely, and no competent archaeologist has since dared to take up the cudgels again on behalf of the Phoenicians in the second millennium B.C.[81] Meanwhile, Beloch went so far (1894) as to deny that the Phoenicians exerted any influence at all on Greece and Greek commerce in the early first millennium B.C.; according to him, Herodotus and Thucydides were either romancing or were misinformed. Beloch's point of view was most recently and most forcibly presented in the second edition of his *Griechische Geschichte* (1913). He maintained (Vol. I, Chapter VII) that there was no evidence whatever, either archaeological or literary (since he considered all contrary statements in

Greek writers as based on "haltlosen Kombinationen"), for admitting the existence of any Phoenician colonies or trading stations in the Aegean region at any period. At most, he would admit only that the orientalizing style of the eighth century and later, as well as the adoption of the Phoenician alphabet (which he attributed to the ninth century), pointed to commercial relations of some kind in the age of the first Greek colonies and of the Greek epics (according to his chronology). In discussing the Phoenicians in the western Mediterranean (Chapter xxii), he went still further: Phoenician colonization in pre-Punic times was very much less important than generally supposed and there is no valid archaeological or literary evidence to carry it back before the seventh century. In other words, the earliest Greek settlements in the western Mediterranean were earlier than (or as early as) the oldest Phoenician factories. Beloch expressed himself skeptically about the official Punic date of the foundation of Carthage (814 B.C.), which he was unwilling to place before the seventh century, or the eighth at the earliest. Biblical references to Tarshish proved nothing, he claimed, for the period before the Deuteronomic redaction of Kings in the sixth century B.C. Other scholars went still further, and even the Phoenician origin of the Greek alphabet was regarded with increasing skepticism. Dussaud expressed the attitude of a whole school of thought when he denied that the Greeks borrowed their alphabet from the Phoenicians and maintained that both obtained it from a common source, which was probably the Minoan script.[82] Subsequent discoveries have brought about a change of view on Dussaud's part, as we shall see.

Unfortunately for the legitimate claims of the Phoenicians, their defense has been too often in the hands of scholarly phantasts. V. Bérard's *Les Phéniciens et l'Odyssée* (1902–3, 1927–28) gathered an enormous mass of material in support of his thesis that "the Phoenicians, coming from the Red Sea to the shores of our sea [the Mediterranean] about the 30th to the 25th century B.C. were from the 16th to the 11th century the principal agents of the spread of Pharaonic influence in the waters of the Levant."[83] It may safely be said that Bérard's influence would have been negligible if it had not been for his great prestige in French intellectual circles and for the fresh enthusiasm of his presentation. The distinguished historical architect and archaeologist W. Dörpfeld went to the most absurd lengths in attributing Greek geometric art to Phoenicians who lived in Greece side by side with the Hellenes during the second millennium B.C.,[84] but since Dörpfeld not only lacked historical judgment but also denied the validity of modern ceramic chronology (!) his views exerted no influence among specialists, though they created much confusion outside the latter's ranks.

Among serious scholars a reaction was inevitable. In 1912 the eminent Danish classical archaeologist, F. Poulsen, published *Der Orient und die frühgriechische Kunst*. In it he collected all accessible archaeological evidence for Phoenician metallurgic and glyptic art, especially ivory carvings. Ivories and metal vases came mainly from the excavations at Calah (Nimrud) in Assyria, from Cyprus, Crete, Olympia in Greece, and from Etruria. From their chronological and geographical distribution, from their common repertoire and technique, as well as from the extraordinary amount of borrowing, mainly from Egypt, but also from Assyria and Syria-Anatolia, he deduced that all these objects were either Phoenician in origin or were made under direct Phoenician influence, in imitation of Phoenician originals. The outbreak of the First World War, before the book (printed at the end of 1912) had become generally known, delayed critical examination of the work and allowed it to be ignored in some quarters. However, subsequent discoveries of rich collections of ivories of the same type at Arslan Tash, published in 1931, and at Samaria (published in 1938), as well as the further study of the Nimrud collection, have brought such cumulative evidence for the correctness of Poulsen's position that only strong partisans can oppose it any longer.[85] We will discuss the chronological development of this category of art below.

In 1929 Eduard Meyer published a brief but important paper on some problems of Phoenician history,[86] followed in 1931 by an extremely valuable detailed treatment in the new edition of his *Geschichte des Altertums*. Meyer examined all available documentary material with his usual acumen and, in general, reached very sound conclusions. However, he seems to have overshot the mark in accepting Timaeus's date for the foundation of Utica near Carthage in 1100 B.C. One serious weakness in his otherwise admirable historical sketch was his neglect of the accumulating archaeological data and his disregard of what archaeologists had contributed to the solution of the question. To be sure, since the conclusions of archaeologists were based on negative evidence, they were not entirely reliable, as we shall see, so Meyer's results could scarcely have been improved by drawing on them.

Recent archaeological research tends to reject the standpoint of Eduard Meyer with respect to the time of Phoenician commercial activity in the Mediterranean and to adhere to the attitude of Beloch, almost wholly on negative evidence. Thus the eminent Catalan authority, P. Bosch-Gimpera,[87] followed closely by Rhys Carpenter[88] and Pierson Dixon,[89] thought that Phoenician trade with Spain began in the eighth century and was at its height in the seventh, when the Phoenician colonies in Spain were established. Shortly after the middle of the sixth century the Phoenicians lost their commanding position in the western Mediterranean and were replaced by the Carthaginians. The foundation of Carthage is placed by these authorities at least a century later than the traditional date, i.e., not before the end of the eighth century. Phoenician penetration of the Aegean is restricted to the eighth century and Carpenter brings the date of the adoption of the Phoenician alphabet by the Greeks down to the end of the eighth century, about a century and a half later than Beloch's date.[90] In his *History of Cyprus* (1940) Sir George Hill declared that "we have no direct or indirect evidence of the presence of Phoenicians in Cyprus before the eighth century."[91] Olmstead reflects the same point of view when he dates the beginning of Phoenician expansion in the western Mediterranean in the ninth century and its climax in the eighth and seventh.[92]

Epigraphic discoveries have, however, changed the situation materially. At the end of 1939, A. M. Honeyman published an archaic Phoenician inscription in the Cyprus Museum, in the study of which the writer had collaborated with him.[93] The writer then studied it anew, with a facsimile copy, and showed that it cannot be later than the ninth century and may even belong to the first half of that century.[94] The stone is local red sandstone. This discovery pushes the date of the effective Phoenician colonization of Cyprus back more than a century, since the Baal-Lebanon dedication can scarcely be dated before *ca.* 750 B.C. and the five-letter graffito on a vase of red bucchero ware[95] belongs epigraphically to about the same time, or somewhat later.

Much more unexpected than this discovery were the results of a careful re-examination of the earliest Sardinian inscriptions, undertaken by the writer after he had repeatedly despaired of any success whatever in this direction.[95a] It turns out that the interpretation of the Nora stone has been hopelessly handicapped in the past by three things: (1) scholars relied on recent copies of the weathered surface, presupposing erroneous underlying characters; (2) correct interpretation would have been almost impossible before the Cyprus inscription and other archaic texts had yielded previously unknown or little-known forms of characters and meanings of previously misunderstood words and phrases; (3) previous students had all wrongly assumed that the inscription was virtually complete, which is not the case at all. On careful examination of photographic reproductions, assisted materially by the oldest facsimile copies by Arri and Euting, the characters prove to be almost identical with those of the Cyprus inscription. The script of the Sardinian inscriptions is rather more archaic and cannot be dated later, unless we assume a most improbable lag. The language of the Nora stone is pure Phoenician, representing exactly the combination of earlier and later elements which we should expect in a document from the ninth century. The stone is local, so there can be no doubt about its local origin. The characters are monumental in size and the original inscription was considerably over a meter in height and about a meter and a quarter (over four feet) in width. The contents strongly suggest a public decree. It is evident that Nora must have been a town of considerable importance in the century before the foundation of Carthage! The two other archaic Sardinian inscriptions are both fragmentary, but enough is preserved to show that their script is even more archaic than that of Nora and may well go back to the beginning of the ninth century. Moreover, the Bosa fragment, though found at a site a hundred kilometers away in a straight line, exhibits the same monumental script (with characters twelve to fifteen centimeters high) as the Nora stone and accordingly should also belong to a public decree. If the writer's interpretation is correct, Nora then bore the Phoenician name "Tarshish," meaning "Smelting Plant, Refinery."[96] What Phoenician refineries of the period were like has been shown for the first time by Glueck's excavation of a great copper refinery of the tenth and ninth centuries, operated by slave labor, at Tell el-Kheleifeh, Biblical Ezion-geber on the Gulf of 'Aqabah.[97] There were doubtless at least as many Phoenician settlements which bore the name *Tarshish* as there were "New Towns" (*Qart-ḥadasht* = Carthage).

Further study of the material in local museums in the western Mediterranean region, systematic excavations in North Africa, Sardinia, and Spain, and in sites of the Early Iron Age in Phoenicia itself, are now greatly increasing the amount of recognizable early Phoenician material.[98] Even now, it is clear that the Spanish ivories of Carmona, which correspond in technique and repertoire with the Phoenician ivories of comparable age, belong to the tenth-eighth centuries rather than to the seventh, where they are usually dated.[99] Of course they may have been exported later to Spain. On the other hand, the famous Praenestine bowl, often dated in the eighth century, belongs in the seventh, as proved both by its artistic relations and by the characters of the Phoenician epigraph.

In 1957 President B. Mazar of the Hebrew University in Jerusalem headed an expedition to study the Phoenician remains of Spain. While the results of their summer's work have not yet been published, I have been authorized to describe them briefly. There are no significant Phoenician remains anywhere in the Iberian Peninsula except along the old trade route from Gader (Cadiz) and the still unknown site of Tartessus up the valley of the Guadalquivir to Seville and thence northward east of the Portuguese frontier to the rich mining regions of northwestern Spain. Along this route the area of Carmona and Jerez southwest of Seville have been particularly rewarding. Among still unexcavated sites are a true *tell* (mound) and a Phoenician temple at its foot. The magnificent finds of Cáceres halfway up the Portuguese frontier have already been published by Antonio Blanco Freyeiro (a pupil of A. Garcia y Bellido).[99a] Among unpublished items are beautiful golden candelabra, with an inscription in Phoenician from the sixth century B.C., discovered in the Guadalquivir Valley. The earliest Phoenician remains in western Spain are dated by Mazar in the ninth century B.C.

The following historical sketch of Sidonian expansion will illustrate the conclusions which we have reached with regard to the solution of the Phoenician problem. As we have pointed out above, there is no reason to suppose that Sidon and Tyre formed distinct states during the period of colonization; it is rather almost certain that Tyre was refounded by the Sidonians in the early 12th century and remained a Sidonian city until the late eighth century B.C., when a separate dynasty was set up at Sidon under Assyrian tutelage.[100] It is clear that Sidon had not attained her later significance in the time of Wenamun, and Tyre is mentioned only in passing (see above). We may safely suppose that the colonial expansion of the Sidonians began after David's destruction of the Philistine Empire about 990 B.C. As long as the Sea Peoples had a strangle hold on both the sea and the Palestinian hinterland, the Sidonians were helpless. It began undoubtedly with Cyprus, where the colony of "New Town," almost certainly Citium, was founded. If the writer's interpretation of Josephus's quotation from Menander of Tyre is correct, the people of Citium rebelled against Hiram I (*ca.* 969–936 B.C.).[101] The Honeyman inscription (see above) at all events proves effective Phoenician penetration in the early ninth century.

It is not necessary to suppose that the Phoenicians established any colonies in the Aegean. The dangers of piratic raids in this region must have discouraged them from serious attempts at economic control; we may rather suppose that they contented themselves with temporary trading "factories" under local Greek protection. On the other hand, we may safely trace their earliest colonizing activities in the western Mediterranean back to the early tenth century. The more important routes were undoubtedly well known to the more adventurous seamen of the eastern Mediterranean, since they had been traversed intensively by the Sardinians, Tyrrhenians,[102] and other Sea Peoples in the late 13th and 12th centuries. As we have seen above, Sardinia was already colonized by the Phoenicians in the ninth century, and there seems no reason to doubt that the smelting plants of Nora dated back to the age of Hiram I, if not earlier. One would expect a period of several generations before the colonies of Nora and Bosa could develop to the point where monumental edicts in stone would be set up. In Sardinia we may safely suppose that the Phoenicians followed in the traces of the Sea Peoples, whose exploitation of their island metals they continued. North Africa and Spain were, however, more remote and in all probability less known. We may, therefore, set up the provisional order of colonization: Cyprus—Sicily (first on such islands as Malta and Motya, in agreement with Thucydides)—Sardinia (Nora and Bosa)—Africa (Utica)—Spain (Gades and Tartessus). By the middle of Hiram I's reign, about 950 B.C., we may suppose that Gades and Tartessus had been founded.[103] It is significant for the probable lack of any local civilization that both these towns received Phoenician names.

Just as the date of the beginning of Phoenician colonization in the west must be pushed back two or three centuries earlier than the dominant view now allows (though a century or two later than Meyer's date), so the date of its close must be raised from the middle of the sixth century to the end of the eighth century B.C. The foundation of Carthage in the late ninth century was the beginning of the end, since the Carthaginians must soon have begun to compete with the mother country—and they were not the only colony strong enough to become a serious competitor. The conquest of Phoenicia by the Assyrian kings of the late eighth and the early seventh centuries proved fatal to Sidonian independence, and the contemporary wave of Greek colonization[104] weakened Phoenician maritime power still further. Finally, the Chaldeans dealt Phoenician maritime ambitions the *coup de grâce* when they captured Tyre in 572 B.C., after a siege of thirteen years.[105] The Greek colonies in the west now entered into the Phoenician heritage. Carthage was not ready, it would appear, to carry the burden of empire for several generations yet. In Tartessus there was a brief, but apparently a brilliant, period of native autonomy under the semi-legendary Arganthonius.[106] In Cyprus local Phoenician dynasties were set up at Citium and Salamis on the eastern coast. But the day of the Phoenicians was over. With the subsequent Canaanite renaissance under Carthage we are not concerned here.

VI. THE DIFFUSION OF PHOENICIAN CULTURE

After this reconstruction of the history of Phoenician expansion, we may profitably turn to survey the development of Phoenician art and the chronology of Phoenician cultural influence on other Mediterranean peoples. Owing to the synthetic character of Phoenician art, which borrowed from elsewhere and continued to borrow new repertoires and new motifs down to the very end of its autonomous existence in the sixth century B.C., it is not only difficult but dangerous to attempt a coherent history of its development. We must content ourselves for the present with classifying the available material according to the evidence furnished by datable groups of homogeneous objects.

The oldest large group of ivories belonging to the Canaanite Iron Age was discovered in 1937 at Megiddo by Gordon Loud, on behalf of the Oriental Institute.[107] These ivories belong to the latest of a series of Canaanite palaces, the last of which was destroyed not long after *ca.* 1135 B.C. (in or immediately after the reign of Ramesses VI).[108] Unfortunately, they do not form a homogeneous group from a single article of furniture or a suite, but represent a miscellaneous collection. Some of the strips of inlay in Pls. 58–61 may go back to the 15th century or even earlier. However, it is clear that the majority of the pieces in the collection belong to the first half of the 12th century, like the model pen case in Pl. 62, which is dated by an inscription to the reign of Ramesses III (*ca.* 1180–1149 B.C.). The remarkable plaque on Pl. 4, bearing a scene which exhibits striking points of contact with the Ahiram Sarcophagus (see above, note 78), is among the latest characteristic pieces and may provisionally be dated *ca.* 1150 B.C., though it may be a little earlier, of course. While Egyptian influence on the Megiddo ivories is strong, it is not nearly so pervasive as it later became, and these pieces, like the roughly contemporary ivories from Enkomi, are excellent examples of the artistic syncretism of Syria in the Late Bronze Age. Such stray objects as have come down to us from the 11th century, like the Ahiram Sarcophagus, still reflect the same artistic tradition.

After a gap of over two centuries we find Syro-Phoenician art well illustrated by the ivories from the Southeast Palace at Nimrud (Calah) in

Assyria, which belong to the outgoing tenth century and perhaps to the beginning of the ninth, as has been shown by Barnett.[109] Resemblances in detail to the finds at Enkomi, Byblos, and Tell Halaf have been pointed out by Watzinger[110] and others; we may add that there are some resemblances to the Megiddo ivories, though not very striking. Closely following this group in point of time are the Samaria ivories and the ivories from Arslan Tash, which are epigraphically and stratigraphically dated to the ninth century, probably to the second half.[111]

In the eighth century the syncretistic tendencies of Iron Age art reach an all-time high, with the fusion of Egyptian and Mesopotamian elements which characterizes the art of the earlier group of silver bowls from Cyprus and Greece and of the bronze shields from Crete. To this period belong the earliest known Greek imitations of Phoenician work, abundant in Crete, Rhodes, Ionia, and illustrated by inferior work on the Greek peninsula itself.[112]

The Saite renaissance in Egypt was accompanied, it would seem, by a new wave of Phoenician adaptation and imitation, best known from the Barberini and Bernardini tombs at Praeneste in Eturia.[113] One of these bowls bears the name of its maker, Eshmunya'id son of 'Ashta, in characters belonging to the seventh century, probably to its latter half. The Egyptian borrowings of this phase do not limit themselves to specific religious groups and decorative motifs as in the Bubastite period (ninth century), but extend to copying whole scenes of action from the walls of tombs and temples, together with quantities of meaningless hieroglyphs. The Barberini group and contemporary finds elsewhere represent the last and least original phase of Phoenician art. Thereafter it lost all claim to autonomous existence and by the early fifth century, if not earlier, it was completely absorbed by triumphant Greek art.

It cannot be accidental that the period when Phoenician art[114] most powerfully affected the Greeks was also the time at which the alphabet was borrowed. Thanks to our steadily increasing knowledge of the development of the Phoenician alphabet, both lapidary and cursive, and to recent discoveries of early seventh (or late eighth) century graffiti at Hymettus,[115] we can speak with a confidence not hitherto possible. The early chronology of Ullman (11th or even 12th century)[116] and others is absolutely out of the question. These scholars reach their conclusions by comparing individual characters, regardless of their period, and striking the highest chronological average, whereas we must, as recently emphasized by Rhys Carpenter,[117] compare whole alphabets taken from actual inscriptions and not eclectically reconstructed. Carpenter, working with insufficient data and basing his conclusions solely on lapidary inscriptions, thinks that the alphabet was borrowed from the Phoenicians toward the end of the eighth century; the writer, with more material and a cursive prototype, would date this event in the early eighth century or possibly the late ninth.[118]

The blows of fate *per Assyrios,* which put an end to the territorial ambitions and the merchant empire of the Phoenicians in the late eighth and the early seventh centuries B.C., brought with them a renewed interest in the literature of the Canaanite past.[119] There was a literary renaissance which may have attained its climax in the sixth century. To this renaissance belongs the enigmatic figure of Sanchuniathon, who collected the religious records and the mythological poems of his people, as we know from a Greek sketch, written in the first century A.D. by Philo of Byblos. To the same period we may perhaps attribute the Tyrian history from which Menander of Ephesus drew material for a Greek adaptation in the third (?) century B.C.

Our ideas about Phoenician religious literature would be exceedingly hazy if it were not for the documents of Ugarit, from the 14th century B.C. The mythological epics of Baal and Anath, of Danel and Aqhat, of Keret, etc., unquestionably reflect a common Canaanite literary heritage, as we can tell both from the many reminiscences of them which we find in Philo Byblius and from their strong literary influence on the Israelites (see above). If we pass over the earliest documents, which illustrate Canaanite influence at the beginning of Israel's history, we find it in the later prophets (but not in Hosea, Amos, the original parts of Isaiah, etc.), especially in Ezekiel, Habakkuk and the exilic parts of Isaiah and Deutero-Isaiah, the Psalms, Proverbs, Job, Song of Songs, etc.—everywhere in works or passages dating in their present form from the period 650–350 B.C. It can now be proved that substantial parts of Proverbs are direct borrowings from Phoenician sources. The case of the Psalms is more difficult, since many of them go back to early Israelite times, and direct Phoenician influence on Israelite music in the age of David and Solomon is increasingly likely. However, some close literary parallels are found in the latter books of the Psalter. There can no longer be any doubt that the Bible has preserved some of the best in Phoenician literature, especially lyric and gnomic poetry. Without the powerful influence of Canaanite literary tradition, we should lack much of the perennial appeal exerted by Hebrew poetic style and prosody, poetic imagery and vivid description of natural phenomena. Through the Bible the entire civilized world has fallen heir to Phoenician literary art.

NOTES TO APPENDIX I

1. The evidence is very complete, consisting of explicit statements in classical writers from Philo Byblius to Stephanus of Byzantium and of coins from Laodicea south of Tyre bearing the inscription *l-l' dk' 'š b-kn'n,* "Belonging to Laodicea which is in Canaan"; see especially Eduard Meyer in the *Encyclopaedia Biblica,* I, p. 638, with corrections by Meyer in *Geschichte des Altertums,* II, 2^2, p. 63, n. 2, and additions by F. M. Th. Böhl, *Kanaanäer und Hebräer* (1911), p. 5.

2. For an account of the previous literature and of the progress of research before his time see Gesenius, op. cit., pp. 1–9.

3. E.g., Albright, *The Archaeology of Palestine and the Bible,* New York, 1932–35; "The Present State of Syro-Palestinian Archaeology" in the *Haverford Symposium on Archaeology and the Bible,* New Haven, 1938, pp. 1–46; *The Archaeology of Palestine,* Harmondsworth, 1949 (latest revision, 1956).

4. See the detailed discussion and refutation by R. Pietschmann, *Geschichte der Phönizier* (1889), ˙pp. 121 ff.

5. See Albright, *BASOR,* No. 71 (1938), pp. 35–40; R. de Langhe, *Eph. Theol. Lovan.,* 16 (1939), pp. 245–327; J. Pedersen, *Berytus,* 6 (1941), pp. 63–104. For Dussaud's views on the Negebite origin of the Phoenicians, see especially his paper "Les Phéniciens au Négeb et en Arabie d'après un texte de Ras Shamra" (*Rev. Hist. Rel.,* 108, 1933, pp. 5–49) and his later discussion, *Les découvertes de Ras Shamra et l'Ancien Testament* (1937), especially pp. 55–63.

6. On this subject see Albright, *JPOS,* 15 (1935), pp. 199 ff.; G. E. Wright, *The Pottery of Palestine from the Earliest Times to the End of the Early Bronze Age,* New Haven, 1937; Albright, *The Archaeology of Palestine,* pp. 49 ff., as well as his chapter on the "Prehistory of Palestine" in the forthcoming first volume of the *History of the Jewish People,* edited by S. Baron, B. Mazar, and E. A. Speiser.

7. Recently there has been a return to the idea that there are numerous non-Semitic place names in early Palestine, best illustrated by various studies of B. S. J. Isserlin and S. Moscati. Since fashions in forming place names change, often radically, over the centuries, and the most purely Semitic parts of Arabia also contain many archaic place names which cannot be explained (though there is also nothing non-Semitic about their formation), I adhere to the view most recently stated in *The Archaeology of Palestine,* pp. 178 ff. For instance, the name of Mount Tabor can now be explained as derived from a **taburru,* "brightness" (cf. Ugaritic *tbrrt,* "brightness," "freedom").

8. The name *'Irqatum, 'Irqata* already appears in the execration texts from the beginning of the second millennium; see Albright, *JPOS* 8 (1928), p. 245, and *BASOR,* No. 81, 18.

9. Gabala (modern Jebeleh) is probably the *Gb'l,* i.e., *Gab'al* (cf. Heb. *gib'ôl*), of the Ugaritic inscriptions. The name *Ugarit* itself is clearly connected with that of the composite mythological figure *Gapnu-wa-Ugâru,* "Vineyard-and-Field," in which the second element cannot be separated from Accadian *ugâru,* "field," which seems ultimately to be a Sumerian loanword, like a number of other common words in Ugaritic Canaanite. The name is to be pronounced *Ugarîtu* (nominative) for older **Ugârîyătu,* with a phonetic development which is regular in Ugaritic. The corresponding South Canaanite form would normally be *Agôrît,* transcribed in Egyptian syllabic orthography as *A-ku-ri-ta* (with the accusative ending, as usual, in Egyptian transcriptions).

10. See Albright, *Voc. Eg. Syl. Orth.* (1934), p. 47, x.a. i.

11. For the low chronology of Mesopotamian history which is employed in this paper, see especially the writer, in a whole series of papers and discussions from *BASOR,* No 77, pp. 25–30, No. 88 (1942), pp. 28 ff., No. 99 (1945), pp. 9 ff., to No. 144 (1956) and 146 (1957), which contain a debate between A. Goetze and the writer. In these papers the now extensive literature is cited. In general, the "Albright-Cornelius" chronology is followed by the Germans, and the "Sidney Smith" chronology (64 years higher), which the writer also held (independently) in *BASOR,* No. 77, pp. 25 ff., is followed by the British and French. American views are very much divided.

12. Cf. *JPOS* 15, p. 210. The detailed comparative study of these alabaster and other stone bowls, begun by Mme. Judith Marquet-Krause (*Les fouilles de 'Ay (et-Tell) 1933–1935* [Paris, 1949], pp. 18 f.), has unhappily never been published.

13. For a partial list of the now available material, including especially inscribed objects, see Rowe, *A Catalogue of Egyptian Scarabs, etc.* (Cairo, 1936), pp. xiii ff. Subsequent publications by Rowe himself and others have greatly extended the list of such material.

14. *JPOS* 15, pp. 212 f.

15. See the references given by the writer, *FSAC* (1940), pp. 319 f., n. 23. For H. Stock's slight modification of the Old Kingdom chronology of A. Scharff, see his *Studia Aegyptiaca* II (1949), and for the close agreement with the writer's own published views since 1920, see *BASOR*, No. 119 (1950), p. 29. This chronology is being increasingly confirmed by comparative archaeology, supported by radiocarbon dates; see especially Helene Kantor and the writer, in R. W. Ehrich's *Relative Chronologies in Old World Archaeology* (Chicago, 1954), pp. 1–33.

16. See *JPOS* 15, pp. 217 ff., abundantly confirmed by subsequent discoveries. See the 1956 edition of the Penguin *Archaeology of Palestine*, pp. 81 ff., for the writer's latest statement of his views.

17. Accadian *Amurrî(y)um* is adjectival from *amurrum*, "west," a Sumerian loan-word (as shown by the form, though the Sumerian pronunciation of the ideographic *MAR-TU* is still unknown).

18. For full bibliographic references to M. Parrot's sensational finds, as well as to the publication of texts by Dossin and others, see the writer's sketches, *BASOR*, No. 67, pp. 26–30; No. 77, pp. 20 ff.; No. 78, pp. 23–31. For the emerging historical picture see the writer's account, *FSAC* (1940), pp. 109, 111 f., 120 ff. There is now a wealth of material for Mari, among which we may mention particularly J. R. Kupper's exemplary monograph *Les nomades en Mesopotamie au temps des rois de Mari* (Paris, 1957). Nearly a score of volumes have appeared in three major series devoted to the site and its inscriptions.

19. See *BASOR*, No. 81, pp. 16–21; 83, pp. 30–36.

19a. In the late 19th century we have Abi-shemu (or Abi) and his son Yapi-shemu-abi. Contemporary with Seḥetepibre', the fourth king of the Thirteenth Dynasty, we probably have Yakin-ilum (*JPOS* 2, 120, where I erroneously identified him with Amenemmes I), followed perhaps by Ilum-yapi (*JPOS* 15, 226) and then by Yantin-Addu of the Mari texts, who is almost certainly to be identified with Entin of scarabs and an inscription (see *BASOR*, No. 99 [1945], pp. 9 ff.). Still earlier we have, perhaps in the late 21st or early 20th century B.C., another Abi-shemu, prince of Byblos (on whom see the writer's review article on M. Dunand's *Byblos II, Texte*, second part, *BASOR*, No. 155). All these names are Amorite.

20. See J. Pirenne, *Journal des Savants*, 1937, pp. 14–17. Some details of Pirenne's treatment must be modified (e.g., his reference to Athribis and some lexical points), but there can be little doubt that he is correct in the main.

21. Cf. provisionally *BASOR* No. 60, pp. 3–6, together with Dunand's subsequent observations, *Mélanges Maspero*, I, pp. 567–71, and *Fouilles de Byblos*, I, pp. 30 (on No. 1140) and 158 (on No. 2334). The publication of all available material in Dunand's *Byblia Grammata* (Beyrouth, 1945) has stimulated several efforts at decipherment, notably on the part of E. Dhorme, but the writer agrees entirely with R. de Langhe's adverse judgment, *Bibliotheca Orientalis*, V (1948), pp. 80–83.

22. See *JAOS* 56 (1936), p. 129, n. 8. Several of the semi-legible signs on the Balû'ah stela have close analogies in the Byblos syllabary.

23. Cf. *JPOS* 15 (1935), pp. 220 f., and Wilson, *AJSL* 1941, pp. 225–36.

24. Ibid., pp. 217, n. 73, 222; Frankfort, *Cylinder Seals* (1939), pp. 259 ff.; Watzinger, *Denkmäler Palästinas*, I, pp. 45 f. In this connection it may be emphasized that Strata E-D at Tell Beit Mirsim and Strata XII-IX at Megiddo have yielded proportionately many more beautiful objects than have any other strata in these sites (we except, of course, occasional hoards like the ivories of the 12th century, on which see below). According to ceramic experts who have examined Palestinian wares of all ages, the Middle Bronze II pottery is unequaled before the Greek period, both in beauty of form and in technical excellence. This is also true of the goldsmith's art and of jewelry, to say nothing of faience, work in metal, etc. We need only refer to the objects found in patrician houses and tombs at Gezer, Jericho, Beth-shemesh, Tell Beit Mirsim, Tell el-'Ajjûl, Meggido, Ugarit to demonstrate our point.

25. The linguistic difference between Amorite as reconstructed from personal names and words preserved in Old Babylonian tablets, especially at Mari, and Canaanite is so slight that far-reaching conclusions are futile. Albrecht Goetze has tried to show that the North Canaanite of Ugarit was really an Amorite dialect (*Language*, 1941, pp. 127–38), but this is again going too far; moreover, the cultural connections of Ugarit are mainly with Phoenicia, not with the Euphrates Valley. That the dialect of Ugarit was in some respects more closely related to the Amorite of the Euphrates Valley than it was to the South Canaanite of Phoenicia proper and Palestine we may well grant. It is also probable that the semi-nomadic East Canaanites (Amorites) swept through the coastal regions of Syria and Palestine, leaving a solid deposit of personal names. Thus, for example, a name like *Yantin-'ammu*, name of a prince of Byblos about 1760 B.C., both of whose elements are characteristically Amorite, the first phonetically, the second semantically (since the use of *'ammu* "clan, kindred," in personal names was characteristic of Semitic nomadic groups), certainly suggests Amorite intrusion of some kind into Byblos (see above, n. 19a).

26. For excellent illustrations see Schaeffer, *Ugaritica* I, pp. 19 ff., 53 ff.

27. See below for several illustrations of this fact. Many names, such as *'Anat-har, Ya'qob-har, 'Abd, Naḥmân*, etc., were already known to be Canaanite-Amorite, but the rest defied explanation and Hurrian or Indo-European theories were current. Now we can add *Samuqena, Khayana, Bablimma* (*Nablimma*), etc., to the list of Hyksos names of Semitic character. The mysterious Ugaritic names ending in *n*, to which the first two of these names belong, turn out not to be Hurrian, as thought by Thureau-Dangin, nor South Anatolian (Luwian), as conjectured by the writer, but simply Canaanite. It may now be demonstrated that nearly all of them have hypocoristic endings, properly *ânu, âna*, which become *yânu, yâna* after an initial element ending in *i* (e.g., *Iliyâna, Shamshiyâna, 'Ammiyâna, Akhiyâna, Nuriyânu, Zukriyâna*), except where there is an initial *ya* in the name, in which case the ending becomes *inu* (*enu*) by dissimilation. Where the initial element ends in a consonant, the ending remains *ânu*. This observation, illustrated by scores of examples, eliminates nearly all of the puzzling names in *n* from the supposed non-Semitic category. On these names see now the observations of B. Landsberger, *JCS* 8 (1954), pp. 56–60, *passim*.

28. Eduard Meyer's skepticism about the Manethonian origin of this datum may now be corrected, since the datum in question is correct.

29. See especially *JPOS* 15 (1935), pp. 227 ff. See most recently the writer's suggestion that the Manda name *Zayaluti* (*Za-a-lu-t/di*) underlies the name of the

founder of the Fifteenth Dynasty, Salitis, just as Amarna *Zilû* ("Tjaru") became Hellenic *Silê* (*BASOR*, No. 146 [1957], pp. 31 f.).

30. Cf. *JBL* 1935, p. 191, n. 51 for the second element. The first element (Biblical "Jacob") is found in personal and place names attested in the 18th and the 15th centuries.

31. *JPOS* 15, p. 229.

32. Ibid., p. 227, n. 107.

33. Ibid., p. 227.

34. Ibid., p. 227, n. 107.

35. Farina, *Il papiro dei re* (Rome, 1938), pp. 49–56. From the literature on the Hyksos period which has appeared subsequently, we may single out H. Stock, *Studien zur Geschichte und Archäologie der 13. bis 17. Dynastie Ägyptens* (1942) because of its comprehensive character. Studies by Winlock and Säve-Söderbergh must be mentioned because of their value in clearing up individual problems. Recent publications by W. C. Hayes and P. Montet (on the Kemose stele) have revolutionized our knowledge of the mid-18th and early 16th centuries in Egypt. A new study which will fully utilize all the rich material which has been accumulating during the past decade is badly needed.

36. The monuments of Apophis I and of Khayana are now quite numerous. The name *Apapa* may be an Egyptianized Canaanite hypocoristic name like *Ababenu* (*Syria*, XVIII, pp. 249 ff.), presumably from an original name beginning with *abu*, "father"; Canaanite *b* often appears as *p* in Egyptian. The name *Khayana* seems to occur at Ugarit; see *Syria*, XIX, 138, line 11, where we find the name *Ḫyn-m*. The name of the last king of the dynasty is at least partly preserved on the Turin Papyrus as reconstructed by Farina, who reads *Ḫȝ-mw-dy*, transcribed by him *Ḫemeṭe*. The writer tentatively proposes a different reading for the second and third hieratic signs: ['*A*?]-*ḫu-ḍu-ri*, corresponding to a Canaanite or Amorite *Aḫu-ṣûrî*, "The Brother is my Rock."

37. According to the Turin Papyrus it lasted 108 years, but there was presumably much overlapping at the beginning and at the end; cf. the writer's discussion, *BASOR*, No. 99 (1945), pp. 16 ff. The arrangement of the kings called "Apophis" is still very difficult; it has been further complicated by the discovery of the Kemose stele.

38. *JPOS* 15, p. 227, with references to Borchardt's publication, according to which *Shȝ-r-k* and an Apophis were respectively contemporary with the grandfather and the father of a Memphite priest who flourished under Amosis I.

39. Cf. *Jour. Soc. Or. Res.*, 1926, pp. 243 ff., 267 f.; *JPOS* 15, pp. 223 ff.; *BASOR*, No. 78, pp. 30 ff.; *BASOR*, No. 146 (1957), pp. 30 ff.; R. T. O'Callaghan, *Aram-naharaim* (Rome, 1948), pp. 149–55 (cf. pp. 56–63). Contrast Landsberger, *JCS* 8, pp. 129 ff., who includes many clearly Indo-Aryan names among Hurrian and other groups.

40. See A. Hrdlička in Guy and Engberg, *Megiddo Tombs*, pp. 192 ff.

41. For literature on this subject see especially *AASOR* XVII (1938), pp. 28 f., n. 2, where necessary references are given. The question has now been admirably treated by Yigael Yadin in *BASOR*, No. 137 (1955), pp. 23–32, with full references.

42. Dossin, *Revue Hittite et Asianique*, fasc. 35, pp. 70 ff.; Albright, *BASOR*, No. 77, p. 31. On the subject of the early history of the horse and chariot in general, see especially J. Wiesner, "Fahren und Reiten in Alteuropa und im alten Orient" (*Der Alte Orient*, 38: 2–4, especially pp. 22–44). However, though this monograph appeared in 1939, the Mari tablets and other recent discoveries have already rendered both Wiesner's data and his chronology antiquated in vital respects. For example, there is still no clear evidence of horse-drawn chariots

in western Asia before the beginning of the second millennium. On Wiesner's views with reference to the relation between domestication of the Bactrian camel and the horse, see R. Walz, *Actes de IV⁰ Congrès International des Sciences Anthropologiques et Ethnologiques,* Vienna, 1952, Vol. III (1956), pp. 203 f., n. 59.

43. See literature quoted in n. 39, above.

44. Dossin, *Syria,* XX, pp. 111 f.; Albright, *BASOR,* No. 77, pp. 30 f.

45. See Andrae, *Die jüngeren Ischtar-Tempel in Assur* (1935), pp. 78 ff., 106 ff., etc., where 13th-century objects imported from Canaan or imitated from Canaanite models are illustrated and described.

46. See Speiser, *Language,* 1936, p. 124.

47. Cf. Schaeffer, *The Cuneiform Texts of Ras Shamra-Ugarit* (1939), pp. 22 f., 38. There has been no detailed report so far.

48. Thureau-Dangin, *Syria,* XV, pp. 137 ff. and Virolleaud, *Syria,* XIX, pp. 131 ff. The Canaanite tablet has not been entirely understood by Virolleaud. It deals with eight and two-fifths talents of wool delivered by (not "to"; cf. the Accadian *ina qâti . . . aṣû* which corresponds exactly to Canaanite *bd . . . ys'a*) Shumeminu to the weavers for the purple industry (*'argamannu,* just as in Hebrew).

49. Speiser, ibid., pp. 121–26. Contrast Bonfante's labored criticism in *Classical Philology,* 1941, pp. 1–20, which substitutes wholly impossible speculations.

50. A brief explanation is in order. In the 1942 edition of this study, I proposed a derivation of the word "Canaan" through Hurrian, suggesting that *kinaḫḫi* was an adjectival formation in *ġġi* from **ikna,* "blue purple," and that Amarna *Kinaḫni* stood for the form with Hurrian determinative, **Knaġġini.* This was a very reasonable explanation as long as there was no really early alphabetic writing of the name. Now we have Egyptian *Kn'n* from about 1430 B.C. (inscription of Amenophis II) and Ugaritic *Kn'n* from 14th-13th century texts, so the Nineteenth Dynasty Egyptian spelling *Kn'n* is not unique. The Hurrian explanation seems to be ruled out, though the ending *n(i)* may still be non-Semitic. We must, therefore, follow B. Mazar, *BASOR,* No. 102 (1946), pp. 7–12, according to whom the word meant originally "merchant," and only secondarily "purple merchant," or modify slightly by assuming a lost Semitic word **kn'* for "murex" and derive the later meanings through "purple merchant."

51. For the date at which Mycenaean ware began to be imported in appreciable quantities into Palestine and Syria see the writer's remarks, *AASOR* XII, § 60, corrected by the revised treatment ibid., XVII, § 87. The recent publication of the pottery from the Fosse Temple at Lachish is in agreement with this general date, as is also Sjöqvist, *Problems of the Late Cypriote Bronze Age* (1940), pp. 194 f. The end of the period is marked by less clear-cut evidence from stratigraphy; decisive is typology, since Mycenaean granary and close styles are entirely missing. For details see especially Mackeprang, *Am. Jour. Arch.,* 1938, pp. 537–59, and Daniel, ibid., 1940, pp. 553 ff., and 286 ff. (on Sjöqvist's views). The results of work since 1946 have not added appreciably to our knowledge of chronology. The publication of A. Furumark's important excavations at Sinda in eastern Cyprus has not yet appeared; together with the finds of Schaeffer at Enkomi they prove that there was an Aegean settlement of proto-Philistine type between the latest date for importation of Mycenaean ware into Syria-Palestine (*ca.* 1225 B.C.) and the invasion of Syria-Palestine by the Sea Peoples *ca.* 1175 B.C.

52. On this pottery, which he calls "Levanto-Helladic," see now Sjöqvist, op. cit., pp. 65 ff., 92 ff., 212. His contention that the Mycenaean ware in Syria and Palestine was made by local colonies of Mycenaean potters is very unconvincing, especially in view of the identity of wares and techniques between "Levanto-Helladic" and

native Aegean pottery (see pp. 65 f.). It is quite possible that there were such colonies in Cyprus (with reference to which Sjöqvist is less than clear) and even in Ugarit (with Schaeffer), but Syrian potteries would have been compelled to use Syrian clays. Ancient potters were not so skilled that they could duplicate exotic wares; numerous examples show that they preferred exterior camouflage to laborious efforts to duplicate materials. The view that Mycenaean vases found in the eastern Mediterranean were actually imported from the Aegean seems still most probable, though it may well require modification with regard to Cyprus (see now especially Sjöqvist, op. cit., p. 212!).

53. Here we must enter a vigorous protest against the theory that Mycenaean pottery was exported *en masse* empty from the Aegean. We must surely assume an active basic trade in perfume; cf. Sjöqvist, op. cit., p. 29, on the similar use of base-ring ware. Of course, open bowls and cups could not be so used but they need much less space. Moreover, it is likely enough that perfume manufacturers in the eastern Mediterranean sometimes ordered empty vases in which to pack their own substitutes for the Syrian market.

54. On Mycenaean influence, and imports at Ugarit see especially Schaeffer, *Ugaritica* I (1939), pp. 72–106.

55. Cf. *AASOR*, XVII (1938), § 77.

56. Cf. Albright, *The Archaeology of Palestine and the Bible*, pp. 99 f.; *FSAC* (1940), pp. 155 f.

57. *AfO* VI, pp. 217 ff. On the institution see further R. T. O'Callaghan, *Aram-naharaim* (1949), *passim*, and especially his "New Light on the *Maryannu* as 'Chariot-Warrior' " in *Jahrbuch für kleinasiatische Forschung*, I, pp. 310–24 (1951).

58. See I. Mendelsohn, *BASOR* 83 (Oct. 1941), pp. 36–39.

58a. The foregoing remarks still hold (with the insertion of "independent" before "crafts and guilds,"), in the writer's opinion, in spite of the discovery of long lists of classes, professions, and crafts in both Ugaritic and Mycenaean Linear B inscriptions, as pointed out particularly by C. H. Gordon. At that time and in those milieus, the economy of each small state was under the direct control of king or notables, who left little autonomy to the representative of crafts and guilds. Hence the strange anonymity of the members of such groups as a rule— a situation which has been discussed by A. Alt and others.

59. Albright, *FSAC* (1940), p. 325, n. 46.

60. On this early literature see especially my treatment of the Oracles of Balaam in *JBL* 63 (1944), pp. 207–33; F. M. Cross and D. N. Freedman on the Blessing of Moses in *JBL* 67 (1948), pp. 191–210, and on the Song of Miriam, *JNES* XIV (1955), pp. 237–50; H. L. Ginsberg on Psalm 29, *Kitvê Ugarit* (1936), pp. 129 ff.; my treatment of Psalm 68 as a list of *incipits* (probably composed for liturgical purposes) of hymns composed orally between the 13th century (or earlier) and the tenth century, in *HUCA* XXIII: 1 (1950–51), pp. 1–39.

61. See especially the writer's programmatic surveys of the evidence in his articles on the Psalm of Habakkuk in the T. H. Robinson Volume, *Studies in Old Testament Prophecy* (Edinburgh, 1950), pp. 1–18, as well as in the paper on the 68th Psalm just cited. In his forthcoming "History of the Religion of Israel" (edited by Louis Finkelstein), he is setting up a stylistic sequence dating for the period between the 13th and the 10th centuries, which agrees exceedingly well with other internal evidence.

62. See Ginsberg, *Orientalia*, VIII, pp. 317 ff.; see also Goetze, *JBL* LX (1941), pp. 353 ff.

63. E.g., the frequent stylistic device of the use of graduated numbers in Canaanite poetry, often as "seven . . . eight," appears also in Hurro-Hittite verse, as pointed out by Friedrich.

64. Cf. the writer's remarks in *The Haverford Symposium on Archaeology and the Bible* (1938), pp. 18 f. On the one hand, Olmstead goes too far in trying to derive the cuneiform alphabet from the early Phoenician in Sprengling, *The Alphabet,* Chicago, 1931, pp. 57–62; and Ebeling goes too far on the other in deriving it from Old Babylonian cuneiform (*Forschungen und Fortschritte,* 1934, pp. 193–94). B. Rosenzweig's recent effort to improve on Olmstead (whom he does not mention), *ZDMG* 92 (1938), pp. 178 ff., cannot be regarded as successful. (It is now certain that the cuneiform alphabet of Ugarit was influenced by the linear alphabet, since several whole and broken lists of signs have been discovered by Schaeffer and published by Virolleaud, *Le palais royal d'Ugarit,* II [1957], pp. 199–203; they prove to follow the familiar Hebrew-Phoenician order of letters without modification except that five additional consonants are interspersed between other letters and that two extra *'aleph* signs and one duplicate *samekh* are added at the end, thus yielding thirty characters. Moreover, as T. O. Lambdin has pointed out to me, the Accadian column in the tablet 19.159 gives the first syllable of the name of the letter in the Canaanite alphabet [*be* = *bêtu, ga* = *gamlu,* etc.]. Two apparent exceptions, *ḥ* and *ṭ,* have their Accadian transcriptions reversed; the supposed *ku* is *ṭu* in a simplified western form, and *ṭi* should be read *ḥe.*)

65. On the problem of the three alephs see especially Friedrich, ibid., 91, pp. 322, and Eissfeldt, *Ras Schamra und Sanchunjaton* (1939), pp. 58 ff.

66. Cf. Dunand, *Mélanges Maspero,* I (1934), pp. 569 ff. (subsequent discoveries have added two more characters to the list of correspondences); contrast the writer, *BASOR,* No. 60, p. 5. (See also the discussion of the correspondences by Dunand in his *Biblia Grammata* [1945].)

67. See especially the excellent treatment of this material by Cross, *BASOR,* No. 134 (1954), pp. 15–24, which supersedes all earlier discussions, including those of the writer. Some additional matter is now available. The writer would now date the Beth-shemesh ostracon about 1100 B.C., in the middle of the time of the Judges.

68. The latest of these inscriptions is certainly the Shechem plaque, which may even come down into the 15th century. The writer expects to publish his own tentative decipherment soon.

69. In general see the writer, *BASOR,* No. 74, pp. 11–23, and in L. Finkelstein's *The Jews; Their History, Culture and Religion* (1949), pp. 15–20. See most recently G. E. Wright, *Biblical Archaeology* (1957), pp. 69–84. The entire question will be discussed in much greater detail in a forthcoming publication being prepared by the writer.

70. On the Sea Peoples and especially on the Philistines and Tsikar or Tsikal see my discussions in *Am. Jour. Archaeol.,* LIV (1950), pp. 166–71; *Archaeology of Palestine* (1956 ed.), pp. 112 ff.; Trude Dothan in *Antiquity and Survival,* Vol. II, No. 2/3 (1957), pp. 151–64; and *Eretz Israel,* Vol. 5 (1958; the Mazar volume), pp. 55–66.

71. In the writer's opinion the Aramaeans of the Assyrian inscriptions from 1100–800 B.C. were North Arab tribesmen who were occupied in settling down in Syria and northern Mesopotamia and who adopted the local Northwest Semitic dialect of the Upper Euphrates region. In other words, the people were in part originally Aramaeans but the language was a later acquisition.

72. For many years the writer has endeavored to find proof of the existence of true Bronze Age cisterns in Palestine, hitherto without success. It is also quite certain that watertight lime plaster has not yet been identified by experts before the Iron Age, all older samples being of gypsum or hydraulic plaster.

73. Cf. Albright, *Archaeology of Palestine and the Bible,* p. 215, n. 75.

74. N. Slousch(z), *Les Hébraeo-Phéniciens*, Paris, 1909. According to him the Phoenicians who colonized the western Mediterranean were mainly of Hebrew origin. This goes much too far, but the Song of Deborah, v. 17, proves that the Danites took service as sailors in the early 11th century (*BASOR*, No. 78, pp. 7 ff.).

75. See Rosen and Bertram, *Juden und Phönizier* (1929), who lay their emphasis mainly on an alleged amalgamation of the Phoenician colonists in the Mediterranean with the Jews in the Hellenistic-Roman period.

76. *Geschichte des Altertums*, II, 2 (2nd ed.), p. 126.

77. It may be, as often thought, that the king of the Ascalonians was a Philistine. Another suggestion, that someone confused the Tsikal (Phoen. **Skl-*) with the Ascalonians (Phoen. *'šqln-*), is very unlikely.

78. On these inscriptions and their date see especially the writer's detailed treatment in *JAOS* 67 (1947), pp. 153–60.

79. On the Wenamun report see the writer's discussion in *Studies Presented to David Moore Robinson* (St. Louis, 1951), pp. 223–31. My insistence that it is basically a contemporary document has been confirmed by J. Černý (*Revue d'Egyptologie*, 6, p. 41, n. 8, etc.), who points out that the external form is that of an official document, not of a literary composition. In this paper I have also shown that the three names of prominent Philistines (so probably), *Wrkdr, Wrt,* and *Mkmr,* are probably to be vocalized *Warkadara, Warta* (i.e., *Warda*), and *Mukmura,* with many Southwest Anatolian parallels (which can now be increased in number by the material published by J. Sundwall, *Kleinasiatische Nachträge, passim*).

80. The meaning was correctly given by the writer in *Vocalization*, p. 18, n. 77, but the etymology there proposed is false. The correct etymology was given *BASOR*, No. 63 (1936), p. 28, n. 27, where an article on the subject was promised. The article in question has not been written, but the conclusions have now been in large part anticipated by Rosenthal, *Orientalia*, 1939, pp. 231 f. and by Brandenstein, *ZA* 46 (1940), p. 87, n. 1. Schroeder (*ZA* 35, p. 49) was clearly right in explaining Assyrian *bît ḫubûri, bît ḫuburni, bît ḫiburni* (the latter two being Hurrianized forms with the Hurrian demonstrative particle -*ni*) as *Proviantmagazin,* "storehouse for grain." With this rendering would agree the Assyrian documentary evidence, the building inscriptions (according to which this building had thick double walls, necessary for insulation against moisture), the Keret epic of Ugarit (in which Keret gets wheat from the *bt ḫbr*), and the references in Proverbs. Hebrew *ḥbr* (for **ḫbr*) has the same meaning in the Maccabean coins, as pointed out by Rosenthal. There were demonstrably two Semitic stems with similar meanings, *ḥbr* and *ḫbr*. Coptic *šbêr*, "companion, partner," bears the same relation to older Egyptian *ḫubûra*, "company, partnership," that Phoenician *mmlkt*, "king," bears to older Canaanite *mmlkt*, "kingdom." Semantic parallels are legion. (On the linguistic cognates of Canaanite *ḫubûr* see further the discussion in *Studies . . . David Moore Robinson*, cited in n. 79, pp. 229 f. B. Mazar has pointed out a series of extremely pertinent Hebrew derivatives in *BASOR*, No. 102 (1946), pp. 9 ff. On the term for "brewery," *bêtu ḫubūri* in Canaanite, see now *Supplements to Vetus Testamentum*, III (Leiden, 1955), pp. 10–12. There is perhaps a popular etymology involved, since one *ḫubūru* appears to be of Semitic origin whereas the word *ḫubūru*, "brewery vat," is apparently Hurrian.)

81. There are of course some exceptions, even among archaeologists of standing, like Dörpfeld (see below), but one would hesitate to apply the term "competent" to a man who had fallen so far behind the main body of scholarship.

82. Dussaud, *Les civilisations préhelléniques* (1910), pp. 296–300.

83. Op. cit., Vol. I (1927), p. 7.

84. See Dörpfeld, *Alt-Olympia* (1935), *passim.*

85. Among classical scholars who support Poulsen's position may be mentioned particularly V. Müller and C. Watzinger; see especially the latter's sketch in Walter Otto's *Handbuch der Archäologie* (1938), pp. 805–12.
86. "Einzelne Fragen der phönizischen Geschichte" (*Sitz. Preuss. Akad.,* 1929, pp. 204–6).
87. "Fragen der Chronologie der phönizischen Kolonisation in Spanien" (*Klio,* 1928, pp. 345–68).
88. Cf. loc. cit., p. 368.
89. *The Iberians of Spain* (Oxford, 1940), pp. 23–27.
90. *Am. Jour. Archaeol.,* 1933, pp. 8–29.
91. Op. cit., pp. 96–104.
92. *History of Palestine and Syria* (1931), pp. 404–6. For still lower dates (agreeing substantially with Beloch) see Myres in the *Cambridge Ancient History, III,* pp. 642 f. (nothing in Spain before the late seventh century; Sardinia occupied about the same time).
93. *Iraq,* VI, 106–8.
94. *BASOR,* No. 83 (Oct. 1941), pp. 14–22.
95. For references see Hill, op. cit., pp. 102 f.
95a. Since my initial study appeared in 1941 there have been criticisms of my readings by Arthur Mentz, A. Dupont-Sommer, and Giovanni Lilliu (for details see my discussion in *Am. Jour. Archaeol.,* LIV [1950], p. 175, n. 50). The two former, both Semitists, have accepted my chronological attribution of the monument, which is all that concerns us here. I adhere to my insistence that the inscription is only a single stone from a much larger inscription of public character.
96. The formation *taf'îl* is common in Accadian and was frequent in Northwest Semitic as well; *taršîš* seems to be derived from Accadian **taršîšu,* from the stem *rašâšu,* "to melt, be smelted," cognate with Arabic *ršš,* "to trickle, etc., of a liquid." This etymology will be discussed in detail elsewhere.
97. Glueck, *The Other Side of the Jordan* (New Haven, 1940), pp. 50–113; *BASOR,* No. 79 (1940), pp. 2 ff.
98. It must be remembered that there have been virtually no systematic, scientific excavations in Spain, aside from the German work at Numantia, that there has been only a little scientific excavation at Carthage and less in other Phoenician sites of North Africa, and that the Sardinian towns which were occupied by the Phoenicians remain archaeologically virgin.
99. Published by Bonsor, *Early Engraved Ivories* (New York, Hispanic Society, 1928). Others have since been found and partly published. There are numerous similarities to the Megiddo ivories of the 13th–12th centuries B.C. and to late Mycenaean motifs. E.g., the griffins in Bonsor's Pls. XIII, XV, XVII resemble 13th-century Aegean griffins, as pointed out at once by the late A. J. B. Wace, when I showed the photographs to him. The helmet of the warrior in Pl. XIII resembles the helmet on the Warrior Vase from Mycenae (H. Bossert, *Altkreta,* Fig. 265). The combs, with animal center and zigzag lines, are remarkably similar, though not identical; Dr. Berta Segall has drawn my attention to similar zigzag decoration on later ivory combs from the Spartan sanctuary of Artemis Orthia (Dawkins, 1929, Pls. 126 ff. and pp. 222 ff.) from the eighth to seventh centuries B.C. Many other details suggest Megiddo and argue for a tenth-century date; e.g., the multiple stamens in Pls. I and XIX, with which cf. my observations on similar treatment of the stamens at Tell Halaf in the tenth century B.C. (*Anatolian Studies,* VI, p. 80, n. 28).
99a. "Orientalia: Estudio de objetos fenicios y orientalizantes en la Peninsula" in *Archivo Español de Arqueologia,* XXIX (1956), pp. 3–51.
100. Sennacherib, Taylor Prism, col. II: 34 ff. For the subsequent reduction of both

Sidon and Tyre to the status of Assyrian provinces, see Forrer, *Die Provinzeintei-lung des assyrischen Reiches* (1921), pp. 65 ff. The province of Sidon was estab-lished about 676 B.C., the province of Tyre in 668.

101. Josephus quotes Menander on Hiram twice: in one case the text reads τοῖς τε Ιυκεοις (ηυκαιοις, ηυκεοις, etc.); in the other it reads ὁπότε τιτυοις (τιτυαιοις, Ιυκεοις, titiceos, etc.). Gutschmid cleverly emended the text to read τοῖς τε 'Ιτυκαίοις, referring to the men of 'Ιτύκη, Latin *Utica*, but this is at best only plausible (against it see Beloch, op. cit., p. 251). The writer proposes what seems to him a much more rational emendation: τοῖς τε κιτίοις, from which the manuscript readings may be derived by assuming only the simplest types of scribal error.

102. It is now hypercritical to reject the identity of the Sardinians and the Etruscans with the corresponding Sea Peoples. With the Greco-Roman *Sardin-, Sardan-,* Phoenician (ninth century) *Šrdn* cf. Egyptian *Ša-ar-di-na, Ša-ar-da-na* (the writer's transcription) and with Greco-Roman *Turs-* (Τυρρ-, *Turs-*) cf. Egyptian *Tu-ur-ša, Tu-ru-ša* (cf. Latin *Etrusc-*). It is not necessary to go into the strong archaeological arguments here, since they are well known. Where the ancestors of the later Tyrrhenians or Etruscans were between the 12th and the eighth centuries is another question, but they may well have settled in Italy as early as the tenth century, in spite of the negative evidence of archaeology, since relevant material still comes almost exclusively from tombs.

103. It is true that the accounts of Solomon's mercantile activities do not refer to Tarshish, but only to a "Tarshish fleet" which was sent to Ophir in the extreme south to bring back gold, silver, ivory, and two kinds of monkeys, both with Egyptian names. Moreover, this expression probably means only "refinery fleet" (see above and note 96), i.e., a fleet which traversed the Mediterranean at regular intervals, bringing smelted ores home from the western mines. The word "Tarshish" appears in extant literary sources only from the seventh century on, but in our earliest references, especially in an inscription of Esarhaddon (*Tar-si-si* [pronounced by the Assyrians *Taršiš*] is the actual reading of the original, not an emendation, as still thought by Hill, *History of Cyprus,* p. 106), it already appears explicitly as the farthest limit of the Mediterranean or of the Phoenician colonial empire. But since the neighboring Gades was believed by the Greeks to vie with Utica in age and since the mines of northern Spain were much more important than those of Sardinia, where a "Tarshish" was established not later than the early ninth century, it is hypercritical to reject a date in Hiram's reign or even earlier for the Phoenician settlement of Tartessus. In this connection it may be observed that the phonetic relation between *Taršiš* and *Tartes-* is almost exactly like that between Phoenician *Qarthad-* and Greek *Karkhad-* (later Ionic-Attic Καρχηδών), "Carthage"; the dissimilation in question has been explained by J. Friedrich. The Greek ending is obviously formed on the analogy of a very widely diffused group of pre-Hellenic place names. Biblical Tarshish was located in Sardinia by W. W. Covey-Crump in *Jour. Theol. Stud.,* 1916, pp. 280 ff., but on inadequate toponymic evidence (Tarshish = Tharros at the mouth of the Thyrsus). (In recent years the writer has become more and more convinced that Tarshish [Assyrian *Tarsisi*] was located in Sardinia, not in southern Spain.)

104. The age of Greek colonization must apparently be lowered somewhat, as a result of the general lowering of the date of late geometric pottery; this fact has been repeatedly stressed by Rhys Carpenter.

105. This date has been fixed by Eissfeldt, *Ras Schamra und Sanchunjaton* (1939), pp. 4–8.

106. Cf. Schulten, *Tartessos* (1922), *passim,* and *Klio,* XXII (1928), pp. 284–91. Schulten's historical methods are generally questionable.

107. *The Megiddo Ivories,* Chicago, 1939.

108. On the date see *BASOR*, No. 78, p. 8; *Am. Jour. Archaeol.,* 1940, p. 548a. Watzinger (in Otto, *Handbuch der Archäologie,* p. 807) seems to have misunderstood the provisional reports of the excavators; at all events he has dated the destruction of the ivory palace a century too late (*ca.* 1050 B.C.) because of an erroneous identification of the fire which destroyed Stratum VI with the fire which ended VII.

109. *Iraq,* II (1935), pp. 179 ff.

110. Op. cit., pp. 807 f.

111. For Samaria see the discussion by Crowfoot and Sukenik, *Early Ivories from Samaria* (1938), pp. 1 ff., 6 ff. For the Egyptian background, which is "all-pervasive" (Crowfoot's term), in the art of the Bubastite period (late tenth and ninth centuries), see Crowfoot's remarks, pp. 49–53.

112. On this material see especially Poulsen, op. cit., and Kunze, *Kretische Bronzereliefs* (1931).

113. C. Densmore Curtis, "The Bernardini Tomb," in the *Memoirs of the American Academy in Rome,* III (1919).

114. Phoenician influence on Greek art extended also to architecture, where it was undoubtedly strong but perhaps in part indirect. There are still serious gaps in our documentation, especially in Phoenicia. The best single illustration of this influence is the Aeolic-Ionic capital, which may be traced back to the tenth century at Megiddo and to the ninth at several Palestinian sites. The early Hellenic parallels with the Phoenician Temple of Solomon have often been noted and pan-Hellenic archaeologists have tried to explain them away by denying the age and authenticity of the account of the Temple in Kings. However, it becomes clearer all the time that it must have been typically Phoenician; see especially Watzinger, *Denkmäler Palästinas,* I (1933), pp. 88–95, and Wright, *Biblical Archaeologist,* IV (1941), pp. 16–31, and *Biblical Archaeology* (1957), pp. 136–45.

115. See Blegen, *Am. Jour. Archaeol.,* 1934, pp. 10–28.

116. Ibid., 1934, pp. 359–81.

117. Ibid., 1933, pp. 8–29.

118. The discovery of Phrygian inscriptions in the great tomb at Gordion attributed to Midas, during the University of Pennsylvania Museum excavations conducted by Rodney Young, has radically changed the situation, since they cannot under any circumstances be later than the beginning of the seventh century B.C. and may easily date back into the last quarter of the eighth. Since Phrygian was unquestionably borrowed from Greek, not directly from Phoenician, we must allow at least a few decades for the diffusion of the Greek alphabet after it was adapted from Phoenician prototypes.

119. See Albright, *FSAC* (1940), pp. 242 ff.; *JBL* LX (1941), pp. 209 f.

Bibliography of W. F. Albright

(FROM 1911 THROUGH MAY, 1958)

1911

Recent Discoveries at Elephantine, *Upper Iowa Academician,* 18–20

1913

The Origin of the Arch, *Scientific American*
Dallalu, *Orientalistische Literaturzeitung* 16, 213

1915

The Home of Balaam, *JAOS* 35, 386–90
The Conclusion of Esarhaddon's Broken Prism, ibid., 391–93
Some Unexplained Cuneiform Words, ibid., 394–98

1916

The Eighth Campaign of Sargon, *JAOS* 36, 226–32
The Assyrian Deluge Epic (unpublished doctoral dissertation)

1918

The Babylonian Sage Ut-napištim rûqu, *JAOS* 38, 60–65
Ninib-Ninurta, ibid., 197–201

Notes on Egypto-Semitic Etymology, *AJSL* 34, 81–98, 215–55
The Solar Barks of Morning and Evening, ibid., 142–43
The Etymology of Še'ôl, ibid., 209–10

1919

Some Cruces in the Langdon Epic, *JAOS* 39, 65–90
Historical and Mythical Elements in the Story of Joseph, *JBL* 37, 111–43

1919–20

The Mouth of the Rivers, *AJSL* 35, 161–95
Notes on Assyrian Lexicography and Etymology, *Revue d'Assyriologie* 16, 173–94
Menes and Narâm-Sin, *Journal of Egyptian Archaeology* 6, 89–98, 295–96; 7, 110
Uttu, the Sumerian God of Commerce, *JAOS* 40, 73–74

1920–21

Gilgames and Engidu, Mesopotamian Genii of Fecundity, *JAOS* 40, 307–35
The Goddess of Life and Wisdom, *AJSL* 36, 258–94

Der zweite babylonische Herrscher von Amurru, *Orientalistische Literaturzeitung* 24, 18

Ein ägypto-semitisches Wort für "Schlangenhaut," ibid., 58–59

Ivory and Apes of Ophir, *AJSL* 37, 144–45

Magan, Meluḫa, and the Synchronism between Menes and Narâm-Sin *Journal of Egyptian Archaeology* 7, 80–86

The Blind Poet of Islam (Review of Nicholson, *Studies in Islamic Poetry*), *Palestine Weekly* 2, 130

1921–22

A Revision of Early Hebrew Chronology, *JPOS* 1, 49–79

Yemê hash-shaḥarût shel ha-'am ha-'ivrî, *Hash-Shilôaḥ* 39, 28–33

A Colony of Cretan Mercenaries on the Coast of Negeb, *JPOS* 1, 187–94

A Revision of Early Assyrian and Middle Babylonian Chronology, *Revue d'Assyriologie* 18, 83–94

The Babylonian Temple-tower and the Altar of Burnt Offerings, *JBL* 39, 137–42

The Supposed Babylonian Derivation of the Logos, ibid., 143–51

The Name *Rebecca*, ibid., 165–66

The Assumed Hebrew Stem *skt*, be silent, ibid., 166–67

The Hebrew Stems *dlḳ, grš, škḥ*, ibid., 167–68

Free Course for the Spade in Palestine, *Sunday School Times*, Oct. 39, 1921, 565–66

Review of the Recueil of the Jewish Archaeological Society, *Ha-'Aretz,* Oct. 1921

The Amorite Form of the Name *Hammurabi*, *AJSL* 38, 140–41

The Earliest Forms of Hebrew Verse, *JPOS* 2, 69–86

A Misunderstood Syrian Place-name —Dana and Tyana, *American Journal of Philology* 43, 74–75

The Origin of the Name Cilicia, ibid., 166–67

Epigraphical Postscript to Sukenik: The Ancient City of Philoteria, *JPOS* 2, 108–9

Palestine in the Earliest Historical Period, ibid., 110–39

Preliminary Reports on Tell el-Fûl, *BASOR* 6, 7–8

Gibeah of Saul and Benjamin, ibid., 8–11

The Excavations at Ascalon, ibid., 11–18

Extracts from Report, *BASOR* 3, 2–3

Extracts from Report, ibid. 4, 2–12

Annual Report, ibid. 5, 9–23

1922–23

The Location of the Garden of Eden, *AJSL* 39, 15–31

The Date and Personality of the Chronicler, *JBL* 40, 104–24

Archaeological Discovery in the Holy Land, *Bibliotheca Sacra* 79, 401–17 (cf. *Review of Reviews* 66, 547)

The Name and Nature of the Sumerian God Uttu, *JAOS* 42, 197–200

The Excavation at Tell el-Fûl, *BASOR* 7, 7–8

One Aphek or Four?, *JPOS* 2, 184–89

Rediscovering Ancient Palestine, *Sunday School Times* 65, Jan. 6, 1923, 7–8

The Epic of the King of Battle: Sargon of Akkad in Cappadocia, *Journal of the Society of Oriental Research* 7, 1–20

New Identifications of Ancient Towns, *BASOR* 9, 5–10

The Danish Excavations at Shiloh, ibid., 10–11

The Hebrew *Nippa"el* in the Light of Comparative Philology, *Jewish Quarterly Review* 13, 503–5

New Light on Magan and Meluḫa, *JAOS* 42, 317–22

Some Additional Notes on the Song of Deborah, *JPOS* 2, 284–85

The *Ṣinnôr* in the Story of David's Capture of Jerusalem, ibid., 286–90

The Principles of Egyptian Phonological Development, *Recueil de Travaux* 40, 64–70

The Etymology of Egyptian *ḥmt*, "woman," ibid., 71–72

Contributions to the Historical Geography of Palestine, *AASOR* 2–3, 1–46

Review of *Annals of Archaeology*

and Anthropology, Vol. 9, *Palestine Weekly* 3, 483

Review of Boylan, *Thoth, the Hermes of Egypt, JPOS* 2, 190–98

Annual Report, *BASOR* 8, 10–21

1923–24

Report on the Tumuli of Mâlhah, *BASOR* 10, 2–3

Eliezer Ben Yehudah, *JPOS* 3, 4–5

The Ephraim of the Old and New Testaments, ibid., 36–40

The Site of Aphek in Sharon, ibid., 50–53

The Sumerian Conception of Giš-Xar—a Correction, *Journal of the Society of Oriental Research* 7, 79

Die Ausgrabungen auf Tell el-Ful, *Palästinajahrbuch* 18–19, 99–100

Some Archaeological and Topographical Results of a Trip through Palestine, *BASOR* 11, 3–14

Ben Yehudah, *Palestine Weekly,* Dec. 7, 1923, 462–63 (translated into Hebrew)

The Site of Mizpah in Benjamin, *JPOS* 3, 110–21

The Babylonian Antediluvian Kings, *JAOS* 43, 323–29

Shinar-Šangar and its Monarch Amraphel, *AJSL* 40, 125–33

Some Notes on the Early Babylonian Text of the Atraḫasîs Epic, ibid., 134–35

The Readjustment of Babylonian Chronology by the Elimination of False Synchronisms, *Journal of the Society of Oriental Research* 8, 51–59

The Town of Selle (Zaru) in the Amarnah Tablets, *Journal of Egyptian Archaeology* 10, 6–8

Some Observations Favoring the Palestinian Origin of the Gospel of John, *Harvard Theological Review* 17, 189–95

The Archaeological Results of an Expedition to Moab and the Dead Sea, *BASOR* 14, 2–12

Annual Report, *BASOR* 12, 9–22

1924–25

Macalister's Operations on the Ophel, *BASOR* 14, 15

Results of the Archaeological Survey of the Ghor in Search for the Cities of the Plain (with M. G. Kyle), *Bibliotheca Sacra* 81, 276–91

Egypt and the Early History of the Negeb, *JPOS* 4, 131–61

Canaanite ḥofšî, "free," in the Amarna Tablets, ibid., 169–70

Contributions to Biblical Archaeology and Philology, *JBL* 43, 363–93

Researches of the School in Western Judaea, *BASOR* 15, 2–11

Account of Hebrew Ostracon from Jerusalem (with Margolis), reproduced with comments by Cook, *Palestine Exploration Fund Quarterly Statement* 1924, 184–86

Excavations and Results at Tell el-Fûl (Gibeah of Saul), *AASOR* 4, New Haven, 1924, 160 pp.

The Administrative Divisions of Israel and Judah, *JPOS* 5, 17–54

The Evolution of the West-Semitic Divinity 'An-'Anat-'Attâ, *AJSL* 41, 73–101

Ha-ḥafîrôt be-Giv'at Sha'ûl, *Journal of the Jewish Palestine Exploration Society* 1, 53–60

The Fall Trip of the School in Jerusalem: from Jerusalem to Gaza and Back, *BASOR* 17, 4–9

The Conquests of Nabonidus in Arabia, *Journal of the Royal Asiatic Society* 1925, 293–95

Philological Method in the Identification of Anatolian Place-Names, *Journal of Egyptian Archaeology* 11, 19–22

Topographical Researches in Judaea, *BASOR* 18, 6–11

To Engedi and Masada, ibid., 11–15

Review of Margoliouth, *The Relations between Arabs and Israelites prior to the Rise of Islam, JPOS* 4, 204–11

Annual Report for 1923–24, *BASOR* 16, 9–15

1925–26

The Agrippan Wall of Jerusalem, *Palestine Weekly* 7, 607–8

Mari on the Upper Euphrates or Eastern Babylonia?, *AJSL* 41, 282–83

Further Observations on the Name 'Anat-'Attah, ibid., 283–85

Further Observations on the Name Yahweh and its Modifications in Proper Names, *JBL* 44, 158–62

Address at Opening of Institute of Jewish Studies, *Yedî'ôt Ha-Makôn le-Madda'ê Hay-Yahdût*, I, 13–14

A Babylonian Geographical Treatise on Sargon of Akkad's Empire, *JAOS* 45, 193–245

Ein zweites Land Mari in Ostbabylonien, *Zeitschrift für Assyriologie* 2, 312

Bronze Age Mounds of Northern Palestine and the Hauran: the Spring Trip of the School in Jerusalem, *BASOR* 19, 5–19

The Third Wall of Jerusalem, ibid., 19–21

The Hebrew Ostracon, *Palestine Exploration Fund Quarterly Statement* 1925, 219

Proto-Mesopotamian Painted Ware from the Balikh Valley, *Man* 26, No. 25, 41–42

From Jerusalem to Baghdad down the Euphrates (with R. P. Dougherty), *BASOR* 21, 1–21

Ea-mummu and Anu-adapa in the Panegyric of Cyrus, *Journal of the Royal Asiatic Society* 1926, 285–90

Notes on Early Hebrew and Aramaic Epigraphy, *JPOS* 6, 75–102

Canaanite *ḥapši* and Hebrew *ḥofšî* again, ibid., 106–8

Drei assyrische Etymologien, *Zeitschrift für Assyriologie* 3, 139–40

Ass. martakal "Haschisch" und amurtinnu "Sidra," ibid., 140–41

Review of Bruno, *Gibeon, JAOS* 45, 181–82

Review of Sellin, *Wie wurde Sichem eine israelitische Stadt,* ibid., 182–84

Review of Simpson, *Pentateuchal Criticism, JPOS* 5, 156–57

Review of Eitan, *A Contribution to Biblical Lexicography,* ibid., 158–59

Review of Gadd, *A Sumerian Reading Book,* ibid., 159–61

Annual Report for 1924–25, *BASOR* 20, 9–16

Review of Dalman, *Hundert deutsche Fliegerbilder aus Palästina, JPOS* 5, 218–19

Review of Eissfeldt, *Die Quellen des Richterbuches,* ibid., 220–22

Review of Schumacher and Steuernagel, *Der Adschlun,* ibid. 6, 111–12

1926–27

An Incised Representation of a Stag from Tell el-'Oreimeh, *JPOS* 6, 167–68

The Historical Background of Genesis 14, *Journal of the Society of Oriental Research* 10, 231–69

Mesopotamian Elements in Canaanite Eschatology, *Haupt Anniversary Volume,* 143–54

The Jordan Valley in the Bronze Age, *AASOR* 6, 13–74

Notes on the Topography of Ancient Mesopotamia, *JAOS* 46, 220–30

The Excavations at Tell Beit Mirsim I-II, *BASOR* 23, 2–14

The Date of the Foundation of the Early Egyptian Temple of Byblos, *Zeitschrift für Ägyptische Sprache und Altertumskunde* 62, 62–63

Aman-hatpe, Governor of Palestine, ibid., 63–64

Another Case of Egyptian û = Coptic ê, ibid., 64

The New Cuneiform Vocabulary of Egyptian Words, *Journal of Egyptian Archaeology* 12, 186–90

The Topography of the Tribe of Issachar, *ZAW* 44, 225–36

The Spoken Arabic of Palestine (with E. N. Haddad), Jerusalem, 1927, iii+42+96 pp.

Notes on the Goddess 'Anat, *AJSL* 43, 233–36

Egypt and Palestine in the Third Millennium B.C., *Sellin Festschrift,* Leipzig, 1927, 1–12

The Babylonian Gazelle God Arwîum-Sumuqan, *AfO* 3, 181–83

The Danish Excavations at Seilûn: a Correction, *Palestine Exploration Fund Quarterly Statement* 1927, 157–58

Professor Albert T. Clay—an Appreciation, *JPOS* 6, 173–77

Review of *The People and the Book, Essays in the Old Testament,* ibid., 178–83

Professor Haupt as Scholar and Teacher, *Haupt Anniversary Volume,* pp. xx–xxxi

Annual Report for 1925–26, *BASOR* 24, 9–17

Review of Bauer, *Die Ostkanaanäer,* *AfO* 3, 124–26

Review of Pedersen, *Israel, JPOS* 6, 222–24

Review of Böhl, *Genesis,* ibid., 224–28

Review of *Vorgeschichtliches Jahrbuch,* Vol. I, ibid., 228–29

Review of Spiegelberg, *Glaubwürdigkeit von Herodots Bericht über Ägypten, JAOS* 47, 91–92

Review of Obbink, *De magische beteekenis van den Naam,* ibid., 93–94

1927–28

Notes on Egypto-Semitic Etymology III, *JAOS* 47, 198–237

The Name of Bildad the Shuhite, *AJSL* 44, 31–36

The Names "Israel" and "Judah" with an Excursus on the Etymology of *tôdâh* and *tôrâh, JBL* 46, 151–85

The End of the Inscription on the Aḥîrâm Sarcophagus, *JPOS* 7, 122–27

Among the Canaanite Mounds of Eastern Galilee, *BASOR* 29, 1–8

A Trial Excavation in the Mound of Bethel, ibid., 9–11

Tarqumuwa King of Mera, *AfO* 4, 137–38

Review of Thureau-Dangin, *Lettres de Ḫammurapi à Šamaš-ḫaṣir, Journal of the Society of Oriental Research* 11, 234

Review of Contenau, *Contrats et lettres d'Assyrie et de Babylonie,* ibid., 234–37

Review of Brawer, *Ha-'Aretz* (Geography of Palestine), *Ha-'Aretz,* Dec. 16, 1927

Review of Hogarth, *King of the Hittites, JPOS* 7, 128–31

Letter from the School in Jerusalem, *American Journal of Archaeology* 32, 117–21

Review of Contenau, *La civilisation phénicienne, JAOS* 48, 76–80

Review of Meissner-Weidner-Ebeling, *Die Inschriften der altassyrischen Könige,* ibid., 90–93

Review of Luckenbill, *Ancient Records of Assyria and Babylonia,* I–II, ibid., 93–95

In Memoriam Paul Haupt, *Beiträge zur Assyriologie und vergleichende Semitische Sprachwissenschaft* 10, No. 2, xiii–xxii

1928–29

The Second Campaign at Tell Beit Mirsim (Kiriath-sepher), *BASOR* 31, 1–11

The Egyptian Empire in Asia in the Twenty-first Century B.C., *JPOS* 8, 223–56

A Royal Stele of the New Empire from Galilee (with Alan Rowe), *Journal of Egyptian Archaeology* 14, 281–87 + 1 pl.

Die Vokalisation der asiatischen Fremdnamen und Wörter in der syllabischen Schrift des neuen Reiches (abstract), *Zeitschrift der Deutschen Morgenländischen Gesellschaft* 7, xlv–xlvi

The American Excavations at Tell Beit Mirsim, *ZAW* 47, 1–18

Progress in Palestinian Archaeology during the Year 1928, *American Journal of Archaeology* 33, 133–41 (= *BASOR* 33, 1–10)

The Second Campaign at Tell Beit Mirsim, *AfO* 5, 119–20

Review of Bezold, *Babylonisches-assyrisches Glossar, JAOS* 48, 177–82

Review of Jirku, *Die Wanderungen der Hebräer im 3. und 2. Jahrtausend v. Chr.,* ibid., 183–85

Ancient Palestine Yields Many Relics, *New York Times,* Sept. 16, 1928

Annual Report for 1927–28, *BASOR* 32, 9–14

Review of Wiener, *The Altars of the Old Testament, JPOS* 9, 50–54

1929–30

A Neglected Hebrew Inscription from the Thirteenth Century B.C., *AfO* 5, 150–52

New Israelite and Pre-Israelite Sites: The Spring Trip of 1929, *BASOR* 35, 1–14

The Anatolian Goddess Kubaba, *AfO* 5, 229–31

Review of Stephens, *Personal Names from Cuneiform Inscriptions of Cappadocia*, JPOS 9, 103–4

Review of Contenau, *Les tablettes de Kerkouk et les origines de la civilisation assyrienne*, AfO 5, 173–74

Review of Yahuda, *Die Sprache des Pentateuchs in ihren Beziehungen zum Aegyptischen* (Hebrew), *Kirjath Sepher* 1929, 195–96

Mr. Harold Wiener, BASOR 35, 22–23

Annual Report for 1928–29, ibid. 36, 10–16

1930–31

The Third Campaign at Tell Beit Mirsim, BASOR 39, 1–10 (cf. BASOR 38, 9–10)

A Millennium of Biblical History in the Light of Recent Excavations, *Proc. Am. Philos. Soc.* 69, 441–61

Excavating an Israelite City, *Presbyterian Magazine,* Dec. 1930, pp. 716–18

Mitannian *maryannu,* "chariot-warrior," and the Canaanite and Egyptian Equivalents, AfO 6, 217–21

Recent Progress in the Late Prehistory of Palestine, BASOR 42, 13–15

Notes on Semitic Proper Names in Bauer and Rostovtzeff, *The Excavations at Dura-Europos*, New Haven, 1931, pp. 115–71 *passim*

Excavations at Jerusalem (Reviews of Macalister-Duncan, *Excavations on the Hill of Ophel, Jerusalem,* Annual of Palestine Exploration Fund for 1923–25, and Crowfoot-FitzGerald, *Excavations in the Tyropoeon Valley, Jerusalem,* Annual of the Palestine Exploration Fund for 1927), *Jewish Quarterly Review* 21, 163–68

Introduction to G. L. Robinson, *The Sarcophagus of an Ancient Civilization,* New York, Macmillan, 1930, pp. xiii–xvi

Note on the Etymology of *Sîq*, "Gorge of Petra," JPOS 10, 179–80

Charles Clermont-Ganneau, *Encyclopedia of the Social Sciences* 3, 554–55

Review of Speiser, *Mesopotamian Origins*, JAOS 51, 60–66

Review of Hertz, *Die Kultur um den persischen Golf und ihre Ausbreitung,* ibid., 67–70

1931–32

The Third Campaign at Tell Beit Mirsim and its Historical Results, JPOS 11, 105–29

The First Campaign of Excavation at Beth-zur (with O. R. Sellers), BASOR 43, 2–13

The Archaeology of Western Asia at the Leyden Congress, ibid., 21–23

The Third Campaign at Tell Beit Mirsim, AfO 7, 56–58

The Site of Tirzah and the Topography of Western Manasseh, JPOS 11, 241–51

New Light on an Important Biblical City, *Discoveries* (Univ. of Pa. Mus.), 2, 3, 1–2

The Discovery of an Aramaic Inscription Relating to King Uzziah, BASOR 44, 8–10

The Archaeology of Palestine and the Bible, New York, Fleming H. Revell, 1932, 233 pp.

The Syro-Mesopotamian God Šulmân-Ešmûn and Related Figures, AfO 7, 164–69

New Light on Early Canaanite Language and Literature, BASOR 46, 15–20

The Seal of Eliakim and the Latest Preëxilic History of Judah, with some Observations on Ezekiel, JBL 51, 77–106

Review of von der Osten and Erich Schmidt, *The Alishar Hüyük, Season of 1927,* JAOS 51, 173–75

Review of Van Buren, *Clay Figurines of Assyria and Babylonia,* ibid., 175–77

Review of Ember, *Egypto-Semitic Studies,* Language 7, 147–50

Friedrich Delitzsch, *Encyclopedia of the Social Sciences* 5, 68–69

Review of Mayer and Sukenik, *The Third Wall of Jerusalem* (Hebrew), *Kirjath Sepher* 1931, 308–9

Notes on Aramaean Personal Names in Johnson, *Dura Studies,* Philadelphia, 1932, pp. 39–40

Review of Böhl, *Das Zeitalter Abrahams,* AfO 7, 197–98

Benjamin Wisner Bacon and Lewis Bayles Paton, In Memoriam, BASOR 45, 2–3

Review of Peet, *A Comparative Study of the Literatures of Egypt, Palestine, and Mesopotamia, JAOS* 52, 51–52

Review of Badè, *Some Tombs of Tell en-Naṣbeh,* ibid., 52–53

Review of Watelin and Langdon, *Excavations at Kish,* ibid., 54

Some New Publications on the History and Archaeology of Palestine, *BASOR* 46, 21–23 [Olmstead, Garstang, Kjaer, Brawer, Albright]

Recent Works on the Topography and Archaeology of Jerusalem (reviews of Mayer-Sukenik, *The Third Wall of Jerusalem,* in English and Hebrew, and Dalman, *Jerusalem und sein Gelände*), *Jewish Quarterly Review* 22, 409–16

Review of the *Quarterly of the Department of Antiquities in Palestine,* Vol. I, *JPOS* 12, 108–11

1932–33

Exilic and Post-exilic Judah in the Light of Palestinian Archaeology, *Actes du XVIIIe Congrès International des Orientalistes,* Leiden, 1932, pp. 202–4

The Excavation of Tell Beit Mirsim, I: The Pottery of the First Three Campaigns, AASOR 12, New Haven, 1932, xxi + 94 pp., 71 pls.

An Anthropoid Clay Coffin from Saḥâb in Transjordan, *American Journal of Archaeology* 36, 295–306, Pl. XII

The Fourth Joint Campaign of Excavation at Tell Beit Mirsim, *BASOR* 47, 3–17 (= *American Journal of Archaeology* 36, 556–64

The North-Canaanite Epic of 'Al'êyân Ba'al and Môt, *JPOS* 12, 185–208

The Chaldaean Conquest of Judah, A Rejoinder, *JBL* 51, 381–82

Palestine in the Light of Archaeology, *Annals of the Amer. Acad. of Polit. and Soc. Science,* Nov. 1932, pp. 184–89

The Chalcolithic Age in Palestine, *BASOR* 48, 10–13

A Set of Egyptian Playing Pieces and Dice from Palestine, *Mizraim* 1, 130–34, Pl. XIV

Archaeological and Topographical Explorations in Palestine and Syria, *BASOR* 48, 23–31

More Light on the Canaanite Epic of Aleyan and Mot, ibid. 50, 13–20

Max Leopold Margolis, In Memoriam, *BASOR* 47, 35–36

A New Decipherment of the Hittite Hieroglyphs (review of Gelb, *Hittite Hieroglyphs I*), *AJSL* 49, 61–66

Review of Robinson and Oesterley, *A History of Israel, JPOS* 12, 251–67

Recent Books on the Archaeology of Palestine, *BASOR* 48, 15–17 [Vincent-Abel, *Emmaus;* Sukenik, *The Ancient Synagogue of Beth-alpha;* E. Grant, *Ain Shems Excavations;* Petrie, *Gaza I;* Starkey-Harding-Macdonald, *Beth-pelet II*]

James Hardy Ropes and Dana Carleton Munro, In Memoriam, ibid., 31–32

Review of Grant, *Ain Shems Excavations, Art and Archaeology* 34, 110

Review of FitzGerald, *The Four Canaanite Temples of Beth-shan, the Pottery,* ibid., 111

Review of Vincent and Abel, *Emmaus, sa basilique et son histoire, American Journal of Archaeology* 37, 192a–93b

Review of Sukenik, *Bet hak-keneset ha-'atiq be-Bet-alfa, Kirjath Sepher* 10, 25

Review of Reubeni, *Shem, Ham, wa-Yefet,* ibid., 28–29

Abraham Kuenen, *Encyclopedia of the Social Sciences* 8, 609

1933–34

The Excavation of Tell Beit Mirsim, IA: *The Bronze Age Pottery of the Fourth Campaign, AASOR* 13, 55–127 (also printed as a separate monograph, Baltimore, Furst, 1933, 72 pp. 27 cuts)

The Archaeology of Palestine and the Bible, second edition (with new Preface and Supplementary Notes, pp. 7–8, 224–39), New York, Revell, 1933

A New Campaign of Excavation at Gibeah of Saul, *BASOR* 52, 6–12

How to Study the Archaeology of Palestine, ibid., 12–15 (also as separate booklet)

A New Hebrew Literature in Cuneiform, *The Jewish Forum,* 1934, 85–88

Soundings at Ader, a Bronze Age City of Moab, *BASOR* 53, 13–18

The Cuneiform Tablet from Beth-shemesh, ibid., 18–19

Light on the Jewish State in Persian Times, ibid., 20–22

Archaeology in Palestine and Syria during 1933, ibid., 22–25

Excavations during 1933 in Palestine, Transjordan, and Syria, *American Journal of Archaeology* 38, 191–99

Archaeological News from Syria, *BASOR* 54, 24–27

The Decipherment of the Hittite Hieroglyphs, ibid., 34–35 (reprinted in *Antiquity* 1934, 453–55)

The North-Canaanite Poems of Al-'êyân Ba'al and the "Gracious Gods," *JPOS* 14, 101–40

Review of Rostovtzeff, *Caravan Cities, Art and Archaeology* 34, 277–78

In Memoriam Melvin Grove Kyle, *BASOR* 51, 5–7

Review of Sellers, *The Citadel of Beth-zur,* ibid., 28–29

Review of Petrie, *Ancient Gaza, JAOS* 53, 285–87

Notes from the School in Jerusalem, *BASOR* 52, 18–20

Selah Merrill, *Dictionary of American Biography* 12, 564–65

The History of Palestine and Syria (reviews of Olmstead, *History of Palestine and Syria;* Kammerer, *Pétra et les Nabatéens*) *Jewish Quarterly Review* 24, 363–76

New Books by Officers of the Schools, *BASOR* 54, 27–28 [Montgomery, Barton, Albright]

Some Recent Publications in Palestinian Archaeology, ibid., 28–30 [Watzinger, Garstang, Engberg-Shipton, Sukenik, Kyle, *Berytus, Abel*]

Review of Hooke, *Myth and Ritual, JPOS* 14, 152–56

1934–35

A Parallel between Vedic and Babylonian Sacrificial Ritual (with P. E. Dumont), *JAOS* 54, 107–28

The First Month of the Excavations at Bethel, *BASOR* 55, 23–25

The Vocalization of the Egyptian Syllabic Orthography, American Oriental Series 5, New Haven, 1934, viii + 67 pp., 37 autographed pls.

The Kyle Memorial Excavation at Bethel, *BASOR* 56, 1–15

The Words for "Year" in Egyptian and Sumerian, *AJSL* 51, 126–27

The Excavation of the Conway High Place at Petra, *BASOR* 57, 18–26

Observations on the Bethel Report, ibid., 27–30

A Summary of Archaeological Research during 1934 in Palestine, Transjordan, and Syria, *American Journal of Archaeology* 39, 137–48

Two Great Discoveries Bearing on the Old and New Testaments, *BASOR* 58, 2–4

Archaeology and the Date of the Hebrew Conquest of Palestine, ibid., 10–18

The Inscription from Gezer at the School in Jerusalem, ibid., 28–29

The Horites in Palestine, *From the Pyramids to Paul* (George Livingstone Robinson Anniversary Volume), New York, 1935, pp. 9–26

Review of Worrell, *Coptic Sounds,* Part I, *Language* 10, 220–24

News from the School in Jerusalem, *BASOR* 55, 25–28

Review of Friedrich, *Ras Schamra, JPOS* 14, 312

John Alsop Paine, *Dictionary of American Biography* 14, 150–51

Annual Report of the Director of the School in Jerusalem, *BASOR* 56, 19–29

News from the School in Jerusalem, ibid., 30–32

Sir John Creswicke Rawlinson, *Encyclopedia of the Social Sciences* 13, 132

Vicomte Olivier Charles Emmanuel de Rougé, ibid., 444

Cornelis Petrus Tiele, ibid., 14, 628

From the School in Jerusalem, *BASOR* 57, 30–32

Recent Books on the Archaeology of Palestine and Syria, ibid., 36–37 [Garstang, Galling, Diringer, Mallon, von Oppenheim]

Review of Woolley, *Ur Excavations II: The Royal Cemetery, American Journal of Archaeology* 38, 607–9

1935-36

The Archaeology of Palestine and the Bible, third edition (revised and enlarged, pp. 7–8, 174–75, 224–43 rewritten), New York, Revell, 1935, 250 pp.

Palestine in the Earliest Historical Period (Presidential Address), *JPOS* 15, 193–234

Some Suggestions for the Decipherment of the Proto-Sinaitic Inscriptions, ibid., 334–40

The Names Shaddai and Abram, *JBL* 54, 173–204

The Ancient Near East at the Congress of Orientalists in Rome, *BASOR* 60, 2–9

Primitivism in Ancient Western Asia (Mesopotamia and Israel), in Lovejoy and Boas, *A Documentary History of Primitivism,* Baltimore, 1935, pp. 421–32

A Supplement to Jeremiah: The Lachish Ostraca, *BASOR* 61, 10–16

The Song of Deborah in the Light of Archaeology, ibid. 62, 26–31

Archaeological Explorations and Excavations in Palestine and Syria (1935), *American Journal of Archaeology* 40, 154–67

Zabûl Yam and Thâpiṭ Nahar in the Combat between Baal and the Sea, *JPOS* 16, 17–20

Review of Abel, *Géographie de la Palestine I, JPOS* 15, 185–89

From the School in Jerusalem, *BASOR* 59, 6–7

Some Notes on Recent Books, ibid., 9–12 [Meek, Mallowan-Rose, Van Buren, Frankfort, Chiera, C. H. Kraeling, Jack, G. L. Robinson Volume, Frank-Alt, Albright]

Review of Eissfeldt, *Molk als Opferbegriff und das Ende des Gottes Moloch, JPOS* 15, 344

The Late James Henry Breasted, *The Palestine Post,* Dec. 5, pp. 4–5

Notes and News from Jerusalem, *BASOR* 60, 11–14

Report of the Director of the School in Jerusalem, ibid., 18–30

Edward Robinson, *Dictionary of American Biography* 16, 39–40

Eli Smith, ibid., 17, 257–58

Moses Stuart, ibid., 18, 174–75

James Henry Breasted, In Memoriam, *BASOR* 61, 2–4

The New Head of the Oriental Institute (J. A. Wilson), ibid., 19

The New Director of the School in Jerusalem (N. Glueck), ibid., 20

Archaeological Notes and News of the School in Jerusalem, ibid., 23–25

Comments on Books Received by the Editor, ibid., 26–31 [Watzinger, Galling, R. W. Hamilton, Lamon, Sukenik, Bar Deroma, ʿArif Bey el-ʿArif, Granqvist, *PJB* 31, Ch. W. Harris, Ben Zevi, Assaf, Montgomery-Harris, H. L. Ginsberg, Gelb, Ingholt, Barnett]

William Frederic Badè (Jan. 22, 1871–March 4, 1936) ibid., 62, 4–5

Additional Note to Bergman, Soundings at the Supposed Site of Old Testament Anathoth, ibid. 25–26

News of the Schools, ibid., 31–33

News of Excavations in Palestine, ibid., 33–34

The Retiring Director of the British School: An Appreciation, *Palestine Exploration Fund Quarterly Statement* 1936, 83–86

Review of Watzinger, *Denkmäler Palästinas, JPOS* 16, 50–58

Review of Phythian-Adams, *The Call of Israel,* ibid., 67–68

1936-37

James Henry Breasted, Humanist, *The American Scholar* 5, 287–99, with frontisp.

The Early Evolution of the Hebrew Alphabet, *BASOR* 63, 8–12

New Canaanite Historical and Mythological Data, ibid., 23–32

Some Recent Archaeological Discoveries, *The Jewish Forum,* Sept. 1936, 205–6

The Canaanite God Ḥaurôn (Ḥôrôn), *AJSL* 53, 1–12

Recent Discoveries in Bible Lands, supplement to Young, *Analytical Concordance to the Bible* (20th ed.), New York, Funk and Wagnalls, 1936, 45 pp.

Ostracon C 1101 of Samaria, *Palestine Exploration Fund Quarterly Statement,* 1936, 211–15

Archaeological Exploration and Excavation in Palestine, Transjordan, and Syria during 1936 (with N. Glueck), *American Journal of Archaeology* 41, 146–53

Review of Alt, *Ursprünge des israelitischen Rechts, JBL* 55, 164–69

Short book notices, ibid., 172–74 [Glueck, Ch. W. Harris, Kohut Volume, Weiser, Bickermann]

Note on Bergman, Anathoth?, *BASOR* 63, 23

From the School in Jerusalem, ibid., 35–37

Review of Galling, *Biblisches Reallexikon, JPOS* 16, 255

Memorial to James Henry Breasted, *Bulletin of the American Council of Learned Societies* 25, 58–59

Review of Mallon-Koeppel-Neuville, *Teleilat Ghassul, American Journal of Archaeology* 40, 389a–90b

Review of Bittel, *Die Felsbilder von Yazilikaya,* and *Prähistorische Forschung in Kleinasien,* ibid., 391a–92b

Article "Explorations and Excavations" *New Standard Bible Dictionary,* third revised edition, New York, 1936

Some Recent Publications, *BASOR* 64, 28–32 [Garstang, Ory-Mrs. Iliffe, Johns, Avi Yonah, Iliffe, Stékélis, Hennequin, Narkiss, Maisler, Solomiac, Z. S. Harris, Parrot, Graham-May, Goetze, Jean, Edgerton-Wilson]

Report of the Director of the School in Jerusalem (with C. C. McCown), ibid., 35–44

Review of Hempel, *Gott und Mensch im Alten Testament, JBL* 55, 311–14

Review of *Werden und Wesen des Alten Testaments,* ibid., 316–18

Review of the *Hebrew Union College Annual* (11), ibid., 321–22

Brief notices, ibid., 322–26 [Eissfeldt, Alt, Würthwein, Munch, Holzhey, E. Hirsch, Schmökel, Tchernowitz, Narkiss, Bergman]

Review of H. L. Ginsberg, *Kitvê Ugarit, Kirjath Sepher* 13, 426–27

From the School in Jerusalem, *BASOR* 65, 37–38

Some New Archaeological Books, ibid. 66, 28–32 [Dura-Europos Volume, Meek, Albright, Dussaud, Cantineau, Goldmann, Winnett, Mallowan, Stein, Thompson-Gadd]

1937–38

Hat-tanakh le'or ha'arke'ologiyah, *Had-Do'ar,* 25 Sivan, 5697, p. 488

Western Asia in the Twentieth Century B.C.: The Archives of Mari, *BASOR* 67, 26–30

A Biblical Fragment from the Maccabaean Age: the Nash Papyrus, *JBL* 56, 145–76

Further Light on the History of Israel from Lachish and Megiddo, *BASOR* 68, 22–26

The Present State of Syro-Palestinian Archaeology, *Haverford Symposium on Archaeology and the Bible,* New Haven, 1938, pp. 1–46

A Revolution in the Chronology of Ancient Western Asia, *BASOR* 69, 18–21

What Were the Cherubim?, *Biblical Archaeologist* 1, 1–3

Archaeology Confronts Biblical Criticism, *The American Scholar* 7, 176–88

The Egyptian Correspondence of Abimilki, Prince of Tyre, *Journal of Egyptian Archaeology* 23, 190–203

The Oldest Hebrew Letters: the Lachish Ostraca, *BASOR* 70, 11–17

Recent Progress in North-Canaanite Research, ibid., 18–24

The Excavation of Tell Beit Mirsim, II: The Bronze Age, AASOR 17, New Haven, 1938, xxiv + 96 pp., 56 pls.

From the School in Jerusalem, *BASOR* 67, 33–36

Some Recent Archaeological Publications, ibid., 36–37 [Garstang, Ben Dor, FitzGerald, Sukenik, Schaeffer, Bauer, Ingholt, Klein, Stephens, Contenau, Cross, ed. Mayer]

Review of *Dura-Europos VI, JAOS* 57, 318–21

Review of Legrain, *Archaic Seal Impressions, American Journal of Archaeology* 41, 497a–98b

Review of Mallowan, *The Excavations at Tall Chagar Bazar,* ibid., 498b–501b

Review of Starr and Butin, *Excavations and Proto-Sinaitic Inscriptions at Serabit el Khadem,* ibid., 501b–2a

Review of Forbes, *Petroleum and Bitumen in Antiquity, Classical Weekly,* Oct. 18, 1937, pp. 18b–19b

Review of Calice, *Grundlagen der ägyptisch-semitischen Wortvergleichung, AfO* 12, 71a–73a

Review of Loud et al., *Khorsabad* I, *JBL* 56, 412–13

Review of Jean, *Le milieu biblique avant Jésus-Christ, III: Les idées religieuses et morales,* ibid., 417–18

Reviews of Torczyner, Buber-Rosenzweig, Coppens, Jirku, Spinner, Malden, Romanoff, ibid., 420–23

Three New Publications of the Schools, *BASOR* 68, 26–27 [R. F. S. Starr, Speiser, Wright]

Review of Woolley, *Abraham, Journal of the Bible and Religion* 5, 182–83

Romain Butin, In Memoriam (with J. A. Montgomery), *BASOR* 69, 4–5

James Llewellyn Starkey, Excavator of Lachish, ibid., 6–7

Review of Waterman, *Preliminary Report of the University of Michigan Excavations at Sepphoris, Classical Weekly,* March 7, 1938, p. 148

The Protosinaitic Inscriptions (review of Grimme, *Altsinaitische Forschungen*), *Jewish Quarterly Review* 28, 333–35

Review of Auerbach, *Wüste und Gelobtes Land,* II, *Kirjath Sepher* 15, 68–70

James Henry Breasted (obituary notice), *Year Book of the American Philosophical Society,* 1937, pp. 338–41

1938–39

The Northwest-Semitic Tongues before 1000 B.C., *XIX Congresso Internazionale degli Orientalisti,* Rome, 1938, 445–50

Was the Patriarch Terah a Canaanite Moon-God?, *BASOR* 71, 35–40

The Chronology of a South Palestinian City, Tell el-'Ajjûl, *AJSL* 55, 337–59

A Hebrew Letter from the Twelfth Century B.C., *BASOR* 73, 9–13

A Reëxamination of the Lachish Letters, ibid., 16–21

The Israelite Conquest of Canaan in the Light of Archaeology, ibid. 74, 11–23

Maps of Bible Lands (with J. O. Boyd), New York, American Bible Society, 1939, iv + 12 pp.

Ceramics and Chronology in the Near East, *So Live the Works of Men* (Edgar Lee Hewett Anniversary Volume), Santa Fe, Univ. of New Mexico Press, 1939, pp. 49–63

Astarte Plaques and Figurines from Tell Beit Mirsim, *Mélanges syriens offerts à M. René Dussaud,* Paris, Geuthner, 1939, I, 107–20

Review of Auerbach, *Wüste und Gelobtes Land,* II, *JBL* 57, 219

Review of Causse, *Du groupe ethnique à la communauté religieuse,* ibid., 219–21

Review of Buber, *Königtum Gottes,* ibid., 221

Review of Gordis, *The Biblical Text in the Making: A Study of the Kethib-Qere,* ibid., 223–24

Review of Noth, *Das Buch Josua,* ibid., 226

Review of Hölscher, *Das Buch Hiob,* ibid., 227–28

Review of Mowinckel, *The Two Sources of the Predeuteronomic Primeval History,* ibid., 230–31

Review of Galling, *Biblisches Reallexikon,* and Dalman, *Arbeit und Sitte in Palästina,* V, ibid., 234–35

Review of Jirku, *Die ägyptischen Listen palästinischer und syrischer Ortsnamen, AfO* 12, 157–59

On Dr. Gordis's Communication, *JBL* 57, 332–33

Addendum to Glueck, "The First Campaign at Tell el-Kheleifeh (Eziongeber)," *BASOR* 71, 17–18

Review of Dussaud, *Les découvertes de Ras Shamra, Antiquity* 12, 370–72

Review of Pfeiffer-Speiser, *AASOR* 16, and of Glueck, *AASOR* 17, *JBL* 57, 435–36

Review of *Haverford Symposium,* and Wright, *Pottery of Palestine from the Earliest Times to the End of the Early Bronze Age,* ibid., 440–41

Notes on Glueck, "The Topography and History of Ezion-geber and Elath," *BASOR* 72, 11–13

Note on the names Ziper and Zineida in C. H. Kraeling, *Gerasa,* New Haven, 1938, p. 489

A. V. Williams Jackson, *Bulletin of the American Council of Learned Societies* 27, 87–89

Review of A. Vincent, *La religion des Judéo-Araméens d'Éléphantine, Jewish Social Studies* 1, 128

Review of De Genouillac, *Fouilles de Telloh,* ii, *American Journal of Archaeology* 42, 590–91

Review of Schaeffer et al., *La septième campagne de fouilles à Ras Shamra (Ugarit),* ibid., 591–92

Review of Lassus, *Inventaire archéologique de la region au nord-est de Hama,* ibid., 592–93

Review of von Soden, *Der Aufstieg des Assyrerreichs, Orientalia* 8, 120–23

Recent Books on the Archaeology, Geography, and History of Western Asia, *BASOR* 74, 25–28 [Guy-Engberg-Hrdlička, Otto, Abel, Maisler-Ben Shammai-et al., Maisler-Ben Dor-Glueck-Klein-Avi Yonah-Narkiss, Ben Zevi, Narkiss, Yeivin, Schofield, E. F. Schmidt, Christian, Gordon, Parrot, ed. Mayer, Schloessinger]

Review of Starr, *Nuzi* ii, *American Journal of Archaeology* 43, 159

Review of Braidwood, *Mounds in the Plain of Antioch,* ibid., 160–61

1939–40

The Babylonian Matter in the Predeuteronomic Primeval History (JE) in Gen. 1–11, part 2 (reply to Mowinckel), *JBL* 58, 91–103

An Aramaean Magical Text in Hebrew from the Seventh Century B.C., *BASOR* 76, 5–11

New Light on the History of Western Asia in the Second Millennium B.C., ibid. 77, 20–32; 78, 23–31

The Ancient Near East and the Religion of Israel (Presidential Address), *JBL* 59, 85–112

Review of Abel, *Géographie de la Palestine,* ii, *JBL* 58, 177–87

Review of Finkelstein, *The Pharisees, Menorah Journal,* 1939, 232a–34b

Review of Simons, *Handbook for the Study of Egyptian Topographical Lists Relating to Western Asia, AfO* 12, 384b–86a

Note on Ben Mordecai, Chezib, *JBL* 58, 286

Some Recent Books on the Near East, *BASOR* 75, 31–32; 76, 14–15 [Grant-Wright, Watzinger, Schaeffer, Z. S. Harris, Berry, James, Przeworski, Garstang, Salonen, Gordon, Friedrich, Speiser, Engberg, ed. Mayer, J. Starr]

Review of Hempel, *Das Ethos des Alten Testaments, JBL* 58, 392–94

Review of Torczyner, *The Lachish Letters, Kirjath Sepher* 16, 310–12

Review of Torczyner, *The Lachish Letters, Asia* 38, 627

Review of Guy and Engberg, *The Megiddo Tombs,* ibid., 39, 306

Article *"Amarna," Universal Jewish Encyclopedia* i, 221

Article "Achaeology," ibid., 459–66

From Letter to A. M. Honeyman, *Iraq* 6, 108

Review of Frankfort, *Sculpture of the Third Millennium B.C. from Tell Asmar and Khafajah, Asia* 40, 166–67

Note on E. G. Kraeling, "Light from Ugarit on the Khabiru," *BASOR* 77, 32–33

Cyrus Adler, In Memoriam, ibid. 78, 3

Archaeology in the Near East (reviews of Glueck, E. F. Schmidt, Loud), *Asia* 40, 280

Note to Engberg, Historical Analysis of Archaeological Evidence: Megiddo and the Song of Deborah, *BASOR* 78, 7–9

Books Received by the Editor, ibid., 36–38 [Koeppel-Senès-Murphy-Mahan, Ehrich, Otto, Rostovtzeff-Brown-Welles-et al., Jacobsen, Eissfeldt, Parrot, Hrozný, Halley, ed. Hitti et al., Goitein]

Tenney Frank (obituary notice), *Year Book of the American Philosophical Society for 1939,* 444–46

Review of the *Hebrew Union College Annual* (12–14), *JBL* 59, 298–302

Review of Yellin, *Ḥiqre Miqra: Yeshayahu, and Ketavim Nivḥarim II,* ibid., 303–4

Review of Mercer, *The Tell el-Amarna Tablets,* ibid., 313–15

Review of Goetze, *The Hittite Ritual of Tunnawi,* ibid., 315–16

1940–41

The Archaeological Background of the Hebrew Prophets of the Eighth Century, *Journal of the Bible and Religion* 8, 131–36

Islam and the Religions of the Ancient Orient, *JAOS* 60, 283–301

From the Stone Age to Christianity: Monotheism and the Historical Process, Baltimore, The Johns Hopkins Press, 1940, xi + 363 pp.

Archaeology and Religion, *Science, Philosophy and Religion; A Symposium,* New York, 1941, pp. 279–306

New Light on the Walls of Jerusalem in the New Testament Age, *BASOR* 81, 6–8

New Egyptian Data on Palestine in the Patriarchal Age, ibid., 16–21

The Lachish Letters after Five Years, ibid. 82, 18–24

Two Letters from Ugarit (Ras Shamrah), ibid., 43–49

Letter of June 6, 1932, to Maurice Dunand, in Dunand, *Fouilles de Byblos,* I, 313, No. 4183

Review of Kenyon, *The Bible and Archaeology, Thought* 1941, 193–95

Tenney Frank (Memorial), *Bulletin of the American Council of Learned Societies* 31, 47–49

Nathaniel Schmidt (Memorial), ibid., 49–50

Review of Glueck, *The Other Side of the Jordan, Asia* 40, 558

Notes to Glueck, The Third Season of Excavation at Tell el-Kheleifeh, *BASOR* 79, 15, 21; Kramer, Ishtar in the Nether World according to a new Sumerian Text, 21, 25; Torrey, A Hebrew Seal from the Reign of Ahaz, 28 f.

Some Recent Books Received by the Editor, ibid., 35–37 [Rowe, Gordon, S. Smith, Van Buren, Heidel, Goetze, Liebmann]

Review of Harris, *Development of the Canaanite Dialects, JAOS* 60, 414–22

Review of Barrois, *Manuel d'Archéologie biblique, Classical Weekly* 34, 45–46

Review of Sethe-Schott, *Vom Bilde zum Buchstaben, Language* 16, 357–58

Notes to Glueck, Ostraca from Elath, *BASOR* 80, 6–9

Note to Wampler, *Triangular Impressed Design in Palestine Pottery,* ibid., 16

Note to Mendelsohn, *Guilds in Ancient Palestine,* ibid., 21

Review of Fernández, *Problemas de topografía palestinense, JBL* 59, 538–43

Review of Fernández, *Commentarius in Librum Josue,* ibid., 543–46

Review of Lamon and Shipton, *Megiddo, I,* and Shipton, *Notes on the Megiddo Pottery, American Journal of Archaeology* 44, 546a–50b

Postcript to W. R. Taylor, A New Samaritan Inscription, *BASOR* 81, 5–6

Postscript to Lewy and Lacheman, A Propos of Criticism in Assyriology, ibid., 22–23

Ostracon No. 6043 from Ezion-geber, ibid. 82, 11–15

Note on Torrey, The Seal from the Reign of Ahaz Again, ibid., 16–17

Notes on Wampler, Three Cistern Groups from Tell en-Naṣbeh, ibid., 25, 31–32, 36, 43

1941–42

New Light on the Early History of Phoenician Colonization, *BASOR* 83, 14–22

The Land of Damascus between 1850 and 1750 B.C., ibid., 30–36

Are the Ephod and the Teraphim Mentioned in Ugaritic Literature?, ibid., 39–42

The Egypto-Canaanite Deity Haurôn, ibid. 84, 7–12

Anath and the Dragon, ibid., 14–17

The Rôle of the Canaanites in the History of Civilization, *Studies in the History of Culture* (Waldo Leland Volume), Menasha, Wis., 1942, pp. 11–50

Two Cressets from Marisa and the Pillars of Jachin and Boaz, *BASOR* 85, 18–27

Archaeology and the Religion of Israel, Baltimore, The Johns Hopkins Press, 1942, xii + 238 pp.

Observations on the Date of the Pottery-bearing Stratum of Mughâret Abū Uṣbaʿ, *BASOR* 86, 10–14

A Teacher to a Man of Shechem about 1400 B.C., ibid., 28–31

The Creation of the Composite Bow in Canaanite Mythology (with G. E. Mendenhall), *JNES* 1, 227–29

Review of Tufnell, Inge, and Harding, *Lachish II: The Fosse Temple, Asia* 41, 393–94

Reviews of Dürr, *Die Wertung des göttlichen Wortes im alten Testament und im antiken Orient;* Clemen, *Die phönikische Religion nach Philo von Byblos;* Stamm, *Die akkadische Namengebung, JBL* 60, 205–12.

Article "Nelson Glueck," *Universal Jewish Encyclopedia* IV, 627

Postscript to I. Ben-Zevi, The Beit el-Mā Samaritan Inscription, *BASOR* 84, 4

Postscript to Sukenik, A Note on the Seal of the Servant of Ahaz, ibid., 18–19

An Authoritative Introduction to Biblical Archaeology, ibid., 19

Books and Monographs Received by the Editor, ibid., 20–25 [Dunand, Stillwell-et al., Ingholt, Noth, Rosenthal, Pedersen, Balázs, Hallock, Kramer, Hyatt, Gordon, Garstang, Seele, Cooney-Riefstahl, Clawson, Tseretheli, Nioradze, Starr, Nilsson, Neuman, Adler, Rosenblatt, Pfeiffer, Morgenstern, Faris]

Samuel Klein, *Jewish Social Studies* 3, 124–25

Review of Gordon, *The Living Past, JBL* 60, 433–34

Review of Gordon, *Ugaritic Grammar,* ibid., 434–49

Article "High Place," *Universal Jewish Encyclopedia* v, 357–58

Article "Hittites," ibid., 402–3

Article "Inscriptions (Hebrew and Aramaic)," ibid., 570

Review of Burrows, *What Mean These Stones?, Asia* 42, 75–76

The Near East Needs the Jews, *The New Palestine* 32, No. 9, 12–13

Review of Adler, *I Have Considered the Days, Thought* 7, 174–75

Notes on Speiser, The Shibboleth Incident, *BASOR* 85, 10–12

Notes on Rowley, The Exodus and the Settlement in Canaan, ibid., 27–31

Note on Glueck, Further Explorations in Eastern Palestine, ibid. 86, 20

Notes on Wright, Two Misunderstood Items in the Exodus-Conquest Cycle, ibid., 32–33

Note on Lacheman, Note on the Word *ḫupšu* at Nuzi, ibid., 37

A New Wall-map of Palestine, ibid., 37–38

1942–43

A Votive Stele Erected by Ben-Hadad I of Damascus to the God Melcarth, *BASOR* 87, 23–29

A Case of Lèse-Majesté in Pre-Israelite Lachish, with Some Remarks on the Israelite Conquest, ibid., 32–38

From the Stone Age to Christianity, third printing (with changes in Preface and some forty lines of text), Baltimore, The Johns Hopkins Press, 1942

Japheth in the Tents of Shem, *Asia* 42, 692–94

A Third Revision of the Early Chronology of Western Asia, *BASOR* 88, 28–36

King Joiachin in Exile, *Biblical Archaeologist* 5, 49–55

Two Little Understood Amarna Letters from the Middle Jordan Valley, *BASOR* 89, 7–17

An Archaic Hebrew Proverb in an Amarna Letter from Central Palestine, ibid., 29–32

Some Notes on the Stele of Benhadad, ibid. 90, 32–34

The Copper Spatula of Byblus and Proverbs 18:18, ibid., 35–37

The Excavation of Tell Beit Mirsim, III: The Iron Age, AASOR 21–22 (with a chapter by J. L. Kelso and J. P. Thorley), New Haven, 1943, xxvi + 229 pp., 73 pls.

Review of Pfeiffer, *Introduction to the Old Testament, JBL* 61, 111–26

Palestine and Auxiliary Immigration Stations, *The Jewish Forum,* July 1942

Palestine in a Brave New World, *The New Palestine,* Sept. 11, 1942, 11–12

Review of Goetze, *Kizzuwatna and the Problem of Hittite Geography, American Journal of Archaeology* 46, 444–46

George Aaron Barton, *BASOR* 87, 4–5

Sir W. M. Flinders Petrie, ibid., 7–8

George Andrew Reisner, ibid., 10

Note on Levi della Vida, The Phoenician God Satrapes, ibid., 32

Note on Marcus, The Word Šibboleth Again, ibid., 39

Some Books Lately Received by the Editor, ibid., 41–42 [Morey, Turner, Steindorff-Seele, Leland Anniversary Volume, Dohan, Maisler-et al., Flight-Fahs, Olmstead]

Elihu Grant, ibid. 88, 3

Some Recently Received Books, ibid., 39–41 [Delougaz-Lloyd, Gelb, Hyslop-Taylor-Williams-Waechter, Worrell, Leslau, Ginsberg, Lieberman, Neuman, Pinson, Hanna, *Berytus*]

Review of Steindorff-Seele, *When Egypt Ruled the East, JBL* 61, 299–305

Remarks on Dr. Stekelis's Late Prehistoric Chronology, *BASOR* 89, 24–25

Article "Mizpah," *Universal Jewish Encyclopedia* VII, 599

Article "Ostraca," ibid. VIII, 333–34

Article "Phoenicians," ibid., 517–19

Contribution to Symposium on the Conference on Science, Philosophy and Religion, *The Humanist* 3, No. 1, 25–26

Reply to Neville Barbour on The Arab Movement, *Asia* 43, 261

Review of Delougaz and Lloyd, *Pre-Sargonid Temples in the Diyala Region,* ibid., 317

Note on Glueck, Three Israelite Towns in the Jordan Valley, *BASOR* 90, 17–18

Books Received by the Editor, ibid., 39–42 [ed. Sukenik, ed. Ingholt, ed. Glanville, Martin, Coppens, Cassuto, Johnson, Filson, Prakken, Waterman, Patai, Rosenblatt, Brill]

1943–44

Palestina ante la incógnita del Nuevo Mundo de mañana, *La Luz,* Buenos Aires, 1943, 79–81

The Furniture of El in Canaanite Mythology, *BASOR* 91, 39–44

The Gezer Calendar, ibid. 92, 16–26

A Tablet of the Amarna Age from Gezer, ibid., 28–30

A Prince of Taanach in the Fifteenth Century B.C., ibid. 94, 12–27

A Vow to Asherah in the Keret Epic, ibid., 30–31

The "Natural Force" of Moses in the Light of Ugaritic, ibid., 32–35

Historical Adjustments in the Concept of Sovereignty in the Near East, *Approaches to World Peace,* New York, Harper and Brothers, 1944, pp. 1–16

Article "Shechem," *Universal Jewish Encyclopedia* IX, 499

Notes on Glueck, Some Ancient Towns in the Plains of Moab, *BASOR* 91, 10–20

Notes on Oppenheim, Assyriological Gleanings I, ibid., 37–38

Publications Recently Received by the Editor, ibid., 44–47 [Burrows, McCown, Crowfoot-Kenyon-Sukenik, Pritchard, Albright, Duell-Gettens, Cooney, Mason, Gelb-Purves-MacRae, Steele, Liebesny, Alexander, Mendelsohn, Gordon]

Notes on Glueck, Ramoth-gilead, ibid. 92, 12–13

A Great Jewish Historian on the Beginnings of Christianity, *Jewish Frontier,* Nov. 1943, 29–30

Article "Sumerians," *Universal Jewish Encyclopedia* X, 102

Article "Tehom," ibid., 187

Article "Tombs of the Kings," ibid., 265

Article "Ur of the Chaldees," ibid., 379–80

Review of Allis, *The Five Books of Moses, JBL* 62, 357–61

Review of Heidel, *The Babylonian Genesis: The Story of Creation,* ibid., 366–70

Review of Worrell, *Coptic Texts in the University of Michigan Collections,* ibid., 373–74

Review of Speiser, *Introduction to Hurrian,* ibid., 374–75

Review of Sbordone, *Hori Apollinis Hieroglyphica, Classical Weekly* 37, 107–8

Review of Coppens, *The Old Testament and the Critics, Theological Studies* 4, 601–3

Review of Smith, *Alalakh and Chronology, American Journal of Archaeology* 47, 491–92

Notes on Oppenheim, Assyriological Gleanings II, *BASOR* 93, 15–16

In Reply to Dr. Gaster's Observations, ibid., 23–25

Publications Recently Received by the Editor, ibid., 25–27 [Ingholt, Mayer-Reifenberg-Maisler-Cassuto, Garstang, Engnell, Lewy, Feigin, Klausner-Stinespring, Marcus, Fritsch, Farmer, Rosenthal]

William Rosenau, In Memoriam, *Johns Hopkins Alumni Magazine* 32, 52

The Place of Minorities in Our Civilization, *The Jewish Forum*, April 1944, 85–86

Palestine Transformed (review of Lowdermilk, *Palestine, Land of Promise*), *The Nation* 158, No. 23, 656–57

The Arabs and the Jews in the Voice of Christian America, *Washington*, 1944, 18–22

1944–45

The Oracles of Balaam, *JBL* 63, 207–33

Early-Bronze Pottery from Bâb ed-Drâ' in Moab: I. Description and Chronology, *BASOR* 95, 3–11

An Unrecognized Amarna Letter from Ugarit, ibid., 30–33

The End of Calneh in Shinar, *JNES* 3, 254–55

The Old Testament and Canaanite Language and Literature, *Catholic Biblical Quarterly* 7, 5–31

The Rediscovery of the Biblical World, in Wright and Filson, *The Westminster Historical Atlas to the Bible*, Philadelphia, Westminster Press, 1945, pp. 9–14

Is the Mesha Inscription a Forgery? *Jewish Quarterly Review* 35, 247–50

A New Hebrew Word for "Glaze" in Proverbs 26:23, *BASOR* 98, 24–25

The Talmud (Invitation to Learning Symposium), *Talks: a Quarterly Digest of Addresses Broadcast over the Columbia Network* 10, No. 2, pp. 15–17

Review of Byng, *The World of the Arabs, Palestine* 1, No. 8, 8–9

Recent Publications Received by the Editor, ibid., 37–42 [Braidwood-Tulane-Perlins-Braidwood, Kantor, Dunand, de Vaux, Glueck, Levi, Riefstahl, Brand, Smith, Hill, Riefstahl, Westermann et al., Maisler, Picard, Lowdermilk, Kramer, Patton, Steinmueller, Wright, Rowley, Thiele, Wach, Patai, Segrè, Marx]

Review of Kramer, *Sumerian Mythology, Thought* 19, 514–16

Review of Kramer, *Sumerian Mythology, JAOS* 64, 146–48

Review of Woolley, *Ur Excavations V: The Ziggurat and its Surroundings, American Journal of Archaeology* 48, 303–5

Review of Wetzel and Weissbach, *Das Hauptheiligtum des Marduk in Babylon*, ibid., 305–6

Review of Starr and others, Nuzi, Vol. I, *American Journal of Archaeology* 48, 306–8

Review of Scholem, *Major Trends in Jewish Mysticism, JBL* 63, 436–38

Review of Davis-Gehman, *The Westminster Dictionary of the Bible, The Westminster Bookman* 4, No. 3, 2–3

Review of Gelb, *Hittite Hieroglyphs, III, JNES* 4, 58–59

Review of Braun, *History and Romance in Graeco-Oriental Literature, American Journal of Philology* 66, 100–4

Review of Winlock, *The Temple of Hibis in El Khargeh Oasis*, ibid., 104

Foreword to Engel-Janosi, *The Growth of German Historicism*, Baltimore, The Johns Hopkins Press, 1944, pp. 11–12

Postscript to Professor May's article, *BASOR* 97, 26

Some Recent Publications Received by the Editor, ibid. 98, 27–31 [Wright-Filson, Maisler, Romanoff, Thompson, Riefstahl, West-Johnson, Lewy, Gelb, Bossert, Güterbock, Landsberger, Lloyd Gehman, Lane-Miller, Cassuto, Neufeld, Scott, Johnson, Steinmueller-Sullivan]

Some Functions of Organized Minorities in Approaches to National Unity,

New York, *Conference on Science, Philosophy and Religion,* 1945, 260–68, 271–72, 274–75

Discussion of papers by Roucek, Shridharani, Allers, ibid., 178–79, 311–12, 517–18

A Tribute to Hebrew University on its 20th Anniversary, *News Bulletin* (Hebrew University) 8, No. 3, 4

Review of *Hebrew Union College Annual* (16–18), *JBL* 64, 285–96

1945–46

An Indirect Synchronism between Egypt and Mesopotamia, *ca.* 1730 B.C., *BASOR* 99, 9–18

A Note on the Name of the Forger of the Moabite Antiquities, *Jewish Quarterly Review* 36, 177

The Chronology of the Divided Monarchy of Israel, *BASOR* 100, 16–22

L'hypothèse négébite des origines canaanéennes, *Actes du XXe. Congrès International des Orientalistes,* Louvain, 1940, pp. 253–56

Cuneiform Material for Egyptian Prosopography, 1500–1200 B.C., *JNES* 5, 7–25

A Brief History of Judah from the Days of Josiah to Alexander the Great, *Biblical Archaeologist* 9, 1–16

The List of Levitic Cities, *Louis Ginzberg Jubilee Volume,* English Section, pp. 49–73

Israel in the Framework of the Ancient Near East, *The Jewish People, Past and Present,* New York, Jewish Encyclopedic Handbooks, Inc., I, 27–47

George Ricker Berry, 1865–1945, *BASOR* 99, 5

Some Publications Received by the Editor, ibid., 21–23 [Sukenik, Braidwood, Ehrich, Levi, Steindorff, Neugebauer, Elmer-Faris, Leslau, Stetson, Bierberg, Reines, Korngrün, Faris, Birnbaum, Roth, Halkin]

Albert Ten Eyck Olmstead (obituary), *American Journal of Archaeology* 49, 358–59

Review of Finegan, *Light from the Ancient Past, Christian Century,* April 10, 1946, pp. 462–63

The River Jordan (review of Glueck, *The River Jordan*), *BASOR* 102, 19

Some Books and Journals Received from Abroad, ibid., 19–22 [Dunand, Mouterde-Poidebard, Langhe, Parrot, Dossin, Jean, *Sumer,* Van Buren, Ravn, Basmadschi, Praag, Ravn, Salonen, *A Topographical-Historical Encyclopaedia of Palestine,* Klein, Vilnay, Glueck, *Bulletin of the Jewish Palestine Exploration Society,* Qóveṣ, Ashkenazi]

1946–47

From the Stone Age to Christianity, 2nd edition (new preface, pp. vii-viii, and pp. 364–67 added), Baltimore, The Johns Hopkins Press, 1946

The Late Bronze Age Town at Modern Djett, *BASOR* 104, 25–26

The Names "Nazareth" and "Nazoraean," *JBL* 65, 397–401

Archaeology and the Religion of Israel, 2nd revised edition (with many changes in detail and several additions), Baltimore, The Johns Hopkins Press, 1946

Survey of Christianity in Palestine and Its Attitude toward the Jewish Question, *Palestine: A Study of Jewish, Arab and British Policies,* New Haven, Yale University Press, 1947, I, 534–53

Review of Glueck, *The River Jordan, Asia* 46, 335

English Abstract of Eichrodt's Review of Fosdick, *Guide to Understanding the Bible, JBL* 65, 205–8

Review of Glueck, *The River Jordan, Journal of the Bible and Religion* 14, 169–70

More Books and Journals Received from Abroad, *BASOR* 103, 14–18 [*Bibliotheca Orientalis,* Dunand, Maisler, Baqir, Lloyd, Borowski, Rowe, Lange-Neugebauer, Polotsky, Tcherikover, Pedersen, Coppens, Cook, Rowley, Haldar, Kapelrud, Nielsen, Messel, Rowley, Danell, Yeivin, ed. Weir, *Revue Biblique, Edoth,* Lichtenstädter]

Review of Torrey, *The Apocryphal Literature, Theology Today* 3, 418–21

Review of Snaith, *The Distinctive Ideas of the Old Testament, The Presbyterian,* Dec. 5, 1946, p. 16

Review of Eichrodt, *Das Menschen-verständnis des Alten Testaments, JBL* 65, 412–14

Review of *Studies in Memory of Moses Schorr,* ibid., 418–21

Review of Vergote, *Phonétique historique de l'Égyptien, JAOS* 66, 316a–20b

Review of Burrows, *An Outline of Biblical Theology, The Westminster Bookman* 6, No. 3, 8–12

Review of De Koning, *Studiën over de El-Amarnabrieven en het Oude-Testament inzonderheit uit historisch Oogpunt, JNES* 6, 58–59

Review of Schaeffer and others, *Xe et XIe Campagnes de Fouilles à Ras Shamra-Ugarit, Rapport sommaire, American Journal of Archaeology* 50, 317–18

Review of Schaeffer and others, *La Huitième Campagne de Fouilles à Ras Shamra-Ugarit, Rapport sommaire,* ibid., 318

Review of Adams, *Ancient Records and the Bible, Crozer Quarterly* 24, 183–84

Egyptian Art at the Walters (review of Steindorff, *Catalogue of the Egyptian Sculpture in the Walters Art Gallery*), *Baltimore Evening Sun,* March 12, 1947

Comment on Recently Received Publications, *BASOR* 105, 12–16 [Reisner, Smith, Parrot, Hare-Porada, *Sumer,* Sachs, Bossert-Cambel, Akurgal, *Revue de la Faculté de Langues, d'Histoire et de Géographie, Syllabus of General Anthropology I,* Ackerman, *Bulletin of the Jewish Palestine Exploration Society, Revue Biblique,* Obermann, Thomas, Vilnay, Rowley, Steinmueller, Steinmueller-Sullivan, Engnell, Nathan-Gass-Creamer, *The Louis Ginzberg Jubilee Volume,* Gordis, Cazelles, Burrows, McGinley]

Note on article by Yigael Sukenik, ibid. 106, 17

Comment on Recently Received Publications, ibid., 18–22 [Childe, Steindorff, *Bulletin of the Iranian Institute,* Schneid, Hudson, Herzfeld, Böhl, Gordon, Labat, Schwartz, Nougayrol, Bea, Speiser, Hyatt, Coppens, Torrey, Edsman, Leslau, Sander-Hansen, *The Jewish People—Past and Present,* Weinreich, Friedenwald, Zlotnik-Allony-Patai, *Edoth, Al-Andalus, Sefarad,* Archer, Jurji]

Notes in *Approaches to Group Understanding,* New York, Harper and Brothers, 1947, pp. 706, 709, 814, 819 f.

Chester Charlton McCown: an Appreciation, *An Indexed Bibliography of the Writings of Chester Charlton McCown,* Berkeley, Pacific School of Religion, 1947, pp. 5–7

1947–48

The Phoenician Inscriptions of the Tenth Century b.c. from Byblus, *JAOS* 67, 153–60

The War in Europe and the Future of Biblical Studies, in Willoughby, *The Study of the Bible Today and Tomorrow,* Chicago, University of Chicago Press, 1947, pp. 162–74

The Old Testament and Archaeology, in Alleman and Flack, *Old Testament Commentary,* Philadelphia, The Muhlenberg Press, 1948, pp. 134–70

Exploring in Sinai with the University of California African Expedition, *BASOR* 109, 5–20. (Also reprinted as *Exploring Sinai with the University of California African Expedition,* with foreword by Wendell Phillips, Baltimore, 1948, 16 pp.)

The Early Alphabetic Inscriptions from Sinai and Their Decipherment, *BASOR* 110, 6–22

Contributions to C. C. McCown and others, *Tell en-Nasbeh,* Berkeley and New Haven, 1947, I, 151 f., 168 f., etc.

Reviews of Koeppel, Senès, Murphy, Mahan, *Teleilāt Ghassūl* II, *Biblica* 28, 308–10

Review of Frankfort and others, *The Intellectual Adventure of Ancient Man, American Journal of Archaeology* 50, 490–91

Review of Gibb, *Modern Trends in Islam, Theological Studies* 8, 519–21

Review of Winlock, *The Rise and Fall of the Middle Kingdom in Thebes, American Historical Review* 53, 85–86

In Memoriam Warren Joseph Moulton, *BASOR* 107, 6–7

Note on article by Yigael Sukenik, ibid., 15

Comment on Recently Received Publications, ibid., 17–23 [Dossin, Goetze,

Sumer, Safar, Mallowan, Porada, Kramer, Landsberger, Kraus, Güterbock, Speiser, Brandenstein, Bossert, *Die Welt des Orients,* Scharff, G. Ryckmans, Ringgren, *Book List* of the British Society for Old Testament Study, Köhler, Buber, Mercati, Mowinckel, Stamm, Haldar, Torczyner, Murphy, *Bulletin of the Jewish Palestine Exploration Society,* Stummer, *Palestine: a Study of Jewish, Arab and British Policies, A Palestine Picture Book,* Thorbecke, Gibb, Rosenthal, Grunebaum, Blumenfeld, *Edoth,* Patai, Appadorai, Rowley]

Review of Steinmueller and Sullivan, *A Companion to the Old Testament, JBL* 66, 467–69

Notes from the President's Desk, *BASOR* 110, 1–3

Some Recent Archaeological and Oriental Publications, ibid., 27 [Gardiner, Huzayyin, Saad, Stock, Leland Volume, Winlock, Parrot]

1948–49

"William Foxwell Albright," *American Spiritual Autobiographies,* New York, Harper and Brothers, 1948, pp. 156–81 (with portrait)

The Rediscovery of Civilizations, *Commentary* 6, 570–77

From the Stone Age to Christianity, 2nd edition, 2nd printing, Baltimore, The Johns Hopkins Press, 1948

The Archaeology of Palestine (Pelican Books, A 199), Penguin Books, Harmondsworth, Middlesex, 1949, 271 pp. + 16 pls.

Are the 'Ain Feshkha Scrolls a Hoax?, *Jewish Quarterly Review* 40, 41–49

On the Date of the Scrolls from 'Ain Feshkha and the Nash Papyrus, *BASOR* 115, 10–19

The So-called Enigmatic Inscription from Byblus, ibid. 116, 12–14

Von der Steinzeit zum Christentum: Monotheismus und Geschichtliches Werden (translation of *From the Stone Age to Christianity,* revised), Bern, A. Francke, 1949 (Sammlung Dalp, Vol. 55), 495 pp.

Review of *Semitic Studies in Memory of Imanuel Löw, Theological Studies* 9, 469–70

Foreword to Detweiler, *Manual of Archaeological Surveying,* New Haven, *ASOR,* 1948, pp. v–vi

Review of McCown ond others, *Tell en-Naṣbeh,* Vol. i, *JNES* 6, 202–5

Editorial Note on the Jerusalem Scrolls, *BASOR* 111, 2–3

Note on article by H. L. Ginsberg, ibid., 26

Recently Received Archaeological Books, ibid., 28–30 [Lloyd, *Sumer,* Friedrich-Meyer,Ungnad-Weidner, Poebel, van der Meer, Gordon, Obermann, Schaeffer, Porada, Borowski, Mode, Kantor, Blake, Dyggve]

Detweiler's *Manual of Archaeological Surveying* and Kelso's *Ceramic Vocabulary of the Old Testament, BASOR* 112, 23

Review of Wambacq, *L'épithète divine Jahvé Seba'ôt: Étude philologique, historique et exégétique, JBL* 67, 377–81

Review of Böhl, *King Hammurabi of Babylon in the Setting of his Time, Bibliotheca Orientalis* 5, 125a–27a

Two Books on Ancient Near Eastern Religion (Obermann and Frankfort), *Jewish Quarterly Review* 59, 291–96

Review of Jirku, *Die ältere Kupfer-Steinzeit Palästinas und der bandkeramische Kulturkreis, American Journal of Archaeology* 52, 469b–70b

Review of Diringer, *The Alphabet: a Key to the History of Mankind, Modern Language Notes* 64, 182–84

A Decade of Middle Eastern Archaeology, *Palestine Affairs* 4, 22–25

Divine Right in the Ancient Near East (review of Frankfort, *Kingship and the Gods), Jewish Quarterly Review* 39, 415–17

Books Recently Received by the Editor, *BASOR* 114, 12–19 [Gardiner, Breasted, Labat, von Soden, Falkenstein, Lenzen, O'Callaghan, Cameron, Duchesne-Guillemin, Tallqvist, Salonen, Holma, Friedrich, Sommer, Bozkurt-Çiğ, Balkan, Bossert, Landsberger, Höfner, Jamme, Willoughby, Alleman-Flack, Bentzen, Rudolph, Nötscher-Staab, Ziegler, Eissfeldt, Elliger, Ginsberg, North, Sukenik, Kahle, Braidwood, Sukenik, de Vaux, Welker, Mesnil du Buisson, Cintas, Stewart]

Review of Thieberger, *King Solomon*, *Jewish Social Studies* 11, 163–64

Review of *Megiddo II: Seasons of 1935–39*, *American Journal of Archaeology* 53, 213–15

Notes on J. C. Trever, Identification of the Aramaic Fourth Scroll from 'Ain Feshkha, *BASOR* 115, 9, 10

Comment on Dr. Lacheman's Reply and the Scrolls, ibid. 116, 17–18

Some Recent Books on Archaeological and Oriental Subjects, ibid., 18–22 [Needler, Starcky-Munajjed, Reifenberg, Perkins, Burton-Brown, Goosens, Schweitzer, Frankfort, Montet, Keimer, Ungnad, San Nicolò, Falkenstein, Oppenheim, Fleisch, Moscati, Dupont-Sommer, Gordon, Hammershaimb, Cohen, Torczyner, Bentzen, Pfeiffer, Rehm, Morgenstern, Sonne, Widengren, Kapelrud, Wace, Hrozný, Bidez, Brockelmann, Bowen, Wittfogel, Widengren, Edsman, Wischnitzer, Obermann, Rosenblatt, Rabinowitz, Hershman, ben Isaiah-Sharfman, Hirsch, Brauer, Löwinger-Somogyi, Robertson-Wallenstein, Wilber, O'Leary, Farès]

Review of Olmstead, *History of the Persian Empire*, *JBL* 68, 371–77

Review of Prijs, *Jüdische Tradition in der Septuaginta*, *Theological Studies* 10, 588–91

1949–50

The Biblical Period, *The Jews: Their History, Culture, and Religion*, ed. Louis Finkelstein, Philadelphia, Jewish Publication Society of America, 1949, I, 3–69. (Reprinted for private distribution by photo-offset, Pittsburgh, The Biblical Colloquium, 1950)

Baal-zephon, *Festschrift Alfred Bertholet*, Tübingen, Mohr, 1950, pp. 1–14

The Psalm of Habakkuk, *Studies in Old Testament Prophecy* (Presented to Theodore H. Robinson), ed. H. H. Rowley, Edinburgh, T & T Clark, 1950, pp. 1–18

A Re-interpretation of an Amarna Letter from Byblos (EA 82), with William L. Moran, S.J., *Journal of Cuneiform Studies* 2, 239–48

Some Important Recent Discoveries: Alphabetic Origins and the Idrimi Statue, *BASOR* 118, 11–20

Les Inscriptions du Sinai et l'évolution de l'alphabet, *Actes au XXIe Congrès International des Orientalistes*, Paris, Société Asiatique, 1949, 100–2

The Judicial Reform of Jehoshaphat, *Alexander Marx Jubilee Volume*, New York, Jewish Publication Society, 1950, English Section, pp. 61–82

Some Oriental Glosses on the Homeric Problem, *American Journal of Archaeology* 54, 162–76

Palestinian Inscriptions, Akkadian Letters, *Ancient Near Eastern Texts Relating to the Old Testament* (with G. E. Mendenhall), ed. Pritchard, Princeton University Press, 1950, pp. 320–22, 482–90

The Chronology of Ancient South Arabia in the Light of the First Campaign of Excavation in Qataban, *BASOR* 119, 5–15

The Origin of the Alphabet and the Ugaritic ABC Again, ibid., 23–24

Rib-Adda of Byblos and the Affairs of Tyre (EA 89), with William L. Moran, S.J., *Journal of Cuneiform Studies* 4, 163–68

Cilicia and Babylonia under the Chaldaean Kings, *BASOR* 120, 22–25

Ha'arke'ologiyah shel Erets-Yisra'el (Hebrew translation of *Archaeology of Palestine*, with contribution by E. L. Sukenik, pp. 231–44), Tel Aviv, 'Am 'Oved, 5711, 1950, 260 pp.

Review of Schweitzer, *The Philosophy of Civilization, The Hopkins Review* 3, No. 2, 45–47

Review of Mendelsohn, *Slavery in the Ancient Near East, The American Historical Review* 55, 347–48

Note to Howie, The East Gate of Ezekiel's Temple Enclosure and the Solomonic Gateway of Megiddo, *BASOR* 117, 16–17

Memorial (James Alan Montgomery), *JBL* 69, xviii–xix

Review of *The Dead Sea Scrolls of St. Mark's Monastery, BASOR* 118, 5–6

Some Recent Archaeological Publications, ibid., 31 [Marquet-Krause, Schaeffer, Goldman, Lacheman]

Current and Forthcoming Publications of the Schools, ibid. 119, 4–5 [Glueck, Brownlee, Kraus, Moran, Kramer, Brownlee, Diringer, Kelso, Clark, Bowen, Pritchard]

Some Recent Publications Received by the Editor, ibid., 24–30 [Cassuto, Steinmueller, Finkelstein, Lieberman, Ferm, Mendelsohn, Michel-Noth-Andrae, Parrot, Bossert-Alkim-Çambel-Ongunsu-Süzen, Akurgal, Dussaud, Reifenberg, Sukenik, Yavis, Reygasse, Legrain, Figulla, Parrot, Dossin, Jean, Kupper, Falkenstein, Steele, Ebeling, San Nicolò, Tallqvist, Salonen, Böhl, Moortgat, Falkenstein, von Soden, Edel, Friedrich, van der Waerden, Stock, Fakhri, Grdseloff, Scharff, Drioton, Vercoutter, Braver, Bodenheimer]

Edward Robinson and Charles Cutler Torrey, ibid. 120, 27–28

Some Recent Publications Received by the Editor, ibid., 28–31 [Granqvist, Sukenik, Galling-Edel-Rapp, Parrot, Bertholet Festschrift, Robinson Volume, Rowley, Noth, Nötscher-Junker-Rehm-Fischer-Stummer-Hamp, Elliger, Heinisch, Hempel, Tobler, Eliot, Blegen-Caskey-Rawson-Sperling]

Review of Gordon, *Ugaritic Handbook, JBL* 69, 385–93

Zur Zähmung des Kamels, *ZAW* 1949–50, 315

1950–51

The Hebrew Expression for "Making a Covenant" in Pre-Israelite Documents, *BASOR* 121, 21–22

Gerhard Kittel and the Jewish Question in Antiquity, *Freedom and Reason, Studies in Philosophy and Jewish Culture in Memory of Morris Raphael Cohen,* New York, Conference on Jewish Relations, 1951, pp. 325–36

The Old Testament and the Archaeology of Palestine, The Old Testament and the Archaeology of the Ancient East, *The Old Testament and Modern Study: A Generation of Discovery and Research* (chs. 1 & 2), ed. H. H. Rowley, Oxford, 1951, pp. 1–47

The Chronology of the Dead Sea Scrolls, Postscript to W. H. Brownlee, *The Dea Sea Manual of Discipline, BASOR Supplementary Studies* 10–12, 1951, pp. 57–60

Review of Kahle, *The Cairo Geniza, American Journal of Philology* 72, 105–6

Some Books Received by the Editor, *BASOR* 121, 23–25 [de Vaux-Steve, Casson-Hettich, Maisler, Ben Dor, Bossert-Steinherr, Landsberger-Balkan, Alp, Akurgal, Stewart, van den Branden, Noth, Rowley, Wright, Johnson, Eissfeldt, Lindhagen, Schmidt, Howie]

Arabia (Archaeological News), *American Journal of Archaeology* 55, 99a–100b

Review of Riis, *Hamā: Les Cimetières à Crémation,* ibid., 106a–7b

Review of Perkins, *The Comparative Archaeology of Early Mesopotamia,* ibid. 209a–10b

Review of Driver, *Semitic Writing from Pictograph to Alphabet, JNES* 10, 217a–22b

1951–52

The Archaeology of Palestine (Pelican Books, A 199), reprinted (with many corrections and editions), Penguin Books, Harmondsworth, 1951, 271 pp.

The Eastern Mediterranean about 1060 B.C., *Studies Presented to David Moore Robinson,* St. Louis, 1951, I, pp. 223–31

De l'âge de la pierre à la chrétienté (extensively revised from the English editions), Paris, Payot, 1951, 303 pp.

The Smaller Beth-shan Stele of Sethos I (1309–1290 B.C.), *BASOR* 125, 24–32

A Catalogue of Early Hebrew Lyric Poems (Psalm 68), *Hebrew Union College Annual,* Cincinnati, 1950–51, 33, part 1, 1–39

A Note on the Chronology of the Second Millennium B.C., *BASOR* 126, 24–26

The Latest Publications of the Schools, *BASOR* 123, 5–8 [Glueck, Burrows, Brownlee, Bowen, Sellers, *Biblical Archaeologist, Journal of Cuneiform Studies,* Tobler, Lacheman, Speiser, Albright]

Notes to articles on the Dead Sea scrolls by Sellers, Beegle, Brownlee, ibid., 26–31

Review of Noth, *Geschichte Israels,* *Erasmus* 4, 489–93

Review of Pritchard, *Ancient Near Eastern Texts Relating to the Old Testament, JAOS* 71, 259–64

James Anderson Kelso, In Memoriam, *BASOR* 124, 12

Recent Books on the Archaeology of Syria, ibid., 30 [von Luschan-Andrae, Collart-Coupel, Lenzen, Abdul-Hak]

Review of Rowley, *From Joseph to Joshua, Gnomon* 23, 397a–98a

Review of Gordis, *Koheleth—the Man and His World, Jewish Frontier,* Jan. 1952, 30–31

Review of Thiele, *The Mysterious Numbers of the Hebrew Kings, Interpretation* 6, 101–3

In Defense of the American Foundation for the Study of Man, *Middle East Journal* 6, 111–12

Note to Murphy, A Fragment of an Early Moabite Inscription from Dibon, *BASOR* 125, 23

Books on the Archaeology of Syria, Arabia, Egypt and Mesopotamia, ibid., 33–34 [*Les Annales Archéologiques de Syrie,* Friedrich, Harris, Tawfiq, Yeḥya, 'Alī, G. Ryckmans, J. Ryckmans]

Review of Velikovsky, *Ages in Chaos,* Vol. I, *New York Herald Tribune Book Review,* Apr. 20, 1952, p. 6

From the Acting President's Desk, *BASOR* 126, 1–2

Books on the Ancient East, ibid., 27–34 [Emery, Groenewegen-Frankfort, Stubbings, de la Ferté, Bennett, Sittig, Angel, Blegen-Caskey-Rawson, Milojčić, Scharff-Moortgat, Wilson, Welser-Stoheker, Thiele, Klausner, Abel, Runes, Weidner, Rowley, Robinson Festschrift, Popper Festschrift, Popper, Nötscher Festschrift, Schwabe Festschrift, Dhorme Festschrift, Dussaud, Kittel, Roberts, Kahle, Nakarai, Touzard, Blake, Nötscher, Junker, Hamp, *The Book of Psalms* trans., Rypins, Unger, Montgomery, Khuri, Cassuto, Mowinckel, Engell, Haldar, Lindblom, Coppens, Eichrodt, von Rad, Ginsberg]

Review of Glueck, *Explorations in Eastern Palestine,* Vol. IV, *JBL* 71, 115–17

Review of Frankfort, *The Birth of Civilization in the Near East, American Journal of Archaeology* 56, 145–47

Review of Crawfoot and Addison, *Aber Gidi,* and Addison, *Sagadi* and *Dan el-Mek,* ibid., 158

Article "Old Testament," American People's Encyclopedia, The Spenser Press, 1952, XIV, cols. 1034–38

1952–53

The Language of the Old Testament, *An Introduction to the Revised Standard Version of the Old Testament,* New York, Thomas Nelson & Sons, 1952, pp. 32–41

The Bible after Twenty Years of Archaeology, *Religion in Life* 21, 537–50

The Old Testament World, *The Interpreter's Bible,* New York, 1952, I, 233–71

Further Observations on the Chronology of the Early Second Millennium B.C., *BASOR* 127, 27–30

The Dead Sea Scrolls, *The American Scholar* 22, 77–85

Notes on the Temple 'Awwâm and the Archaic Bronze Statue, *BASOR* 128, 38–39

The Chaldaean Inscriptions in Proto-Arabic Script, ibid., 39–45

Kessler Foundation Lectures, *The Wittenberg Bulletin* 49, No. 8, 2–15

The Chronology of the Minaean Kings of Arabia, ibid., *BASOR* 129, 20–24

The Bible, *Literary Masterpieces of the Western World,* Baltimore, The Johns Hopkins Press, 1953, pp. 3–20

New Light from Egypt on the Chronology and the History of Israel and Judah, *BASOR* 130, 4–11

The Traditional Home of the Syrian Daniel, ibid., 26–27

Israel, an Archaeological Treasure House, *Israel: Life and Letters,* May–June 1953, 8–11

Review of Coon, *Caravan: The Story of the Middle East, The Middle East Journal* 6, 347

Review of Lamb, *Theodor and the Emperor: The Drama of Justinian,* New York *Herald Tribune Book Review,* Aug. 3, 1952, p. 5

Some Recently Received Books on the Near East, *BASOR* 127, 31–35 [Finegan, Schaeffer, Furumark, Maisler, Rostovtzeff, Detweiler-Perkins-Welles, Saad, Coon, Ringbom, Kenyon, *Interpreter's Bible*, Engnell-Fridrichsen-Reicke, Hatch, Baron, Rowley, Gordis, Kraeling, Smalley, Obermann, Danby, Klein, Leslau, von Soden, Jean, Dossin, Kramer, Landsberger, Salonen, Schmidtke, Neufeld, Laroche, Steindorff, Säve-Söderbergh, Jamme, Ryckmans, Ingholt-Starcky-Schlumberger]

Review of Montgomery, *A Critical and Exegetical Commentary on the Book of Kings, JBL* 71, 245–53

Some Recently Published Books, *BASOR* 128, 46 [Marmardji, Hill, Levy, Young, Khadduri, Abdallah-Khuri-Graves, Field]

From the President's Desk, ibid. 129, 1–3

Books Received by the Editor, ibid., 27 [Bossert, Gurney, Friedrich, Gaster, Cross-Freedman]

Review of J. Ryckmans, *L'institution monarchique en Arabe méridionale avant l'Islam, JAOS* 73, 36–40

From the President's Desk, *BASOR* 130, 1–3

Correspondence with Professor Einar Gjerstad on the Chronology of "Cypriote" Pottery from Early Iron Levels in Palestine, ibid., 22

1953–54

Mit-teqûfat ha'eben ve'ad han-Noṣrût (Hebrew translation of *From the Stone Age to Christianity* with new preface and additions), Jerusalem, Achiasaf, 1953, xii + 306 pp.

Dedan, *Geschichte und Altes Testament* (Albrecht Alt Festschrift), Tübingen, 1953, pp. 1–12

Syrien, Phönizien, und Palästina, vom Beginn der Sesshaftigkeit bis zur Eroberung durch die Achämeniden, *Historia Mundi,* Bern, Francke, 1953, II, 331–76

Archaeology and the Religion of Israel, third edition (with new preface and additional notes, pp. 223–30), Baltimore, The Johns Hopkins Press, 1953, 246 pp.

Archaeological Excavations and the Bible, *Scopus* 8, No. 1, 6–7

Dwarf Craftsmen in the Keret Epic and Elsewhere in North-west Semitic Mythology, *Israel Exploration Journal* 4, 1–4 (Hebrew translation below)

'Ômenîm gammadîm ba'alîlat Ḳeret ûbimiqômôt aḥerîm bamitologiya haṣ-Ṣafôn-ma'rab-Šemît (Hebrew translation of Dwarf Craftsmen in the Keret Epic and Elsewhere in North-west Semitic Mythology), *Erets Yisra'el III* (Cassuto Memorial Volume), Jerusalem, 1953, pp. 58–59

Some Observations on the New Material for the History of the Alphabet, *BASOR* 134, 26

The Judeo-Christian View of Man (Radio lecture), *Man's Right to Knowledge,* New York, Columbia University Press, 1954, pp. 16–24

Notices of *Studies Presented to D. M. Robinson,* Vol. I, and Jack Finegan, *The Archaeology of World Religions, Book List* (Society for Old Testament Study) *1953,* No. 10, 68

Review of Diringer, *The Alphabet, American Journal of Philology* 74, 449–50

Note on article by Rabinowitz, A Hebrew Letter of the Second Century from Beth Mashko, *BASOR* 131, 24

Books Recently Received by the Editor, ibid., 27–34 [*Historia Mundi,* Clark, Braidwood, Cornelius, Moscati, Coates, Brodrick, Cooper, National Geographic Society, Barrois, Garstang, Dussaud, Friedrich, Dunand, Woolley, Wiseman, Kapelrud, Eissfeldt, Al-Yasin, Braidwood, Parrot, Jean, Gelb, Bauer, Bergmann, Çiǧ-Kizilyay-Kraus, Sollberger-Ebeling, Falkenstein-von Soden, Haldar, Proosdij, Weidner, Hayes, Smith, Weill, Davis, May, Noth, Würthwein, Robert-Tricot, Bentzen, Schneider, Junker, Nötscher, Köhler, Wright, Eichrodt, Vriezen, Young, Mace, Rowley, Dupont-Sommer, Rowley, Driver, Reicke, Habermann, Marcus, Brand]

Editorial Note, ibid. 132, 2–3

Some Recent Publications, ibid., 46–47 [Tufnell-Murray-Diringer-Dupont-Sommer, Jamme, Rhodokanakis, Ziegler, Kraeling]

Israel-Prophetic Vision and Historical Fulfillment, *Land Reborn* 5, pp. 1, 3, 16

Review of Braidwood, *The Near East and the Foundations for Civilization,* *American Anthropologist* 56, 143–44

Review of Diolé, *Four Thousand Years under the Sea,* New York *Herald Tribune Book Review,* June 6, 1954, p. 6

Article "Gebal," *Entsiqlopediya Miqra'it,* Jerusalem, 1954, II, cols. 404–11

Review of Howells, *Back of History,* New York *Herald Tribune Book Review,* June 20, 1954, p. 5

1954–55

The Archaeology of Palestine (Pelican Books, A 199), third revised printing, Penguin Books, Harmondsworth, 1954, 271 pp.

A Survey of the Archaeological Chronology of Palestine from Neolithic to Middle Bronze, *Relative Chronologies in Old World Archaeology,* ed. R. W. Ehrich, Chicago, 1954, pp. 28–33

Notes on Ammonite History, *Miscellanea Biblica B. Ubach,* Montserrat (Spain), 1954, pp. 131–36

The Bible after Twenty Years of Archaeology (1932–52), reprinted from Religion in Life with four pages of additional notes, Pittsburgh, The Biblical Colloquium, 1954, 17 pp.

Northwest-Semitic Names in a List of Egyptian Slaves from the Eighteenth Century B.C., *JAOS* 74, 222–33

On the Early South-Arabic Inscription in Vertical Columns, *BASOR* 138, 50

Review of Graves and Podro, *The Nazarene Gospel Restored,* New York *Herald Tribune Book Review,* July 18, 1954, p. 8

Review of Toynbee, *A Study of History,* Vols. VII–X, Baltimore *Evening Sun,* Oct. 14, 1954, 3 cols., editorial page

Foreword to Trever, *Cradle of our Faith,* 1954, p. xi

Comment on Arnold Toynbee and the Jews, *Jewish Frontier,* Feb. 1955, 23

Review of Hrozný, *Ancient History of Western Asia, India and Crete,* *American Anthropologist* 57, 166–67

Three New Books of General Interest, *BASOR* 137, 39 [Pritchard, Phillips, Trever]

Reply to letter of Professor Zeitlin, *Israel Speaks,* Apr. 22, 1955, 5

1955–56

Inscriptional Material from New Testament Jericho and Khirbet en-Nitla (with A. Jeffery), *AASOR* 29–30, 53–56

The New Assyro-Tyrian Synchronism and the Chronology of Tyre, *Mélanges Isidore Lévy, Annuaire de l'Institut de Philologie et d'Histoire Orientales et Slaves,* Brussels, 1955, XIII, 1–9

Some Canaanite-Phoenician Sources of Hebrew Wisdom, *Wisdom in Israel and in the Ancient Near East* (Rowley Festschrift), *Supplements to Vetus Testamentum,* Leiden, 1955, III, 1–15

Contributions to William C. Hayes, *A Papyrus of the late Middle Kingdom in the Brooklyn Museum,* Brooklyn, 1955, pp. 94–99

Recent Discoveries in Bible Lands (revised), supplement to Young, *Analytical Concordance to the Bible,* New York, Funk and Wagnalls, 1955, 51 pp.

L'Archéologie de la Palestine (revised translation of *The Archaeology of Palestine*), Paris, Les Éditions du Cerf, 1955, 93 pp. + 16 pls.

New Light on Early Recensions of the Hebrew Bible, *BASOR* 140, 27–33

The Son of Tabeel (Isaiah 7:6), ibid., 34–35

Die Religion Israels im Lichte der archäologischen Ausgrabungen (revised and enlarged edition of English edition), Munich, Reinhardt, 1956, 268 pp + 12 pls.

Notes on Psalms 68 and 134, *Interpretationes ad Vetus Testamentum pertinentes Sigmundo Mowinckel septuagenario missae,* Oslo, Forlaget Land og Kirke, 1955, pp. 1–12

Further Light on Synchronisms between Egypt and Asia in the Period 935–685 B.C., *BASOR* 141, 23–27

The Archaeology of Palestine (Pelican Books, A 199), revised reprint, Penguin Books, Harmondsworth, 1956, 271 pp.

Recent Discoveries in Bible Lands (reprinted with additions), Pittsburgh, The Biblical Colloquium, 1956, 136 pp.

Recent Discoveries in Palestine and the Gospel of St. John, *The Background of the New Testament and its Eschatology* (C. H. Dodd Anniversary Volume), Cambridge, University Press, 1956, pp. 153–71

Not likely to Change Beliefs (Symposium on the Dead Sea scrolls), *The New Republic*, April 9, 1956, pp. 19–20

Israel—Prophetic Vision and Historical Fulfillment, *Israel: Its Role in Civilization*, ed. Moshe Davis, New York, 1956, pp. 31–38

The Biblical Tribe of Massa' and Some Congeners, *Studi Orientalistici in Onore di Giorgio Levi della Vida*, Rome, 1956, I, 1–14

Review of *The Idea of History in the Ancient Near East*, ed. Dentan, Baltimore *Evening Sun*, July 21, 1955, 1 col., editorial page

Article "Palestine: History: Old Testament Period," *Encyclopaedia Britannica*, XVII, 124b–27b

Review of Wilson, *The Scrolls from the Dead Sea*, New York *Herald Tribune Book Review*, Oct. 16, 1955, p. 3

Recent Books on Archaeology and Ancient History, *BASOR* 139, 14–25 [Pritchard, *Historia Mundi*, Hrozný, Frankfort, Akurgal, Tahsin-Özgüç, Ingholt, Lane, Mallowan, Ghirshman, Wheeler, Ehrich-Kantor-Albright-Braidwood-Perkins-McCown-Goldman-Weinberg-Ehrich-Ward, Weidner-König, Driver, *Les Annales Archéologique de Syrie: Revue d'archéologie et d'histoire syriennes*, Schaeffer-Nougayrol-Boyer-Laroche, Dussaud, 'Ali, Rathjens, Wissmann, Höfner, Caskel, Hayes, Reisner-Smith, Hughes, Vandier, Caminos, Mekhitarian, Anthes, Dunham-Chapman, Davies-Bull-Hall, Cintas, Berthier-Charlier, Février, Landsberger, Landsberger-Hallock-Schuster-Sachs, Parrot-Kupper, Bottéro-Finet, Crawford, Schmökel, Goodenough, Birnbaum, Avigad, Kadman, Marucchi, Davies, Atiya]

Review of Aldington, *Lawrence of Arabia*, and Armitage, *The Desert and the Stars*, Baltimore *Sunday Sun*, Nov. 13, 1955, p. 12

Review of Burrows, *The Dead Sea Scrolls*, New York *Herald Tribune Book Review*, Dec. 11, 1955, p. 4

Review of Ceram, *The Secret of the Hittites*, ibid., Jan. 8, 1956, pp. 1, 12

Review of Wilson, *The Scrolls from the Dead Sea*, and Burrows, *The Dead Sea Scrolls*, *The American Scholar*, 1956, 247–48

Review of Cottrell, *The Mountains of Pharaoh*, New York *Herald Tribune Book Review*, April 29, 1956, p. 5

Some Books Received by the Editor, *BASOR* 142, 35–39 [Alt, Böhl, C. H. Dodd Anniversary Volume, Mowinckel Festschrift, Pedersen Festschrift, Rowley, Tur-Sinai, *Semitica*, Vincent-Steve, Avi-Yonah, Dunand, Grollenberg, Wilnay, *Hebrew Encyclopaedia Biblica, Eretz-Israel*, Yonah-Yeivin-Stekelis, Parrot, Metzger, Horn, Albright, Cornelius, Ubach Festschrift, Weller Festschrift]

Review of Kramer, *From the Tablets of Sumer*, New York *Herald Tribune Book Review*, June 24, 1956, p. 4

Article "Archaeology, Biblical," *Twentieth Century Encyclopedia of Religious Knowledge*, Grand Rapids, 1955, I, 65–73

1956–57

The Significance of the Dead Sea Scrolls, *Chemical and Engineering News*, Sept. 3, 1956, p. 4256

A Note on Early Sabaean Chronology, *BASOR* 143, 9–10

The Nebuchadnezzar and Neriglissar Chronicles, ibid., 28–33

The Date of the Kapara Period at Gozan (Tell Halaf), *Anatolian Studies VI* (Garstang Festschrift), pp. 75–85

Stratigraphic Confirmation of the Low Mesopotamian Chronology, *BASOR* 144, 26–30

Northeast-Mediterranean Dark Ages and the Early Iron Age Art of Syria, *The Aegean and Near East: Studies Presented to Hetty Goldman*, New York, 1956, pp. 144–64

The High Place in Ancient Palestine, *Supplements to Vetus Testamentum,* Leiden, 1957, IV, 242–58

New Material for the Egyptian Syllabic Orthography (with T. O. Lambdin), *Journal of Semitic Studies* 2, 113–27

From the Stone Age to Christianity, reprinted as Anchor Book (with new introduction, pp. 1–23, and chronological table, pp. 404–9), New York, Doubleday & Co., 1957, 432 pp.

Review of Petrie, *City of Shepherd Kings,* and Mackay and Murray, *Ancient Gaza V, Bibliotheca Orientalis* 13, 164–65

Review of Toynbee, *An Historian's Approach to Religion,* Baltimore *Evening Sun,* Sept. 11, 1956

Some Books Received by the Editor, *BASOR* 143, 34 [Sukenik-Avigad, Barthélemy-Milik, Yadin, Elliger, Nötscher]

Albrecht Alt, *JBL* 75, 169–73

Review of Pope, *El in the Ugaritic Texts,* ibid., 255–57

Review of North, *Sociology of the Biblical Jubilee, Biblica* 37, 488–90

Review of *Studia Orientalia Ioanni Pedersen Septuagenario A.D. VII Id. Nov. Anno MCMLIII a Collegis Discipulis Amicis Dicata, JAOS* 76, 233–36

Review of Dentan, ed., *The Idea of History in the Near East,* ibid., 236–39

Review of Zeitlin, *The Dead Sea Scrolls and Modern Scholarship, The American Historical Review* 62, 103–4

John Garstang, In Memoriam, *BASOR* 144, 7–8

Note on Cross, Lachish Letter IV, ibid., 26

Some Books Received by the Editor, ibid., 38–39 [Vermès, Dupont-Sommer, Wilson, Burrows, Brecher-Avrunin, Smith-Metzger, de Vaux, Hartman-Skehan, Robert-Tricot-et al., Kuhl, Kraeling, Rudolph-Eissfelt, Tur-Sinai, de Vaux, Cazelles, Myers]

Review of Bibby, *Testimony of the Spade,* New York *Herald Tribune Book Review,* January 20, 1957, p. 3

Review of Goneim, *The Lost Pyramid,* ibid., February 17, 1957, p. 3

Review of Coon, *The Seven Caves, Natural History,* March 1957, p. 116

Review of Keller, *The Bible as History, Saturday Review,* March 9, 1957, pp. 31–32

Note to Jamme, On a Drastic Current Reduction of South-Arabian Chronology, *BASOR* 145, 30–31

1957–58

Die Bibel im Licht der Altertumsforschung (revised translation of the 1955 edition of *Recent Discoveries in Bible Lands*), Stuttgart, Calver Verlag, 1957, 148 pp.

L'archeologia di Palestina (Le Piccole Storie Illustrate, 4), (translation of the 1956 edition of *The Archaeology of Palestine*), Florence, Sansoni, 1957, 346 pp. + 16 pls.

The Refrain "And God Saw ki tob" in Genesis, *Mélanges bibliques rédigés en l'honneur de André Robert,* Paris, 1957, pp. 22–26

The Results of Recent American Archaeological Research in South Arabia, *Proceedings of the Twenty-Second Congress of Orientalists Held in Istanbul,* Vol. II, Leiden, 1957, pp. 94–98

Zur Chronologie des vorislamischen Arabien, *Von Ugarit nach Qumran* (Otto Eissfeldt Festschrift), Berlin 1958, pp. 1–8

Was the Age of Solomon without Monumental Art? *Eretz-Israel* V (Mazar Volume), Jerusalem, 1958, pp. 1*–9*

Comments on Professor Garber's Article (with G. Ernest Wright), *JBL* 77, 129–32

The Seal Impression from Jericho and the Treasurers of the Second Temple, *BASOR* 148, 28–30

An Ostracon from Calah and the North-Israelite Diaspora, ibid. 149, 33–36

Recent Progress in Palestinian Archaeology: *Samaria-Sebaste III* and *Hazor I,* ibid. 150, 21–25

Specimens of Late Ugaritic Prose, ibid., 36–38

Articles "Hadatta," "Hamat," "Haran," *Entsiqlopediya Miqra'it,* Jerusalem, 1958, III, cols. 41–42, 193–200, 301–3

Article "Assur (Assyria)," *Entsiqlopediya Ivrit,* Jerusalem, VII, cols. 359–75

The Bible as History, *Jewish Heritage,* I, pp. 5–8

Nelson Glueck as Archaeologist, *Hebrew Union College Bulletin* 10, No. 1, 7

Foreword to Lily Edelman, *Israel: New People in an Old Land,* New York, 1958, p. 7

Recent Books on Assyriology, *BASOR* 148, 30–31 [Landsberger-Hallock-Jacobsen-Falkenstein, Gelb, Finet, Balkan, Salonen, Sachs-Schaumberger, Gelb, Cığ-Kızılyay-Salonen]

Chester Charlton McCown, In Memoriam, ibid. 149, 3–4

The Assyrian Open-Court Building and the West Building of Tell Beit Mirsim, ibid., 32

Some Recent Books on the Ancient Orient, ibid., 37–38 [Gordon, Gray, Pope, van Selms, Aisleitner, Fronzaroli, Bottéro, Greenberg, Kupper, Johnson, Widengren, Mowinckel]

Robert Henry Pfeiffer, In Memoriam, ibid. 150, 3–4

Address in Honour of Otto Eissfeldt, *Von Ugarit nach Qumran* (Otto Eissfeldt Festschrift), Berlin, 1958, pp. xiv–xvi

Dead Sea Scrolls, The American People's Encyclopedia Year Book, 1958, Chicago, 1958, cols. 409–10

Editor-in-Chief of R. L. B. Bowen, F. P. Albright et al., *Archaeological Discoveries in South Arabia,* Baltimore, The Johns Hopkins Press, 1958, Prefatory Note, p. xi

Reviews of Yadin, *The Message of the Scrolls,* Howlett, *The Essenes and Christianity,* Stendahl, ed., *The Scrolls and the New Testament,* New York *Times Book Review,* Nov. 10, 1957, p. 32

Review of Cross, *The Ancient Library of Qumran and Modern Biblical Studies,* ibid., April 20, 1958, p. 12

Review of Cottrell, *Lost Cities,* New York *Herald Tribune Book Review,* Aug. 11, 1957, p. 3

Review of Schreiber, *Vanished Cities,* ibid., Aug. 18, 1957, p. 4

Review of Lissner, *The Living Past: Seven Thousand Years of Civilization,* ibid., Nov. 17, 1957, p. 4

Review of Burrows, *More Light on the Dead Sea Scrolls,* ibid., June 15, 1958, p. 6

SUBJECT INDEX